THE RUSSIAN TRADITION

Tibor Szamuely was born in Moscow in 1925 into a well-known Hungarian family. He went to school briefly in England, but his family returned to Russia in the mid-1930s. (His father was a victim of Stalin's Great Purges.) He served in the Soviet Army and studied at Moscow University but was arrested in 1951 and spent some time in a labour camp. Later he taught at Budapest University, becoming its Vice-Chancellor in 1958. In 1964 he was able to bring his family to England where he taught at the University of Reading until his death in December 1972.

'His understanding of the Russian mind and ways was profound, and his ability to convey this understanding in vivid prose is well demonstrated here.'   Harry Shukman, *TLS*

'A wealth of scholarship, deployed with great literary skill, with wit, eloquence and notable impartiality.'
                                        Colin Welch, *Daily Telegraph*

'Abounds in brilliantly illuminating summaries of complicated situations and ideas, and in graphic illustrations from little known sources.'
                                        Leonard Schapiro, *Sunday Times*

'Immense vigour, panache and erudition . . . rich and stimulating . . . packed with swift illuminations and disturbing insights.'   Edward Crankshaw, *Observer*

THE
RUSSIAN TRADITION

Tibor Szamuely

Edited and with an Introduction by
ROBERT CONQUEST

FONTANA PRESS

First published in England in 1974 by
Martin Secker & Warburg Ltd
Fontana Press edition first published in 1988
by Fontana Paperbacks,
8 Grafton Street, London W1X 3LA

Printed and bound in Great Britain by
William Collins Sons & Co. Ltd, Glasgow

FOR NINA

CONTENTS

Introduction by Robert Conquest   ix

PART I   THE RUSSIAN STATE TRADITION

1   The Sleeping Past   3
2   The Mongol Heritage   13
3   Independence and Despotism   30
4   The State over Society   49
5   The Institutionalization of the Autocracy   65
6   Interpretations: Feudal and 'Asiatic'   99
7   The Petrine Watershed   122
8   The Eighteenth Century: Enlightenment and
    Enslavement   149
9   Alexander I and Nicholas I   173

PART II   THE RUSSIAN REVOLUTIONARY TRADITION

10   The Intelligentsia   189
11   Early Revolutionaries: the Decembrists to Herzen   240
12   The Second Generation: Chernyshevsky   282
13   Nihilists   302
14   Nechaev and the Conspiratorial Principle   332
15   Going to the People   367
16   Tkachev and the Roots of Leninism   388
17   Back to Politics   435
18   Discipline and Terrorism   455
19   The Marxist-Populist Dialectic   502
20   Towards the New-style Absolutism   526

Notes   567
Index   583

INTRODUCTION

The death of Tibor Szamuely in December 1972 at the early age of forty-seven was the severest possible loss to all interested in the study of the world's political cultures.

Dr Szamuely was born in Moscow in 1925 into the well-known Hungarian Communist family: his uncle and namesake was a celebrated figure in the Hungarian Revolution of 1919. He came to England as a young boy and spent some time at Bertrand Russell's Beacon Hill School. However, his family returned to Russia in the mid-thirties, and his father Gyorgi Szamuely disappeared in Stalin's great purge when Tibor was eleven years old.

He served in the Soviet Army, and then went to Moscow University, where he took his doctorate, but in 1951 he was arrested and spent some time in labour camp in the Vorkuta area. He was later allowed to go to Hungary, where he taught at Budapest University, becoming its Vice-Chancellor in 1958. He and his wife were allowed to visit England, while leaving their children behind as hostages, in the early sixties, and he at once impressed British historians generally and students of Russia in particular with the profundity of his knowledge and the breadth and balance of his political judgments. He was sent to Ghana to lecture, this time being allowed to take his family to what was then a pro-Soviet dictatorship, and was able to bring them to England in 1964, since when he taught at Reading University and at the same time played a prominent part in public controversy on a variety of subjects.

It is difficult to realize that he was only in this country for eight years, so great was the impact he made on our public and academic life. In particular, of course, he established himself as one of the world's most outstanding commentators on the Soviet scene. Though he had contributed widely and effectively not only in the learned periodicals but also in journalism and on television, he had not at the time of his death published a book. We are fortunate that *The Russian Tradition* was nevertheless completed before he died.

It demonstrates, as his less formal work has demonstrated in less complete manner, the quite unrivalled grasp which he had not only on the history and the culture of Russia, but on the histories and cultures of the West and of the rest of the world. When it comes down to it, it is only by the profoundest knowledge and feeling, the most powerful exercise of the intellect and the imagination, the broadest combination of erudition and common sense, that the modern world, or any part of the modern world, can be fully understood and presented. Many people have possessed one or other of these qualities, without a sufficient admixture of the others. This broader grasp is an extreme rarity; it is also an urgent necessity. For those of us who cannot attain it, it is the greatest good fortune that there was a man who could.

There can be few enterprises more valuable today than to instruct the West in the nature of the culture of its major rival; and by none could it have been better done. It is curious, among the vast amount of current writing on world affairs, how much otherwise informed and sensible analysis there is which is yet seriously, sometimes fatally, weakened by the absence of a more than sketchy or superficial grip on all that has moulded the most decisive and deep-set characteristics of the Russian state and the Russian revolutionary movement.

A knowledge – a genuine knowledge – of Russia is (let us insist again) essential to all who seek to understand the world as it is today. This book establishes in full depth, and the broadest historical perspective, the great essentials of that tradition which renders Russia and the Russian state what they are. It is one of those books which are for expert and non-expert alike, readily conveying this extraordinarily important and extraordinarily neglected material to the ordinary intelligent reader, while at the same time forming a solid and original contribution to the literature.

Tibor Szamuely had certain personal advantages. His Hungarian family, though of Communist belief, was yet rooted in the European culture; and he even (as we saw) spent a period of his childhood in England. At the same time, it was in Russia that he had his upbringing, that he went to school, to university, to the Army, to labour camp. But apart from this wealth of personal experience, he was virtually unique in that he had also, as we have said, actively and profoundly studied and understood both the Russian and the Western political cultures. Erudite Russians, even when wholly sympathetic to the ideas of the West, and wishing to bring their country into the civic tradition of Europe, have yet often given the impression of being outside observers with insufficient understanding of the nature of Western history, and inclined to project upon the West a rather more Utopian pattern than is justified – but above all, a simpler, a more schematic pattern.

On the other hand, many views on Russia have been propounded in the West by men of intelligence and erudition, to whom nevertheless that country was a historical phenomenon not fully grasped with all the resources of intellect and sensibility. They saw it, too often, from a Western point of view – not necessarily in the sense of merely regarding the Western culture as preferable (indeed, Dr Szamuely does that), but in the sense that whether they approved or not, their Russia was an extrapolation of what they had already learned and experienced elsewhere. It was, for them, a Western society aberrant in many particulars but still basically 'European', or it was a strange society whose nature was nevertheless to be understood by political theories which had been developed on the basis of a study of the West. Marx, of course, was one of those who imposed on Russian history (as on world history in general) a theory originally developed to cover the periods and the areas with which he was best acquainted: that is, the previous century or so in Western Europe. Marx, it is true, hedged to some extent, deployed his concepts with a certain flexibility not to be seen to any extent in later Marxist writings. But his basic categories – and in particular that of 'feudalism'

– confused the issues to a very high degree, and still confuse them. As to the 'Marxism' which prevailed in the Russian Revolution, Dr Szamuely shows that it bore about as much relation to the original study of Western society as the 'Christianity' of the T'ai-Ping did to that of Thomas Aquinas.

But this was the fruit of a Russian history which, at least since the time of the Mongols, had been of a type totally unlike that of any other country. And century-long habits are not to be changed by fiat. It is Dr Szamuely's theme, which he develops so effectively, that the circumstances of the past seven centuries in Russia had produced an order in which society as a whole had become totally dependent upon the state, and moved according to the subjective decisions taken by the state leadership. Moreover, the almost complete lack of any autonomous social and civic phenomena led to the absence of ideas of political adjustment and give-and-take among the state's opponents as well: so that these central peculiarities of Russian history produced the practice and principle of absolutism, of rule by decree, not only in the established order, but equally in the revolutionary tradition which opposed it.

Western revolutionaries recognized this. As Rosa Luxemburg put it in a curious passage, long before the Revolution:

> In Lenin's over-anxious desire to establish the guardianship of an omniscient and omnipotent Central Committee… we recognize the symptoms of the same subjectivism that has already played more than one trick on socialist thinking in Russia…
>
> Knocked to the ground, almost reduced to dust, by Russian absolutism, the 'ego' takes revenge by turning to revolutionary activity. In the shape of a committee of conspirators, in the name of a non-existent Will of the People, it seats itself on a kind of throne and proclaims it is all-powerful. But the 'object' proves to be the stronger. The knout is triumphant, for tsarist might seems to be the 'legitimate' expression of history.
>
> In time we see appear on the scene an even more

'legitimate' child of history – the Russian labor movement. For the first time, bases for the formation of a real 'people's will' are laid in Russian soil.

But here is the 'ego' of the Russian revolutionary again! Pirouetting on its head, it once more proclaims itself to be the all-powerful director of history – this time with the title of His Excellency the Central Committee of the Social Democratic Party of Russia.

There was indeed another trend in Russia, a genuine tendency towards Europe and the idea of a civic order. By the time it was extirpated following the October Revolution, it had not had long enough to match either the roots or the power inherent in its twin rivals. All the same, around 1910 it looked possible that a constitutional and civic development might after all come about. The younger generation, even among the intellectuals, were turning from the ideas of both Nicholas II (born 1868) and Lenin (born 1870). The Russian Enlightenment, as Pasternak pointed out, depended upon the development of a 'middle class open to occidental influences, progressive, intelligent...' – but, alas, unused to politics, unpractised in the exercises of power. Dr Szamuely ends his book with the appearance of Lenin, who was to abort this shaky promise and restore – in a different form – the Russian Tradition.*

Dr Szamuely powerfully helped to change the Western mind in the direction of truth rather than preconception, of reality rather than illusion. *The Russian Tradition* will contribute even more powerfully to this achievement. Of his personal qualities I have written elsewhere, and here I would only mention the good humour, the panache, the kindness, the unpretentiousness, the honesty which, so apparent in his private affairs, were also part and parcel of his intellectual and public influence.

He had not, at the time of his death, carried out the final

---

* As we see today, the struggle between that despotic tradition and the civic developments which alone can modernize the country continues; and readers of this book will have a powerful and realistic grasp of the profound difficulties facing such a change. (RC, 1988.)

revision of his typescript. I have made a few cuts, of no great length, at points where there were repetitions which he himself would certainly have pruned; I have transposed one passage to what seemed to be a more suitable position; and I have added an occasional note where I know he had intended to do the same.

I would wish, as Dr Szamuely would have wished, to acknowledge the quite incomparable editorial contribution of Mr John Blackwell.

Acknowledgements are due to the editor of *Survey*, in which chapters 19 and 20 originally appeared.

ROBERT CONQUEST
1973

Part I

THE RUSSIAN STATE
TRADITION

CHAPTER 1

The Sleeping Past

1

In the summer of 1839 a French nobleman went on a journey to Russia. He was the Marquis de Custine, already well known as the author of several lively books of travel. As a devoted Royalist, whose father and grandfather had both died on the guillotine, Custine was an admirer of the Russian political system; indeed he went there, as he himself put it, 'to seek for arguments against representative government'. His background and parentage assured him an easy entry into the most exalted circles: the Emperor himself honoured him with several private conversations.

Custine returned from his travels a bitter enemy of Tsarist autocracy and 'a partisan of constitutions'. He wrote one of the most famous and influential descriptions of Russia ever to be published; Herzen, the renowned Russian revolutionary, called it 'beyond doubt the most fascinating and the cleverest book ever written by a foreigner about Russia'.[1] Custine's most important observations and conclusions sound oddly familiar today:

> The political state of Russia may be defined in one sentence: it is a country in which the government says what it pleases, because it alone has the right to speak . . .
>
> In Russia, power, all unlimited as it is, entertains an extreme dread of censure, or even of free speech . . . I compare, with a wonder mixed with fear, the disorder of ideas that reigns among us, with the absence of all private views, of all personal opinion – the blind submission, in short, which forms the rule of conduct among all, whether

3

heads or subordinates, who carry on the administration of affairs in Russia . . .

In Russia fear replaces, that is, paralyses thought . . .

Here reserve is the order of the day, just as imprudence is in Paris. In Russia secrecy presides over every thing; a silence that is superfluous insures the silence that is necessary . . .

The corps diplomatique, and the Western people in general, have always been considered by this Byzantine government and by Russia in general, as malignant and jealous spies . . .

A traveller who would allow himself to be indoctrinated by the people of the country, might overrun the empire from one end to the other, and return home without having surveyed any thing but a series of façades. This is what he should do in order to please his entertainers . . .

The observer can inspect nothing without a guide: never being alone, he has the greatest difficulty in forming his judgment upon his own spontaneous impressions; and this is what is desired. To enter Russia you must, with your passport, deposit also your right of opinion on the frontier . . . You obtain no other permission than that of expressing before the legitimate authorities the admiration which politeness, prudence, and a gratitude of which the Russians are very jealous, demand . . .

I marvel at the prestige which the Russian government exercises over minds. It obtains silence, not only from its own subjects – that were little – but it makes itself respected, even at a distance, by strangers escaped from its iron discipline . . .

In Russia, on the day that a minister falls from favour, his friends become deaf and blind. No one dares to remember that he is living, nor even to believe that he ever had lived. A man is as it were buried the moment he appears to be disgraced. Russia does not know to-day if the minister who governed her yesterday exists . . .

Nor in this country is historical truth any better

respected than the sanctity of oaths ... even the dead are exposed to the fantasies of him who rules the living ...

When the sun of publicity shall rise upon Russia, how many injustices will it expose to view! – not only ancient ones, but those which are enacted daily will shock the senses of the world.[2]

Custine's final, comprehensive conclusion was the harshest indictment of all: 'If ever your sons should be discontented with France, try my receipt; tell them to go to Russia. It is a useful journey for every foreigner: whoever has well examined that country will be content to live anywhere else.'[3]

Almost exactly a hundred years later, in 1936, after a great social revolution had transformed the face of Russia, another Frenchman undertook the same journey, a writer of far greater eminence than Custine: André Gide. Gide did not merely approve of the new Russian political system – for many years he had been the foremost Western literary champion of the Soviet Union. Before his trip he had regarded Russia not as just another country, not only as a dynamic and rapidly developing society, but as the tangible materialization of a beautiful vision: 'Who shall say what the Soviet Union has been to us? More than a chosen land – an example, a guide. What we have dreamt of, what we have hardly dared to hope, but towards which we were straining all our will and all our strength, was coming into being over there. A land existed where Utopia was in the process of becoming reality.'[4]

Gide's journey was a triumphal progress. Everywhere he went he was acclaimed by rapturous throngs. He was showered with honours, even to the unique distinction of becoming the first non-Communist foreigner to stand next to the Soviet leaders on top of Lenin's tomb. It would have been only human of Gide to feel his lonely and unpopular stand gloriously vindicated, yet he returned to France with his faith in ruins. The tragic and agonized book he wrote sounds almost a paraphrase of Custine:

Stalin's effigy is met with everywhere; his name is on

every tongue; his praises are invariably sung in every speech . . . Is it adoration, love, or fear? I do not know; always and everywhere he is present . . .

In the USSR everybody knows beforehand, once and for all, that on any and every subject there can be only one opinion . . . Every morning *Pravda* teaches them just what they should know and think and believe. And he who strays from the path had better beware! So that every time you talk to one Russian you feel as if you were talking to them all . . . Nobody can differ from anybody else . . .

What is wanted now is compliance, conformity. What is desired and demanded is approval of all that is done in the USSR, and an attempt is being made to obtain an approval that is not mere resignation, but a sincere, an enthusiastic approval. What is most astounding is that this attempt is successful. On the other hand the smallest protest, the least criticism, is liable to the severest penalties, and in fact is immediately stifled. And I doubt whether in any other country in the world, even Hitler's Germany, can thought be less free, more bowed down, more fearful (terrorized), more vassalized . . .

Nobody dared risk himself, before knowing what to think . . .

What really interests them is to know whether we admire them enough. What they are afraid of is that we should be ill-informed as to their merits. What they want from us is not information but praise . . .

The Soviet citizen is in an extraordinary state of ignorance concerning foreign countries. More than this – he has been persuaded that everything abroad and in every department is far less prosperous than in the USSR. This illusion is cleverly fostered . . . For them, outside the USSR the reign of night begins . . .

After so many months, so many years of effort, one had the right to ask oneself – will they now at last lift up their heads? They are more than ever bowed down.

After a hundred years the final lesson drawn from a visit to Russia remained identical: 'As it always happens that we recognize the value of certain advantages only after we have lost them, there is nothing like a stay in the USSR (or of course in Germany) to help us appreciate the inappreciable liberty of thought we still enjoy in France.'[5]

Two Frenchmen, a century and a revolution apart – two practically indistinguishable descriptions. They might almost have been travelling companions.

2

However celebrated these two books soon became, however violent the enraged reaction of the Russian government and its foreign friends to their publication, there was nothing really exceptional about their contents. The observations quoted above could easily be matched from any of the scores of descriptions of Russia published in the West over the past 400-odd years. It is the very consistency of these two books, their basic points of similarity with other writings on Russia, far removed from them in time, that is so extraordinary: the fact that twenty years after the 1917 revolution Gide had been struck by the same social phenomena that Custine recorded back in the days of Nicholas I, and that had indeed deeply impressed almost all Western visitors to Russia, starting from Baron Sigismund von Herberstein, Ambassador of the Emperor Maximilian of Germany, in 1517.

This is the first highly significant feature of all these descriptions of Russia, past and present: the astonishing durability of certain key social and political institutions, traditions, habits, and attitudes; their staying power, their essential stability amidst the turbulent currents of violent change, chaotic upheaval, and sudden innovation.

The other striking aspect of these travellers' reports is the profound dissimilarity, invariably noted by their authors, between the customs and institutions of Russia and those of the Western European societies with which they were familiar. Since 1917 it has become a truism that Russia is developing along lines fundamentally different from the broad societal pattern of what is usually called the Western world. But it is insufficiently realized that this is not just a comparatively recent attitude of wonder at a revolutionary society that has made a decisive, irrevocable break with the past and has embarked on a unique experiment: for many centuries now Russia has been viewed, by Russian and foreigner alike, as something basically different from the norms and standards of the West.

Most incomprehensible and alien of all, pervading and colouring every Western description of Russia, was the awesome sway of an omnipotent State exercising unlimited control over the persons, the property and the very thoughts of its subjects. It was not adherents of parliamentary democracy and majority rule, but faithful servants of the monarchs of absolutist Europe who felt this to be a phenomenon beyond the compass of their experience.

Baron von Herberstein was the first Westerner to describe the incredible power of the Russian autocrat: 'In the sway which he holds over his people, he surpasses all the monarchs of the whole world . . . He uses his authority as much over ecclesiastics as laymen, and holds unlimited control over the lives and property of all his subjects: not one of his counsellors has sufficient authority to dare to oppose him, or even differ from him on any subject. They openly confess that the will of the prince is the will of God, and that whatever the prince does he does by the will of God . . . In short they believe that he is the executor of the divine will.'[6]

Giles Fletcher, the cultivated and perceptive Ambassador of Queen Elizabeth I of England, saw things in much the same way: 'The state and forme of their government is plaine tyrannicall, as applying all to the behoofe of the prince, and that after a most open and barbarous manner . . . Concerning the principall pointes and matters of state, wherein the soveraintie consisteth (as the making and annulling of publike lawes, the making of magistrates, power to make warre or league with any forraine state, to execute or to pardon life, with the right of appeale in all matters, both civill and criminall) they doo so wholy and absolutely pertain to the emperour, and his counsell under him, as that hee may be saide to be both the soveraine commaunder, and the executioner of all these.'[7]

Adam Olearius visited Russia as Ambassador of the Duke of Holstein almost a century and a half after Herberstein, after the country had trembled on the brink of total ruin and disintegration during the so-called 'Time of Troubles', yet the picture of the State was unchanged: 'The politick Government of Muscovy is Monarchical and despotical . . . No Master hath more power over his slaves, than the Great Duke hath over his subjects, what condition or quality soever they be of . . . No people in the World have a greater veneration for their Prince than the Muscovites, who from their infancy are taught to speak of the Czaar, as of God himself, not onely in their acts and publick assemblies, but also in their entertainments and ordinary discourse.'[8]

The next two centuries brought greater changes to Russia than perhaps even to the nations of Western Europe, yet for the Marquis de Custine the foundations of Russian society had remained intact. And another century later, after the greatest revolution of our times had ruthlessly razed the Tsarist system to the ground, and carried out what was announced as the most profound social transformation in the whole of recorded history, André Gide, to his intense sorrow, once again found the Leviathan of the Russian State clutching its helpless subjects in an ever-tightening grip.

For all these observers, and for many others as well, Russia appeared to be a society whose basic principles were totally alien to all Western concepts. Striving to make this vast empire intelligible to their compatriots, they could find no familiar parallels to the extraordinary way of life they were describing. Instead, they had to turn to the Bible and to the ancient authors for illustrations most nearly resembling the state of affairs in Russia. Olearius even combined both types of object lesson, declaring that 'Muscovy may be numbered among those States, whereof Aristotle speaks, when he sayes there is a kind of Monarchy among the Barbarians which comes neer Tyranny,' and also: 'we may say of the Great Duke, what the Prophet Daniel sayes, of the King of Babylon, That he put to death whom he would, and saved whom he would.'[9]

There can be no doubt that pre-revolutionary and non-Marxist Russian thinkers, writers, poets, historians, sociologists, would not have accepted the idea of the Russian past having been just a part of a single, uniform, homogenized European experience. In no other country did the intellectuals, almost to a man, pass their lives in tortured reflections on their people's past and in apprehensive speculation as to its future. They knew their story to have been sombre and tragic – they also knew it to be essentially different from that of Europe. Whether they gloried in this difference and strove to perpetuate it, like the Slavophiles, or yearned for a decisive break with tradition, like the 'Westerners', all alike recognized that Russia had merely been in Europe, but not of it. From the first appearance of the Russian intelligentsia the problem of Russia and Europe, Russia and the West, lay at the heart of every controversy, of every social theory, of every political movement.

For the Russian intelligentsia was acutely conscious of a basic fact that has today been largely forgotten or is passed over in silence in the name of a worldwide brotherhood of man: every country of modern Europe either was at one time a province of the Roman Empire, or received its religion from Rome. Russia is the sole exception. Russia is the only country of geographical Europe that owed virtually nothing to the common cultural and spiritual heritage of the West.

The famous 'Russian soul' was to no small extent the product of this agonizing uncertainty regarding Russia's proper geographical, social, and spiritual position in the world, the awareness of a national personality that was split between East and West. This perpetual dilemma received perhaps its finest literary expression in 'The Scythians', Alexander Blok's last great poem, written just three months after the October Revolution had swept away the old order of things:

10

Yes – we are Scythians! Yes – we are Asiatics,
With slanting and rapacious eyes!

And a few lines later, addressing Europe:

We shall turn to you
Our Asiatic face!

Three times in the course of her history has Russia undergone vast upheavals that broke the yoke of custom, and imposed upon her patterns derived from the West: under Peter the Great, after the peasant reform of 1861, and as a result of the 1917 revolution. Every one of these transformations was greeted abroad as the long-awaited Europeanization of Russia. But of these three onslaughts on the Russian past it was only the second that aimed at the introduction not merely of Western customs and technology, but of a 'Western' system of social relationships. Perhaps significantly, it was the one attempt that remained, by and large, unsuccessful. By way of contrast, the great convulsions of the eighteenth and twentieth centuries achieved all their aims and had lasting results – their 'Europeanizing' aspect, however, remains highly ambiguous, to say the least.

Speaking forty years after the inauguration of the 'Era of the great reforms' and only a decade before it was to be overwhelmed by the tidal wave of war, Russia's greatest historian, Vasily Kliuchevsky, made a profound comment on the nature and the fate of all attempts at transforming his country: 'Having decided that Russia has now abandoned the old foundations of her life, society has adjusted its historical ideas in accordance with this assessment . . . Not so long ago we thought: why look back, when there is so much to be done, and such a bright future before us? Today we think: what is there to learn from our past, when we have broken all our ties with it, when our life has irrevocably shifted onto new foundations? But an important point has been overlooked: lost in admiration for the way in which the Reform has been transmuting the Russian tradition, we have shut our eyes to the way in which the Russian tradition has been transmuting the Reform.'[10]

Of all the burdens Russia has had to bear, heaviest and most relentless of all has been the weight of her past.

CHAPTER 2

The Mongol Heritage

The factor that has probably contributed most towards shaping Russia's history has been her geographical position. It is worlds apart from that of Western and Central Europe: instead of the great variety of natural features and climates, of the comparative isolation of one region from another by mountain ranges and other natural barriers, of the long and indented coastline of Europe, Russia offers a picture of a vast, unbroken, unchanging and unending plain. She possesses no barriers either to expansion or to invasion. Her seas are landlocked and not easily accessible, her sole ocean icebound. Her climate varies little, her soil is either poor or gets insufficient rainfall. Her physical features, in fact, resemble Asia far more than they do Europe.

From the point of view of Russia's history the decisive feature of her geographical environment has been the absence of natural frontiers. This has led, on the one hand, to the expansion of the Russian people over one-sixth of the world's land surface and, on the other, to a history of armed struggle against invaders that for length, intensity and ferocity has no parallel in the annals of any other nation. It was this ceaseless and merciless struggle that gave birth to the Russian State.

Russia had no frontiers: for many centuries she was herself *the* frontier, the great open, defenceless dividing-line between the settled civilized communities of Europe and the nomadic barbarian invaders of the Asian steppes. One of the keys to the understanding of Russian history is the fact that for a thousand years, until the end of the eighteenth century, she was always a frontier country.

The concept of the frontier as a decisive factor in the shaping of a specific civilization is of comparatively recent standing, and has justifiably gained wide acceptance in connection with the history of the United States of America. F.J. Turner, who, practically single-handed, created the idea of the frontier as a force of history, has written of America (and, curiously, his remarks are, in a certain sense, apposite to the history of Russia as well): 'The larger part of what has been distinctive and valuable in America's contribution to the history of the human spirit has been due to this nation's peculiar experience in extending its type of frontier into new regions . . . The frontier is the outer edge of the wave – the meeting point between savagery and civilization . . . The American frontier is sharply distinguished from the European frontier – a fortified boundary line running through dense populations. The most significant thing about the American frontier is, that it lies at the hither edge of free land . . . What the Mediterranean Sea was to the Greeks, breaking the bond of custom, offering new experiences, calling out new institutions and activities, that, and more, the ever-retreating frontier has been to the United States directly, to the nations of Europe more remotely.'[1]

The Russian frontier came into being a full thousand years before the signing of the Declaration of Independence; the 'savagery' it beat back, or failed to beat back, was not that of a few scattered Indian tribes, but of great armies and mighty kingdoms; and, not surprisingly, the customs, experiences, institutions and activities it called forth were usually diametrically opposed to their American counterparts. But its importance for Europe has been all the greater for not being cut off by a broad expanse of ocean. For Russia herself the frontier has been the paramount formative factor of her history. To quote S. M. Solovyov, the great nineteenth-century Russian historian: 'Russia is a border state; it is the European frontier with Asia. This frontier position of Russia has naturally had a decisive influence on her history.'[2]

There were two aspects to Russia's position as a frontier country: one was her unremitting struggle against recurring waves of powerful nomadic invaders, and the other the continuous process of opening up and colonizing the vast spaces of Eastern Europe and Northern Asia.

These two closely connected aspects of Russian history were very different from anything in the European experience. Europe, too, has had its fair share of barbarian invasions – Huns, Saracens, Vikings, Magyars, Mongols – and the part they played in its development is well known. But these were all sudden attacks by invaders who appeared unexpectedly out of nowhere, sacked and pillaged for several years, and then, after being defeated in a single pitched battle – Châlons in 451, Tours in 732, Lechfeld in 955 – or for reasons of their own, they either departed just as suddenly as they had come, or settled down and became like anybody else. For Russia, the cruel relentless struggle never abated: it was a permanent part of her life for most of her history. The death of the Great Khan Batu saved Europe from the Mongols: Russia lived under Mongol rule for 250 years. And Russia had no friends to come to her aid, to organize crusades against the common enemy, as was done against the Moors or the Turks – on the contrary, her western Christian neighbours were only too happy to make use of her misfortunes for their own aggrandizement. She was on her own: a wretchedly poor country pitted against the greatest military forces of the age.

The age-long colonizing activity of the Russian people was also greatly different from anything known to European nations. Throughout the Middle Ages large parts of Western and Central Europe, too, were being gradually settled: marshes drained, forests cut down, agriculture established. The scale of this effort, involving many peoples, and carried out under comparatively favourable climatic, political and technological conditions, was, however, dwarfed by the sheer size of the territory confronting the Russian people, the meagreness of their resources and the bleakness of their circumstances.

Nor can a comparison be drawn with European colonization overseas. For the Russians this was not a question of a few adventurous spirits shaking the dust of the homeland off their boots and sailing away to newly discovered continents: it was a gigantic national enterprise, lasting for centuries, and involving the constant migration and remigration of their people to new lands, first to the North and the East, later to the South and the West. It was the very stuff of their history. 'Migration, the colonization of the country,' wrote Kliuchevsky, 'was the central fact of our history, which was more or less closely connected with every other fact.'[3]

To gain an idea of the human effort this entailed, one should try to imagine thousands of American overland migrant parties or South African Great Treks simultaneously on the move, in an unending procession lasting for several centuries, in conditions of incredible severity, equipped with the most primitive of technologies, burdened with an ever harsher and more oppressive social system, while all the time straining every nerve to fight off powerful invaders and extend their land in armed conflict. There was no romance, no Wild Western glamour about this immense undertaking: through many generations millions of unknown men toiled and died, their effort unsung and all but forgotten today in their native land, bequeathing nothing but their misery and a few more square feet of land redeemed from the hostility of man and nature.

This was a national experience and a national existence radically different from that of the West; it created a social and political system, a national character, a mentality, a way of life, utterly dissimilar to the patterns evolved in Western and Central Europe.

The divergence originated at an early stage.

The first Russian State, established with its capital in Kiev towards the end of the ninth century, bore a close resemblance to the state formations then being set up in Western Europe. It ruled over a considerable territory, and possessed large and wealthy cities, important waterways, a flourishing foreign trade – and a culture derived not from Rome, but from Byzantium. By present-day standards it seems to have been in certain respects a more civilized society than some that existed further to the west: for instance, it had neither capital nor corporal punishment (for free men), nor the institution of judicial torture. Though its life-span coincided with the heyday of Western feudalism, Kiev Russia was not a feudal society: it had no vassalage or system of service-based conditional fiefs; land was held in unconditional, allodial possession; fighting-men were free to enter and leave the prince's service at will; the bulk of the peasants were also free.

Among the features that set Kiev apart from most contemporaneous European states, mention should be made of one that was later to acquire considerable significance: the widespread prevalence of slavery. While not on the scale of Greece or Rome, Kiev was nevertheless a slave-holding society. It conducted a brisk slave trade with Byzantium; indeed, slaves seem to have been the staple of its foreign commerce.

The history of Russia as the history of a nation engaged concurrently in colonization and in defending itself from nomadic incursions has its origin in the Kievan period. Situated as it was on the far edge of European civilization, and at the end of the great swathe of steppe which stretched unbroken to the heart of Central Asia, and had been since time immemorial the domain of warlike nomadic peoples and the route along which they irrupted into Europe, the Kievan state had been engaged in perpetual warfare since its foundation. Khazars, Pechenegs, Polovtsy – one wave followed the other.

It was a losing struggle. Although the Kiev princes of the house of Rurik succeeded in inflicting a number of military defeats on the assailants, the constant pressure of the nomadic world grew ever harder to bear. The fabric of society began to break up. Gradually the population started to move to less exposed country, and by the end of the twelfth century the centre of gravity of Russia (or Rus, as it was called) had shifted decisively to the North-East – there to remain.

Conditions of life in the newly settled territories were very different from what they had been in the South. This was a forbidding land of forest and marsh, where hard work could eke out only the barest of subsistences for peasant and lord alike. North-Eastern Rus became – and for long remained – a country of thousands of tiny, self-contained, scattered peasant communities, existing largely in isolation, using their primitive implements to clear small patches of subsoil amidst the great forests, and, having exhausted them, moving on again along the banks of the numerous rivers. Cities declined and trade dwindled.

This first great colonizing effort of the Russians had other important consequences: as the new lands had not previously been the property of any of the Slavonic tribes that made up Rus, and as the migration itself had proceeded along non-tribal lines, the inevitable effect was to throw the ancient system of complex tribal relationships into utter disarray and, indeed, it was soon obliterated without trace. Post-Kievan Russia, therefore, offered no basis for the development, or even the existence, of that intricate network of clannish, tribal, and regional loyalties which was such a characteristic feature of medieval Western European societies, and which, surviving until the onset of the industrial era, proved a powerful obstacle to the encroachments of centralization and absolutism. Nor were conditions in the new North-Eastern Russia favourable for the establishment of feudal relations. It remained, at that early stage, a free society, for land was in abundant supply, while labour remained scarce, and as yet no force existed which was capable of binding the peasants to the soil and of preventing their free movement.

This was the so-called apanage period of Russian history, when the idea of a common homeland was honoured only in the breach, when Rus had disintegrated into a dozen or so separate territorial entities. In theory, these were only the apanages of princes of the house of Rurik – that is, of members of a single family – but in actual fact they were completely independent states, perpetually at war with each other, connected only by their jealousies, their petty spites, and a shifting system of alliances that easily changed to hostility and fratricide. In the middle of the twelfth century even the fiction of the seniority of the Grand Duke of Kiev, as repository of the idea of national unity, was eliminated: the Grand Duke of Vladimir now became *primus inter pares*. His, however, was a purely honorary title: outside his own apanage it conferred less power than even that of the Holy Roman Emperor, and it rotated, according to a curious Russian custom, from one brother to another, and then in turn among the next generation of princes, in strict order of seniority.

There can be little doubt that, had this evolution continued unchecked, Russia would have irrevocably split up into several fully sovereign national states having no more in common than do those of the Western and South Slavs. In 1237, however, this process was brought to a sudden halt.

In that fateful year the Mongol army, the most fearsome instrument of war yet devised, having conquered the greater part of Asia, crossed the Volga and descended upon the disunited, squabbling Russian principalities. In the course of a lightning campaign Russian resistance was ferociously crushed, and the Mongols (or Tartars, as they were usually called in Russia) became undisputed masters of the whole country. The Tartar yoke, that was to press so heavily upon the Russian people for the next 250 years and decisively to influence the further course of their history, had been firmly established.

'The Tartars were unlike the Moors: having conquered Russia, they gave her neither algebra nor Aristotle,' wrote Pushkin. The great poet was right: culturally the effect of the Mongol conquest, together with that of the changed physical environment of Russian society, was to put Russia back several centuries – during precisely that crucial period when the European New Learning flowered into the Renaissance. But the Mongols, though ignorant of algebra, Aristotle and the finer things of life, were able to give Russia something of more lasting importance: a political and administrative system, a concept of society, quite unlike anything that was to be learned in the West.

The Mongols were rather different from other hordes of Asiatic horsemen that had ravaged Europe during the preceding millennium. They had not only a superb military organization, created by Genghis Khan, one of the supreme military geniuses of all time, but a state that, despite its size, was far more efficient than any contemporary European administrative system. They also possessed a very definite set of socio-political ideas.

The Mongol empire was, in fact, a state grounded on an ideology, an early example of a phenomenon to which the world has since become accustomed; it was not just a state among other states, but, to use an apt description, an *imperium mundi in statu nascendi*, a World-Empire-in-the Making. Its object was the establishment, by means of a series of wars, of a system of universal peace and of a worldwide social order based on justice and equality. After having achieved this, writes Vernadsky, 'the price for the security of mankind would be permanent service to the state on the part of each and all; this would establish an orderly way of life and social equality. The rich would serve the state to the same extent as the poor; and the poor would be protected from injustice and exploitation by the rich.'[4] These ideas were embodied in the great Mongol law code, the Yasa, which uncompromisingly laid down the fundamental principle: 'There is equality. Each man works as much as another; there is no difference. No attention is paid to a man's wealth or importance.'[5]

The Mongol concept of society was based on the unqualified submission of all to the absolute, unlimited power of the Khan. Every member of society was allotted from above his specific position, to which he was bound for life, and which he could never desert, on pain of death. The Khan was not only invested with unquestioned authority over the lives of his subjects: he was also sole owner of all the land within his domains, and all other persons could hold land only on conditions of temporary tenure. In his role as supreme land proprietor the Khan stood as the embodiment of the principle that all the land in the empire of the Mongol World-Conqueror was to be devoted to the interests of the State, i.e. of the entire community.

Such then was the social and political system imposed upon a prostrate Russia by the merciless conqueror. (The westernmost Russian principalities remained free from the Tartar yoke; vulnerable and defenceless, they came within the sphere of influence of Poland and Lithuania, by whom they were soon swallowed up and whose fate they shared. Their further development hardly influenced the general course of Russian history, and does not, therefore, concern us in this context.)

The 250 years of the Tartar yoke have remained in the collective memory of the Russian people as a period of tragedy and humiliation. It was to have profound and lasting results.

The first and most important effect of Mongol rule was the re-establishment of national unity, the foundation of a unified Russian national state. On this point there is general agreement even among the most patriotic non-Communist Russian historians. Karamzin, the father of modern Russian historiography, wrote: 'Batu's invasion overthrew Russia . . . but upon further examination we discover that the calamity was a blessing in disguise, that the destruction contained the boon of unity . . . Another hundred years or more might have passed in princely feuds. What would have been their result? Probably the doom of our country . . . Moscow, in fact, owes its greatness to the Khans.'[6]

A hundred years later Kliuchevsky passed the same judgment on the Tartars as the true unifiers of Russia: 'Had they [the princes] been left completely to themselves they would have smashed Rus up into disjointed, permanently hostile, patrimonial fragments. However, at that time the principalities of Northern Russia were not independent domains, but tributary *uluses* [provinces] of the Tartars. Their princes were called slaves of the "free Tsar", as the Khan of the Golden Horde was styled in our country. The Khan's rule gave at least the semblance of unity to the patrimonial patches of the Russian princes, that had been growing ever smaller and drawing ever further away from each other . . . Fear of the Khan's wrath restrained the bullies; on many occasions devastating strife was prevented or stopped at the Khan's pleasure, or, in other words, by his arbitrary fiat. The Khan's rule was the hard Tartar knife that cut through the knots into which [the princes] had entangled their country's affairs.'[7]

In their dealings with subject populations the Mongols proved masters of the methods of indirect rule. The unending internecine warfare which the Russian princes were eager to

21

continue, even in the hour of national disaster, could not be countenanced by the new rulers; the surly and disputatious princelings had to be kept in check; peace was to be maintained, taxes gathered, and the conqueror's laws upheld. The simplest and most effective way of achieving these aims was to delegate certain powers to trustworthy agents chosen from among the princes themselves. Conclusive proof of fidelity and devotion to the Khan's interests was graciously rewarded by a *yarlyk*, or patent, to the Grand Duchy of Vladimir and to seniority among Russian princes. There was no shortage of contenders for the honour, but soon all were superseded by the one that was least scrupulous and most imaginative: the Khan's favour became the first stepping-stone in the rise to power of what was then perhaps the tiniest of Russian principalities – Moscow.

Moscow owed its extraordinary future to two factors: its geographical location, and the qualities of its rulers. It was situated not only in the geographical centre of North-Eastern Russia, but also at the heart of its waterways, the sole system of communications: between the Volga and the Oka, with comparatively easy access to all parts of the country. As for its princes, they were composed of a mixture of qualities unique among the headstrong and not particularly bright descendants of the house of Rurik: ambitious, ruthless, unprincipled, cunning, tortuous, grasping, miserly, cautious to the point of cowardice – yet at the same time persevering, shrewd, frugal, devout and patriotic.

All these qualities were possessed in full measure by the true founder of the dynasty, Ivan I, nicknamed 'Kalita', or 'Moneybags' (1325–41). He founded his fortunes – and those of his successors and of the Russian national state as well – by a policy of total subservience to the Mongol overlords. The rewards were substantial. When in 1327 Moscow's principal and far stronger rival, the prince of Tver (whose father had earlier been murdered in the Khan's capital by Ivan Kalita's brother with a callousness that had shocked even the Tartars), rose in arms against the Tartar yoke and called upon all the Russian princes to follow his example, Kalita eagerly accepted the Khan's commission to lead the punitive expedition that savagely suppressed the uprising. The Khan thereupon awarded him the coveted title of Grand Duke of Vladimir. From that moment Kalita never looked back. The Metropolitan, head of the Russian Church, moved his residence to Moscow, thereby conferring a much-needed spiritual aura of national unity upon the Grand Duke, who promptly – and gratuitously – added 'of all Russia' to his title. The Tartars did not object: indeed, with their own empire starting to split up, they thought it more convenient to keep the unruly Russian princes in check through the agency of a single delegate.

In return for services rendered, Kalita and his successors persuaded the Tartars to grant them the exclusive right of collecting taxes on the Horde's behalf, and also supreme judiciary authority over all the Russian princes. These prerogatives, added to the prestige of the national religious centre, became powerful levers in the Moscow Grand Dukes' ceaseless campaign, aimed first at rounding out their dominions and later at unifying the Russian principalities under their rule. They used their powers wisely. Ever careful to retain the Khans' trust, they were able to guarantee a lengthy period of peace and stability, during which the people of North-Eastern Russia could start to recover from the overwhelming shocks and the fearful bloodletting they had sustained.

Having realistically appraised Russian military weakness, the Grand Dukes of Moscow sought to attain their ends by all means short of war: obsequiously toadying to the Khans, building up a full treasury by careful husbandry and financial juggling, and always acquiring new lands, by any method available. When the situation seemed propitious, they were even capable of leading an army into battle against the Tartars (1380) – only to revert, as soon as circumstances changed, to their traditional policy.

From the first there was a good deal of give-and-take between the Tartars and Moscow. The Grand Dukes entered with gusto into the maze of internecine Mongol intrigue, backing various contenders to power, and always emerging with something to show for their pains. In 1392, for instance, the grateful Khan of the Golden Horde rewarded Moscow for its support against Timur with the gift of four principalities, including Nizhny-Novgorod, one of the largest of all. And what Moscow once acquired she never again relinquished.

For the suffering Russian people ethical considerations meant very little. In the rise of Moscow they saw their only hope of deliverance from the Tartar yoke, and in the Grand Dukes the symbols of national unity. Although at times their sycophantic grovelling before the Mongols seemed too much for injured national pride to bear – the Grand Duke Vasily II, father of Ivan the Great, even had his eyes put out for overdoing it – on the whole it did them no harm, and never prevented the rapid growth of their popularity and influence. Most Russian historians, too, warmly approve of the methods employed by the Moscow Grand Dukes. Wrote Karamzin: 'The princes crawled on their knees at the Orda [Horde], but returning thence with a gracious yarlyk of the Khan they commanded with greater boldness than they used to do in the days of our political independence . . . The Moscow princes took advantage of this attitude and situation, and, uprooting little by little all the survivals of the ancient republican [i.e. democratic] order, established genuine autocracy.'[8]

Karamzin touches here upon the fundamental aspect of the period of Mongol rule: it led not only to the establishment of a unified Russian state, but to a remoulding of Russia, of its society, its political and administrative system, along lines far removed from those of the pre-Mongol era. It can be said with truth that Russia was really conquered twice: first by the Mongol army, and then by the Mongol State idea.

This was a process going far deeper than the familiar phenomenon of a vanquished people mastering the conqueror's methods in order to avenge their defeat. At the time of the Mongol invasion Russia was in the melting-pot: the old Kievan order had dissolved, and in the changed conditions of the north-eastern frontier a new society was slowly coming into being.

The Mongol conquest, with its carnage and destruction, and the imposition of a harsh alien rule, served to break up the old fabric even more thoroughly. In this reign of chaos the rise of Moscow meant more even than the appearance of a power capable of liberating and reuniting the Russian land; it meant, as Karamzin saw, the gradual, hesitating evolution of a new and genuinely revolutionary concept of society, of government, and of administration, a concept in many vital respects patterned upon the system of the Mongol empire. In Vernadsky's words:

> The Mongolian state was built upon the principle of unquestioning submission of the individual to the group, first to the clan and through the clan to the whole state. This principle was in the course of time impressed thoroughly upon the Russian people. It led to the system of universal service to the state which all without differentiation were forced to give. Under the influence of Mongolian ideas the Russian state developed on the basis of universal service. All classes of society were made a definite part of the state organization. Taken altogether, these ideas amount to a peculiar system of state socialism. The political theory developed into a finished plan later, in the Moscow Kingdom and the Russian Empire; but the basis of the idea of state service was laid down during the period of Tartar domination.[9]

The Muscovy that emerged from the fragments of the old Rus, amid the break-up of the Mongol empire, bore hardly any resemblance to the free society of Kiev. Continuity had been broken, and Muscovy was a successor state of the Golden Horde, inheriting from the Khan, together with his claims for leadership in the Mongol-Turkic sphere, his title of Tsar. This was recognized by the Tartar tribes themselves, who bestowed upon the ruler of Muscovy the appellation of 'White Tsar' – the traditional title of the Khans of the Golden, or White Horde. As the eminent Slavist Nicholas Trubetskoy put it: 'The Russians inherited their empire from Chingis-Khan.'[10] Berdyaev is even more direct: he calls Muscovite Russia 'a Christianized Tartar kingdom'.[11] It is hard to resist quoting one more authority – that of Dr Karl Marx. In the only one of his major works that has never yet been published in the Soviet Union, although it has appeared several times in the West, Marx wrote: 'The bloody mire of Mongol slavery, not the rude glory of the Norman epoch, forms the cradle of Muscovy, and modern Russia is but a metamorphosis of Muscovy ... Kalita's whole system may be expressed in a few words: the machiavellism of the usurping slave ... It is in the terrible and abject school of Mongolian slavery that Muscovy was nursed and grew up. It gathered strength only by becoming a virtuoso in the craft of serfdom. Even when emancipated, Muscovy continued to perform its traditional part of the slave as master.'[12]

The basic Mongol principles of unqualified submission to the State, and of the universal, compulsory and permanent state service of all individuals and classes of society, gradually permeated the Muscovite social structure. So too did the Mongol (and typically Oriental) attitude to property. Speaking of the origins of the Russian system of *pomestie*, or conditional service landholding, the nineteenth-century historian Gradovsky pointed out that

> *pomestie* land-holding presupposes a supreme owner who possesses the land as inalienable property. In the early period of our history Russian society was incapable of evolving such a concept of a supreme landowner: at that time the Russian prince was considered ruler, but not owner of the land. The concept of the prince as supreme landowner arose only in the Mongol period. The Russian princes, as representatives of the Khan, enjoyed within their apanages the same rights as the Khan commanded throughout his dominion. Later the Russian princes came into full possession of these rights through inheritance from the Khan; this inheritance undermined the principle of private property.[13]

The Mongols bequeathed to Muscovy not only their conception of society and of the state, but also the system of

26

government and administration that had served them so well, and that was so admirably fitted to the needs of a large, expanding and powerful state. This applies particularly to those two most important fields in which the administrative practice of the Oriental despotisms – taken over by the Mongols – was so markedly superior to that of feudal Europe: military affairs and finance.

In military organization the Russians proved apt pupils (allowing for the basic difference between Mongol light cavalry and Russian armies composed of both heavy horse and infantry regiments): the system of a unified and centralized army based on universal conscription, the structure of the army, its strategy and tactics – all these were derived from the Mongols. So was another feature of Russian government invariably remarked upon with surprise by all early Western visitors: the extremely efficient service of posts and intelligence, known under its Tartar name of *yam*.

Even greater was the debt Muscovy owed the Tartars in the sphere of finance and taxation. The Mongol principle of universal taxation became the cornerstone of the Russian financial system, supplemented by such traditional Oriental methods as arbitrary confiscation. The pervading Mongol influence on Russian financial policy is reflected most vividly in the Turko-Tartar names of many important Russian fiscal institutions, such as *kazna, kaznachei* – treasury, treasurer; *tamga* or *tamozhnia* – customs office; *kabak* – licensed tavern; *kabala* – debt-slavery, and so on. The Russian word for money itself – *den'gi* – is derived from the Tartar, as were the denominations of the most widely used Russian coins: *kopeika* (kopeck) and *altyn*.

The Mongol system of universal taxation could not have been achieved without the institution of the periodic population census; this was begun by the Khans and continued thereafter by the Muscovite State – several centuries before the rudimentary administrative apparatus of the Western European countries was capable of undertaking a census to cover a far smaller territory (with the single and special exception of Domesday Book). Mention should also be made of certain less admirable, although by no means unique features of Mongol government, now taken over and stringently applied by the Muscovite State, such as capital punishment, corporal punishment and judicial torture (interestingly, the Russian words for executioner – *palach* and *kat* – are both apparently of Tartar origin).

The infiltration of Russian society by Mongol concepts and practices was a gradual and insidious process that covered a long period of time. It took place unnoticed – all the more so since it achieved full fruition well after the destruction of the Tartar yoke – and without any conscious design, as a by-product of the Russian people's desperate struggle for national survival. Strangely enough, in that most critical period of Russia's history this struggle was conducted chiefly by diplomatic and political means – what little warfare there was happened almost exclusively between Moscow and other Russian principalities. The military might of the Mongols, fearsome even in their decline, could not be openly challenged until Russia was re-unified. And so for one and a half centuries the successors of Ivan Kalita patiently and laboriously, overtly and covertly, by stealth and by force, carried on his policy of 'collecting the Russian lands'.

By the end of the fifteenth century the task was fulfilled – with the notable exception of the lands taken over by Poland and Lithuania. But that could wait. In 1471 Moscow annexed the largest and wealthiest of the Russian states: the republic of Novgorod. A few years later Tver fell, obdurate to the last. The Russian lands were united once more, and in 1480 Grand Duke Ivan III, or the Great, proclaimed the end of the Tartar yoke and Muscovy's complete independence of the Mongols.

This new Russia was a world apart from the first unified Russian state of Kiev. 'The very foundations of Muscovite society were different from those of the Kievan age,' remarks Vernadsky:

Throughout the Mongol period the foundations of the old social order – the free society – were gradually and persistently chipped away without at first affecting the façade. At the time when Ivan III announced Russia's emancipation from the Mongol power and conquered Novgorod, the framework of the new structure was all but ready and the new order, that of a service-bound society, became clearly noticeable . . .

In the Tsardom of Moscow of the sixteenth and seventeenth centuries we find an entirely new concept of society and its relation to the state. All the classes of the nation, from top to bottom, except the slaves, were bound to the service of the state . . .

The regimentation of the social classes which started during the Mongol period and was originally based on the Mongol principles of administration, was carried further and completed by the Muscovite government. Autocracy and serfdom were the price the Russian people had to pay for national survival.[14]

The reign of Ivan III, the first autocrat of all the Russias, began a new era of Russian history. Out of the blood and the agony of Mongol subjugation the Russian State had been born.

CHAPTER 3

Independence and Despotism

The three centuries that followed Russia's proclamation of full sovereignty were for her people a period of unremitting and relentless armed struggle, such as no other nation has had to endure in modern times, of warfare that tied down all their energies and taxed their strength to the utmost limits. This was an endless series of inconclusive wars against enemies who never faded away; of conflicts which do not come within the familiar categories of aggressive and defensive wars, or fall into the snug pigeon-holes of just and unjust wars. They can be called neither wars of territorial aggrandizement nor of resistance to aggression; neither colonial nor national liberation wars; neither civil nor foreign wars; aimed neither at achieving unification nor at attaining natural frontiers. They were none of these – for they were all of these. They constituted the fierce struggle of a nation placed on the frontier between Europe and Asia, on the great dividing line between settled and nomadic society, between Christian, Moslem and pagan; of a poor, but hardy and resourceful nation which had been pushed out of its homeland into the inhospitable environment of northern forest and Arctic waste, and which, despite fearful difficulties, wished to retain its distinctive civilization; the struggle of a nation that felt it had been assigned by Providence and by nature to the stupendous task of colonizing and settling a wilderness far greater in size than the whole continent of North America, and also to retrieve its ancient lands, of which it had been dispossessed by Catholic and Infidel. This combination of national purpose, moral fervour, self-defence, and everyday struggle for a bare existence, was the driving force behind the Russian people's travail. The state of never-ending war gave their society its distinctive form.

The armed struggle was waged, most often simultaneously, on three fronts: in the West, the South, and the East and South-East. Most difficult and, for a long time, least successful, was the contest with the traditional western enemies: Poland-Lithuania and Sweden. In the 200 years between the end of the Tartar yoke and the accession of Peter the Great, Russia fought six wars with Sweden and twelve with Poland-Lithuania. Altogether they lasted for about eighty-five years; all except one or two were either unsuccessful or inconclusive, and two were disastrous: the enormously costly Livonian war of 1558–83, which ended in ignominious defeat, and the so-called 'Time of Troubles' at the beginning of the seventeenth century, when Moscow itself was occupied, and Russia seemed to have disintegrated once again. There was, on the whole, very little to show for two centuries of armed conflict and heavy sacrifice; in 1700 Russia's western borders were much what they had been under Ivan the Great: precarious acquisitions in the Ukraine were largely cancelled out by territories lost around the Baltic. In the long run, however, the western battlefields proved the most profitable of all, since it was here that Russia finally realized that without Western methods and European technology she would never be a match for her much smaller and potentially far weaker neighbours.

Stalemate in the West was partly compensated for by rapid and resounding triumph in the East and South-East. By the end of the fifteenth century the Golden Horde had finally broken up into the three independent Khanates of Kazan, Astrakhan and Siberia. They did not last long: in the 1550s, in the course of two well-executed campaigns, Ivan the Terrible destroyed the Khanates of Kazan and Astrakhan and annexed their territory to Muscovy. The road was now clear for the colonization of the vast spaces of the middle and upper Volga, the Ufa and the Kama, and for a mass migration of Russian peasants to these new and more fertile lands.

Beyond Kazan lay Siberia. For the Cossack adventurer Yermak Timofeyevich the first sight from the Ural mountains of the endless sea of forest, stretching for thousands of miles to the Pacific, was as exhilarating an experience as the view from Darien had been for Balboa on the other side of the globe. The conquest, exploration and colonization of Siberia is an epic story comparable only to that of the conquest and settlement of the New World. It still awaits its Prescott or its Parkman.

Within fifty or sixty years tiny, intrepid bands of Cossacks had traversed the length and breadth of Siberia, founding towns, villages, forts, trading posts. Yermak crossed the Urals in 1581 – a hundred years later Russia was already engaged in her first conflict with China over territories at the mouth of the Amur river. Muscovy had become an empire bestriding two continents.

But it was in the South that the interminable, cruel war was fought which for 300 years drained Russia's life-blood, and left an indelible mark upon the whole pattern of her existence. The Mongol onslaught had ravaged Southern Russia with a destructive fury that effectively erased practically every vestige of the flourishing Kievan civilization. The great expanse of fertile steppe between the Dnieper and the Volga was once again the undisputed domain of the nomadic horseman. For hundreds of years fierce Tartar and Turkic tribes roamed the steppes, attacking Russian settlements almost at will. Behind them stood the formidable power of the Crimean Khanate and of its suzerain, the mighty Turkish Empire.

Every year massed hosts of Tartar cavalry would swoop out of the steppes, penetrating deep into Russian territory. Moscow itself was captured and sacked several times, the latest being in 1571, when Ivan the Terrible was at the height of his powers. These constant devastating raids had one object: slaves. Year after year an unending procession of young Russians disappeared into the Crimea. An eye-witness account tells of an old money-lender in Perekop, the gateway to the Crimea, who, after having for many years seen countless thousands of slaves pass by his house, incredulously asked one of them whether there was still any inhabitant left in his land.[1]

Perhaps no other historical experience has left as lasting an impression on the folk-memory of the Russian people as the horrors of this interminable struggle against the slavers and killers of the South. For centuries the steppe remained a source of constant menace, a land of terror, death, destruction and degradation. It was called the Wild Plain, or, as we would say today, the Frontier; the greater part of this region is now called the Ukraine, which is but another word for Frontier (*ukraina* or *okraina*).

Until the seventeenth century the effective frontier passed along the Oka river, less than a hundred miles from Moscow. As long as it existed, like a terrible gaping wound through which Russia's strength poured out, there could be no stability, no peace. The closing of the southern frontier and the establishment of security from Tartar incursion became, and remained until the end of the eighteenth century, the all-important, overriding object of the Russian State.

This task demanded a total, unremitting and ruthless concentration of all national resources, both human and material, that for scope and intensity is probably unparalleled, over a comparable period of time, by any other nation. Russia's struggle with the Tartars comes nearer to the modern concept of total war than anything else in pre-twentieth-century European history.

If we consider the size and the general backwardness of the country, the scattered nature of its settlement, and the almost complete absence of roads, we can only marvel at the quality of organization and the degree of efficiency achieved. Every year at the beginning of spring the fighting-men would arrive, fully equipped, at their call-up points, from there to take up their assigned stations along the frontier. Service lasted until late autumn, when the steppes became impassable. This routine would be repeated, year in and year out, for a man's whole lifetime. As every foreign observer noted with surprise, there could be no question of haggling over the terms and duration of service, or of abrupt departure when the brief period came to an end, as was the rule in feudal Europe: military service was obligatory and permanent, and non-appearance or insubordination were punished with the utmost severity. As Herberstein wrote: 'In war time they do not serve in annual rotation, or by turns, but each and all are compelled . . . to go to battle.'[2] And war time was all the time.

The permanent army that defended Russia from the Tartars throughout the sixteenth and seventeenth centuries was divided into six regiments, and usually consisted of up to 65,000 men.[3] To gain an idea of the colossal effort this entailed one would do well to compare it with medieval European military practice. When in 1467 the German Emperor gathered an army for an all-out offensive against the Turks, drawing upon all the forces of his numerous vassals, he succeeded in mustering 18,500 men – out of a population considerably larger than that of sixteenth-century Russia.[4] At the battle of Crécy the King of France (also with a population larger than Russia's) commanded the most numerous army yet seen in feudal Europe: 12,000 men.[5] And finally, in the greatest combined military effort of the Middle Ages, the First Crusade, which was sustained on a tremendous wave of enthusiasm, the force that passed into Asia Minor numbered not more than 25–30,000 men.[6]

All the examples cited above were but short-lived spurts of energy, that left their begetters utterly exhausted. Russia, on the other hand, had to raise and maintain an armed force, much larger than these European armies in absolute figures and greater still in relation to her resources, not just for an isolated campaign, but for three hundred unbroken years – while at the same time conducting an endless series of wars against more highly developed western neighbours, and also colonizing a country the size of a continent. For above all she needed firm control of the steppes, at whatever price, since without that there could be no national existence.

By the early sixteenth century a defensive line of wooden fortresses and fortified towns was established along the Oka river from Nizhny-Novgorod to Serpukhov, Tula and Kozelsk. Slowly, mile by mile, year by year, at terrible cost to themselves, the Russians pressed southwards. Around the middle of the century Ivan the Terrible set up a new line of fortifications about one hundred miles to the south, between the Volga and the Desna. Still further in the heart of the steppes ran what we would call today an early-warning system of isolated blockhouses and mobile patrols. Another half-century of uninterrupted savage fighting went by – and Russia's armies, closely followed by a tide of peasant settlers, reached a line from Voronezh through Belgorod to the Dnieper; a third screen of fortifications was erected along it. But the greater part of the Wild Plain was to remain for a long time to come an untamed and hostile no-man's-land.

Hardly anything can give a more vivid illustration of the vital importance and the prolonged nature of this struggle, as well as of the essentially frontier nature of Russian life throughout most of her history, than a list of the foundation dates of the more important towns established in various newly colonized regions of the vast empire. In Siberia, thousands of miles from Moscow, in the most inaccessible places and the bleakest of natural environments, the principal towns had already been established in the late sixteenth and early seventeenth centuries: Tiumen 1586, Tobolsk 1587, Obdorsk (at the mouth of the Ob river) 1595, Narym 1596, Tomsk 1604, Yeniseisk 1619, Krasnoyarsk 1628, Yakutsk 1632, Nizhne-Kolymsk (on the Arctic Ocean, at the mouth of the Kolyma) 1644, Okhotsk (on the Pacific) 1649. The frozen tundra, although in some cases a distance of two years' travel, proved easier of access for Moscow than the rich and fertile lands at her doorstep, for the greatest and most important cities of Central Russia were only being founded in the wild steppes at the same time, or even later than these far-flung and practically useless outposts of Siberian empire: Orel 1564, Kursk 1586, Voronezh 1586, Saratov 1590, Belgorod 1593, Tambov 1636, Simbirsk (Ulyanovsk) 1648, Kharkov 1655, Penza 1666. For many years they continued to retain their character of fortified advance posts in a still largely unsubdued countryside.

The grim struggle against the Tartar hordes dominates Russia's history. Generations of Russians have regarded this centuries-long mortal combat as a struggle for the protection of European civilization; to quote Alexander Blok once more, the West was able to develop its arts and industries in peace because:

> We, like obedient slaves,
> Have held a shield between the hostile races
> Of Mongols and of Europe.

This is, of course, a poetic assessment, interesting mainly as an indication of Russian feeling on the subject: one can hardly expect consideration for the salvation of Europe to have been a mainspring of Muscovite policy. But as regards the long-range effects of this struggle on Russia's general development *vis-à-vis* Western Europe, one can only endorse Kliuchevsky's words: 'If one thinks of the amount of time and the material and spiritual forces consumed in this wearying, violent and painful pursuit of the cunning steppe predator, one can hardly ask what the people of Eastern Europe were doing while Western Europe was achieving its triumphs in industry and commerce, in social life, in the arts and the sciences.'[7]

The threefold tasks of defence, reconquest and colonization, set before the Russian people by the geographical position and the historical development of their country, had to be met with limited and widely dispersed resources, and by a nation standing at a low level of natural economy. These grave disadvantages, added to the multiplicity and the strength of her enemies, could be successfully counterbalanced only by the evolution of a political and social system capable of fully mobilizing Russia's scanty and scattered resources, and of converting them into effective national power.

'Compelling national need,' wrote the famous Russian historian Paul Miliukov, 'resulted in the creation of an omnipotent State on the most meagre material foundation; this very meagreness constrained it to exert all the energies of its population – and in order to have full control over these energies it had to become omnipotent.'[8] A political system arose that was based on the unquestioning obedience and unlimited submission of the subjects; on the principle of the obligations owed by each and every subject to the State, obligations that were ruthlessly exacted without being compensated for by the grant of any rights or privileges whatsoever; on the impressment into the State's service of all the creative forces of the nation, and on the sacrifice of private interest to the State's demands. 'The Muscovite state,' says Kliuchevsky, 'in the name of the common welfare, took into its full control all the energies and resources of society, leaving no scope for the private interests of individuals or of classes.'[9]

The State was no bloodless abstraction: its awesome sway and majesty were embodied in the person of the autocratic ruler – styled, beginning from Ivan the Terrible, Tsar of All the Russias. The Tsar combined the symbols of terrifying power with very real and extremely effective authority over the lives and welfare of every one of his subjects, regardless of degree or rank. The position of the Tsar (or the State) was one of unique strength: he was the sole and exclusive wielder and source of power, for all authority in the country emanated from him; he shared power with no one. In addition to this he held an unrestricted monopoly of organization at all levels; non-governmental bodies did not exist, and there was no opportunity, either within the government or outside its system, for the development of rival centres of power capable of limiting, balancing or checking the authority of the ruler. In Muscovy power was indivisible.

This concept of government was evolved over a period of more than two centuries, in the very special circumstances under which Moscow 'gathered the Russian lands', liberated the country from the Tartar yoke, and set about organizing its defence and expansion. Before these events the authority of the Russian princes had been limited and conditional; the ancient aristocracy, the boyars, possessed full and unrestricted title to their lands, and indeed both they and the members of the warrior class were free to transfer their allegiance from one apanage prince to the other, without let or hindrance, and retain their property situated within the domain of their former liege lord. Under the Grand Dukes of Muscovy these customs came to an abrupt end.

The annexation by Moscow of all the independent Russian principalities meant the disappearance of possible alternative suzerains; renunciation of allegiance to the ruler of the embattled national state was now equated with high treason and apostasy. Every inhabitant of the realm became not only the sovereign's subject, but, by an easy and entirely logical transmutation, his bondsman as well.

This vitally important change in the traditional ruler—subject relationship stemmed in large part from a curious parochial principle, evolved in Muscovy at an early date, and applied until the eighteenth century to the whole of the vast empire collected by the house of Kalita:

> The state was regarded, not as the integral unity of the nation and its government, but as if it were no more than the royal household, into which were included, under the heading of household effects, the various classes of population of the royal patrimonial estates. Therefore the people's welfare and the interests of state were subordinated to the dynastic interests of the landowner, and the laws themselves were in the nature of domestic instructions issued by the Kremlin manor-house to regulate the work of the subordinate regional administration. Chiefly, however, they laid down the rules according to which the inhabitants were to fulfil their obligations towards the state.[10]

The fusion of sovereign and of patrimonial landowner was, in fact, none other than the political system described by Jean Bodin as seigneurial monarchy: the concept underlying the despotical empires of the Orient. According to a number of

Russian historians, it was the development of this concept that distinguished Moscow from the other Russian principalities, and that largely ensured its victory.

The evolution of the prince's authority in the direction of unrestricted despotic rule was part of the general rapid growth of regimentation of every aspect of the nation's life that followed emancipation from the Tartar yoke. This seemingly paradoxical phenomenon is to be explained primarily by the mounting complexity of the eternal tasks confronting Russia. 'The foreign policy of the State demanded an ever-growing extension of the nation's resources,' wrote Kliuchevsky. ' . . . The sole domestic expedient consisted of continuously increasing the power of the State, at the expense of the freedom of the community, in contracting the field of private interests in the name of interests of State. Therefore each new reform of this order was accompanied by some further sacrifice of the people's welfare and freedom.'[11]

Russia's astonishing growth within the course of less than 300 years – from a pitiful dependency of the Mongol Khan (whose very existence was completely unknown to Europe) at the accession of Ivan III, to a mighty world power under Peter the Great – was achieved without any corresponding real increase in her resources. It had called for an unparalleled national effort, for a total concentration of every ounce of the nation's strength. It was effected by investing the State, i.e. the Crown, with unlimited despotic powers. Small wonder then that for Russians and foreigners alike the country's greatness became synonymous with despotism. Karamzin declared firmly that 'Russia had owed her salvation and her greatness . . . to the unlimited authority of the monarchs.'[12] One of the shrewdest and most experienced of eighteenth-century British diplomats, Sir George Macartney, Ambassador to Russia in the 1760s, wrote in a dispatch: 'To despotism Russia owes her greatness and her dominions, so that if ever the monarchy becomes more limited, she will lose her power and strength in proportion as she advances in virtue and civil improvement.'[13]

After Russia, by superhuman exertions, had won herself a position where she was feared and respected among the Great Powers of Europe – and it is often forgotten today that this happened not after the Second World War, but at the beginning of the eighteenth century – it became customary to attribute the unlimited powers wielded by her sovereigns to all her past rulers, going back in time practically to the beginnings of the Kievan state. For this belief there is no foundation in fact.

The synthesis of the Muscovite seigneurial system, of Mongol despotism and of Byzantine Caesaropapism, in the distinctive form of Russian autocracy, can be said to have first emerged, after a lengthy period of germination, in the middle of the sixteenth century. More than any other man, it owes its crystallization, both in theory and in practice, to Ivan the Terrible. Whatever posterity may have had to say about Ivan – and its judgment has tended, with every reason, to be a harsh one – there can be no denying the fact that he was a great innovator, even a great revolutionary in the field of government. Ivan left an imprint on Russia that 400 years have failed to erase.

Ivan, a man of considerable education, expounded his views on autocracy, at great length, in one of the most remarkable political documents of Russian history: his correspondence with Prince Kurbsky, a former favourite, who had fled to Lithuania to escape the Tsar's wrath (thus becoming probably the first Russian political defector). From the safety of the West Kurbsky bitterly attacked the Tsar in print, accusing him of having renounced Russia's ancient political traditions, of ruling arbitrarily, without seeking the advice of the boyars, of reducing all to the level of slaves etc. Stung to the quick, Ivan replied in even more abusive terms. Very cleverly, but in complete contradiction of the facts, he set out to prove that he was only following in the footsteps of his ancestors, each of whom, since time immemorial, had possessed absolute, unlimited power; he also gave an entirely new interpretation of the title of autocrat: previously it had only meant a sovereign ruler in his own right, independent of any suzerain – now, for the first time, Ivan took it to mean an absolute, despotic ruler, governing his country as he saw fit, with no bounds set to his authority over his subjects, their lives and their property. Indeed, he made it eminently clear that his subjects, however high their station, were no better than slaves, and their property – his to take at any time he deemed fit.

Rejecting Kurbsky's accusations, he wrote impassionedly:

Is this then the sign of a 'leprous conscience', to hold my kingdom in my hand and not to let my servants rule? And is it contrary to reason not to wish to be possessed and ruled by my own servants? And is this 'illustrious Orthodoxy' – to be ruled over and ordered about by my own slaves? . . .

And as for the godless [i.e. foreign] peoples – why mention them? For none of these rule their own kingdoms. As their servants order them, so too do they rule. But as for the Russian autocracy, they themselves [i.e. the autocrats] from the beginning have ruled all their dominions, and not the boyars and not the grandees . . .

And is this 'darkness', for the tsar to possess his kingdom and for his slaves slavishly to fulfil his orders? How, pray, can a man be called autocrat if he himself does not govern . . .?

And we are free to reward our slaves, and we are also free to punish them . . .

Hitherto the Russian masters were questioned by no man, but they were free to reward and to punish their subjects; and they did not litigate with them before any judge . . .

Am I vainglorious, in that I order my slaves, who are subjected to me by God, to carry out my wishes?[14]

In a country without any basic constitutional laws, where for centuries no attempt was made to define the political system, the structure and functions of government, or even the

41

relationship between government and subjects, the writings of Ivan the Terrible remained until comparatively recent times the most forthright and authoritative exposition of the all-embracing powers of the Russian State, embodied in the person of the autocratic monarch. It was a new and revolutionary concept of government, which, although already partially realized in practice, was undoubtedly foreign to the political system that had existed in ancient Rus. Needless to say, Ivan's doctrine of the State as legitimate proprietor of all that lay or moved within its territories had hardly anything in common with Western theories of the divine rights of kings, theories that derived from an entirely different system of social relationships.

Ivan IV was his own ideologist, but the case he propounded should by no means be regarded as the special pleading of a power-mad despot. His doctrines enjoyed wide support within the literate segment of the public, and especially in Church circles. Similar arguments are to be found in much of the theological and political writing of the time; the case for unlimited autocracy was put forward most cogently by Ivan Peresvetov, Russia's first political theorist. In his pamphlets, explicitly addressed to the Tsar and written a few years before the latter himself took up the pen, Peresvetov argued persuasively for a far-reaching remoulding of the Russian policy on the pattern established in the Turkish Empire. The superiority of the Turkish system was proved by one incontrovertible fact: the taking of Constantinople, an event that had made a profound and lasting impact on Russia. Peresvetov was convinced, as was his royal master, that the principal cause of the fall of Constantinople had been the limited nature of the Byzantine Emperor's authority. Not so the Turks – and the Russians should draw the obvious inference: 'Should they but combine that Turkish rule with the Christian faith, and the very angels would descend amongst them.'[15]

Of all the admirable features of the Turkish political system, one in particular was repeatedly stressed by Peresvetov: the permanent use of terror as the mainstay of the monarch's authority. 'If the king is gentle and timid upon his throne,' he wrote, 'his kingdom weakens and his fame declines. If the king is terrible and wise upon his throne, then his kingdom grows and his fame resounds through every land ... If the people are not kept in great dread they will never obey the laws. As a horse without a bridle is under its rider, so is a kingdom without dread under its king.'[16]

These were sentiments after the Tsar's own heart. 'The rule of a Tsar,' he wrote to Kurbsky, 'because of the folly of the most wicked and cunning men, calls for fear and suppression and bridling and extreme suppression.'[17] Ivan was nothing if not consistent, for during his reign the calculated use of terror – swift, widespread, unpredictable and relentless – for the first time became the main instrument of Russian government.

In a country as vast, as sparsely populated and as turbulent as Russia, with vague frontiers and poor communications, with meagre resources and unstable social relationships, engaged in a life or death struggle for national existence, sheer physical terror – 'fear and suppression and bridling and extreme suppression' – seemed the most efficacious method of sustaining law and order, implementing necessary reforms, intensifying the national effort, and obtaining the unconditional submission of every subject to the will of the State. Ivan set a high standard for his successors.

In their perennial campaign to rehabilitate Ivan, and incidentally to prove the conformity of the Russian historical process to the general stages of European development, Soviet historians have consistently belittled the well-authenticated horrors of his reign, and portrayed him as a typical medieval monarch, no harsher than other strong rulers, such as Philip le Bel, Louis XI, Richard III or Henry VIII. This suggestion does not bear scrutiny. Ivan IV succeeded to the throne of a state that had already been unified and centralized; he was compelled neither to defend his title to the throne, nor to combat a powerful and independent Church, nor to put down the private armies of rebellious nobles. The enemies of his country and of his reign were all external – yet simultaneously with his foreign wars he conducted what can only be described as a ceaseless military campaign against his own subjects.

His policy was a strange mixture of farsightedness and paranoia – a combination frequently reproduced by his successors through the centuries. Ivan carried the process of gathering the Russian lands to its logical conclusion by killing off the greater part of the boyars: the old apanage princes, their descendants, families and courts. This labour of love was not limited, as were similar actions of Western European centralizing monarchs, to the execution of a few obstreperous and over-powerful vassals, for it invariably flowed over into the frenzied massacre of thousands of innocuous house-servants, slaves, tenants or anybody else who had been somehow connected with the object of the Tsar's insane suspicions.

The most hideous example of the new doctrine of mass-murder as an act of State policy was the tragic fate of Novgorod. In 1570 the Tsar, for some inexplicable reason, became doubtful of the loyalty of this magnificent and opulent city, Russia's sole important centre of international trade (no proofs of treasonable dealings have ever been discovered). Descending upon it out of the blue, he proceeded to subject the city – one of his own valuable possessions – to a systematic sack, rapine and pillage that exceeded the most grisly savageries of the invading Mongols. Thousands, perhaps even tens of thousands of peaceful inhabitants were put to death by various fiendish methods born in the fertile imagination of their lawful sovereign: impaling, flaying alive, boiling, roasting on spits, frying in gigantic skillets, evisceration and most mercifully, drowning. Novgorod never recovered, and Russia herself was the loser.

With every due allowance for his occasional fits of homicidal mania, Tsar Ivan's policy was undoubtedly one of calculated frightfulness. In the specific conditions of Russia, where Western methods of government were plainly impracticable, a certain amount of bloodletting, sufficiently lurid to catch the imagination, went a very long way towards instilling the fear of God, and of the Tsar, in the mind of even the most dull-witted of his subjects. It was the best method for producing fear, and fear was the surest basis of obedience.

The chief instruments of Tsar Ivan's terroristic policy were the *Oprichniki*, the first political police in Russia's history. This body of 6000 picked cutthroats was established with the general purpose of extirpating even the most insignificant seeds of disloyalty, and with the more specific aim of physically destroying the ancient boyar families. In carrying out their task they showed neither squeamishness nor lack of enthusiasm; so successful were they that after a few years' intensive activity the Tsar could afford to have the most prominent *Oprichniki* themselves consigned to an appropriately painful death. They left a name that was never to be forgotten, and one of the most lasting of Russian traditions.

The institution of the political police, with their black uniforms and even more terrifying dog's head emblems, was only a part of a still more ambitious enterprise of the Tsar's, namely the establishment of a genuine, full-blooded police state covering almost half the country. Russia was divided into two parts, and in the half that was called *Oprichnina* the ancient customs and laws were officially declared suspended, and the Tsar was able to rule in full accordance with his doctrines. This peculiar experiment of a state within a state was not long-lived, but it marked a significant stage in the consolidation of the Russian system of despotic government.

For all the unique extravagances and aberrations of his reign, Ivan the Terrible was by no means a transient phenomenon in Russian history. In a largely illiterate community a very effective yardstick towards measuring a monarch's place in the history of his country is provided by the image he engraved in the people's collective memory. The impression left by Ivan the Terrible, recorded in countless legends, ballads and folk-songs, was far deeper than that made by any other Tsar (the reputation of Peter the Great was much more of a literary than a popular effort). The most significant aspect of this is that Ivan's reputation was, on the whole, a highly favourable one: neither that of an ineffectual and pious despot, as with the early Romanovs, nor of a tobacco-consuming and foreigner-besotted Antichrist, like Peter, but of the Dread Tsar – stern and harsh, as befitted the times, but always with the best interests of the nation at heart. This is all the more remarkable because the record of the latter part of Ivan's long reign was one largely of failure, engendering stresses and tensions that were soon to explode in the cataclysm of the Time of Troubles.

The Russian political system and the general condition of the country were such that even his notoriously meek successors could on occasion be just as vicious and cruel, although their atrocities never had the sombre and awe-inspiring grandeur of Ivan's reign of terror. Whatever his reputation in the West, it was not because of his all too familiar cruelty that the Dread Tsar remained for his people the greatest of their rulers: he was, in the fullest sense of the word, the father of his country, the man who had conquered the evil Mongol overlord, given his people unlimited territories for settlement, and laid down the firm foundation on which the Russian State was reared.

It was in the reign of Ivan IV that the previously blurred outline of a State commanding the totality of powers, with unlimited and unquestioned authority over every subject, took on clear and definite shape. The rudimentary elective institutions of local and central government, that had somehow still lingered on, were now deprived of all genuine content. With the complete centralization of the administrative structure local elected bodies and their officers were transformed into State officials, bureaucrats whose duty consisted no longer in running local affairs, but in executing the orders of the central administration, and who were obliged to fulfil these duties under pain of direst punishment. As for the ancient Popular Assembly – the *Zemsky Sobor* – from now on it became, in Kliuchevsky's words, nothing but 'a conference between the Government and its own agents ... In sixteenth-century Muscovy it was considered that the people had no business electing the representatives of their own will, but that God had for this end specially provided an eternal authority: the Government and its servants, and it was these who constituted the real State. In other words, the people had no right to a will of their own, but were obliged to think in accordance with the will of the authorities that represented them.'[18]

The final death of Russia's vestigial representative bodies was a development in no way comparable to the eclipse of Western European parliamentarianism in the sixteenth and seventeenth centuries. Absolute monarchy was not nearly as absolute as its name implied. In Tudor England the importance of Parliament had temporarily decreased, yet even under Henry VIII debate remained fairly free, and the Commons actually rejected a number of measures desired by the government, and amended others. In France the *Etats-Généraux* withered away, but the local *parlements* and similar bodies flourished, retaining and even extending their wide powers, and not infrequently refusing to obey the royal will. The same applies to Spain, the Netherlands, Sweden, and other European nations.

In Russia the only rights that remained were those of the State, and these were total and limitless. Giles Fletcher provides a vivid eye-witness description of the *Zemsky Sobor* at work. Although by no means a believer in popular sovereignty, Queen Elizabeth's Ambassador was clearly shocked by what he saw, 'for to propound bils what every man thinketh good for the publike benefite (as the manner is in England), the Russe parliament knoweth no such custome nor libertie to subjects'. He drily adds that after the court official had read out the law proposed by the Tsar, the assembly would be asked for their assent, 'which they used to do without any great pausing . . . For as touching any lawe or publique order of the realme, it is ever determined of before any publique assemblie or parliament bee summoned.'[19]

From one end of the enormous country to the other the monarch had become the sole and undisputed source of laws and regulations, appointments and dismissals, rewards and punishments, taxes and impositions; he was master over war and peace, life and death. In the words of Adam Olearius, another dumbfounded representative of Western so-called absolute monarchy: 'He is not subject to the Lawes; he onely makes them, and all the Muscovites obey him, with so great submission, that they are so farre from opposing his will, that they say, the Justice and word of their Prince is sacred and inviolable. He onely creates Magistrates, and deposes them, ejects them, and orders them to be punished, with absolute power.'[20]

The centralized autocratic State held every aspect of the nation's life within its grip. There was no room left for the autonomous activity of either individual, local community, or social class. The position is best summed up in Kliuchevsky's brilliant phrase: 'The State waxed fat, while the people grew lean.'[21] For centuries this was to remain the basic pattern of Russian history.

CHAPTER 4

The State over Society

1

Faced with tasks of overwhelming complexity, for which their available resources were clearly inadequate, the Russian people and their leaders had slowly and laboriously fashioned an instrument that would be capable of meeting the manifold challenge: a State stronger than the society above which it was raised. In its turn the State inevitably proceeded to mould the structure of society in accordance with its specific requirements. 'In Russia the State had an enormous influence on the social structure,' wrote Miliukov, 'whereas in the West it was the social structure that determined the system of government ... The primitive condition of Russia's economic "basis" caused the hypertrophy of the "superstructure" of the State and ensured the strong counter-effect of this superstructure upon the "basis" itself.'[1]

The transformation of the Russian social structure into a system where all became compliant and powerless dependants of the State was consummated primarily through the organization of the nation's defence. Defence was the *raison d'être* of the omnipotent State; its most vital task was the creation, under extremely unfavourable conditions, of an optimally efficient system for the mobilization of the nation's scattered human and material resources. The method evolved was one based on the bondage of the entire population, on the *pomestie* system of service lands, and on serfdom.

The government's paramount concern was with the establishment and maintenance of an immense standing army for permanent duty on the southern frontier and for service against Russia's western enemies. Fighting-men were available,

49

since the courts of the old apanage princes had always disposed of large numbers of servitors who had no inclination for seeking a meagre livelihood in the inhospitable forests of the North-East; the problem was how to support them. In a country with an economy as primitive as Russia's, payment, either in money or in kind, was out of the question. Of one commodity only did she possess an abundant supply, and that was land. The essential nexus between landholding and State service became the cornerstone of Russia's military organization, and, by the same token, of her social structure as well.

The practice of remunerating the monarch's fighting-men by grants of land conditional upon service was started by Ivan III. It was a most convenient method: land was there for the taking, and since the newly colonized territories had never belonged to any of the original East Slavonic tribes, the State's property rights were unchallenged. The conditional service landholding was called *pomestie*; the landholder was the *pomeshchik*.

The granting of service land exclusively in the newly colonized territories was in itself, however, insufficient to meet the requirements of the State. On the one hand, this did not necessarily guarantee the warriors' permanent presence in those regions where it was most needed, while on the other hand, it contributed nothing towards the more important task of mobilizing for defence the resources of the already settled, and richer part of the country.

The greater portion of the land in the Russian principalities gathered together by Moscow had belonged to the old aristocracy, the boyars – the apanage princes, their numerous relatives and descendants – who held it as *votchina* land, in absolute and unconditional ownership. Within a relatively short space of time, however, the rulers of Muscovy, basing themselves on the principle – inherited from the Khans – of their supreme ownership of all the land in the realm, and fully utilizing their monopoly of armed force, had irreversibly demolished the very idea of full, allodial private landownership.

A few years after the annexation of Novgorod Ivan III began

this process by simply dispossessing eight thousand landowners of the principality, who were compensated by grants of *pomestie* in outlying parts of his kingdom. The lands thus requisitioned were assigned, on conditional military tenure, to trusted serving-men from Moscow. This two-way resettlement lasted for some years, and was followed by similar sweeping actions in the other former apanage principalities: Riazan, Pskov, Tver, etc. They involved vast population movements, the forcible eviction, dispossession and deportation of virtually the whole landowning class, the creation of a new class of conditional landowners, and the establishment of a novel and highly significant principle of landholding – derived exclusively from the State and depending wholly upon service rendered to the State. Although the concept itself was not yet in existence, this was in fact none other than the nationalization of the land.

The inception and rapid development of the *pomestie* system became, as many Russian historians have pointed out, one of the most momentous events in the country's history, a genuine revolution in its political, social and economic life. It was largely effected, as so much else, in the reign of Ivan the Terrible, through the agency of the *Oprichnina*, and its killings, tortures and exiles; the government made short work of the remnants of boyar independence, and achieved the virtual assimilation of allodial *votchina* property to *pomestie* holding.

The basic principles of the new system, as finally evolved in the seventeenth century, were simple and straightforward. All land was service land (or, as Max Weber called it, 'liturgical' land – in the original Greek meaning of the word 'liturgia' as compulsory service in the interests of the community). Everybody who served the State had the right, and indeed the obligation, to hold State land, and conversely, all landholders were *ipso facto* servants of the State. None outside the ranks of the 'Sovereign's serving-men' had the right to hold land, under any conditions whatsoever.

This did not, however, mean the establishment in Russia of a new ruling class or privileged estate. On the contrary, the introduction of the *pomestie* system marked the degradation of the erstwhile 'free serving-men', the *pomeshchiki* or noblemen (*dvoriane*, from *dvornia* or house servants), to the status of 'the Sovereign's slaves', as they called themselves, bound in perpetuity to the service of the centralized State. There was no question of service being voluntary: a number of laws were passed (1550, 1558 and 1672), expressly prohibiting serving-men from selling themselves into slavery in order to avoid life-long compulsory military service – a loophole that had apparently been frequently utilized. This was no feudal contract of mutual fealty, no act of vassalage or commendation. The landholding nobleman was tied to the State by bonds of compulsion; he owed it a life-long obligation of service, but received no privileges in return. By the end of the sixteenth century, remarks Miliukov, 'the former free servant finally became enthralled; his relationship to the government became completely compulsory'.[2] He was granted land not as a fief, but as an act of grace, based on the suzerain's absolute sovereignty, and for the exclusive purpose of supporting himself and his family during his service. Previously the ruler had rewarded his fighting-men *for* their service, now they were being remunerated *in order to enable* them to carry out their obligations towards the State. Land was granted only for actual service; in case of the holder's death or disability it reverted to the State, which conferred it either on his sons (if any), or his son-in-law, or on anyone else it deemed fit. But the nobleman's obligations towards the State transcended the principle of mere repayment for the land he had received: in those cases when he was in a position to support himself without a *pomestie* (if, for instance, he owned an allodial *votchina* – before that form of property was abolished), he still could not contract out of his unquestioned duty of faithfully serving the State for the term of his natural life. In other words, the new Russian aristocracy of serving nobility that emerged during the sixteenth century was nothing but a peculiar class of soldier-serfs, bound to their condition in perpetuity by the all-powerful State.

This represented a critically important dissimilarity between the social structures of Russia and of Europe. Muscovy, as

Plekhanov noted in his *History of Russian Social Thought*, 'diverged from the Western nations by reducing to bondage not only the lower, peasant class, but the upper, serving class as well . . . In the conditions then prevailing in Muscovy the serving-man could not but become a slave, even under a ruler personally disinclined to tyranny.'[3] In the West, of course, the long-drawn-out struggle between the monarchy and its powerful vassals also ended in the victory of the centralizing forces. But what a totally different picture that victory presented: the aristocracy retained a uniquely privileged position, no restrictions were placed on its property rights – rather the contrary, and, the very notion of its compulsory service, to say nothing of its bondage, was inconceivable. Indeed, with the rapid development of the economy, kings made haste to do away with their military dependence on the lords by engaging mercenary armies.

In Russia the aristocracy was not merely subdued or tamed: having been deprived of every privilege and even of its basic right of full landownership, it was left unreservedly at the mercy of the State that had placed it in bondage. This situation was by no means unforeseen by, or unwelcome to the government: Peresvetov, for example, had strongly urged the general introduction of the *pomestie* system upon Tsar Ivan IV, arguing that as a result of this the Tsar would be free 'to torment his nobles to his heart's content, and to make game of his boyars as if they were children; the nobles will fear him, and never dare to spin their wicked plots against him'.[4]

The sad fate of the ancient Russian aristocracy and the means by which it was encompassed were described with great accuracy by that alert and perspicacious observer, Dr Giles Fletcher. Having taken away their patrimonies, the Tsar instead 'gave them other landes of the tenour of *pomestnoy* (as they call it), that are helde at the emperours pleasure, lying farre of in an other countrey; and so removed them into other of his provinces, where they might have neyther favour nor authoritie, not being native nor well knowen there . . . In the end he made them not onelie his vassals, but his *Kolophey* [i.e.

53

kholopy, or slaves], that is, his very villains or bondslaves. For so they terme and write themselves in anie publike instrument or private petition which they make to the emperour. So that now they holde their authorities, landes, lives and all at the emperours pleasure, as the rest doe.'[5]

The only substantial element missing from Fletcher's excellent description is the fact that this exotic social, political and military system was based on undoubtedly Oriental models. The *pomestie* was a Russian copy of the Byzantine *pronoia* and the Turkish *timar.* And although with the passing of time, under the influence of human nature and for reasons of administrative convenience, the land gradually came to be treated as the *pomeshchiks'* hereditary property, their rights were never really transformed into full private ownership, that could be alienated without restriction to the buyer of their choice. Always the State loomed above them, with its undefined yet tangible overlordship. It was not just a bizarre atavism that made Nicholas II, the last Russian Tsar, describe his occupation in the 1897 census returns as 'Master of the Russian land'.

The *pomestie* became a crucially important factor in the development of the distinctive Russian system of society. By the introduction of its two main elements – land nationalization, and unlimited governmental authority over the persons of the landholders – the State had become not only independent of society, but overwhelmingly powerful in relation to it. Within this rigid scheme of things no rival power-centre could arise; no opportunity existed for the emergence of a class similar to the feudal aristocracy of Europe, which could serve as a counter-weight – or at least a check – to the ambitions of the centralized State. The new serving aristocracy, created by State fiat, with no traditions or roots among the people, possessing neither corporate privileges nor landed property, could not even dream of challenging the long-established and strongly entrenched authority of the Muscovite State. It was not, nor could it ever become, a genuine landed aristocracy in any accepted meaning of the word, since its position was based not on landownership, but on State service, and its powers, such as they were, derived exclusively from the State. It was not treated as a separate estate of the realm (the very idea being foreign to Russian society), nor could it develop a real corporate spirit: it remained throughout Russian history an atomized, inert mass, with no secure institutions, traditions, or privileges that could stand between its individual members and the omnipotent State. Nor could the new nobility become a class of landlords, a squirearchy. Its members were far too busy serving the State to be able to devote the necessary attention to running their estates or to evolving a manorial economy. This detachment of the Russian nobles from the land, and the weakness of property in general, was further fostered by the peculiar Russian law of inheritance, which provided neither for primogeniture nor for entail, and led to the permanent splitting-up of estates and to the further fragmentation of landed property.

To the end the Russian aristocracy remained a class of serving nobility, occupied with their State duties, weak politically, legally and economically, incapable of playing an important independent role in the life of their country.

The pressing demands of defence and colonization thus caused the establishment of a serving nobility of conditional landholders; this in turn inexorably led to the reduction of the peasantry – the vast majority of the population – to a condition of servile bondage that became in many of its aspects indistinguishable from classical slavery. The origin and development of Russian serfdom presents a vague and hazy picture, because, like so much else of Russian social history, it was never at any stage defined in the concise language of law. It developed in a nebulous, random and often contradictory fashion. In the famous words of Alexander Radishchev, the first Russian revolutionary, serfdom was 'a grim monster, savage, gigantic, hundred-mouthed, and bellowing' – but a monster that was shapeless as well as hideous.

Up to the sixteenth century the Russian peasant, as opposed to the numerous category of slaves or *kholopy*, was, by and large, free. He tilled the landowner's fields, but he was a free man, able to move at will – provided he was not in debt to his master.

Freedom from debt, however, became increasingly more difficult to achieve, for the land was poor, and the return it offered insufficient to repay, with interest, the odd loan received to set up a homestead or to tide the peasant over a bad patch. The peasant debtor began to be transformed imperceptibly into a debt-slave – a condition at first understood to be purely temporary, but gradually hardening into permanent bondage.

The decisive impetus towards serfdom came with the introduction of the *pomestie* system, simultaneously with the beginning of the reconquest of the South and with the opening-up to colonization of the great empty spaces of the East and the South-East. These events had two important consequences. On the one hand, grants of *pomestie* were now made largely in territories as yet free of inhabitants. At the same time a spontaneous mass migration of peasants began to the rich black soil of the Don and the Volga, so extensive as to threaten the settled regions of the country with depopulation.

Land, never an object of particular value in Russia, was practically worthless without peasants to work it. The landholders vied in enticing each other's tenants away, settling their debts and granting them new loans. In exchange they usually extracted an obligation by which the peasant renounced in perpetuity his own and his descendants' rights to leave the service of his new master. In other words, he lost his status of freeman, and became, to all intents and purposes, a bond slave. Yet this was not easy to enforce, with the lure of the open spaces ever tempting the peasant to pull up his stakes and start a new life further on in the limitless steppe. A new master and a fresh loan would always await him, and no questions asked.

The government viewed these developments with increasing alarm. The growing shortage of labour and its continuing freedom of movement not only posed the danger of decisively shifting the country's population balance, but could well make impossible the object of the *pomestie* system: the creation of a permanent military class supported by land grants from the State. Inability to provide service land with a permanent supply of labour was bad enough, but Moscow was perhaps even more apprehensive about the mounting tendency for peasants to renounce their condition and to join the ranks of the chattel slaves. If allowed to continue unchecked, this process would have brought down the whole financial structure of the country, based as it was upon the heavy taxation of the non-serving majority of the free population. The State tax – *tyaglo*, or burden – had been introduced during the period of the Tartar yoke as a means of collecting the tribute demanded by the Horde, and continued, growing ever heavier, by the Tsars after independence. It was assessed not upon individuals, but upon land, with payment shared between the peasant tenants. *Kholopy*, however, being by definition the full legal property of their masters, were exempt alike from the rights and the obligations of the Tsar's subjects, and therefore constituted a dead loss to the State.

The mass transference of free peasants into a non-*tyaglo*-paying condition had to be stopped, and a solution found that would take into account the interests alike of the State and of the landholding serving nobility, or in other words – reducing these categories to their common denomination – meet both the fiscal and the defence requirements of the State. The solution evolved in the sixteenth and seventeenth centuries consisted of the imposition of the Statute of Bondage, or of serfdom, as it is commonly called in the West – although Russian serfdom cannot be properly equated with the corresponding Western European institution, however close the seeming resemblance between them.

From the middle of the sixteenth century the government began to restrict the peasants' freedom of movement from one master to another; in the last years of the century all such movement was finally and completely prohibited: the peasants were now bound to the land.

This was probably the most important single development in the history of Russian society. Not only did it vitally concern the great bulk of the population: it created an entirely new set of relationships between the State and the two main classes of society – the nobility, and the peasantry.

'The state created serfdom as a means of assuring itself of a reliable source of revenue in a situation in which land was plentiful but labour was scarce, and agriculture was the principal source of income,' says a distinguished American scholar.[6] Fiscal considerations undoubtedly provided the main incentive for the introduction of serfdom by the State; this system ensured the government's stable administrative and financial control over the whole country to a degree that could not, at that stage, have been achieved by any other means. Yet the social and political consequences of serfdom were immeasurably greater than any mere improvement of bureaucratic efficiency or increase in the State's revenues. It signified the reduction of the nobility to final impotence, for whereas in the West the establishment of serfdom had been the direct result of the enfeeblement and even the disintegration of the centralized State and of the corresponding aggrandizement of the territorial magnates, in Russia it was instituted and sustained at the command of, and in the interests of, a State already wielding the totality of power. It also transformed the peasantry, the bulk of the country's population, into a class probably without parallel in any other society: into the category of 'tax-paying slaves' (*tyaglye kholopy*).

For the State this was a tidy and definitive method of harnessing the full manpower potential of a backward, poor, and underpopulated country for the solution of formidable national tasks. By the middle of the seventeenth century, partly because of the intense labour shortage caused by the Time of Troubles, the previous sharp distinction between full slaves and free peasants had been erased: both of these had merged into the new class of serfs.

The serfs constituted a social class founded on a unique dichotomy. On the one hand – and this is what has made the problem a source of considerable bafflement – they were regarded as full-fledged subjects of the Tsar, and therefore quite different from the category of slaves that they had largely superseded. They enjoyed no rights – nor did anyone else – but in serving the masters to whom they had been bound in perpetuity they were essentially discharging their obligation towards their supreme proprietor, the State: feeding and supporting the State's serving-men, and thus making it possible for the latter to spend their lifetimes in combating the nation's enemies. In the eyes of the government the serfs occupied the same legal position as the land on which they worked: they were assets belonging to the State, but temporarily ceded into private ownership as a reward for military service. This official view was put forward very clearly in the reign of Peter the Great by Pososhkov, the first Russian political economist: 'The land they [the *pomeshchiki*] all occupy belongs in eternity to the Tsar, and is granted to the *pomeshchiki* temporarily, for their support . . . The *pomeshchiki* are not the peasants' permanent owners, and this is why they do not take much care of them; the peasants' direct proprietor is the Autocrat of all the Russias, and their [the *pomeshchiki's*] ownership is but temporary.'[7]

In a weird and uniquely Russian way the serf continued to possess certain attributes of an equal member of society. Until the middle of the eighteenth century he took the oath of allegiance to the Tsar, and could complain to the authorities about the treatment he received at the hands of his master. After the reforms of Peter the Great he was liable for military service. Yet at the same time he was a chattel slave, in the fullest sense of the word, indeed doubly so – a slave both of the State and of his master.

The evolution of serfdom into a peculiar form of full slavery was greatly facilitated by the vagueness and equivocality of the serfs' legal position, and by the complete absence of legislation regulating the relationship between serf and master. As Miliukov remarked, 'the ambiguity of relationships constituted the essence of our serfdom'.[8] In these circumstances it was perhaps inevitable that the ancient and well-established Russian tradition of slavery should gain a new lease of life, and that the customs and methods of a slave-holding society should gradually have been transposed to the new and indeterminate institution of serfdom.

The serf was bound to his master unconditionally. The only limitation the State set on the *pomeshchik*'s authority over his serf was to ensure the peasant's continued ability to pay his tax – the basis of the Russian financial system. The serf had to be given a plot of land to establish his obligation to pay *tyaglo* – it was in this way that former *kholopy* were transformed into serfs. Previously the peasant had payed *tyaglo for* the tax-bearing land that he tilled; now, in the conditions of a service-bound society, he was compulsorily attached to a plot of land *in order to be in a position* to pay tax.

In every other respect the landowner's powers soon became absolute and unlimited. He could, and did, raise his demands upon the serfs' labour at will. Already in the seventeenth century he treated them as his chattels: they were taken off the land (if substituted by another tax-payer), transferred to household service, separated from their families, exchanged, and even sold. The master acquired the right to try his serfs, to torture them, to incarcerate them in his own gaol, to impose upon them the full range of punishment, including death: he was disciplined for killing a serf only if the dead man had belonged to another master, in which case the victim was to be replaced. The serf's property rights closely resembled the Roman law concept of *peculium*, according to which the master might allow his slave to possess a certain amount of property that he could treat as his own, but in the eyes of the law this property always continued to belong to the master.

For foreign observers there was never any doubt that Russian serfdom was equivalent to what the West had known as slavery, the difference being that, unlike Greece or Rome, in Russia the vast majority of the population belonged to this category. In the sixteenth century, Fletcher reported: 'This may truly be saide of them, that there is no servant nor bondslave more awed by his maister, nor kept downe in a more servile subjection, then the poore people are, and that universally, not only by the emperour, but by his nobilitie, chief officers and souldiers

. . . Concerning the landes, goods, and other possessions of the commons, they answer the name – lie common indeed without any fence against the rapine and spoile, not only of the highest, but of his nobilitie, officers and souldiers.'[9] By Olearius' day the situation had become even worse: 'Masters dispose of their slaves as they do of any other moveable; nay, a father may sell his son, and alienate him, for his own advantage.'[10]

However, these reports touched upon only one aspect of the problem, and could not convey the extremely complex and contradictory nature of the phenomenon of Russian serfdom. The serf became in actual fact little better than a chattel slave, yet he always remained a subject of the Tsar. The *pomeshchik*, however unlimited his authority, held only secondary rights to the person of his serf, rights that were derived from the primary owner, the State. He was at once proprietor and guardian of his serf. As such, he had to perform a variety of functions. In his capacity of slaveowner he alienated the serf's labour, and, if necessary, even his body for his own personal needs. In his capacity of guardian he simultaneously assumed the duties of government representative, exercising responsibility for, and control over the fulfilment by the serf of his State obligations; of magistrate, meting out justice to the serfs, and conveying their grievances to the appropriate governmental authorities; of police inspector, responsible for upholding law and order, and for the good behaviour of his serfs; and of tax-collector, charged with gathering the full amount of taxes assessed upon his serfs by the State, and with delivering it to the exchequer. Performing the manifold obligatory duties of his office, the landowner gradually developed into a State official, holding a key position in the country's administrative system. 'The landowning class,' says Kliuchevsky, 'became a nationwide police and fiscal agency of the state exchequer; from a rival it was transformed into an employee.'[11]

Despite the extreme centralization of the Russian administrative system, it was able to operate with any degree of efficiency only by delegating some of its functions to non-professional (and non-voluntary) auxiliaries like the serving nobility, and to compulsory associations set up for the joint performance by groups of subjects of their duties towards the State. The most important of these associations was the village community, the *obshchina* or *mir*.

The village community occupies a very special place in Russian social history, not only for the great part it played in the everyday lives of the people, but because in the *Weltanschauung* of the nineteenth-century Russian intelligentsia, in the voluminous writings of their social and political thinkers, and in the theoretical projections of the revolutionary movements, it acquired a mystique and a significance entirely separate from its actual functioning. The community came to be exalted as the repository of the ancient democratic virtues and the innate socialistic tendencies of the Russian people, as a unique form of collective life that, having miraculously survived through the centuries, set them apart from other, less spiritual and more grossly materialistic nations. The reality, as established in the late nineteenth century by a number of brilliant Russian historians, beginning with Chicherin, was somewhat less exciting.

The *obshchina*, it transpired, did not go back into the hoary mists of antiquity, but was a comparatively recent institution, dating approximately from the sixteenth and seventeenth centuries. It was a compulsory fiscal group, created, if not on the direct initiative of the State, then at least with its active encouragement, to ensure the orderly payment of *tyaglo* by its members. It was based upon the principle of the joint performance by its members of their tax-paying duty, on the collective responsibility, and indeed under the collective guarantee of the community as a whole. To cope with its task the *obshchina* gradually gained wide-ranging powers: it distributed the tax obligation among its members, enforced payment, prevented members from escaping (which would have meant a corresponding increase in the tax burden of the remaining peasants); later it became responsible for supplying recruits, administering punishments, exiling lazy or criminal members to Siberia, etc. Its most important function became the management of the village's economy, the provision of the wherewithal to pay tax by assigning each member a plot of land (itself called a *tyaglo*), roughly commensurate with the size of his family. The community periodically reapportioned the land among its members, and it was this feature that, perhaps more than any other, fired the imagination of the early social scientists.

The Russian village community was a remarkable institution. It gave the wretched serf a certain feeling of security, it enabled him to cast off his individual identity (something he could hardly have had much use for), and blend into a tight circle of his fellows, indistinguishable one from the other, huddled together for warmth and protection, sharing a common fate. He called it the *mir* – the world, the universe – and that is exactly what it was for him. It was democratic in a primitive way – decisions were taken at general assemblies of all members – and Wittfogel has aptly called it a Beggars' Democracy, for it was the democracy of men who could not even call their bodies their own, and for whom it meant all the difference between brutish and degraded slavery, and a semblance of human dignity.

The *obshchina*, in short, constitutes another peculiarly Russian paradox. It was an autonomous peasant community, running its own affairs with no outside interference, on democratic and egalitarian lines, wielding considerable authority – but every single one of its members was the landowner's chattel, to be bartered or sold with impunity. The reason why it could reconcile the seemingly irreconcilable, and endow a slave with the right to take independent decisions, was because in reality it represented the basic administrative unit of the country, the vital cog on which, in the final analysis, the Russian economic and financial system turned. The village community could lead an existence and play a part independent of the landowner, even though it was composed entirely of his bond slaves, because its principal function was service to the State, the common master of lord and serf alike. This has been admirably summed up by Miliukov: 'The Russian *obshchina* is a compulsory organization that imposes upon its members a collective responsibility for the regular discharge of the payments and obligations that have been placed upon them, and which achieves this regularity by adjusting each member's paying capacity to the obligations he carries.'[12] The *obshchina* was the agency through which the State could mobilize the energies and resources of the peasant serfs towards the solution of its tasks.

It was within the *obshchina* that the Russian serf's dual nature, at once the *pomeshchik*'s slave and the Tsar's subject, was most clearly manifested. He was no less a slave for this – if anything, his load became even heavier – but he was not wholly his master's private property. Above them both towered the State. The paradoxes and contradictions of the Russian social structure all stemmed from the single, overriding fact that this was a society, every class and every individual member of which was bound, in one form or another, in perpetual service to an all-powerful State.

CHAPTER 5

The Institutionalization of the Autocracy

The institutions of the *pomestie* and of 'tax-paying slavery', or serfdom, were the twin levers by means of which Russia was transformed into a service-bound society. It was a long and painful process, which can be said, very roughly, to have taken place in three main stages. The first two were the reign of Ivan IV, in which the foundations of the system were laid down, and the Time of Troubles (1605–13), when for a few fearful years it seemed as if the State itself had dissolved in chaos and anarchy. The third stage was one of reconstruction and completion: the pieces were picked up, sorted out, rearranged, and assembled in a durable structure of society that was to last, with surprisingly little basic change, for more than two centuries. This was achieved in the reigns of the first two Tsars of the new Romanov dynasty, particularly in that of Alexei Mikhailovich (1645–76); the system was reduced to order in the first Russian Code of Laws, or *Ulozhenie*, which was adopted in 1649 and remained in force until 1833.

The *Ulozhenie* was urgently needed. What little law there was had crumbled and disappeared in the whirlwind of the Time of Troubles. The election of a new dynasty had solved one crisis, but began another: continuity had been broken, the vitally important tradition according to which all Russia constituted the patrimony of the descendants of Rurik had been shattered, and this in turn had gravely undermined the principles of customary law. Moreover, Russia had embarked on a series of practically never-ending wars against her much more highly developed western neighbours, which, coming so soon after the disasters of the beginning of the century, and added to her continued struggle against the emboldened southern nomads, taxed her meagre resources to the utmost limits. Order had to be established, and society regimented, in a much more systematic way than before.

The adoption of the *Ulozhenie* marks a turning-point in Russian history. In the words of the *Cambridge Economic History of Europe*, from that day 'begins modern history, or the period of the *Polizeistaat*, continuing until 1861 and, politically speaking, even until 1905'.[1] The *Ulozhenie* summed up and institutionalized the principal social development of the preceding one and a half centuries: the rigid division of Russian society into watertight hereditary categories, each member of which, together with his descendants, was bound to a lifetime's service of the State in the condition and station in which the Code found him.

The famous nineteenth-century Russian historian Boris Chicherin formulated the essence of the *Ulozhenie* most succinctly: 'This meant the bondage not of any one particular estate, but of all the estates as a whole; it meant the imposition of a State burden upon everyone, whoever he might be. All without exception were obliged to serve the State for the term of their lifetimes, each in his allotted place; serving-men on the field of battle, and in civil administration; tax-bound individuals, whether townspeople or peasants, by discharging the various services, taxes and duties that had been laid upon them. The landowners' peasants also fulfilled their duty to the State, over and above this . . . by serving their masters, and thus making it possible for them, in turn, to perform their own compulsory State service.'[2]

The main object of the 1649 Code was the final and complete subjugation of society to the State, achieved by chaining each and every subject in eternity to one particular social station, and compelling them, in this cramped position, to serve the State in accordance with their qualifications, and regardless of their private interests. It established the division of the population into three main classes, each subdivided into numerous strictly defined categories and sub-categories: the serving-men, meticulously graded into 14 sections, from royal councillor to lowliest musketeer; and tax-bound men, classified into 7 categories of townspeople and 4 of peasant serfs; and, finally, the non-*tyaglo*-paying men, divided into the fast-dwindling group of freemen, and into 4 varieties of full slaves.

The *Ulozhenie* was definitely weighted in favour of the serving nobility. This was in recognition of the leading part they had played in putting an end to the Time of Troubles, in the liberation of Moscow from the Poles, in the suppression of peasant and Cossack uprisings and in the election of the Romanovs to the throne. In the early, unsettled years of the new dynasty the nobility exercised a considerable say in the affairs of State. However, with the steady return to normality, the gradual reconstruction of the administrative machinery, and the progressive reassumption by the State of the full range of its unlimited powers, the serving nobility, which had been the chief architect of recovery, but which possessed neither vested privileges nor property rights nor corporate organizations, nor even the will to change their status with regard to the State, inevitably relinquished their temporary position of eminence and relapsed into their familiar role of unquestioning obedience. They did this undoubtedly with a strong feeling of relief and satisfaction at the successful completion of a particularly arduous spell of duty. Nevertheless the first Romanovs, although they soon reverted to autocratic rule as to the manner born, felt the necessity of rewarding the nobility for their past service, and of recompensing them for the increased military burden. The *Ulozhenie* therefore, while finally eliminating full *votchina* right, acknowledged the *pomestie* to be hereditary, together with the obligations attached to it. The ultimate property rights to the land remained, as before, vested in the State, but the landowners' security of tenure had palpably increased.

The balance of Russian society was such, that an improvement in the standing of any one of its interlocking elements could be achieved only by a corresponding deterioration in the position of another. For the peasantry the *Ulozhenie* brought the final legalization of a serfdom that was in most respects indistinguishable from slavery. This verbose, imprecise, contradictory and exceedingly vague document defined nether the peasants' duties to the State, nor their obligations towards the landlords, nor did it attempt to delimit the authority respectively of State and *pomeshchik* – which was perhaps just as well, for even the best European legal minds could hardly have found the precise legal terms to describe the status of someone who was at once a chattel slave, to be bought or sold or lost at cards, and also a full-fledged citizen, owing allegiance and service to his sovereign. What was made abundantly clear – and this proved quite sufficient – was that the peasant had now been bound to his station in perpetuity, with no hope of alleviation.

The peasant was placed in threefold bondage: he was bound to the person of the landlord and to his descendants; he was bound to the soil; and he was bound to his tax-paying estate. Within this triple relationship it was the peasant's bondage to the landlord that soon came to dominate over all else; the State washed its hands of its 'subject', as long as his *tyaglo* was duly paid in. The serf was in bondage to the landowner not as a consequence of being bound to the land, but in a purely personal relationship; indeed, he was bound to the land only insofar as this was necessary to enable him to fulfil his State obligations as a tax-payer.

The *Ulozhenie* also established a new and separate social category: that of townspeople. In view of the enormous part played by the cities and their inhabitants in the history of Western Europe, this might be thought to have been a development of considerable importance. It was not – for the cities of Russia had very little in common with their Western counterparts, those dynamic, opulent and privileged concentrations of commerce, finance, industry and culture, in which modern industrial civilization was born.

Russian cities were few in number and small in size; they were poor, built entirely of wood, and held no privileges whatsoever. Founded as fortresses, they soon acquired the functions of administrative and military centres (the Kremlin – *kreml'* or fortress – famous today the world over for its associations with Moscow, was actually a feature of almost every ancient Russian city). The tradesmen and artisans who catered to the needs of the court and of the military and civil officials, and who established their own settlements (*posady*) outside the fortress walls, remained peasants burdened by all the attributes of peasant status: personal bondage, *tyaglo* and collective responsibility. This degraded position, with its complete lack of security, either of profit or of person, was certainly not conducive to the development of commerce and industry, or to the accumulation of wealth. Giles Fletcher, as the representative of a nation deeply concerned with trade, deplored the absence of incentives and the sad consequences of this state of affairs: 'This maketh the people (although otherwise hardened to beare any toile) to give themselves much to idleness and drinking: as passing for no more than from hand to mouth . . . because the people, being oppressed and spoiled of their gettings, are discouraged from their labours.'[3] This was so much the case that in the course of the sixteenth century and during the Time of Troubles the flight of townspeople to the steppe, and their voluntary conversion to full slavery, resulted in a further marked decline of the cities and of the revenues accruing from them to the State.

The *Ulozhenie* solved this problem by subjecting the townspeople to direct State bondage and to the strictest of regimentation. All private landowners were deprived of their holdings; the towns, together with their suburbs, became Crown property, administered directly by the government. Townspeople were bound irrevocably and in perpetuity to their various callings and to their *tyaglo*; any burgher who attempted to escape from State bondage by selling himself into slavery, or even who merely married into another estate, automatically incurred the death penalty. They were allowed, or, rather, obliged to ply their trades and crafts – in order to be able to pay taxes. The merchants, i.e. members of the highest of the seven categories of townspeople, were officially impressed into State service: they were obliged to serve as tax farmers, customs officers and licensees of State pot-houses, in other words to become State employees and to combine their vocations of private entrepreneurs with those of government fiscal agents.

By establishing a rigid, immutable and hereditary membership of the estate of *posad*-dwellers, or townspeople, the 1649 Code of Laws effectively debarred the Russian cities from fulfilling the historical functions of the European city, and from playing a leading part, or indeed any important part in the economic and social development of their country. Without the fermenting influence of the city Russia was destined to remain a backward peasant nation. For the next 200 years her towns retained their almost exclusive character of administrative centres, inhabited largely by officials, and with a minority population of burghers (*posadskie*) engaged in purveying to the material well-being of the State bureaucracy. In 1701 the only considerable city, Moscow, consisted of 16,000 households: 7500 households of State officials, 1500 of clergy, and only 7000 households (44 per cent) of townspeople as such – almost all employed in court service. By the middle of the eighteenth century the country had a total of 202 towns, but only 214,000 burghers (out of a population of approximately eighteen million), and even of these only a handful, 40,000, were engaged in trade.[4]

Unlike Western Europe, where large-scale industry was established on the basis of existing crafts, and where cottage industry grew by stages into manufactures, in Russia what industry there was developed outside the towns, and independently of existing handicraft skills. Most important of all – industry, when it came, was manned by peasants: not by peasants who became working men, as elsewhere, but by peasants who remained peasants. When in 1632 the first Russian factory – an iron-foundry – was established near Tula by a Dutch concessionaire, the State ensured a permanent and uninterrupted supply of labour by the simple expedient of allocating to it, in perpetuity, the peasants of a whole administrative district (*uyezd*). This marked the birth of a new social category of 'factory peasants', which was to expand considerably in size, without merging with townspeople and without its members divesting themselves of the status, the background, the mentality, or the way of life of peasant serfs.

Until the emancipation edict of 1861, therefore, Russian cities could not become the natural foci of their country's economic and social development. Their population was left to stagnate within the iron bonds of State serfdom and stringent discipline: effectively cut off from industry, burdened with a hinterland that subsisted on natural economy, deprived of privileges, opportunities, and even of the vital inflow of the nation's most enterprising, vigorous, non-conformist and dissatisfied elements, for whom – with very few exceptions – the only remaining escape route led to outlawry in the empty steppe or the trackless forest.

There could never be room in Russia for the emergence of a Third Estate.

There was not, in fact, room for the emergence of any force independent of the State. The heart of the *Ulozhenie* was the principle that every individual belonged first and foremost to the State, and that no one therefore had the right even to renounce his personal liberty, for nobody was his own master. Kliuchevsky put this essential concept very well indeed: 'A free individual, bound to the State in a relationship of *tyaglo* or service, could not repudiate his liberty, and by this means rescind at pleasure the obligations placed upon the free individual by the State: the individual should remain exclusively in the possession and in the service of the State, and could not become the property of anybody else ... In forbidding the individual to enter into any dependent relationships the State was not trying to protect him as a human being or as a citizen, but only preserving him for itself as a soldier or taxpayer. The State was not prohibiting personal slavery in the name of freedom, but transforming personal freedom into slavery in the name of the State interest.'[5] The extraordinary feature of this system was the fact that, by some arcane method of early Russian double-think, the very statute which prohibited personal slavery became at the same time the legal basis for the reduction of the majority of the country's population to what can only be described as chattel slavery. But, although the peasants could be bought and sold with impunity, they were not slaves, for in relationship to the State that owned them both, the landowner was no freer than the serf, the serf not more servile than the master.

To be sure, each had to carry burdens of differing weight, and the serf's lot was incomparably the harder. This was the most characteristic aspect of Muscovite society: it recognized neither the free individual nor the privileged estate, but consisted of social categories distinguished one from the other by the nature of the State obligations carried by each. 'The political system of Muscovy was founded on the distribution among the classes only of duties, divorced from rights ... State obligations became the basis of social divisions, the essential indications of rank or class.'[6] In other words, the difference between the classes boiled down to the difference between various types of State slavery. Where no one was free, no one class of society could be regarded, or could be allowed to regard itself, as slaves.

The fact that every individual was held in full bondage by the State, and that, regardless of social status, he was no more than the Tsar's *kholop*, was very well understood by the Russians themselves. As witness Herberstein: 'All confess themselves to be Chlopos, that is, serfs of the prince.'[7] Or Olearius: 'No Muscovite, what quality soever he be of, but makes it his brag, to be the Great Duke's Golop, or Slave ... The Great Duke speaking to them uses the same expression, treating them in all things like slaves, as far as Whips and Cudgels can do it, which is but consonant to their own acknowledgement, that their persons and estates are God's and the Great Duke's.'[8]

Despite the manifest monstrous injustices of the Russian socio-political system, in this one sense, in the equal absence for all of rights and privileges *vis-à-vis* the State, Russian society can be, and was, regarded as a community based on the principle of equality. As Karamzin was to put it approvingly, nearly two centuries after the *Ulozhenie*: one right, and one right only, was held by every subject of the Tsar – the right to call himself a Russian.[9]

A State constructed on principles such as these was a phenomenon far removed from the types of polity then being evolved in Europe. Berdyaev has described it in uncompromising terms: 'The Orthodox Tsardom of Muscovy was a totalitarian State.'[10] Without, at this stage, going into the accuracy or otherwise of this statement, it is necessary to point out that, however thorough and widely extended the control exercised by the State over the lives, occupations and property of its subjects may have been, it was not, nor could it become, either total or ubiquitous. Given the sheer size of the country, its lack of adequate communications, and the extremely primitive level of its material conditions, the facilities for imposing a total and ubiquitous control were simply non-existent. Moreover: such a degree of control, even if attainable, would have been quite unnecessary; the State could achieve its objectives merely by perpetuating the atomization of society and preventing the emergence of organizations capable of challenging its powers.

The State exercised this control through an inflated, oppressive and predatory bureaucracy.

The administrative apparatus of the bureacratic State had had to be largely rebuilt in the aftermath of the Time of Troubles: not only was its authority gravely undermined, but account had also to be taken of the increased importance of the serving-men. This led to a temporary recrudescence under the first Romanov Tsar, of the ancient institution of the *Zemsky Sobor*. But, despite the severe shocks it had recently sustained, the Russian social system was by now so strongly entrenched that even in these favourable circumstances the *Zemsky Sobor* never became anything more than a pliant tool in the hands of the government. Its members regarded their deliberations, aimed at advising the government, not as a right or a privilege or a civic duty, but as an additional form of obligatory State service, to be rendered as unhesitatingly (and on pain of the same dire punishments) as their military duties. Lacking all real foundations, this anachronistic survival of a bygone age soon died a painless and unlamented death, leaving the centralized State in sole possession of the field. 'The re-established system of government delivered the country into the hands of an all-powerful bureaucracy, over whose abuses there could be no effective control.'[11] For the next 300 years the Russian people were handed over to the tender mercies of a harsh and grasping bureaucratic machine.

Fear of officialdom and dissatisfaction with its workings was being expressed from very early on. At the 1642 *Sobor*, a group of noblemen from the Southern provinces eloquently complained: 'And we are being ruined not so much by the Turkish and Crimean infidels, as by the pettifogging Muscovite officials, by injustices and unjust magistrates.'[12] There was no legal recourse against the misdeeds of the often inefficient and usually harsh and corrupt bureaucracy; the only hope of redress lay in the personal intervention of the Tsar, who was above the laws, and had absolute power over their executors and victims alike. From time to time the autocrat of all the Russias would indeed smite down one or another of his agents, making public examples of bad, peculative, and oppressive officials, or merely of loyal executors of unpopular decrees. This was done, as Fletcher noted, not out of a sense of justice, but in order 'that the emperour may seem to mislike the oppressions done to his people, and transferre the fault to his ill officers'.[13] The transference of popular discontent to scapegoats marked out by the government became one of the most lasting of Russian political traditions, one which was to outlive the monarchy itself. The supreme ruler was never, could never be at fault: his benevolent intentions had been distorted by wicked or dishonest men.

Another much-favoured Russian method of statesmanship that had its origin in the Muscovy of the *Ulozhenie* was also aimed at establishing the elaborate fiction of popular approval of the Tsar's decrees. This was the tradition of announcing of each State edict that it had been passed in response to spurious petitions coming from all sections of the population. In Kliuchevsky's words: 'To speak on behalf of the whole land was a habit of the Muscovite government . . . The petition from "people of all degrees" became a stereotyped formula with which they justified every important government action . . . This official counterfeit of the people's will became a kind of political fiction, which has, in certain cases, continued to exist to this day.'[14] (These remarks were first published in the last years of the Tsarist regime: old habits die hard.)

The principal functions of the central government and its bureaucracy were the organization of national defence and the collection of revenue; the unimpeded fulfilment of these tasks, in a country with a widely scattered and restless population, required the establishment of a strong apparatus of coercion. The time-honoured institution of the Russian political police, as we have seen, had its origins in Ivan IV's *Oprichnina*. During the reigns of his successors the Office of the Sovereign's Word and Deed (*Slova i dela gosudareva*), under different names, led a full and active existence. We have it on first-hand authority that the Tsar's secret agents accompanied every Russian embassy abroad (usually under the guise of minor officials), and vigilantly watched for the slightest sign of disloyalty; they were also included in the retinues of provincial governors, military commanders, and other important personages.[15]

The job of the political police was made much easier by the habit of total submission to the State, inculcated among the population, and most vividly expressed by the purely Oriental posture of prostration before the monarch and his representatives, and also by the unique Russian tradition of the application of corporal punishment to all subjects, whether of high or low degree. In feudal and post-feudal Europe immunity from vile and ignominious punishment was the basic and unquestioned prerogative of the nobility and gentry; a nobleman could be, and often was executed, but to flog him, to deprive him of his honour, would have been an unthinkable crime against the very moral foundations of society. In Russia, on the other hand, where every subject was considered to be the ruler's property, flogging was applied impartially and indiscriminately to members of all estates. It was only in 1785 that Catherine the Great first granted the Russian nobility immunity from flogging. They were again deprived of this precious privilege by the Emperor Paul, but had it restored under his son Alexander I (1801). Even priests, the servants of God, were flogged in Russia until 1796, their wives – until 1808, their children – until 1839, while junior members of the clergy, and monks, were submitted to corporal punishment until 1863.

This may seem a small detail, yet what an expressive picture it paints of a completely disfranchised society, where there was no protective integument of custom, law or privilege between the citizen and the State, and where even the highest in the land walked as naked and defenceless to the whims and humours of his royal master as did the most wretched slave.

The ubiquitous system of internal security was complemented by the strictest security watch on Russia's western frontiers. Muscovy presents an example, with no European and very few Asian parallels, of what today would be called a closed society not only in the rigid regimentation of her people, but also in the sense of a society effectively shuttered to any foreign, particularly Western, influences. It is quite clear that the object of this control was to prevent Russians from gaining any idea of life in the West, and thus from making any possibly unfavourable comparisons.

From the time when, in 1486, a wandering German knight, Nicholas Poppel, accidentally strayed into Muscovy, and returned to tell his master, the German Emperor, of a hitherto unknown mighty Christian kingdom, lying beyond Poland and Lithuania, very few foreigners were allowed into the domains of the Tsars. There were occasional diplomatic missions, some merchants (mainly English), and a sprinkling of specialists under contract to the government: soldiers, physicians, apothecaries, architects, and highly skilled craftsmen. They were not expected to mingle with the population, and had to live apart from them, in strictly segregated and closely watched settlements on the outskirts of Moscow.

As for those Greek Orthodox churchmen who, after the conquest of Constantinople and the Balkans by the Turks, hopefully flocked to Moscow as to the sole surviving bulwark of Orthodoxy – many of them, becoming disillusioned or having backed the losing side in the ferocious theological disputes, found it practically impossible to receive permission to leave the country and return to the infidel-ruled homelands towards which they were now far more kindly disposed. Such, for instance, was the fate of one of the most celebrated sixteenth-century Orthodox theologians, Maxim the Greek. When, after a few years in Moscow, he began to ask for leave to go back to the monastery of Athos, he was instead incarcerated in a Russian monastery and kept there until his death, despite a constant stream of supplications, and even the personal intervention on his behalf of the Patriarch of Alexandria. The officials who investigated his case told him quite frankly why he could never be allowed to leave the country: 'This we fear: thou art a sage man, and thou hast lived amongst us; here thou hast seen both the good and the bad, and when thou returnest there, thou wilt tell all.'[16]

For native Russians foreign travel was prohibited altogether. Muscovite hatred and suspicion of foreigners and foreign influence bordered on the pathological. At all costs Russians were to be prevented from falling under the pernicious and heretical spell of the West. The policy of forcible seclusion from Europe was carried out for several centuries with no little success. Exceptions were rarely made; even diplomatic missions were preferably staffed with foreigners employed by the Russian government, and the few Russian envoys had to leave their families behind as hostages, to be tortured and executed in case of defection. As Prince Kurbsky, himself a refugee, wrote to Ivan IV: 'You shut up the kingdom of Russia – in other words, free human nature – as in a fortress of hell; and whoever goes from your land to foreign countries . . . you call a traitor; and if he is caught on the frontier, you punish him with various forms of death.'[17]

Foreign observers of the Russian scene never ceased to marvel at this unheard-of encagement of an entire people. They were in no doubt as to its reasons. According to Giles Fletcher: 'That they may be fitter for the servile condition wherein now they are, and have neyther reason nor valure to attempt innovation . . . they are kept from traveling, that they may learne nothing, nor see the fashions of other countries abroad. You shall seldome see a Russe a traveller, except he be with some ambassadour, or that he make a scape out of his countrie. Which hardly he can doo, by reason of the borders that are watched so narrowly, and the punishment for any such attempt, which is death if he be taken, and all his goods confiscate.'[18] Adam Olearius, the other principal source of our knowledge of Muscovy, was no less emphatic: 'To continue them in this lownesse of spirit and to keep them from feeling that liberty which other Nations about them enjoy, the Muscovites are, upon pain of death, prohibited to go out of the Countrey, without the Great Duke's expresse permission.'[19]

The authorities were fortified in their stern resolve to prevent their people from falling into temptation by the unfortunate results of an experiment undertaken by Tsar Boris Godunov in 1603: four young noblemen were sent to study in England, and all refused to return – one, indeed, became an Anglican clergyman. In the next twenty years the Russian government sent several missions to London to demand the return of the refugees; fortunately for the latter, the tradition of political asylum was already sufficiently well-established for the Russian claims to be met with firm refusals.[20]

As a result of this curious episode controls became even more rigorous, and the Muscovite fear of the irresistible seductiveness of the Western way of life grew into an obsession. In 1664 came the defection of the bright young secretary of the Russian mission to Sweden, Grigory Kotoshikhin; in his famous description of Russia he had this to say on the subject of foreign travel: 'They do not send their children to study the sciences and customs of foreign countries, for they fear that, having discovered the faiths and customs of these countries, and the precious liberty that prevails in them, they would begin to depart from their faith and to join others, and would lose all intention and thought of returning to their homes and their relatives. And therefore, as regards travel, so, with the exception of those who are sent on the Tsar's orders, or to trade with wayfarers, no Muscovite is allowed to go anywhere on any business whatsoever.'[21]

Under Peter the Great this attitude to travel abroad changed considerably, yet, except for a brief interlude, it was to remain to this day a much sought-after and valued privilege, to be bestowed or withheld by a government that was ever watchful over the true interests of its subjects (which invariably coincided with the interests of the State), ever careful to protect them, even from themselves.

The evidence adduced from Russian documentary records and from a number of trustworthy eye-witness accounts presents a bleak picture of Muscovite society: regimentation, arbitrariness, insecurity, and isolation. This would be a true picture, but an incomplete one. No less important to a proper understanding of the Russian tradition is the fact that the Russian people regarded their national state and their social system with a feeling of pious reverence and blind faith that went beyond simple patriotism, and that posed an insoluble puzzle to the foreign observers who have, over the centuries, approached Russia with the yardsticks of European rationality and common sense. As Tyutchev put it, in a verse that every educated Russian knows by heart:

> Russia cannot be fathomed by the mind,
> Or measured by a common yardstick:
> She has a stature all her own –
> Russia can be but *believed in*.

Among those many peculiar features of Russian life that transcend the earthbound European comprehension, it has been perhaps most difficult of all to understand the mainsprings of the Russian people's devotion, not just to their country, but to their State, and to the socio-political system it embodied. This was a complex emotion, composed of diverse strands, and rendered practically unintelligible to the outsider by a thick overlay of mysticism, exaggeration and idealization; it was held in much the same way by the illiterate peasant serf and by the highly sophisticated and widely travelled poet; it became a vital ingredient of Russian life at a time when patriotism or nationalism were feelings still practically unknown to most Western European peoples.

Two of the factors that determined the Russians' attitude towards their State can be fairly easily pinpointed. One was their acute consciousness of the fact that only a powerful and rigidly centralized State, in full control of the nation's every resource, could ensure national survival. Another was the largely artificial, centuries-old isolation from Europe, and the resulting ignorance and fear of the outside world: a feeling very similar to that which led the early cartographers to decorate uncharted seas with the legend 'Here be monsters'.

The combined influence of these two ineluctable facts of life could well have led to the appearance, at an extremely early state, of the concepts of fatherland, national feeling, and patriotism. It cannot, however, account for the ecstatic rapture, the exaltation bordering on idolatry, with which Russians of all classes learned to regard their country and their State. Instead of 'my country, right or wrong', it was 'my country – never wrong'. The Russians' insufferable self-righteousness, their unshakable conviction of moral superiority, the self-glorification that they carried to ridiculous lengths: these conspicuous national traits (combined as they were with many highly attractive characteristics) would have been less galling to foreigners had they not seemed so groundless, so utterly divorced from the harsh realities of Russian life. It has been hard for outsiders to realize that Russian national feeling is a spiritual emotion largely detached from the mundane things of life, that for centuries past Russia has meant for her people much more than just a country to be loved and defended: 'Russia' was a state of mind, a secular ideal, a sacred idea, an object of almost religious belief – unfathomable by the mind, unmeasurable by the yardstick of rationality.

One of the cornerstones of what became known as the 'Russian idea' was a profound belief in Russia as the embodiment of a society based on equality and justice, where, in the final reckoning, no man was greater than his neighbour, and where only a single will could prevail. This may seem the supreme paradox, but it was precisely the system of universal bondage and disfranchisement of the whole population that was held up, indeed brandished, as the conclusive proof of the unique virtue of the Russian State, and of its incontestable superiority to all its neighbours.

Every Russian, whatever his station, was an equal member of a close-knit community headed by a patriarchal absolute ruler. This high-flown principle – expressed most simply by an unknown serving-man during the Time of Troubles, 'The sovereign feeds everyone, whether great or small'[22] – was not just a blind belief forcibly instilled in a brutish and illiterate populace, but a reasoned and sincerely held conviction. Consider, for instance, the Muscovites' reply to the Polish officers who were promising them liberty if they would but transfer their allegiance to the King of Poland; it was recorded by the flabbergasted Poles themselves: 'You cherish your liberty, and we – our bondage. What you have is not liberty, but licence: the powerful man robs the weak, he can take away his land and even his life, and under your laws it would be difficult indeed to bring him to justice. The litigation would last for years, and some there are who could never be punished. But in our country even the greatest boyar cannot oppress the lowliest commoner: the Tsar metes out justice and punishment at the first complaint. And if the Tsar himself commits an unjust act, his will must be done, for it is easier to suffer a grievance from the Tsar than from one's fellow, by reason that he is master of us all.'[23]

The extravagant idealization of Russian society as an

exceptional temporal community founded on the ideals of brotherhood, equality and social justice, became, in one form or another, the essence of the 'Russian idea'. It may have been only a myth, it was treated with ridicule and incredulity in the West, but, as myths sometimes do, it became one of the most potent forces that have shaped – and are still shaping – Russian history.

The man who probably contributed most to its development was Jurij Križanić, a seventeenth-century Croatian scholar. Križanić can be rightfully included among the most influential European political writers of his time, for it was he who first expounded the ideas of Panslavism, of Slav nationalism, and of Slavonic unity under the leadership of Russia, the greatest Slavonic nation. He spent twenty years in Muscovy, fifteen of them in Siberian exile – like so many other foreign admirers of Russia – but miraculously survived to return to the West with his faith in Russia, if anything, further strengthened by his experiences. His treatise on Russian politics is a powerful and closely argued justification of the Muscovite socio-political system; the only critical remarks were concerned with the removal of the foreign influences that had lately crept in, to sully the pristine grandeur of the traditional principles.

According to Križanić, unlimited autocracy constituted the basis of the Russian polity: 'Absolute autocracy is the Moses' rod by means of which the sovereign Tsar can perform all the necessary miracles. Under such a system of government any errors, shortcomings or distortions can be easily corrected, and all manner of beneficial laws introduced. We shall receive this blessing in the spirit it deserves if we submit in everything to the sovereign Tsar as to God's Victory.' Thus the Tsar, as supreme proprietor of all the country's wealth, and with 'unlimited powers over the will, the lives and the minds of his subjects', was in a position to prevent the emergence of an oppressive minority raised above the bulk of the population – as had happened in Western Europe, deprived of the blessings of autocracy. The Tsar should use his absolute power to eliminate his country's military and economic backwardness, but, most emphatically, not at the price of changing her system, or of following Western patterns. Indeed, in Križanić's opinion, Russia's isolation from Europe – the greatest boon conferred on her by geography and by autocracy – should be made even more complete: 'Next to autocracy itself the most valuable of our traditions is the closing of the frontiers, i.e. the prohibition to foreigners of facile access to our country, and the prohibition to our people of wandering outside the borders of the realm without important reason. These two customs are the two legs, the twin supports of the kingdom, and they must be strictly observed. The heart and soul of this kingdom is the closing of frontiers, and this should be reinforced by the expulsion of all foreigners.'

Križanić made a point-by-point comparison between Russia and the West, and, apart from her low level of education and scientific knowledge, Russia passed the test with flying colours. The learned Croat became the first to set down in writing the Russian national ideal of a just and equitable society – a society, moreover, that existed not in some unattainable Utopia, but in the here and now, in the wide Russian spaces, under the benevolent eye of an omnipotent government. In the benighted countries of Western Europe, he declared, a tiny ruling class lived 'extravagant, luxurious and indolent lives . . . of profligacy, gluttony and effeminacy; they wallow in their feather beds and sleep until midday . . . Many nobles and townspeople live in indolence and luxury, like Sardanapalus of ancient times, or like fattened swine that are of no use to anybody in the world.' At the same time their toiling masses suffered oppression, starvation and misery.

What a striking contrast to this horrifying state of affairs was provided by the Russian people, who, having no class divisions or unproductive social groups, cheerfully and purposefully turned their energies, each in his own place, towards the furtherance of the common good:

No one is allowed to live in indolence, and no one can be freed from public service: at the court, in the departments of State (*prikazy*), in military campaigns . . .

No one can live for himself, i.e. no one is born to live exclusively for himself and to care only for his own pleasures. Every person must have an occupation that is useful also for all other people, and earn his own bread by it. And such labour in the common good, by which one earns or otherwise deserves one's bread, is called 'duty' . . .

The peasants, the artisans and the merchants produce everything needful to support and feed all the Tsar's subjects . . . The rulers, the boyars and the warriors sit in judgment, wage wars, protect the public peace, the health, life and the honestly gained possessions of all subjects . . . The ecclesiastics, the bishops and the priests, supply everybody with spiritual comfort, with light and learning. The monks and nuns pray to God for everybody's sins . . . He that does not serve the public weal in husbandry, in the crafts, in the army, or in office is to be treated as a good-for-nothing, of use only to himself.[24]

Muscovite Russia, a backward and poor country with a social system of regimentation and general State bondage, enforced by terror and strict seclusion from the outside world, was rapturously described by Križanić in terms of a socialistic society, based on equality and collective endeavour in the common cause. This greatly amused the sophisticated, liberal-minded, Westernized pre-revolutionary Russian historians. Today, however, one cannot be quite so sure . . .

This version of Russian society was no more than the Russian people's traditional image of the ideal social order inherent in their nation and their form of government, an image that served as justification for the wretchedness of their lives. It appeared over and over again, in the folklore of the masses and in the writings of the educated classes. Ivan Pososhkov, the most important political theorist of the eighteenth century, went even further in defining the principles of this peculiar autocratic State socialism: 'No men should pass their days in indolence, and eat their bread in idleness. God has not given us bread merely for us to devour it like worms, and to turn it into rust. If we wish to eat bread we must bring some benefit to God and to our Tsar and to our brethren and to ourselves – otherwise we shall be like unto the useless worm ... All governors should see to it that nothing is wasted anywhere, and that no men eat bread in idleness, but that all do labour and bring forth fruits.'[25]

This passage is most enlightening, for here Pososhkov, practically in so many words, formulates the famous maxim 'He who does not work, neither shall he eat', that is today enshrined in Article 12 of the Soviet Constitution. These words are the more remarkable in that they were written by a man who can by no stretch of the imagination be considered a socialist, a Utopian visionary, or even much of a reformer, but by a devoted supporter and admirer of Tsar Peter the Great, and a staunch believer in the excellence of the Russian system of society and of government.

Russia, wrote Križanić and Pososhkov and a host of lesser luminaries, was the embodiment of social justice and genuine equality, and reflected these ideals in her peculiar social and political structure, so different from, and so superior to, anything existing outside her borders. This, briefly, was the quintessence of the 'Russian idea'. But, in a non-ideological age, this belief, however deep, was in itself insufficient to create the Messianic fervour, the near-adoration with which Russians regarded their country and their Tsar. The religious element that suffused the 'Russian idea' was provided by the Orthodox Church.

The Church occupied a very special place in Russian life, and Russian Christianity had a flavour that was all its own. It was not that the Russians were more devout than Western Christians – the opposite was often the case – but that religion did not mean quite the same thing to them. Whether they were as single-mindedly pious as many Russian and foreign writers have described them is open to doubt, but there can be no dispute about the fact that in the course of their country's history Christianity became for them synonymous with Russia herself.

From the point of view of the present inquiry, the three salient features of the Russian Church were its national character, its identification with and glorification of the State, and the Messianic outlook that it engendered and fostered.

The Church became the visible symbol of national unity during the apanage period, when Russia had broken up into feuding principalities, without even the ties of a common vassalage to preserve the semblance of princely co-operation. Only the Orthodox religion remained undivided. It acquired a new importance under the Tartar yoke, when, amid the suicidal bickering of the Russian princelings, now little more than the Khan's placemen, it provided the sole rallying-point for outraged national feeling. The transfer of the Metropolitan see to Moscow proved a vital factor in the successful unification of the Russian land by the house of Kalita. The centuries-long struggle against the Tartars was as much a religious crusade as a national war; national survival became indistinguishable from the preservation of Christianity.

It was in this, the darkest period of Russian history, that the very words 'Russian' and 'Christian' became blended with each other to the point of interchangeability. This has left a unique linguistic trace: Russian seems to be the only language in which one word (in the variants of *khristianin* and *krestyanin*), stands for both 'Christian' and 'peasant'. Until the revolution the usual way of addressing groups of people was not 'Russians', or 'Citizens', or 'Fellow-countrymen', but 'Christians' or 'Orthodox'.

The fusion of nationality and religion was not created solely by the identification of the national cause with a religious ideal; it was just as much a result of the isolation of the Russian Orthodox Church from Western Christianity, and of the elevation of its own national brand of Christianity to the position of the only true faith. Christianity had been brought to Russia from Byzantium, and for four and a half centuries it developed under the intense influence and the close supervision of the

Eastern Church. In the course of their struggle for national and religious survival the Russian people came to defend the tenets and rites of their faith with a stubbornness and fanaticism that far outdid the worldly attitudes of the Mother Church. And when in 1439 the Eastern Empire, hard-pressed by the Turks, turned in desperation for aid to Rome, and at the Council of Florence agreed to a reunion with the Catholic Church, the Muscovite government promptly denounced the 'apostatic treaty', and confined one of its co-signatories, the head of the Russian Church, Metropolitan Isidor, to imprisonment in a monastery.

Fourteen years later Constantinople fell to the infidels, and the Muscovites congratulated themselves on their foresight, for what clearer indication could there be of God's wrath against the perpetrators of this heinous betrayal of the true faith? The hapless Byzantine clergy soon renounced their backsliding, but the damage had been done, and the impious Greeks were from then on treated in Moscow with grave suspicion, though not quite with the same abhorrence as the Catholics and, somewhat later, the Lutherans. The Orthodox nations of the Balkans had all been overwhelmed by the Mohammedan Juggernaut, and Russia was now on her own: the sole citadel of the Christian faith, beleaguered by a world of infidelity, heresy and apostasy.

Just as the State had clamped down its borders against all intercourse with a feared and hated Europe, so too did the Church turn its back upon a Western Christianity that was, in its firm conviction, inspired by Satan. The isolation and introversion of Russian Orthodoxy, its parochialism, its unyielding resistance to foreign influence and to all change, even the abysmal ignorance and virtual illiteracy of much of its priesthood and the stagnation of its theology: all these became virtues to be gloried in. It was both a national institution and the only true Church in the world, and therefore doubly blessed; this provided the grounds for the nationalistic exclusiveness, the narrow-mindedness, and the self-righteous bigotry that characterized the Russian Orthodox Church. It regarded itself, says Kliuchevsky, 'as the only truly orthodox church in the world, and its interpretation of the Divine Will as the only correct one. It regarded the Maker of the Universe as its own Russian God, who could not belong, and was not even known, to anyone else. It substituted its ecclesiastical province for the Universal Church. Having complacently convinced itself of this, it elevated its local ceremonial into a sacred mystery, and its religious ideas into the inviolable standard of theology.'[26]

With the rise of Moscow, Church and State inevitably became one. This was not merely a consequence of the identity of national and religious interests, but a reflection of the fundamental fact that within a system where the State had become the absolute master of all social forces, no possibility existed for rivalry between Church and State, for the struggle between temporal and spiritual power, between Emperor and Pope, King and Prelate, such as fill the pages of medieval European history. 'A society which provided unique opportunities for the growth of the governmental machine left no room for the growth of a politically and economically independent dominant religion.'[27] Religion could not remain independent, but was itself integrated in the power system. The priesthood, just like any other social category, was bound in perpetuity to its State service, which in this particular case happened to be ministration to the spiritual needs of the Tsar's subjects. Although the enthralment of the clergy, like so much else in Russian life, was never actually laid down in law, their slavish subservience to the government astonished all foreign observers. As noted already by Herberstein at the beginning of the sixteenth century, 'they all obey, not only the commands of the prince, but all the boyars sent by the prince'.[28]

But the total subordination of the Church to the State, and the fusion of the two in the person of a single quasi-theocratic ruler, was not just a measure of expediency, enjoined by the government, but a relationship implicit in the thinking and the structure of the Church itself. Byzantium bestowed its religion upon Russia, and with it the doctrine of Caesaropapism, which was to prove its most lasting heritage. In Russia, as in Byzantium, no line of demarcation existed between the spheres of ecclesiastical and political power; the ruler not only supervised, and strictly enforced, the maintenance of ecclesiastical discipline, but even controlled matters of doctrine; government officials took an active part in the administration of ecclesiastical affairs, and churchmen were entrusted with purely political duties.

In Russia, however, the ideas of Caesaropapism took much deeper and stronger root than in the Eastern Empire itself: partly by reason of the greater political stability of the Muscovite State, but chiefly as a result of their coalescence with the concepts of nationality and of the autocratic State. Both in the popular mind and in the teachings of the Church, Russia became identified with Christianity, its cause with the cause of God, its State power with the power of God. 'There was no concept of a secular state in Russia, no concept outside Christianity and its purposes.'[29] Not only did Christianity and Russia become synonymous, but also the State and the faith.

Russian Orthodox theologians went far beyond Western Church teachings on the subjects' duty of obedience, or even on the divine right of kings: the Tsar was for them the visible manifestation of the Divine Order, the Vicar of Christ, and, as such, not only autocratic temporal prince, but supreme spiritual ruler as well, possessing God-like powers. This has been called the 'theory of theocratic absolutism'; it was first formulated in the reign of Ivan III by the most famous of Russian theologians, Joseph of Volok: 'In his mortal form [the Tsar] resembles all men, but in his power he is like unto Almighty God.'[30] Joseph of Volok saw the Tsar as the supreme ecclesiastical authority, with special responsibility for preserving the purity of Church doctrine and for enforcing Orthodoxy.

The Tsar of Muscovy came to be surrounded by an atmosphere of religious worship that was truly Oriental in character, with Byzantine ceremonial, resounding incantations, hyperbolic praise, and grovelling obeisance. But there was nothing insincere or hypocritical about the adulation showered upon the ruler of all the Russias: his power really was, to all intents and purposes, as unlimited and as terrifying as that of the Almighty. Elaborate church rituals invested it with divine mystery, but for the Russian people the Tsar's authority had always had magic qualities. They called him 'Little father Tsar', as they called their country 'Little mother Russia' – thus expressing a mystical and tender relationship of wedlock and parenthood between sovereign, country and people.

The Russian language is justly famous for the extraordinary wealth of its proverbs. Many of them express the people's belief in the Tsar and in the Almighty, as in the two co-equal and interdependent mighty powers that be: 'God in the heavens, the Tsar on earth'; 'One God, one sovereign'; 'God's will and the Tsar's justice'; 'There can be no world without God, and no order without the Tsar'; 'There is no one, but God and the sovereign'; 'One sun shines in heaven, and the Russian Tsar on earth'; 'All are in the power of God and the sovereign'; 'Without a Tsar the land is a widow'; 'Only God and the sovereign know'; 'Our souls are God's, our bodies the Tsar's'; 'The Tsar is God's overseer'; and so on.[31] In Russian eyes, the direct relationship between the prince and the deity was a far more profound and mystical one than anything conceived of in the West and expressed in such platitudinous and politically inspired formulas as 'His Most Christian Majesty' or 'Defender of the Faith'. The prince was the representative of God and the tangible symbol of Godhead, and not merely an anointed Caesar; through him the aura of sanctity was transmitted to the State which he also incarnated, and, *mutatis mutandis*, to the Russian people as a whole.

This belief underwent severe strain in the middle of the seventeenth century, when Patriarch Nikon's revision of ecclesiastical ritual and of the text of the Slavonic Bible led to the lasting Church crisis known as the Schism (*Raskol*). A large body of believers and a significant number of priests utterly refused to accept the new-fangled conceits, in which they detected the Devil's handiwork. The Orthodox Church was split from top to bottom, and the Schism was never to be healed.

The breakaway minority, the so-called Old Believers, although they soon started to split up into ever smaller sects, were united in their fierce determination to have no dealings with the

Antichrist now reigning triumphant in the official Church and the State. They constituted not only the most devout and the most literate, but also the most enterprising and most courageous segment of the population: the pioneers, the fur-traders, the settlers of the Siberian wilds, the Cossacks. They renounced the State and all its works, but they were not rebels – only fanatically religious Russian peasants searching for God. Fleeing from the government's savage persecutions, they moved deeper and deeper into the impenetrable forests, the frozen wastes of the North or the boundless steppe of the South; when escape was impossible, they often resorted to mass self-immolation. In the first thirty years of the Schism not less than 20,000 people burned themselves in this way; some of the largest of the 'conflagrations' numbered up to two and a half thousand victims. For the Old Believers, with their peculiarly Russian single-mindedness, there could be no half-way house: one either belonged to the State body and soul, or one killed oneself rather than be defiled by its touch.

The Schism was to remain, until the advent of the nineteenth-century revolutionary movement, and then of Bolshevism, the most remarkable episode in the Russian people's age-long quest for the terrestrial City of God. Many historians see in its tragic events the beginning of that disastrous and unbridgeable split between the State and a part of its subjects, that was to become such a significant feature of later Russian development.

The Schism also resulted in the final renunciation by the official Orthodox Church of any lingering ideas regarding its supremacy in spiritual matters, and in its ultimate humiliating decline to the level of a Department of State. (Ex-Patriarch Nikon himself had ample opportunity to reflect on this in the solitude of the monastic cell in which he had to spend the last fifteen years of his life.) With the most godly part of the Christian community in open rebellion against its teachings, the Church now depended on the police arm of the government to uphold its diminished moral authority, and to chastise the sectarians. The priesthood, largely ignorant, slothful, and slightly esteemed by their flock, walked in as much fear of their royal master's wrath as any other poor sinner.

But the fervent faith of the Russian people in their country, as the unique embodiment of social justice and of the only true Christian faith, remained unimpaired. Indeed, the Schism itself had had its roots in the widespread fear that Nikon's reforms would somehow damage the purity of Orthodoxy, and thus render Russia unworthy of her messianic task. The vision of the Apocalypse was more scorching than the flames into which the Schismatics hurled themselves and their families. For herein lay the inner mystery of the 'Russian idea': the conviction that Russia had been entrusted with the divine mission of resuscitating the world by sharing with it the revelation that had been granted to her alone.

This mystical conception owed much less to any inherent Russian saintliness than to the emergence of a unified Russian State as the sole bastion of Orthodoxy in a depraved world. Two great events, the fall of Constantinople, and Russia's deliverance from the Tartar yoke, as the historian Dyakonov pointed out, 'prepared the ground for a new political dogma, namely that the Grand Duke of Moscow and of All the Russias should assume the position that had been previously held in the universe by the Emperor of Byzantium'.[32] The new doctrine found its most perdurable expression in the idea of Moscow as the Third Rome – the natural inheritor, to the end of time, of Rome and Constantinople as the centre of Christendom. In 1510 the monk Philotheus composed his celebrated address to the Tsar: 'Know then, O pious Tsar, that all the Orthodox Christian realms have converged in thy single Empire. Thou art the only Tsar of the Christians in all the universe . . . Observe and hearken, O pious Tsar, that all Christian Empires have converged in thy single one, that two Romes have fallen, but the third stands, and no fourth can ever be. Thy Christian Empire shall fall to no one.'[33]

The doctrine of 'Moscow, the Third Rome' evolved into a highly complex national and religious philosophy, capable of various, and often differing interpretations. In its simplest form it provided the basis for the Russian government's perennial pretensions to the leading place among the nations of the world. Already in the reign of Ivan the Terrible the incipient national megalomania had reached a stage where not only the monarchs of Poland, Sweden, England and France, but even the German Emperor were, one by one, declared unfit to be treated as equals by the ruler of Muscovy; and finally even the Turkish Sultan was deposed from the lonely eminence which he had previously been allowed to share with the Tsar. It should be noted that these delusions of grandeur, coinciding, as they did, with the nadir of Russian fortunes in the field, caused more amusement than annoyance among the European courts.

However, with the growth of Russia's military might, her sweeping claims to worldwide moral and political leadership became a source of constant anxiety. Western statesmen and journalists tended to dismiss the 'Russian idea', ecstatically advanced by Russian spokesmen in spiritual justification of their country's foreign policy, as so much hypocritical mumbo-jumbo, on a par with, if somewhat weirder than 'The white man's burden', 'civilizing mission', or 'Manifest Destiny'. Karl Marx, ever on the alert to warn Europe against the peril of Russian encroachment, was nearer the truth when he sought for the roots of Russian expansionism in the remote past; he wrote of 'that bold synthesis which, blending the encroaching method of the Mongol slave with the world-conquering tendencies of the Mongol master, forms the life-spring of modern Russian diplomacy'.[34]

Yet the conviction that Russia occupied a special place in the world was by no means confined to the Russian government, nor did its main importance lie in the production of excuses for an aggressive foreign policy. It was shared, in one form or another, and in varying degrees of intensity, by every segment of the Russian people. It was for them the vindication of a social and political system that would otherwise have been unbearable.

Over the centuries the 'Russian idea' developed into an exotic amalgam of emotions that struck vibrantly upon the high-strung chords of the Russian soul: deep national feeling, a sense of belonging to a nation set apart from others by its own history; mystical devotion to an Orthodoxy of which Russia was the sole champion, and which was somehow more spiritual than any other Christian Church; faith in the God-given system of autocracy whereby prince and people were fused together into a single integral entity; the conviction that the individual's duty towards the State, the community, transcended all other obligations, and provided the main justification for his existence; the idea that collectivism – the famous principle of *sobornost'*, or communality – was nobler than individualism; the assumption that idealism and other-worldliness were inherent in the Russian national *Weltanschauung*, in contrast to the gross materialism of the Western scheme of values; the notion that equality, even if achieved at the lowest of material levels, formed the essence of justice, and was, as such, infinitely preferable to any non-egalitarian system; a deep-rooted concern with the abstract ideas of justice and equity expressed most vividly in the selfless and tireless quest for a just and godly society, for the terrestrial City of God; the conviction that suffering was inseparable from purity, and that the Russian people's centuries-long ordeal had been a cleansing fire, from which they were to emerge with enhanced virtue and spirituality; consciousness, to the point of exaggeration, of the profound difference between Russia and the West; the messianic fervour that imbued the 'Russian idea', the conviction that the Russian nation was a 'God-bearing people' (*narod bogonosets*), entrusted with the mission of sharing with others the revelation of unity and of true freedom which had been vouchsafed to them alone, and of redeeming the world from the bonds of individualism and materialism.

This involved and mystical system of ideas grew out of the much simpler beliefs that had been passed on through many generations of unlettered peasants. It achieved its ultimate degree of refinement – without, however, losing anything of its original substance – in the writings of the nineteenth-century Slavophiles. In his fine poem 'To Russia', the Slavophile poet/philosopher and theologian Alexei Khomyakov reminded his people of the fate that had overtaken such purely terrene empires as those of Rome, of the Mongols, and of Albion (which last he believed to be already convulsed in its death agonies). But Russia's destiny was a different and far more glorious one: Almighty God had rewarded her for her 'humility', her 'childlike simplicity' and her unquestioning faith with the supreme task of 'Preserving for the world the treasure/Of noble sacrifices and pure deeds,/Preserving the sacred brotherhood of nations,/The life-giving vessel of love,/And the inheritance of burning faith and justice.'

> Hearken unto Him, and embrace
> All nations with thy love.
> Divulge to them the mystery of freedom,
> And shed upon them the radiance of faith.
> Then will thy sublime glory
> Place thee above all mortal peoples.

This was the concept of Holy Russia, of a nation destined to redeem all others, and to lead them towards a great moral Truth. Konstantin Aksakov wrote: 'The history of the Russian people is the only history in the world of a Christian people ... not only in its profession of faith, but also in its life, or at least in the aspirations of its life.'[35] His words were taken up by Konstantin Leontiev: 'Russia has a strange political destiny: whether it is a happy lot or an unhappy one, I do not know. Her interests have *in some way a moral tendency* towards supporting the weak, the oppressed. And all these weak, all these oppressed are her partisans ... I understand that even the Moslems and Hindus of India have prophecies in favour of the "Urus" and in disfavour of the "Ingles". Such is the curious political destiny of this *despotic* Russia ... I believe that Russia, destined as she is to head a new oriental State organization, must also give the world a *new culture*, and to replace by this new Slavonic-Oriental civilization the *dying* civilization of Romanic-German Europe.'[36] The 'Russian idea' was fast growing into a universal idea.

Holy Russia, cleansed by her tribulations, was uniquely

equipped to lead the world out of the morass of disunity, egoism, doubt, and materialism in which it was floundering: the message found its most influential interpreter in Dostoevsky:

> Our great people were brought up like beasts; they have suffered tortures ever since they came into being, throughout the millennium of their existence – tortures such as no other people in the world could have endured, because they would have disintegrated and perished, whereas our people merely grew stronger and became more compact amidst their misfortunes . . .
>
> We Russians possess two dreadful powers, worth all others in the world – the unity, the spiritual indivisibility of the millions of our people, and their closest communion with the Monarch . . .
>
> In every significant moment of our historical life the issue has invariably been determined by the people's spirit and view, by the Tsars of the people in sublime communion with the latter . . .
>
> Here we have something universal and final, which, though by no means solving *all* human destinies, brings with it the beginning of the end of the whole former history of European mankind . . .
>
> Russia, in conjunction with Slavdom, and at its head, will utter to the whole world the greatest word ever heard, and that word will precisely be a covenant of universal human fellowship . . . The Russian national idea, in the last analysis, is but the universal fellowship of man . . .
>
> The genuine social truth resides in no one else but our people; their idea, their spirit contains the living urge of universal communion of men.[37]

Even in the nineteenth century few Russians saw the irony of the most enslaved nation in Europe showing mankind the way to full liberation and to genuine spiritual and physical unity. Still less could this be expected of earlier ages. Indeed, the very incongruity between the 'Russian idea' and Russian reality seemed somehow to strengthen the people's faith in their country and its political system. However cruel life became, however harsh the injustices that had to be endured, however helpless the individual felt himself – nothing could shake the peasants' basic conviction in the righteousness of their State.

This is not to say that the peasants were necessarily content with their lot: on the contrary, the history of Russia contains probably more peasant rebellions than that of any other country. The recurrent uprisings, however, apart from a few Cossack movements, were never directed against the Tsar or the principle of absolute autocracy, but against evil officials and oppressive landowners, who were believed to be thwarting the sovereign's will. To be sure, similar rationalizations were not unknown, though hardly frequent, in Western European *jacqueries*. The singular feature of almost all Russian peasant movements was that they were actually conducted in the name of the Tsar, with the object of establishing the ideals of social justice embodied in his person. Moreover, they were in many cases led by pretenders to the throne, by impostors who had assumed the identity of any mysteriously deceased monarch or heir to the throne (at no period of Russian history was there ever a shortage of discreetly murdered royal personages). Appearing suddenly in some remote province, the pretender would announce his miraculous salvation from the wicked courtiers and landowners who had plotted to kill him because of his love for the people, but had been foiled by Providence. Without the principle of legitimacy few rebellions would have got off the ground.

The most famous of these impostors, the two False Dmitrys of the Time of Troubles, have even secured a place in Russian chronological tables as False Dmitry I and II. Emelian Pugachev, the leader, in the late eighteenth century, of the greatest and most widespread peasant rebellion, not only passed himself off as the Emperor Peter III, assassinated ten years earlier with the connivance of his wife, but even bestowed upon his closest adherents the titles and dignity of the highest officials of the court of St Petersburg.

The myth of the 'people's Tsar' proved to be the most potent of weapons for stirring up insurrections. Even throughout the nineteenth century the rapidly burgeoning revolutionary organizations of the intelligentsia, in their attempts to gain popular support, were time and again compelled to resort to deceit, to the pretence of acting in the name of the Tsar and against the bureaucracy which had suppressed and falsified the royal will.

The Russian people's almost religious devotion to their country, their deep-rooted faith in autocracy and in its superiority to any other system of government, played a vital part in the shaping of the national character and of the national way of life. As Karamzin pointed out with great approbation: 'Our ancestors, while assimilating many advantages which were to be found in foreign customs, never lost the conviction that an Orthodox Russian was the most perfect citizen and Holy Rus the foremost state in the world. Let this be called a delusion. Yet how much it did to strengthen patriotism and the moral fibre of the country!'[38]

This conviction did more than just strengthen the nation's moral fibre: it provided a poor and sorely pressed country with the cohesion and stability which external and internal pressures could never have achieved by themselves.

CHAPTER 6

Interpretations: Feudal and 'Asiatic'

In the course of the sixteenth and seventeenth centuries Russia had largely evolved its distinctive and durable social and political structure. For a general description of this traditional Muscovite system one could hardly better the following:

> It had three main peculiarities. First, *the military structure of the state*. Muscovy was Great Russia in arms, fighting on two fronts: in the West for national unity, in the south-east for Christian civilization, and in both places – for her very existence. The second peculiarity was the *compulsory*, extra-legal nature of internal administration and the social structure, with sharply separated estates. Administration was carried on by bodies acting under constraint: at the top – by the serving men, at the bottom – by elected representatives of the estates. The estates were distinguished not by their rights, but by the obligations assigned to them. Everybody was obliged either to defend the State or to work for the State, i.e. to feed those who defended it. There were commanders, soldiers and workers, but no citizens, for the citizen had been transformed into either a soldier or a worker, who was to defend the State or work for it, under the leadership of his commander . . . The third peculiarity of the Muscovite state structure was *a supreme authority with an indefinite, i.e. unlimited sphere of action, and with an undetermined relationship towards its own subordinate parts.*[1]

In the preceding pages an attempt has been made to trace the development of this singular system, to analyse the factors that brought it into being, and to describe its working and the nature of its component elements. A clearer understanding of all these points would be facilitated by comparing the Muscovite social system with some other types of society existing contemporaneously with it in Europe and Asia. The object of such an exercise should not be the enunciation of moral judgments or the assessment of the relative worth of various types of society in accordance with the student's personal scale of ethical values. Nor should it be carried out merely in the interests of sociological tidiness, with each social system, neatly packaged and labelled, popped into the appropriate pigeon-hole. The proper purpose of such a comparative analysis is to provide a deeper insight into the nature of Muscovite society by establishing its institutional framework and its relationship to other basic societal patterns. Such an inquiry is essential to the whole problem of continuity and change in Russian history, down to the present day.

Of later it has become customary for Western writers, Marxist and non-Marxist alike, to place Russian society within the general framework of feudalism, and to call the system that existed in Russia until 1861 'feudal'. This attitude is part and parcel of the general unilinear approach to the development of human society; the approach that emphasizes a supposed fundamental similarity between the various stages of growth through which all civilizations (to use a common expression) have passed, are passing, or should have passed – were it not for the intervention of extraneous forces.

In keeping with this, the concept of feudalism has been expanded and reduced to a denominator sufficiently low to enable it to embrace practically all non-savage, pre-industrial traditional societies, from the Andean Indians to the West African Hausa to the Tibetans. Somewhere in this comprehensive structure Russia, too, is safely ensconced. For latter-day Soviet Marxist-Leninists, with their rigid vision of five consecutive 'modes of production', this interpretation is the ark of the covenant; reservations would be out of place in a doctrinal system of such stark single-mindedness as theirs.

These considerations do not, in themselves, invalidate a 'feudal' reading of Russian history – the *argumentum ad hominem* is a treacherous pilot. But if the classification of Russian society as 'feudal' is to be of any value for the student, the terms of reference must be precisely defined. First the concept of feudalism should be made clear, and then its applicability determined, not vice versa.

What, in fact, was the actual content of this much abused concept of feudalism, and what were its distinctive features? Feudalism, in the proper meaning of the word, was the socio-political system which prevailed in Western Europe, particularly in France, England, the Low Countries, the greater part of Germany, Italy, and Christian Spain, throughout the Middle Ages, achieving its full flowering between the ninth and the thirteenth centuries. Europe was not a unified entity, and feudalism was by no means a unitary system: indeed, one of its conspicuous qualities was the very diversity of its manifestations. Yet there undoubtedly existed certain basic characteristics held in common by the various feudal societies, the sum of which provides the best description of this type of polity – and the presence of which can be the only real criterion for the classification of any society, European or non-European, as feudal.

Marc Bloch, one of the greatest twentieth-century authorities on the subject, defined the basic features of feudalism: 'A subject peasantry; widespread use of the service tenement (i.e. the fief), instead of a salary, which was out of the question; the supremacy of a class of specialized warriors; ties of obedience and protection which bind man to man and, within the warrior class, assume the distinctive form called vassalage; fragmentation of authority – leading inevitably to disorder; and, in the midst of all this, the survival of other forms of association, family and State . . .'[2]

On the face of it there would seem to be considerable resemblances between classical Western feudalism and the Muscovite social system. One is immediately struck by the prevalence in both types of society of service land tenure, in combination with the military tenants' far-reaching authority over a subject and unfree peasantry. This fact has often been advanced as conclusive proof of the basic identity of the two systems, or, at the very least, of their adherence to a common societal pattern. Upon closer examination the resemblance is seen to be no more than a superficial and misleading one.

A comparative analysis of European feudalism and the Muscovite social system should start with the role of the State. This was a question of vital importance for both – in a diametrically opposite way. The development of the feudal order was a direct result of the breakdown of the State, of its inability to perform its natural functions, chief among them being the organization of defence. In a period of uncertainty, lawlessness and imminent chaos, people turned for protection not to an impotent government, but to the local strong-man. The weak sought the protection of the strong, the powerful sought that of the still more mighty. Throughout most of the feudal age the central government was feeble; where a relatively strong State did exist, as in post-Conquest England, its powers were severely circumscribed. A political and social system grew up, where private law had taken the place of public law, in which public duty had become private obligation.

The extreme fragmentation of authority formed one of the most characteristic features of the feudal order; the dispersion of power often reached a stage where the territorial magnate was all but independent of his ruler. Effective government was largely confined to the local level, where public authority had been transferred into a private possession. The king's writ, like that of any other feudal lord, ran only through his own personal estate. The central government, such as it was, could rely only on the income from the royal estates; taxes were levied on very rare occasions, and then only by consent.

Social relationships and loyalties were by nature neither political nor constitutional, but personal. 'There began to be built up a vast system of personal relationships whose intersecting threads ran from one level of the social structure to another ... The most characteristic feature of the civilization of feudal Europe was the network of ties of dependence, extending from top to bottom of the social scale.'[3] This network of personal relationships inevitably found its legal expression in a tortuous maze of codified safeguards, conditions and guarantees: of agreements, contracts, charters, privileges, parliaments and so on.

At the bottom of this system of personal ties, and of the whole feudal order, lay the relationship between lord and vassal. Most students of feudalism consider vassalage to have been its essential element. According to two of the greatest of English historians, Maitland and Pollock, 'What is characteristic of the "feudal period" is not the relationship between letter and hirer, or lender and borrower of land, but the relationship between lord and vassal, or rather it is the union of these two relationships.'[4] This has been put even more categorically in a recent authoritative discussion of feudalism: 'Feudalism is primarily a method of government . . . in which the essential relation is not that between ruler and subject, nor state and citizen, but between lord and vassal.'[5]

The cornerstone of the vassal relationship, of its complex structure of commendation, homage, investiture, immunity, etc., and of the powerful mystique of knighthood and chivalry, was the fief: a piece of land (or other source of revenue) granted by suzerain to vassal in return for the latter's contractual obligation of service. 'Feudalism is a regime based on the legal recognition of the connection, compulsory for both parties, between the vassal's service and the suzerain's grant to him. At the basis of this regime lies a contractual but indissoluble bond between service and land grant, between personal obligation and real right.'[6]

It is at this point that an affinity has been claimed to exist between European feudalism and the Russian *pomestie* system. Yet in reality nothing could be further apart than the *pomestie* – land granted by the State as an act of grace to enable its serving-man to fulfil his compulsory duty of unlimited and unconditional service, with no reciprocity of obligations – and the fief, based on a strictly private agreement, and on a limited contractual relationship between the lord (himself often the vassal of someone else's vassal) and his vassal. The principle of mutual rights and obligations, meticulously defined under contract, distinguished European feudalism from every other type of human society. Beyond the contract there could be no service, nor even loyalty; non-fulfilment of his obligations by the lord automatically relieved the vassal of his duties. To quote Bloch once again: 'The obedience of the vassal was conditional upon the scrupulous fulfilment of his engagements by the lord. This reciprocity in unequal obligations ... was the really distinctive feature of European vassalage ... Vassal homage was a genuine contract and a bilateral one. If the lord failed to fulfil his engagements he lost his rights.'[7]

The legal concept of termination of obligations as a result of the violation of the contract of vassalage by either side, was fully applied to the relationship between the king and his vassals. The bond between the sovereign and his people, just as any other, was considered to be based on contract, and a royal transgressor was expected to pay the usual penalty. The Sachsenspiegel, a famous thirteenth-century German law-code, declared flatly: 'A man may resist his king and judge when he acts contrary to law and may even help to make war on him ... Thereby, he does not violate the duty of fealty.'[8] The acknowledged legal right of resistance to the government, the right of rebellion if the king forfeited his vassal's loyalty by breaking their mutual contract, went even further: medieval customaries recognized cases in which the aggrieved baron's own liege vassal could lawfully wage war against the king in support of his lord. The principle of inviolable legal contract, embodied in the king's coronation oath, was clearly understood and widely accepted; in Aragon, for instance, a famous formula laid down that subjects would only obey the king as long as he performed his obligations, 'and if not, not'. Long after feudalism disappeared the idea of contract as the basis for relationship between State and subjects was to exert a powerful influence on the development of European political thought and constitutional law.

The system of vassalage, of reciprocal contractual obligations, of immunities (the magnates' rights to jurisdiction over the inhabitants of their territories, based on the exclusion thence of the king's representatives), led inevitably to the growth of a powerful landed aristocracy, a class of semi-independent magnates (or barons), with private armies, private courts, private taxation. Their fiefs soon became hereditary, and they were in a position to enforce upon a weak State the principles of entail and primogeniture, and thus ensure the lasting strength of landed property. The vassals set up their independent organizations, or corporations, to protect and enhance their fixed hereditary rights; these developed into autonomous centres of power, and breeding-places for the strong corporative feeling that distinguished the European nobility. The king was obliged to take counsel from his vassals – counsel which not infrequently went very much against the grain – and often compelled to act upon it.

There is an unavoidable dichotomy in any assessment of the historical role of the medieval European aristocracy. On the one hand, they unquestionably represented a force for anarchy, and in extreme cases (e.g. Poland), for chaos. Yet it is arguable that far more important in the long run was the fact that a potent and privileged aristocracy constituted the strongest of checks upon the powers of the State, and that in this capacity it made a decisive contribution towards the evolution of democratic processes. De Tocqueville saw in the aristocracy, in its institutions and privileges, the chief rampart against the rise of despotism. And one can hardly dispute the essence of this argument, even after every reservation is duly made. The most celebrated of feudal documents, Magna Carta, which was imposed upon King John by his rebellious barons in order to strengthen their – real or imaginary – traditional corporative rights, became in time the rallying-point for every English democratic and revolutionary movement, from Pym to the Chartists. (This phenomenon has created an insoluble quandary for Soviet medievalists, torn between their glorification of the strong centralized State and its 'positive role', and their automatic obeisances to the 'great landmarks of liberty' –

wrested, alas, from an enfeebled State by the 'forces of feudal reaction'.)

Even where the central government retained considerable powers, the king represented but the apex of the hierarchical pyramid that was feudal society. His authority was limited not only by the nobility, but by a number of other institutions and vested interests, all stemming from the very nature of the feudal order: by the position of the Church as a parallel and independent authority, frequently stronger than the State itself, and, from the eleventh century, locked with the latter in a combat that gravely weakened both; by the rich and powerful cities, loaded with privileges, at once allies and enemies of the government, and profiting from both situations; by strong local loyalties that had endured since the pre-feudal era, and were enshrined in tradition and codified in regional charters of autonomy and privilege; by the government's own interest in the development of commerce and industry, which, even under so-called absolute monarchy, served as a built-in check against despotic tendencies.

These and similar factors, combined within the characteristic corporative structure of feudal society, constituted a durable institutional bulwark against autocracy. Feudalism, with all its injustice and inequality, was essentially what would today be called a pluralistic society – in contrast to monolithic despotism. This feature was well understood at an early date. Jean Bodin wrote: 'Take away corporations and communities, and you ruin the State and transform it into a barbaric tyranny.'[9] His view has been supported by a present-day scholar, and no admirer of the aristocratic principle, Geoffrey Barraclough: 'In Western European experience democratic practice has resulted from the action of estates and – on the continent, if not in England – of provincial groupings, fighting for their "rights".'[10]

Just as great a contrast between the two types of society under discussion as that pertaining to the powers of the State and the position of the nobility and other privileged categories, is provided by the relative status of the lower classes of population, the enserfed peasantry. In Russia, as has been shown above, the peasants were actually tax-paying chattel slaves, to be bought and sold, given away, lost at cards, or even deprived of life at their master's whim. Their bodies might belong, in the final analysis, to the Tsar, and their souls to God, but as human beings they stood outside the law; they were not merely unfree, but un-people.

The position of the peasant in feudal society was so utterly different as to make nonsense of the accepted practice of applying to both the same term: 'serf'. He was unfree and personally dependent on his lord, but cannot by any stretch of the imagination be described as a chattel. He was subject solely to the jurisdiction of the lord, but this jurisdiction was exercised in accordance with local custom and the law of the land. Both his rights and his obligations were precisely defined and codified. His property rights were limited, but he could bring civil suits (even against his lord, in certain specified instances); in criminal cases he stood trial before the common courts; he was expected to fulfil certain civic duties, such as participation in a coroner's jury; he partook of the privileges contained in the charters granted to his village; and so on.

In contrast to the Russian peasant, whose bondage was established by the State and enforced by the State, the peasant in feudal Europe stood in a private relationship to his lord. Of considerable importance also was the different scale of values that prevailed: in Western Europe the precious commodity was not manpower, but land, always in short supply. The position in Russia was almost exactly reversed, with all the consequences that this entailed.

Even from this brief and necessarily condensed account of the feudal order it becomes obvious that traditional Muscovite society, with its bureaucratic police State based on the absolute and indivisible authority of the supreme ruler and on the compulsion of unconditional and unlimited service of all subjects in the community's interest, with a serving nobility in place of a landed aristocracy and with chattel slaves instead of serfs, with neither vassalage nor contract, and lacking any institutional or societal safeguard against despotism, can be described as feudal only by depriving the concept itself of any real meaning. Whatever the incipient developments of the pre-Mongol era may have been (and there seems little doubt that these bore certain feudal characteristics), the Russia that was gathered together by Moscow never knew feudalism – just as she had no experience of such vitally important factors of European history as the Investiture Contest, the Renaissance, the Reformation or the Counter-Reformation.

Beginning from Karamzin, the founder of modern Russian historiography, and until well into the twentieth century, serious Russian historians consistently rejected the applicability of the concept of feudalism to post-Mongol Russia. Of particular value is the opinion of Pushkin, who was not only Russia's greatest poet, but a considerable student of history in his own right. Moreover, he possessed a profound intuitive understanding of his people and of their past. Pushkin wrote: 'We never had feudalism, the more is the pity . . . It must be realized that Russia never had anything in common with the rest of Europe, and that her history requires ideas and formulas that are different from the ideas and formulas deduced by Guizot from the history of the Christian West.'

The only important non-Leninist Russian historian to have written of Russian feudalism (at the turn of the century), was Pavlov-Silvansky, but he confined his 'feudal' analysis, in the main, to pre-Muscovite Rus. His writings have, naturally, been made much of by Soviet historians, who quote them as proof – the more conclusive for having been adduced by a 'bourgeois' historian – of the fundamental identity of Russian and Western European development. Yet Pavlov-Silvansky himself gave a vivid description of late seventeenth-century Muscovite society in terms that are simply not comparable to any Western social or legal concept: 'The basic principle of the Russian social structure in the Muscovite era was the total subjugation of the individual to the interests of the State. The external circumstances of the life of Muscovite Rus, her stubborn struggle for existence against her eastern and western neighbours, demanded the extreme exertion of the nation's resources.

Russian society was permeated by the readiness of every subject to serve the State to the best of their abilities, and to sacrifice themselves in the defence of the Russian land and of the Orthodox Christian faith . . . All classes of the population were bound either to service or to *tyaglo*, in order that "each shall stand firm and unwavering in the station to which he has been bound and at the disposal of the Tsar".[11] Hardly the description of a feudal or post-feudal country of Western Europe!

But if Muscovy manifestly refuses to conform to the pattern of feudalism, is there any other general institutional framework into which her peculiar system can be seen to fit?

Already the first Western visitors to Russia were struck by the numerous seeming affinities between that country and the great Asiatic empires that were then becoming ever better known to Europeans. Fletcher compares the government of Russia with that of Turkey, Olearius with Persia, others still with China. This opinion became widely accepted, and for a long time dominated Western thinking about Russia. Custine, equipped with a knowledge of the very considerable results achieved by his day in the fields of sociology and comparative government, spoke quite straightforwardly of Russia as of 'a community governed on the principles which directed the most ancient states named in the annals of the world . . . the patriarchal tyranny of the Asiatic governments'.[12]

Whether or not this approach was correct, it at least had the inestimable advantage of providing the observer with a definite frame of reference for his interpretation of Russian society. In those more happy times Russia was never thought of as an inscrutable enigma: to be sure, she was an entity quite different and standing apart from Europe, but then so were a majority of the countries of the globe. The concept of One World was yet to come.

The idea that the whole of mankind is progressing along closely similar lines of development towards a more or less identical future, and that the only real difference between peoples and societies lies in the respective stages of this historical process attained by each at a given time, is one of comparatively recent standing. Prior to our modern age, from the time when, as a result of the Renaissance and the great voyages, the European mind broke out of its spiritual and geographical shackles, the realization of the uniqueness and singularity of Western European development pervaded all serious writing on social and political theory. It was generally accepted that the great civilizations of the East, the ones that were by then only a memory as well as the still flourishing empires of Asia, represented a common socio-political system that was far removed from the principles of social organization being evolved in the West. Scholars might have differed in the relative importance they attached to one or another characteristic feature of this Oriental system, or in the theories they developed to explain its genesis and its remarkable stability, but on several points there was general agreement: that the great empires of the East constituted a specific, integral species of human society; that this type of society was based on a series of concepts not merely different from, but in many cases directly opposed to those that had been developed by Western European civilization; that this was the oldest type of society known to man, and that it was dominant over the greater part of the globe.

Among the first to take cognizance of this phenomenon, which today is usually called Oriental despotism, was Jean Bodin, one of the founders of modern political science. Bodin classified it as *monarchie seigneuriale*, a type of monarchy based on the principle of its subjects' unlimited submission and total dependence on the State; none had any rights, none were free to dispose of their property or even of their persons. This view was more or less accepted by such widely divergent thinkers as Bossuet and Locke.

The most detailed, lucid and influential exposition of Oriental despotism was made by Montesquieu in his celebrated *Esprit des Lois*. According to his scheme, of the three types of government – republican, monarchical and despotic – it was the despotic variety that held sway over all the lands between Turkey and the East Indies. This was a system of government 'in which a single person directs everything by his own will and caprice', where mankind is 'all upon a level', and 'all are slaves'. The fundamental principle of despotic government is universal fear: 'In despotic states, the nature of government requires the most passive obedience; and when once the prince's will is made known, it ought infallibly to produce its effect. Here they have no limitations or restrictions, no mediums, terms, equivalents or remonstrances; no change to propose: man is a creature that blindly submits to the absolute will of the sovereign.' Montesquieu put his finger squarely on the prime economic aspect of this system, pointing out that in despotic states no laws on property exist, that 'the lands belong to the prince' – who is by the nature of things heir to all his subjects.[13]

It should be noted that Montesquieu often cited Russia as a typical example of the despotic state – along with China, Persia, Turkey, India, Ceylon, Java etc.[14]

The concept of Oriental despotism as a type of polity based on principles completely different from and, indeed, repugnant to those of Western Europe, was further developed by the classical economists: James Mill, Richard Jones and John Stuart Mill. But perhaps the most expressive description of this system as exemplified by China, was made by Hegel, who saw as the principal problem the relationship between the individual and the State:

> In China we have the realm of absolute equality, and all the differences that exist are possible only in connection with the administration, and in virtue of the worth which a person may acquire, enabling him to fill a high post in the Government. Since equality prevails in China, but without any freedom, despotism is necessarily the mode of government . . .
>
> The Emperor is the centre, around which everything turns; consequently the well-being of the country and people depends on him . . . There is no other legal power or institution extant, but this superintendence and oversight of the Emperor . . .

111

In China the distinction between slavery and freedom is necessarily not great, since all are equal before the Emperor – that is, all are alike degraded . . .

And though there is no distinction conferred by birth, and every one can attain the highest dignity, this very equality testifies to no triumphant assertion of the worth of the inner man, but a servile consciousness.[15]

The concept of Oriental despotism was followed up and fruitfully expanded by Hegel's most famous ex-disciples: Marx and Engels. As early as 1853 they saw that there was something about the social order of the Oriental despotisms. It did not fit into any of the categories through which, they had confidently asserted, all societies cyclically evolve – primitive communism, ancient society (i.e. slaveowning), feudal society, capitalist society and socialist society. As Engels put it, 'But how does it come about that the Orientals did not arrive at landed property, even in its feudal form? I think it is mainly due to the climate together with the nature of the soil . . . artificial irrigation is here the first condition of agriculture.' Thus, he and Marx argued, the primitive village communities had needed the State simply as a provider of water. That is to say, it did not 'represent' any specific exploiting class: insofar as there was exploitation, it was by the State itself and its bureaucratic caste. 'An Oriental government,' Engels added, 'never had more than three departments: finance (plunder at home), war (plunder at home and abroad), and public works . . .' They adduced several other main factors to account for its extraordinary longevity and immobility: the dispersed condition of the population living in isolated, identical village communities; the staying power and inertia of the natural economy that was the economic foundation of society; and – a paramount feature – the concentration of landed property in the hands of the State, and the absence or exceeding weakness of private property in land.

The Founding Fathers never managed – scarcely even tried – to solve the problem presented by this recognition of the fact that their unilinear scheme, based on Europe, was thus falsified. In the preface to Marx's *The Critique of Political Economy* he says, it is true, 'in broad outline, the asiatic, the ancient, the feudal, and the modern bourgeois modes of production can be indicated as progressive epochs in the economic system of society'. This rather trivial sleight of hand did not, of course, solve the problem: taken literally the sentence is untrue according to the Marxist, or any other, scheme. And otherwise he avoided the problem.

The unilinear view of historical development was by no means confined to Marxist thought. Like the latter, it was born of the nineteenth century – that magnificent age when Europe bestrode the globe, and the industrial capitalist system seemed monarch of all it surveyed. In the prevailing intellectual atmosphere of heady self-confidence, liberal humanitarianism and unbounded faith in progress and improvement, what more natural than to view the self-evidently successful European pattern as the prototype for the development of human society, and to regard other, less fortunate 'backward' peoples as having fallen behind or got caught in a groove at some stage in this passage. This generalization of the European experience was also closely connected with the rise of modern sociology and its quest for a unified pattern of societal development, and also with the widespread influence of Darwinism, which, when applied to the evolution of human society, led to the concept of certain scientifically inevitable stages of growth.

The argument about the 'Asiatic' mode of production has always been troublesome to Marxists.[16] Since the Russian Revolution, in particular, discussion of it has been almost totally repressed in Russia itself – partly, no doubt, because it would allow flexible-minded Marxists the existence of a category not covered in the original Marxist scheme, so that a new one still could be devised for a post-capitalist Russia which was not yet recognizably socialist by any earlier standards.

Even nearer the knuckle, though, was the idea that the 'Asiatic' bureaucratic despotism itself bore very strong resemblances to the condition of the Soviet Union. But more broadly, it has been suggested that Asiatic despotism is the most fruitful concept to be applied to Russia throughout its post-Mongol history.

In recent years a powerful case has been made by Professor Karl Wittfogel for the classification of Russia in this way. Like Marx, he tells that 'Even in its simplest form, agrohydraulic operations necessitate substantial integrative action. In their more elaborate variations, they involve extensive and complex organizational planning . . . The effective management of these works involves an organizational web which covers either the whole, or at least the dynamic core, of the country's population. In consequence, those who control this network are uniquely prepared to wield supreme political power . . . The hydraulic State is a genuinely managerial State. This fact has far-reaching societal implications. As manager of hydraulic and other mammoth constructions, the hydraulic State prevents the nongovernmental forces of society from crystallizing into independent bodies strong enough to counterbalance and control the political machine.'[17]

The hydraulic works and the life-giving water that flowed through them constituted the property of the State; the soil itself, and all its inhabitants, either belonged to, or were rigidly controlled by the State. In China, for instance, a famous poem of the Chou dynasty (1122–256 B.C.) had it that:

> Everywhere under vast Heaven
> There is no land that is not the king's
> To the borders of those lands
> There are none who are not the king's servants.[18]

This was a bureaucratic police state which recognized no checks or limitations on the ruler's absolute authority, where the laws offered no guarantees to the subjects; it demanded, and received, total and unquestioning submission from everyone, including the most important officials and territorial magnates, for whom there could be no security, either of tenure, of possessions or of life itself. Terror – secretive, unpredictable, undefined by law – was an indispensable weapon of governmental policy. The State had a monopoly of armed forces;

all adult males were expected to toil, to fight and to pay whenever the State willed it. Private landed property was weak and insecure, and its representatives, deriving their authority from the State, bore a much closer resemblance to government functionaries than to landowners in the European sense of the word.

Obviously there is a marked similarity between this socio-political system and that of traditional Russia. Would it then be justified as Wittfogel does, to equate Russian society with Oriental despotism? For such a conclusion to be meaningful a simple inventory of parallels is not enough. Mention must be made of the points of divergence between the two patterns, and the differences appraised and weighed against the analogies.

From the point of view of social structure the most significant discrepancy concerned the relative position of the peasantry, which everywhere comprised the vast bulk of the population. Whereas in Russia by the beginning of the seventeenth century the majority of peasants had been reduced to a condition that soon acquired the characteristic features of chattel slavery, in the great despotic empires of the Orient personal slavery never played an important part. There the commoners, including the peasants, all 'share a negative quality: none participates in the affairs of the state apparatus. They also share a positive quality: none are slaves.'[19] Today most authorities agree that in these societies slave labour was but of minor auxiliary importance, and confined mainly to the household, the court, the government office, workshop and mine. The tiller of the soil was personally free, or, to put it more precisely, was held in bondage, like everybody else, directly by the State. This was inherent in the nature of the economy: irrigation agriculture required the constant toil, care and devotion of which a slave, or a Russian serf, would have been incapable. In Russia, on the other hand, the facts of life: the unsettled frontier, the wild open spaces, the shortage of manpower, the ceaseless warfare – all made the Statute of Bondage inevitable.

But this distinctive feature, however important, can by itself hardly invalidate the great number of facts pointing to a fundamental affinity between the Muscovite system and that of Oriental despotism. The chief stumbling-block to their identification lies elsewhere: in the simple fact that Russia never possessed a hydraulic economy or a 'hydraulic State', that her agriculture was not based on irrigation or flood control, that waterworks of any kind, whether for production or for transportation, were probably of lesser importance for Russia than for any other country – not only of despotic Asia, but even of feudal and post-feudal Europe.

This crucial flaw in the argument for Russia's classification as an Oriental despotism has already been pointed out: 'The basic error of Wittfogel consists in failure to distinguish between the hypothesis (1) that large-scale irrigation necessitates despotism and (2) that all cases of despotism are products of this type of agriculture. This confusion leads him to include Russia and Turkey in the category of "hydraulic societies", which is clearly absurd, since neither of these countries knew irrigation on a large scale.'[20]

Wittfogel, it is true, attempts to overcome this obstacle by referring to the Tartars, who, in the course of their centuries of rule, introduced into Russia the methods and concepts of Oriental despotism, which they, in turn, had acquired from the Chinese: 'Tartar rule alone among the three major Oriental influences affecting Russia [the other two being Byzantine and Turkish] was decisive both in destroying the non-Oriental Kievan society and in laying the foundations for the despotic state of Muscovite and post-Muscovite Russia.'[21]

But this explanation actually begs the question. Tartar rule, as has been shown above, was undoubtedly a factor of vital importance in the break-up of the old fabric of society and the reshaping of Russia in the new Muscovite mould. From the Mongols Moscow inherited not only its claim to dominion over the Russian lands, and not only the methods of Oriental statecraft, of military organization, finance, etc., but also the very ideas which lay at the heart of its system of government: the conception of universal compulsory service, of the unquestioning submission of the individual to the State; the idea of the prince as the supreme landowner; very probably too, the dream of a world empire based on the principles of justice and equality – the 'world-conquering tendencies of the Mongol master' of which Marx spoke.

For a system of government, however, that was so utterly alien from all earlier Russian tradition, to have taken root and flourished with such intensity, the force of example, the mere acessibility of the tools, could not have been sufficient. After all, Hungary and the Balkan countries remained under Turkish rule for periods, in some cases, far exceeding the duration of the Tartar yoke, yet none of them emerged from thraldom as Oriental despotisms. This will not do – as in murder investigations, not only opportunity and method, but motive also has to be established. There had to exist in Russia a particular concatenation of circumstances that required, necessitated or called for the introduction of this socio-political system, and that ensured the rationality and success of its operation – or, to use the Toynbeean terms, there had to have existed a 'challenge' which evoked an appropriate 'response'.

What then were the compelling factors that drove Russia, a country where 'hydraulic' conditions were non-existent, towards the development of a system which was in its main features indistinguishable from that of Oriental despotism? Two such factors existed.

The first is the simple fact that throughout nearly the whole of written history, from the first great civilizations of the East to the beginnings of the Industrial Age, despotism was the only form of government capable of holding together and administering large territorial entities. Any looser form of organization embracing considerable areas would have dissolved within a short space of time, as so often happened. It was not in the least fortuitous that the first systems of limited, even democratic, government sprang up in the Greek city-states – those alien specks on the edge of the vast land-mass of Asia – or that a type of pluralistic society should have evolved in the infinitesimal (by Asian standards) feudal States of Western Europe. Such methods were totally unsuitable for running a far-flung empire, and that is what Russia had become. Her sheer size, her giant, shapeless, frontierless bulk, irresistibly spilling over into the unsettled heartland of Asia, set Russia decisively apart from the nations of Europe. In evolving and consolidating her despotic system Russia was actually only conforming to the normal pattern of life that had always been preponderant throughout the globe; it was the European countries which were the anomalies: tiny mammals in a world of fearsome dinosaurs.

But the exigency that called forth the Muscovite variety of Oriental despotism was more pressing than the mere demand for effective administration. The socio-political system of the great Asian empires had been created by the paramount need for building and maintaining the waterworks upon which the very lives of their peoples depended. Russia knew nothing of this, yet for centuries she too had been confronted by a task which, though different in nature, was for her just as much a matter of life and death: national survival depended upon the permanent mobilization and organization of all her meagre resources for defence, war and colonization, on a scale beyond the European comprehension. Despotic government, with all its implications, was the instrument she shaped to cope with the everlasting emergency. The ideas may have been brought in from the outside, but the necessity was terrifyingly real.

From the very beginning, as has already been mentioned, foreign visitors were struck by the uncanny resemblance between Russian institutions and those of the Oriental despotisms. Some even suggested a deliberate policy of emulating the methods of Oriental government. Fletcher, for instance, wrote: 'The manner of their government is much after the Turkish fashion: which they seeme to imitate as neare as the countrie, and reach of their capacities in pollitique affayres, will give them leave to doo.'[22] Fletcher seems to have hit the nail on the head for, unbeknown to him, this is precisely what the Russian governments of the sixteenth, seventeenth and early eighteenth centuries were being urged to do by their most influential political writers. Peresvetov's belief in the supernatural power of a Russia that would combine Orthodox

Christianity with Turkish custom has already been quoted. Križanić was only slightly less emphatic: 'Reason tells us that the Turks have a number of excellent institutions, which deserve to be copied (although not all).'[23] Even Pososhkov, the ideologist of the Westernizing reforms of Peter the Great, declared: 'It is profitable to study and to apply the Turkish laws, which are clearer and more just than those of the Germans.'[24] These may or may not have been fair judgments; their significant feature is their authors' appreciation of the substantial affinity between Russia and Turkey (invariably coupled with a strong denunciation of the West).

Later generations of Russian historians tended, not without reason, to approach this problem somewhat gingerly. The famous nineteenth-century philosopher Pyotr Chaadayev appears to have been among the first to describe Russia as 'an oriental despotism supported by an oriental cult'[25] (it was for views of this nature that the government had him declared insane). Towards the end of the century, however, the 'Oriental' interpretation of the traditional Russian system of State and society began to gain considerable currency. Chicherin stated unequivocally: 'Oriental despotism served as the model for Russia.'[26] Kliuchevsky, although more cautious by nature, repeatedly stressed the basic identity between the Russian and Oriental types of despotism. A few random examples should suffice. Justifying Ivan IV's fears for the safety of his family after his death, Kliuchevsky speaks of the 'usual fate of rival princes in Oriental despotisms'. In the course of his analysis of the sixteenth-century Muscovite social structure he finds it necessary to draw attention to the points at which it diverged from the typical Oriental configuration (incidentally, by over-emphasizing the amorphous nature of Oriental society Kliuchevsky seems to have exaggerated the actual difference). Finally, and most tellingly of all, Kliuchevsky describes the basic aspects of Russian government and society *of the mid-eighteenth century* as 'characteristic features of states of an Oriental Asiatic structure, even if decorated by a European façade'.[27] Miliukov, the last of the eminent pre-revolutionary historians, left no doubt as to his views: compelling national necessity, he wrote, 'gave the Muscovite government the means to establish a centralized state of the Oriental type, i.e. military force'.[28]

The conviction that the traditional pre-1861 Russian socio-political system, in many of its vital features, approached very near to, or could even be identified with, Oriental despotism, was by no means confined to liberal 'bourgeois' historians. It was also held (before they were strapped into the strait-waistcoat of uniformity) by a number of the most outstanding Marxist students of the Russian past – no doubt under the influence of the strong views expressed on the subject by Marx himself. In his brilliant account of the *History of Russian Social Thought*, Plekhanov returns to the problem over and over again: 'Throughout many centuries Russia was moving further and further away from Western Europe, and approaching nearer and nearer to the Orient. . . . By the time that settled Russian Europe finally succeeded in defeating nomadic Asia her own socio-political relationships had become very similar to those prevailing in the Asiatic despotisms. In other words, Europe had defeated the "Asiatics" only by herself becoming Asia . . . During the century that followed the Time of Troubles the internal conditions of Muscovy became more and more those of the great Oriental despotisms.'[29] Trotsky too, in his best-known historical work, largely subscribed to this opinion. Speaking of the primitiveness and backwardness of Russia's economic development, he commented: 'Here we were nearer to India than to Europe, just as our medieval cities were nearer to the Asiatic than the European type, and as our autocracy, standing between the European absolutism and the Asiatic despotism, in many features approached the latter.'[30]

Today hardly a hint of 'Oriental' analogies is allowed to pierce the massive ideological armour encasing the spotless official Soviet view of Russian history. Indeed, the very idea of a separate social system of 'Oriental despotism' or 'Asiatic mode of production', once so fruitfully developed by the Founding Fathers themselves, has been obliterated, erased from memory, made into an 'un-concept'. (Quite recently, beginning with 1965, there have been a few hesitating attempts to revive Marx's ideas on this subject: they have met with unjustified official disapproval.) Many Western scholars too, though for entirely different reasons, prefer to seek out and to stress the underlying sameness of the stages of all nations' economic, political, social and cultural development. Whatever the humanitarian merits of the case, it has hardly been conducive to a proper understanding of the Russian past: rather the opposite.

CHAPTER 7

The Petrine Watershed

Russia's modern history was inaugurated by Peter the Great.

In the history of no other nation has a single individual made an impact as shattering, and as lasting, as the impression left upon Russia by her first Emperor. It is strikingly reflected in the fact that since his day Russian history has been regarded as falling into two parts: pre-Petrine and post-Petrine. Nowhere else is this the case: for other nations the great turning-points of the past are provided by impersonal events – wars, conquests, revolutions, reformations – and even the most important historical figures have to be content with Ages, Epochs or Eras – Elizabethan, Victorian, Jeffersonian, Napoleonic, Wilhelmine. Only Russia adjusts her whole chronology around one man. This is the measure of Peter's greatness.

His colossal figure, straddling Russia ancient and modern, represents a fascinating compound of contradictions. Peter dominates his country's history because, to an extraordinary degree, he combined within his own person all the conflicting tendencies, the seemingly incompatible extremes of a Russia poised between Europe and Asia, between barbarism and civilization, between semi-Tartar Muscovy and European Great Power status. In a very definite sense, Peter *was* Russia.

Physically he was a giant of a man, standing nearly seven feet tall, possessed of Herculean strength, and with an inexhaustible fund of energy – yet from his youth he was afflicted with a nervous ailment that made his head shake uncontrollably, and at several critical moments of his life he was seized by fits similar to epilepsy. Throughout his reign his principal, all-absorbing preoccupation was with military matters: he created a modern army and Russia's first navy, he fought for twenty-one years against Sweden in what was the longest continuous

122

European war of the past 300 years, taking part in all its major engagements, besides personally leading armies against Turkey and Persia; indeed, it was by constant and eventually victorious warfare that he transformed Russia into a powerful factor in European politics. Yet he remained to the end of his days a most unmilitaristic man (in contrast to his adversary, Charles XII of Sweden), with no particular stomach for fighting, displaying neither outstanding military ability nor conspicuous courage, and on one occasion (in 1711) causing, by his own and his generals' gross incompetence, the ignominious defeat of the Russian army, escaping Turkish captivity only by acceptance of humiliating terms and by bribing the Grand Vizier with his wife's jewellery.

He introduced Western customs and costumes into Russia, cutting off beards and banning all external manifestations of the traditional past, modelling his court upon that of Versailles – yet in barbarism and cruelty he could outdo even Ivan the Terrible himself: personally beheading rebels, torturing his disloyal son with his own hands. Whenever he had the time he would work, seriously and devotedly, as a common labourer, mastering more than a dozen skills, striving in vain to set an example to his slothful courtiers – yet he was always acutely conscious of being the autocrat, the divine ruler of his country, with unlimited powers over life and property. He was a great educator, prizing knowledge above all else, forcing his subjects to acquire Western learning; establishing the country's first secular schools; founding an Academy of Sciences; employing the most eminent European scholars – yet he never became fully literate in his own language, and often astonished foreigners both by his proficiency in some fields of knowledge and by his total ignorance of others. He was a deeply religious man – yet delighted in organizing blasphemous spectacles of the utmost depravity. Frugal, abstemious, even parsimonious by nature, he would suddenly burst out in Gargantuan debauchery for weeks at a time, resulting not infrequently in the drunken death of one or another of his cronies.

Peter's attitude to his country poses the most important and

123

probably the most difficult problem of all. He was a great patriot; his single-minded belief in Russia's dazzling future developed into an obsession; every one of his actions was motivated by concern for the nation's greatness, strength and well-being; he was the first Russian ruler to regard himself as standing in a relationship of service to the country. Yet to achieve the aims he had set for his nation he ruthlessly drove it to the breaking-point of human endurance; he profligately squandered the country's human and material resources; and, while trampling upon hallowed and cherished national traditions, he revived the most archaic and basically anti-national one of all: the concept of the country as the Tsar's patrimonial possession, to be disposed of according to his sovereign will. He destroyed the hide-bound, ossified, servile conventions of Muscovy – only to impose upon Imperial Russia a regimentation that was even harsher and more rigid. Although in many ways, by the standards of his time, a humane and enlightened man (as shown, for instance, by his charitable treatment of the Old Believers), he created a regime of terror that was perhaps worse – because more efficient – than anything seen before: in this respect too, he broke with the incompetent, obsolete methods of the past, and his fear-inspiring *Preobrazhensky Prikaz*, with the monstrous Prince Romodanovsky as torturer- and executioner-in-chief, became the model for all future Russian secret police institutions.

And, supreme paradox of all, although Peter was closer to his people than any other monarch of European history – spending his life among them, eating their food, speaking their language, being acclaimed as the People's Tsar, the Muzhik-Tsar, the Workingman-Tsar – during his lifetime and for long thereafter he was probably personally the most hated of all Russian Tsars.

Such are some of the puzzling features that go to make up this extraordinary man, 'this mighty lord of fate' – in Pushkin's inspired words – who 'with an iron bridle reared Russia upright, high above the abyss'. Peter's character, his prodigious labours, the nature of his transformation of Russia: these are riddles set by him for future generations. They have not been satisfactorily solved to this day.

It was not for want of trying. For two and a half centuries the reign of Peter the Great has been the most controversial period of Russian history, and it shows no signs of losing that position. Even in the present age of unparalleled revolutionary upheaval the Petrine Reform continues to dominate the Russian past and, in a vital sense, the Russian future as well, for within it are contained all the essential elements of the age-old Russian dilemma: the problems of continuity and change, of tradition and innovation, so often expressed in the contraposition of Russia and the West, or (since Peter) of Moscow and St Petersburg.

This debate was never a matter of dispassionate inquiry by rival schools of cloistered historians, but from its very inception within Peter's lifetime it has raged in the forefront of Russian political life. For two hundred years the Petrine Reform remained as a peculiar touchstone for every Russian political and social movement, as the acid test of their intentions. The approach to Peter constituted the line of division between opposing ideological tendencies. The whole history of Russian political and social thought can be seen as the history of the development of contrasting views of the Petrine Reform, as the history of the attitudes of various political currents – conservative, liberal, reactionary, revolutionary, reformist, Populist, Slavophile, Westerner, Socialist – towards the legacy of Peter the Great.

A detailed examination of this legacy must of necessity fall outside the scope of the present inquiry, but Russia's past would be unintelligible without a brief description of its principal aspects.

Probably the most striking feature of the Petrine Reform is its complete lack of design or even of premeditation; the haphazard way in which it developed, branching out, seemingly at random, into ever newer fields of activity, stumbling alike upon unsuspected problems and adventitious solutions. When Peter took over the country's administration in 1694 (he had succeeded to the throne in 1682, at the age of ten), not only did he have no plan of reform, it is doubtful whether the idea itself had ever entered his mind. But as a boy, during the regency, first of his strong-willed half-sister Sophia, and then of his weak and silly mother, he had been allowed to run wild, acquiring neither the traditional education nor the Byzantine inhibitions expected of a Tsar of Muscovy. It was with an open mind and an eager and undulled intelligence that he took up his royal duties. The direction of his life and the course of Russian history were changed decisively by the diverse experiences of the first years of his reign: two indecisive and immensely costly military expeditions against the Turks; a lengthy journey through Western Europe, opening up a hitherto undreamt-of world of material achievement of trade and industry, of science and technology, of a civilized and refined way of life; a number of assassination plots and attempted uprisings by disgruntled adherents of the old order of things – ruthlessly put down, and powerfully reinforcing Peter's innate hatred of Muscovite traditions; and, most important of all in its traumatic effects, Russia's ill-prepared and bungling entry into a war with Sweden, then at the zenith of her power, resulting in a series of disastrous defeats, from which Peter emerged as a universal laughing-stock, and the gallant Charles XII as the toast of Europe.

The Swedish war was both the midwife and the hard school-master of Petrine Russia. Peter himself was free with his acknowledgments: after the victorious conclusion of the war he likened his country to an exceptionally dull-witted and backward child, forced to attend school for three times the normal seven-year period before it finally succeeded in passing its examinations.

It was the military reform that provided the heart, the fountain-head, the driving force of all Peter's manifold activities: the urgent necessity to establish a permanent standing army, organized, trained and equipped along the most modern European lines. Everything undertaken by the great Tsar, whether in administration, education or economics, was, in a very direct sense, derived from or consequential upon his single-minded battle for the creation of an efficient military machine.

126

The traditional Muscovite system of the *levée en masse* – the annual mobilization of the country's fighting-men for service on the southern frontier – was becoming inadequate even for its protective functions, since, instead of Tartar raiding parties, it was now increasingly faced by the hardened professionals of the Turkish army. Against the highly trained armies of the European Powers, with their sophisticated equipment and the revolutionary military techniques evolved in the campaigns of Gustavus Adolphus, Condé and Turenne, it was less than useless. This was amply proved throughout the seventeenth century, further evidence being provided by the rout of Peter's army at Narva, in the first engagement of the Northern War (1700).

The initial steps towards the establishment of a regular army had already been taken by the governments of Peter's predecessors – his father Alexei Mikhailovich, his brother Fyodor and his half-sister Sophia – but they had been half-hearted ones at best. Peter threw himself into the task with unbelievable energy and a total disregard for accepted conventions. He first set up two Guards regiments, the Preobrazhensky and the Semenovsky, to serve both as models and as officers' training schools for his new army; they were composed, from privates up, exclusively of noblemen, and no one could receive an officer's commission without having first served in the ranks. Around this nucleus new regiments of the line were established with incredible speed, the old irregular formations being disbanded to provide the manpower, with only a fraction preserved for auxiliary duties. No expense was spared, either human or material: foreign experts and soldiers of fortune were employed on a lavish scale, and the battlefield became the new army's principal training-ground. Either they learned their lesson, or they perished. To ensure the permanence and the rapid growth of his armed forces, and to offset the fearful battle-losses and the wastage caused by incompetent leadership, poor communications and lack of supplies, Peter introduced a regular system of conscription, with an annual call-up, with compulsory life-long and year-round service for the nobility, and with every *pomeshchik* obliged to supply a certain number of peasant recruits, in a fixed proportion to his total muster of serfs.

Besides establishing a standing professional army, Peter created a navy for the first time in Russian history. Nothing delighted this ruler of a land-locked and ice-bound empire more than the open sea. The Navy was his first and strongest love, and he himself became Russia's most expert sailor, navigator, shipwright and jack of all seafaring trades.

By 1725, the year of his death, Peter commanded a well-trained and battle-tested professional army of over 200,000 regular soldiers and about 100,000 irregulars, the largest in Europe: an army which had eventually demolished the might of Sweden and, for the first time, carried the Russian colours into the heart of Europe; he also possessed a large and efficient navy, which had secured mastery of the Baltic. By force of arms, by dint of fearful sacrifice, imposed upon her from above, Russia had become a Great Power. No one counted the human cost: there were always more men where the others came from. As regards finance, the military budget now consumed fully two-thirds of the vastly increased volume of State expenditure.

For Russia to accomplish the foreign policy aims set before her by Peter, to achieve the Great Power status commensurate with her size and population, to break out to the sea, and through the sea to the great world outside, the old military machine had had to be scrapped and a new one fashioned. But in order to provide the armed forces with a steady and uninterrupted flow of trained manpower, money and supplies, the old social, economic and administrative system had to be drastically overhauled. So it was that the exigencies of his life and death struggle with Sweden led Peter, step by inexorable step, towards the transformation of Muscovy into the Russian Empire – just as the Muscovy he was reshaping had herself been moulded by the circumstances of her mortal combat with the Tartars.

One thing led to another – usually without design, often without deliberation, sometimes by chance. Backed by the unlimited powers of the State, Peter could afford to rush through his reforms at top speed: hurried decisions acquired the sanctity of law, stopgap measures endured as permanent regulations, casual ideas became basic policies for future generations.

The new standing army and navy required a strong social foundation, a new type of serving military class; therefore the status and functions of the nobility had to be changed and so, inevitably, had the relative position of other classes of society. The armed forces needed up-to-date equipment, arms, financing, therefore industry had to be established, the fiscal system reformed, new burdens laid upon the people. These novel and complex tasks called for newfangled organizational methods; therefore a brand-new administrative structure had to be devised. Both the army and the civil administration urgently needed large numbers of educated and technically trained people; therefore a system of education had to be started from scratch, and doors thrown wide open to foreign contacts. And so on and so forth, until the whole fabric of Russian life had seemingly been changed beyond recognition.

In the sphere of social relationships probably the most significant effect of the Petrine Reform was a distinct change in the position of the nobility. Although much has been made of the cases in which Peter appointed men of extremely humble origin to high office, it was in general a matter of course that the executors of his policy, both at NCO and at officer level, on whom the success of the entire venture depended, were to be supplied by the serving nobility; it was to the regulation of their status that the Tsar first applied himself, in the fitful interludes between campaign or commissariat duties. Towards the latter, more tranquil and legislatively most productive part of his reign, this resulted in a far-reaching alteration of the Russian social structure.

Like so much else of Peter's achievements, the new position of the nobility was fraught with contradictions. On the one hand, their obligations to the State had been sharply increased, and their dependent and duty-bound status strengthened. Indeed, the nobility came to stand for a category more of *employment* than of *social class*; a person's inclusion within its ranks was to depend on his official position rather than on his genealogy. The requirements of the military reform were the determining factor: military service became not only obligatory, but also life-long and strictly regulated. It began actually at the age of ten, with five years' compulsory education, followed by a period of service in the ranks in one of the Guards regiments, after which came either a term of further study abroad, or an officer's commission, or – less frequently – an appointment in the civilian branch of government. This pattern, broken only by rare periods of leave, would last until terminated by death, senility, or physical disablement. Non-compliance, or non-appearance for service – as laid down by Ukases passed in 1714 and 1722 – entailed automatic outlawry and liability to summary execution, forfeiture of all rights, and confiscation of all property, half of which was to pass to anybody, even to a serf, who denounced or apprehended the truant.

The introduction of a strictly regulated scheme of military service, with orderly promotion by merit through all ranks, marked the transformation of the Russian nobility from a caste-bound hierarchy, based on family and social standing, into a homogeneous militarized bureaucratic class, where (at any rate theoretically) the only thing that mattered was distinction gained in service. The Muscovite aristocracy had always been a serving nobility, but in the olden days rank was equivalent with birth: the traditional Muscovite system had been that of *mestnichestvo*, or the order of precedence, whereby each nobleman's rank and station was immutably ordained and defined with mathematical precision in accordance with the exact position occupied by his forebears within the military hierarchy, neither lower nor higher. Thus if, as sometimes happened, nobleman A, appointed to serve under the command of nobleman B, was able to prove that his (A's) family had never been subordinate to B's ancestors, but had occupied the same, or perhaps an even higher rank, the offending order would be rescinded, and A would receive an appointment equal or superior to B's. For a Muscovite nobleman nothing could be more important than the punctilious safeguarding of his family's traditional place in the order of precedence: it was, after all, the only possession that he could unreservedly call his own.

Ivan IV's *Oprichnina* struck the first blow at *mestnichestvo*. During the seventeenth century it gradually fell into desuetude, and was abolished in 1682, a few years before Peter took over the reins of power. But the concept, and the habits it had bred, proved hard to demolish: it needed a Peter for this to be achieved. In 1722 the famous Table of Ranks refashioned the whole structure of State service and of the nobility along symmetrical lines of almost classical severity. They were to last, practically unchanged, for nearly 200 years. The complete bureaucratization of the serving nobility was finally accomplished: genealogical ranks and ancient pedigrees were replaced by grades of State service. The Table enacted the creation of the three separate, parallel and closely interlocking categories of military, civilian and court service; each was divided into a rigid scale of fourteen classes, from lowly subaltern to Field-Marshal, from clerk to Chancellor. Only by starting at the bottom could one reach the top (this, at least, was the conception). Ancient lineage and pride of family were now worth little in themselves: social position was determined by service rank. Moreover, since promotion was based on merit and length of service, and as the eight highest ranks could by law be occupied only by noblemen, it naturally followed that any commoner who reached the eighth class automatically acquired a patent of hereditary nobility. The government could now regulate, to its heart's content, not merely the social standing and official position of every nobleman, but even the most minute details of his everyday life; for instance, a special edict prescribed the exact quality and price of suitings that he was permitted to use: for the first five ranks – not above 4 rubles per *arshin*; for the next three – up to 3 rubles, and for the rest – not more than 2 rubles per *arshin*. Not for nothing was this embodiment of the bureaucrat's fondest dreams called the 'regulated' (*regulyarnoye*) State!

Yet, and herein lay the basic contradiction of his policy, while forcing the nobility into the rigid confines of his grand design,

Peter at the same time took the first steps along the road that was to lead to the establishment of a privileged estate and, within fifty years, to the emancipation of the nobility. It was an inexorable process, and, once again, its starting-point was the Petrine military reform. In the new scale of priorities the paramount place belonged to the category of highly trained professional fighting-men, which was perforce synonymous with the nobility. Come what may, their social and economic position had to be buttressed, though, as was well understood, stopping considerably short of granting them any real independence of the State. This was the object of the momentous Ukase of 1714 which made the *pomestie* hereditary and indivisible, to be bequeathed intact by the *pomeshchik* to any one of his sons. Like all Russian legal documents, it was imperfectly conceived, ambiguously expressed, vague and verbose in style; it has been interpreted as transferring full property rights to the landlords, and as instituting a Western-style system of entail and primogeniture. In reality the new law did nothing of the kind: the question of property rights was evaded, land remained service-bound, and the *pomestie* did not by right revert to the eldest son. What it actually decreed was that the ancient allodial *votchina* principle of inheritance should now apply to *pomestie* lands. This was *per se* a development of the highest significance. 'The combination of legal features of the *pomestie* and the *votchina* created a new and unprecedented type of landholding, which can be characterized as *hereditary, indivisible, and service-bound in perpetuity*, and which was linked to the owner's perpetual, hereditary and corporate service.'[1]

The principle of indivisibility of landholding might have become decisive for the evolution of a strong propertied aristocracy, as was the case in Western Europe; but, being completely alien to Russian custom, it did not long survive its author. Very soon after his death (typically, without the law itself ever being struck off the statute book) things returned to their old, happy state, under which estates were constantly being split up, breeding an impoverished nobility and engendering a depressed agriculture. However, despite the transient nature of Peter's 'majorat', the acquisition by the nobility of hereditary rights to their estates, in conjunction with their visibly increased importance within the State system, their greatly enhanced educational opportunities, and the creation of their own élite military units, inevitably led to the growth of a corporative spirit, to demands for full emancipation and for transformation into a uniquely privileged social estate.

As the nobility rose in importance and privilege, so did the peasantry sink still lower in the social scale. The peasants provided the raw material for Peter's great undertaking – the cannon-fodder, the tax-payers, the navvies and builders – and they were to become its chief victims. With the single-mindedness and the utter disregard for sacrifices that characterized all his actions, Peter carried the work of the 1649 *Ulozhenie* to its logical conclusion. He sought to achieve three aims: to satisfy the needs of the State; to keep the nobility happy; and to fashion a structure of society as neat as that of a man-of-war.

His policy, as embodied in a series of Ukases over the last ten years of his reign, was remarkably consistent. *Kholopy* (personal slaves) finally and irreversibly merged with serfs into a single servile category, every member of which was alike bound to the person of his master, and obliged to pay taxes. The field of operation of the Statute of Bondage was considerably broadened: the various intermediate groups that had previously, in the muddle and confusion of traditional Muscovite government, evaded its full application and preserved a modicum of independence – remote husbandmen of the European North and Siberia, landless members of serfs' families, impoverished serving-men with no serfs of their own, minor ecclesiastical and monastic hangers-on, etc. – were now brought under its full application. Most of these, in conjunction with other groups, went to form a new category of bondsmen, finally evolved during Peter's reign, and numbering anything up to half the total peasant population: that of *State serfs*, standing in the same relationship towards the State as landlords' serfs to their masters. State serfs fulfilled a variety of uses, not least as part of the largesse liberally bestowed upon royal favourites of the moment (and often taken away again with the same princely nonchalance). The State was, however, less harsh a taskmaster than the individual landowner, and their position, miserable as it was, came to be greatly envied by the unfortunate private serfs.

The process of simplification of servile relationships was more or less completed by the establishment, beside the two main categories of State and *pomeshchik*'s serfs, of the condition of factory serf. The origins of this group have already been described; their numbers and importance were to grow rapidly, with the increasing pace of Peter's forced industrialization.

For all serfs, old and new, the reign of Peter the Great marked a tangible change for the worse. Although their precise legal status remained as obscure and undefined as before, although they were never officially termed chattel (being tax-payers, they hardly could be so designated), the borderline between serfdom and full slavery had been effectively crossed, both in legislation and in practice. Indeed, in private and governmental correspondence, as in polite conversation, peasants were now frequently called slaves (not by the obsolete, patriarchal appellation of *kholop*, but by the harsh Biblical word *rab*), although there existed no legal foundation for this practice; it was in fact directly contrary to all the norms of ancient Russian law, which prohibited the imposition upon slaves of State obligations. But it was no more than a statement of fact: as a result of the Petrine Reform the peasants lost what few rights they had still retained, such as the right to lodge complaints against their master; the landlord's powers became unlimited, extending even to the freedom to interfere in their most intimate private affairs.

Most important of all, the government now finally recognized the landowners' right to sell their peasants without land, though this too, never found any expression in law. In 1721 the all-powerful autocrat of all the Russias, the man who had bodily carried his country from one age into another, confessed himself impotent to do anything about this evil practice: in an official letter about the sale of human beings in the market-place, he asked the Senate, lamely, 'to prohibit at least their being sold retail, as cattle are sold'.[2] The prohibition was duly enacted – without having the slightest effect. How could it, when Peter himself had instituted and encouraged the sale of recruits to the army?

The indefatigable labours of the great Tsar had profound and manifold effects on the Russian social structure, but it was the more visible manifestations of change that caught the imagination of his contemporaries and of later generations, at home and abroad alike. Peter had Europeanized Russia, it was proclaimed, and as proof of this fact there towered the mighty monuments to his reign: a European-type army and navy; an industry newly established on European models; a new secular culture, patterned along Western lines, and itself becoming an integral part of the culture of Europe. There was much else, of smaller importance perhaps, but no less striking to the beholder: periwigs and knee-breeches, tobacco and rum, titles and ribbons, the minuet and etiquette, Governors and Senators. And above all else, St Petersburg, his 'window into Europe'. All in all, it was an unparalleled achievement.

This was undoubtedly Europeanization on a grand scale – yet while Russia was becoming Europeanized, the European elements which now infused her had been very definitely Russified. In part this was a logical and inevitable development: recent history has furnished us with abundant experience in this respect. Russia was the first in the long line of countries that have sought to modernize themselves by transplanting and adapting the institutions and customs evolved in the specific and highly peculiar circumstances of Western Europe. Embedded in alien soil, these either perish or take on some of the properties of their new surroundings – sometimes becoming unrecognizable in the process. In Russia's case, however, there was more to it than the necessary modification of foreign experience in accordance with native tradition: all the evidence shows that from the very beginning Peter's approach to the task of Europeanization was one of hard-headed pragmatism. An intensely practical man, he cared only for practical results: Russia had to become a great military Power, and to hold her own against any combination of her neighbours. She had the size, the population, the potential wealth, and, above all, the State organization; what was needed was European efficiency and European technology. That was all, as far as he was concerned; for the rest, Europe remained an object of hostility and distrust. Peter expressed his attitude to the West with the utmost clarity and bluntness; on one occasion he told an intimate companion: 'We shall need Europe for a few decades, and then we can turn our backside to her.'[3]

Nowhere was this utilitarian approach more evident than in Peter's main contribution to the Russian economy: the establishment of an independent home industry. It was, by the nature of things, an artificial creation, forced upon an unwilling nation; in a country with neither capital nor entrepreneurs, working men nor consumers, supply nor demand, the State had to forge these ingredients itself. Russian industry was brought into being by the State for its own needs, in accordance with its decision to overcome Russia's backwardness and military weakness. The driving force behind the Petrine industrialization plan was not private profit, but compulsion. 'Under Peter,' wrote Kliuchevsky, 'factories and works were not true private enterprises, run solely in the interests of their proprietors, but became State operations, conducted by the Government through its obligated agents, the guild-merchants. In return for this service the industrialist could exercise the nobleman's privilege of acquiring villages with serf labourers for his factory . . . The establishment of a factory or the formation of a company became a compulsory service, a form of obligation, and the factory or company approximated to State institutions . . . In his factories and companies Peter combined the compulsoriness of the enterprise with the monopoly of production.'[4]

Unlike the mercantilist governments of Western European 'absolute monarchies', which merely supervised certain aspects of their countries' industrial development, in Russia, it could be said, the State actually managed industry – either directly, as with the bulk of heavy industry, or through the agency of nominated merchants, many of whom became 'capitalist entrepreneurs' only under duress. The State owned the country's natural resources – timber, metal ores, etc. – and it alone could undertake their exploitation. Concealment of mineral deposits or obstruction to the establishment of industrial enterprises automatically entailed flogging or death.

The factories, mills, mines, collieries, industrial and commercial companies set up under Peter the Great were mechanical, and rather inferior, copies of corresponding European establishments; they were usually situated at great distances from the old handicrafts centres, and owed little or nothing to the long-standing Russian tradition of skilled craftsmanship. The new industries received every conceivable support from the government: they were assured of a monopoly market; high tariffs and other devices excluded foreign competition; a permanent and unstinted supply of slave labour was guaranteed by the assignment to them in perpetuity of the inhabitants of whole districts and by the employment of convict labour. The State not only protected them: it was itself practically their only customer; only in 1809, for instance, were textile manufacturers permitted to accept orders from private clients. Yet despite this hot-house atmosphere, or perhaps because of it, and despite the natural aptitude of the Russian working man, year after year, decade after decade Russian factories continued to produce goods of poor quality, at outrageously high prices. Being a capitalist under compulsion was not a popular occupation, and few of Peter's seedlings reached maturity: of the hundreds of industrial establishments set up during his reign, by 1780 only twenty-two had survived.

Yet, with all these failures, in its main essentials Peter's industrial policy represented a striking success: Russia now had her own mining and manufacturing industry. And, by adding a new dimension to the business of government, it enhanced still further the authority and the coercive power of the State – thus conforming to the general pattern that emerged with ever greater clarity out of the chaos, the toil and the turmoil of the Petrine Reform.

The overall aim of the Reform has been summed up as being 'to stimulate the country's social forces and governmental institutions to intense activity in the interests of the State'.[5] It had been carried out by the State, and its benefits were to accrue to the State. Russia's increased military and economic might meant the increased power of the State, which now clutched society even more relentlessly in its grip. Gone was Muscovite semi-patriarchal regimentation, which, harsh and barbarous though it had been, was nevertheless tempered by its own bumbling inefficiency. In its place stood the 'regulated State' of the Russian Empire, where modern European methods of (relatively) competent administration had been applied to the service of Leviathan. The task of bureaucracy had been much simplified by the Table of Ranks and the streamlining of the servile system, but it was also in the reign of Peter the Great that Russia made one of her most lasting contributions to world civilization by the introduction of the internal passport, without which no subject, whether nobleman or serf, was allowed to move around the country. Vernadsky has commented forcefully on this basic aspect of the Petrine Reform: 'It would not be an undue modernization to suggest that Peter intended to establish what is now termed a totalitarian state.'[6]

As a person Peter was in some ways the opposite of either a martinet or of a power-hungry tyrant: a very human, impulsive character of extremely simple tastes. Much of what he did was desperately needed. But Russia's whole previous development imposed not only the Reform itself, but the shape it took and the methods used to implement it. As Miliukov remarked, 'a reform that was truly essential, it *unavoidably* manifested itself, could not but manifest itself in the form of personal, arbitrary compulsion exerted over the masses of the population'.[7] This was well understood by Peter; indeed, he knew of no other way in which the stupendous goals he had set his country could be reached. In 1723, less than two years before his death, looking back upon the agonizing path they had traversed together, the Emperor wrote: 'Our people are like children, who would never of their own accord decide to learn, who would never take up the alphabet without being compelled to do so by their teacher, who would at first feel despondent. But later, when they have finished their studies, they are grateful for having been made to go through them. This is evident today: *has not everything been achieved under constraint*? Yet now one hears gratitude for much that has already borne fruit' (my italics).[8]

Force, repression, discipline, and dire punishment were the means by which Russia was modernized. Her productive forces were developed by becoming still further enslaved. This paradox, central to an understanding of the Petrine Reform and of much else of Russian history, was probably best expressed by Kliuchevsky: 'The whole of Peter's reforming activity was animated by the idea of the necessity and the omnipotence of imperious compulsion: he hoped by force alone to press upon the people the benefits they lacked . . . Therefore, while zealous for the people's welfare, he strained their labour to the utmost limits, and spent human resources and lives profligately, unsparingly . . . The Petrine Reform was a struggle between despotism and the people, between despotism and the people's torpor. He hoped by means of harsh governmental measures to evoke initiative and enterprise among an enslaved society, and through the agency of a slaveholding nobility to install European learning in Russia. He wanted the slave, while remaining a slave, to act consciously and freely. To achieve the joint action of despotism and liberty, of education and slavery – this is the political equivalent of squaring the circle, which we have been trying to solve for two centuries, since Peter's day. It is still unsolved.'[9] Have the last fifty years brought the riddle any nearer to solution? One wonders.

The price paid by the Russian people for this first essay in modernization was stupendous. They were decimated alike by war, forced labour, famine, revolt and repression, and mass exodus to the outlying wilderness. The construction of St Petersburg, Peter's 'Paradise', his 'Northern Palmyra', erected in record time on a desolate stretch of marshland at the mouth of the Neva river, took a particularly heavy toll of life; not for nothing was it said that the new capital had been built on the bones of Russian serfs. The cost of Peter the Great is best reflected in population figures. Towards the end of the seventeenth century Russia had largely recovered from the losses of the Time of Troubles, and by 1678 her population reached the figure of sixteen million. In the next twenty years it grew still further. Yet by the end of Peter's reign, in 1724, it had fallen to thirteen million: a drop of about 25 per cent![10] Even Russia's Second World War losses pale beside this figure.

But the hecatombs of human sacrifices at the altar of innovation were never held against Peter by future generations of Russian reformers or revolutionaries (or by anybody else, except perhaps the people, and no one was ever really interested in what *they* thought). On the contrary, one of the most important consequences of the Petrine Reform was the fact that its manifest success instilled within the Russian progressive camp the firm conviction that in their country any fundamental changes could be carried out only from the top, by the forcible action of the State itself. For many, as we shall see, this attitude – and the disregard for human sacrifice that it entailed – became an article of faith. The Populists idolized Peter and his actions: Belinsky hoped for the coming of a new Peter the Great; for Chernyshevsky Peter symbolized the ideal patriot; and even Lenin, while essentially opposed to crowned heads of any description, spoke approvingly of the way in which Peter had smashed barbarism by barbaric means.

In canonizing Peter the Russian intelligentsia was actually canonizing the State, of which he was the embodiment. As a result of his policies the State was even more firmly in the saddle than ever before. All non-governmental institutions, however feeble, insignificant or rudimentary, were now finally engorged. Even the Orthodox Church, that faithful servant of the throne, seemed to the autocrat to have remained much too independent – and over-addicted to tradition as well. He solved the ecclesiastical problem as abruptly and unceremoniously as any other: the Church was incorporated into the body of the

State administration, the Patriarchate abolished and replaced by a governmental institution – the Holy Synod, headed by a Chief Procurator, a State official appointed by the Emperor, and roughly equivalent to a Minister of Church Affairs. Peter explained the reasons for this reform with the utmost frankness in his new Church Regulation: 'A conciliar administration cannot threaten the country with the riots and disorders that occur under a single ecclesiastical ruler. For the common people, not knowing the difference between the spiritual and the autocratic power, and being impressed by the greatness and fame of the supreme pastor, think him a second sovereign, equal or even superior in power to the autocrat, and believe the Church to be another and higher State . . . But when the people shall see that the conciliar administration has been established by monarchal decree and the decision of the Senate, they will abide in meekness and abandon all hope of the Church's support for their riots.'[11]

Church and State were one, and no room was left for ambiguity regarding their relationship. When, soon after the establishment of the Synod, a deputation of the clergy petitioned Peter to appoint a Patriarch, the Emperor drew out his dirk, bared his chest and smiting it a mighty blow, declared: 'Here is your Patriarch!'[12] That effectively settled the problem for as long as monarchy existed in Russia. It also provided a perfect illustration for one of the basic differences between Russian despotism and Western European 'absolute monarchy': the Russian ruler, with every justification, considered not only 'L'Etat, c'est moi', but 'L'Eglise, c'est moi', too.

Nor surprisingly, it was in the reign of Peter the Great that the glorification of the despotic State became the overriding theme of official propaganda. Indeed, it is only from this time on that one can speak of *official propaganda* at all, in the sense of a massive and intensive ideological campaign mounted by the government and directed at influencing and conditioning the minds of its recipients. There was no hypocrisy about it: the glorification of the State and the deification of the sovereign were carried out with enthusiasm and passion, and considerable ability, by the 'new men' of the reign, totally devoted to the Reform of which they were the loyal executors – 'Peter's fledglings', as they were called. For the first time in Russian history a group of quasi-official ideologists appeared near the seats of power, with the express purpose of buttressing the system of autocracy and the policies of its government with a convincingly argued set of ideas for both home and foreign consumption. This was the so-called 'Learned Regiment', with Feofan Prokopovich, Bishop of Pskov and author of the Church Regulation, as its acknowledged leader and most brilliant representative. Feofan, in a happy, if somewhat exaggerated turn of phrase, called Russia 'Peter's statue'; according to him 'the Russian people are by nature such that they can be secure only under autocratic lordship, and were they to assume the recipe of any other kind of government their further unity and well-being would be made impossible'.[13]

A sophisticated and historically well-grounded argument in favour of despotic rule was made out by another famous ideologist of the time, V. N. Tatishchev, the first Russian historian. He declared that a democratic system, or 'popular rule', could exist only in countries that were small in size and secure against attack. Large, but similarly secure nations could choose aristocratic governments. 'But great states that are not secure against their neighbours cannot exist and retain their integrity but under a despotic ruler.'[14]

Arguments on the purely rational level have never carried great weight in Russia, not even with their authors: they have always been oddly intermingled with semi-mystical ideas of other-worldliness and spirituality, of the unique moral superiority of the Russian people and their form of government and society. It was in the reign of Peter the Great, which combined a powerful Westernizing drive with the final consummation of age-old theocratic tendencies, that the curious synthesis of Western rationalism and Russian spirituality, that was to become so characteristic of Russian progressive thought, first came into being. An excellent example of this is provided by the already quoted writings of Ivan Pososhkov, who combined a theoretical turn of mind with utter devotion to the great Emperor and active participation in various aspects of his Reform. In the Soviet Union Pososhkov is extolled as the founder of Russian political economy, equal or even superior to the Western European mercantilist school in depth of analysis. This claim is not worthy of serious consideration; Pososhkov's writings are of interest chiefly for the insight they afford into the ideas of the man who has been called the first representative of the Russian intelligentsia. His politico-economic magnum opus not merely deifies the Tsar, in the best Oriental traditions: it endows him with God-like powers to establish the laws of economy, the value of currency, etc., simply by royal command – something other, less fortunate nations could never dream of achieving:

The Tsar is the judge, and he is like unto God . . .

As God rules over the whole earth, so does the Tsar have power over his domains . . .

We revere our monarch as we revere God, we guard his honour with our lives and obey his will most zealously . . . And therefore it is not the coins' weight that has currency among us, but the royal command.

Among foreigners kings have less power than the people, and therefore their kings cannot do anything of their own will. Power resides with their subjects, especially the merchants . . .

We are ruled by the most puissant and absolute of all monarchs, and not by any aristocrat or, God forbid, democrat. Therefore it is not silver or copper that we value: we feel veneration and awe only for His Imperial Majesty's mighty title.

So powerful with us is the word of his Most Serene Majesty that were he to order the lowliest copper coin to be struck with the denomination of One Ruble then in the market-places it would have the immutable value of one ruble forever and ever.[15]

Then and later, nothing could be more typical of the Russian *intelligent*, equipped with the new European-style education and at the same time laden down by the weight of ancient folkways, than this touching faith in the unlimited ability of an autocratic State, provided for the Russian people by Divine dispensation, to solve even the most intricate of problems by stern fiat. There were to be many variations on this theme.

The ever-intensifying conflict between the Western elements ruthlessly introduced by Peter the Great and the traditional patterns of Russian life became a determining feature of society. It was present in the actions of the Reformer himself, but that was only the beginning. Before Peter, Muscovite society, like any other, had had its share of sharp divisions and stresses, economic and social; it knew misery, slavery, cruelty, oppression. But, for all that, it had constituted a single organic community of people whose lives, however great the distance between their stations, had all fallen within a single overlying pattern; who spoke the same language, conformed to the same standards of thought and behaviour, and had felt themselves tied to each other by the same fate. Indeed, as we have seen, Russians attached an extraordinary importance to this mystic unity, which they regarded as the basis of the 'Russian idea'.

The Petrine Reform put an end to this state of affairs by splitting Russian society into two parts: the Westernized upper classes, and the masses, whose way of life became ever less distinguishable from that of the population of the great Asian empires. The bifurcation, the effects of which became fully felt in the course of the eighteenth century, was of a far more profound nature than the class divisions of European nations – the Two Nations of Disraeli. The nobility, for whom the acquisition of European learning and manners had at first meant a harsh duty, imposed under duress and approached with resignation and an ill-concealed loathing, soon discovered that it could also provide a source of wealth, of advancement and of unfamiliar pleasures. But since the education, the concepts, the habits, the amusements, the very food, clothes and houses, that were prescribed for the nobility in Petrine and post-Petrine Russia, had been imported wholesale from Western Europe, and lacked any roots in Russian national tradition, the chasm between the educated classes and the people grew to be practically unbridgeable. Herzen has a brilliant description of these products of Westernization: 'Foreigners at home and foreigners abroad, idle onlookers – spoiled for Russia by their Western prejudices, and spoiled for the West by their Russian habits – they constituted a strange kind of intelligent superfluity, and lost themselves in their artificial life, in sensual pleasures and in an intolerable egoism.'[16] They can even hardly be said to have spoken a common language with the people: the nobility now used either French or German, or a clumsy and unbeautiful lingo top-heavy with undigested foreign words and phrases. In neither case was their conversation intelligible to the people. (It is for the titanic feat of creating a new Russian literary language, subtle, powerful and up-to-date, and common to all classes of the population, that Pushkin, apart from his poetic genius, enjoys his unique place – at once national hero and national poet – in the Russian consciousness.)

A curious process took place in Russia as a result of the Reform, a process that in a way resembled a foreign conquest *in reverse*: whereas, for instance, in England Norman baron and Saxon peasant gradually grew closer, in time evolving a common nation, a common language, a common culture, in Russia the nobility and the peasantry, already separated by rigid social barriers, rapidly came to inhabit what were, to all intents and purposes, different worlds alien and incomprehensible one to the other. Observant foreigners would often remark on the strange similarity between Russia and some of the European overseas colonies, with the serving and landowning nobility in the part of colonists and colonial administration, and the enserfed peasants in that of the natives. The comparison was not altogether far-fetched: for one and a half centuries after the Reform the way of life and the social position of the 'educated classes' moved ever closer to the European models they admired and sought to emulate, while the multi-million peasant masses sank deeper into the morass of brutishness and an Asiatic general slavery. The tragic alienation between Occident and Orient, one of the most pregnant features of modern world history, had been in a very definite sense reproduced within the confines of a single nation.

The State, too, had changed; 'Holy Russia', revered as the abode of righteousness, had given place to the Russian Empire, a very different proposition indeed. The government and its bureaucracy was becoming Germanized and foreign to the mass of its subjects. Alienation was setting in; under the stress of forced and indiscriminate Europeanization the mystical bonds between Tsar and people were gradually becoming strained. But there was still a long way to go before they finally snapped.

Such were some of the more important elements of the Petrine Reform. They left hardly a single aspect of Russian life untouched; some achieved results almost immediately, while others needed generations to reach fruition; by no means all were beneficial. Yet their cumulative effect was such that by the time the Emperor died, worn out by his superhuman labours, it seemed as if a gigantic whirlwind had passed from one end of the country to the other. To the onlooker Russia presented the aspect of an entirely different country.

But was that really the case? Had Russia undergone a genuine revolutionary transformation? Had the old, semi-Tartar Muscovite Russia really been swept away for good and all, and replaced by a shining, brand-new, model European State? This was asserted by no less an authority than Voltaire himself. But, nevertheless, was it true?

In the protracted controversy over the historical significance of the Petrine Reform its revolutionary character was taken for granted by opponents and supporters alike. The conservative critics of the Reform – represented at their most cogent, at the end of the eighteenth and the beginning of the nineteenth centuries, by Prince Shcherbatov's powerful and nostalgic pamphlet 'On the Impairment of Morals in Russia', and by Karamzin, who declared in his 'Memoir on Ancient and Modern Russia' that Peter had transformed Russians into citizens of the world by stopping them from being Russians – deplored the

Reform for having broken, decisively and irreversibly, with the Russian tradition. So did the nineteenth-century Slavophiles. Peter's literary champions, the so-called 'Westerners', acclaimed it for exactly the same reason.

Since the rise, towards the end of the last century, of the critical school of Russian historiography this view can no longer be accepted. Particularly today, when a wide range of experiments in Europeanization, conducted in a number of countries within our own lifetimes, has convincingly demonstrated the variety of ways in which the old wine of social structure and custom can be poured practically unchanged into the new bottles of modern technology, ideology and administration. The Petrine Reform was no more than its name implied: a reform, and a much-needed one at that. Of course, it did far more than simply attire the Russian Old Adam in European finery: by shaking up Russian society, by introducing efficient and up-to-date methods, by equipping Russia with the military and economic might she so sorely lacked – and achieving all this by main force – Peter not only preserved the most salient features of traditional Muscovite society, but actually strengthened and reinvigorated them. The stranglehold of the despotic, centralized State was made even tighter, arbitrary rule elevated into the basic principle of government, society yet more rigidly regimented, the burden of obligatory State service made even heavier, the Statute of Bondage strengthened and made still harsher. In truth, Westernized Russia was in many respects more 'Russian' than before.

Once again, this process has been most eloquently and searchingly summed up by Kliuchevsky:

> Peter accepted the previously established relationships and mores as he found them; he did not inject new principles into them, but only re-grouped them in new combinations, adapting them to changed circumstances. He did not revoke existing law, but only modified it in accordance with the new requirements of the State . . .

The new order was compounded of the old relationships . . .

Peter's social measures reveal an unconscious tendency to reproduce in his innovations the echoes of the past . . . Now Russian society finally received the shape into which the Muscovite legislation of the seventeenth century had sought to mould it . . .

[The Reform] was a revolution not in its aims and results, but solely in its methods and in the impression it created upon the minds and feelings of contemporaries. It was a convulsion rather than an upheaval.[17]

This analysis has only been strengthened by the results of more recent research. It was largely accepted – usually with the appropriate terminological changes – by Marxist interpreters of the Russian past. In his History – one of the earliest, and best, attempts at a general description in Marxist terms, and today the object of official Soviet disapproval – Plekhanov reinforced it: 'In his Europeanization of Russia Peter developed to its final, logical conclusion the condition of complete helplessness of the population *vis-à-vis* the State that is characteristic of Oriental despotism.'[18]

CHAPTER 8

The Eighteenth Century: Enlightenment and Enslavement

It can be said, in a certain sense – and this is no more paradoxical than a number of other features of his reform – that by Europeanizing Russia in the way he did and with the methods he used, and thus infusing new blood and new life into the traditional Muscovite system, Peter probably retarded the genuine, radical Europeanization of his country. In at least one highly important respect he took a definite, and significant, retrograde step, by reverting to the most ancient, and already obsolete, concept of Muscovite patriarchal despotism, which regarded Russia as the unconditional private property of her Tsar, to be willed or otherwise disposed of in accordance with his sovereign wish. In 1722, after having had his only son and heir executed, Peter announced a new Law of Succession: the principle of primogeniture – originally established by the Grand Dukes of Moscow, successfully defended by them against the prerogative of the Khans, and used to good account in their struggle for Russia's unification – was now abolished as a 'most evil custom', and replaced by the principle 'that it should always remain at the will of the reigning sovereign to leave his inheritance to whomsoever he wishes'.[1]

Whatever the Emperor's intentions, the actual results of this measure proved disastrous. In the political sphere it inaugurated a period of unparalleled confusion. To appreciate the full abnormality and the extent of the ensuing disarray one should bear in mind that previously, despite the turbulent nature of so much of Russian history, the Russian throne had for centuries

149

enjoyed a stability and a continuity hardly matched by any other European country. During the 400 years between the accession of Ivan Kalita and the death of Peter the Great (excluding only the fifteen years of the Time of Troubles), Muscovy had been ruled by fifteen sovereigns, each one of whom had ascended the throne peacefully and legally, and had in due course died of natural causes. By way of contrast, of the eight monarchs who ruled Russia as Peter's successors until the end of the eighteenth century, only *two* achieved the throne legally, and for neither of them was the promise of this happy augury borne out – both were murdered: Peter III with the connivance of his wife, and Paul with that of his son. Every one of the other six monarchs was brought to power by an armed coup d'état.

Peter's Law of Succession cannot be regarded as the sole reason for the continuous instability of the throne. Even after it had been revoked and the principle of primogeniture restored (1797) Russia maintained her new-found tradition: only one of her last five emperors died of unquestionably natural causes (Alexander III). As for the rest: Nicholas I committed suicide, Alexander II was assassinated, Nicholas II was massacred together with his family, and the mystery surrounding the true circumstances of the death of Alexander I has not been penetrated to this day.

It is hardly likely that these events constituted a purely fortuitous chain of coincidences. They should rather be seen as symptoms of the general instability of governmental institutions and social relationships caused by the workings of the Petrine Reform. Tradition had been undermined, but not supplanted, by the haphazard and largely superficial innovations. Russia was in a state of flux, with old and new opposing and interpenetrating each other. And since the country possessed only one genuine institution, that of monarchy, it was only natural that the generally unsettled state of affairs should be reflected in constant violent changes in the occupancy of the throne.

Instability at the top was largely caused by the social forces unleashed by Peter, for which no place could be found within the traditional structure of the State. After Peter's death, in the chaotic transitory conditions of an unfinished and unplanned reform, authority came to be vested in the armed forces and their élite, the regiments of the Guards. The coups d'état that established or terminated the eight reigns between 1725 and 1801 were all carried out by the Guards; the throne, and with it the State itself, became the plaything of ambitious cliques of courtiers, and the prize was his who succeeded in securing the support of the Guards. Biron, the all-powerful favourite of the Empress Anne (1730–41), called them Janissaries – both aptly and prophetically, as it transpired, for soon afterwards he was himself turned out of bed, beaten up, bundled into a blanket, and deposited in a dungeon, swiftly and efficiently, by members of yet another Guards conspiracy.

Underlying the new phenomenon of the successive Guards coups d'état was a basic shift that had taken place in the social system: the supremacy of the Guards meant the supremacy of the nobility, for the Guards regiments were no more than the nobility in arms. For the first time in their long history the Russian nobility were united in an exclusive, close-knit organization, within which a new corporate spirit, a sense of common interest, could at last arise. By the nature of things, their ascendancy could last only as long as the Guards regiments continued to be composed entirely of noblemen – as soon as the other ranks began (towards the end of the eighteenth century) to be filled by peasant recruits, this anomalous situation came to an end. Moreover, the heady air of new-found authority and influence proved altogether too much for the Russian nobility, unaccustomed as they had previously been to any other role but that of faithful servant of the government: excessive greed and a precipitate haste in the achievement of their selfish ends, without regard for the consequences, considerably shortened the span of their domination. But it was good while it lasted.

The eighteenth century, and particularly the seventy years that separated the reigns of Peter the Great and Paul I, was the century of the nobility. It was a grand saturnalia of aristocratic depredation; the erstwhile humble serving-men, raised by the Petrine military reform to a pinnacle of pre-eminence, now gorged themselves on privileges and possessions extorted willy-nilly from an enfeebled and dependent government. They sought three main objects: the ending of compulsory service, full rights of ownership of landed property, and the final enslavement of the peasantry. All were achieved – or so it appeared at the time – but in the final reckoning it was the nobility who had to pay the price for the resultant dislocation of the Russian social system.

In 1731 the *pomeshchik* became full proprietor of his estate. In 1736 the compulsory life-long service of the nobility was cut down to a term of twenty-five years. The right to hold serfs became the exclusive privilege of the hereditary nobleman. 'To own human beings, to possess slaves, was regarded as the supreme privilege, as a princely status which served as compensation for numerous political and social disadvantages.'[2] Finally, on 18 February 1762, only a few months before his wife's lover knocked out his muddled brains with a footstool, the Emperor Peter III signed a manifesto granting 'every member of the Russian well-born nobility his freedom and liberty'. Compulsory service was abolished; one of the two main classes of Russian society had been officially emancipated.

This was one of the great turning-points of Russian history. Hardly anyone realized at the time that by triumphantly asserting their independence of the State the nobility were encompassing their own eventual and inexorable downfall. They sought to emulate the privileged position of the Western European aristocracy – but their title to lands and serfs was based not on ancient feudal rights secured in law, but solely on their unremitting military service to the State. Once they had wriggled out of their obligations their property rights became illegal, and they themselves superfluous. The nobility had chosen to contract out of the traditional Russian social system, and as a result, lacking as they did any legal or otherwise generally accepted basis for their authority, their privileges, their possessions, or even their continuing existence as a class, became in the long run more dependent on the State than ever before. With time came a growing realization: sixty years later Pushkin, ever acutely conscious of his position as a nobleman, wrote of the 1762 manifesto as of something 'of which our ancestors had felt so proud, but of which they should much rather have felt repentant'. The peasant masses had arrived at this conclusion even earlier. The nobility, they felt, had voluntarily forfeited their rights, or been deprived of them by the State, it did not really matter which, and the logical next step should in equity be their own emancipation and endowment with the land tilled by them since time immemorial. And when they discovered that their expectations were not to be fulfilled, they rose in 1773 under the leadership of Emelian Pugachev, in the greatest of Russian peasant rebellions.

But for the time being the nobility felt secure. The accession to the throne of Catherine the Great (1762–95) inaugurated what was to be their short-lived Golden Age. Gradually they began to taste the pleasures of freedom, of the indolent provincial life, and of lording it over vast numbers of slaves. The government expected compulsory service to be replaced by service out of a sense of duty. Old habits did indeed die hard, and for many noblemen any way of life other than State service was inconceivable. But even those among them who departed for their estates with a sigh of relief, or who decided against entering State service to begin with, could never really grow accustomed to their new-found liberty. For one thing, the burden of their fiscal, administrative and police responsibilities towards the State with regard to the serfs in their possession had greatly increased: they were glorified overseers rather than rural squires. 'Instead of a country gentleman the nobleman became a police inspector, instead of a landowner – a slaveowner.'[3]

In other respects, too, the nobility were not left entirely to their own devices. In 1775 Catherine carried out a reform of local administration: elected bodies of the nobility, with their own officers, were now set up in each of the country's fifty governments (*gubernii*) and in the lower administrative units;

they received a limited autonomy with regard to local affairs, the administration of justice, public works, charitable institutions etc. There was no danger of the new bodies overstepping the narrow confines set them from above: they were firmly subordinated in all matters to the Governor and to a host of other appointed officials sent out by the central administration. Still, at first it was quite a change. Some foreign observers of the Russian scene became very excited – as they have frequently tended to do since – over the magnitude and the confidently expected far-reaching consequences of this innovation. The usually level-headed Frenchman Masson wrote in his *Mémoires secrets sur la Russie*, that 'sooner or later these assemblies of the nobility will sound the signal for revolution'.[4] Bedazzled by the 'enlightened' splendour of the court of St Petersburg, with its chatter of Voltaire and Diderot, he can be excused for having overlooked the enormous staying power of the Russian State tradition.

The Empress Catherine, who fancied herself as a Philosopher-Queen, and paid bountiful pensions to the men of the French Enlightenment, toyed with the idea of introducing certain European institutions into her own country – though not at the cost of weakening the autocracy. She was inspired to her reform of local government by the works of Blackstone. As happened so often, European seedlings exhibited a stunted growth in the bleak light of Russian reality.

Very soon things fell into the familiar pattern, and elective officials became indistinguishable from appointed ones. The authorities themselves recognized this: the names of approved candidates were handed down from above to the obedient 'voters', elected officers of the nobility were included into the Table of Ranks and received their own distinctive uniforms, and voting itself became an obligation to be shirked only at the risk of dire penalties. Gradually the noblemen who remained outside the direct military or civil service of the centralized State were transformed into local government officials. Some grumbled that this was but another form of the compulsory service from which they had recently been freed, but the vast majority were perfectly content – even relieved – to carry on in their subservient relationship to the State in one form or another. Most would have felt lost without it: as Miliukov put it, 'the *pomeshchik* continued to live, as before, in the conviction that the government *must* give him an appointment and must guarantee his livelihood'.[5] Besides, many felt, somewhat uneasily, that only continued service justified their retention of full property rights to lands and serfs.

The high point of privilege was reached in 1785, when Catherine issued her Charter of the Nobility, which once again solemnly relieved them of any obligation to enter the military or civil service of the State, exempted them from corporal punishment, conscription, and taxation, and laid down the principle that a nobleman could be tried only by a court of his peers. At the same time similar, though much more limited, corporative rights were bestowed upon the merchants and other top categories of townspeople.

The fatal defect of the favours showered upon them so liberally, as the nobility were to find out very soon after the passing of their benevolent 'Little Mother', lay in the fact that their preservation depended entirely upon the goodwill of the State, i.e. the monarch. Despite all the concessions it had made, the State emerged from the succession of post-Petrine political crises, just as it had after the Time of Troubles, like a giant refreshed. Its real powers had in no way been curbed, and indeed, with the thoughtlessly self-inflicted weakening of the nobility's political and military importance, had actually been enhanced. The main reason why the nobility had not used their ascendancy to curtail the real powers of the State was undoubtedly the existence and further growth of the system of serfdom.

For the most striking feature of eighteenth-century Russian social history was the great expansion and intensification of peasant bondage at the precise moment when, with the emancipation of the nobility, it finally lost any vestige of moral, political or legal justification. The peasants, well aware of the historical basis for their subjugation, looked forward expectantly to a speedy liberation and entry into possession of 'their' lands: instead, they received reduction to full slavery.

The manifesto of 1762 meant that 73 per cent of the tax-paying population were handed over, in return for the landowners' guarantee of their taxes, into the worst form of servitude known in Europe since the days of the Roman Empire. During the reign of Catherine the Great the system of peasant bondage was extended into the newly conquered Ukrainian territories and the Cossack lands. Wealth began to be calculated in 'souls'. The nobility used their privileged position to lay their hands – by award, extortion, peculation or bribery – upon vast numbers of State serfs. The appropriation of peasant 'souls' became a headlong scramble. This practice had been started by Peter the Great, who handed out the comparatively modest total of 177,000 serfs to his underlings (it was actually multiplied several times over by the illegal depredations of favourites like the fantastically corrupt Menshikov). Under his successors the custom swelled into an orgy: Kiril Razumovsky, 'president' of the Academy of Sciences and brother of the Empress Elizabeth's lover, received 100,000 serfs. Catherine, who marked her accession to the throne by largesse totalling 18,000 serfs, altogether in the course of her reign distributed about one million peasants among her various favourites – Potemkin alone receiving over 200,000. The coronation of Paul I was celebrated by 100,000 human 'gifts'. In 1796, the year that represents the high-water mark of Russian serfdom, out of a total population of thirty-six million the number of *male* serfs in private ownership was 9,790,000, and of *male* State peasants – 7,276,000.[6] By normal demographic standards this gives a total of over 90 per cent of the Russian people in private and State bondage!

Parallel with this went a rapid worsening of the actual conditions of bondage. A bare list of the principal Imperial edicts is sufficient to show the obliteration of the last feeble restraints upon the rapacity and arbitrary licence of the *pomeshchiki*: 1741 – peasant serfs no longer to take the oath of loyalty to the monarch; 1747 – the time-honoured custom of selling peasants without land finally acknowledged in law; 1760 – the *pomeshchik* granted the right to exile offending peasants to Siberia; 1765 – the *pomeshchik* allowed to sentence peasants to convict labour (the dreaded *katorga*) at his own discretion; 1767 – any attempt by serfs to lodge complaints against their masters to be automatically punished by convict labour in the Nerchinsk mines (the Russian government had abolished the death penalty from motives of humanity, but this was no less efficacious than the scaffold).

Suddenly, in the beginning of the enlightened reign of Catherine the Great, that favourite of the French *philosophes*, it dawned upon the authorities that serfs had in actual fact become slaves. This was in large measure due to the pedantic German mind of the Empress herself. The Russian tradition of legal ambiguity and political double-talk remained, of course, in full force, and neither at this nor at later stages were any moves taken to have the transformation of peasants into chattel property established in law (it could hardly be otherwise, since they had remained tax-payers), but the Empress believed in calling a spade a spade. Her famous Instruction to the abortive Commission for preparation of a new legal Code (1767), ecstatically acclaimed by every European progressive worth his salt, consistently spoke of landlords' peasants as 'slaves', and regarded their belongings as the property of their masters. Even franker was a rather ironical letter (for originally she had been a genuine opponent of serfdom), written by Catherine during the deliberations of the Commission, which had rapidly degenerated into a free-for-all fight for additional 'souls': 'If a serf cannot be regarded as a person, it follows that he is not human; in that case please to call him a brute – this should serve to increase the fame of our humanity.'[7] There is no indication that the Empress's sarcastic remark had the slightest effect upon either the voracity of the 'deputies' – who took her at her word – or the adulation of her Western liberal admirers, whose faith nothing could shake.

One basic fact cuts across the fog of equivocations: the Russian bondsman had become an object of civil law, with the status of personal property, of 'chattels personal'. Of particular interest in this respect is the question of the master's right to kill his slave with impunity. There seems little doubt that such a right was generally accepted in practice, although neither formulated nor denied in law. At least since the middle of the eighteenth century the courts simply refused to accept cases against *pomeshchiki* accused of murdering their own serfs 'in the absence of clear decrees on this score'.[8] One of the problems which the 1767 Commission was expected to solve was: 'What should be done when serfs die as a result of their *pomeshchik*'s beating?'[9] No answer was apparently forthcoming. Every year hundreds and thousands of slaves were murdered by their masters, yet only in a very few cases of extreme cruelty on a mass scale were the perpetrators, upon the personal intervention of the monarch, brought to book and condemned . . . to do penance in church for their sins. The single notorious exception was the fiendish noblewoman Saltykova, who, after quite openly torturing up to a hundred slaves to death with every sadistic refinement at her command, was sentenced to a particularly harsh form of life imprisonment upon the express order of the humane Empress.

It is instructive to draw a comparison between Russian 'serfdom' and a similar, but far better known contemporaneous institution, whose essence has never been palliated by specious euphemisms – Negro slavery in the United States of America. It would be no exaggeration to say that the legal and social positions of Russian and Negro slaves roughly corresponded. Both were chattels; both could be bought and sold – if need be, separately from their families; neither enjoyed any legal, political or civil rights; neither could own property (though in practice both sometimes did); the offspring of both were slaves in perpetuity; in both cases a free person entering into marriage with a slave automatically became a slave; and so on.

To be sure, there were divergences – often more apparent than real – and it is these that have blinded most observers to the basic identity of the two institutions. Negro slaves were outside civil society, whereas Russian slaves were regarded, in some weird fashion, as subjects of the Emperor, even though they no longer took the oath of loyalty: they were liable to military service (which meant in reality their expropriation by the State for a term of twenty-five years), and they paid taxes. This actually may very well have made their lot worse – neither 'privilege' was exactly popular – but it did give them a vague sense of human dignity and even patriotism, something their Negro fellows lacked. Besides, the Russian slaves had the collective life, the warmth and the rudimentary security of the *obshchina*. The economic conditions of their lives were different, too: Negro slaves worked as a rule on plantations, but in Russia the usual forms of slave labour were *barshchina* (compulsory work on the landowner's fields), and *obrok* (quit-rent), although from about the middle of the eighteenth century a plantation type of economy was steadily spreading in Russia, under which the peasants no longer spent part of their time on their 'own' plots, but worked full-time on the *pomeshchik*'s land, in return for which he fed and clothed them.

The most important difference was also the most obvious one: the colour of the Russian slaves' skin was the same as that of their masters.

In one vital, and rather surprising, respect the legal status of the Negro slave was superior to that of his Russian counterpart. We have seen above that under Russian legal theory and practice a *pomeshchik* was not accountable for murdering a slave. In contrast to this, after the American Revolution all Southern States passed laws imposing the death penalty for the murder of a slave. Deliberate cruelty, even if not resulting in the victim's death, was also considered a crime. True, the law was only enforced in a fraction of such cases, but its very existence had a salutary effect on many potential Simon Legrees. State laws extended a degree of protection to Negro slaves in other respects, too: slaveowners could be fined for giving their slaves insufficient food and clothing, or for abandoning aged and infirm bondsmen. Some States regulated the slaves' hours of labour.[10] Once again: the law was honoured in the breach far more than in the observance, and convictions were rare. But in Russia even these flimsy legal safeguards were missing

– as were the American provisions for the trial by jury of slaves accused of capital crimes.

A remarkable consistency, even identity, can be found between the rationalization put forward by American and Russian exponents of slavery. In the United States a massive literary effort went into justifying the South's 'peculiar institution'. A Northern sympathizer declared that the slaves 'find themselves first existing in this state, and pass through life without questioning the justice of their allotment, which, if they think at all, they suppose a natural one'. In the words of an educated Southerner, slavery was 'a system which proclaims peace, perpetual peace between the warring elements. Harmonizing the interest betwixt capital and labour, Southern slavery has solved the problem over which statesmen have toiled and philanthropists mourned from the first existence of organized society.' Senator James H. Hammond was convinced that 'our slaves are the happiest . . . human beings on whom the sun shines'.[11] The greatest and most eloquent defender of Southern slavery, John C. Calhoun, summed up all these arguments: 'Many in the South once believed that slavery was a moral and political evil. That folly and delusion are gone. We see it now in its true light, and regard it as the most safe and stable basis for free institutions in the world.'[12]

Russian slavery was buttressed by much the same arguments: as against the upheavals and the misery of capitalism, it gave security to the slave and stability to the whole of society. Besides, the slave knew no other way of life anyway. 'Russian peasants,' declared the eighteenth-century historian General Boltin, 'do not regard their condition of slavery as an unhappy one . . . They cannot conceive of any better condition, and that which they do not know they cannot desire: human happiness is a creature of the imagination.'[13]

Whatever may have been the innermost thoughts of the Dixie slaveowners, there can be no doubt that the Russian ruling class (and many others besides), nurtured for generations on the idea of Russia's incontestable moral superiority to the West, were genuinely convinced of the beneficial effects of their own system of slavery. Even Pushkin, the most generous and noble-hearted of men, passionately defended its social and humanitarian advantages:

> The complaints of English factory workers make one's hair stand on end. What revolting tortures, what inconceivable agonies! What cold barbarism at one pole, and what terrifying poverty at the other! It seems that the English workingman is the most miserable being in the world . . .
>
> In our country everything is quite different. Obligations are not onerous. The tax is paid by the community; *barshchina* is regulated by law; *obrok* is not crushing . . . Look at the Russian peasant: is there even a trace of servility in his walk or in his speech? . . . In Russia there is no one without a house *of his own*. The mendicant who goes out to beg leaves behind him a house *of his own*. Abroad there is nothing like this. Everywhere in Europe a cow is a sign of luxury; in our country not to have a cow is a sign of terrible poverty . . . The life of the peasants is improving from day to day, in accord with the spread of education. Everyone realizes that the peasants' welfare is closely dependent upon the welfare of the *pomeshchiki*.[14]

America, despite Negro slavery, was in general a free society; in Russia peasant slavery was but one facet of a whole nation enchained alike by its government and its beliefs. There only the slaveowner's voice was heard. Only once was this idyllic uniformity disturbed: in 1790 Alexander Radishchev, with incredible courage, privately printed his *Journey from Petersburg to Moscow* – a searing indictment of the horrors of peasant slavery, every word of which contradicted the lying picture of social harmony presented by Russia to the world. The infuriated Empress, the book's first reader, had all 850 copies confiscated and destroyed; the author received the death sentence (the fact that capital punishment had been officially abolished never counted for much in Russia), 'mercifully' commuted to ten years' *katorga*. More than a century had to pass before the book could first be legally published in Russia – forty-five years after the abolition of slavery. Yet the memory of Radishchev's bold defiance lived on to haunt Russia: Pushkin's article quoted above was one of many 'refutations' of a 'non-existent' book, written by a condemned State criminal.

One can hardly concur with the idea of the *moral* superiority of the Russian socio-economic order, but in one vital respect it always enjoyed a very definite advantage over the free, or 'open' society of the West: by keeping dirty linen unwashed and every skeleton firmly locked in its cupboard, the Russian government and its accomplices in this conspiracy of silence effectively prevented true understanding of the nature and consequences of the system of nationwide chattel slavery, glossed over as patriarchal serfdom, from entering the consciousness either of the outside world or of its own people. (To a large extent this still holds true: Soviet historians, though usually eager to expose the evils of Tsardom, are even more anxious to prove the identity between the development of their country and that of Western Europe – the very word 'slave', once in general and unaffected use, has disappeared from the pages of Russian historical treatises, uniformly replaced by the respectable 'serf'.)

The most surprising aspect of this was the general indifference of Russian nineteenth-century writers to the actual workings of slavery. Although most of them were strong opponents of bondage, they wrote about it sparingly. Apart from a few scattered, and sometimes quite Arcadian references (and, of course, Radishchev), the only realistic descriptions of peasant life under bondage are to be found in a few of Turgenev's *Sportsman's Sketches*, some chapters from Goncharov and Saltykov-Shchedrin, and some of Nekrasov's poems. And much of this concerns slave house servants, whose life – just as in the American South – was somewhat untypical of the great peasant masses. Even such an untiring revolutionary fighter for emancipation as Herzen, when it came down to describing the actual scenes of slavery he had himself witnessed as a youth, did so with something of the indulgent air of a well-meaning Southern gentleman reminiscing nostalgically about Sambo and

Sukey on the old plantation. Only towards the end of the century, with the appearance of the so-called Populist writers, did a large body of literature about peasant life begin to appear – but this was already after emancipation. The truth of the matter is that the great Russian novelists wrote marvellous books about the nobility, the intelligentsia, petty officials, merchants, clergymen – about everybody but the enslaved and much-suffering 90-odd per cent of their people.

It is difficult to explain this incuriosity on the part of men with generally highly developed social consciences, who felt sincere indignation over the sufferings of the Balkan Christians, of English working men and even – yes . . . of Negro slaves. Fear of censorship and repression had the least to do with it. Probably most important was the alienation between the educated classes and the peasantry, the impossibility for a gentleman of bridging the gulf, of entering into the peasants' life and comprehending their mentality, of understanding what slavery was really about. To this must be added a strange distaste towards dragging out something of which they were all deeply ashamed, but which was somehow or other mystically tied up with the great moral Truth which Russia was at some time in the future going to announce to the world. Be that as it may, the fact remains that for Negro slavery we have at our disposal vast quantities of detailed descriptions, whereas of the life of Russia's slave peasantry we know next to nothing.

And here we have approached the crux of the matter. For Negro slaves, about whose tragic plight so much had been written, never made up more than one-fifth of the total population of the United States; on the eve of the Civil War they constituted only one-eighth. Even in the slave States (including the District of Columbia), in an 1860 population of 12,302,000 there were only 3,954,000 slaves.[15] In Russia, as we have seen, at the height of the system more than nine-tenths of the population were in bondage. If it has been remarked, so often and so truly, that Negro slavery warped the historical development of the United States and created the gravest of still unsolved social problems, with how much more justice might this not be said of Russia, where slavery was general, where it lasted at least as long, and where it came to an end almost simultaneously with that of the Negro?

For one and a half centuries slavery remained the central, dominating problem of Russian life, the pivot around which all else moved, the factor that determined the whole pattern of society. From a by-product of Russia's peculiar social structure it had become the *raison d'être* for its continued existence. Serfdom-slavery, originally established by the all-powerful State, now provided the main impulse for preserving the State's unlimited powers intact. Slavery was the reason why the nobility, during their brief period of ascendancy, confined themselves to seating and unseating a succession of occupants of the throne, without making any attempts at curbing the actual authority of the autocrat. On the contrary: the power of the State was guarded most jealously.

Only once did the organizers of a coup d'état have the temerity to circumscribe the absolute royal prerogative; their venture ended in miserable failure. In 1730, upon the death of the youthful Peter II, power was left in the hands of a small group of Russia's most ancient noble families, constituted into a Supreme Privy Council; they invited Anne, Duchess of Courland, Peter the Great's niece, to assume the throne, with the stipulation that she sign a set of conditions effectively limiting her authority. When Anne, having signed the articles, arrived in the capital she was faced by a revolt of the nobility, represented by the Guards and the top ranks of the civil service, demanding that she renounce the pledge extorted from her by the grandees, *and restore unlimited autocracy*. Which she graciously condescended to do. The main leaders and ideologists of this curious rebellion, conducted in the name of renunciation of rights already granted, were Peter's 'fledglings', the members of his 'Learned Regiment': Feofan Prokopovich, Tatishchev, Kantemir. The motives for their behaviour are quite clear: however much they may have preferred a degree of limited freedom, the existence and the further extension and intensification of serfdom imperatively demanded the retention of a State with full control over the lives and property of all its subjects. This was why the frequent political convulsions of the eighteenth century did not result in any weakening of the State, but only in a number of weak (if vicious) monarchs. Neither could the emancipation of the nobility have this effect: charter or no charter, the price paid for the servile status of nine-tenths of the population was the subjection of the remaining one-tenth to the State.

The eighteenth century is famous as the age of European absolute monarchy, of 'enlightened absolutism' and of a little Versailles in every great and small capital of Europe. Russia, still somewhat ill-at-ease in her brand-new court attire of a Great Power, was warmly welcomed into the charmed circle. Indeed, such Russian rulers as Peter, Elizabeth and Catherine, particularly the latter, are still regarded as shining exemplars of the enlightened absolute monarch. But in reality Russia was no more an absolute monarchy (in the European sense) than a feudal society. Western 'absolutism', even at its height, was never truly absolute: for one thing, authority was everywhere split, to a greater or smaller degree, between the political and the ecclesiastical power; it was limited by strongly established privileged classes, by provincial autonomies and local charters, by powerful economic interests, by accepted traditional customs and such recognized rights as those of petition or of non-political association. The rights of the individual may have been an unrecognized abstraction, but the rights and the effective powers of the various social groups constituted a formidable force.

Not even after the granting of the Charter of the Nobility did anything faintly resembling such a system make its appearance in Russia. The nobility could be deprived of their new-found privileges at the stroke of a pen – as Paul I was to show. The most eminent exponent of European absolutism, Bossuet, would hardly have approved of Russian autocracy. Firm believer in the Divine Right of Kings though he was, in his 'Politique' Bossuet was at pains to draw a sharp dividing line between *absolute* and *arbitrary* government. Under arbitrary government – a regime that he regarded as *barbare et odieuse*

– all subjects were serfs or slaves of the supreme power, with no really free men among them; private property was absent, for everything in reality belonged to the prince; the ruler had unlimited powers over not only the property, but also the lives of his subjects; the only law was the arbitrary will of the monarch. A very far cry, he thought, from the France of the Sun-King.[16] But, we may reflect, a tolerable likeness of 'enlightened' eighteenth-century Russian society, where, to quote a Russian historian: 'the whole social structure of the State, from top to bottom, was marked by the brand of bondage. All social classes were enslaved. The imperial court of an Anne or an Elizabeth – modelled upon Western lines, dazzling foreigners by its splendour and brilliance, the principal medium for the introduction of European manners to Russian society – was in actual fact nothing but a vast serf-holding estate.'[17]

Probably the best description of Russian reality in the St Petersburg period was given by Alexander Herzen:

Even in the worst periods of European history, we encounter some respect for the individual, some recognition of independence, some rights conceded to talent and genius. Vile as were the German rulers of that time, Spinoza was not sentenced to transportation, Lessing was not flogged or conscripted. This respect not merely for material but also for moral force, this unquestioning recognition of the individual – is one of the great human principles in European life . . .

We have nothing similar. With us the individual has always been crushed, absorbed, he has never even tried to emerge. Free speech with us has always been considered insolence, independence – subversion; man was engulfed in the State, dissolved in the community . . .

With us slavery increased with education; the State grew and improved but the individual reaped nothing from it; on the contrary, the stronger the State, the weaker the individual. European forms of administration and justice, of military and civil organization, developed with us into a kind of monstrous and inescapable despotism . . .

With us authority feels freer, more self-confident than in Turkey or Persia, nothing restrains it, no past of any kind; it has repudiated its own past and is not concerned with that of Europe. It has no respect for national principles, it knows no universal culture, and it fights against the present.[18]

Nevertheless, Western governments and public opinion alike began to assume that Russia was a state much the same as any other absolute monarchy, only considerably larger, rather more backward, and consequently mysterious. To a certain extent this was due to ignorance of Russian conditions, and to the remarkably thoroughgoing way in which Russian educated society had adapted itself to the *forms* of European life. Much more telling, however, was the unremitting conscious effort of the government itself to implant, both abroad and at home, the image of a well-ordered society that had chosen its political system partly out of necessity, and partly for its manifest advantages. It was Catherine the Great, the most intelligent and best-educated of Russia's eighteenth-century rulers, who first grasped the practical and educational importance of assigning to Russian autocracy a definite frame of reference within the generally accepted sociological scheme of the Enlightenment. In her 'Instruction' she produced not only a sophisticated analysis of Russian despotism, but also a shrewd programme for its successful operation – something that had become necessary by reason of the country's new Great Power respectability and the emergence of an educated public opinion:

The sovereign must be autocratic, for no other form of government but that which concentrates all power in his person is compatible with the dimensions of a State as great as ours. Only swiftness of decision in matters sent from distant realms can compensate for the slowness caused by great distances. Any other form of government would be not merely harmful, but utterly ruinous for

Russia. But public opinion has already long entertained the idea that European States differ from Asiatic ones by the subjects' freedom with regard to their Governments. It is imperative therefore to define freedom as it may exist in an autocratic State. The aim and object of autocratic governments is the glory of their subjects, of the State and of the Sovereign. And national pride creates, among a nation ruled autocratically, a sensation of liberty that is no less conducive to great deeds and to the welfare of the subjects, than liberty itself.[19]

In other words, Russia, by her sheer size, could only be governed autocratically (or despotically), but it did not follow from this that her people should necessarily be lacking in the initiative, enterprise or ardour thought to pertain to members of freer communities. Only in her case the stimulus for the development of these admirable traits would have to come not from personal interest or from unlimited opportunity, but from national pride, from a profound identification of the individual with the glory and grandeur of the State. To this end Catherine proposed to utilize to the full every available means of education and instruction, and in particular to mobilize the literary talents of Russia's writers. In one of the many pseudonymous – but easily recognizable – articles she wrote for the literary journals published at her instigation, the Empress laid down a firm line to be followed by all Russian practitioners of letters:

The well-meaning author should treat of vices sparingly, lest he offend against sensibility by some ill-chosen example, but when presenting his discourses to the public he should set them a model in the person of a hero graced with various virtues, *viz.* moral rectitude and integrity. He should describe the firm guardian of faith and justice; praise the patriot burning with love and loyalty to his sovereign and his people; depict the peaceful citizen, the sincere friend, the faithful confidant.[20]

This was apparently the first appearance in Russia of the

literary doctrine of the 'positive hero' – so familiar by now – according to which the writer's calling was to mould human souls into conformity with the dictates of the State. Under Catherine's benevolent guidance the arts flourished, and poets and playwrights outdid each other in singing her praise, to the sweet accompaniment of a shower of money, sinecures and honours. But the enlightened 'Little Mother' had other means in store for dealing with writers rash enough to transgress her literary rules: Radishchev was sentenced to *katorga*; Novikov spent many years in the dungeon from which he was only freed by the death of the Empress; Knyazhnin died under torture at the hands of the dreaded Sheshkovsky, chief of Catherine's secret police.

The fostering of national pride became a policy of State. Intense nationalism set in as a reaction to the earlier fashion, often carried to ludicrous extremes, of compulsorily admiring and copying everything foreign. Or, to be more accurate, the two attitudes intertwined into that curious mixture of admiration and hatred, envy and contempt, superiority and inferiority, that has so often characterized the Russian attitude towards Europe. Their standing in the world had to be measured by Western yardsticks, even while stressing their differentness, yet to feel truly proud of their country they had to be assured that they were not merely as good, but even better than 'abroad'. Now that Russia had become universally respected, even feared, it was axiomatic that Europe was effete, played out, convulsed by insoluble social problems. What a happy contrast was provided by the state of affairs in the Russian Empire, and how refreshing that this proof of Russian superiority could always be cited – without fear of contradiction at home – in reply to various ill-mannered slanderers!

The nationalistic orgy of denigration of Western Europe was started by the famous playwright Denis Fonvizin. In his widely read travel notes he drew the most satisfying comparisons between Russia and the West: 'Contemplating the condition of the French nation, I have learned to distinguish between liberty by law and genuine liberty. Our people do not possess the first, but they abundantly enjoy the second. The French, on the contrary, though endowed with the right to liberty, live in downright slavery ... Everything in our country is better, and we ourselves are more of a people than the Germans.'[21] This refrain, so very much in consonance with traditional Russian feelings of moral supremacy, was taken up by a many-voiced chorus, exposing and condemning the evil ways of the West. A considerable number of books by English and French authors, criticizing the social structure of their countries, and describing the appalling conditions of the lower classes, were lovingly translated and reproduced in Russia, always with the suitable moral lesson expatiated upon at length. For instance, the first volumes of L. S. Mercier's *Tableau de Paris*, with their grim picture of French working-class life, had hardly appeared from the press in France when they were already thrust into the hands of the Russian reading public; General Boltin and other authors used copious quotations from them to emphasize the idyllic life of the Russian peasantry. The utilization of condemnatory works freely published in the West became the stock-in-trade of the literary defenders of Russian despotism; the advantage of this method lay in the impossibility of any rejoinder or counter-evidence ever being published in Russia.

Of even greater value for the Russian government was the strong moral support provided by a number of Western, particularly French, progressive thinkers. The love affair between Russian 'enlightened despotism' and the French *philosophes* constitutes one of the most bizarre episodes in the history of European progressive thought. Voltaire canonized Peter the Great, and Diderot performed the same service for Catherine. No doubt the moneys and pensions lavished upon them were not entirely without effect. Certainly the Empress, a shrewd and cynical judge of human character, played upon their vanity, cupidity and credulity, achieving all her aims while leaving the savants happily convinced of having bested the Semiramis of the North at every turn. But the extremely favourable attitude adopted towards Russia by men otherwise renowned for the acerbity of their critical judgments is really explained by their delight in having at last found the enlightened monarch, the Philosopher-King (or Queen) who was going to put their cherished social theories into practice. Russia, they felt, was ideally suited for this great experiment: as a backward country with an undeveloped society she represented a *tabula rasa*, a virgin territory where there were no fossilized feudal remnants to hamper the bold projector; besides, her despotic system was in this case a positive blessing, for it would enable the wise monarch to establish the Kingdom of Reason by simple word of command. The dismal outcome of their fallacious hopes could have been profitably studied by the eager theoretical devotees of a later Russian despotism.

The fall of the Bastille provided a rude awakening both for the men of the European Enlightenment and for the 'enlightened despot' on the Russian throne. The last years of her reign were marked by a headlong retreat from the sublime idea of combining slavery with liberalism. For the Russian nobility the real shock came with the death of their benefactress and the enthronement of her son Paul (1796). Suddenly it transpired that the hard-won improvements in their legal and political position had been built on sand. The new Emperor transferred his intense hatred of his mother and all her works to the social class so favoured by her. Among his first acts was the revocation of most of the concessions contained in the Charter of the Nobility; with unconcealed satisfaction he restored flogging for noblemen condemned of criminal offences, for good measure adding branding and the tearing-out of nostrils. The pendulum had swung again, and now it was the turn of the peasants to gather some crumbs from the Imperial table: Paul decreed that *barshchina*, the peasants' compulsory work on the landlord's land, should not be allowed to exceed three days in the week. There was no question of the new Emperor's policy being pro-peasant: it was just that he refused to countenance the idea of the existence of any permanent privileged groups, estates or classes. All must once again be equal in their complete lack of rights. 'In Russia,' Paul explained to the Swedish Ambassador, 'only he is great with whom I speak, and only while I am speaking to him.'[22]

These were, of course, the actions of a wilful and half-mad despot, but their significance goes well beyond the grotesque figure of their author: they provided definite proof of the fact that, despite all the events of the preceding century, the power of the State was still as unlimited, as utterly dependent upon the quirks and fancies of its holders, as ever it had been in the history of Muscovy. This revelation was further underlined by the realization that the only feasible (one is almost tempted to add, constitutional) way of ensuring a change in policy was by murdering the Emperor. The assassination of Paul I, carried out in March 1801 with the knowledge of his son Alexander, inspired Madame de Staël to utter her immortal and profound epigram: 'En Russie le gouvernement est un despotisme mitigé par la strangulation.'

It was no more than the truth. Although Alexander hastily restored most of his grandmother's decrees, the damage had been done, and Russia could never be the same again. In Europe ancient thrones were falling and historical boundaries being uprooted; in the baleful glow from the West the transitory nature of Russia's social and political institutions stood out stark and clear. Catherine's make-believe of spurious liberalism and meaningless legislative declarations – symbolized by Potemkin's famous villages – had largely disappeared. The shattering events of the French Revolution, combined with the latest turns in their country's chronic political crisis, compelled the Russian educated class to take stock of political realities, probably for the first time in their history. It was a terrifying sight: a country with neither laws nor institutions; with no guarantees for either individuals or classes. Continuity had been broken, but nothing substituted in its place. For a whole century government had been a matter of makeshift expedients. What legislation there had been was of the most transient nature, unable even to survive the change from one reign to another. Everything had a provisional air about it: impermanence and instability became the essential characteristics of Russian life.

CHAPTER 9

Alexander I and Nicholas I

The more unreal the existing Russian laws and institutions appeared the greater grew the importance of the one factor that had remained constant through all the turbulent upheavals, and whose reality and effective power nobody could doubt: the autocratic State. At the height of the masked ball the hour of midnight had struck, and now all who had eyes to see discovered that naked, untrammelled despotism was the only genuine and lasting institution that Russia possessed.

All hopes were now pinned on the young Emperor, reared by his grandmother on the rich milk of the European Enlightenment. Alexander ascended the throne bursting with good intentions, and, supported by a small group of earnest young aristocrats and officials, began to make plans for a complete transformation of the Russian socio-political system. As has happened so many times in Russian history, expectations ran high.

The leading part in these activities was played by M. M. Speransky – a man of low origin, a gifted, incorruptible and experienced administrator, and probably the most brilliant Russian statesman of the nineteenth century. In the course of several years Speransky, who had become the Emperor's closest and most trusted collaborator, prepared a number of papers for his royal master, containing a detailed analysis of Russian society and a programme of far-reaching reforms. For a century and a half Speransky's papers, kept under strict lock and key, have been the subject of rumour and conjecture. It was only in 1961 that they were first published in their entirety. They constitute beyond doubt the most valuable of all existing source materials on Russia's past. For they were drawn up, not for propagandistic publication by some dissenter with an axe to

173

grind, nor by a biased foreigner lacking real knowledge of the country, but in absolute secrecy – for the Tsar's eyes only – by the Tsar's most loyal and devoted servant, who combined a first-rate legal brain with an extensive practical knowledge of administration and government, and with a personal understanding of the life of the people. Speransky's description of the Russian social and political system at the beginning of the nineteenth century must be regarded as an unimpeachable source, as the most authoritative and truthful picture that we can ever hope to possess. It deserves an extensive quotation:

[Russia is] the vastest Empire in the world, inhabited by many tongues, renowned for her might, her slavery, the diversity of her customs, and the instability of her laws . . .

Since the days of Peter the Great the history of Russia has consisted of the continuous oscillation of the Government from one plan to another. This instability, or rather, this absence of firm principles is the reason why today our system of government lacks any definite form, and why many institutions, although perhaps excellent in themselves, collapsed almost as soon as they were established . . .

[Under Catherine the Great the Government] wished to enjoy all the advantages of despotism together with all the glory of philosophical ideals . . . It can be said that our laws were written in Athens or in England, but our system of government borrowed from Turkey . . .

The fundamental principle of Russian government is the autocratic ruler who combines within his person all legislative and executive powers, and who disposes unconditionally of all the nation's resources. There are no physical limits to this principle . . .

Russia is today . . . at the stage when the supreme autocratic authority, combining within itself all the forces of the State, is in full possession of the liberties of its subjects, both political and civil . . .

When the powers of the sovereign authority are

unlimited, when the forces of the State are combined within the sovereign authority to such an extent that no rights are left over for the subjects – then such a State exists in slavery and its government is despotical . . .

A State thus composed, whatever superficial constitution it may have, whatever may be asserted in its Charters of the Nobility or of the Towns, and even if it has two Senates and as many legislative Parliaments – such a State is a despotism . . .

Under autocratic rule there can be no Code of Laws, for where no rights exist there can be no constant balance between them. What these governments call Codes and laws are nothing but the arbitrary decisions of the sovereign authority, prescribing to the citizens their duties for a certain period of time, i.e. until the autocratic will chooses to change or otherwise circumscribe them . . .

Governments without political foundations can have no stability . . .

In the present state of affairs one cannot discern even the first elements indispensable for a monarchical government. Indeed, how can a monarchical government of the kind we have proposed be founded in a country where half the population exists in a state of complete slavery, where this slavery is linked to almost every part of the political structure and to the military system, and where this military system is necessitated by the length of the frontiers and by the political situation . . .?

The Charter of the Nobility [bestowed upon the noblemen] a slave's privilege: it empowered them to impose the weight of the chains they carried upon other, even weaker beings. What interests have the nobility in common with the people? Are not their main advantages based on the exclusive right to own lands and men as physical property? Is not the estate and the person of the nobleman dependent on the Sovereign's autocratic decree . . .?

In no other State do political words stand in such contrast

to reality as in Russia . . . Outwardly we seem to have everything, but actually nothing has any material foundation . . . What, in fact, is the nobility itself, when their persons, their estates, their honour, are all dependent – not on the law, but solely on the autocratic will? Is not the law itself dependent on this will, which alone creates it? Can it not elevate and degrade noble families at pleasure? Is it not this will alone that establishes courts, that names the judges, that gives them their rules, and that revokes or confirms these rules, as the fancy strikes it? Does it not comprise the exclusive source of honour and distinction? Is not this autocratic will, according to the letter of the law, the possessor of all the State's wealth, of all lands, of all properties, and even of all rights of property as such? For are not private property rights merely enjoyed under permission, and are not their owners but tenants (*usufruitiers*)?

I wish someone could point out to me the difference between the peasants' subservience to their *pomeshchiki* and the nobility's subservience to the Sovereign, or could show that the Sovereign's powers over the *pomeshchiki* are not identical with those the *pomeshchiki* wield over their peasants?

In short: instead of all the pretentious divisions of the free Russian people into the absolutely free classes of nobility, merchants, etc., I can find only two conditions existing in Russia: the Sovereign's slaves, and the *pomeshchiki*'s slaves. The first can be termed free only with regard to the second, but actually there are no truly free men in Russia, except beggars and philosophers.

With the people divided in such wise with regard to the throne, how can one even dream of any ordered system of government, or of any basic laws . . .?

People complain about the confusion and complexity of our civil laws. But how can these be corrected and established without firm fundamental laws of State? What is the use of laws assigning property to private individuals, when property itself has no firm basis in any respect whatsoever? What is the use of civil laws, when their tablets can at any time be smashed upon the first rock of arbitrary rule? People complain about the confusion of our finances. But how can finances be set in order in a country without public confidence, without any laws for regulating the financial system? People complain of slowness in the progress of education and of industry. But where is the stimulus to come from? Of what use is education to the slave? It could only make him perceive even more clearly the full wretchedness of his condition.[1]

It is impossible to overrate the significance of Speransky's analysis. In the clearest and most concise way, and backed by an unquestioned authority, he shows that in nineteenth-century Russia – for all the sound and fury of the preceding centuries, despite the Time of Troubles, the Petrine Reform and Catherine's 'enlightened despotism' – the basic, essential features of the socio-political system were still practically unchanged from what they had been three hundred years before, during the reign of Ivan the Terrible – or even earlier, when they had first confronted and confounded the Baron von Herberstein. The State was still omnipotent, it still exercised unlimited control over the lives and property of all its subjects, it was still, in fact as in law, the real owner of everything and everybody within its boundaries. If anything, as a result of the Petrine Reform and of the final enslavement of the peasantry, it had become even stronger. So much for those modern historical treatises, whether by Soviet Marxist or Western non-Marxist authors, that strive to tell us how fundamentally similar – if only slightly slower – Russia's historical development had been to that of Western Europe!

Even Speransky's conservative opponents, in their bitter struggle to prevent the implementation of his plans, fully agreed with him regarding the absence in Russia of any laws or institutions outside the autocrat's sovereign will. Karamzin, the most articulate of these, boldly pointed out to the Tsar that, being human, he possessed no practical means of limiting autocracy for the future: 'But let us assume that Alexander actually prescribes royal authority some kind of statute based on the principles of public good, and sanctions it by a sacred oath. Would such an oath be capable of restraining Alexander's successors unless it were strengthened with other means, means which in Russia are either unfeasible or dangerous? No, let us be done with schoolboy sophistries.'[2]

Once again, despotism won: after a characteristically lengthy period of vacillation the Emperor decided against change. Speransky himself suffered the usual fate of the would-be reformer: disgrace and exile. His projects were buried in the secret archives. The high hopes of the new reign waned and vanished. Alexander increasingly came to be identified with reactionary policies: a stricter censorship (first officially established by his father), a viciously retrograde University Statute, the tightening-up of police powers, the rise to eminence of a junta of religious mystics and ferocious disciplinarians headed by Count Arakcheev. Besides, there were the ever-multiplying delights of foreign affairs to take his mind off Russian realities. The glory of Russia's victory over Napoleon and of her Emperor's primacy within the Concert of Europe proved an excellent justification for the preservation of the status quo.

Alexander the Blessed (for such was his official title) bequeathed to his successor a crisis of instability heightened by the *immobilisme* of the last period of his reign. Even the succession to the childless Emperor was unprovided for. For a whole month the populace was regaled by the unedifying spectacle of a government at wits' end over which of the deceased's two brothers to acknowledge as lawful monarch, and taking the oath of loyalty to both, one after the other. This period of total confusion was chosen by the officer members of the 'Decembrist' revolutionary conspiracy as the moment to strike. The attempt failed, and its merciless suppression provided a fitting introduction to the reign of Nicholas I (1825–55).

The age of Nicholas I represented in many ways the pinnacle

of achievement for the Russian monarchy, the full realization of age-old traditional tendencies. Never in its whole history was it as powerful both at home and abroad.

For forty years, from the downfall of Napoleon to the débâcle of the Crimean War, Russia dominated Europe to an extent greater even than that attained immediately following the Second World War. Russian diplomacy seemed ubiquitous, and Russia towered above all in her self-appointed role of the 'Gendarme of Europe'. Of the other Great Powers, Prussia and Austria were practically client-States – indeed, the Austrian Emperor owed his throne to Russia's crushing of the Hungarian Revolution of 1848-9. France was systematically browbeaten, and on at least two occasions lived in fear of an imminent Russian invasion. Turkey was contemptuously dismissed by the Tsar as the 'Sick Man of Europe', fit only to be carved up. England alone, secure in the consciousness of her naval and industrial might, seemed immune from the fear that gripped everyone else – although a considerable body of British public opinion was convinced that their country, too, shaped her foreign policy in obedience to the dictates of the puissant Tsar, and regarded Palmerston as little better than a paid Russian agent.

This was the Russia visited by the Marquis de Custine, who returned from his travels with a terrifying impression: 'The Russian people will surely become incapable of anything except the conquest of the world. I always return to this expression, because it is the only one that can explain the excessive sacrifices imposed here upon the individual by society ... Since I have been in Russia, I take a gloomy view of the future reserved for Europe ... I stand close by the Colossus, and I find it difficult to persuade myself that the only object of this creation of Providence is to diminish the barbarism of Asia. It appears to me that it is chiefly destined to chastise the corrupt civilization of Europe by the agency of a new invasion. The eternal tyranny of the East menaces us incessantly.'[3]

Events were to disprove de Custine's sombre forecast, but it was widely accepted over a long period. In 1835 Alexis de Tocqueville published the first volume of *De la démocratie en*

Amérique, with his famous prediction of a world dominated, a century from then, by the two Superpowers of Russia and the United States; we do not perhaps sufficiently appreciate that at the time the startling part of this prophecy was that concerning the United States: the position already achieved by Russia made her future role seem all too assured.

Within Russia the defeat of the Decembrist uprising determined the course of internal policy for the thirty years of Nicholas's reign. Society was put into a deep freeze; Peter's idea of a 'regulated State' had been finally consummated. Nicholas made it into a fully-fledged police State – probably mild enough by present-day standards, but inhumanly thoroughgoing by those of any less enlightened age. One of the first of the new Emperor's acts was the establishment, under the Third Section of the Imperial Chancellery, of the most efficient secret police in pre-1917 Russian history, complemented by a uniformed Corps of Gendarmes. The country was covered by a comprehensive network of police spies and informers. Rigid military discipline, sustained by all-pervading fear, became the order of the day. Nicholas was famous for the fixed stare with which he could reduce anyone to a state of petrification. Seventy million people cowered beneath it.

The great satirist Saltykov-Shchedrin later graphically represented the Russia of Nicholas I: 'A desert landscape, with a gaol in the middle; above it, in place of the sky, hung a grey soldier's greatcoat.' The climate of those grim years is best conveyed by the Populist writer Gleb Uspensky: 'Never to stir, even though one might have longed to do so; never to show that one had any thoughts; never to show that one was not afraid; always, on the contrary, to show that one was "scared", terrified – even though one had no cause to be frightened: such were the habits bred by those years in the Russian public. One must be permanently afraid: this was the basic rule of life. As for everything else, it might exist, but then, again, it might not exist, and anyway, who cared about everything else – it could only lead one into trouble. This was the atmosphere that pressed upon the public, that throttled its mind and its ability to think

. . . There was no one who believed that man had an intrinsic right to live – on the contrary, it was this belief that had been killed in the public . . . The atmosphere was full of terrors; "You are done for!" shrieked the sky and the earth, the air and the water, men and beasts. And all shrank and bolted from trouble into the nearest hole.'

The writers were the only elements who persisted in spoiling the beautiful symmetry of the barracks square which the Emperor tirelessly sought to impose upon Russia. For this was the beginning of the great period of Russian literature, which miraculously flowered in that most inclement climate. Its history reads like a martyrology: Russia's two greatest poets, Pushkin and Lermontov, killed within five years of each other in duels instigated by the authorities; Dostoevsky on the scaffold, hearing his death sentence commuted to *katorga*; the poets Shevchenko and Polezhaev sentenced to serve in military punitive battalions; the country's most original philosopher, Chaadayev, wrongfully declared insane; the historian Kostomarov exiled to Siberia, and so on (not to mention the brilliant galaxy of convicted Decembrist poets). One always had to be made of stern stuff to become a genuine writer in Russia.

Police omnipresence was only the most conspicuous feature of Nicholas's authoritarian regime. For the first time the bureaucracy was in complete and undivided control of the country. Russia had become a bureaucratic autocracy. 'By the middle of the century,' wrote Kliuchevsky, 'Russia was governed by neither aristocracy nor democracy, but by the bureaucracy, i.e. by a crowd of individuals of heterogeneous origin, acting outside society and lacking any definite social complexion, and joined together only by the table of promotion.'[4] The *chinovnik*, the government official, became the most characteristic figure of Russian life. The bureaucratic machine seemed to have discovered the secret of perpetual motion: spewing forth an ever-mounting volume of papers, multiplying in size at a geometrical rate, feverishly producing new departments and sub-departments for yet more hosts of underpaid and corrupt officials. At the centre of the elephantine mechanism sat the *chinovnik*-in-chief: Nicholas himself, a model of unsleeping industriousness, busily inaugurating fresh schemes for additional and more perfect institutions, desperately trying to keep the minutest details under his personal control, yet gradually being snowed under by an infinity of papers. 'Russia', he once declared, 'is really ruled not by the Emperor, but by the departmental chiefs.'[5] Ruled and plundered, we may add: for bribery, embezzlement, peculation of every kind were now a part of everyday life. Gogol's authority should alone be sufficient for this statement.

The triumph of the featureless State bureaucracy symbolized the end of the nobility's role as governing class. It remained important for the State only as a prime source of manpower for the colossal administrative apparatus. Gone was the power and the glory of the days of Catherine the Great; the nobility had been first diluted, and now drowned, in the ocean of officialdom. In the words of a prominent administrator of the reign, it was now no more than 'dough from which the State could bake bureaucrats'.[6]

The nobility was itself fully bureaucratized: its corporative and local self-government bodies were transformed into State institutions, elective service was officially equated with State service, and all noblemen were required to wear the uniform of the Ministry of the Interior.

The decline of the nobility constituted a fact of profound social importance. It was brought about by a variety of causes. Their vital *political* position as the warrior class of Russian society had been first undermined by the Petrine Reform, and then voluntarily abrogated by the emancipation decree of 1762 – without having been replaced by any other constitutional status. *Socially* the nobility had been adulterated and demoralized by the developments of the eighteenth century: the succession of upheavals, the rapid rise and extinction of many noble families, the meteoric rise to eminence and ennoblement of royal favourites of the lowliest extraction. Their *economic* position had gravely deteriorated: agricultural productivity remained low, but Europeanization and the new hectic style of court life had proved an expensive business, and fortunes were rapidly dissipated; by the end of Nicholas's reign two-thirds of *pomeshchik* slaves were mortgaged.[7] Curiously it was the Decembrist conspiracy, in which so many scions of Russia's best families had participated, that administered the coup de grâce to the nobility's governing-class status. Nicholas, haunted to the end of his life by the terrible memory, could neither forgive nor forget, and extended his distrust to the whole social stratum from which the Decembrists had come.

The traditional balance of Russian society, with State, nobility and peasantry each fulfilling their allotted roles, had been irreparably upset. The waning of the nobility meant that the bureaucratic State now directly confronted the enslaved peasantry. No other social forces counted; there was no middle class to speak of – in the middle 1850s townspeople comprised a bare 4,700,000 out of a total population of 74,000,000[8] – and the intelligentsia was only just emerging. A new balance of society had to be established.

From the end of the eighteenth century the peasant problem had become central to every aspect of Russian life. The pressing need for peasant emancipation was borne in upon everyone with ever-growing clarity. From a legal point of view there was nothing to prevent the government from carrying this out by a stroke of the pen: since no legislation existed *enslaving* the peasants, none was needed to emancipate them. But it would have meant a fearful wrench, a complete transformation of Russian society, a perilous leap into the unknown, and every monarch from Catherine the Great to Nicholas I, although personally favouring the abolition of slavery, hesitated and retreated from taking the fateful step. As Karamzin, a fervent supporter of slavery, put it: 'From the point of view of political stability it is safer to enslave men than to give them their freedom prematurely.'[9]

But what was 'prematurely'? When was the right time – if there was any? And would it not actually be safer from the point of view of political and economic security to liberate the slaves? But how were they to be liberated: with land or without land? And how were the *pomeshchiki* to be compensated? These were the questions that occupied a succession of governments. A number of intermediate steps were taken: in 1803 *pomeshchiki* received the right to manumit slaves with land; in 1816–19 peasants in the Baltic regions were liberated without land; under Nicholas I a series of measures led to the gradual emancipation of State serfs and to an amelioration in the conditions of *pomeshchik* bondage. Over the years innumerable governmental committees had produced countless projects of reforms. And yet the government vacillated before taking the irrevocable plunge.

It needed the disaster of the Crimean War, which finally exposed the hopeless inadequacy of Russia's obsolete social system and exploded the illusion of her irresistible might, to set the cumbersome wheels rolling. On 19 February 1861, ninety-nine years to the day after the emancipation of the nobility, personal slavery was abolished, and the peasants received their liberty, together with part of the land – against heavy redemption payments over a long period of years.

Too little, too late. The traditional mould of Russian society was shattered, but the prerequisites for a new evolution had not been established. The State still held everyone in its iron grip. And the sense of deepening crisis, far from being dispelled, became still stronger. The terrible crime of transforming the people, the 'God-bearing people', into chattel slaves, had not been redeemed. The Russian social system, once passionately believed in as the embodiment of justice, had been broken when one class wickedly amassed property and privilege while the other was loaded with chains. Injustice still reigned, but a day of atonement would come. For in Russia justice was the essence; without justice there could be no Russia.

Such were the ideas expressed ever louder, inarticulately and eloquently, with hope and with dread, by progressive and by reactionary, in every class of society. They are to be found in the works of practically every national writer, from the beginning of the nineteenth century onwards. Russian literature, remarked Berdyaev, 'is the most prophetical literature in the world; it is full of presentiments and predictions; its distinctive attribute is anxiety over an approaching catastrophe.'[10] When reading the great Russian poets and novelists one can hardly escape the overhanging feeling of heavy foreboding, the sense of peering into a dark abyss from which there is no salvation. Again and again there appear the tortured visions of the horrors in store for a people who depart from the path of righteousness. The Four Horsemen of the Apocalypse thunder through the sky, and revolution, anarchy, death and an inhuman tyranny rule the land.

In 1830 the sixteen-year-old Lermontov set down the fearful prediction in one of his most powerful poems:

> A year will come for Russia, a dark year
> When Royalty no more their crown will wear,
> The rabble who loved them once will love forget,
> For Blood and Death will richest feast be set;
> The fallen law no more will shield the weak,
> And maid and guiltless child in vain will seek
> For justice. Plague will ride
> Where stinking corpses fill the countryside,
> And flapping rags from cottages demand
> Help none can give, while Famine rules the land.
> Dawn on thy streams will shed a crimson light;
> That day will be revealed the Man of Might
> Whom thou wilt know. And thou wilt understand.
> Wherefore a naked blade is in his hand.
> Bitter will be thy lot; tears flood thine eyes,
> And he will laugh at all thy tears and sighs.

Three-quarters of a century later, on the eve of the first Russian revolution, Alexander Blok described an almost identical vision:

> 'Is all calm with the people?'
> 'No. The Emperor has been killed.
> Someone speaks of new freedom
> Out in the public squares.'

'Are they all ready to rise?'
'No. They are numb and they wait.
Someone has told them to stay;
They wander about and they sing.'

'Who is then installed in power?'
'The people wish for no power.
The civic passions are torpid:
It is heard that someone is coming.'

'Who is he, the people's subduer?'
'Dark and evil and cruel:
The monk at the door of the cloister
Glimpsed him – and lost his sight.

'He drives to unknown abysses
The people, as if they were herds . . .
He drives with a staff of iron. . . .'
'O God! We must flee from the Judge!'

For some, Revolution meant the coming of Antichrist, for
others – the Day of Judgment. But most would have agreed
that, in one way or another, a cataclysmic upheaval was
inexorably approaching.

Part II

THE RUSSIAN REVOLUTIONARY TRADITION

CHAPTER 10

The Intelligentsia

The history of the Russian revolutionary movement is the history of the Russian intelligentsia. The two are inseparable. The Russian revolution was the product of the intelligentsia, and revolution was the intelligentsia's *raison d'être*. In no other European country did a social stratum exist that remained, through three or four generations, exclusively and specifically devoted to the idea of revolution. For the bourgeoisie of the Western countries revolution was but a means to an end; for the Russian intelligentsia it was the be all and end all of their existence. The revolutionary movement was staffed, supported and trained by the intelligentsia; it received its ideas, its ethos, its system of values, its world-outlook and its way of thinking from the intelligentsia. In the words of a famous critique, published a few years before the revolution: 'The Russian revolution was a movement of the intelligentsia. The spiritual leadership belonged to the intelligentsia, with its *Weltanschauung*, its traditions, tastes, and social habits ... The intelligentsia supplied the revolution with all its ideological resources, all its spiritual equipment, together with its active fighters, its leaders, its agitators and propagandists. It was the intelligentsia which spiritually shaped the instinctive aspirations of the masses, which fired them with its enthusiasm, which was, in a word, the nerves and the brains of the gigantic body of the revolution. In this sense the revolution is the spiritual offspring of the intelligentsia, and its history is therefore a historical judgment on this intelligentsia.'[1]

The Russian intelligentsia was an instrument of destruction; unlike the European bourgeoisie it had no constructive purposes, neither was it equipped to fulfil any such tasks. The consummation of its sole object automatically entailed its own

189

self-destruction. The old order died, and the old intelligentsia died with it. But the new order created by the revolution, while publicly disowning and physically destroying its progenitor, inherited, and further developed, the essential traditions, political and moral, social and ideological, of the intelligentsia: in the same way as it inherited, and enlarged upon, the centuries-old State tradition of the regime it had supplanted. In this life after death, in this incorporation of its ideas and its values within the living body of present-day Russian society, the intelligentsia has made a cardinal contribution to the staying power and the stability of the Soviet system. There is every justification for saying that 'no class in Russian history has had a more momentous impact on the destinies of that nation or indeed of the modern world'.[2]

What, then, was the Russian intelligentsia? The word itself first appeared in the 1850s, at about the time when the emergence of a now social stratum began to be somewhat uneasily acknowledged; it was coined by the now all but forgotten novelist Boborykin, and rapidly acquired wide currency through the novels of Turgenev. Since then it has been naturalized in practically every one of the world's languages and, as a result, having been transposed to social circumstances very unlike those for which it was initially created, the original, Russian sense of the word has become largely obscured.

Not that a clear definition of the term would ever have been easy to achieve. One of the favourite occupations of the Russian intelligentsia had always been the absorbed study of itself, and only very rarely did any of the countless essays in self-analysis produce identical answers. In the course of this endless debate, however, certain salient features of the problem gradually grew clearer.

For one thing, the intelligentsia was undoubtedly a definite social category; although never officially recognized as such, it was plainly differentiated from the other classes of Russian society. But it was a class that could not be defined by any of the traditional criteria of rank, status, property, birth or privilege: it consisted of men and women of the most diverse social origins, who held no rank, possessed hardly any property, and enjoyed no privileges. Neither can it be compared to such other essentially classless concepts as 'bureaucracy' or 'meritocracy' – for the simple reason that its members had voluntarily opted out of any form of either State service or of what is today called the 'rat-race'.

A conspicuous attribute held in common by every member of the intelligentsia, and one which singled them out from the overwhelming majority of their countrymen, was the possession of an education. Yet here it is important to dispel the misconception – widely held outside Russia – that the term 'intelligentsia' was more or less equivalent to 'the intellectual community' or 'the educated class', or in other words, that the Russian *intelligent* corresponded to the European 'intellectual'. This was never the case. A significant proportion of the intelligentsia consisted of people who were, at best, semi-educated, by either European or Russian standards: failed students, lapsed seminarians, auto-didacts etc. At the same time a large part, probably the greater and most highly civilized part, of the educated class – higher civil servants, university professors, engineers, scientists, many professional people – were never regarded as belonging to the intelligentsia, either by themselves or by others. They had forfeited this right by entering into the service of the State or the pursuit of Mammon, both of which constituted *per se* disqualifying factors.

Strange as it may seem, the Russian intelligentsia can only be defined as a social category based upon criteria not of class, but of consciousness, upon a certain set of moral, ethical, philosophical, social and political values, upon a particular attitude towards the political and social system of their country. This attitude was one of sharp and uncompromising hostility. The *intelligent* was, above all, an enemy of Tsarist autocracy and of all its works. His hostility could, and did, take a variety of forms, but it was ever-present, and it was this basic characteristic which set the intelligentsia apart from all other strata of Russian society. It could be said that the intelligentsia was not so much a class as a state of mind.

In Russia itself this distinctive hallmark of the intelligentsia gradually acquired general recognition. Only a few years after the word itself had made a first appearance we find Ivan Aksakov, the famous Slavophile, describing the intelligentsia as 'the self-aware people', and explaining that it 'is neither an estate, nor a guild, nor a corporation, nor an association . . . It is not even a gathering, but rather the aggregate of the vital forces issuing from the people.'[3] Miliukov, the liberal historian and politician, was another champion of the intelligentsia's great destiny; not being a poet, however, he expressed the heart of the matter in more mundane terms: 'Almost from its inception the Russian intelligentsia has been hostile to the governmental system.'[4]

It was only after the revolution and the final eclipse of the old Russian intelligentsia that a broader historical assessment of its character and influence could be made. Berdyaev found a reasoned form of words for a comprehensive definition: 'The intelligentsia bore a strong resemblance to a monastic order or a religious sect, with its own extremely intolerant morality, with its obligatory world-outlook, with its own customs and traditions, even with its own peculiar physical appearance . . . an ideological, and not a professional or economic grouping, made up from different social classes . . . united solely by ideas, namely, ideas of a social character.'[5]

The Russian intelligentsia was a social stratum composed of those politically aroused, vociferous and radical members of the educated classes who felt totally estranged from society, who rejected the social and political system of Tsarist autocracy, and who single-mindedly nurtured the idea of the imperative downfall of that system – who, to use a Russian expression common at the time, had taken a 'Hannibalic oath' of opposition to the State.

The alienation of the intelligentsia from society was to a great extent inherent in the country's rudimentary social structure: between the two great divisions of nobility and peasantry there existed no middle class similar to that European bourgeoisie of which the Western intellectual community formed an integral, well-protected and vital offshoot. Unlike the West, Russia had no interest groups capable of giving strength, support and substance to the intellectuals' protest, of acting as a channel between them and the body politic. Lacking the natural paternal environment of an established bourgeoisie (which even the most rebellious Western intellectuals have found so difficult to shake off), the Russian intelligentsia was at once more democratic and more rootless than its European counterparts could ever aspire to be. It had neither a place nor a stake in the existing order of things – no material or social interests fettered its revolutionary ardour. It was truly *déclassé*, a genuine intellectual proletariat, homeless and unprotected, isolated from the ruling class by its radicalism and from the peasantry by its education. Both chasms were unbridgeable. Estranged and disaffected, it came to inhabit a world of its own, a peculiar world of internal emigration, a State within a State. In a sense, the only home it could claim as its own, and in which alone it could feel happy, was its mental vision of the ideal society of the future. And the more it was persecuted by the forces of governmental repression, the more impenetrably it sealed itself up in this spiritual refuge.

The alienation of the Russian intelligentsia has frequently been explained in the West by a relative 'overproduction' of intellectuals, whom it was impossible to accommodate within the country's backward and rigid social structure: by insufficient 'social mobility' and the unsatisfactory 'circulation of élites'. There seems little justification for this argument. Actually, since the days of Peter the Great, the social structure, however backward, was more flexible and less caste-bound than, for instance, that of contemporary England, with greater opportunities of successful careers in the State service (the only kind there was) for talented and ambitious men of humble origin. There are innumerable examples of this (quite apart from the meteoric careers of many eighteenth-century royal favourites, whose rise was often due to adventitious factors): Speransky, the outstanding statesman of the nineteenth century and first minister of Alexander I, was the son of a village priest; General

Yevdokimov, who accomplished the conquest of the Caucasus in the 1850s and became a Count, was the son of a serf; Professor Pogodin, the leading historian of the mid-nineteenth century and the official ideologist of autocracy, and Nikitenko, the long-time liberal professor of literature at St Petersburg University and prominent civil servant, were both serfs' sons. The tradition persisted until the very downfall of Tsarism: General Denikin, the leader of the anti-Bolshevik White armies in the Civil War, was also the son of a serf. Nor should it be forgotten that I. N. Ulyanov, the inspector of schools of Simbirsk *guberniya*, who achieved general's rank in the civil service and a patent of hereditary nobility, was the son of a serf – and became the father of the leader of the Russian revolution, Lenin. In fact, the 'generals' of the progressive intelligentsia were, as a rule, of a higher social origin than any of the above-named (and many other) faithful servants of the Tsar.

There is nothing surprising in the existence of a comparatively high degree of social mobility in Tsarist Russia: in a bureaucratic empire, with no intrinsically privileged classes, where in the eyes of the autocrat all his subjects were essentially equal and where service to the State constituted the sole real yardstick of social position, advancement by merit could be easier than in countries with complex social structures and ancient and jealously guarded class privileges. The *intelligent* was alienated primarily not because it was impossible for him to fit into the existing social structure, but because he himself rejected the idea of serving a system founded on injustice, oppression and misery.

During much of the nineteenth century the only field open to the educated Russian who had opted out of official society but who wished to serve his people and to advance his ideals was that of literature and the periodical press. The rise of the intelligentsia coincided with the great flowering of Russian literature and literary criticism. Tsarist censorship, for all its evil reputation, was a bumbling and permissive body compared to its Soviet successor – and the so-called 'thick journals', the monthly literary and political reviews, became the breeding-ground, the school, the natural habitat of the most radical and influential part of the intelligentsia. The writer and, even more, the literary critic acquired a position and a historical importance that has no parallel in any other country or age. The radical editors and critics of nineteenth-century Russia – Belinsky, Herzen, Chernyshevsky, Dobrolyubov, Pisarev, Lavrov, Mikhailovsky – became the ideologists and the natural leaders of the intelligentsia. It is impossible to exaggerate the influence their writings have had, not only upon the Russian revolutionary movement, but upon the evolution of the Soviet society of our day.

It was Vissarion Belinsky, often called the Father of the Russian intelligentsia, who in 1847 first formulated – in his famous Letter to Gogol – the very special importance of the writer in Russia:

> The character of the Russian public is determined by the state of Russian society: fresh forces are stirring to break out – but they are crushed down by tyranny, they can find no outlet, and are only capable therefore of producing dejection, weariness and apathy. In literature alone, despite our Tartar censorship, is there life and forward movement. That is why we esteem so highly the profession of letters, why literary success comes so quickly even to slight talent. And that is why particular attention is paid to every liberal trend, even in the case of inferior talent, and why the popularity of great poets rapidly declines when they enlist, whether sincerely or not, in the service of 'autocracy, Orthodoxy and national character' [an allusion to Pushkin] ... And our public is right: they see in Russian writers their only leaders, protectors and saviours from the desolation of autocracy, Orthodoxy and national character. That is why they are always ready to forgive a writer for an inferior book, but they will never forgive him a harmful one.[6]

Russian literature was expected to carry a profound social message, and it usually did. Better than any learned treatise, it has preserved for posterity a vivid picture of the life and ideas of the Russian intelligentsia who were its first reading public – before it had swept across Russia's frontiers to conquer the world.

It was through the medium of literature that the men who became the forerunners of the radical intelligentsia – Radishchev and Novikov – acquired their fame. And it was in the pages of literature that the *intelligent* made his first recognizable appearance – as that distinctive Russian character, the 'superfluous man'. This favourite hero (or rather, to use a modern term, anti-hero) of so many of Russia's greatest writers – Pushkin's Onegin, Griboyedov's Chatsky, Lermontov's Pechorin, Turgenev's Rudin, Goncharov's Oblomov – typifies the young man of education and sensibility who is unwilling to accept the harsh realities of Russian life and unable to find a place within it. He is estranged from society, which he loathes and despises, but is incapable of any positive action, either by personal weakness, or because of political and social restrictions, and instead fritters away his life in senseless frivolity, melancholia and indolence. These young men were in many ways attractive characters, often reminiscent of their Western contemporaries, but there was about them none of the relentless ambition of Julien Sorel or Rastignac, the wholesome innocence of David Copperfield, the romantic passion of Heathcliff. They were, in the fullest sense of the word, superfluous men, and they wander through Russian fiction vainly seeking a purpose in life, true rebels without a cause.

The 'superfluous men' of Russian literature all came from the ranks of the nobility. So too did the first generation of the intelligentsia. In the early years of the nineteenth century the nobility were the only people with the means and the leisure, not merely to obtain an education, but to enable them to devote their lives to less mundane occupations than the pursuit of a career and the support of a family. Writing was only beginning to emerge as a gainful profession, and within the intelligentsia – as, indeed, within the revolutionary movement – the non-noblemen were few and far between. (One such was the doctor's son Belinsky.)

This first, aristocratic generation of the intelligentsia, who appeared on the Russian scene in the 1840s, became known later as the 'Men of the Forties', or, after the publication of Turgenev's *Fathers and Sons*, as the 'generation of the Fathers'. It was a remarkable group – probably the most talented creative generation of Russia's history. A brilliant constellation of novelists, playwrights, poets, critics, scholars, philosophers – many of them soon to win worldwide acclaim – suddenly erupted to light up the gloom of Nicholas I's police State. There was nothing dogmatic or uniform about them: espousing a wide diversity of political and social views, they were at one only in their hostility towards the existing order, and particularly in their implacable hatred of serfdom. They were a high-minded and rather romantic set, much influenced by Germany and the idealistic philosophy of Fichte, Schelling and Hegel, attached to the concept of art for art's sake, devoted to Humanity, Beauty and Reason.

However large the Fathers loom in the history of Russian civilization, they played only a secondary role in the development of the intelligentsia proper. Their spiritual ascendancy was short-lived: a bare decade later it faded away before the onslaught on a new type of *intelligent*, very different both in social origin and outlook.

One of the earliest symptoms of the changes germinating within Russian society – and one which, significantly, coincided with the humiliation of the Crimean War and the crisis of the slave-holding autocratic system – was a marked shift in the social composition of the student body in the universities. From being selected predominantly among youths of aristocratic extraction it came to be made up more and more of so-called *raznochintsy*, 'people of diverse rank': sons (and later daughters) of clergymen, peasants, petty officials, army officers, artisans, tradesmen – who had become divorced, by virtue of their education (or inclination), from their fathers' social station, and could no longer fit into the official estate system. Russian universities, which were still comparatively novel institutions (the first was founded in 1755), had never resembled the privileged aristocratic corporations of Oxford or Cambridge. They had always been much easier of access for the 'lower classes', and were arguably the most democratic of any Russian institution. In the second half of the nineteenth century the majority of university students came from needy families: up to three-quarters were supported by the State or by grants from charitable organizations. However – as was to be expected under the circumstances – the student-*raznochinets*, instead of being grateful and counting his blessings, brought with him a deep sense of the injustices of Russian life, which usually went beyond mere personal resentment of an impoverished and miserable existence, and rapidly turned into hatred of the existing order and uncompromising rejection of all its basic assumptions. Having gone up to university (particularly in the great centres of Moscow and St Petersburg) the student was able, for the first time in his life, to meet large numbers of young men of similar background and kindred frame of mind; he eagerly absorbed the legal and illegal radical periodicals now appearing in ever growing number; he made the acquaintance of a variety of exciting radical theories, both foreign and Russian; he began to feel acutely the necessity and imminence of social and political changes. The universities became hotbeds of sedition, rebellion and disaffection; they retained this character for the next half-century. Out of them sprang the Revolution, and the old reactionary Joseph de Maistre was vindicated for having warned, in the beginning of the nineteenth century, that the real danger would come not from the Russian peasants, but from an eventual '*Pougatchev d'université*'.

By the 1860s the *raznochintsy* had coalesced with the radical young *déclassé* noblemen into a clearly defined social group, united by a particular set of social attitudes, conscious of being different from the rest of society. It had, in fact, repudiated society, and, both individually and as a group, broken off all ties with it. The *raznochintsy* became the core of the stratum then beginning to be known as the intelligentsia. Being composed of 'people of diverse rank', it belonged to all classes and to none; it originated within the people and yet stood outside it; it was part of society and yet remained an extraneous element within the body politic; it was the first social group in Russian history to become free of the State. It felt, therefore, not without reason, that it had every right to represent the whole of society, and to assume the task of curing Russia's ills.

Such then were the 'Men of the Sixties', or the 'generation of the Sons'. In most respects they stood poles apart from the 'Fathers', upon whom they transferred much of their general animosity towards society: jeering at their cult of art for art's sake, disparaging their lofty ideals, upbraiding them for half-hearted liberalism, taunting them for their comfortable lives. The poor 'Fathers' – bewildered, indignant, and yet in their hearts agreeing with many of the accusations – were soon chased from the field or, at best, consigned to the sidelines. The Sons had devoured their Fathers.

The intensely dramatic confrontation between two generations of the intelligentsia, so closely related one to the other and yet so different, was transposed into the central conflict of much of the Russian fiction of the day. It has been immortalized by two of the greatest Russian novelists.

In Turgenev's *Fathers and Sons*, Bazarov the nihilist – intended by his author as a caricature but enthusiastically acclaimed as their model by the young *raznochintsy* – delights in humiliating his hosts, a family of well-meaning, liberal-minded, cultured 'Men of the Forties':

> The day before yesterday I saw him reading Pushkin. Explain to him, please, that that's no earthly use. He's not a boy, you know; it's time to throw up that rubbish. And what an idea to be a romantic at this time of day! Give him something sensible to read. [Translated by Constance Garnett]

Dostoevsky's comments are more profound. In *The Possessed* Stepan Trofimovich Verkhovensky, the old liberal idealist (actually modelled on Granovsky, the famous progressive historian of the 1840s) and father of the monstrous Pyotr

Verkhovensky, not only expresses his disgust at his son's theories, but also confirms the basic affinity between them and his own views:

> You cannot imagine what wrath and sadness overcome your whole soul when a great idea, which you have long cherished as holy, is caught up by the ignorant and dragged forth before fools like themselves into the street, and you suddenly meet it in the market unrecognizable, in the mud, absurdly set up, without proportion, without harmony, the plaything of foolish louts! No! In our day it was not so, and it was not this for which we strove. No, no, not this at all. I don't recognize it . . .
>
> The fundamental idea is a true one, but that only makes it more awful. It's just our idea, exactly ours; we first sowed the seed, nurtured it, prepared the way, and, indeed, what could they say new, after us? But, heavens! How it's all expressed, distorted, mutilated! Were these the conclusions we were striving for? Who can understand the original idea in this? [Translated by Constance Garnett]

Stepan Trofimovich was right: it was the ideas of his generation which were being followed up by the Men of the Sixties, however unfamiliar and frightening they may have seemed to their seniors. The fierce conflict between generations was to be repeated over and over again – the Men of the Sixties were followed by 'Men of the Seventies', and they in turn by those of the Eighties; new political tendencies regularly appeared and just as regularly split along age lines. But through all these vicissitudes the continuity of the basic world-outlook of the Russian intelligentsia stands out sharp and clear. Despite the ferocious feuds, certain fundamental premises were held in common by every generation of the intelligentsia.

Underlying all else, and colouring their distinctive approach to every social, political or theoretical problem, was a deep-rooted and constant sense of guilt. Guilt was the driving force that cleaved off the intelligentsia into a separate group, the cement that held them together throughout the better part of a century. An overwhelming sense of guilt permeates much of nineteenth- and early twentieth-century Russian writing and political thought; it produced the famous *l'ame Slave*, the interminable soul-searchings, the self-lacerations, the tortured disquisitions on right and wrong, that did so much to entertain the Western readers of Russian novels, and to puzzle them by disappearing after the revolution. It was an emotion born of the single most important feature of Russian life: the unjustified and unnatural enslavement, in the condition of human chattels, of the vast majority of their Christian fellow-countrymen by a handful of aristrocratic landowners. Gradually the idea began to sink in that every Russian of education and leisure was an accomplice in a crime unparalleled in its enormity – a crime, moreover, that had been committed against a people with a unique historical destiny. The only way in which an honourable and decent man could make amends was by devoting his whole life to the expiation of this crime.

Atonement for serfdom became the collective mission of the intelligentsia. Not for nothing did their first generation, the Men of the Forties, become known as 'repentant noblemen'. But the liberation of the serfs in 1861 and the concurrent change in the social composition of the intelligentsia did not imply the completion of this mission. On the contrary: the obligation to make reparation to the people for their centuries of suffering was taken over with even greater fervour by the *raznochintsy*, animated, as they naturally were, by a stronger fellow-feeling for the lower classes. The advantages they enjoyed seemed to them even more illogical and shameful; they could be justified only by being used to wipe out the evil past. The intelligentsia's moral responsibility for expiating the sin committed against the people was clearly formulated by Nikolai Mikhailovsky:

We have come to realize that our awareness of the universal truth and of universal ideals could only have been reached at the cost of the age-old suffering of the people . . . We have come to the conclusion that we are the people's debtors . . . We may argue about the size of the debt or the best method of repayment, but this debt weighs down on our conscience, and return it we must.[7]

The overpowering guilt-complex of the Russian intelligentsia, its obsession with the ideas of collective sin and social redemption, engendered a general outlook which can only be described as eschatological, and which was held in common, in one form or another, by every school of thought. 'A certain other-worldliness, an eschatological vision of the City of God, of the coming kingdom of justice (under various socialist pseudonyms), and an urge to save mankind – if not from sin then from suffering – constitute the immutable characteristics of the Russian intelligentsia.'[8] To read the works of any of the nineteenth-century ideologists is to recapture some of the flavour of the apocalyptic writings of the Old Believers at the time of the great Schism and after: their fearless rejection of the State as the embodiment of Antichrist (or of an evil social order), and their uncompromising faith in the advent of a kingdom of righteousness and justice. Nothing less than this could recompense the people for their inhuman sufferings.

The messianic vision of the just society which animated the writings and actions of the nineteenth-century Russian intelligentsia was an (often unconscious) revival of the traditional 'Russian idea'. During the 'Westernizing' St Petersburg period of Russian history, the faith in Russia's unique destiny had lost much of its hold over the governing class; all the greater the intensity with which it was taken up the new social stratum which saw as their only purpose unyielding opposition to official State and society. Russia, by her immeasurable suffering, had earned the right and acquired the understanding to show Mankind the path to its future. There were serious differences of opinion regarding the precise nature of this path, but on the great regenerative mission of the Russian people all were at one. Even Mikhailovsky, the most Western-minded and 'liberal' of the men who shaped the intelligentsia's *Weltanschauung*, wrote: 'We believe that Russia can lay down a new historical path, different from that taken by Europe.'[9]

For all the sophistication and brilliance of the nineteenth-century Russian ideologues, theirs was in essence an almost religiously held belief in a coming millennium – a millennium, moreover, which they, like the chiliastic theologians of an earlier age, expected to arrive quite suddenly, almost miraculously. Only in their case the millennium was to be achieved not by the intervention of some supernatural agency, but through the great historical cataclysm of violent revolution. The most important contribution of the Russian intelligentsia to our present-day system of moral values has been their cult of 'revolutionism', their idealization of revolutionary acts, and their enshrinement of the 'revolutionary fighter' as the supreme folk-hero of our age. The attitude of unreserved admiration for the revolutionary deed is today by no means confined to Communist movements, the direct inheritors of the views of the nineteenth-century Russian *intelligent*: it is – in striking contrast to the climate of opinion of past ages – almost as widespread among those 'progressive' Western middle classes who would, in fact, have most to fear from actual revolution. This 'cult of revolutionism' was undoubtedly the creation of the Russian intelligentsia; in 1917 it erupted on the world scene, to become the most potent mass influence of the twentieth century. The term 'revolutionary' continues to carry only the noblest connotations. Nowhere is this more evident than in the study of the history of Russia herself: in the words of a Western scholar, 'radical convention still demands that we should study the history of the Russian intelligentsia as an epic struggle of brave and enterprising reformers against an obtuse tyranny which went on crushing them until successful revolution crowned their efforts to crush *it*'.[10] And although they themselves were also crushed in the process, this had no discernible effect upon the obdurate revolutionism of the pathetic survivors of the Russian intelligentsia.[11]

The acceptance of revolutionary upheaval as the only solution to their country's problems sprang from the intelligentsia's rejection of the existing order, on the one hand, and their messianism, on the other. It was an unqualified attitude, attractive in its simplicity: the question was one of total evil or total good. In mid-nineteenth-century Russia there were no signs of a possible half-way house between the two; the path from the one to the other could lead only through total destruction. The kingdom of absolute justice was attainable, but it would come only as the result of a gigantic cataclysm. The mentality of the radical intelligentsia took on an apocalyptic hue; the exultant expectation of an inevitable catastrophe became one of its most characteristic features. No matter that a social convulsion might well bring new suffering in its wake – as long as it ended the existing order. This longing for a catastrophe that would sweep away the wickedness and injustice of Russian life distinguishes, in particular, the social outlook of Chernyshevsky, the most influential of the radical ideologists. In Chernyshevsky's diary we find his views expressed with great intensity of feeling:

> Here are my thoughts about Russia: an overwhelming expectation of the coming revolution, a longing for it – even though I know that for a long time, perhaps for a very long time nothing good can come of it, that maybe for a long time to come it can only lead to even greater oppression. Does it matter? The man who is not blinded by idealization, who is capable of deducing the future on the basis of the past, and who glorifies certain [revolutionary] epochs of history, despite all the evil they initially created – such a man cannot be scared off by apprehensions of this nature. He knows that nothing else is to be expected, and that peaceful and calm development is impossible. Far better that I should be seized by convulsions, for I know that without convulsions there could never have been a single forward step made in history.[12]

The 'revolutionism' of the Russian intelligentsia manifested itself in a variety of forms. The majority were never more than ineffectual dreamers, revolutionary Walter Mittys, but their radical contingent – largely nurtured on the writings of

Chernyshevsky – not content with passive expectation of the cataclysm, threw themselves into actively promoting its arrival. But, even when not carried to its logical conclusion, the basic attitude of 'heroic defiance', of constantly challenging the existing order, of joyfully hoping for the inevitable revolution, of justifying its excesses and canonizing its heroes, was held in common to the very end by every self-admitted member of the intelligentsia – even when their external way of life came more and more to resemble the comfortable bourgeois existence of the Western middle classes. The evergreen revolutionary romanticism of the progressive Russian *intelligent* was the source of his invincible contempt for so-called 'small deeds' – i.e. any kind of social, philanthropical, educational etc. activity which was aimed merely at improving the people's lot and reforming the existing system of society – and of the cult of violence (of violence in a progressive cause, that is), to which he invariably subscribed.

The intelligentsia's idealization of revolutionary action at any price distinguished them from the first. Nikitenko, the well-known liberal professor of literature, remarked upon this propensity, and its probable outcome, in his diary under April 1862:

> A terrible fate is being prepared for our country by all these ultra-progressives. And what is it they want? Instead of gradual reforms, instead of rational development, they want a violent transformation, a revolution, which they are trying to induce artificially. The blind fools! As if they didn't know what kind of revolution is the only possible one in Russia! They want to posture on the stage, they want to play at making history – but inevitably they will be the first to be ground down by history and swept away in its maelstrom.[13]

It would be an error to ascribe the romantic messianism and the faith in revolutionary violence to simple bloody-mindedness, or to isolation from more sophisticated Western ideologies, or – as is often done – to an intense desire to assume the leading role in society. There is no ground to impugn their motives, which invariably, and quite sincerely, were of the highest. Nothing could be more alien to them than sordid worldly considerations, whether of ambition or aggrandizement. They wanted nothing for themselves; what they sought, with a single-mindedness and a readiness for self-sacrifice that was probably unequalled since the Age of Religion, was the happiness of all.

By 'the happiness of all' they meant the happiness of 'the people'. The elusive concept of 'the people' constituted the heart of every doctrine that held sway among the intelligentsia. Although the term 'Populism', strictly speaking, refers to one particular – albeit the most influential – current of thought in Russia, it can be fairly stated that almost every section of the intelligentsia shared in the extravagant idealization of 'the people'. In whatever philosophical theory it was decked out, this remained at bottom an irrational feeling, an almost mystical belief in 'the people' as the repository of some profound truth of life, some eternal verity that would cleanse the intelligentsia themselves, corrupted as they were by worldly education and material goods. 'The people' became a highly coloured icon that bore little if any resemblance to the actual peasantry; it was worshipped with religious fervour, and its absolute and everlasting happiness became the object of the intelligentsia's hopes and endeavours.

But worship at the altar of 'the people' went hand in hand with a deep-rooted conviction that 'the people', left to themselves, were incapable of overthrowing oppression and achieving the just society. This was a curious attitude, combining deification with a marked condescension towards the object of idolatry; 'the people', for all their mystic virtues, were regarded as an immature mass, whose salvation could only come from outside. Devotion to an idealized concept of 'the people' was blended with an almost aristocratic contempt for the actual down-to-earth, prosaic propensities of the real people – whenever the *intelligent* came into contact with them – and a disbelief in their political maturity. From Herzen on, the radical intelligentsia maintained that the people were indifferent to politics and incapable of independent political action. Chernyshevsky developed this idea in one of his widely read articles:

> This is how all changes occur in the State, whether for better or for worse: the mass of the population knows nothing and cares about nothing except its material advantages, and rare indeed are the cases in which it even suspects any relationship between its material interests and political change. This indifference of the mass is the main factor which makes possible the very idea of changes in political life ... The mass is simply the raw material for diplomatic and political experiments. Whoever rules it tells it what to do, and it obeys.[14]

Here we have a striking example of the dichotomy which characterized the intelligentsia's attitude to the people: Chernyshevsky, its outstanding radical spokesman, a man who was to spend twenty-seven years in prison and remote exile without wavering in his devotion to the Populist cause, expressing his patronizing disdain for the people for whom he sacrificed his life! The undercurrent of supercilious contempt for the peasants' absorption with petty material cares was skilfully presented by Turgenev in the character of Bazarov, that archetypal *intelligent*. Speaking to his liberal friend Arkady, Bazarov explains: 'You said, for instance, today when we passed our bailiff Philip's cottage – it's the one that's so nice and clean – well, you said, Russia will come to perfection when the poorest peasant has a house like that, and every one of us ought to work to bring it about ... And I felt such a hatred for this poorest peasant, this Philip or Sidor, for whom I'm to be ready to jump out of my skin, and who won't even thank me for it.' In his infrequent encounters with peasants Bazarov affects a sneering, derisive tone: 'Come, expound your views on life to me, brother; you see, they say all the strength and future of Russia lies in your hands, a new epoch in history will be started by you – you give us our real language and our laws.' Such was Bazarov's attitude, and Bazarov is by no means a malicious caricature – on the contrary, in the Soviet Union today he is cherished as the noblest and truest literary representation of the democratic Populist *raznochinets*.

Turgenev, who knew the actual life of the peasants far better than any radical ideologue, fully appreciated the breadth of the gulf separating intelligentsia from people. He realized, as the intelligentsia were never capable of doing, that the peasants repaid them for their condescension with hostility and a kind of inverted contempt; Bazarov, he says, 'did not in his self-confidence even suspect that in their eyes he was all the while something of the nature of a buffooning clown' (tr. by Constance Garnett). It was this convoluted relationship, composed of such discrepant and contradictory elements, which contained the seeds of the tragedy of the Russian intelligentsia.

The intelligentsia worshipped at the shrine of 'the people', but they also remained convinced that the people could never achieve salvation on their own: an exterior agency was needed to guide them to their goal, all the more so since the people had no conception of where their real interest lay. Their simultaneous love for, and mistrust of, the people bore a curious resemblance to the ideas of Rousseau: 'Left to themselves, the People always desire the good, but, left to themselves, they do not always know where that good lies. The general will is always right, but the judgment guiding it is not always well informed. It must be made to see things as they are, sometimes as they ought to appear to them.'[15] Phrases such as these could have come from the pen of almost any of the spiritual leaders of the Russian intelligentsia, even though the influence upon them of Rousseau, and of the French Enlightenment in general, was meagre.

There was never any doubt as to the identity of the people's self-appointed guide to a happy future. To quote Plekhanov: 'In all our revolutionary calculations the intelligentsia has played the part of the benign Providence of the Russian people, of a Providence that is capable at will of turning the wheel of history in any desired direction.'[16]

The intelligentsia were always profoundly conscious of their unique historical role. But, however passionately they desired to put an end to oppression and injustice, however great their sense of guilt before the people, in most cases it was not humanitarian compassion for the actual sufferings of the people that impelled then along their path. Humanitarianism and philanthropy were, indeed, favourite objects of derision. Charity or brotherly love had very little, if anything, to do with their attitude – what they believed in, what they trusted, were not flesh-and-blood human beings, but ideas. For the most part, it was not the sight of actual human suffering which led them to espouse revolutionary doctrines, but rather the study of revolutionary theory which opened their eyes to the existence of social injustice and cruelty. The primacy of ideology was fundamental to the intelligentsia as a whole. Indeed, one of their most characteristic features was a penchant for translating every practical problem into an abstract point of doctrine, for raising specific concrete issues to the level of universal laws. They compounded a lovable, unselfish impracticality with a rigidly doctrinaire and uncritical approach to questions of dogma. They lived for ideas, and in the strange illusory world of nineteenth-century Russia ideas would often become substitutes for reality.

Theory invariably took precedence over practice, and principles – over actuality. They erected a fortress of principles, to protect their forces and to prepare them for the onslaught against autocracy and oppression. These principles were absolute and unyielding; on them there could be no compromise, no concessions. Throughout her history Russia had been a country of extremes: absolute power and total servitude, unlimited despotism and uncontrolled anarchy. Irreconcilability was the basic principle of public life. Nothing could be more alien to the Russian tradition than the idea of politics being the art of the possible. True to the soil that had nurtured them, the intelligentsia saw their historical mission in the attainment of the Absolute: absolute freedom, absolute equality, absolute happiness. Anything less than the Absolute was inconceivable; pragmatism was an invention of the devil. The idea that – as

Burke once put it – absolute liberty, like other mere abstractions, was not to be found, would have been simply incomprehensible to the Russian *intelligent*. He was engaged in the pursuit of the maximum; it was all or nothing.

This was not based primarily on some innate totalitarianism of the 'Russian soul', but rather on the reasoned conviction that Russia's specific circumstances allowed of no solution short of the maximum. As Herzen wrote in 1851 in his Open Letter to Jules Michelet (*The Russian People and Socialism*):

> We are too oppressed, too wretched to make do with a half-liberty. You have your commitments to consider, your scruples to restrain you – but we have none of this, no commitments and no scruples – it is merely that for the moment we are powerless.[17]

The maximalism of the Russian intelligentsia was expressed in their unceasing and overwhelming concern with the ultimate objective of a perfect society, and their lack of interest in the intermediate stages and practical measures which were to lead to this consummation. It would probably be fair to say that the ultimate object *was* their sole practical aim. In these politics of utopianism the more extreme tendencies were invariably victorious – the comparative moderates, even though they might have disagreed with the extremists, could not but feel ashamed of their own moderacy, and tried to make up for it by defending the extremists and justifying the extremism with which they themselves were in disagreement. Under all circumstances the Russian *intelligent*, whatever his views on particular questions of detail, had to be opposed to the government: that was the unwritten law. *Pas d'ennemi à gauche* became the guiding political principle of every member of the intelligentsia. When the absolute happiness of mankind was the object, and implacability the order of the day, any wavering, any idea of compromise or half-way measures, any notion of co-operation with the authorities were at best despicable cowardice, at worst – an unspeakable betrayal of all that was sacred and good. And the 'moderates', brought up as they were within the same ideological framework, inwardly agreed with this assessment of their behaviour, and hated themselves for being moderate.

For the ideologues of the radical intelligentsia moderation was the supreme crime. In the words of Chernyshevsky's biographer Yury Steklov: 'towards all those who displayed weakness, half-heartedness, readiness to enter into compromises with Tsarism, Chernyshevsky felt at best contempt. For the most part, however, he treated them with the same hatred that he turned against the representatives of Tsarism, because in his opinion it was these moderate elements who constituted the most reliable prop of the regime – by immobilizing active struggle against it.'[18]

The Russian intelligentsia – subjected to unceasing harsh persecution by the authorities, preoccupied with the search for the theoretical formula of a truly just society, contemptuously rejecting any solution that fell short of absolute perfection – lived in an atmosphere of the utmost spiritual intolerance. How could it be otherwise, when – as they were convinced – the future of mankind hung in the balance, when the fate of generations yet unborn depended on the results of their doctrinal arguments, when the difference between two formulations might well spell the difference between absolute happiness and untold misery for all? Intellectuals the world over attach great importance to theoretical concepts – that, after all, is their métier – but the Russian intelligentsia's attitude to ideas was of a very different nature: ideas were for them the magic force which would change the world, the medium which contained the secrets of the future. Revolutionary messianism provided unpromising ground for tolerance of the other man's view – particularly in Russia, where tolerance had always been in extremely short supply – and the Russian intelligentsia was, from beginning to end, remarkably conventional in its automatic radicalism. Faith in progress, revolution and 'the people' became the hallmark of the new conformism, and anyone who disagreed was self-evidently an enemy of the human race, to be branded and hunted down by the progressive intellectual establishment – just as they themselves were persecuted by the Tsarist authorities. The obverse side of the *intelligent*'s love for mankind was his hatred for those who, by disagreeing with his ideas, were malignantly obstructing progress to the shining future. However mild and amiable the *intelligent* might personally have been – and most of them were the kindliest of men – faith called for hatred, and ideological purity for constant vigilance. Heretics were subjected to intense moral pressure: they were boycotted by friends and acquaintances, submitted to campaigns of calumny, vilified as government agents, often driven to the point of suicide. (Cruellest of all were the persecutions of erring political prisoners by their companions in detention or exile.) That humane and liberal observer, Professor Nikitenko, wrote bitterly in his diary about the spiritual intolerance of the progressive intelligentsia:

> The spirit of intolerance and the tendency to intellectual and moral tyranny is the ulcer of our so-called progressive society . . . Every kind of despotism is odious, but worst of all is the despotism of so-called extreme liberalism. This shackles not only the body, not only corporeal life: it strives to penetrate one's innermost being and to put fetters on one's convictions, one's thoughts and conscience.[19]

The violent, slanderous style, the personal attacks, the character-assassination that were such marked features of the savage literary polemics between various schools of thought within the intelligentsia (and that were inherited and given international currency by the Communist movement) expressed, better than anything else, the almost religious fanaticism, the devotional fervour which pervaded the intelligentsia. This burning spirituality – deeply rooted in the national character and the historical past of the Russian people – was composed of a number of varying strands: the effects of constant police persecution; isolation from other sections of the community; an other-worldly frame of mind; an obsession with guilt and quasi-religious penance for age-old sins; blind faith in the power of abstract doctrine; apocalyptic visions of gigantic social upheavals and a messianic faith in the advent of a kingdom of justice.

> Fanatics have their dreams, wherewith they weave
> A paradise for a sect.

Far more potent was the dream of a paradise for the whole human race.

Imbued with this outlook, the intelligentsia itself represented something in the nature of a revolutionary priesthood, a subversive monastic order. Its way of life was founded on a genuine asceticism, an aversion to worldly riches, a scorn for the ordinary 'bourgeois' creature comforts. Self-abnegation became second nature; the Russian *intelligent* was easily recognizable by his utter and un-selfconscious disregard for material considerations, his fecklessness and impracticality, his indifference to appearances and his cheerfully disorganized existence. Chekhov in particular has preserved for posterity his ungainly figure – the unkempt, ill-fitting suit – the straggling beard, strewn with shreds of tobacco – the untidy room, littered with books – the negligence and improvidence – the undivided absorption in the problems of mankind and the unconcern with personal afffairs.

The intelligentsia regarded this hand-to-mouth existence as an admirable and highly moral condition. In part it reflected their voluntary renunciation of conventional values – it also went a long way towards satisfying the search for martyrdom which, whether consciously or not, underlay so much of their activity. In autocratic Russia martyrdom, in prison or exile, was not difficult to come by; it was accepted not merely courageously, but often, it seemed, eagerly. The cult of suffering, the idea of the necessity of sacrifice – sacrifice of oneself no less than of others – formed a vital element in their ethos. Suffering cleansed one, brought one nearer to the tormented people; the sacrifice of personal happiness, of the best years of one's life, and, if need be, of life itself, was the price that had to be paid for the achievement of a new Golden Age; only through suffering and sacrifice could the guilt of privilege ever be expiated. Herzen expressed the views of every progressive *intelligent* when he proudly declared:

> Does Russia inevitably have to go through all the phases of European development, or will her life conform to other laws? I categorically deny the inevitability of these repetitions ... The Russian people will not have to undertake this arduous road once again ... for we have already performed this oppressive work on their behalf. We have paid for their future on the gallows, with convict labour, dungeons, exile, ruin – with the unendurable life that we lead.[20]

Herzen was, by Russian standards, a moderate man and this was a comparatively moderate statement. But if one reads even a small part of the great volume of writings devoted to the glorification of what was usually called – without any hyperbole – the 'martyrology of the Russian intelligentsia', and calling for newer suffering, fresher sacrifices – and is aware, as we are, of the subsequent fate of the Russian intelligentsia, one cannot help feeling that they were impelled by some strange kind of collective death-wish, that unconsciously perhaps they felt that the sole reason for their existence was their self-destruction. This suspicion had, indeed, already been expressed by some of the intelligentsia's critics well before the 1917 revolution.

A great deal can be explained by the singular age-composition of the Russian intelligentsia: the extreme youth of most of its members. Whichever generation of the intelligentsia we are speaking of – whether it is the Men of the Forties, the Sixties, the Seventies, or of later decades – we are chiefly referring to the intellectual *youth* of the time. In large measure this applies to the spiritual leaders and ideologues: Dobrolyubov died at the age of twenty-five. Pisarev at twenty-seven, Belinsky at thirty-seven; Chernyshevsky, revered as the grand old man of the progressive movement, had his active career cut short at the age of thirty-four by his arrest: Mikhailovsky reached the peak of his influence when in his early thirties.

This applied, to an even greater extent, to the rank and file of the intelligentsia. At all periods of its history it was a predominantly youthful group. Indeed, its most typical, most vociferous, and most active members were always the university students. In Russian classical fiction the *intelligent* is usually represented by the student; for the police, at any rate, 'subversive' was practically synonymous with 'educated person', and this, in turn, with 'student'. It could hardly be otherwise: the generation of the sixties, the *raznochinets*-intelligentsia, was a product of the universities. And, on the other hand, in the vastness of Russia, where an educated man would often find himself separated by hundreds of miles from the nearest 'cultural centre' and even from any kind of intellectual conversation (a prime necessity of life for him), the compact groups of students in the handful of university cities constituted the only sizeable concentrations of intelligentsia, the only mass readership for the 'thick journals', the only mass audiences for radical ideas, the only ready material for actual revolutionary conspiracies. The university students' domination within every radical movement, and even within the intelligentsia as such, was natural and inevitable. Besides, the Russian student was by his nature the most alienated of men (with women it was even more so, since their further education frequently entailed a complete and lasting break with their families). 'Student life' was a specific and clearly defined sub-culture within the general Russian way of life, with its own traditions, customs, morals, rituals, heroes and folk-lore (particularly songs); it became the most authentic expression of the unworldliness of the Russian intelligentsia – here impecunity and fecklessness were the highest virtues, and what property there was usually came to be held in common, in the so-called 'communes' which served as models for the members of the revolutionary circles, and later – of the revolutionary parties. The *beau idéal* of the intelligentsia was the 'eternal student': unshaven, unkempt, unclad, underfed, he would cling on to university life for as long as possible, attending no lectures, passing no examinations, but taking a leading part in every radical activity – until this precarious existence was cut short by prison or consumption.

Inescapably the intellectual climate of Russia came to be established by the youth. They set the fashion, they dictated the trends. And in order to hold this audience, to win them to their views, to march with the times, the rival ideologists of the various schools of thought pandered to the tastes of the youth, fawned upon them, flattered them, obsequiously assured them of their pre-eminence in Russian life. This flagrant elevation of the youth to the position of intellectual pace-setter was viewed with grave anxiety by many of the more thoughtful people in public life. Professor Nikitenko described this tendency, as epitomized by one of the radical journals of the day:

> Young people are being incessantly taught that sensual pleasures and interests are preferable to any moral considerations, that schoolboys should concern themselves not with learning, but with so-called modern problems; that everyone senior to them in age, position, experience or knowledge is retrograde, incapable of any progress, practically an idiot, and therefore unsuited not only to the education of the young, but to any kind of activity in any intellectual, literary, scholarly or political field. The sole strength, support and hope of society – they are told – is in them, the young people, before whom everyone else must fall silent and humble themselves . . . The journal is concerned not so much with the reconstruction of society on the basis of a new system as with the destruction of all systems. It strives to demolish every authority – of government, morality, faith, science – and indeed the very principles of government, morality, faith and science do not exist for it.[21]

One generation of students succeeded another, but the exceptional position of the student community and of the young intelligentsia remained unchanged. Fifty years later a celebrated collection of political essays, published under the title of *Milestones* (*Vekhi*) followed up Nikitenko's remarks:

Everybody who is concerned with the future cares deeply about our young generation. But to become spiritually dependent upon it, to curry favour with it, to cringe before its opinions, to take it as our yardstick – only proves the spiritual malaise of our society.[22]

These alarming diagnoses of the state of society in backward, Tsarist Russia, made respectively a half-century and a full century ago, would sound strangely familiar to the present-day citizen of any of the highly developed Western democracies. The mindless cult of youth, the installation of youth as the supreme arbiter and touchstone of popular trends and intellectual fashion, is becoming a general worldwide phenomenon of our times. Like so much else in our lives, this modish convention has its origins in pre-revolutionary Russia. For the *Weltanschauung* of the Russian radical intelligentsia, which has since 1917 acquired – posthumously – an unparalleled international influence, decisively reflected the youthful characteristics of those for whom and by whom it was fashioned. It reveals all the familiar qualities, the strengths and the weaknesses, of youth through the ages. On the one hand the enthusiasm and energy of youth, its boldness and exuberance, selflessness and optimism, generosity and idealism, its spirit of revolt, intellectual curiosity, and general high-mindedness. But also the flaws that go to make up the essence of youth: the self-assurance and the inexperience, the arrogance and the credulity, the impatience and the implacability, the ruthlessness and the fanaticism, the inflexibility, the firm belief that for every ill there exists a ready-made and effective nostrum.

There was about the Russian intelligentsia, its leaders and its ideas, an air of arrested juvenility, of rawness and immaturity. This detracted nothing from their importance – if anything, it made their activities even more dangerous. And it also endowed the *intelligent* with those maddening and endearing qualities which have fascinated generations of readers of the Russian novel.

When suddenly faced with life in all its intricate variety, youth is prone to view it through the prism of abstract values, to pass judgments and seek for solutions on the basis of moral categories. This single-minded youthful approach was shared by the Russian intelligentsia as a whole. To be one of them was to be a 'terrible simplifier'. Every problem, every institution, every proposition was reduced to a moral issue. An abstract concept of 'justice' was the sole criterion: is a thing 'just', or 'unjust'? is it 'good' or 'bad'? – was the question. And if the concept under analysis was deemed to be unrighteous from the standpoint of social justice and the eventual happiness of mankind, then it would be ruthlessly consigned to what later came to be called 'the rubbish-heap of history'.

Youth is ordinarily no respecter of persons, reputations, authorities or traditions – enthusiastic iconoclasm was the stock-in-trade of the radical *intelligent*. In the world that surrounded them – a world of evil, of injustice and oppression – they found very little deserving of preservation. Bazarov spoke for all of them when he exclaimed: 'I shall be quite ready to agree with you when you bring forward a single institution in our present mode of life, in family or social life, which does not call for complete and unqualified destruction' (tr. Constance Garnett). The glittering vision of a just society called for the denial and (prospectively) for the annihilation of every value, institution and idea connected with the hideous old world around them. The great anarchist Mikhail Bakunin had coined the slogan '*Die Lust der Zerstörung ist auch eine schaffende Lust*' [The passion for destruction is also a creative passion], which became the ideological justification of Nihilism – that *ne plus ultra* of total denial. (The term itself was coined by Turgenev in a far from approbatory sense.) To quote Bazarov once more : 'We act by virtue of what we recognize as beneficial. At the present time negation is the most beneficial of all – and we deny ... everything.'

Nihilism as a *political* tendency involved only a comparatively small group of people (and will be discussed in detail in a later chapter), but nihilism as a *moral* attitude played a dominant part in the intellectual make-up of the intelligentsia as a whole.

It was expressed in the wholesale radical negation of all existing moral, spiritual, aesthetic and other values, in the denial of the existence of absolute values as such. The intelligentsia refused to recognize any absolute standards of judgment – these were replaced by the single moral criterion of 'the interests of the people'. Only that was accepted as valid, useful and even valuable, which conformed to the ideologues' concept of the people's good. Everything else was worthless and quite possibly harmful as well. Berdyaev has described the ideological basis of this peculiar moral utilitarianism:

> The intelligentsia, for example, does not care whether Mach's theory of knowledge is true or false – what concerns it is whether or not this theory is beneficial to the idea of socialism, whether or not it will promote the interests of the proletariat. The intelligentsia is concerned, not with the reasonability of metaphysics or the existence of metaphysical truths, but solely with the question of whether metaphysics might injure the interests of the people, whether it might distract them from the struggle against autocracy and from their service of the proletariat. The intelligentsia is willing to embrace any philosophy – upon the condition that it endorses their social ideals, and will unthinkingly reject any philosophy, even the most profound and truthful system, which could be suspected of an unfavourable, or simply of a critical attitude towards these traditional feelings and ideals.[23]

Long before Lenin the Russian intelligentsia had rejected the very concept of objective truth or absolute value. In their eyes concern for such abstract ideas was tantamount to betrayal of the progressive cause; at best, it meant the dissipation of intellectual resources which should properly have been concentrated upon furthering the people's good. Nothing could be permitted to distract attention from this sole overriding object. Ordinary, instinctive human feelings – love of family, affection for kith and kin, patriotism etc. – became objects of derision. They were to be replaced by the single, all-purpose moralistic criterion. Belinsky first formulated this new approach:

> To love one's country really means a passionate desire to see in it the realization of human ideals, and to promote them as far as one's strength permits. Any other kind of patriotism turns into a Chinese thing, love of one's kind merely because it belongs to one. Peter the Great, blasting his own son with curses, declaring he would rather have a stranger's son but a good son – than his own, but a worthless creature: there is an enviable example.[24]

Belinsky was, of course, aware that Peter had not merely cursed his son, but – after torturing him with his own hands – had sentenced him to death. This then was the shining example of devotion to a progressive cause which the intelligentsia were called upon to emulate. Belinsky's radical followers, both before and after the 1917 Revolution, did their best to live up to his ideals.

The most characteristic – and probably most durable – aspect of the Russian intelligentsia's utilitarian outlook was its approach to culture. Art, literature, philosophy, science, were all firmly subordinated to the great social and political goals. There could be no independent realm of the spirit; the belief in art for art's sake, in pure science, or in knowledge for the sake of knowing was impermissible and positively harmful, since it somehow implied indifference to the sufferings of the people. Culture as such was a purely utilitarian concept: it meant improving the health, the material well-being and the educational level of the people. Literature was approvable only insofar as it fulfilled the functions of educating the people or exposing the evils of Russian society. The pursuit of beauty, the search for eternal verities, or the study of history – conducted for their own sakes – had no place in this austere scheme of things. The most influential exponent of stark utilitarianism – acclaimed in the Soviet Union as the forerunner of Marxist-Leninist aesthetics – was Dmitry Pisarev, the brilliant radical ideologue of the sixties:

I am delighted to see the shrivelling away of our imaginative literature as a symptom of the growing maturity of our intellect ... In this day and age, when everyone should be wide awake and working away to his full ability, it is shameful and reprehensible to let one's thoughts dwell in the dead past, with which every decent person should have long ago severed any connection ... I utterly reject the notion of the arts having in any way promoted the intellectual or moral advancement of mankind.[25]

The only thing that counted was utility, and the sole touchstone of utility was alleviation of the people's sufferings. Or, in Bazarov's words, 'You don't need logic, I hope, to put a bit of bread in your mouth when you're hungry. What's the object of these abstractions to us?'

One can understand the reasoning behind this attitude, and even, up to a point, sympathize with it. Tsarist Russia – backward, poor, illiterate, oppressed, brutalized – was faced with such a multitude of problems that the well-meaning individual, despairing of progress, could be excused for treating all non-essentials as harmful distractions. The train of thought was quite clear: whatever advanced the achievement of social justice was good, whatever impeded it in any way was bad. It all seemed very simple and consistent.

In this atmosphere of utilitarian morality the idea of the end justifying the means was accepted unquestioningly, even enthusiastically. Not only by the active revolutionary groups – that goes without saying – but by the radical intelligentsia as a whole. Given their ideological and ethical premises, and the actual condition of Russia, it could hardly be otherwise. The great cause of the liberation of the people and the establishment of a kingdom of justice on earth sanctified everything done in its name. Devotion and sincerity provided full absolution.

Like so much else in the intelligentsia's ethos, the philosophical rationalization of the question of ends and means was supplied by Chernyshevsky. He was, as usual, completely honest and matter-of-fact about it: 'Perhaps the means required by the cause are evil – but if one regards them as evil one should never take up the cause itself. If one renounces the means then one should also reject the cause that cannot be sustained without those means.'[26] In one of his most celebrated passages (often quoted admiringly by Lenin) Chernyshevsky gave a comprehensive exposition of his views on political morality:

> The highroad of History is not the sidewalk of the Nevsky Prospekt: it passes all the way through open fields, dusty and muddy; at times it cuts across marshes or forests. If one shrinks from getting covered with dust and dirtying one's boots, then one should never enter into public activity. This is a salutary occupation if one is really inspired by the idea of the good of mankind, but it is not a particularly cleanly occupation. However, there are different ways of defining moral purity.[27]

This undoubtedly became one of the essential guiding principles of the Russian intelligentsia, shared alike by comparative 'moderates' and by revolutionary extremists. It constitutes the cornerstone of present-day Communist morality. But Chernyshevsky, abundantly blessed with the courage of his convictions, went even further: he became, as his biographer Steklov admiringly remarks, the originator of the unique Russian concept of 'the worse it is – the better'. Put in its simplest terms, this means that the interests of the cause sometimes require that the condition of the country and the people deteriorate still further, in order to hasten the desired consummation. Men who were prepared to sacrifice themselves for their principles saw nothing wrong in having others – vast numbers of others, if need be – suffer for the sake of the same principles. Activated, as they were, by a doctrinal love for mankind in the abstract, they often positively welcomed the prospect of a little additional misery if that were necessary to bring the day of rejoicing any nearer. The worse things became, the better it was for the cause. Chernyshevsky was, for instance, greatly disappointed by the

1861 edict which emancipated the serfs *with land;* he would much rather have seen them deprived of land altogether, 'since in his opinion only this could have aroused the lethargic mass of the people and kindled within it a movement that would have swept away the old order once and for all, and really granted the people both land and liberty'.[28] Chernyshevsky was nothing if not consistent: while the reform was still in preparation he deplored the passing of the Iron Tsar, Nicholas I, who 'would have made an end of it much faster' – and many years later, in Siberian *katorga,* he declared to his comrades that 'it would have been far better if the extreme reactionaries had had their way over the reform and liberated the peasants without land: then there would have been an immediate catastrophe'.[29] The 'people', in other words, whether they liked it or not, should forgo any immediate alleviation of their condition in the name of perfect future happiness. No principle of Russian radicalism has been adhered to more faithfully than this one.

Chernyshevsky remained to the end the great patron saint of the Russian intelligentsia. His ideas were gospel, his every utterance a revelation; Lenin himself ranked the influence of Chernyshevsky's teachings second only to that of Marx. The intelligentsia fell completely under his sway – but the true creators of Russian culture regarded his views with abhorrence (while acknowledging the manifest integrity of their author). One of the most significant facts about the intelligentsia is the unwavering hostility towards it of nearly all the great nineteenth-century novelists. These men of sensibility, compassion and humanity could never control their dislike of the 'New Men' of the sixties (as Chernyshevsky had called them), with their joyless utilitarianism, their dogmatic intolerance, their fanatical devotion to a messianic vision, their contempt for accepted standards of morality and their indifference to the actual sufferings of living human beings. Distaste for the radical intelligentsia was by no means confined to avowed conservatives like Dostoevsky or Tyutchev: the unanimity of Russian men of letters on the subject was truly remarkable. Turgenev, for instance, wrote indignantly: 'Never has Russian literature, prior to the invasion of the seminarians, pandered to whippersnappers with the object of gaining popularity. All who love Russian literature and cherish its honour should do everything possible to deliver it from these vandal parsonets.' Tolstoy was of the same opinion: 'I utterly ignore and I intend ever to ignore all so-called postulates and categorical imperatives . . . Belinsky has spawned imitators who are loathsome. Not only in our literary criticism, but also in our literature, even in society at large the idea has been implanted that to be bitter, spiteful and angry is most tasteful. But I find it vile.'

In the cases of Turgenev and Tolstoy genuine disgust for the new intelligentsia *Weltanschauung* was perhaps not entirely free from a certain aristocratic hauteur towards the *raznochintsy*, the 'seminarians' and 'parsonets' (direct references to Chernyshevsky and Dobrolyubov, with their clerical background and religious education). This, however, cannot apply to the plebeian – and mild-natured – Chekhov, yet he shared their views most vehemently: 'I have no faith in our intelligentsia – hypocritical, false-hearted, hysterical, unmannerly, lazy.'

Taken together, these comments – and countless others in a similar vein – form a powerful indictment. Yet they never had the slightest effect: the intelligentsia and its ideologues were impervious to criticism from men for whose opinions they had scant respect (even though they recognized, and often deplored, their literary talents). The novelists, poets and playwrights of Russia were dismissed as irrelevant, except insofar as their works exposed the harsh realities of life and helped to inculcate the civic virtues. The *intelligent*'s contempt for spiritual culture was truly catholic; notable, for example, is the disesteem in which he held all the really original Russian philosophers: Chaadayev, Khomyakov, Konstantin Leontiev, Vladimir Solovyov, Sergei Trubetskoy (the Soviet regime, faithful to its origins, has simply consigned these names to oblivion).

The only field of intellectual activity – apart from radical journalism and revolutionary theorizing – which the intelligentsia regarded as beneficial was that of the natural sciences. It is no exaggeration to say that they all worshipped at the shrine of science. The nineteenth century was everywhere an age of unlimited faith in science – in Russia it evoked a quasi-religious fervour. Science afforded the miraculous means for transforming Russia; science contained within it the sum of human knowledge; anything non-scientific was *per se* worthless; the test of any theory was its conformity to 'scientific' laws; science was new, modern, powerful, *real*; science denied every traditional concept, every old-fashioned view, every conservative assumption. 'Science, and science alone, is capable – regardless of historical events – of awakening public opinion and of moulding the intelligent leaders whom our nation requires,' wrote Pisarev.[30] Science became the handmaiden of Nihilism.

True to their utilitarian principles, the ideologues of the intelligentsia, headed by Chernyshevsky, narrowed down the tasks of science to popularization and scientific education. Russia, they believed, did not possess the resources for independent scientific research, and to squander the country's intellectual forces on this would have been an intolerable luxury. But the achievements of European science must be made available for all, to destroy superstition, to break down the people's regrettably anti-social attitudes, to imbue them with revolutionary fire. 'The popularization of science,' wrote Pisarev, 'is the most important world-wide task of our age. A good popularizer, especially in Russia, can be of far greater use to society than the talented researcher.'[31]

For the nineteenth-century European rationalist science was king – for the Russian intelligentsia it was also God. They were, of course, atheists almost by definition: religion represented the most malevolent of superstitions, to be combated with the same intense ferocity and dogmatism that the Church itself had displayed in its suppression of heresy. But pure intellectual rationalism was foreign to the Russian nature: it gave no moral satisfaction, it inhibited fervour and excluded faith. There was a strong mystical streak that required an object of veneration, even if the object was nothing more than the mental process of reasoning itself. Science became the secular religion of the Russian intelligentsia. Its philosophical expression was a rather primitive materialism. The Men of the Sixties were all ardent followers of the mechanistic, 'vulgar' materialism of Büchner, Vogt and Moleschott, with its reduction of all biological and social phenomena to the basic categories of mechanics, and its explanation of the brain producing thought in the same way as the gall-bladder produces gall. It may seem strange that this most unspiritual of theories should have evoked fanatical exaltation, but for the Russian *intelligent* it opened up limitless vistas of a brave new scientific world, whose guiding principles of absolute justice would be based on the immutable laws of nature. Messianism and scientism blended into a potent brew. In the seventies it was further fortified by the addition of social-Darwinism and of the positivism of Comte and Spencer. Uncritical belief in the magic powers of all-inclusive scientific and materialistic theories, the idea that the methods and laws of the natural sciences could be applied with the same degree of certainty and scientific objectivity to the study of human society, was a hallmark of the intelligentsia well before the appearance of Marxism on the Russian scene.

The optimistic rationalism of nineteenth-century Europe presented them with the ideological means for dethroning God and replacing Him by Man. From the West came the idea of the infinite perfectibility of Man, of boundless and uninterrupted progress, of all the world's ills being rooted in external factors – and therefore curable by enlightened human intervention. All these scientific – and pseudo-scientific – rationalizations strikingly confirmed the home-grown attitudes of the radical intelligentsia. Since men were self-evidently not responsible for the troubles that beset them, Russia's every problem would be solved by the destruction of the Tsarist autocracy and the establishment of a perfect social order. Q.E.D.

But for all the fervid acceptance of these ideas in Russia, the basic assumption of European rationalist thought was unreservedly rejected. The European schools of utilitarianism and positivism were based on the *individual*, his rights, liberties and freedom of initiative. In politics they were libertarian, in economics laissez-faire. Bentham's famous principle of 'the greatest happiness of the greatest number' meant a maximum of individuals enjoying a maximum of pleasures, minus a minimum of individuals afflicted with a minimum of pains. Spencer saw the chief aim of life in the achievement of individual happiness through the free exercise of the human faculties, and the principal duty of government – in refraining from interference with the laws of nature. The guiding concept of Western utilitarianism was that of utility based on human self-interest. Even John Stuart Mill (like Bentham and Spencer, extremely influential in Russia), for all his recognition of the importance of social controls, laid his main stress on the freedom of the individual and on governmental non-interference.

None of these ideas made any significant impact on the *Weltanschauung* of the Russian radical intelligentsia. Whether moderate or extremist, Westerner or Slavophile, Populist or socialist, when it came to the relationship between the individual and society they remained faithful to the centuries-old 'Russian idea': the interests of the individual must be subordinated, in one degree or another, to those of society. This is the crucial point at which Russian progressive thought sharply diverged from its Western counterpart (though one would hesitate to say this about present-day Western 'progressivism', increasingly converging with Russian *étatisme* and regimentation). To quote Ivanov-Razumnik, the eminent historian of Russian social thought: the intelligentsia 'regarded the State, and society and its interests, as infinitely more important than the interests of the living human being, of the individual'.[32]

Chernyshevsky's clear-cut injunction laid down a principle that had already gained general acceptance: 'The citizen is obliged to renounce some of his aspirations in order to assist in the attainment of other aspirations, loftier and more important to society.'[33] Or, as Pisarev wrote: 'All members of society *must*, each in his own place, be of service to society.'[34] The ideal social order envisaged by the radical intelligentsia was to be one in which the interests of society invariably took precedence over the individual, where indeed the individual was actually expected to sacrifice himself in the name of the common good. In this case 'the greatest happiness of the greatest number' meant the general happiness and well-being of organized society, as construed by its leaders. Every member of the just society would have to accept limitations upon his freedom of action and of choice – or, in other words, a curtailment of his personal liberty.

The establishment of restraints upon the absolute freedom of the citizen has, of course, always been a prerequisite for the orderly existence of any type of human society, and the precise demarcation of the borderline between individual liberty and public interest is a major concern of every government. But this was not the argument employed by Russian radical ideologues, since their approach to the problem was very different from that of European political radicalism. The intelligentsia as a whole remained throughout its history essentially indifferent to those questions of constitutionalism, of individual liberties and civil rights, which had dominated the political movements of the European middle classes. The rule of law was for them a meaningless abstraction, and the whole libertarian, legalistic and constitutionalist approach was irritably regarded as a red herring which could only divert attention from the issues that really mattered.

No other ideological feature demonstrates more convincingly than this the extent to which the Russian intelligentsia and their leaders, for all the radicalism and revolutionism, were moulded by the Russian tradition. Throughout the centuries the ideas of legality and liberty, of the rule of law and the rights of the individual, had been outside the compass of Russian experience. They were to remain beyond the perception of the class uniquely dedicated to the transformation of Russian society. In this connection it is worth mentioning that the whole voluminous corpus of Russian political literature, from Radishchev to Lenin, contains not a single work on legal theory, constitutionalism, the rights of man, the natural law, or kindred subjects. This was all considered to be so utterly irrelevant and unimportant that no progressive man would ever give it a thought (characteristically, the only people who ever did take an interest in these problems were a handful of zealous State officials like Speransky, Pogodin or Chicherin). The significance of this void becomes apparent when one recalls that in the West legal theory – in the broadest sense – has been the central preoccupation of almost every important political writer since the Renaissance. Grotius, Milton, Hobbes, Locke, Puffendorf, Montesquieu, Rousseau, Leibniz, Beccaria, Kant, Hegel, Bentham, J. S. Mill, Tom Paine, the authors of *The Federalist Papers* – the list, if prolonged, would include nearly every political theorist of the last four hundred years. Yet none of the eminent ideologues of the Russian intelligentsia ever attached importance to these topics.

The great libertarian and legal issues, when they were ever mentioned at all, were referred to only in the negative sense: to show how irrelevant they were to the problems facing Russia. The messianic vision of a perfect society blended into the old idea of Russia's peculiar moral superiority over the West. There was contempt for the pettifogging legalism of the small-minded European jurists, scorn for the paltry political liberties and the namby-pamby constitutional paragraphs that could never ensure full freedom from every type of injustice and oppression. Herzen, for instance, was convinced that the absence in Russia of legal rights and guarantees represented a positive advantage, for it meant that the old order could be that much easier destroyed, without getting involved in a tangled network of clauses, laws and privileges. And anyway, what was the vaunted European system of laws, but another and more sophisticated mode of injustice? As he declared to Jules Michelet:

How can you expect us to have any respect for the praetorium in which you administer your Barbaro-Roman justice, for those gloomy, oppressive vaults, where no light or air ever penetrates, rebuilt in the Middle Ages and then patched up by the enfranchised Third Estate? What goes on in them is possibly better than the robbery that goes

on in the Russian courts but could anyone maintain that
it had anything to do with justice?[35]

Herzen's contempt for Western legal forms was shared alike
by the 'radical' Westerners and the more 'conservative'
Slavophiles. What Europe had – as they all used to say in one
way or another – was mere 'external justice': an orderly catalogue
of rights and obligations, cold, impersonal and aloof, entirely
unconcerned with the physical happiness or the moral welfare
of the individual – to say nothing of his role as a useful member
of society. What Russia wanted, what indeed the Russian
demanded, was genuine, warm, 'internal' social justice. It was
an article of faith for the intelligentsia (not entirely unfounded
in fact) that the Russian people were endowed with a 'broad
nature', expansive and generous, a nature which it was
impossible to restrict within the narrow confines of legalistic
formulae. What Russia needed was not legal guarantees or
constitutional rights, but an atmosphere of confidence and trust,
an organic unity of the whole people. In the words of the
Slavophile Konstantin Aksakov: 'There is no need for any
guarantee! Every guarantee is evil. Where it exists, there can
be no virtue. It were better that life in which there is no virtue
should collapse than that it should be shored up with the aid
of evil.'[36] The same idea was presented by the famous radical
satirist Saltykov-Shchedrin in his widely popular dialogue 'The
trousered boy and the trouserless boy'. The trousered German
boy – well-fed, well-mannered, well-meaning, and unbearably
dull – is describing his way of life to his little Russian friend
– gay, cynical, reckless, foul-mouthed, and trouserless. His farm-
labourer parents, the German boy explains, have a precisely
drawn-up contract with the local landowner, under which they
have to fulfil a certain amount of work in return for a specific
payment. He is interrupted by the trouserless Russian boy: 'I
knew it, Wurst! I always knew that you'd sold your souls to
the Devil for a farthing!'

No, said the Russian intelligentsia, ours will not be the way
of soulless legal guarantees. Constitutions were unimportant

and political liberties meaningless. The only thing that really mattered was the *social* nature of the State, and all other trivial juristic considerations should be waived in the interest of establishing a truly just and moral social order. They would not be fobbed off by the farthings of legality.

Chernyshevsky's argument sounded extremely convincing:

> Liberalism might be attractive to someone who is lucky enough to be free from material want. Freedom is a very pleasant thing. But liberalism interprets freedom in a very narrow, purely formal way. It sees freedom in abstract right, in paper permissions, in the absence of legal bans. But liberalism does not understand that legal liberty can be important only when the individual possesses the material means to make use of this liberty . . . In most countries the majority of the population is illiterate; not having had the money to obtain an education and not having the money to give their children an education, how on earth can they value the blessings of free speech? Can they value, can they utilize the right of parliamentary debate . . . ?
>
> All the constitutional minutiae have precious little meaning for the man who has been deprived of the physical means and the intellectual development needed to savour these political desserts.[37]

Chernyshevsky, of course, represented the extreme wing of the radical intelligentsia. But these ideas were generally accepted by almost all factions, right until the 1917 revolution – when they became embodied in the substance of the Soviet State. Even the 'moderate' Mikhailovsky, long execrated in the Soviet Union as the epitome of perfidious bourgeois liberalism, wrote, a whole generation after Chernyshevsky:

> Freedom is a wonderful and seductive thing, but we do not want freedom if, as has happened in Europe, it will only increase our age-old debt to the people. By saying this I am giving expression to one of the most deep-seated and heartfelt sentiments of our time . . . European history

and European science have convinced us with the utmost clarity that freedom as an absolute principle is a bad guide . . . We have become convinced that so-called full economic freedom in reality means nothing but unrestrained licence for the large economic forces and veritable slavery for the small forces. As for political freedom, we have discovered that it really is a sun, but only a sun, and although this may be of immense importance in the economy of the terrestrial world, it stands only for very little in the peculiar economy of human ideals. Political freedoms are incapable of changing the relationships between the existing forces within society.[38]

The radical intelligentsia regarded constitutionalism, the rule of law, political liberty, free speech etc. as luxuries ('political desserts'): pleasurable to enjoy, but far from essential, and indeed potentially mischievous – inasmuch as they might easily seduce the 'people', distract their attention and weaken their moral fibre. First things first, and the first and most important thing was undoubtedly the establishment of 'genuine freedom': full social and economic equality. Equality was all; as long as it was assured nothing else really mattered. Such trifling details as the nature, the laws and institutions of the new State could easily be settled at the appropriate moment, but for the time being were to be swept impatiently aside. To quote Chernyshevsky once more: 'The democrats [i.e. the radicals] intend to destroy the ascendancy of the upper classes over the lower, by reducing the power and the wealth of the upper classes, on the one hand, and by granting greater importance and increased welfare to the lower orders, on the other. How precisely the laws are to be changed in this direction, and the new structure of society organized, is a matter of almost total indifference to them.'[39]

It was a noble aim – but it was coupled with disdain for liberty and legality, and a wilful blindness towards any other consideration except that of equality. The doctrine of egalitarianism coloured the outlook of almost every segment of the intelligentsia. This was essentially a doctrine of distributive justice; it hardly ever went beyond plans for the distribution of existing wealth. Indeed, in their view, true justice – as opposed to European legalistic legerdemain – *was* distribution. Ideas about the organization and development of production were nebulous in the extreme. In many ways this attitude was a projection of the intelligentsia's asceticism; it also had a great deal to do with the plain fact that the production of material values was a field of life completely foreign and unknown to its members.

Egalitarianism determined the position of the intelligentsia with regard to the bourgeoisie – the new class which had appeared in Russia after 1861, and was rapidly growing in wealth and influence. It was a position of unqualified rejection, of hatred and contempt bordering on the pathological. Capitalism, far from being seen as a solution to Russia's problems, was proscribed as wicked and immoral by every ideological school: the Slavophiles hoped to bar its progress by resuscitating the traditional values of patriarchal Muscovy, while the Westerners (and particularly their revolutionary wing) saw a system of Russian Populist socialism as the only possible alternative. Uncompromising opposition to capitalism, hatred of the bourgeoisie and the bourgeois way of life, abhorrence of the principle of private property, were features of Russian political thought deeply rooted in the country's historical past. The anti-bourgeois feeling of the intelligentsia was composed of diverse elements: the heritage of the 'Fathers', with their aristocratic scorn for money-grubbing activities; remoteness from practical life and inexperience of systematic work; other-worldliness and disregard for material goods; fear of corruption. Essentially, however, it boiled down to the not unjustified apprehension that the development of capitalism would harden inequalities that already existed, and create new and even more acute injustices.

The main charge raised against Western-style industrial capitalism was that it led inevitably to the development of an impoverished proletariat. It was at this point that Russian radical thought diverged most sharply from Marxism. Where Marx and Engels, while tirelessly excoriating the evils of capitalism, saw it as a carrier of progress, a predestined revolutionary phase in the evolution of mankind, and acclaimed the proletariat as the chosen builder of the socialist society – the earlier Russian intelligentsia viewed both bourgeoisie and proletariat with unrelieved gloom. The very words struck terror into their hearts. They were haunted by the dread spectre of a pauperized, uprooted proletariat. Its appearance would mean not only the perpetuation of inequality on a monstrous scale, but, more important still, the disruption of the mystical fellowship of the 'people'. It was a dire prospect. 'Pauperism is nothing but a type of slavery,' wrote the radical critic Varfolomei Zaitsev, 'and the proletarian is practically indistinguishable from a slave.'[40] With this postulate everybody concurred. Anything was better than such a fate, and nothing should be left undone that might prevent it. The horrors of industrial capitalism (part real, part imagined) fulfilled the same function within the intelligentsia's world-outlook as the lurid portrayal of Hell did in medieval Christian theology: as a means of striking fear into the heart of the sinner, and of steeling his resolve to avoid the infernal regions at any price. The frightful menace of capitalism and pauperization also impelled many to take a kindlier look at Russian reality; however bad it might be, it still possessed certain inestimable advantages, which had to be preserved. As Chernyshevsky said in one of his most famous pronouncements: 'For a democrat our Siberia, in which the common people enjoy well-being, is far better than England, where the majority of the population endure great want.'[41] Of what consequence were England's famed laws and liberties when the basic criterion of justice and happiness were material well-being and equal distribution?

The ideologues of the intelligentsia saw, with praiseworthy clarity of mind, that the principles of egalitarian justice could not but come into conflict with the ideas of political liberty and personal freedom. As Mikhailovsky had pointed out, the concept of freedom inescapably included the freedom of exploitation. They faced this prospect without flinching: their choice was never in doubt. The guidelines of the new way of life would have to be laid down and enforced; the people would have to be educated in their observance; until such time as education took hold, society would have to be protected from anti-social activities, and its members – from themselves. Without going into the tiresome details, it was clearly understood by most that these functions would have to be fulfilled by a benevolent, enlightened, but necessarily authoritarian government. An authoritarian State system, governing Russia in accordance with the principles of humanity, equality and social justice, was seen not as an unpleasant, though unavoidable necessity: it was the focal component of the future social order. The central task of government was to care about the *moral* welfare and the *moral* education of the citizen, to inculcate in him the moral precepts evolved by the intelligentsia. Western liberalism, with its renunciation of the task of moral guidance, its vaunted tolerance of even the most wicked and dangerous opinions, its indifference to the moral life of its people, evoked disenchantment and disgust. It was utterly wrong, a grave dereliction of duty, to pass on these responsibilities to the conscience of every individual member of society.

With the exception of the comparatively minor Bakuninite current of pure anarchism, the dominant Russian ideological and social influences were all *étatist* and authoritarian. Slavophiles and Westerners, each in their own way, were State-centred. Khomyakov, the leading Slavophile ideologue, wrote for instance:

All the benefits of social autonomy, a free Press, independent science, security of individuals from arbitrary violence, all these will lead to nothing, if at the head of the state there does not stand an unrestricted living integrity of conscience, feeling its own responsibility to God and to History, unswayed by human prejudices and temptations.[42]

Not, one would think, a far remove from the writings of

Peresvetov, Križanić or Pososhkov, separated from the Slavophiles by periods of over one, two, or three centuries. Yet it would be fallacious to suggest that these familiar echoes of the Muscovite tradition merely symptomatized the Slavophiles' obsessive nostalgia for the olden times. No less extreme a 'Westerner' than Chernyshevsky himself had written in his diary at the outset of his literary career:

> You long for equality, but can there be equality between the weak man and the strong, between the man with means and the man with none, between the man of intellect and the man whose mind is undeveloped? No, if you are to allow struggle between them, then the weak, the poor, the ignorant will certainly become a slave. Therefore I believe that the only good form of government is dictatorship, or, better still, a hereditary unlimited monarchy – but one that is aware of its mission, of having been established to stand above classes and particularly to champion the oppressed.[43]

There is nothing surprising in the fact that a man like Chernyshevsky – with his unshakeable views on the overriding importance of equality and social justice, the need to employ all means to achieve these aims, and the irrelevancy of constitutional and libertarian principles – should have arrived fairly early at the necessity of a benevolent dictatorship. He remained faithful to this conclusion throughout his political life, and played an immense part in inculcating it among the intelligentsia as a whole. He soon recovered from his temporary enchantment with monarchical institutions – but his republicanism was always of the dictatorial variety. One can only admire the relentless logic and the intellectual honesty with which he (like many other Russian thinkers of lesser stature) pursued his ideas to their ineluctable conclusion. What a contrast he provides to certain Western 'progressive' intellectuals, who worship at the altar of egalitarianism, yet refuse to recognize that their dream of levelling out incomes, social status, education, and everything else, can only be realized by an arbitrary dictatorial government. Chernyshevsky and his followers, down to the present day, have never harboured any illusions about this.

I have attempted to describe and analyse the physical and ideological make-up of the curious stratum that dominated Russian intellectual and social life in the half-century preceding the revolution, that provided the breeding-ground, the men and the ideas for the revolutionary movement, and that contributed more than any other group to the downfall of the old order and the establishment of the Soviet regime. Rootless, estranged from society, embittered – it lived for its apocalyptic vision of a Utopian future, based upon theory and brought about by violence.

The intelligentsia was a strange and disturbing presence in the nineteenth-century world of confident progress, prosperity, and solid bourgeois values. When Europe first discovered it, through the medium of the Russian novel, it aroused wonder and amusement. Naturally so: the West had known the disaffected intellectual, the revolutionary idealist, either as isolated individual or as member of small conspiratorial groups. The idea of a whole social stratum of alienated intellectuals or quasi-intellectuals living for the overthrow of the existing order was singular in the extreme, and explicable only by the mysterious vagaries of the Russian soul. A century later it does not seem far-fetched to suggest that the pre-revolutionary Russian *intelligent* was in many respects a precursor of that phenomenon of our time known to the social scientist as *twentieth-century mass man*.

The appearance of 'mass man' as a definite, perhaps even definitive feature of modern society is usually linked to the turbulent aftermath of First World War and revolution. The essential qualities of 'mass man' have been comprehensively described by Hannah Arendt in her *Origins of Totalitarianism*: the sense of superfluousness, the break with normal social ramifications and conventions, the feeling of being outside the body politic; fury against the powers that be, the conviction that government and authority are inherently evil, stupid, dishonest; contempt for bourgeois values and hatred of the bourgeoisie itself; rejection of conventional standards of thought and behaviour; disdain for material well-being and security, the feeling of having nothing to lose; indifference to the petty problems of everyday life, and an overriding interest in discovering lasting ideal solutions for society, based upon the principles of equality and righteousness; 'the radical loss of self-interest, the cynical or bored indifference in the face of death or other personal catastrophes, the passionate inclination toward the most abstract notions as guides for life, and the general contempt for even the most obvious rules of common sense'; the infatuation with violence and force as means of solving the problems of society.[44]

Mass man is usually, and reasonably, described as the basic material of the great totalitarian mass movements of our century. The Russian intelligentsia – that curious microcosm of mass, collectivist society – became the vehicle for the first and by far the most important of these movements. This development may not have been inevitable – it was certainly not accidental.

For a short time at the turn of the century it did seem as if the intelligentsia might find new avenues for self-fulfilment, might become integrated into the changed Russian society that was evolving under the influence of reforms and of rapid capitalist development. But even at that stage, when they had begun to evince a certain hesitating interest in 'small deeds' and pragmatical works, the intelligentsia as a whole continued to proclaim their devotion to the cardinal tenets that had set them apart from the rest of society: extremism, intolerance, maximalism, irreconcilability with the existing order, doctrinaire faith in theory, idealization of violence, dedication to revolution, indifference to the means used in achieving their aims. This was affirmed approvingly only four years before the First World War by the acknowledged leader of the moderate wing, Paul Miliukov, in an article wherein he re-stated the intelligentsia's claim to leading the nation in accordance with their own ideas of what was good for the nation:

The intelligentsia's break with the traditional ideas of the masses is a constant law for *any* intelligentsia, if it is to retain its position as the most progressive segment of the nation, and to fulfil its inalienable function of criticism and intellectual leadership.[45]

Nevertheless, in the early years of our century there were definite signs that the intelligentsia was changing. Autocracy was in retreat, a middle class had appeared, and with it the genuine possibility of social, political and economic progress along what one might call European lines. 1917 nipped this process in the bud.

The Russian intelligentsia – that erstwhile collection of ineffectual, disgruntled, Bohemian doctrinaires – was transformed into the prime historical mover of our age by its acquisition of Marxism. The theory of Marxism was of a level of sophistication immeasurably higher than anything they had known before. Much of it was never properly understood. But certain of its key elements – hostility to the bourgeoisie, egalitarianism, the apotheosis of revolution, and particularly the fervent messianism – were remarkably consonant with the traditional beliefs of the intelligentsia. And, most important of all, Marxism gave them the *scientific* certitude for which they longed. Marxism swept through the ranks of the radical intelligentsia like wildfire. They embraced it with greater ardour and wholeheartedness than any class in any other country of the world. The 'proletariat' took the place of the 'people', and two varieties of messianism, Russian and Marxist, coalesced. The most potent force of the twentieth century was born. 'Bolshevism,' says a distinguished Western student of Marxism, 'evidently stems from the traditional messianic and universalist outlook of the Russian revolutionary intelligentsia which fastened upon Marxism as an instrument of its own will to "change the world".'[46]

As an intellectual, social, artistic, literary or scientific force the Russian intelligentsia proved to be singularly uncreative. It produced only one thing: the Russian revolutionary movement. That was sufficient to change the course of world history.

CHAPTER 11

Early Revolutionaries: the Decembrists to Herzen

The Russian revolutionary movement was born on 14 December 1825, under a merciless hail of grape-shot on Petersburg's snow-swept Senate Square. This first engagement lasted only a few hours; after the opening salvoes the freezing and bewildered ranks broke and ran. The Decembrists were scattered, but out of the confusion and the despair, the heroism and the blood a vital new tradition was forged. The idea of revolution had come to stay: Russia was never again to be free of its presence. For this we have the authority of the greatest of them all, Vladimir Ilyich Lenin: 'The Decembrists aroused Herzen. Herzen developed his revolutionary agitation. This was caught up, expanded, strengthened, tempered by the revolutionary *raznochintsy*.'[1] The fourth generation of revolutionaries, as Lenin concluded in 1912, was the Bolshevik Party he had created. It was to carry the cause to final victory. And five years later it did.

The Decembrists took the first steps on the road to 1917. But their enterprise, although it established a line of descent and a sense of continuity, does not, strictly speaking, come within the mainstream of Russian revolutionary development. The Decembrist movement stands alone in Russian history: it had no sequel. Created by aristocratic officers, it was neither populist nor ideological in character. Superficially it bore a (much commented upon) resemblance to the numerous military coups d'état of the preceding century. Like them, it was an attempt by a conspiratorial group of Guards officers to overthrow the government and the monarch at a moment of grave dynastic crisis. This, however, would be a misleading impression.

Before 1825 insurrection in Russia had been a matter of either chaotic and furious peasant uprising, or of highly professional court conspiracy. Neither was aimed at fundamental changes in the structure of State and society. The Decembrist plot represents the dividing-line between the traditional forms of rebellion against the constituted authority and the modern revolutionary movement. The Decembrists were recruited from the ranks of the nobility – many, indeed, came from the highest stratum of aristocratic society. Among them we find the names of Russia's most ancient and proudest families: Trubetskoy, Bestuzhev, Volkonsky, Obolensky, Tolstoy, Golitsyn, Naryshkin, Shchepin-Rostovsky. They had been endowed at birth with every gift and privilege that a Russian Providence had at its command: family connections, the best of educations, great wealth, vast estates, numerous serfs, boundless prospects. They were all launched on brilliant careers; many had had outstanding records in the war of 1812–14, some were already commanding regiments or had even attained general officer's rank. They possessed everything that mortal could desire. And they threw it all away – gaily, defiantly, never regretting their action even in the long, tragic years of Siberian penal servitude that were to follow. This was the stuff of high romantic legend. For all the superficial similarity, it had nothing in common with the sordid coups d'état of the eighteenth-century praetorians.

The Decembrists were aristocratic revolutionaries – but they wanted to destroy autocratic, slave-holding Russia and to establish a new and more just society. They were the last of their line, and the forerunners of a very different type of rebel. Theirs was not a homogeneous movement: they neither sought nor achieved any identity of views, discipline was practically non-existent, and the whole enterprise remained extremely amateurish, to say the least. Yet, in a broad sense, it did display certain features which were to recur, again and again, in future generations of Russian revolutionaries.

The men of 14 December 1825 possessed, in the highest degree, those heroic qualities which went such a long way towards creating and nourishing the sanctity of the Russian revolutionary myth: selflessness, courage, manliness, devotion – and a readiness to meet death. They could have come out of some Greek legend. Herzen voiced the sentiments generally felt by Russians, whether of his generation or ours, when he called them 'a phalanx of heroes ... Paladins forged of purest steel from head to foot, a band of warriors who had consciously embarked upon certain death'. But, more even than these personal attributes, the strongest bond between the Decembrists and later revolutionaries was their common hatred of the institution of peasant slavery, or serfdom. The Decembrists may not have been the first of the Russian 'repentant noblemen', but they were certainly the first who tried to do something about it.

What precisely was to be done about the peasants remained unclear, beyond a general acceptance of the principle of immediate emancipation. The members of the secret societies which constituted the 'Decembrist' movement, like all who came under the influence of the French Enlightenment, were much given to the drawing and redrawing of intricate schemes for the construction of a more perfect human society. Of these manifold, often immature, plans only one possesses genuine historical significance: the detailed draft constitution called *Russkaya Pravda*, after the most ancient code of laws of Kievan Rus. It was drawn up by Colonel Pavel Pestel, the head of the 'Southern Society' (one of the two main branches of the movement), and undoubtedly the most remarkable of the Decembrist leaders. Prestel combined great force of character and resolution (properties not excessively conspicuous in many of his colleagues) with a powerful intelligence and a wide range of reading. He represented the extreme radical wing of the conspirators, and his dominating presence ensured the pre-eminence of his own particular brand of revolutionary idea. For Pestel the abolition of slavery and of the Statute of Bondage was 'the holiest and most urgent task' confronting the envisioned revolutionary government. Anyone who, by word or deed, would oppose or even criticize this measure, 'is to be put under arrest and subjected to the severest punishment, as an enemy of the country and a traitor'.[2] Although it was not every Decembrist who shared Pestel's ruthless determination, all alike saw the abolition of serfdom as the cornerstone of their programme.

And here we first encounter the tragic paradox that was to bedevil, and decisively influence, the Russian revolutionary movement at every stage of its history: it remained estranged and remote from the Russian people whose cause it had espoused, but who responded to it with indifference, suspicion and even hostility. Contemporary evidence bears this out quite convincingly. When, in the morning of 14 December, the news spread through St Petersburg that part of the troops lined up in Senate Square had refused to take the oath of allegiance to the new Emperor Nicholas I, a huge crowd gathered to watch further developments. But there is nothing to suggest that the bystanders showed any sympathy with the rebels – rather, the contrary. And after the attempt was crushed, the general attitude of the lower classes displayed a pattern that was to become familiar throughout the nineteenth century: hostility towards the noblemen (later – the intelligentsia) concerned, distrust of their motives, glee at their discomfiture. Countless police informers reported peasants as saying, to quote only one such account: 'At last they've started to hang the nobles and send them to *katorga*. Pity they haven't flogged at least one, and made him level with us. But never mind, sooner or later the nobles will get what's coming to them.'[3]

The Decembrists themselves were resigned to the impossibility of gaining any mass support; even when they led their soldiers into an unheard-of act of defiance and rebellion, they did it without disclosing their true aims, but instead relied upon their authority as military commanders, and upon their misleading explanation to the men that Nicholas was a usurper and that the oath should be taken to the 'rightful Tsar' – his elder brother Constantine. (The conspirators had struck at a moment of extraordinary governmental and popular confusion, caused by the sudden death of the childless Alexander I and the renunciation of the throne by the heir-apparent,

Constantine, in favour of Nicholas – an announcement made only *after* many had already sworn allegiance to him.) It can be plausibly argued that prevailing conditions – rigorous police surveillance, on the one hand, and the abysmal ignorance of the masses, on the other – forced the Decembrists to adopt this subterfuge. However, it boded no good for the success of their enterprise. And, once having entered upon the path of 'warranted' deception, they did not stop there: on the eve of the fatal day they instructed their men to shout 'Long live Constantine! Long live the Constitution!', telling them that 'Constitution' was the name of Constantine's wife (in Russian, which has no articles, *'Konstitutsiya'* can be fairly easily made to sound as if it were the feminine form of *'Konstantin'* – to illiterate peasants, that is). In this regard the Decembrists, the most modern-minded and European-influenced of their contemporaries, were only reviving an ancient popular tradition: the tradition of the impostors, of false pretenders to the throne and feigned upholders of autocratic legitimacy. From their time on the methods of justified dissimulation and benevolent ruse; of lack of candour; of utilizing the ingrained beliefs and prejudices of the unlettered masses; of concealing the movement's true goals – all of these with the highest of motives – have been freely resorted to by the various factions of the modern Russian revolutionary movement.

In nineteenth-century Russia a revolutionary party, or even an oppositional grouping, was inevitably a conspiracy. Originally this had little to do with the personal inclinations of the participants: most of them would have preferred it otherwise, and it was a long time before conspiracy became an end in itself as well as a means. The conspiratorial tradition began with the Decembrists. Many of these gifted, sensitive, patriotic young men had taken part in the Napoleonic Wars, the march through Europe and the subsequent occupation of France. For the first time in Russian history a large body of educated men had come into direct and prolonged contact with the outside world; with a world, moreover, that had for twenty-five years been shaped by the tremendous events and ideas of the French Revolution. The effect was overwhelming. The country which they had defended so bravely became for them a source of shame and sorrow, its government the incarnation of evil. The necessity for a radical transformation of the Russian State was becoming apparent even before the army had returned home. In the next ten years the young officers passed inexorably through every stage of disaffection and rebellion: from friendly conversation to political discussion; to illicit association; to revolutionary conspiracy; to plans of regicide; to armed revolt. The road ended in Senate Square.

Conspiracy breeds its own atmosphere, its own mentality; it creates its own inescapable laws. It is a world in which the toughest men become the leaders, where conviction grows into fanaticism, and well-meaning liberalism is replaced by firmness and authority. Secret societies, whatever their origin, have everywhere tended to become authoritarian – in a country like Russia they could not be anything else. The Decembrists initiated the modern Russian revolutionary movement, and with them we first enter the curious world of authoritarian rebels. This is by no means to say that all the dissident officers subscribed to a dictatorial vision: a wide variety of political ideals were represented within their ranks, from English-style constitutional monarchy to out-and-out Jacobinism. By far the most influential, systematic and workmanlike was the programme of Colonel Pestel. It contains in embryo many of the essential ideas of later and very dissimilar schools of revolutionary thought.

Pestel's *Russkaya Pravda* was nationalistic, authoritarian, egalitarian and crudely socialistic (even though the last word had itself not yet been invented). It was uncompromising in its devotion to virtue and justice: the two basic constitutional principles which were to be enforced by a government possessing virtually unlimited powers. This document, with its medley of progressive European ideas and traditional Russian concepts, makes strange reading today.

The new Russia was to be centralized, unitary and indivisible; no hint of federalism could be tolerated; Poland might be granted independence, but only on condition of complete subservience to Russia; Moldavia, the Caucasus, parts of Central Asia and Mongolia were to be annexed. All non-Russian peoples were to be Russified: no other language but Russian would be allowed, and everyone made to become a Russian. This achieved, every citizen would enjoy full equality: social ranks, titles and privileges were to be abolished, and taxes shared equitably among all. The country's administrative structure was to be based on the *volost'*, the lowest territorial unit; the population would be divided among them, with every citizen attached to his *volost'*, which he would be forbidden to leave without special permission. The *volost'* was to be self-sufficient politically, militarily and economically; and to dispose of all the land within its borders, part of which would constitute the State domain, with the rest parcelled out among the inhabitants.

This was no arcadian dream of an association of autonomous phalansteries, for above them all was to tower the mighty State with its omnipresent bureaucracy. The revolutionary government's sphere of action would be all-encompassing, and include not only the direct management of all political and economic affairs, but also the strict supervision of the citizens' morals and the details of their everyday lives. It would brook no opposition. 'Any teaching, doctrine or occupation at variance with the laws and the rules of pure morality, and thereby introducing even more corruption and temptation, must be absolutely prohibited . . . All private societies established with some specific object must be absolutely prohibited, whether they be overt or covert – for the first are superfluous and the second harmful'[4] (a particularly nice touch, this, in a draft constitution drawn up by the leader of a subversive secret society).

To put it bluntly, Pestel was planning the installation – after the overthrow of the monarchy – of a benevolent, egalitarian and virtuous police State. Indeed, he paid a great deal of detailed attention to the creation of an efficient police force, progressively raising its strength from 47,500 to 112,900 men.[5] In the free Russia of which he dreamed, oppression, injustice and violence would be abolished, and men and women would lead happy, carefree lives – but they had to be regimented, for their own good. It was difficult for him to see how Russia could be governed otherwise. The mating of revolutionary conspiracy with the Russian State tradition could hardly be expected to bring forth a democratic growth, either in Pestel's day or generations later.

Had the Decembrists been less preoccupied with drawing up grandiose blueprints for the distant future, and more with planning their dispositions for the actual uprising, the enterprise might have had some chance of success. As it was, they went into action unprepared and unorganized, without even the faintest of notions as to what their next steps were to be. They proved no match for Nicholas. It was an unprecedented case, and retribution fell swift and harsh. Five men were hanged (Pestel, Ryleev, Muraviev-Apostol, Bestuzhev-Riumin, Kakhovsky), twenty-five sentenced to *katorga* for life, another sixty-two to various terms of *katorga*, and twenty-nine sent into exile or reduced to the ranks. Specially severe conditions were devised for the prisoners (not as severe as those of Soviet labour camps, of course, but these were still far off in the future). A bare handful of broken men survived until the onset of a new reign and the amnesty of 1856.

The conviction and execution of the Decembrists produced a lasting shock that really has no equal in modern Russian history. The educated classes were paralysed by horror and fear – it was a long time before this paralysis eroded. Nothing like it had ever happened before: the offenders became un-persons, their very names expunged from the public memory. The events of 14 December were not to be mentioned in public, even disapprovingly: the first *official*, violently biased account of the uprising could only be published by the Imperial printers thirty years later, after the death of Nicholas I. In part it was this grim interdict that made the punishment itself seem inhumanly cruel; but the brilliant social position and great promise of the accused, the glamour of their personalities, also had a lot to do with it. Whatever the reasons, the fact remains that for generations of Russians – even for those out of sympathy with the revolutionary cause – the Decembrists' sentences represented a uniquely ferocious act of governmental injustice. Their savage punishment became one of the most emotive legends of the Russian progressive movement; their martyrdom – a constant rebuke to the government, and a cause that called for vengeance. This feeling of abhorrence of a blatant wrong has also coloured the approach of most Western students. Even one of the fairest and most level-headed of British historians could write recently that 'Nicholas I suppressed the amateur military revolt, and with quite needless cruelty sentenced its leaders to death and its mildest helpers to the Siberian mines'.[6]

The general belief in the wickedness of the punishment is difficult to sustain. Though the penalty was certainly harsh and vindictive, it can hardly be called disproportionate. The Decembrists stood convicted of the gravest crimes in the calendar: high treason; mutiny; rebellion; intended regicide; the assassination of the St Petersburg Governor-General; and so on. These would have automatically entailed the death penalty in any country of the globe (even in present-day permissive Britain some of them are still capital crimes). To quote just one of many cases, only five years earlier, in 1820, London had been the scene of the so-called 'Cato Street conspiracy' led by Arthur Thistlewood, to murder the entire Cabinet. The plotters were caught before they had actually done anything; five ringleaders were hanged, the rest transported. Public disapproval was directed not at the court, but against the conspirators; Thistlewood and his accomplices have not, on the whole, been treated as unjustly victimized martyrs.

One cannot help feeling that there was something artificial in the general indignation at the severity of the Decembrists' sentences, which continued unabated for over a century. It was symptomatic of the mounting hysteria of Russian public life, and tells us a great deal about the abnormal relationship between society and government. It is also highly indicative of the attitude – then as now – of enlightened Western public opinion towards the Tsarist regime.

Martyrdom was the Decembrists' essential contribution to

the revolutionary cause. The seeds of their rebellion were stamped out with great thoroughness; the idea of a republican military conspiracy died with them; apart from vague rumours and official reports, the public knew nothing about their plans and ideas for nearly a hundred years. But they left something far more important: legend, mystique, inspiration. Every revolutionary movement, every oppositional trend that appeared in Russia was to swear fidelity to the memory and the ideals of 'the martyrs of the 14th December'. The tradition began with Herzen: in 1826, at the age of fourteen, accompanied by his still younger friend Ogarev, he hiked to the highest spot of the Sparrow Hills, overlooking Moscow, and there the two boys solemnly vowed to devote their lives to struggle against the power that had murdered the Decembrists. When, thirty years later, Herzen began the publication in London of the first Russian revolutionary periodical, *Pole Star*, its every issue was decorated by the profiles of the five executed Decembrist leaders. And, another fifty years later, the completely unromantic and unsentimental Lenin chose the title and motto for his first illegal Marxist newspaper, *Iskra* or *The Spark*, from a famous line by a convicted Decembrist poet:

> Out of the spark will come a conflagration.

Never were truer words spoken.

Some historians have maintained that the Decembrists, instead of advancing the cause of Russia's progress, unwittingly retarded it – by instilling an overwhelming fear of revolution in the young Tsar, and thus impelling him upon the path of extreme reaction. There seems to be little basis in fact for such a supposition. It is true that the memory of the events of 14 December haunted Nicholas to the end of his days; whenever he was confronted, in later years, by some evidence of revolutionary or even mildly liberal activity, the Emperor would exclaim furiously: 'My friends of the 14th December are at it again!' But Nicholas hardly needed additional proof to convince him of the abominable wickedness of liberalism: the Decembrist uprising could, at most, do no more than strengthen the fixed beliefs of the stern military disciplinarian who so unexpectedly became autocrat of all the Russias.

It was an inauspicious beginning to a curiously ill-starred reign, at the end of which official Russia found itself bankrupt in ideas and denuded of policies, face to face with the same spectre of rebellion that the Iron Tsar had spent his life in exorcizing. The thirty years' reign of Nicholas I saw Russia at the pinnacle of her power and influence in international affairs – and ended in the ignominious military collapse of the Crimea. It was a period of the most savage censorship and persecution of writers – and of an unparalleled flowering of Russian literature. An age of triumphant reaction and unbridled police repression – during which every conceivable variety of revolutionary movement and subversive idea made their first appearance in Russia. Behind the imposing façade of the 'Gendarme of Europe' Imperial Russia was in decline, while the revolution was beginning to gather strength.

It was a long time before any of this could become apparent even to the most perspicacious of observers. For many years after the events of 14 December Russia remained cowed and silent, frozen into a seemingly immutable mould. The country – so it was said – was united once more around a firm and far-seeing autocrat, the seeds of treason had been extirpated, and even Pushkin, whose closest friends were among the Decembrists, devoted his poetic genius to extolling the virtues of their royal gaoler. This happy state of affairs was temporarily achieved by a combination of coercion with skilful appeals to national feeling and the traditional 'Russian idea'. To combat the baneful influence of seditious foreign doctrines Russia was, for the first time in her history, supplied with an official ideology: in 1833 Count S. S. Uvarov, the Minister of Education, expressed its essence in the famous formula of 'Orthodoxy, autocracy and national character'. For nearly a century this remained the slogan of political obscurantism, the affirmation of unquestioning devotion to the political system. But far from establishing the basis for a rejuvenated spiritual unity of all classes of Russian society, the appearance of Uvarov's credo became merely the opening shot in the fierce battle of ideologies that was to dominate Russian history.

The lines began to be drawn within the next decade, as Russia slowly recovered from the numbing shock of 1825 and its aftermath. A new generation grew up, with an outlook and a background very different from that of the Decembrists, yet the issues that confronted them were the same. Nothing had changed, nothing had been solved, all the old problems were still there. The rift between the 'European' and 'Asiatic' elements of Russian life had become even more profound. The sense of impermanence, of a nation living in a temporary makeshift structure, hastily constructed of incongruous materials and inexorably falling into decay, was now stronger than at any time since Peter the Great, the architect of the Russia of St Petersburg. Change could no longer be resisted: as so many times in Russian history, this was to be irrefutably proved by war. Few doubted the necessity and imminence of fundamental changes. What direction were they to take? what should the Russia of the future be like? These were the all-important questions that in the 1830s and 1840s gave rise to new ideological and political trends in opposition to the official dogma of 'Orthodoxy, autocracy and national character'.

Literature represented the only available field of independent political activity, and it was within the lively literary salons and poetic circles of Moscow and St Petersburg that new ideas made their first appearance. In the early stages it was difficult to draw political distinctions between their authors: alike intensely high-minded and idealistic, deriving their inspiration from the writings of the great German philosophers, primarily Schelling and Hegel. Gradually, through the haze of theoretical arguments and metaphysical concepts, the battle-lines began to grow clear. By about 1845 the new generation of the Men of the Forties was broadly divided into two main groupings: Slavophiles and Westerners.

The Slavophiles emerged somewhat earlier than their opponents. To the end they remained much more of a homogeneous group, with a more coherent and uniform philosophy. They also lasted less long: having largely kept aloof from the unruly body of *raznochinets*-intelligentsia, Slavophilism soon became a minority current which petered out, with the exception of a few individual writers, in the 1870s. Yet in the long run it is arguable that the Slavophiles' contribution to the course of Russian history may well have been greater than that of the Westerners.

Slavophile ideology – as expressed in the writings of men like Kirevsky, Khomyakov, Samarin, the brothers Konstantin and Ivan Aksakov – bears, on the surface, a marked similarity to Uvarov's doctrine of 'official nationalism'. This fact has become the basis for the widely held misconception of the Slavophiles as obscurantist die-hards, supporters of the Tsarist bureaucracy and upholders of serfdom, reactionary opponents of progress and nationalistic enemies of the West. Yet in reality their interpretation of the concepts of Orthodoxy, autocracy and national character provides a sophisticated, romantic and original view of Russia's past, as well as of her prospects and place in the world.

For the Slavophiles Russian civilization – or rather, the idealized image of pre-Petrine Russian society – represented a unique world phenomenon: independent of all foreign influences, with its own indigenous cultural roots and highly original traditions. Traditional Russia had always constituted a separate world of its own, founded on pure spirituality and true Christian ideals, with a patriarchal society and a communal way of life. Her system of government – unlike that of Western Europe – was founded not on force and violence, but on mutual agreement. Autocracy represented the harmony of interests of all classes of society. The benign Muscovite social order had no need of legal guarantees; their very concept was alien to the Russian soul: justice and equality for all were secured by the mystical 'internal truth' embodied in the Muscovite State, and expressed in the traditional ideals of asceticism, other-worldliness, and abnegation of personal interests in the name of a higher purpose.

Traditional Russian society, according to the Slavophiles, was essentially *homogeneous* and *monolithic*. 'All classes and species of the population,' wrote Konstantin Aksakov, 'were imbued by a single spirit, a single faith, by identical convictions, uniform concepts, by the self-same devotion to the public weal.'[7] Herein lay the source of what was for the Slavophiles the most distinctive feature of Russian life: the communal principle, the idea of collective effort for the benefit of all.

This was how it had been for centuries. But there came a day when the Garden of Eden was destroyed, and the Russians fell from their state of grace. In the Slavophile scheme of things the role of Satan was filled by Peter the Great. Peter had demolished the patriarchal idyll; with his ungodly hand he had wrenched the ship of State from its secure mooring and turned it towards the turbulent waters of Western civilization. The government had broken its faith with the people, and the symbol of this betrayal was the alien new capital of St Petersburg. Deprived of its sources of spiritual strength, the nation had lost its traditional sense of unity: the introduction of an outlandish administrative structure and a foreign system of education had created an abyss between the educated and uneducated classes, the rulers and the people. Disharmony, injustice and inequality reigned in Russia.

The country could be revived and its social ills cured only by a return to the spiritual and communal traditions of the old Russia. Orthodox Holy Russia must be restored, with her national autocracy, her ancient representative institutions and her communal way of life. But her Westernized ruling class was unsuited for this task - only the people, the great homogeneous mass of the peasantry, had preserved the beneficent autochthonous principles, and educated men of goodwill must find their way back to the people, must dissolve themselves in the mass. Only thus could Russia - and her intelligentsia - experience a mighty spiritual resurrection, a resurgence of the national will.

Russia, having rediscovered her soul, would fulfil her promise and accomplish her historical mission of redeeming the other, less fortunate nations of the world, through the universal ideas of Orthodoxy and community. The end product of the Slavophile vision was Russian messianism.

The Slavophiles were romantic idealists and, as such, opposed to rationalism and materialism. They were basically uninterested in politics: the Russians, they thought, were an unpolitical, non-state-oriented people, concerned exclusively with their inward spiritual life. They were by no means enemies of European culture – most were highly cultivated men, liberal humanitarians who detested the bureaucratic regime of Nicholas I – but they saw the greatest menace in the dehumanizing effects of bourgeois civilization and its cult of private property. Quite simply, they believed that Russia, with her spiritual integrity and unique traditional values, was superior to the West – for all its material abundance. As Dostoevsky put it, 'Our destitute and unorganized land, aside from its upper stratum, stands as one man. All the eighty millions of its population represent such a spiritual unity as is, of course, non-existent – and cannot exist – anywhere in Europe.'[8] This was to be Russia's message to the world.

The ideological conflicts of mid-nineteenth-century Russia abound in paradoxes. For instance, the Slavophiles, for all their glorification of Russia's uniqueness, were actually under the strong influence of contemporary European schools of thought: their counterparts were to be found among the German and, to a lesser degree, the French Romantics. On the other hand, the Westerners, who advocated a break with the past and a transformation of their country along what they regarded as Western lines of development, were in the main extremely hostile to the capitalist path, and convinced that Russia should at all costs avoid this disagreeable fate by somehow striking out on her own. Most of them knew little of the realities of Western life, and what they knew they largely disliked. The Westerners, too, believed that Russia was different and that, however much she had to change, she was to remain essentially different from Europe: better, purer, nobler. In fact, it would be no exaggeration to say that the Westerners diverged from the Slavophiles not so much over the question of Russia's exceptionality, as in their hostility to religion, their materialism and rationalism, their faith in science and modernization – and their attitude to Peter the Great. Soviet historians are therefore not entirely unjustified when they depreciate the differences between Westerners and Slavophiles, and reclassify the members of these groups in accordance with their attitudes to the revolutionary movement, into 'liberals' and 'democrats'.

It was the Westerners who provided the ideological – and even, to some extent, the organizational – wellspring of the nineteenth- and twentieth-century Russian revolutionary movement. From them stemmed the radical intelligentsia, its ideas and attitudes. But the extremism of their descendants had little in common with the moderate views of the early Westerners: earnest, humane, scholarly men, enlightened admirers of Western values and fastidious enemies of Russian barbarism, men like Chaadayev, Stankevich, Granovsky or Turgenev. The man who did most towards shaping the *Weltanschauung* of the Russian intelligentsia and transforming Westernism into the rebellious temper of an age was Vissarion Belinsky, the arbiter of literary taste for his own and succeeding generations: Hegelian aesthete turned radical doctrinaire, whose passionate intolerance of evil and oppression earned him the nickname of 'furious Vissarion'.

As the founder of Russian literary criticism Belinsky became the first to lay down the guidelines of the national literature: the ideas of the writer's commitment, of the civic responsibility of literature and its social role as the principal medium of instruction and enlightenment, of the primacy of content over form. (Belinsky himself, endowed with a subtle and acute aesthetic sense, would sometimes compromise with his own principles to make allowances for literary genius – an example ignored by his less gifted followers.) From his time onwards literature came to be regarded by the intelligentsia as first and foremost a weapon in the social struggle, and the writer – as front-line fighter against autocracy. The radical critic became chief of staff or, at the very least, operations planner.

But Belinsky was no mere literary critic, no Russian Hippolyte

Taine. For him and for his numerous admirers the advancement of letters increasingly took second place to the social transformation of their country. Belinsky's Westernism, which had at first been indistinguishable from the well-meaning, vaguely liberal views of the enlightened *habitués* of Moscow's progressive literary salons, was gradually converted into an unequivocal rejection of the Russian social order. From a Europeanizing reformer he became a proponent of root and branch change – of change, moreover, that could only be accomplished through a violent convulsion, by means of force. The idea of coercing Russia into the modern world in the name of her future greatness, of forcibly transforming her social system in the interests of the people – if necessary, even against her own will – became Belinsky's principal contribution to the development of Russian radical thought.

There was never any doubt in his mind about the best way of achieving the desired goal: this revolutionary democrat, this passionate foe of injustice and oppression found his ideal in the superhuman figure of Peter the Great. 'For me,' wrote Belinsky, 'Peter is my philosophy, my religion, my revelation in everything that touches Russia. He is the example to great and small, to all who want to get things done, to be of use in any way.'[9] The great autocrat who had ruthlessly remoulded Russia with blood and iron was, to the father of Russian radicalism, a 'divine Heracles', 'hero and demi-god', 'the eternal lodestar of the Russian people', who 'with his mighty hand thrust Russia into world history, showed her the way to her future world pre-eminence, and thus changed the eventual fate of the whole world, of all mankind'.[10] The strange fascination exerted by Peter the Great, by his policies and methods, over several generations of Russian revolutionaries, was first felt by Belinsky. A potent tradition had been established.

The more that Belinsky ruminated on his country's future, the firmer became his conviction that modernity and social justice could only be installed by an omnipotent government which was determined to achieve the good of society by main force – like Peter – regardless of the wishes of the people themselves, who could hardly be expected to understand their elevated purpose. His ideal was not the benevolent autocrat, not the enlightened absolute monarch of the French *philosophes*, but the ruthless autocrat, the revolutionary despot. The iron-willed autocrat with the best interests of his country at heart was for Belinsky the ideal instrument of Russia's transformation. The concept had already been formulated at an early stage of his career:

> Peter provides clear proof that Russia will never be able of herself to develop liberty and civic spirit: she will receive both from her Tsars, just as she has already received so much from them. True, we still have no rights, we are still slaves, so to speak, but this is because we must still remain slaves. Russia is only an infant yet; she requires a nanny – a nanny devoted to her charge, and yet ready to chastise it for misbehaviour. To grant the infant full freedom would mean to ruin it – in our country's present state, to grant her a constitution would ruin Russia . . . The autocratic government gives us complete freedom to think and meditate, but limits our freedom to speak loudly and to interfere in its affairs . . . Wine is beneficial to adults who know how to profit by it, but it is disastrous for children – and politics is a heady wine which in Russia could become a deadly narcotic.[11]

Belinsky soon lost his faith in monarchy; he became a convinced republican, a proponent of the violent overthrow of existing institutions. But his basic philosophy of history, his belief in the essentiality of imposing change from above, under duress, remained unchanged. The State was the only possible instrument of progress, and the career of Peter the Great provided the model for Russia's future modernization. Belinsky's detailed justification of the imposed revolution shaped the pattern of a whole century of Russian radicalism. It deserves quotation at length:

Our history was different from that of Europe, and our

humanization had to be achieved in an entirely different way . . .

With us everything had to be started from the top downwards and not from the bottom up, for at the time when we felt the need of budging from the spot on which we had slumbered for centuries, we already saw ourselves on the height that others had taken by storm. Of course it was not the people who saw themselves at this height . . . but the government, and that in the person of one man – its Tsar. Peter had no time to waste: for now it was no longer a matter of securing Russia's future greatness, but of saving her in the present . . .

Peter had no time to wait and tarry . . . He could not sow and wait calmly until the scattered seed would germinate, sprout and ripen: he cast the seed forth with one hand and wished to reap its fruit at once with the other, in violation of the customary laws of nature and probability – and nature forsook for him her eternal laws, and possibility turned for him into magic. The new Joshua, he stopped the sun in its path, he made the sea disgorge its ancient possessions, he called forth a magnificent city from the marsh. He understood that half-measures would not avail and were merely a hindrance; he understood that fundamental revolutions in things that had developed over the centuries could not be accomplished by halves, that one had to do either more than could possibly be done or nothing at all . . . This was how he fought his war against ignorance: having drawn up his whole people to face this enemy, he cut them off from any chance of retreat or flight. Be useful to the State, learn – or die: such was the motto inscribed in blood on the banner of his struggle with barbarism . . .

As for the sacrifices involved in the creation of Petersburg – they were redeemed by necessity and by their result. With his deeds Peter was writing history, and not a novel; he acted as a Tsar, not a family man. His reform was a harsh ordeal for the people, a difficult and grim time. But when and where were great upheavals accomplished peaceably, without distress for their contemporaries . . .?

Yes, it was hard for the people to climb off their sleeping berths on the stoves and come forth to such labour and struggle. It was not the nation's fault that it had grown up untutored, and then in adulthood found it too toilsome to sit down and learn. But, worst of all, it was incapable of understanding either the sense or the aim or the use of the changes that were being forced upon it by the iron, implacable will of the herculean Tsar.[12]

These paragraphs contain Belinsky's credo, the central part of his theoretical and political legacy: an impassioned hymn of praise for the unlimited use of force, wielded from above by an absolute government without regard for the wishes and convenience of its subjects – but applied wisely and well, in the interests of the people and the country. In this basic belief he never wavered; a few months before his death, in 1848, when already in the last stages of consumption, he wrote to a close friend: 'When and where has a people ever liberated itself? Everything has always been achieved by personalities. . . Russia needs a new Peter the Great.'[13]

In Belinsky's writings we are for the first time confronted by the crucial paradox of Russian radicalism: its sincere concern for the people's plight, combined with a profound (if usually less outspoken) contempt for the people themselves. The conviction that the much-loved people were too backward to be able to understand their own good, and that they therefore had to be forced into the Elysian Fields by beings of a superior intelligence – a self-appointed intellectual élite or a single leader of superhuman stature – found its expression in the extravagant cult of Peter the Great. Largely under Belinsky's influence a significant proportion of the radical intelligentsia – republicans and democrats to a man – became worshippers at the shrine of what Herzen called 'Peter-the-Greatism'. It was an odd sort of radicalism.

The source of Belinsky's immense intellectual influence was

neither the originality of his ideas nor the forcefulness of his style: it lay in the fact of his having been the first Russian socialist. To be sure, his was a rather shallow socialism; it owed nothing to Marx or Engels – he does not even seem to have been aware of their existence – and consisted mainly of bits and pieces of French Utopianism. Its impact, however, was out of all proportion to its intellectual profundity. Beginning with Belinsky socialism of one form or another, home-grown or imported, came to dominate the world-outlook of the Russian revolutionary movement.

Socialism was brought to Russia in the 1840s; it arrived as a revelation, a solution, a signpost to the future. Suddenly the word was on everyone's lips – it became the subject of polite conversation in fashionable society, and of earnest nightlong discussion among high-toned university students. A new dimension was added to the argument of Westerner and Slavophile. At first the government was not overly concerned by the new ferment of ideas: philosophical fads, like literary tastes, were regarded as harmless as long as they did not take the form of political challenge to the existing order. The police only changed this attitude when they discovered, fairly soon, that secret socialistic societies were springing up in the capitals and elsewhere. By far the most important of these was the St Petersburg circle established and led in the late forties by the minor nobleman and junior official Mikhail Petrashevsky – the first Russian socialist group.

In the West the Petrashevskists are known chiefly – if at all – through the subsequent literary career of one of their number: Dostoevsky. In Russian history they occupy a somewhat more prominent place: theirs is the first chapter in the long story of ideological conspiracy. As conspirators the Petrashevskists were, even by Russian standards, pretty ineffectual. They regularly met for lengthy philosophical discussions; they compiled and published a *Pocket Dictionary of Foreign Words used in Russian*, of a pronounced but cleverly disguised subversive nature; they expounded and propagated the Utopian socialist views of Charles Fourier, and, emulating him, dreamt of covering

Russia with a network of egalitarian co-operative communities or *phalanstères* – but the only *phalanstère* they actually established, on Petrashevsky's own estate, was, alas, burnt down by the mistrustful peasants. Although the Petrashevskists, subscribing as they did to a certain basic set of common beliefs, were ideologically much more homogeneous than the Decembrists, one can hardly speak of uniformity or even consistency with regard to their political platform. Their group contained within itself not only the ideological seeds of most of the future revolutionary movements but also many of the men who were to play leading parts in them. Petrashevsky's Fourierism proved to be but a passing phase in Russia. His more lasting influence lay not in any original ideas he may have had, but in his popularization of socialism and his introduction to Russia of the works of a number of early European socialists.

The dominating personality among the Petrashevskists was not so much their nominal leader as the powerful figure of Nikolai Speshnev – regarded by Pokrovsky, the official Bolshevik historiographer, as the 'only communist' among them,[14] and by the same token, the first Russian communist of all. The description does not seem unjustified. He advocated the establishment of a Central Committee, the application of 'Jesuitical' conspiratorial methods, and the preparation of a peasant uprising which would lead to the institution of a revolutionary dictatorship and the reorganization of Russian agriculture in large-scale collective farms! A precocious young man, well ahead of his time. His co-conspirators seem to have been rather frightened of Speshnev; certainly they were vastly impressed by him. Dostoevsky in particular saw him as being of superhuman stature, as the embodiment of evil on a spectacular scale: Speshnev became the prototype of Stavrogin, the daemonic revolutionary leader of *The Possessed*.

More than twenty years – the lifetime of a generation – had elapsed between the Decembrists and the Petrashevskists, twenty years during which the Russia of Nicholas I, growing ever more arrogant, had assumed for itself the role of Gendarme of Europe and arbiter of its destinies. The unexpected reappearance, after years of quiescence at home and martial glory abroad, of an underground revolutionary organization was carelessly laughed off by the government; its participants were treated much more leniently than the Decembrists, having their death sentences commuted to terms of penal servitude. Yet the Petrashevskist circle was soon to be recognized as the ominous harbinger of a new type of revolutionary movement that would unremittantly grow in intensity until finally, seventy years later, it brought the whole edifice of Tsardom crashing to the ground. The Decembrists and the Westerners, Belinsky and Petrashevsky, separately and in conjunction, constituted the introductory phase of this mighty orchestral composition. The creation of its central theme, out of a blend of disparate strains, was largely the work of Alexander Ivanovich Herzen.

Herzen was the commanding figure of nineteenth-century Russian radicalism. Lenin himself, in the rather simplified sketch of Russian revolutionary development quoted above, sees Herzen's activity as the focal point of the whole process. Of Chernyshevsky alone can it be said that his actual influence among the intelligentsia exceeded Herzen's – but the ideas he propagated were derived in the main from Herzen. Herzen's subtle and original mind, his polished style, encyclopaedic knowledge and cosmopolitan outlook invest him with an aura of intellectual brilliance that is noticeably lacking in the much more narrow-minded, pedestrian and plain-spoken Chernyshevsky. Although Herzen's immense personal popularity was short-lived – like so many other idols after him, he was toppled from his pedestal and denounced as a *fainéant* by the jeering youths of the succeeding generation of intelligentsia – his ideas remained to form the ideological core of the Russian revolutionary tradition.

Herzen is often thought of as the Westerner *par excellence*. It is not hard to find the reasons for this: how else to regard the man who spent so much of his life in Europe, the Swiss citizen and London householder, the admirer of Western democracy and European civilization, equally at home in half a dozen European countries, languages, cultures? His outlook was universal, his interests transcended national boundaries, his way of life – that of a wealthy and cultivated man-about-town. Everything about Herzen, from his distinguished appearance to his refined literary tastes, seemed to set him off from the strange and uncouth Russians with whom Europe was beginning to become familiar. Yet the truth is that, unlike many of his countrymen who did their utmost to divest themselves of their Russianness in exchange for an imperfectly understood and ill-fitting Europeanization, Herzen never succumbed to the lure of Western culture, never subscribed to the belief in the superiority of the West, never renounced his faith in Russia's special and separate path of development. On the contrary: the more he saw of the West, the better adjusted he became to the Western way of life – the greater grew his dislike of European bourgeois civilization and European capitalist progress. As a youth in his own country he had been a Westerner; as a mature political thinker and writer in exile he became more and more of a Slavophile. And above all else he was a socialist. It was through a fusion of the three ingredients of Westernism, Slavophilism and socialism that Herzen founded the uniquely Russian philosophy of Populism (*Narodnichestvo*): the ideological basis of the nineteenth-century revolutionary movement. Herzen succeeded, so to speak, in squaring the circle: he adapted the European concept of socialism to Russian conditions, and showed for the first time that backward Russia was actually riper for socialism than industrialized Europe. It was a momentous discovery.

In 1847 Herzen left his country for a journey to the West; the visit soon turned into a permanent exile that lasted until his death in 1870. In Russia Herzen had nurtured his hatred of Tsarism and serfdom for twenty years, ever since the execution of the Decembrists. He had studied the German philosophers and French socialists, and taken an active part in the literary circles and philosophical arguments of the thirties and forties. He had even dabbled in subversive politics, for which he had been punished – rather leniently, by Russian standards – by two terms of provincial exile. And now, at last, he had turned his back on autocracy and slavery, and was heading for Western Europe, for France and Italy, the promised lands of the Jacobins and the *Carbonari*. Being a man both wealthy and prudent, he had naturally provided for the material well-being of himself and his family – Dostoevsky was undoubtedly referring to Herzen when he sneeringly wrote that 'our landowners sold their peasant serfs and proceeded to Paris to publish socialistic magazines'.[15] Yet there was nothing discreditable in this practical-mindedness: Herzen had come to Europe for a definite purpose, and he was not going to let himself be deflected from it by petty financial worries. His purpose was, quite simply, to study the theory and practice of the European revolutionary movements, and to utilize their experience towards the overthrow of the Russian social and political order.

Like others of his generation – the Men of the Forties – Herzen was a romantic both temperamentally and intellectually. His love affair with Europe was lived out with the tragic intensity of a great passion: ardent longing, rapturous meeting, bitter disenchantment. For Herzen Europe had been a splendid vision, an image of Russia's future, representing freedom, human dignity, the rule of law and the rights of man. Although his reading of Western socialist authors had already implanted the seeds of doubt, and caused him to dissent from the uncritical enthusiasm of Westerner friends like Granovsky, he had cast all reservations aside as he set out on his journey. He travelled like an impatient lover – impatient above all to embrace Paris, the capital of revolutions, the dream-city of every Russian radical. In his autobiography, *My Past and Thoughts*, Herzen has left a moving description of his first meeting with Paris:

And so, I really am in Paris, not in a dream but in reality – for this is the Colonne Vêndome and the Rue de la Paix.

In Paris ... This word has for me meant hardly less than the word 'Moscow'. I have dreamt of this moment since childhood. Then let us hurry to see the Hôtel de Ville, the café Foy in Palais-Royal, where Camille

Desmoulins tore off a green leaf and attached it to his hat instead of a cockard, crying 'à la Bastille . . .!'[16]

The awakening was rude and rapid: when measured up to a far-fetched romantic vision reality seemed even more sordid than it actually was. Instead of liberty Herzen found exploitation, instead of human dignity – poverty and servility, instead of the rights of man – the arrogance of a power-hungry and vulgar bourgeoisie. The seal on his disillusionment was set by the Revolution of 1848, which broke out less than a year after his arrival in the West. It found him in Italy, and from there he made haste to Paris, hopes rekindled. What he saw fell far short of the ideal, but still – he promised himself – it might turn out to be the dawn of a new age. Then came the June insurrection of the Paris workers, drowned in blook by General Cavaignac. Thousands were massacred, thousands more imprisoned and transported. The homicidal frenzy of the French bourgeoisie exulting in the triumph of the forces of 'law and order' filled Herzen with horror and repugnance; the shock of June 1848 became the great turning point of Herzen's revolutionary career. He was never able to rid himself of the bloodstained apparition. It meant the end of his hopes. In *My Past and Thoughts* Herzen quotes an old French song:

> Te souviens-tu . . .? mais ici je m'arrête,
> Ici finit tout noble souvenir,

and adds: 'These *accursed* days mark the beginning of the last period of my life.'[17]

The question of whether Herzen's exaggerated despair did or did not prove to be as unjustified as his original extravagant hopes is irrelevant to our present inquiry. What mattered was that, while Herzen's faith in revolution remained unchanged, and indeed his socialistic convictions were greatly fortified, his whole attitude to Europe underwent a profound change. Not that he ever turned his back on European culture, literature, science: far from it; he continued to believe that Russia had much to learn in these respects from the West. But more and more he came to regard the European cultural heritage as precisely that – a heritage, an object perhaps of great value, but essentially a thing of the past. As the years passed and the high hopes of 1848 dwindled and faded away, to be replaced by an orgy of soulless money-making and flashy bourgeois ostentation, Herzen became convinced that Europe's day was over. Europe had no future: it was tired, worn out, decrepit. It was paralysed and rendered incapable by its own great past: 'Europe is sinking because it cannot get rid of its cargo; its hold is crammed with the treasures accumulated in a long and perilous passage.'[18] Old age and vast wealth had led to conservatism, immobility and stagnation.

For Herzen the most repellent aspect of contemporary European civilization was its domination by the bourgeoisie. The great revolutions, he declared, had led to the unequivocal triumph of the bourgeoisie in every field of life; the middle classes had imposed their ideas, their values, their morals upon the rest of society. Everything and everyone was now subservient to their interests. And what was even worse – the downtrodden and oppressed masses were themselves seeking to emulate their bourgeois masters. Unlike Marx, who welcomed the onset of the capitalist system as a mighty victory for progress, indispensable towards the establishment of socialism, Herzen viewed the new social order as an unmitigated evil from which there was no escape, no recovery. The rule of the middle class symbolized the end of Europe's greatness.

There was something irrational, almost hysterical in the way the ordinarily reasonable Herzen incessantly denounced the bourgeoisie and all its works. He was not the first Russian progressive thinker to do so: the anti-bourgeois tradition had been founded by Belinsky, and its roots lead back even further in time. But it was Herzen's immensely popular and influential writings which led to its general adoption; detestation and fear of capitalism, abhorrence of the bourgeoisie and contempt for the middle-class way of life became cardinal tenets of the intelligentsia *Weltanschauung* and the Russian revolutionary movement – down to the present day. Before Herzen the word *meshchanin* – the equivalent of *Bürger* or burgess – carried only one meaning: that of townsman, or member of the artisan or trading class; *meshchanstvo* was a collective noun which meant nothing more than the estate of townspeople, or middle class. Since the middle of the nineteenth century, however, largely under Herzen's influence, *meshchanstvo* has more and more come to stand for sordid narrow-mindedness, selfishness, philistinism – for ignoble opposition to all the high spiritual values; *meshchanin* described the bearer of these reprehensible instincts. Today the original Russian words for 'bourgeois' and 'bourgeoisie' survive in common usage only as terms of opprobrium.

Whether Herzen's denunciations of the European bourgeois order contained traces of the aristocrat's scorn for the Third Estate is beside the point; there is no mistaking the sincerity of his convictions:

> The middle class is the ideal towards which Europe is hastening, towards which the lower depths are rising . . . The *bourgeoisie* is the last word of a civilization founded on the absolute autocracy of property; it is the democratization of the aristocracy and the aristocratization of democracy . . . The German peasant is the bourgeois of husbandry, the worker of all countries is the bourgeois of the future . . .
>
> We see before us a civilization based upon a landless proletariat, upon the unconditional right of property . . .
>
> It is time we reached the sober and humble conclusion that bourgeois society is the final form, the adulthood of Western civilization; bourgeois society concludes the long series of dreams, it puts an end to the epic of growth, the romance of youth – to everything which has brought so much poetry and so many troubles into the lives of the nations.[19]

It may at first sight seem strange that a Russian revolutionary should devote so much attention to condemning a social order which, as he himself readily admitted, was for all its faults infinitely preferable to the one against which he was fighting. As Herzen's biographer caustically remarks, the debate on the depravity of capitalism conducted by the Russian exiles in Paris was 'a controversy not without its comic aspects among the subjects of a monarch who gave them much better things to worry about than the "moral" corruption of France'.[20] But it was for them a debate of the highest relevancy to the problems they faced. Central to Herzen's thought was the question of his country's future path. Before coming to the West he had been firmly convinced that Russia's best hope lay in her social and political reconstruction along broadly European lines. His experiences and observations, and above all the numbing shock of 1848, led to a drastic revision of the earlier Westernist assumption. Europe was effete, worn-out; the bourgeois order was inhuman and disgusting. Russia should never travel this road to Calvary. She would have to work out her salvation in her own way.

Having turned away from the West, discouraged and disillusioned, Herzen looked at his native land with a new appreciation. Might it not be that Russia, a country manifestly different from any other – situated as she was at the convergence of East and West, combining elements of each yet belonging to neither – a nation with no historical memory beyond a series of dynastic changes – unencumbered by the dead weight of traditions, institutions or possessions – a youthful giant who had hibernated through the centuries of European evolution and was only approaching maturity when Europe had already grown senile – a people with a changeless and timeless way of life, upon whose consciousness history had never impinged: might it not be that this nation, far from following the example of an impotent and corrupt West, was actually uniquely qualified to discover a new and better road of historical development? With every year Herzen tended more and more to answer the question in the affirmative.

This evolution of Herzen's views undoubtedly brought him close to the Slavophile conception of Russia's historical destiny. But a kindred strain of thought had always existed within the general intellectual current of Westernism as well. Already in 1830 the first great Westerner, Pyotr Chaadayev, had declared: 'We have never gone together with other nations; we do not belong to any of the great families of mankind, neither to the West nor to the East ... We belong to those nations which do not yet seem to constitute a necessary part of mankind, and who are destined in the future to teach the world some great lesson.'[21] It was not a novel proposition: for centuries the unique character of Russian civilization had been generally recognized by political writers of all schools, and had formed the basis for a widespread conviction of the country's messianic destiny. What Herzen did was to harness this conviction to the cause of revolution.

In countless newspaper articles, addresses, books, essays and letters Herzen developed a doctrine that combined the Westerners' belief in the inevitability of change and modernization with the Slavophiles' faith in Russia's superior virtues – and his own commitment to socialism. Incessantly he preached the lesson of Russia's advantages over Europe:

Russia is an Empire still in its youth; a building that still has about it the smell of fresh plaster, where everything is experimental and in a state of transition, where nothing is final, where people are always making changes, many of which are for the worse but all of which are at least changes ...

We are simpler, we are healthier, we are incapable of any sickbed fussiness over food, we are no lawyers, no bourgeois ... We are placed more freely than the West with regard to the idea of the near future – let us then make use of this. Long struggles and arduous victories enfetter the West, confine it to what has already been achieved: much of this is still treasured, even though it is now quite useless. But we have achieved nothing, and therefore have nothing to preserve ... We are in some respects further advanced and freer than Europe precisely because we have lagged so far behind it.... The extreme contradictions of our disordered existence, the lack of stability in all our legal and constitutional notions, make possible on the one hand the most unlimited despotism, serfdom and military settlements, and on the other hand create conditions in which such revolutionary changes as those of Peter I and Alexander II can be easily achieved. The man who lives *en garni* [in furnished lodgings] finds it much easier to move than the man who has settled down in a house of his own . . .

In Russia nothing bears the mark of stagnation or death, which one constantly and monotonously finds in the unvarying repetitions of one and the same thing, from generation to generation, among the old nations of the West . . . In Russia there is nothing final or petrified; everything there is still in a state of flux, of preparation . . . In his way of life the Russian approaches the new social organization much closer than any European people . . .

I do not regard bourgeois society as the ultimate form of the Russian social order, the social order to which Russia aspires . . . The Russian people, sprawled out *between* Europe and Asia, belonging in a strange relationship of cousinhood to the family of European nations, was the only one to play almost no part in the long family chronicle of the West . . . But why then should a nation which has developed independently, under completely unlike conditions, with a way of life based upon entirely different principles – why should such a nation have to repeat the European bygones, *knowing, moreover, only too well what the result of this would be* . . .?

In the suppressed and slumbering energies of the Russian people, in the estrangement between people and State, in the constricted and ill-fitting conventions into which Russian life has been forced, we have more than a *tabula rasa*: we have *a guarantee* of our unique future development . . . This nation is nearer to the achievement of an economic, i.e. a social upheaval than Roman-feudal, bourgeois-industrial Europe . . . That which in Europe can only be accomplished by a series of catastrophes and shocks, can in Russia develop out of what already exists . . .[22]

Out of the disparate ingredients of Westernism and nationalism, Slavophilism and socialism, Herzen was fashioning a new theory of revolution. It had very little in common with the doctrines being concurrently elaborated by his fellow-exile, Dr Karl Marx (Marx had nothing but the most profound contempt for what he regarded as Herzen's unscientific and nationalistic effusions). It was not universal but exclusive, based not on class but on *the people*. In Herzen's scheme the Russian people as a whole – unlike the class-racked societies of Europe – constituted a single revolutionary force, confronting an alien and rootless monarcho-bureaucratic structure. Herzen appears to have been the first to discover the concept of *proletarian nations*: 'Russia stands in the same position with regard to the Western world as the proletariat: she has received nothing but misfortune, slavery and shame. And therefore both these disinherited hope for a common resurrection in a social revolution.'[23] Europe was old and capitalistic, Russia young and proletarian: an imaginative notion that was to have many imitators.

But it was not solely the youthfulness, the destitution and the underdevelopment of the Russian people that led Herzen to believe in their peculiar ripeness for socialism. Their greatest advantage over the Western nations lay in the possession of a unique traditional institution, salvaged from the past thanks to the absence of either feudalism or capitalism: the village community, the *obshchina* or *mir*. Herzen transformed the *obshchina* into the cornerstone of Russian Populism. Curiously enough, the Russian revolutionary movement owed the discovery of the village community to a conservative Prussian Junker, Baron August von Haxthausen. Having been commissioned by the government of Nicholas I to undertake a study of agrarian relations in European Russia, Haxthausen, after lengthy investigations, and with true German pedantry and scrupulous scholarly precision, produced a vast three-volume work entitled *Studien über die inneren Zustände, das Volksleben und insbesondere die ländlischen Einrichtungen Russlands.* The first two volumes appeared in German and French in 1847, and created an instant sensation. Haxthausen, armed with the most up-to-date methods of European social science, had shown that the village community, with its distinctive system of communal tenure, collective responsibility and regular re-distribution of the land, was since time immemorial the central factor of Russian peasant life. In a sense, of course, the existence of the *obshchina* had always been known; it was much remarked upon by – among others – the Slavophiles. But it was only after the publication of Haxthausen's findings that Russian educated society – with its customary inordinate faith in foreign authorities – really became convinced of the special significance and extraordinary nature of this institution.

The *obshchina* immediately became a bone of contention, each ideological tendency claiming it for its own. The official champions of 'Orthodoxy, autocracy and national character' triumphantly advertised the *obshchina* as the key to the striking stability of Russian society, which no amount of subversive agitation would ever be able to undermine (this was essentially the view of Haxthausen himself). The Slavophiles, for their part, were greatly encouraged by this weighty testimony to the virtues of pre-Petrine patriarchal institutions, and enthusiastically subscribed to the Russian version of the German Romantics' mystical *Volkstum.* (It was left to a later generation of Russian historians to establish the much more recent, and State-inspired, origins of the village community.) But it was upon Populist ideology that the discovery of the Russian peasant's devotion to collective property and primitive socialism made the greatest impact.

For Herzen the existence of the *obshchina* – revealed, by a happy coincidence, at the very moment of his disillusionment with the West – clenched the argument. It had now been proved *scientifically* (a most important point!) that Russia, in spite, or rather because of her backwardness, was historically far better prepared for the acceptance of socialism than those highly developed European nations for whom the concept had originally been created.

The Russian peasant has no real knowledge of any form of life but that of the village commune: he understands about rights and duties only when these are tied to the commune and its members. Outside the commune, there are no obligations for him – there is simply violence . . . The commune has preserved the Russian people from Mongol barbarism, from Imperial civilization, from the Europeanized landowners and from the German bureaucracy: the organic life of the commune has persisted despite all the attempts made on it by authority, badly mauled though it has been at times. By good fortune it has survived right into the period that witnesses the rise of Socialism in Europe. For Russia this has been a most happy providence . . .

The peasants have remained faithful guardians of the national character, which is based on *communism,* i.e. on the regular division of the fields according to the number of workers and the absence of private landownership . . . The Russian people, crushed by slavery and the Government, cannot follow in the footsteps of European nations and repeat their past revolutions. These were revolutions exclusively of the cities, and anything of that nature would instantly fracture the foundations of our communal system. The opposite is the case: the coming revolution will take place on more native ground . . .

We have none of the Western man's blind prejudices which paralyse and deprive him of half his faculties. Our people's life is based on the village community, with division of the fields, with communistic landownership, with elected administration and equal responsibility for each worker (*tyaglo*) . . . The threshold on which Europe has tripped up is for us practically non-existent. The natural unaffectedness of our rural way of life, the precarious and unestablished nature of economic and legal concepts, the vagueness of property rights, the absence of bourgeoisie, our own extraordinary adaptability: all these represent a position superior to nations that are fully constituted and tired . . . The only thing that is conservative on our shifting, unsettled soil is the village community – that is, the only thing deserving preservation . . . I believe, with all my heart and mind, that it is our door on which history is knocking . . .

The word *Socialism* is unknown to our people, but its meaning is close to the hearts of Russians who have lived for ages in the village community and the workman's *artel* . . . I boldly repeat that the mere fact of communal landownership and partition of the fields justifies the assumption that our untilled black earth is *more capable* of germinating the seed brought from Western fields – more capable by reason of its component elements, and because on it have piled up less rubbish and all kinds of ruins than on Western fields.[24]

In the course of the 1850s Herzen had developed all the main elements of his political philosophy: the decrepitude of the West and the unsuitability for Russia of the European example; the unmitigated evil of the capitalist path, which was at all costs to be avoided; the advantages, from the point of view of socialism, inherent in Russia's peculiar past; the people's instinctive devotion to a socialistic way of life, embodied in the timeless institution of the *obshchina*. By a process of completely rational speculation he had arrived at a semi-mystical deification of The People as the natural socialist, the repository of unsullied communal virtue, the guarantor of a comparatively easy transition to a paradisial future. Populism was launched on its way.

The trouble with Herzen's apotheosis of the people was that it had evolved as a purely cerebral exercise. His actual knowledge of the people was minimal; never having studied peasant life and the peasant mentality at first hand, his understanding of these subjects was derived in the main from books. To this should be added the effect of the long separation from his country – always a cruel experience for the soulful Russian. But even apart from the additional impediment of foreign exile, it was this lack of any practical knowledge or understanding of the cult-object – the peasantry – that was to characterize the whole outlook of the Populist intelligentsia. It is hard to resist the inference that otherwise they could scarcely have worshipped with quite the same degree of blind devotion – or doctrinal detachment.

This however does not apply to all educated and progressive-minded Russians. Quite a few enlightened and eminently literate landowners had spent much time among their peasants, and in the process acquired a thorough understanding of their way of life and a genuine love and compassion for them – though stopping short of idolatry. Their conclusions regarding 'peasant socialism' and the *obshchina* could hardly disagree more with Herzen's. One such landowner was Herzen's closest friend and lifelong revolutionary collaborator, Nikolai Ogarev. Ogarev spent several years on his estate, daily rubbing shoulders with the peasants; his account of the actual workings of the 'socialistic' communal system is harsh and realistic:

The habit of slavery, acknowledged by legislation, has given us a form of legality without any law, a form of legal procedure without justice, and the communal way of life, which is a mere form of equality. Our *obshchina* represents the equality of servitude. Our communal meeting is an assemblage where everyone is both executioner and victim, both envier and envied; the *mir* is an expression of the envy of all against one, of the community against the individual. In the West the idea of equality presumes the equal well-being of all, but the equality of the *mir* requires that all be equally miserable. As a result of the whole communal, administrative and judicial system the *mujik* (or rather, the Russian in general) is unable to comprehend the possibility of a man not belonging to something, of a man simply existing by himself.[25]

Ogarev's description of rural community life bears no resemblance whatsoever to the idyllic image of harmonious co-operation and dignified egalitarianism conjured up by Herzen and his Populist followers. But it certainly tallies with the picture of brutality, spite, ignorance and general degradation drawn by every nineteenth-century novelist who wrote about the Russian village. The greatest of these, and probably the best authority on the Russian peasant that we will ever have, was Turgenev. As an intimate friend of Herzen's he did his utmost to keep the exile informed about the situation in their country. Turgenev was what would today be called a hard-headed progressive: although himself a staunch opponent of autocracy and slavery and a supporter of the people's interests, he strongly disagreed with Herzen's idealization of the peasant as instinctive Socialist. In a letter, written in 1862 and published anonymously, Turgenev castigated Herzen for what he saw as the latter's utter misinterpretation of Russian realities:

The people before whom you genuflect is a conservative *par excellence* and carries within himself the seeds of the self-same bourgeoisie ... I fear that in future we shall alternate between abasing ourselves before the people, and deposing the people; between extolling his beliefs as sacred and incomparable, and condemning them as miserable and demented ... Ah, old friend, believe me: the only firm base for live revolutionary propaganda in Russia is the minority of the educated class. At any rate, *you* have no other public ... You, the enemy of mysticism and absolutism, now mystically genuflect before the Russian sheepskin coat, in which you see the great blessing and the novelty and the originality of the future social formation – in one word, *das Absolute*, the very same *Absolute* which you ridicule in philosophy ... Having filled young minds with the over-fermented beer of your socio-Slavophile ideas, you then let them go out, tipsy and hazy, into a world where they will inescapably trip up at the first step.[26]

The charge of misleading the young generation was a grave one; whether it was justified or not, there was no denying the fact that Herzen's tremendous influence upon the educated class – greater probably than that of any other Russian political theorist before him. Considering the prevailing conditions of strict censorship and universal police surveillance, one can only marvel at the widespread popularity of his ideas. Indeed, that they managed to get through to Russia at all was a remarkable achievement, and eloquent proof of the vast changes set in motion in the mid-1850s. It took a cruel military defeat, and the providential death of the tyrant, to transform the prophet without honour in his country into the recognized leader of public opinion.

Herzen had embarked upon his campaign of enlightening and influencing the Russian public in 1853, with the establishment of his 'Free Russian Press in London' and the publication of the first revolutionary pamphlets and broadsheets. For a time it seemed as if the new venture would prove just another ephemeral and futile émigré enterprise: the outbreak of war, with its accompanying wave of patriotic feeling in Russia, effectively closed down even the scanty channels of communication that had previously existed. And then – without warning, as if by a miracle – the whole scene was transfigured. The news of Nicholas's death had the same effect upon Herzen as the first report of the February revolution in Paris, seven years earlier. Once again hope ran high for a new and better era. Nothing could ever be the same; the new reign would surely see the consummation of the high hopes that had been crushed thirty years before, on Senate Square. In 1856 Herzen began publishing a periodical called *Pole Star* – the title of a famous literary almanac of the early 1820s, edited by some leading Decembrist *littérateurs*. A year later, on 1 July 1857, he put out the first issue of a new political supplement. It was called *Kolokol* – The Bell.

Kolokol became one of the most astonishing phenomena in the history of Russian, possibly even of world journalism. Its publisher had already spent ten years in foreign exile, cut off from public opinion and out of touch with events in his country; it appeared abroad, in a distant capital, without any organized means of entering Russia, let alone of being distributed there; its importation into the country was rigorously banned, customs officials used every means at their disposal to keep it out, and anyone caught reading it was automatically liable to prosecution. And yet for five or six years it remained the most influential organ of Russian public opinion. Every person of consequence, and anyone interested in current affairs, read it regularly; to be unaware of the contents of Herzen's latest editorial was to reveal oneself as both ignorant and retrograde; it is said that a copy of every issue, fresh from the press, was laid by unknown hands on the desk of the Emperor himself, who often learned from *Kolokol* of scandals and abuses about which he had not been informed. In all, 245 issues were published over the journal's ten-year life; at its peak it circulated in about 2500 copies – a figure that would have been regarded as high even for a legal domestic publication. Never had a Russian revolutionary held such an audience.

The fantastic success of *Kolokol* was due not merely to Herzen's intellectual and literary ability, but – primarily – to the unprecedented developments within Russia herself. During the first years of the new reign the country lived in a constant state of buoyant optimism. The mood of the time – not unlike that of a century later, after the death of another and greater tyrant – is vividly conveyed in the memoirs of a prominent Populist, Nikolai Shelgunov: 'This was an amazing time, a time when everyone suddenly wanted to think, to read and to learn, and when everyone who had any mind of his own desired to express it openly and loudly. The mind, hitherto lost in slumber, stirred, quivered, and began to work. It acquired a powerful impetus – and it was confronted by huge problems. We were not concerned with the present day: what was being discussed and decided was the fate of generations to come, the future destinies of Russia – everything depended on the nature of the reforms that would finally be adopted.'²⁷

The past was done away with, and anything seemed possible. New laws, new measures, new appointments followed each other in swift succession. The end of serfdom was at last in sight. And there, in London, was the man who had foretold it all and who was now explaining, in measured tones and elegant phrases, what the whole thing was about and where it was leading to. No wonder that for many of the thousands of Russian tourists who now spilled out into Europe a visit to Alexander Ivanovich was the high-point was their journey, as well as an earnest of their progressive convictions (it was mainly these travellers who supplied Herzen with his inside information, and also transported *Kolokol* into Russia).

For a time Herzen was himself infected by the general air of glad anticipation. He addressed several Open Letters full of well-meaning advice to the young Tsar. When in late 1857 Alexander II publicly announced his intention of emancipating the serfs, Herzen saluted him reverentially: 'Thou hast conquered, O Galilean!' This mood did not last long – but Herzen's short-lived honeymoon with the 'Liberator-Tsar' later became the chief instrument of his downfall from the acknowledged position of leader of the progressive movement, the main weapon in the furious attacks launched against him by a new and frighteningly unfamiliar generation of Populist intelligentsia. Yet there was nothing illogical or inconsistent in his attitude. What he strove for was peasant communal socialism; this, he believed, was fairly easy to achieve, because of Russia's peculiar social and economic system, and if there was a chance of the job being done by means of a 'revolution from above' (as the Tsar himself had called it) – well, that made things even simpler. Unlike the great majority of his Populist followers Herzen, though inclined to theoretical solutions, was no doctrinaire; he was never fascinated by the inevitability of revolution or violent social upheaval, nor did he particularly care for the idea of bloodshed. Partly under the influence of his long sojourn in the West, he remained a humane and broad-minded man, strongly addicted to the principles of personal liberty and local self-government, an opponent of Jacobinism, dictatorship, centralization and revolutionary terror. To be sure, a temporary revolutionary dictatorship might prove necessary, but the less of it there was, the better.

Herzen's somewhat ambiguous approach to revolutionary violence becomes apparent if we measure him by the time-honoured Russian test of his attitude to Peter the Great. Like every other Russian ideologue, he returned over and over again, at various stages in his career, to the problem of the Petrine Reform. Throughout the greater part of his life his basic attitude remained roughly the same: admiration for Peter's revolutionary transformation of Russia, approval for his programme of Europeanization, recognition of the necessity for violence – and an involuntary repugnance for the methods employed. In 1843 Herzen wrote in his diary:

Peter I was a revolutionary ... He belonged to the new Europe, he implanted it like a barbarian, but he impelled the government onto a track very different from that of the European dynasts: better or worse as the case may be, but certainly different. His was a material, explicit yoke – not rooted in the past, revolutionary and tyrannical, outrunning the country in order to make her develop not in freedom, but under the lash; Europeanism externally, combined with the total absence of humanity on the inside ... The whip and the axe were instilling humanism in Russia.[28]

In 1857, at the height of his revolutionary agitation, Herzen wrote in *Revolution in Russia*: 'Russia has once had a fundamental revolution: it was made by one man – Peter I ... Peter carried within himself alone that unforeseen, new Russia which he brought into being, sternly and harshly, against the will of the people, sustained by his autocratic powers and personal force.'[29] No trace here of the undisguised relish with which Belinsky – or Chernyshevsky and many other Populists after him – described the use of violence and brute force in modernizing

Russia, no intimation that a self-appointed intellectual élite should compel the people to do what was best for them, whether they liked it or not.

Essentially it was this dislike of compulsion and of the State that set Herzen apart from the archetypal Populists: the *raznochintsy*, the Men of the Sixties. He always remained a libertarian, an anti-Statist, almost an anarchist; believing the Russian people to be 'un-political', he himself took little interest in political solutions for the country's problems. Politics, he believed, would in fact only distract attention from the sole task that really mattered: the establishment of a just and free socialist society. But towards the end of his life Herzen began to realize that the ideas he had evolved and propagated over twenty years – the rejection of the Western road, the concept of peasant socialism based on the *obshchina*, the idealization of the 'people' – had been taken over and shaped into the ideological basis of a political movement with whose aims and methods he felt very little affinity. His was a tragedy that was to be repeated many times in the history of the Russian revolutionary movement. Herzen had produced the fundamental social theories of Populism; the emergence of Populism as the comprehensive socio-political ideology of a powerful political movement was largely the work of Nikolai Gavrilovich Chernyshevsky.

CHAPTER 12

The Second Generation: Chernyshevsky

It would be hard to imagine two men less similar than Herzen and Chernyshevsky. Although the most important and prolific period of both their creative lives was that of the 1850s, they belonged to different generations. Chernyshevsky, born in 1828, was Herzen's junior by sixteen years. But it was not simply a matter of years: the two men belonged to contrasting periods of Russian history – Herzen to pre-Reform Russia, Chernyshevsky to the post-1861 era. Herzen represents the Men of the Forties, Chernyshevsky the *raznochintsy* of the Sixties. From whatever angle of personality or background we examine them, the dissimilarity is striking. By origin and upbringing the one came from the wealthy landowning nobility, the other from a humble provincial clergyman's family. One lived the life of an affluent gentleman of leisure, journeying through Europe, hobnobbing with the great; the other lived in constant drudgery, striving to make ends meet, hardly ever travelling outside Russia – and spending his last twenty-five years in penal servitude and remote exile. One wrote easily and elegantly, the other in a pedestrian and verbose style. One was broad-minded, libertarian, unprejudiced, moderate; the other sectarian, intolerant, conspiratorial, extremist. Not unnaturally, there was never any mutual personal sympathy, yet they were both Socialists. Between them they came to typify the fusion of the two component elements of Russian Populism. But in the years to come the dominating influence was Chernyshevsky's.

The secret of Chernyshevsky's spell over the minds and imaginations of young Russians of his own and succeeding generations is at first sight difficult to understand. He had hardly any personal charm, his books were dull, his ideas possessed little originality, and he himself was singularly unconcerned about his personal popularity or public appeal. Yet, with the sole exception of Lenin, no man had a greater or more enduring influence upon the development of the Russian revolutionary movement – and hence, arguably, upon the course of world history. During the short period of his active political life he became the recognized leader of the radical intelligentsia – his departure from the scene transformed him into their oracle and inspiration.

To the European reader Chernyshevsky seems destined to remain a mystery. Were one to plough through the interminable dreary expanses of his prose – and such an undertaking would require fortitude and devotion of the highest order – one would hardly emerge with much more than infinite exhaustion and a feeling of bewilderment: could this really be the *oeuvre* that launched a thousand revolutionary enterprises and served to change the face of our world? Indeed it is – only it has never travelled well. Unlike the works of any other political philosopher of comparable stature (including such compatriots as Bakunin, Kropotkin or Herzen), nearly all Chernyshevsky's writings have remained untranslated and unread in the West, despite the huge publicity given them by the Soviet government since 1917. (The only foreign lands where Chernyshevsky gained converts to the revolutionary cause were the then strongly Russophile Balkans.) His works, his ideas were suited to meet the specific problems of an exceptional type of society at a particular moment in time – and fashioned to reach a very uncommon kind of reader. But this was all he ever aimed at, and among his chosen audience his success was phenomenal. The Russian intelligentsia, as has already been said, represented a state of mind, and Chernyshevsky's writings fitted it exactly, in form and content alike. In order to receive his message, to absorb it and to transform it into action, one had to be a member of that strange community, one had to be on the same wavelength. And, of particular importance, the appearance of Chernyshevsky's message coincided in time with the entry of the intelligentsia upon the historical stage; Chernyshevsky gave it the ideological charge which set it on its way. The charge has not been exhausted yet.

So powerful was the magic of Chernyshevsky's writings that what in a Western publicist would have been a disability became in Russia a source of strength. He was primarily a literary critic, it was through the medium of critical articles and book reviews that his ideas reached the public, and he has long been regarded as the greatest among the brilliant array of Russian literary critics. Yet he possessed none of Belinsky's infectious passion, of Herzen's stylistic grace, of Dobrolyubov's penetrating power of analysis, of Pisarev's mordant wit. What is even stranger, one feels that he had no genuine love for, or understanding of, literature as such. In 1854 the promising young critic had been invited to join the staff of the literary monthly *Sovremennik* (The Contemporary) by its publisher-editor, the famous radical poet Nekrasov. Within a short time Chernyshevsky, a man of immense industry and application, had taken over most of the editorial work from the indolent and dissipated poet – much to the latter's relief. As his closest collaborator Chernyshevsky installed his intimate friend Nikolai Alexandrovich Dobrolyubov, a youth with a clerical background similar to his own, who was then only eighteen. Taking advantage of the changed political atmosphere of the new reign, the two made *Sovremennik* into the most powerful and hard-hitting organ of radical opinion that had yet existed in Russia. Whereas Herzen's appeal was directed mainly at the country's Westernized 'establishment', *Sovremennik* became the rallying centre for the emerging generation of young *raznochintsy*. It spoke their language and expressed the ideas towards which they were groping; the journal became the gospel, and Chernyshevsky and Dobrolyubov the idols of the Men of the Sixties – the determinant generation of Russian revolutionaries.

Nekrasov was not unhappy about his journal's increased popularity and circulation; nor did he necessarily disagree with Chernyshevsky's political views. But what caused him mounting discomfort and distress was the bitter, vituperative, uncompromising tone adopted by the journal, and its palpably dogmatic, even hostile attitude towards the purely artistic aspect of literature. Unable to contain his misgivings, he wrote to Turgenev: 'Chernyshevsky is an able and useful fellow, only extremely one-sided; he feels something like hatred, or rather contempt towards imaginative literature, and in only one year he has managed to impress the journal with the stamp of monotony and narrow-mindedness.'[1] Turgenev, originally well-intentioned towards Chernyshevsky, now needed no convincing: having been several times savagely attacked by *Sovremennik*, he expressed his indignation in no uncertain terms. Meeting Chernyshevsky, he bluntly informed him that 'You are a common snake, while Dobrolyubov is a cobra'.[2] For Turgenev this was not just a matter of a personal affront – his apprehensions went much deeper. He explained them in a conversation with friends: 'Dobrolyubov's articles display the inquisitorial method of ridiculing and besmirching every enthusiasm, every noble impulse of the writer's soul; he worships materialism and emotional aridity, and insolently jeers at poetry.'[3] To Tolstoy he wrote: '*Sovremennik* is in bad hands – of this there can be no doubt.'[4] As for Tolstoy himself, he had already told Nekrasov, in the vigorous language of the former Guardsman: 'This bedbug-smelling gentleman [Chernyshevsky] is a public disgrace.'[5] Much to Nekrasov's unhappiness, soon after Chernyshevsky took over *Sovremennik* the two greatest Russian novelists of their time broke off all connections with the journal.

Vanity and touchiness are qualities by no means foreign to men of letters, and the discord between Chernyshevsky and his country's leading writers could be explained away by such factors were it not for the fact that Chernyshevsky constantly displayed an astonishing insensitivity to literature as such. It was not just the sneering and condescending tone of many of his reviews: quite simply, he was an abysmally bad judge of literary values. In 1877, for instance, in a letter from Siberia, he delivered the following comprehensive verdict: 'Russian literature is still very poor. Our famous poets, Pushkin and

Lermontov, were no more than feeble imitators of Byron – this nobody would deny. We are very proud of Gogol. But he is an insignificant figure compared to Dickens or Fielding or Sterne, to say nothing of such humorists as Rabelais or Voltaire.'[6] This judgment was passed during the greatest period of Russian literature, a period which for sheer concentration of genius can only be compared with the Elizabethan Age, when Tolstoy and Dostoevsky – to name but two – had just written their finest novels; coming from an eminent literary critic and a sincere patriot, it is an incredible statement.

And here we are face to face with the mystery of Chernyshevsky. In any other country this complete lack of aesthetic perception would instantly have disqualified him as a literary critic. In Russia, on the contrary, it was precisely his unconcern for literary values, his strictly utilitarian approach and his impatience with what he regarded as entirely irrelevant considerations that made him the supreme interpreter of Russian life and literature for the youthful and radical intelligentsia. They had had enough of their elders' preoccupation with Art and Beauty; they wanted to be rid of these frills and fancies, and to get to grips with the cruel world of injustice and misery that surrounded them. In Chernyshevsky they found their natural leader, the codifier of their moral laws, the omniscient authority on every problem of life. From this pinnacle no one could topple him: neither disgruntled authors nor political police.

Many Western students have been baffled by the incongruous spectacle of an eminent literary critic who was oblivious of the central nature of artistic creation. But the main reason why non-Russians find it difficult to gauge the full extent of Chernyshevsky's influence upon his country's social and intellectual development lies elsewhere. However strange it may sound, Chernyshevsky's impregnable dominance over the hearts and minds of the Russian intelligentsia was established primarily not through his critical essays or his ponderous philosophical and sociological writings but through a novel. Called *What Is to Be Done?*, it was, by any reckoning, one of the most appallingly bad novels ever published, either in Russia or in any other country. The plot is implausible, melodramatic and mawkishly sentimental, the characters lifeless and artificial, the composition primitive, the language wooden, and the whole suffused with an unbearably condescending didacticism. And yet, from its first appearance and down to the present day, it has been the most popular, widely read and potent work of Russian fiction, eclipsing anything written by the greatest masters of the novel.

What Is to Be Done? was written in 1863, in prison. As it was a work of fiction the affable censor passed it without a second thought – swayed partly by its palpable mediocrity – and *Sovremennik* promptly published the latest work of their ex-editor, then undergoing interrogation on charges of high treason and sedition. The book created an instantaneous sensation. It swept the board. The few critical voices which drew attention to its inadequacy were drowned by a massive adulatory chorus. Never had Russia known literary success on such a scale – and never was Chernyshevsky's conviction of the unimportance of talent or literary mastery more strikingly confirmed. *What Is to Be Done?* became the Bible of the radical intelligentsia, of the *raznochintsy*, of Russian youth in every succeeding generation. It gave them their beliefs, their morals, their ideals. It instilled in them the idea of an inevitable revolution, and it educated the men who were to carry it out. In the turbulent half-century that followed the publication of Chernyshevsky's novel, practically everyone who joined the revolutionary movement – whether Populist or Marxist, propagandist or terrorist, supporter of the peasantry or of the working class – was profoundly influenced by it. And for much of this time, it must be added, the novel was officially banned (the censors had soon realized their mistake).

'For Russian youth,' wrote the famous anarchist Pyotr Kropotkin, 'the novel came as a revelation; it became their programme . . . None of Turgenev's novels, not one of the works of Tolstoy or any other writer ever had anything like the widespread and deep influence of Chernyshevsky's novel upon Russian youth. It became the banner of Russian youth.'[7]

Even more valuable is the opinion of the ordinarily calm and level-headed Plekhanov, who, besides being the founder of Russian Marxism, enjoys a distinguished reputation as a historian and literary critic:

> Is there anyone who has not read and re-read this famous work? Is there anyone who was not attracted by it and who has not become, under its beneficial influence, purer, better, sounder and braver . . .? From it we have all derived both moral strength and faith in a brighter future.
>
> Our obscurantists have often pointed out the novel's lack of artistic merits, its manifest tendentiousness. On the face of it these strictures are justified: the novel is indeed extremely tendentious and has very few artistic merits. But can anybody name at least one among the most brilliant and truly artistic works of Russian literature which, in the degree of its influence upon the moral and intellectual development of the country, might rival *What Is to Be Done?* Nobody could name such a work, because there has never been, and probably never will be anything like it. From the first appearance of the printing press in Russia and down to the present day no publication has ever had a success similar to that of *What Is to Be Done?*[8]

The novel made large numbers of young men and women choose revolution as their vocation. And not only in Russia – it had a similar effect upon the youthful intelligentsia of the Balkan nations. The Serbian conspirators, who in June 1914 assassinated the Austrian Archduke Franz Ferdinand and thus precipitated the First World War, were virtually nurtured upon it. According to one of their number, 'Chernyshevsky's *What Is to Be Done?* was passed from hand to hand. Whole pages from it were copied and learned by heart.'[9] Such famous leaders of the Bulgarian revolutionary (and later Communist) movement as Dimitr Blagoev and Georgy Dimitrov have described how their whole lives were changed by reading Chernyshevsky's novel.

What is the secret of the perennial fascination exercised by the novel upon a certain type of person living in a particular environment? At first glance the book appears to be concerned mainly with that favourite subject of progressive nineteenth-century authors: the emancipation of women from their age-old social, economic and sexual shackles. But Chernyshevsky was highly skilled in the traditional Russian art of using an innocuous-sounding text to convey a variety of covert meanings, easily comprehensible to those who possessed the necessary key. To the initiated, *What Is to Be Done?* was a novel about socialism and socialists. The socialist society of the future is described in dream-sequences interposed into the main body of the book. It is a heart-warming if somewhat banal picture: a society without inequality, injustice or want; where everything is held in common, and people work short hours in flourishing co-operatives; where the land is covered with lush gardens and beautiful glass palaces, and the air resounds with songs and laughter. For the Western reader, long familiar with joyous Utopian fantasies, nothing to get excited about; for the Russian – the first electrifying glimpse of the promised land. Yet this alone cannot explain the novel's impact.

It was Chernyshevsky's description of the socialists, the revolutionaries and future revolutionaries – the 'New Men', as he called them – that hypnotized the young generation of intelligentsia. Once again, to the Western reader the New Men appear as humourless, smug, priggish fanatics; Russians saw in them a heroic cohort of dedicated, self-sacrificing pioneers of the future. Chernyshevsky's heroes – and especially his favourite, the superman Rakhmetov, who mortified his flesh by sleeping on planks studded with nails, and ate huge quantities of meat to gather strength for the liberating struggle – became the ideal prototypes upon whom generations of young radicals consciously modelled themselves. Within a few short years the New Men had stepped out of the pages of the novel into real life: acquiring flesh and blood, they established secret societies, distributed leaflets, threw bombs, went to the people, trudged to Siberia, ascended the scaffold. They became the men and women of the Russian revolutionary movement. Never has nature imitated art more successfully – and with more pregnant consequences.

To understand the Russian revolutionary, whether Populist or Bolshevik, to comprehend the workings of his mind and to grasp the motives for his behaviour, it is important to have a picture of Chernyshevsky's New Men. They were, needless to say, paragons of virtue – or at least aspired to that condition. They were also – and this was their most important feature – part of an intellectual and moral élite, elevated by nature and their own exertions far above the common run of human being. But they loved ordinary people, whose sorrows they shared, and whom they were going to lead to a brighter and happier future. A few random excerpts from this extraordinary book convey the true flavour of Chernyshevsky's revolutionary *Übermenschen*, those self-proclaimed heroic beings of whom, in their various incarnations, the world has since seen and heard so much.

Chernyshevsky welcomes them as harbingers of a new type of man: 'Kind men and strong, honest and able – it is not long ago that you first began to appear amongst us, but already there are many of you and your number is fast increasing.' 'Each one of them is a courageous, unwavering, unyielding man, capable of tackling a job in such a way that it would never slip out of his hands.' He particularly admires their uniformity: 'They are all cast in the same mould', with them 'everything is cast in the same mould.' They live by their own rules: 'They have their own understanding of everything: of morality, of comfort and sensuality, of good and evil.' Asceticism is a cardinal virtue; as Rakhmetov said, explaining his total abstinence from every pleasure of the flesh, 'This is how it should be. We demand the full enjoyment of life for every man – and we must prove by our lives that we demand this not for ourselves, not for the satisfaction of our private appetites, but for the whole of mankind; that we speak out of principle, not partiality, from conviction, not personal desires.' The discerning reader is left in no doubt as to their main principle: 'the compelling necessity that fills their lives' is the coming revolution, or, as Chernyshevsky calls it out of deference to the censor, 'the common cause'.

Endowed with these exceptional qualities, equipped with an unflinching singleness of purpose, Chernyshevsky's New Men were to constitute a dedicated élite of intellectual and moral leaders of the people, removed 'high above the common run of men', 'superior beings, unapproachable by the likes of you or me'. 'They are still few in numbers, but the lives of all thrive thanks to them; without them life would wither and grow stale; they are few, but thanks to them men can breathe – without them we would suffocate. The mass of good and honest people is limitless, but such men are few; within the mass they are as the caffeine in tea, as the bouquet of a noble wine; they give it its strength and its aroma. They are the flower of the flower of men, the motor of motors, the salt of the salt of the earth.' This was a new race, a race of supermen, called forth to liberate the people and to lead them to salvation: 'In a few years, in a very few years they will be implored: "Save us!" – and whatever they say will be obeyed by all.' And then gradually, step by step, the new demiurgic leaders would raise the rest of humanity, the common herd, up to their own level – and all men, liberated from the shackles that had weighed them down, would become akin to these God-like beings: 'Then this separate species will no longer exist, since everyone will belong to it, and people will hardly believe that there was once a time when it represented an exceptional type of man and not universal human nature.'

This was the essence of Chernyshevsky's message: the need for a new revolutionary élite – ascetic, self-aware, dedicated and disciplined – that would alone be able to lead the Russian people towards the promised land of justice and equality. *What Is to Be Done?* taught the intelligentsia the virtues of socialism; it told them that they were to provide leadership and tutelage, but always unselfishly, in the best interests of the people, and only until such time as the people themselves would be capable of running their own affairs. Its impact was overwhelming: at the outset of the new and bewildering era inaugurated by the recently published Emancipation Decree, it boldly proclaimed the final objective and mapped out the uncharted course ahead. And its spell was vastly reinforced by the fact that it had been written by a man cut off for ever, behind prison walls, from his family and friends, a man who had himself made the supreme sacrifice for the cause.

What Is to Be Done? nurtured three or more generations of Russian revolutionaries; Chernyshevsky's other writings, published legally, and at great length, in *Sovremennik* provided them with a basic Populist body of doctrine. Its main theoretical feature was the thesis (originated by Herzen) that Russia could, and should, avoid the capitalist stage of development and leap directly from her present condition into socialism. 'Is it inevitable,' asked Chernyshevsky in the guarded style imposed upon him by the censor, 'is it inevitable that a social phenomenon should pass, in the life of each society, through every single point of its development? Might it not, under favourable circumstances, leap from the first or second stage direct to the fifth or sixth, omitting all the intermediate stages?'[10] He answered the first question with a resounding No, the second with a no less resounding Yes. Western capitalism, he repeatedly declared, was a system even more evil, fraught with even greater hardships and misery for the masses, than the state of affairs in Russia. Why, was not the Russian peasant, who could at least boast of a full belly, better off than the undernourished and overworked English factory-hand? Proletarianization was not an acceptable solution.

Fortunately the means of salvation were at hand. Chernyshevsky, like Herzen, saw in the *obshchina* Russia's invaluable advantage over the West, the earnest of her speedy transition to socialism:

It is not easy to renounce even an insignificant portion of whatever one has grown used to, and in the West the individual has already become accustomed to the illimitability of private rights ... In the West a better economic order is associated with sacrifices, and therefore its introduction is a matter of great difficulty ...

But that which in one country seems a Utopia, exists in another as a fact of life ... Those habits, the inculcation of which into the people's life appear inordinately difficult to the Englishman or Frenchman, already exist for the Russian as an actual fact of his people's life ... The popular mass continues to regard the land as communal property. The state of affairs which the West is now endeavouring to attain along a lengthy and arduous path, still prevails in our country – in the majestic popular custom of our village life ...

Changes in our economic system are inevitable. But whatever these transformations, may we never dare to lay a finger on the sacred and beneficial custom bequeathed to us by our past, the precious heirloom which alone richly recompenses us for all the past misery: may we never dare infringe upon the communal holding of land. Today the prosperity of the agricultural classes of Western Europe depends entirely upon their acquisition of this boon. Their fate should serve us as warning.[11]

Yet although Russia was situated in a uniquely favourable position with regard to socialism, which she would undoubtedly achieve sooner than the capitalist West, the socialist millennium would not arrive by itself. It could only come about as the result of a cataclysmic upheaval, a violent revolution. Here it was that Chernyshevsky parted company with Herzen. Force, and force alone, was in his conviction the midwife of the new society. In Russia, of course, this could never be said openly: to convey his meaning Chernyshevsky had to substitute 'revolution' by euphemisms like 'the common cause' or 'certain periods of history' or 'great historical events'. It was quite sufficient for anyone initiated into the arcana of Russian radical thought.

Chernyshevsky's impassioned belief in the violent overthrow of the existing order, even at the cost of widespread suffering and anarchy, was best reflected in his diaries. Here is a fairly typical extract:

> Perish, and the sooner the better; let the people enter unprepared into their rights: they will prepare themselves much faster in the course of the struggle, but until you [the Tsarist regime] have fallen they can never become prepared . . . Let there be oppression of one class by another – then the struggle will begin, then the victims will realize that they are being oppressed under the present system, but that there can be another system, under which they will no longer be oppressed . . . Better anarchy *d'en bas* than *d'en haut*, because then at least there can be no such inhuman relationships – understand, not actions, but relationships, which is far more important.[12]

The doctrine of a necessary revolution from below was a startling innovation in Russian political thought. It had been held by neither the Decembrists nor Herzen – the possibility of a peaceful transformation from above was at that time entertained even by 'wild men' like Bakunin. But there was no room for compromise in Chernyshevsky's scheme of things: with relentless perseverance he drove the idea of revolution into the minds of his ever-growing circle of disciples and admirers. By every means at his disposal – veiled references in scholarly articles, stormy debates at endless intellectual tea-parties, quiet conspiratorial meetings with obscure young students – he hammered the lesson home. The intelligentsia was small in size: at that stage it was sufficient for his message to get through to a few thousand young men and women already eagerly awaiting some such message. And get through it did: from Chernyshevsky's day onwards the belief in the unique cleansing properties of violent social upheaval took firm root in the fertile soil of nineteenth-century Russia. The revolutionist principle became the central article of faith in the creed of the Populist intelligentsia.

The principle of revolution for the people and of the people – but not by the people. It was to be carried out on the people's behalf by the élite of 'thinking individuals', the New Men. The idea of anarchy *d'en bas*, of a vast elemental peasant insurrection like those of Pugachev or Stenka Razin, was an appealing democratic concept, but Chernyshevsky, the first great Russian revolutionary realist, had no illusions about the ability of the downtrodden, illiterate, superstitious peasant mass to effect a geniune transformation of the political, social and economic scene. 'The mass of the population knows nothing and cares about nothing except its material advantages,' he wrote. 'This indifference of the mass is the main factor which makes possible the very idea of changes in political life . . . The mass is simply the raw material for diplomatic and political experiments. Whoever rules it tells it what to do, and it obeys.'[13] Clearly, therefore, the leading role of the revolutionary élite was by no means over once the old order had been overthrown. On the contrary, its most important task – that of directing the nation's efforts towards the construction of a new society – would only just have begun. The new state would be enlightened, egalitarian, socialistic, plebeian, and possess all manner of agreeable features into the bargain – but there was no question of it remaining, for a considerable time, anything but authoritarian (even if benevolently so). Chernyshevsky's views on the political structure of the post-revolutionary State, as expressed in numerous pronouncements – particularly in the latter period of his life – were well summed up by his biographer, Steklov: 'The minority that identifies its cause with the cause of the people must take advantage of favourable circumstances to seize state power, to institute a revolutionary dictatorship, and to utilize the powerful mechanism of State in the interests of the popular masses.'[14] Such a revolutionary dictatorship, assured of popular support, would then, by a series of decrees, establish socialism and gradually transform the nation's outlook and way of life.

In view of Chernyshevsky's quite explicit (and already quoted) attitude to individual liberty and political rights – which he regarded as no more than 'political desserts' – it is somewhat odd that in the West he should often be treated as a devoted libertarian. Indeed, the most eminent Western student of Russian Populism, Professor Franco Venturi, declares that Chernyshevsky 'remained constant in his love of liberty',[15] and unswerving in his opposition to despotism, of whatever variety. 'Liberty', however, means many things to many men, and Chernyshevsky's usage of the word was undoubtedly different from ours. When he spoke of liberty he was little concerned with nebulous – and, to him, irrelevant – concepts of individual rights or legal guarantees: he meant freedom from class oppression. To describe Chernyshevsky's political views as libertarian in any meaningful sense of the word is to misrepresent them.

What the student is up against here is a phenomenon that has become increasingly familiar in our age of specious 'consensus' and superficial 'convergence': the general acceptance by widely dissimilar political systems and schools of thought of identical terms of reference, which accordingly come to bear a variety of discordant and often incompatible meanings. 'Democracy', 'freedom', 'peace', 'liberation', 'independence', 'revolution', are among the first that spring to mind. This semantic confusion has often been reflected in assessments of Chernyshevsky and his Populist followers. Chernyshevsky called himself a democrat, and 'revolutionary democrat' is the way he has usually been described since in Russian literature. To the Western reader the designation, although entirely correct, can easily prove misleading. The concept of democracy, as generally interpreted and implemented in Western societies, has at its heart one or another of such closely related principles as government by consent; government by persons freely chosen by, and responsible to, the governed; the sovereignty of the people; majority rule. Or, in other words, the theory and practice of responsible parliamentary government, based on universal suffrage and evolved, in its various forms, over the past two centuries. But this is by no means the only tenable definition of democracy.

When Chernyshevsky referred to himself and his adherents as democrats he was using the word in its original Jacobin sense. Democracy for him meant much the same as it had for Rousseau, Robespierre and Saint-Just, namely the expression of the General Will, directed at the achievement of the Common Good, the ultimate realization of which was to come in the Republic of Virtue. The Common Good, of course, was not expected to coincide with the private interests of all individual members of the community; these would have to be overridden in the name of the General Will. Jacobin democracy, unlike parliamentary democracy, was primarily concerned not with liberty, but with equality. The two principles were far from identical. The furtherance of the General Will inevitably entailed dictatorship – in Robespierre's words, 'the despotism of liberty against tyranny' – which would force the people, if need be, to enjoy the Common Good, which they might otherwise be incapable of comprehending.

This was democracy of a sort: the variety that has been aptly described in our days by J. L. Talmon as 'totalitarian democracy'. One cannot but conclude, with all due allowance for the distinctive Russian influences, that Chernyshevsky's social and political views fall into a broadly similar pattern. But being much more of a practical politician (and possibly also of an honest thinker) than Rousseau, Chernyshevsky made no attempt to evade the crucial issue of who was going to interpret the General Will and lay down the guidelines of the Common Good. His answer was commendably explicit and to the point: the function of leadership would be exercised by the revolutionary minority, the New Men.

Indeed, Chernyshevsky's concept of democracy specifically excluded the traditional libertarian beliefs of enlightened Western liberalism. His most venomous assaults were reserved for liberal reformers and their objectives of political freedom, deliberately designed to hoodwink the masses into accepting continued class exploitation: 'Without them, without these men who have so assiduously established their reputation as liberals and democrats, the reactionaries would have been helpless.'[16]

Liberalism, reform, compromise, humanitarianism, philanthropy – Chernyshevsky transformed these words into terms of contempt, synonyms for treachery, symbols of moral degradation.

Chernyshevsky had no time for liberalism: the realization of his eschatological vision could only come through violence and sacrifice. Like other Russian radicals before him, he found supreme inspiration in the titanic feats of the 'crowned revolutionary', Peter the Great.

> For us the ideal patriot is Peter the Great; we find our highest ideal of patriotism expressed in the passionate, boundless devotion to the good of the country, which inspired the life and animated the actions of this great man ... Every Russian must seek to promote, to the limit of his abilities, the work that was begun by Peter the Great. This cause still requires, and will long continue to require, the entire intellectual and moral faculties of our country's most gifted sons. A Russian who possesses both mind and heart can never become anything other than a patriot in the mould of Peter the Great.[17]

These lines bear eloquent testimony to one principal mainspring of Chernyshevsky's revolutionary activity: his intense patriotism. He sought the perfect socialist society not only because he wanted to better the lot of suffering mankind – he wanted it for *Russia*, for the *Russian* people, for *his* people. His was the most quintessentially national among all the great figures of the nineteenth-century revolutionary tradition. Unlike the Decembrists or the Westerners, he did not derive his ideology from abroad; unlike Herzen, he spent all his life in Russia; unlike Bakunin, he was never concerned with foreign revolutionary movements; unlike many of the Men of the Sixties, he abhorred national nihilism. He was a doctrinaire, but his doctrine was Russian.

The secret of Chernyshevsky's lasting influence upon Russian political development lies partly in the authentic national quality of his writings. There were other reasons as well: his ideas appeared at exactly the right moment, when Russia had reached a great watershed in her history; as the perfect embodiment of the intelligentsia, by origin, upbringing and outlook, he could become the most faithful interpreter of their thoughts and emotions; the philosophy of Populism, largely formulated by him, unquestionably fitted Russian reality far better than any other competing ideology. The personal example set by Chernyshevsky – the immeasurable devotion to the popular cause, the stoicism with which he faced his judges, the willing acceptance of martyrdom – was itself an invaluable contribution to the revolutionary mystique. He endowed the revolution with its most potent legend. The writings of the critic Chernyshevsky could be freely attacked – the ideas of the martyr Chernyshevsky became sacrosanct. For the Russian intelligentsia Chernyshevsky's tragic fate was marked by the stigmata of sanctity. It placed the seal of inviolability upon his authority. Even the liberals and the moderates, the objects of his vitriolic abuse, all had to recognize his paramountcy. To do otherwise, to disavow his teachings, meant accepting the judgment of the Tsarist tyranny, meant *objectively* allying oneself to 'the dark forces of reaction' – and that, of course, would be unthinkable.

It was a fateful choice. By embracing the martyred Chernyshevsky as the symbol of their common cause, the intelligentsia as a whole, including its moderate wing, was inexorably led, step by step, towards acceptance of the man's doctrines. This was a portent of the future, a foretaste of every undignified capitulation to radicalism that was to be made by the intelligentsia in the next fifty or sixty years. Inherent in the intelligentsia was the conviction that any enemy of the regime, whatever his views, was by definition an ally, to be supported, justified, defended. If ever an occasional doubt arose regarding the true nature of some such 'ally's' ideas or the possible consequences of their implementation, the dilemma would be soon resolved: nothing mattered but the overthrow of the Tsarist regime.

For hundreds of thousands of men and women, reading Chernyshevsky became a revelation, an emotional experience that changed the course of their lives. One of these readers was a seventeen-year-old schoolboy in the little town of Simbirsk, Vladimir Ulyanov. Years later, in conversation with a fellow-revolutionary, Lenin described the profound impression made upon him by *What Is to Be Done?*: 'It had fascinated my brother and then it fascinated me. It completely reshaped me . . . This is a book that gives one a charge for a lifetime.'[18] Upon the young Lenin it certainly produced an effect that never wore off. The influence of *What Is to Be Done?* can clearly be traced in many of his later writings, particularly in his lyrical descriptions of the future socialist society. When in 1902 he produced his most important book, in which for the first time he laid down the organizational principles of the Bolshevik Party, he published it under the same title as Chernyshevsky's novel. Indeed, much of what he said there about the new type of dedicated professional revolutionary reads almost like a more level-headed and systematic representation of Chernyshevsky's New Men.

Throughout his life Lenin's attitude to Chernyshevsky bordered on hero-worship. He invariably spoke of Chernyshevsky with a genuine love and admiration usually missing from his more matter-of-fact references to Marx; any aspersion cast upon his idol would call forth his utmost displeasure. His most cherished possessions included Chernyshevsky's portrait and a set of collected works, which he frequently reread and often quoted with great reverence. For Lenin, Chernyshevsky was 'the greatest representative of Utopian socialism in Russia', 'the all-Russian revolutionary democrat'.[19] He was the model whom every revolutionary should strive to emulate:

> Chernyshevsky was a much more consistent and militant democrat [than Herzen]. The spirit of class struggle emanates from his works. He was uncompromising in unmasking the treachery of liberalism . . . Despite his Utopian socialism he was a marvellously profound critic of capitalism . . .

But Chernyshevsky was not only a Utopian socialist. He was also a revolutionary democrat: he succeeded in influencing all the political events of his time in a revolutionary spirit, despite the blocks and obstacles of censorship, by conveying the idea of a peasant revolution, of a mass struggle for the overthrow of all the old authorities.[20]

With his unerring political instinct Lenin had grasped, probably better than anybody else, the vital and truly original aspect of Chernyshevsky's revolutionary doctrine. A Bolshevik colleague, Vorovsky, recorded some of his remarks on the subject:

Chernyshevsky's greatest virtue lay not only in showing that every right-minded and decent person is obliged to become a revolutionary, but in something even more important: in describing what the revolutionary had to be like, what rules he had to adhere to, how he should advance towards his aim, by what methods and means he was to achieve its fulfilment.[21]

A better assessment of Chernyshevsky's contribution to the Russian revolutionary tradition could hardly be made. Chernyshevsky's main ideas – the necessity of violent revolution, Russia's readiness for revolution, the leadership of an élite group of dedicated revolutionaries, the perniciousness of liberalism and political democracy, the justification of means by ends – were to have greater influence upon Russian historical development than those of any man before him. His works became the primer of revolutionary theory and practice for generations of rebels from the intelligentsia.

CHAPTER 13

Nihilists

On 19 February 1861, after lengthy meditation in the seclusion of his study, Emperor Alexander II signed the Emancipation Decree. Under its terms twenty-three million peasants received their personal liberty and full equality of status with every other Russian subject. The nearly century-old argument about emancipation with or without land had ended in a compromise: the former serfs were granted the larger part of the land they had worked, but only at a price considerably higher than its actual market value. This was justified by the necessity to compensate the *pomeshchiki* for the loss, not so much of the land itself, as of the gratuitous labour rendered them since time immemorial. The huge sum involved was to be advanced to the landlords by the State, which would then recover it from the peasants by means of fixed annual 'redemption payments' over a period of years. There were a great many other details of a highly technical nature in the decree, but at that moment, it seemed, only one thing mattered; the Statute of Bondage was no more, slavery had finally been abolished.

To the Emperor himself, to educated Russian society, to the bewildered peasants and to a gratified outside world, the act of 19 February marked the dawn of a new era of progress and prosperity – away from the gloomy Muscovite past and on to the sunlit uplands of European civilization. The rapturous mood of the day was expressed by the famous historian Pogodin, himself a former serf: 'Russians, fall on your knees! Send up your prayers to God! Give thanks to God for this supreme, incomparable joy, for this unprecedented universal emotion, for this magnificent new page that adorns our national history!'[1] It was the miracle that all Russians had been eagerly awaiting, and like any other miracle it was expected to transform everything around it in a trice. And when it became apparent that the millennium was not to be achieved overnight, disillusionment set in.

Yet after the exaggerated expectations had faded away, as the years passed and Russia haltingly and uncertainly moved along the path of modernization, it became ever clearer that the Emancipation Decree had indeed inaugurated a new era. By any standards other than those of Russia's requirements the changes instituted during the next decade, the 'Epoch of the great reforms', made up an impressive aggregate. Potentially the most significant of these reforms was the introduction of a structure of limited local self-government; district and provincial assemblies or *Zemstvos*, elected by a complicated system of three electoral colleges of the nobility, townsmen and peasants. Although their authority was restricted to such prosaic activities as public health, famine relief, education, road-building, etc., the *Zemstvos* – and the similarly constituted city *Dumas* – gradually grew in importance as the sole semi-independent areas of public life, the breeding-grounds of liberal and reforming sentiment.

The legal reforms of the 1860s introduced, for the first time in Russian history, a modern judiciary system based upon West European models. Its most important provisions were trial by jury, the irremovability of judges, an orderly structure of appeals courts, and the establishment of an independent Bar. The army reform did away with the barbaric system of selective conscription for a term of twenty-five years, replacing it by six years' universal military service. A number of other measures were adopted: the abolition of corporal punishment and the branding of convicts; the granting of a degree of autonomy to the universities; the alleviation of censorship.

The reforms of Alexander II, even the emancipation of the serfs, can hardly be said to have brought about a radical transformation of Russian society and its traditional political system. But after the decades of hopeless immobility, after the centuries of Muscovite stagnation behind a pseudo-European façade, a genuine start had at last been made. Unlike the reforms of Peter the Great, this time the government was not merely grafting European technological and administrative methods on to a changeless social order; what was being changed was the very fabric of society. Time was needed, time for the reforms to take root, time for the new class structure to emerge, time for industrial development to burgeon and for semi-Asiatic ways of life to be overcome. And time, as many felt even then, was the commodity of which Russia had the shortest supply of all.

19 February 1861 inaugurated Russia's period of capitalist development. It was to last fifty-six years, almost to the day. This was an eventful period, filled with activity of every kind, rich in achievement, during which Russia progressed far more rapidly than in the whole preceding century and a half. Yet over this doomed age, over its people, its events, its literature, its successes and failures, there hangs the pervasive atmosphere of a desperate race against time. Were one to define the dominating theme of these last fifty-six years of pre-revolutionary Russia, it would be in terms of a race between modernization and revolution. Which would happen first: the reconstruction of the country along modern, broadly European capitalist lines – or the revolutionary cataclysm so often forecast? The problem was posed, sharp and clear, alike by the revolutionaries, who constantly stressed the imperative necessity of forestalling capitalism and constitutionalism, and by the more prescient among the Imperial statesmen, men like Pobedonostsev, Witte and Stolypin.

Today, when everyone knows the answer to this all-important question, we can see most of the personalities and events that filled the public stage of Russian history between 1861 and 1917 for the irrelevances that they turned out to be. To say this is not to reflect upon the ability or the good intentions of the public figures, the merits of their activities, or the contemporary significance of political events in Russia. But from the point of view of the present day, nothing of this matters in the slightest; neither the voluminous legislation, nor the famous statesmen, the governmental transactions, the power struggles, the great political *causes célèbres*, the whole pomp and circumstance of a mighty empire. It is a vanished world, an object of purely antiquarian curiosity. There are no parallels in modern European history for the totality of its eclipse. Even the French *ancien régime* did not disappear with so little trace. The past is of importance to us primarily because it has shaped the present; we look to history for an explanation of the world in which we live. Just as the palaeontologist puts together the fossilized bones of extinct animals in order to find their place in the evolutionary tree, so the historian sifts his facts to establish the lines of continuity in the development of human society. The nearer we approach our own age, the more obvious the relationships become. Probably the only exception to this is the Russia of the recent past, of the period between reform and revolution: it was an evolutionary dead end, with no continuation.

For the last half-century of its existence the Russian Empire was locked in a mortal struggle with the revolutionary movement. At the time this appeared to be only a very minor – indeed, almost unknown – aspect of its life, completely overshadowed by far more momentous happenings. It seemed ridiculous to think of these tiny groups of young people, constantly harassed by the police, divorced from reality, lacking all contacts and influence, as a menace to the stability and order of one of the most powerful countries in the world. Yet from the vantage-point of the present what really mattered then in Russia were not the imperial manifestoes but the illegal leaflets, not the cabinet ministers but the revolutionary propagandists, not the court cabals but the terrorist groups, not political and social progress but the development of revolutionary ideology. Goliath may have been a very imposing giant, but it was David who won, and who then went on to found his own dynasty.

This dénouement was possibly not quite as unexpected in Russia herself as in the outside world. For many years the air had been filled with prophecies, either gloomy or exultant, regarding the inevitability of a great historical catastrophe. A large part of the educated class, namely the radical intelligentsia, growing ever more disaffected, was convinced that Russia's problems could only be solved by root and branch revolution. To them everything that happened in Russia since 1861, indeed beginning with the Emancipation Decree itself, supported this conviction. They could never be placated – not that anyone in government ever thought it necessary to placate them. The ceaseless struggle between government and revolution was a fight to the finish; it was conducted out of sight, deep underground, only rarely erupting to the surface in the form of some successful assassination attempt or muted political trial. But the outcome of this secret war, this ludicrously mismatched encounter, was to be of far greater importance to the world than any of the spectacular and much-publicized military contests that attracted international attention in those years.

Ironically, it was the emancipation of the serfs, the fulfilment of the age-old progressive dream, that really launched the Populist movement. Too many hopes had been pinned to the reform, too much had been expected of it too rapidly for its actual advent to produce anything but a feeling of disenchantment and letdown. With expectations keyed up to an ever-rising emotional pitch ever since the young Emperor had first proclaimed his intention of emancipating the serfs, public opinion was deeply disappointed by the hard terms imposed upon the peasants, and incensed by the heavy-handed manner in which the decree was proclaimed – after a fortnight's delay, with extraordinary police precautions and large military forces patrolling the major cities. The government, it was felt, had now shot its bolt – and failed. It had had its chance, and now nothing more could be expected from that quarter. Other ways and means would have to be devised.

The main battle-lines of a war that was to go on for decades were drawn within a few months of the Emancipation Decree. In September 1861, for the first time in Russian history, the St Petersburg students openly proclaimed their defiance of the regime. The trouble started over new university regulations, but the students' meetings and manifestoes soon took on a radical political colour. When, after a few hectic days, the authorities closed down the lecture-rooms, the students paraded in orderly fashion through the streets of the capital. Such a thing had never happened before, and many foreign onlookers thought it to be the beginning of a revolution (as, in a sense, it was). The authorities vacillated between concessions and punishments, and meanwhile the new-found student leaders – some of them closely connected with Chernyshevsky and *Sovremennik* – kept the place in an uproar for many months. Although the majority of the students soon felt that they had had enough, it was impressed upon them that breaking ranks was equivalent to betraying the cause of progress and supporting the forces of reaction. St Petersburg University remained closed down for the better part of two years, and the radical student *raznochintsy* scored their first success.

The most significant feature of the Russian students' strike was the wholehearted support it enjoyed among the intelligentsia of the capital. By that time the prevailing climate of opinion was already such that any political action against the government, whatever its nature and cause, attracted automatic approval. Some of the professors – all high-ranking government officials – even banded together in a 'free university' to enable the rebellious students to continue with their studies – until they themselves were denounced as liberal traitors by their inconsiderate charges.

The general mood was well described by Professor Nikitenko, a not unsympathetic observer. In his diary he noted that all the country's institutions of higher education, in the capitals and provinces alike, sided with the revolutionary outbreak. 'All the liberal theoreticians and journalists are also on their side . . . This is a symptom of the revolutionary fever that has taken possession of numerous facile and effusive minds. It is a perfectly understandable phenomenon, but it should be opposed intelligently and energetically, otherwise it will lead to anarchy.' A few days later he remarked: 'To speak ill of the government, to accuse it of every possible crime, has become the fashion today.'[2] Once established, this fashion remained unchanged for over half a century.

September 1861 was an important landmark in the

development of revolutionary Populism – in more ways than one. The student disorders in St Petersburg coincided with the appearance of the first illegal proclamation which sweepingly rejected emancipation from above, together with the Tsarist regime and all its works, and went on to call for peasant revolution led by the intelligentsia. Its author was Mikhail Mikhailov, a young poet and associate of Chernyshevsky's, who had travelled to London to get it printed at Herzen's Free Russian Press. The proclamation was entitled 'To the Young Generation', and it was the young generation whom – again, for the first time – it addressed as 'the men who can save Russia', 'its real force', 'the leaders of the people'. It was very much a young man's handiwork: daring, fiery, unrestrained, full of bold generalizations. But for all the impetuosity of its style, and despite the shortness of the time that had elapsed since the reform, 'To the Young Generation' already contained most of the essential ideas that would make up the political platform of Populism. Central to its approach was the proposition – breathtakingly novel at the time, but soon to become the keystone of Populist doctrine – that the peasant reform was pernicious *not* because it had not gone far enough in advancing the peasants' interests, but because, in a sense, it had gone *too far* as it was: because the object of the reform had been to ensure Russia's progress along the Western, capitalist path. To prevent this outcome a revolution was urgently necessary – a revolution that would stop the spread of capitalism and enable Russia to develop along its preordained socialist course:

They want to turn Russia into an England and to feed us on English maturity. But has Russia anything at all in common with England . . .? No, we don't want English economic maturity – the Russian stomach cannot take it . . . Let Europe carry the cross. And anyway, who can say that we should follow the path of Europe . . .? Why shouldn't Russia achieve yet another order, unknown even in America? We not only can but must achieve something different. There are principles in our life completely unknown to Europeans ... We are a backward people, and in this lies our salvation. We must thank destiny that we have not lived the life of Europe. Its misfortunes, its hopeless situation are a lesson for us. We do not want its proletariat, its aristocracy, its governmental principles, its imperial power ...

Europe does not understand, cannot understand our social aspirations, therefore Europe cannot be our teacher in economic questions. No one goes as far in negation as we Russians. And why is this? Because we have no political past, we are not bound by any tradition, we stand on virgin soil ... Unlike Western Europe, we are not afraid of the future: that is why we move boldly forward to the revolution, why we long for it. We believe in our own fresh forces, we believe that we are destined to introduce a new principle into history, to utter a word of our own, and not merely repeat the European past. Without faith there is no salvation, and we have immense faith in our strength.

If in order to achieve our ends, to divide the land between the people, we would have to kill a hundred thousand landowners, even that would not frighten us. Besides, this is not really such a terrible thing.[3]

After this thunderous peroration the rest of the manifesto sounded somewhat anticlimactic. It contained demands that were already becoming familiar: nationalization of the land, equality of rights, elected authorities, freedom of speech, the transformation of the incipient middle class into peasants, etc. The Populists never went in much for detailed descriptions of their new society. What mattered was the destruction of the old, and on this basic point Mikhailov gave a clear lead. 'To the Young Generation' went further than anything ever written before in Russia: taking Herzen's ideas on the exceptional nature of Russia for its point of departure, it carried them to their logical conclusion of the necessary revolution aimed at preventing the spread of capitalism.

But however shocking Mikhailov's call to revolution must have sounded in the euphoric aftermath of the peasant reform, within a year it was to be superseded by a far more inflammatory and significant publication. In May 1862, a large number of copies of a revolutionary manifesto signed 'Young Russia' (the name by which it has come to be called) began circulating in the capital and various provincial centres. Its tone and contents were such as to make everything that had gone before seem no more than playful banter. The police were at their wits' ends: their first suspicions fastened on Chernyshevsky, then they instituted frantic investigations into every known subversive or radical grouping – all to no avail. They never did succeed in discovering the authorship of 'Young Russia'. Had they done so they would probably have received a considerable surprise.

The story of the manifesto is almost as astonishing as its contents, and provides an unusual insight into the state of affairs prevailing in the Russian Empire. It was written not by any celebrated critic of the regime, but by a completely unknown nineteen-year-old student called Pyotr Zaichnevsky; the reason why he was never caught out was that he had written it in the safest of all places – in a Moscow prison where he was serving a short sentence for revolutionary propaganda. In those far-off days of almost Arcadian simplicity, when prisoners were allowed to go for walks into town accompanied only by a readily bribable guard, there was no problem about smuggling a manuscript out of prison. Nor did Zaichnevsky's friends have any difficulty in getting the manifesto printed at one of the many small private printing-presses with which Russia abounded.

Zaichnevsky could hardly have foreseen the sensational effect of his pamphlet upon radical opinion, nor its profound influence upon the future development of the revolutionary movement. With this one inspired publication he single-handedly founded a political tradition of the utmost importance: the revolutionary trend known as 'Russian Jacobinism'.

We know too little about Zaichnevsky to be able to explain

either his prescience regarding the future, or the peculiar ferocity of his fancies, or the ruthless realism with which this callow youth analysed the inevitable course of revolution. Among his contemporaries there was none who could match him in any of these qualities. He remains a man of mystery – like so many of the shadowy figures moving silently and inscrutably beneath the glittering surface of official Tsarist Russia. But there is nothing mysterious about his message. Coldly and precisely, in the simplest of terms, his manifesto propounded the necessity for the seizure of power by a small and well-disciplined revolutionary group, which would thereupon proceed, first to massacre all its actual and potential opponents, secondly to establish its own undisputed dictatorship over the country, and thirdly to reorganize Russia's economic and social system along socialist lines. Truly, a most precocious young man.

A brief résumé of 'Young Russia' can convey at least some of the authentic flavour of this extraordinary document. It begins by flatly rejecting, not only the peasant reform as such, but the very idea of the possibility of any kind of reform in Russia. There was no room for compromise between the ruling classes – including the liberals – and the people:

> There is only one escape from this monstrous, oppressive condition which is grinding down our people and demanding of them the sacrifice of their finest representatives, and that is revolution, bloody and merciless revolution, revolution which will radically transform each and every foundation of our present society and destroy the supporters of the existing order. We are not afraid of it, even though we know that a river of blood will flow, that there will be many perhaps innocent victims; we foresee all this, and nevertheless we welcome its approach. May it come at last! How we have longed for it!

This grim chant of exultation was immediately followed by some very matter-of-fact calculations regarding the most effective ways and means of achieving the object so passionately desired. Like many other Russian revolutionaries, Zaichnevsky was a strong believer in the method of 'justified mystification', or, to put it more bluntly, deceit. His whole manifesto was, in a sense, a skilful imposture, appearing, as it did, in the name of a non-existent group called Young Russia. Part of the document was devoted to an account of a 'meeting', allegedly held on 7 April 1862, of a totally fictitious 'Central Revolutionary Committee', and of the decisions adopted thereat. One of these consisted of a bitter attack on Herzen, who was accused of having betrayed the revolutionary cause: a harbinger of the denunciatory campaign that was to develop in the next few years. Because of Herzen's faithlessness, the proclamation declared, *Kolokol* was no longer to be trusted, and a new revolutionary paper would have to be established; its principal task would be regular information on the 'provincial committees' and rank-and-file members of the 'revolutionary party'.

In England this elaborate tissue of fantasies would be laughed off as a high-spirited student's hoax. But this was not England, and in Russia, as Zaichnevsky and many others were convinced, very little was needed to spark off the inevitable explosion. The most likely cause, declared 'Young Russia' (not unreasonably, as events were to show), would be a foreign war: 'A war will break out, recruits will be needed, loans will have to be floated, and Russia will soon reach bankruptcy. And it is at this point that some insignificant incident will ignite the revolt!' The new order created by the revolution would be republican, democratic and socialistic: a federation of autonomous regions based on agricultural communes. It would be governed by a freely elected National Assembly in conjunction with the regional assemblies. All land would be nationalized, with its cultivation entrusted to the agricultural communes. Industry and trade would also be nationalized, children were going to be brought up collectively, and the institutions of marriage and the family abolished. Poland would be granted independence, while the other national majority areas could choose between independence and remaining within the federated Russian Republic.

Zaichnevsky, however, made it quite clear that this delightful picture was no more than a blueprint for the distant future. Immediate reality was going to be a good deal harsher – and here one is entitled to speak of the genuine originality of his ideas:

> We know that it will not be possible to carry out this part of our programme at once. The revolutionary party which, if successful, will stand at the head of the Government must certainly preserve the present centralization of the country's political system, if not of its administration. By this means it will be enabled to introduce new foundations of economic and social life within the shortest possible time. It must seize the dictatorship into its own hands and stop at nothing. Elections to the National Assembly must be carried out under the influence of the Government, which will immediately make sure that no supporter of the present regime manages to get in – that is, if any of them remain alive.

Never before had a Russian revolutionary argued the necessity for the dictatorship of a minority group with the object of carrying out by force the socialist transformation of the country's political, economic and social system. Zaichnevsky had no illusions as to the method by which this could be achieved – the most memorable lines of his manifesto were those which conjured up a vivid and frightening picture of the ruthless terror, the mass bloodbath to be unleashed by the purifying revolution. The lasting impact of 'Young Russia' was largely based on these grisly yet, to many of the radical intelligentsia, strangely satisfying descriptions:

> We will be more consistent than not only the miserable revolutionaries of '48 but even the great terrorists of '92. We will not falter even if we see that the overthrow of the present regime will require the spilling of three times as much blood as was shed by the Jacobins in the 1790s . . .!

Soon, very soon the day will come when we will unfurl the great banner of the future, the red banner. And with a mighty cry of 'Long live the Russian Social and Democratic Republic!' we will move on the Winter Palace to exterminate all its inhabitants. It may be that it will be sufficient to exterminate only the imperial family, i.e. a mere one or two hundred people. But it may also happen, and this is more likely, that the whole imperial party will rise as one man behind the monarch ... In this case, with full faith in ourselves and our strength, in the support of the people and in the glorious future of Russia, which destiny has ordained shall be the first country to realize the great cause of Socialism, we shall utter the battle-cry: 'To your axes!' and then – then kill the imperial party without pity, just as they do not pity us today! Kill them in the squares, if the dirty swine dare to show their faces there, kill them in their houses, kill them in the narrow alleys of the towns, kill them in the broad avenues of the capitals, kill them in the villages!

Remember: anyone who is not with us then is against us, whoever is against us is our enemy, and enemies should be exterminated by every possible means.[4]

The homicidal fury of 'Young Russia's' call for a mass slaughter of all opponents of the revolution certainly struck a new note in Russian political debate. Yet, curiously enough, although at the time it met with only limited support among the intelligentsia, neither did it evoke any feeling of moral revulsion. The general opinion seemed to be that here was an interesting and original argument, perhaps a bit strong in places, but outspoken and sincere, and therefore a worthwhile contribution to the progressive cause. Its numerous readers found nothing bizarre about either the extravagance of its language or the openly dictatorial trend of its programme.

Mikhailov's and Zaichnevsky's publications, which appeared almost simultaneously, were probably the two most influential (though not necessarily most famous) illegal manifestoes of the nineteenth-century revolutionary movement. But whereas 'To the Young Generation' had formulated the basic tenets of the generally accepted Populist creed, 'Young Russia' struck out in a somewhat different direction. In broad terms, Mikhailov stood for the mainstream of Populism while Zaichnevsky represented its 'Left wing' (if one can use the term 'Left' with regard to a movement which had no 'Right'). And in an intellectual and political atmosphere where being radical was of the essence and no limits were set to revolutionism, it is not surprising that many of Zaichnevsky's ideas soon acquired a considerable degree of acceptance – all the more so since they merely drew the logical and practical inferences from the prevailing Populist theoretical assumptions.

There can be no doubt as to the historical significance of Zaichnevsky's platform, with its novel blend of socialism, discipline, centralization, dictatorship and political terror. The Bolsheviks, no mean judges of revolutionary radicalism, were generous in their acknowledgments to the founder of Russian Jacobinism. Pokrovsky called his manifesto 'the first document of Russian revolutionary socialism', which 'already contained many features of the future proletarian revolution'. One of these was singled out for especial mention by the official Leninist historiographer of the revolutionary movement, 'an exceedingly prophetic feature: the dictatorship of a revolutionary party possessing full power and in no hurry to introduce federalism'. All in all, concluded Pokrovsky, Zaichnevsky's manifesto was 'a model Bolshevik offensive'.[5] High praise indeed!

Other early Communist historians stressed the elements of continuity in Zaichnevsky's ideology – not only with the future, but with the past as well. Steklov, for instance, regarded it, with every justification, as the first open expression and further development of Chernyshevsky's revolutionary principles. '"Young Russia",' he wrote, 'was the only illegal publication of the early 1860s which reflected Chernyshevsky's real views . . . Thus, it was fully in the spirit of Chernyshevsky that the proclamation condemned the criminal dynasty to collective extermination . . . The proclamation did no more than proclaim the principles which Chernyshevsky had gradually evolved in his articles. The sole difference was that he had had to express himself cautiously, through hints and allusions . . . Reading the proclamation Chernyshevsky must have recognized his own ideas, his own most cherished thoughts.'⁶

Russian Jacobinism, together with the rest of the broad current of Populism, was certainly descended from Chernyshevsky. Although they themselves chose the name deliberately, the 'Russian Jacobins' show few signs of having been influenced by the original French Jacobins or such later disciples as Buonarotti or Blanqui – beyond a general belief in the virtues of revolutionary dictatorship and terror. As convinced élitist conspirators they were, on the whole, unsympathetic to the genuine plebeian democratic streak in Jacobinism. But it was a good name: bold and unambiguous, well calculated to produce the desired effect.

Zaichnevsky's own contribution to Russian Jacobinism was by no means confined to the composition of its founding manifesto. As his authorship of 'Young Russia' remained unknown until the end of his life, he was soon out of prison and on the move again, spending the next thirty years mainly under police surveillance or in 'administrative exile', going from one place to another, never settling down anywhere for long. And wherever he went he spread his own peculiar brand of revolutionary ideology. Openly contemptuous of the ineffective Populist propagandists and opposed in principle to the method of individual terrorism increasingly favoured by the underground revolutionary groups, Zaichnevsky never wavered in his belief that a tight-knit, disciplined, centralized illegal party must be established against the day when it could seize power in the land. Despite the difficulties he succeeded in setting up a number of small 'Jacobin' circles in various parts of the country. Many years later one of his early disciples, Maria Oshanina, described his organizational principles as follows: 'He was, as one said at the time, a "centralist". All revolutionary activity must be perfectly planned beforehand by a "centre", made up of people who are dedicated body and soul to the revolution, and superior to the average in quality.'[7]

Ruthless extermination of the enemies of the revolution, and the creation of a dedicated and centrally directed élite to carry out a carefully conceived plan for the seizure of power – these were the main points of Zaichnevsky's message. At the time it achieved only a very limited circulation, but Zaichnevsky's powerful personality and cogent arguments left a deep imprint on the development of Russian radicalism – and on the many young people whom he had converted to revolution. Although he himself died in 1896, a few years before the foundation of the Bolshevik Party, a number of his followers subsequently joined the Leninist ranks. It was an entirely logical step to take.

The appearance of Zaichnevsky's and Mikhailov's manifestoes marked the transformation of Populism from a set of theoretical doctrines into an active revolutionary movement. But the dividing-line between the two aspects of the Populist phenomenon never really became clear-cut: Populism remained, in one form or another, the generally accepted world-outlook of the intelligentsia as a whole, while at the same time providing a programme of revolutionary action for a variety of successive political movements. It is this close relationship between the two nevertheless divergent functions of Populism that has given rise to a certain amount of confusion in later studies of the Russian revolution. Could the term be meaningfully applied alike to the disputatious student, the muckraking novelist and the bomb-throwing terrorist? Some scholars have solved the problem by narrowing Populism down to a more or less clearly defined political movement, while others treat it primarily in terms of a more generalized ideological attitude. Yet to detach the minority of Populist activists from that broad natural environment of the Populist intelligentsia which engendered it, supported it, replenished its ranks, admired it and often followed its lead, is to confuse the issue. Perhaps the closest analogy to the relationship between the revolutionary conspirator and the Populist *intelligent* is provided by the communion between clergy and believers within the Christian

Church. Certainly Populism – the ideology of alienation from the Russian State – provided its followers with a faith, a way of life, a sense of community, a system of morals. And like the early Christians, the first generation of the Populist intelligentsia constituted a tiny subversive cell within the body politic, determined to overthrow the mighty Empire and to establish the Kingdom of Heaven upon its ruins.

To their contemporaries the Men of the Sixties, the youthful *raznochintsy* who suddenly erupted on to the stage out of nowhere, filling the air with the clamour of controversy, seemed to represent a new and rather frightening species of humanity. Nobody could remember seeing or hearing of them before 19 February, but here they were – disgruntled, disaffected, jeering at reform, denying everything, mocking the established order, contemptuous of authority, denigrating tradition, talking of revolution, preaching hatred, professing materialism yet indifferent to material goods, cynical yet strangely idealistic. Into a Russia which was attempting to Europeanize itself upon the orders of the autocratic State they brought the spirit of negation and rebellion. By the heterogeneity of their social background, by their very rootlessness, they symbolized Russia's crisis of identity, the dislocation of the national life and the abnormality of social relationships. They brought with them a great ferment of ideas – some admirable, many half-baked at best, all aimed at undermining the foundations of Russian society. 'The passion for destruction,' they would repeat after Bakunin, 'is also a creative passion.' And most of all they were fired by a passion for discussing their ideas.

Thanks to the great Russian novelists, we know more about the Populist intelligentsia of the sixties than about any other group of people in Russian history. Turgenev in particular was both fascinated and repelled by these 'New Men'. In *Virgin Soil* he gave an inimitable description of the atmosphere prevailing at their get-togethers:

Like the first flakes of snow, swiftly whirling, crossing and recrossing in the still mild air of autumn, words began flying, tumbling, jostling against one another in the heated atmosphere of Golushkin's dining-room – words of all sorts – progress, government, literature; the taxation question, the church question, the woman question, the law-court question; classicism, realism, nihilism, communism; international, clerical, liberal, capital; administration, organization, association, and even crystallization! It was just this uproar which seemed to rouse Golushkin to enthusiasm; the real gist of the matter seemed to consist in this, for him ... [Translated by Constance Garnett]

But for many of these young men the gist of the matter certainly did not consist of insubstantial intellectual debate. The Men of the Sixties were made of sterner stuff than the ineffective dreamers of the Forties, the generation of the Fathers. They were impatient for action, contemptuous of liberal half-measures, convinced of the impossibility of peaceful change, intolerant of accepted opinions and suspicious of everyone who disagreed with them. They were socialists, nurtured on the heady wine of Chernyshevsky, assured of Russia's glorious predestination. Their emergence as a political force was heralded, figuratively speaking, by a fanfare of trumpets: the disturbances at St Petersburg University and the publication of two explosive pamphlets addressed specifically to them – 'Young Russia' and 'To the Young Generation'.

All this soon became a source of acute anxiety, not only to the authorities but also to a number of well-meaning liberal spirits. Professor Nikitenko viewed the situation with unrelieved pessimism:

Does not all this signify a process of degeneration – this general commotion of minds, the rapidly growing and alarming discord in social relationships, the demoralization, the senseless enthusiasms of young intellects and the dull inactivity of mature intellects – this universal ferment, this fever of ambitions devoid of any title to distinction, this delirious obsession with theories which have hardly

319

impinged on their minds and have certainly not been sustained by either analysis or testing?[8]

Now that the first exhilaration of reform had passed, Nikitenko's fears were shared by many other liberal Westerners. Something strange was obviously happening in Russia, something they had not reckoned with. The reaction of government circles was, naturally enough, even more drastic. The retrograde majority of the ruling class, particularly the now-serfless landowners, had not been happy with the peasant reform to begin with. Of course, the autocrat's will was law – that went without saying – but if the reform was seen to have had disastrous consequences, might there not be a chance of turning the clock back?

It was a tense and unquiet time. The first two years after emancipation were marked by a notable degree of restlessness among the peasants, culminating in a number of uprisings. Naturally, these were put down by armed force, with much bloodshed – this was how it had always been. But the peasants were the least of the government's worries: the student strike was still on, and in May 1862, to add to the suspense, a series of mysterious large-scale fires occurred in various parts of the capital. Fires were common happenings in Russia's wooden cities, but in this case the hand of arsonists was clearly discernible. The culprits were never found – their identities remain unknown to this day. To the distraught police, however, it seemed a reasonable assumption that one and the same hand was responsible for the fires, the inflammatory proclamations, the student disorders, and possibly even other disturbances still further afield. They decided to strike – hard.

Centuries of experience had taught the Russian secret police one all-important lesson: in order to quell political unrest it was necessary to catch the people behind it and withdraw them from circulation, after which peace and harmony would once more reign undisturbed. With their network of informers and *agents provocateurs*, discovering the malefactors presented no problem. Mikhailov had already been arrested and sent off to exile (and an early grave). Now the time had come to eliminate what they regarded as the main centre of subversion: in July 1862 the publication of *Sovremennik* was suspended and Chernyshevsky himself taken under arrest. After two years in the grim Peter-Paul Fortress (during which he wrote *What Is to Be Done?*) Chernyshevsky was sent up for trial. The prosecution had made out a strong case; he was sentenced to fourteen years of penal servitude (reduced by the Tsar to seven) with subsequent banishment for life. During these two years the police succeeded in rounding up several hundred students and other young *raznochintsy* suspected of sedition, among them the members of a rather nebulous Populist secret society called *Zemlya i Volya* (Land and Liberty), headed by a close collaborator of Chernyshevsky's, Nikolai Serno-Solovievich.

The police were satisfied and so was the government. Subversion had been suppressed, and now the authorities could turn their undivided attention to great affairs of State without being distracted by a lot of foolish and rebellious young men. But for the first time in the history of the police, this most venerable of Russian political institutions had completely misjudged the situation. The opponent confronting them was no longer a conspiratorial group like the Decembrists or Petrashevskists, fairly easy to unmask and render harmless. It would be a long time before the fact sank in, but at some point at the beginning of the decade a decisive change had occurred: a combination of several factors – the emergence of the *raznochinets*-intelligentsia, the development of Populist ideology, and the emancipation of the serfs – had produced, not the customary conspiracy, but a clearly defined *social class* standing in outright opposition to the regime, dedicated to its downfall, and providing a permanent breeding-ground and sympathetic milieu for a succession of ever newer and more widespread revolutionary movements. The Men of the Sixties had come into their own.

The members of this first – and formative – generation of the radical intelligentsia are widely known in the West as 'Nihilists'.

They adopted the name themselves, in admiring imitation of Bazarov, the self-proclaimed Nihilist hero of Turgenev's *Fathers and Sons*. It is one of the many paradoxes of the Russian revolutionary movement that this rather unpleasant literary character who became the model for countless young radicals was deliberately intended by Turgenev as a satirical presentation of the New Man (with his pet aversion, Dobrolyubov, serving as the prototype). When the novel appeared in 1862, literary critics both of Left and Right (including Chernyshevsky) were almost unanimous in treating it as a take-off of the fledgling intelligentsia. But a strange thing happened; the very qualities which Turgenev set out to lampoon in Bazarov were seized upon enthusiastically by the radical youth as representing the most desirable attributes of every right-thinking person. Nothing could have demonstrated more strikingly the complete breakdown of communications between the generations, the gulf that had suddenly divided the formerly dominant intellectual and literary community from their unfamiliar and, to many, frightening progeny. In no time large numbers of Bazarovs sprang forth in the capitals and throughout the country – studiously neglectful of their appearance, denying authority, questioning every accepted moral or social norm, contemptuous of ideals and beauty, proclaiming Nihilism, or, in other words, a belief in nothing save science, materialism, revolution and the People.

Bazarov's transformation into the patron saint of the radical intelligentsia was largely due to the influence of the remarkable young man who, while never achieving Chernyshevsky's stature, succeeded him in the role of arbiter of progressive ideas – Dmitry Ivanovich Pisarev. 'From the very first appearance of Bazarov,' wrote Pisarev, audaciously contradicting every other Left-wing literary pundit, 'he engaged all my sympathy, and he continues to remain my favourite.'[9] An extremely young man himself, only turned twenty in 1861, Pisarev proved – on this as on other occasions – that he understood the peculiar radical temper of his contemporaries far better than anyone else who presumed to speak for them. His was a short and tragic life.

Unlike most ideologues of the intelligentsia, Pisarev came from the landowning nobility; he was arrested at about the same time as Chernyshevsky and spent four and a half years in the Peter-Paul Fortress, where he wrote the greater part of his critical and theoretical works; in 1868, shortly after his release, he was drowned while bathing. Judging by the achievement of these few years, he possessed probably the most penetrating intelligence and certainly the most brilliant literary style of all the great Russian radical thinkers of the nineteenth century.

Pisarev's influence upon the world-outlook of the intelligentsia was out of all proportion to the comparatively slender size of his *oeuvre*. If we can speak at all of any specific body of Nihilist doctrine, then it is contained in his writings. Its dominating theoretical principle was that of utilitarianism – Pisarev's most signal contribution to the mainstream of Populism and to the Russian revolutionary tradition. It was an austere and joyless doctrine, according to which the sole criterion for judging the value of any action or product of the human mind was its direct contribution to the material well-being of mankind. The concept of well-being was construed in the most literal sense possible, and everything which lay beyond it was proclaimed out of bounds for any decent person concerned with the plight of his fellow-creatures:

> The object to which all our thoughts and all the actions of every honest person are directed is the solution of the inescapable problem of hungry and unclad people. Beyond this nothing exists that is worthy of anxiety, thought or trouble. But this problem is in itself so vast and so complex that its solution requires all the available powers of the human intellect, the application of every ounce of human energy and love, and of every resource of human knowledge. There can hardly be anything left over for other aims.[10]

Neither Belinsky nor Chernyshevsky, for all their belief in the criterion of social utility, had ever put the matter in such stark and uncompromising terms. Here then was a philosophical basis for a new code of morality, appealing to the intellectual pretensions of the radical *raznochintsy* as well as to their innate generosity and sense of purpose: only that which could directly contribute towards feeding and clothing the people was of importance to society; anything else was a useless waste of time, and, by inference, harmful. In this new scale of values everything was subordinated to the harsh reality of the struggle for existence (significantly, Darwin had just irrupted on to the Russian scene): materialism and science, particularly applied and popular science, were good – abstract ideas and art, particularly art for art's sake, were bad. To buttress this up Pisarev evolved what he called the 'theory of the economy of intellectual force': 'Those individuals who by their position are enabled, and by their nature are willing, to indulge in intellectual work, must expend their forces with the utmost prudence and calculation, i.e., they must undertake only such assignments as are of real benefit to society.'[11]

Unlike Chernyshevsky, Pisarev's critical writings show unmistakable signs of a discriminating and fastidious aesthetic sense, so it must have been by a deliberate effort of the will that he managed to subjugate all considerations of beauty and form to the nakedly utilitarian principle of the social content of literature and art. Nobody did more to inculcate this principle in the thinking of the Russian intelligentsia. It became an integral part of the revolutionary tradition, first of its Populist and later of its Leninist strains, and when today in the USSR Pisarev is acclaimed as one of the forefathers of modern Soviet aesthetics one well understands what they mean.

To the delight of his own and subsequent generations of the intelligentsia Pisarev made short shrift of the classics – with the exception of those works which, like *Fathers and Sons*, had actively contributed to the material progress of mankind. Poetry, and especially Pushkin, came in for his most virulent attacks. 'Our little Pushkin' was how he usually referred to the poet. 'Pushkin's place,' he declared, 'is not on the desk of the contemporary worker but in the dust-filled study of the antiquary.' 'In this so-called great poet I have exposed to my readers a frivolous versifier, enmeshed in his petty prejudices, absorbed in the contemplation of his petty personal feelings, and completely incapable of analysing and understanding the great social and philosophical problems of our age.'[12]

This was Nihilism at its purest: a bleak doctrine of fanatical asceticism and self-mortification, rejecting the past in the name of the future, renouncing pleasure for the sake of saving the world. Pisarev provided the ideological justification for the new barbarism that now swept through the ranks of the youthful Populist intelligentsia, to the bewildered dismay of the older generation of cultivated liberals – of both Westerner and Slavophile persuasion. In the graceless hands of his followers, who lacked both his learning and his literary gifts but made up for these deficiencies by the intensity of their devotion to the cause, Pisarev's intellectual Nihilism became a philosophy of unqualified denial of all existing values. Its logical corollary was the further growth of their self-confidence, the intensification of their belief in the special mission of the 'self-aware' élite. They were the carriers of science and progress, theirs was the task of transforming and leading society. Utilitarianism, revolution and dictatorship became complementary ideas.

Nihilism was no passing fad. In time, with the emergence of newer and ever more exciting political currents, the name itself fell into disuse (in Russia much earlier than in the West) but the ideas, the way of life associated with it exerted a potent influence upon every generation of Russian intelligentsia. The ideologues of Nihilism were assured of a large and admiring audience; what they said or wrote was accepted almost religiously by the strangely conformist 'New Men'. Best known (or most notorious) of these ideologues was Varfolomei Zaitsev, regarded by contemporaries as the archetypal Nihilist. Zaitsev has achieved literary immortality, of a kind, as the original of Shigalev, the gruesome doctrinaire of tyrannical socialism in Dostoevsky's *The Possessed*. Dostoevsky may well have been unfair to Zaitsev personally – as Soviet literary historians tell us – but the man's own writings certainly do conjure up a rather terrifying figure.

Zaitsev was much cruder than Pisarev, in style and substance alike – but then, so were his readers, and his blunt exposition of Nihilist attitudes possibly had a greater impact at the time than Pisarev's literary sophistication. In the field of culture he enriched the thinking of the intelligentsia by such dicta as 'Any artisan is more useful than any poet, just as any positive number, however small, is greater than zero'; or 'Utility and art are mutually exclusive concepts, and in the present state of society anything that is of no use to it is also dangerous'.[13] But his principal contribution was in the field of politics; no Russian writer before him had ever revealed quite the same degree of contempt for the common people whose interests he was championing, quite the same measure of detestation for democracy or freedom. Zaitsev put forward his views with unparalleled frankness – the Men of the Sixties regarded hypocrisy as the most heinous crime of all:

> Outside the upper and middle classes, the rest of the nation, the so-called people, live in a state of existence close to that of any Kaffir or Kurd. One might think that in such a country the question of democrats or democracy could never even arise. But the brazen democrats do not let themselves be deterred by such trifles ... They wish to be democrats, whatever happens – they are unconcerned with the fact that the aristocracy and bourgeoisie can only be succeeded by beasts in human form ... The people are rude and obtuse, and consequently passive; this is not their own fault, of course, but it is so, and any initiative of theirs would be terrifying ... Therefore prudence dictates – in defiance of the grandiose pedestal upon which the democrats have lifted the people – that energetic action be taken against them, because a people as backward as the Italians [to speak of some other nation while actually referring to Russia was a common subterfuge] is incapable of acting in accordance with its own interests. If it has

been accepted as necessary to impose education forcibly upon the people then I fail to understand how a false diffidence about this democratic nonsense can prevent us from realizing the necessity of forcibly endowing the people with another benefit, no less important than education, and without which the latter is impossible – namely, freedom.[14]

Perhaps, after all, Dostoevsky was not really mistaken when he took Zaitsev as the model for Shigalev, whose cardinal principle was: 'Starting from unlimited freedom, I arrive at unlimited despotism.' Shigalev's vision of the future certainly resembles Zaitsev's: the people 'have to give up all individuality and become, so to speak, a herd, and, through boundless submission, will by a series of regenerations attain primeval innocence, something like the Garden of Eden'. The fictional 'Shigalevism' had quite a lot in common with the genuine 'Zaitsevism'. Both reflected the intelligentsia's tormented search for truth in a world which they could not accept.

The intelligentsia were forged in the literary-political battles of the sixties. Chernyshevsky, Mikhailov, Zaichnevsky, Pisarev, Zaitsev – Socialism, Populism, Jacobinism, Nihilism – denial of the past, hatred of the present, direction of the future – sacrifice for the people and contempt for the people – conspiracy, violence, terror, dictatorship – justice, equality, benevolence, righteousness: these were the teachers, the concepts, the words that ran riot among the young *raznochintsy*. They were the élite, the hope of the future – this they knew firmly – and now at last they had all the answers. Towards those who thought otherwise they felt nothing but derision and bitter acrimony.

It was inevitable that there should be a parting of the ways between the new radical intelligentsia and some of the older generation of revolutionaries. The most prominent of these was Herzen. For several years already he had followed developments in Russia with increasing unease. However much he tried to understand the New Men, his basic devotion to constitutionalism and the liberal values made this impossible. The Jacobins and the Nihilists, with their cult of bloodshed in politics and boorishness in personal relations, horrified him. The circulation of *Kolokol* was rapidly falling: in the changed situation Herzen's exhortations, which had sounded daring beyond belief only a few years ago, now seemed irrelevant and even slightly comical. His popularity suffered its first heavy blow (apart from his short-lived approval of the peasant reform) as a result of the Polish uprising of 1863 – Herzen warmly supported the Poles' liberation struggle, whereas Russian public opinion, including most of the radicals, adopted a nationalistic line. But more was to follow: Herzen's public criticism of the Nihilists and their first conspiratorial and terroristic organizations was taken in exceedingly bad part. Who is this refined nobleman – they asked – with his liberal views and elegant life, with his vast wealth, derived from the sufferings of his serfs, to criticize us, who struggle and sacrifice all for a new Russia? The first great wave of Russian revolutionary emigration now poured into Western Europe, and as a result of personal contact repressed rancour flared into open hostility (unalleviated by Herzen's generous hand-outs to the impecunious young Nihilists).

War was declared in the spring of 1867 in a pamphlet printed in Switzerland by Alexander Serno-Solovievich, the brother of Chernyshevsky's imprisoned disciple. His attack was couched in terms of the vicious personal abuse that had already become *de rigueur* in Russian revolutionary circles. 'Yes,' he sneered, 'the young generation has understood you. Having understood you, it has turned away from you in disgust – and you still dream that you are its guide, that you are "a power and a force in the Russian state", that you are a leader and representative of youth. You our leader? Ha! Ha! Ha! The young generation has long outstripped you by a whole head in its understanding of facts and events . . . You are a poet, a painter, an artist, a story-teller, a novelist – anything you please, only not a political leader and still less a political thinker, the founder of a school and a doctrine.' Bitterly, Serno-Solovievich went on to castigate

Herzen for his 'blood-stained wealth', to revile him as a 'paper snake' and a 'corpse'. The young Nihilists were particularly infuriated by Herzen's claim to have fought side by side with Chernyshevsky, their idol and martyr. 'So you were the complement of Chernyshevsky! You marched shoulder to shoulder with Chernyshevsky! Such an idea I never expected even from you . . . Between you and Chernyshevsky there never was and never could be anything in common. You are two opposite elements which cannot exist side by side . . . Chernyshevsky founded a genuine school, he educated people, he brought up a whole phalanx of people – but where, I ask, are your followers? In what respect then, Mr Herzen, have you complemented Chernyshevsky?'[15]

Herzen was deeply shaken. Much more than wounded vanity was involved; he apparently realized that Serno's invective, crude as it was, expressed the feelings not just of one man, but of a whole generation. An unbridgeable chasm separated him from the revolutionary and radical movement to whose emergence he had dedicated a lifetime in exile. He voiced his anger in a private letter to Bakunin, calling the Nihilists 'scoundrels' and 'ignoramuses', and qualifying their behaviour as 'son-of-a-bitchism'. 'He [Serno-Solovievich] is insolent and mad, but what terrifies me is that the majority of the youth is *the same*, and that we have all helped them to become *such*.'[16]

The process of Herzen's disenchantment with revolutionary Populism had begun earlier, under the impact of events in Russia, but the personal onslaught against him undoubtedly speeded it up. Somewhere, he felt, at some stage things had gone wrong. Gradually, step by step, he was impelled to revise his own previous views, as well as some basic ideas advanced by others but implicitly accepted by himself. The results of his re-examination of the old verities were set out in Herzen's last important work, an Open Letter 'To an Old Friend' (Bakunin), written in 1869, only a few months before his death:

Violence and terror are used to spread religions and policies, to found autocratic empires and indivisible republics; violence can destroy and clear the ground – but no more. Peter-the-Greatism can never carry a social upheaval beyond the prison equality of Gracchus Babeuf or the communist *corvée* of Cabet . . . I do not believe in the previous revolutionary solutions . . .

The popular masses themselves . . . are suspicious of the persons who advocate an aristocracy of science and issue calls to arms. And, mind you, these preachers come not from the people, but from the schools, books, literature, from a life spent in abstractions. These old students have moved further apart from the people than its enemies . . . That is why they believe it possible to begin the economic upheaval with a *tabula rasa*, by reducing to ashes the whole historical terrain, not realizing that this terrain, with all its strips and tares, represents the very foundation of the people's life, the totality of its moral values. The people is a conservative by instinct . . .

Great revolutions are not achieved by unleashing evil passions . . . I do not trust the sincerity of men who prefer destruction and brute force to development and compromise . . . A savage and unrestrained explosion will spare nothing . . . The rampant spirit of extermination will destroy, together with the boundary signs, all those landmarks of human progress that men have created since the beginning of civilization.[17]

The tragic figure of the old revolutionary stood alone, reviled and rejected by the young people on whom he had pinned his hopes. Sensing his own responsibility for the unforeseen turn of events ('we have all helped them to become *such*'), Herzen wished to render a last service to the revolutionary cause; to warn the new generation against the ineluctable results – as he saw them – of their actions, and, by implication, against accepting his own former theories. The beliefs of a lifetime lay in ruins. No longer with the *tabula rasa*, the blank surface uniquely equipped for carrying out socialist experiments, a thing to be gloried in: socialism would have to grow organically and naturally out of the whole historical development of the Russian people. No longer was the Russian peasant a natural Socialist: he was, on the contrary, a conservative by instinct, and this factor would have to determine the country's rate of progress. And, above all, there must be a profound disbelief in the doctrinal solutions of a self-appointed élite, divorced from the people and from life, relying on violence and force for the materialization of their visions.

Herzen became the first in that long line of Russian revolutionaries, stretching from his day to ours, who at some stage of the struggle were to be thrust aside by the pressure of new events, new men, new ideas; and who from these unfamiliar vantage-points would make anguished reappraisals of the past and sombre forecasts for the future. None of them would heed their predecessors' cries until it was too late, and their own warnings would go unnoticed by the men who were to join their company at subsequent turnings in the revolutionary road. Much of what they would say was to sound strangely similar to Herzen's last writing.

CHAPTER 14

Nechaev and the Conspiratorial Principle

Herzen's disenchantment and final break with the Populist *raznochintsy* was caused by much more than wounded pride. Things were brought to a head by startling news about the practical political activities of the new radicals: in 1866 an illegal group, headed by Ishutin and Karakozov, carried out the first attempt on the life of the Tsar. Their undertaking electrified Russia and marked the beginning of a new phase in the development of the revolution.

The Ishutin group can be treated almost as a textbook example of a Populist conspiracy. It displayed every characteristic feature of these organizations: unbounded self-sacrifice and devotion to socialist principles, unscrupulousness in method and the extensive use of deception, belief in the necessity for action and the virtue of violence. The degree of mystification instituted by Ishutin was such that it has never been possible fully to establish the structure of his group; according to some accounts, it consisted of an outer circle called 'The Organization' and an inner core termed, simply and expressively, 'Hell', the main function of which was to keep a vigilant watch on the rank-and-file members of the conspiracy. Other participants have, however, denied the existence of these two separate bodies. To complicate matters still further, Ishutin – a rather sinister young man with a positive genius for Machiavellism – had convinced his comrades that their organization was actually run by a 'European Revolutionary Committee', a vast regicidal conspiracy with branches in every country of Europe. In the name of the revolution the conspirators were to renounce every worldly interest, every human feeling, every moral scruple. As

Ishutin himself put it, 'The member of "Hell" must live under an assumed name and break off all his family ties; he must never marry, he must part from all his old friends – in a word, he must devote his whole life to one exclusive aim: the good of his country. For this he must renounce all personal pleasure, replacing it by hatred and detestation of evil – a feeling he must learn to enjoy.'[1]

The need for principles such as these was self-evident to young revolutionaries nurtured on the writings of Chernyshevsky and his followers. The futility of legalism and the fallaciousness of brotherly love had been proved by the miserable effects of the peasant reform. Other methods were needed, and in an autocratic police State one could not afford to be too squeamish about them. Among the fund-raising projects discussed by the Ishutinites were holding up the post, robbing a merchant, and even a proposal by one of their number, Fedoseyev, to poison his own father for the sake of the legacy. Hardly any of this was ever actually accomplished, or even attempted – though not because of any moral scruples. On the principle of the ends justifying the means all were agreed. But, quite simply, they did not know how to go about making a revolution.

What the Ishutinites lacked in the way of practical ability they made up for by the directness of their views. A revolution was imperative; it had to come as soon as possible, in order to forestall the development of capitalism and constitutionalism. Ishutin himself admitted at his trial that he had been filled with apprehension by rumours about the formation of a secret liberal party with purely political aims: 'If this society were to win, then things would be a hundred times worse for the Russian people than they are today. They would immediately think up some constitution, and insert Russian life into a Western frame. Such a constitution would be supported alike by the middle and upper classes, as it would guarantee personal freedom and provide an impetus for industry and commerce; but it would not guarantee us against the development of pauperism and a proletariat – rather, it would accelerate this process.'[2] The general view (shared by a much wider section of the radical intelligentsia) was that the Tsar deserved death as a punishment for having emancipated the serfs and thus obstructed the course of revolution.[3]

There was no place for paltry political liberties in the Ishutinites' vision of the future. After the revolution (to be achieved in some still undetermined manner) power would pass to the (largely nonexistent) revolutionary party, 'The Organization', which was to establish a dictatorship and nationalize the economy by a series of socialist decrees. The dictatorship would be of considerable duration; within its system the 'inner party', or 'Hell', was to retain supreme political control over the government and its leaders, remedying errors by occasional assassinations. By a combination of these methods the new government would ensure prosperity, justice and equality for all – excepting, of course, the enemies of the revolution.

But, however satisfying their lengthy discussions of the shape of things to come, and heartened though they were by Ishutin's tales of a mighty international conspiracy, some members of the group felt that talking was not enough. Action was needed: a beginning had to be made. The most determined proponent of action was Dmitry Karakozov, a twenty-five-year-old law student. Assassinating the Tsar, most of the group agreed, was the best way of starting the revolution. Very well then, Karakozov told his somewhat sceptical comrades, he would do it. Having purchased a pistol, he travelled from Moscow to St Petersburg, and on 4 April 1866 he fired a shot from close quarters at the Tsar, who was taking his regular stroll in the park. Luckily for Alexander, one of the bystanders, a peasant named Komissarov, had the presence of mind to knock Karakozov's hand upwards: the bullet missed, and the would-be assassin was immediately apprehended.

Karakozov's shot marked the beginning of a new era in Russian political life, and the appearance of a new method of struggle. It was the first time that a direct attempt had been made against the life of the Emperor; from then on assassination plots multiplied, and Alexander II gradually came to lead the existence of a hunted man – an existence shared by many high dignitaries of his empire. But at that moment the news of Karakozov's deed struck the country with the force of an unprecedented horror. To the revolutionaries' disgust, the popular masses were engulfed in a great wave of patriotic and monarchical sentiment. Clearly, the centuries-old tradition of unquestioning loyalty and veneration for the Tsar had remained intact. Besides, this was Alexander II, the 'Liberator-Tsar', the author of the Emancipation Decree. The rumour rapidly spread among the peasants that the wicked deed had been the work of the landowners, seeking to avenge themselves for the loss of their slaves. Huge demonstrations took place, particularly in the towns, and quite a few students got beaten up by the infuriated populace. It was, all thought, an obvious manifestation of Divine Providence that a man of the people, a simple peasant, had been chosen to save the Tsar's life. Komissarov became a national hero: ennobled, lionized, and given every opportunity to drink himself into a state of permanent stupor – which he promptly proceeded to do.

The intelligentsia itself was far from unanimous in its attitude to this first terrorist outrage. Nekrasov wrote a fulsome ode upon the Emperor's miraculous deliverance, and Herzen issued a stern condemnation of the method of individual terror in general, and Karakozov's act in particular. This was the actual cause of Serno-Solovievich's venomous attack and of the final rift between Herzen and the young Populists. For, whatever the state of popular feeling, and however great the shock administered to their elders, the New Men – the *raznochintsy*, the students, the youthful followers of Chernyshevsky – exulted in Karakozov's heroic act. That was the stuff true revolutionaries were made of! Karakozov, Ishutin and the rest of their schoolboyish group became an inspiration, a legend, an integral part of the revolutionary mystique. The only regret was that their attempt had failed.

The conspirators were tried by jury. Karakozov was condemned to death and hanged, Ishutin's death sentence was commuted to penal servitude for life (he died on *katorga* a few years later), the others received varying terms of penal servitude or exile. It was widely alleged that the accused had been tortured in prison. The allegation – like a similar rumour concerning the Decembrists – was entirely untrue, but for the radicals it became another black mark in their indictment of Tsarism.

The Karakozov affair had grave repercussions on both government policy and revolutionary tactics. To the government it signified the impossibility of achieving any measure of real accommodation with the radical intelligentsia and the futility of all attempts at reconciliation. The period of liberal reform came, by and large, to an end. Reaction now took over. As a first step towards the restoration of proper respect for authority, *Sovremennik* was finally closed down. Censorship was tightened up. Predictably, university and secondary-school students bore the brunt of the new repressive wave. Large-scale arrests and expulsions were carried out as a matter of course. But the changes were intended to go deeper. Ten days after Karakozov's shot Count Dmitry Tolstoy, well known for his extreme conservative views, was appointed Minister of Education, and immediately proceeded to introduce a series of markedly retrograde measures. In particular, the secondary-school curricula were drastically revised: a significant increase in the teaching of Greek and Latin was accompanied by a corresponding decrease in the natural sciences (thus fully confirming the intelligentsia's belief in the progressive properties of science and the reactionary nature of the humanities).

The government's new policy was termed by its opponents, somewhat grandiloquently, the 'White Terror' – a mild kind of terror by present-day standards, yet nevertheless a nasty shock after the comparatively relaxed atmosphere of the preceding decade. In the long run, however, the reversion to traditional methods was undoubtedly counter-productive: the radical intelligentsia, after an initial scare, became even more hostile to the system than ever before, and began to look much more kindly upon assassination, regicide, and other extreme forms of action which it had only recently repudiated and condemned.

The events of 1866 helped bring home two main lessons to the Populist revolutionary faction. One was the necessity for tighter organization, stricter discipline, better planning: the Ishutinites' open trial had shown up the group's incompetence and the pathetic amateurishness of Karakozov's attempt. The other was the realization, perhaps for the first time, of how remote they all were from the real people, of how dissimilar the masses' actual feelings were to the idealized accounts of the literary journals. Bridging the chasm between intelligentsia and people, teaching the peasants what was best for them, would obviously require long hours of patient work by armies of dedicated men and women. But for this neither time nor people were available. The revolution could not wait – and, once again, the only solution was intensified conspiracy.

It was the Karakozov affair and its bitter aftermath that prepared the ground for the emergence of the most extraordinary figure in the whole history of the Russian revolutionary movement: Sergei Gennadievich Nechaev. During his own lifetime Nechaev became a legend: a man of mystery, inspiring horror, fascination, awe and reverence; dominating, almost hypnotizing everybody he met; preaching a gospel of revolt such as had never been heard before, and imposing it upon others by sheer force of character; a shadowy presence, seen by few – known to all. The name, even when not pronounced, was never far from men's minds. His baleful influence, his demonic character cast a spell which even death could not break. Nearly a century after his death Nechaev remains the focus of unending violent political controversy. Every other revolutionary figure of the past has long since been weighed up, appraised, categorized and fitted into his own little historical niche – Nechaev alone has defied classification. He is not yet a part of history: although repeatedly exorcized, anathematized, denounced, hushed up – his restless spirit still haunts the victorious revolutionary feast. He was the only man besides Lenin to give his name to a specific political tendency within the revolutionary movement – *Nechaevshchina* or Nechaevism – and it is still a term full of meaning in a world so very different from his own. More books have been written about him than about any other pre-Leninist Russian rebel, among them one of the greatest novels in the language. Yet the riddle of Nechaev is still largely unsolved. The historical roots and ideological sources of Nechaevism are sufficiently discernible, the facts of his life are well documented, his influence has been painstakingly appraised – yet the man himself still eludes us.

Sergei Nechaev was born in 1847. Of all the prominent Men of the Sixties, his was probably the most genuinely proletarian background: his father had been a serf, and later worked as a waiter. Even more unusual was the fact that Sergei himself had, as a child, worked for some time in a factory. (In the first post-revolutionary years, when Nechaev's reputation was at its highest, Soviet historians explained his extreme radicalism in terms of his class origins.) With the help of friends, and with his own boundless energy, he managed to acquire an education of sorts, and at the age of nineteen appeared in St Petersburg as a primary-school teacher of religious knowledge – of all unlikely subjects. Shortly afterwards he enrolled as an external student at the university – and entered upon his true vocation of revolutionary conspirator.

Nechaev eagerly sought contacts with radical circles, and found them without much difficulty. In Russia nothing could have been simpler, even in a period of repression. His driving ambition, his urge to dominate, his ruthless and single-minded devotion to the cause, the air of mystery with which he contrived to invest himself even at that early stage, soon brought him to a position of prominence among the awestruck and rather innocent youngsters who surrounded him. The group which he joined professed the principles of 'Russian Jacobinism'; this fully accorded with his own inclinations. In particular, he struck up a relation of comradeship (friendship was not a thing Nechaev ever believed in) with the young journalist Pyotr Tkachev, who was later to become the theoretician of Russian Jacobinism.

In 1868-9 Nechaev, together with Tkachev, drew up a *Programme of Revolutionary Action*. Although this document does not seem to have achieved much more effect than any other of the numerous revolutionary manifestoes circulating almost freely around the capital, it already bore the hallmark of Nechaev's peculiar brand of revolutionary activism. Many of the elements of Nechaevism were already present, if not yet in a fully developed form.

The revolutionaries' task was formulated clearly: 'Social revolution, as our final aim, and political revolution as the only means of achieving this aim.' Revolution was inevitable, it went on, but the task of the 'revolutionary prototypes', or organized revolutionaries, was to speed up this process in every possible way. Organized, planned conspiracy was all-important; without it the revolution could never succeed. What was needed at this stage was 'to create the largest number of "revolutionary prototypes" and to develop in society the consciousness of an eventual and inevitable revolution as a way of achieving a better order of things'. But what were the 'revolutionary prototypes' to be like? How were they to be different from the already familiar 'type', the members of revolutionary student conspiracies? Here, for the first time, we see the authentic Nechaev touch: 'Those who join the organization must give up every possession, occupation or family tie, because families and occupations might distract members from their activities.'[4] This was going well beyond Chernyshevsky's concept of the 'New Men'; what the *Programme* invoked was a selfless élite of 'professional revolutionaries', as they later came to be called.

Nechaev's activities, together with those of the other members of his group, soon came to the attention of the police, and in the beginning of 1869 he disappeared from the scene. Such things happened quite often, and nobody ever asked any questions when some good comrade suddenly vanished from his usual haunts, but Nechaev's departure was executed with an artistry that was all his own, and in a manner that contained a foretaste of subsequent events. A crumpled note from him, addressed to his friends, was left lying in a street where it was sure to be found by some student. The note said that he was being taken to prison and had seized an opportunity to throw it out of the police van, unnoticed by his guards. Nechaev's bravery and resourcefulness generated considerable admiration; a little later this was followed by an even more daring exploit: it became known that he had escaped from prison and was making his way illegally to the border. The whole elaborate story, however, had been deliberately concocted by Nechaev. There was not a word of truth in it. But it had achieved its aim: Nechaev's revolutionary reputation was now established. Now he could really go abroad and embark upon serious political activity. At the end of March 1869, Nechaev arrived in Switzerland.

His arrival electrified the Russian émigré community. Ever since the Karakozov affair the Russian political exiles had been living in a state of ill-suppressed excitement, constantly waiting for the news of another great revolutionary upsurge. And now here was this remarkable young man, come to seek their assistance on behalf of the embattled underground movement at home. Every door was open to Nechaev, but no one embraced him more fervently than the grand old man of Russian and European revolution, the apostle of rebellion, Mikhail Bakunin.

Bakunin had become a revolutionary long before Nechaev was even born. His life read like a story of high romance, startling even against the background of a romantic age: the barricades of 1848, the Russian fortress, escape from Siberia, plots and imbroglios in half a dozen European countries. The world press – to say nothing of countless police forces – followed his doings with constant attention; no name was regarded with greater fear by the well-fed bourgeoisie of mid-nineteenth-century Europe. But the years had taken a heavy toll and now, at fifty-five, age, together with a series of disappointments, was beginning to tell. The old lion was dispirited: there had been fewer and fewer successes of late, and his bitter battle against Marx for control of the International, while doubtless exhilarating, was a poor substitute for genuine revolutionary struggle. Nechaev, with his news of a Russia in ferment, could not have come at a more opportune moment. Actually, during the thirty years since he had left Russia, Bakunin had never shown any special interest in his country's affairs, not even in the development of the revolutionary movement at home – when he was handed over by Austria to the Tsar's police in 1850 his main concern, understandably, had been to get out of Russia as soon as possible. A true internationalist, he saw the whole world as his battleground, and Russia as no more than one sector of the great struggle against tyranny. He never wrote much about Russia, and what did appear from his pen showed little understanding of the country and its problems. And, although every Russian revolutionary revered the name of Bakunin and felt proud to be his countryman, his actual political or ideological influence upon the radical intelligentsia was insignificant. However great the respect in which he was held, he had hardly any real followers in Russia, and although in the West he still remains the best known of all Russian revolutionaries before Lenin, his impact upon Russia cannot be compared with that of Herzen or Chernyshevsky or even a host of lesser names.

The meeting between Bakunin and Nechaev ushered in one of the most bizarre episodes in Russian revolutionary history. On the one hand the ageing, semi-legendary leader of an international conspiracy, hero of a thousand worldwide exploits, passionate, warm-hearted, commanding; on the other the young rebel with unconventional ideas, cold, enigmatical, powerful, pitiless, probably even a little mad. For all the difference in temperament and political outlook, they were bound by a fanatical dedication to the cause of revolution and destruction. And both were masters of deception and mystification, of Machiavellian ruses and intricate fabrications. Both were magnetic, masterful personalities, with the ability to inspire confidence and devotion. In a partnership of two such men one had to achieve a dominating position. And the younger man won. 'Bakunin had never before met anyone whose talent for make-believe surpassed his own. Above all, he had never met anyone who possessed his own singular taste for inventing political societies of which he was the commander-in-chief, and whose rank and file scarcely existed outside his own imagination.'[5] Bakunin fell completely under Nechaev's spell; for a time the two became inseparable, and Bakunin's immense prestige and influence were placed unreservedly at the service of his new friend.

In the course of the next few months Bakunin and Nechaev, working in collaboration, produced a number of revolutionary manifestoes and political statements of the utmost importance and influence. They also published the first issue of a new periodical called *Narodnaya Rasprava* (People's Summary Justice). Despite countless efforts by a variety of students, it has proved impossible to establish the precise authorship of these documents or the extent of the individual contributions of each of the two authors. Some appeared anonymously, others were signed by either Bakunin or Nechaev. They certainly represented a weird blend of incongruous, often contradictory ideas: Bakunin's anarchism, his faith in a spontaneous, elemental revolutionary explosion, found its strangest expression in the apotheosis of the Russian brigands, of the members of a romanticized criminal underworld, as the only true revolutionaries in the country:

> In Russia the brigand is the only true revolutionary – a revolutionary without phrases, without bookish rhetoric, an irreconcilable, indefatigable and indomitable revolutionary, a popular, and not a class revolutionary . . . The brigands of the forests, towns and villages, scattered throughout Russia, together with the brigands confined in the innumerable prisons of the empire – these constitute a single, indivisible, tight-knit world, the world of the Russian revolution. In this world, and in it alone, there has always been revolutionary conspiracy. Anyone in Russia who seriously wants to conspire, anyone who wants a people's revolution, must go into this world.[6]

There was much more of the same extravagant and rather childish stuff in the manifesto *How the Revolutionary Question Presents Itself*. It certainly helps to explain why Bakunin, for all his great reputation, never had any real influence upon the serious-minded young men and women brought up in the intellectual discipline of Chernyshevsky and his followers. Nechaev, however, possessed a very different outlook, and soon Bakunin's confused ranting about brigandage and outlawry began to be replaced by cold and methodical, almost Jesuitical instructions regarding organization, conspiracy and subversion. Even Bakunin's cherished ideas on the virtue of total destruction acquired a much more businesslike shape in the new manifesto, *Principles of Revolution*. Ishutin's 'Hell' and Zaichnevsky's 'Young Russia' had taken over from Bakunin's anarchism:

A real revolution requires individuals who do not march at the head of the mob and just hand down their orders, but who are concealed within the mob itself and imperceptibly link up one mob with another, while at the same time inculcating into the movement – also inperceptibly – a unified tendency, a single spirit and character. This is the only type of preparatory organization that makes any sense and fulfils a genuine need. The men of the real popular revolution, when they appear, shall make themselves known, and unite and organize in the course of the action . . .

The extermination of prominent personages who symbolize governmental or economic oppression must begin with individual acts. This work will then be facilitated by the spread of panic among the doomed class of society. Actions such as those initiated by Karakozov and others will increase and multiply, and gradually develop into collective movements of the masses . . . only without any idealism, which can only impede proper action, and which should be replaced by grim, cold, ruthless consistency . . . We must unreservedly give ourselves over to destruction, to ceaseless, unremitting, relentless destruction, which will mount in a crescendo until nothing of the existing social forms will be left undestroyed.[7]

The strange partners set out to translate their principles into action. Both were highly imaginative masters of deception, which they regarded as one of the most effective methods of revolutionary conspiracy. Bakunin, moreover, was endowed with an infinite capacity for self-deception as well, while Nechaev was certainly never taken in by anybody, least of all himself. It was thus a mismatched alliance from its very inception, but it did produce results – of a kind. A string of spurious manifestoes appeared, in the name of assorted non-existent organizations. Typical of these was a proclamation, 'To the Officers of the Russian Army', signed by Bakunin. It informed all and sundry of the existence *within Russia* of a powerful and widespread secret organization – disciplined, centralized, and utterly obedient to its Committee. The organization's members are expected to renounce everything they may have held dear: property, power, influence, fame. 'Like the Jesuits – only with the object not of enslaving but of liberating the people – every one of them has even renounced his own free will.' The sacrifice of independent thought and will is imperative, for every member belongs no longer to himself but solely to the organization. 'Only the strictest and most absolute discipline . . . can establish a genuine organization and create the collective revolutionary force that, basing itself upon the elemental power of the people, would be capable of defeating the formidable might of the State.' With a great show of artlessness, Bakunin announced that he was writing this proclamation upon orders from the Committee in Russia, though its actual composition had been kept secret even from him. But, he reassured his readers, 'the organization is firmly established and has such strong roots among the people that the forces of reaction are powerless to destroy it'. And finally, a flesh-creeping word of warning: 'Entry into the organization is open to all, but withdrawal from it is impossible . . . He who is not with us is against us. You may choose.'[8]

Needless to say, there was not a word of truth in the whole fantastic rigmarole. Whether Bakunin had believed Nechaev's stories or had merely given rein to his infantile taste for blood-and-thunder mystery, the crude hoax deceived nobody. Not a soul applied for admission to his 'organization'. But Nechaev was working, methodically and inexorably, towards the establishment in reality of just such a secret organization as Bakunin had described at his instigation. The concept itself was not new: from the Petrashevskist Speshnev to the Ishutinites, it was always held, to a lesser or greater degree, by almost every Russian revolutionary circle. Yet it was Nechaev who carried the idea of a Machiavellian, utterly immoral, ruthless and dedicated revolutionary conspiracy to its extreme logical conclusion. He formulated his principles in what is probably the most famous and certainly the most astonishing document in the history of the nineteenth-century Russian revolutionary movement, the *Revolutionary Catechism*, drawn up with Bakunin's participation. Here at last was a revolutionary code that took all the nebulous notions, the unspoken desires and euphemistic phrases of the past twenty years, and expressed them in such a way as to scare off all but the hard core of truly fanatical believers. It deserves to be quoted at some length. Here are a few of the 'rules by which the revolutionary should be guided'.

PARAGRAPH 1 The revolutionary is a lost man. He has no interests of his own, no affairs of his own, no feelings, no attachments, no belongings, not even a name of his own. Everything in him is absorbed by a single, exclusive interest, a single thought, a single passion – the revolution.

PARAGRAPH 2 In the very depths of his being, not just in words but in deeds, he has broken every tie with the civil order and the whole educated world, with all laws, conventions, generally accepted conditions and morals of this world. He will be an implacable enemy of this world, and if he continues to live in it, that will only be so as to destroy it the more effectively . . .

PARAGRAPH 4 He despises public opinion; he despises and hates existing social morality in all its demands and expressions. For him moral means everything that facilitates the triumph of the revolution; everything that hinders it is immoral and criminal . . .

PARAGRAPH 6 Hard with himself, he must be hard towards

others. All tender and debilitating feelings of family, friendship, love, gratitude and even honour must be stifled in him by a single cold passion for the revolutionary cause. For him there can be only one pleasure, one consolation, one reward and one satisfaction – the success of the revolution. Day and night he must have only one thought, one purpose – merciless destruction. Working tirelessly and cold-bloodedly towards this aim, he must always be prepared to die and to destroy with his own hands anything that stands in the way of its achievement . . .

PARAGRAPH 8 . . . The measure of friendship, devotion, and other obligations towards a comrade is determined solely by the degree of his usefulness to the cause of all-destroying practical revolution . . .

PARAGRAPH 12 The acceptance into the organization of a new member, after he has already proved himself not in words but in deeds, cannot be carried out otherwise than unanimously . . .

PARAGRAPH 14 With the object of ruthless destruction the revolutionary can, and very often must, live inside society, pretending to be someone very different from what he really is. The revolutionary must penetrate everywhere: into all the lower and middle classes, into the tradesman's shop, the church, the aristocratic house, into the bureaucratic and military world, into literature, into the Third Department and even into the Winter Palace.

The whole of the 'filthy' Russian social structure was to be divided into six categories. The first, comprising the most energetic, intelligent, and therefore dangerous members of the ruling class, would be exterminated without further ado. The members of the second group could be allowed to live on for a little while longer, in the expectation that they themselves would 'by a series of savage acts drive the people into an unavoidable rebellion'. The third category consisted of 'high-placed swine' without either brains or energy; these should be ensnared, deceived, blackmailed; their 'dirty secrets' should be ferreted out by the revolutionaries, who would thus acquire control over their wealth, power and influence. The fourth category – the 'liberals' – were to be subjected to the same treatment, and then used as tools for the disruption and demoralization of society. The fifth was the category of 'revolutionary chatterboxes' (meaning all revolutionaries whose ideas happened to differ from those of Nechaev): these should be incited to reckless actions, in the course of which most would perish (and good riddance), whilst a few might redeem themselves. Finally, there came 'Women', the majority of whom were to be treated (or, rather, mistreated) similarly to the males in categories three, four and five – but a select group was to specialize in seducing and trapping key members of the ruling class. In other words, glorified prostitution in the revolutionary cause.

The concluding paragraphs of the *Revolutionary Catechism* are given over to Bakunin's beatific vision of all-encompassing destruction – but with the addition of a distinctive dose of the cynical ferocity peculiar to Nechaev:

PARAGRAPH 22 The association has no other aim but the fullest emancipation and happiness of the people, i.e. the toiling masses. As we are convinced that this emancipation and happiness can only be achieved through an all-destroying popular revolution, the association will use every means in its power to foster and spread those wrongs and those evils which will finally break the patience of our people and force them to a general revolt.

PARAGRAPH 23 By 'popular revolution' the association does not mean a regulated movement on the classical Western pattern, which is always kept in check by respect for property, traditions and those social structures called 'civilization' and 'morality' ... The only revolution that can save the people is one that destroys every element of State organization root and branch, that annihilates all State traditions of order and all classes in Russia.[9]

Now there was nothing more for Nechaev to do in

Switzerland. He had achieved all his aims: the principles of his revolutionary organization had been formulated, Bakunin's unstinting support was assured. In August 1869, armed with a membership card of a non-existent 'World Revolutionary Union' signed by Bakunin, a copy of the *Revolutionary Catechism*, a rubber stamp with the name of the new organization – *Narodnaya Rasprava*, and a large sum of money extorted from the ailing Herzen under false pretences, Nechaev returned to Russia. His plan was quite simple: to establish an organization that would carry out a popular revolution on 19 February 1870 – the ninth anniversary of peasant emancipation. What is more, he probably believed he could do it. He failed to get his revolution – but even in failure he shook Russia as nobody had shaken it since the Decembrists.

Moscow became Nechaev's centre of operations. Here, in the course of a few months, re-establishing old contacts and creating new ones, he set up a tight-knit, strictly disciplined conspiratorial group, completely subservient to himself, and consisting largely of students from the Agricultural Academy and the Technological Institute. They were told that they now formed a part of the Russian section of the World Revolutionary Union: an international order numbering four million members, with branches in every country of the world, ready to rise simultaneously at a word from its leaders – of whom Nechaev himself was one. Their guiding principles were those of the *Revolutionary Catechism*; by precept and example Nechaev set them an almost unattainably high standard of unscrupulousness in the name of the revolution. To transform the students into a really revolutionary body, he used to explain, it was necessary to make the government persecute them as harshly as possible: expel them from universities, send them to prison or exile, drive them frantic by its cruel and unjust actions. 'Only then will they become steeled in their hatred towards the foul government and society . . . Only then will our student body produce genuine revolutionaries.'[10]

Nechaev certainly did his best towards this end. He was even less fastidious in his treatment of political opponents within the revolutionary underground. The most dangerous of these, Natanson, he had got arrested by having a parcel of subversive literature sent to him from Zurich through the mail. Another enemy, one Kolachevsky, was rendered harmless by an ingenious expedient: as he was leaving his house someone stuck a packet of proclamations in his hand – a moment later he was 'caught red-handed' by a group of Nechaev's men disguised as gendarmes, who took him off to an hotel, and there, under threat of instant imprisonment, forced him to sign a bond in the sum of six thousand rubles.[11]

These months probably marked the summit of Nechaev's extraordinary career. He was feared and adored, mysterious and omnipotent. Paradoxically, it was his ruthlessness which brought about his downfall. One day he summoned several of his fellow-conspirators and informed them that another member of the organization, the agricultural student Ivanov, was a traitor who had to be liquidated immediately. We shall never know whether Nechaev really believed the story or whether he had merely invented it in order to tie the others together inexorably by the bond of a crime committed in common. But for the spellbound disciples there was no question of doubting the leader's word or hesitating to fulfil his command. The very next evening Nechaev, together with three others, murdered the unfortunate Ivanov.

A few days later the body was discovered. The police immediately sensed a political motive. Nechaev escaped to Switzerland; the rest of his group were arrested, together with a large number of people incriminated in one way or another in Nechaev's activities. The public trial of the 'Nechaevites' became a worldwide *cause célèbre*. The documentary evidence was, naturally, printed in full, and for the first time in Russian history the most inflammatory revolutionary broadsheets were faithfully reproduced for all to see, at government expense, in the decorous pages of the *Official Gazette*. The *Revolutionary Catechism*, in particular, created an indescribable sensation. The authorities decided to publish it in the belief that this testimonial to (as they saw it) total immorality, which had served as the ideological justification for a brutal murder, would cause a profound moral revulsion even among the most radical section of the intelligentsia. In the short run this object was probably achieved – to many it seemed as if Nechaev had hopelessly compromised the revolutionary cause. But, as with the Karakozov affair three years earlier, once the initial shock had worn off and the sordid details were forgotten, what remained was Nechaev's fascinating personality and selfless dedication. True, he had been somewhat over-zealous, perhaps injudicious in his methods and too extreme in his formulations – but he had done it all in a good cause: in the common cause, in fact. And so the end result was that Nechaev's widely publicized ideas entered into the public domain, to be studied, discussed, digested.

Nor was this the end of Nechaev himself, not by any means. He had reappeared in Switzerland as the hero of a great revolutionary exploit and the head of a vast underground organization, with the additional romantic aura of a man relentlessly hunted by the Russian secret police. Good men and true in many countries rallied to the defence of the man who had had the courage to commit murder in the name of progress (or so they thought). Bakunin proudly embraced his belaurelled disciple. Again they would work together towards the destruction of the old order. But the fond hopes were very soon dashed. Nechaev was now determined to organize the émigré revolutionary forces, under his own leadership, by applying the same methods and principles as in Russia. At first Bakunin saw no reason to object – were these not, after all, their joint principles? – but the aged sorcerer proved no match for his steely apprentice. Nechaev, as always, sought complete domination and total obedience; to ensure it he started blackmailing Bakunin, using various unsavoury titbits extracted secretly from the latter's papers. Bakunin, who throughout his life had exhibited an unmatched lack of scruple in dealing with others, was shattered by this unexpected development. For a while he submitted to Nechaev's dictates – then the humiliation became too great to bear. With great difficulty he succeeded in breaking free from the young man's hypnotic influence. The partnership was at an end.

In a letter to a close associate, written a few weeks after the breach, Bakunin described Nechaev's character at length, with a mixture of horror and awe. It is probably the best portrait in existence, drawn up by the man who had had more opportunities for studying Nechaev than anybody else:

> Nechaev is one of the most active and energetic men whom I have ever met. When it is a question of serving what he calls 'the cause', he does not hesitate or stop at anything and is as pitiless with himself as with everyone else . . . He is a dedicated fanatic, and at the same time an extremely dangerous fanatic. To join with him can only lead to results fatal for all . . . After the terrible shock of the catastrophe of the secret organization in Russia he has gradually convinced himself that a serious and indestructible society can only be founded on the policies of Machiavelli and the system of the Jesuits: for the body – only violence; for the soul – lies.
>
> Truth, mutual trust, genuine solidarity, can exist only among the dozen people who make up the society's *sancta sanctorum*. All the rest are to serve as a blind weapon, as soulless material in the hands of these dozen men who are in agreement among themselves. It is allowed, indeed it is even a duty, to cheat them, to compromise them, to rob them, if need be to have them killed. This is the meat of conspiracy . . . In the interests of the cause he is impelled to gain full possession of your personality without your knowledge. To achieve this he will spy after you and will try to appropriate all your secrets . . . If you introduce him to your friend, his first aim will be to sow dissension, scandal and intrigue between you, in one word, to make you quarrel. If your friend has a wife or daughter, he will try to seduce her and get her with child, in order to snatch her from the power of conventional morality and force her into a protest against society. All personal

ties, all friendships, all connections of any kind are for him evils which must be destroyed, for otherwise, if left to exist outside the secret organization, they would become an influence detracting from the unified force of the organization . . .

Without knowing it, he is a man of boundless ambition, as he has completely identified the revolutionary cause with his own person. But he is not an egoist in the common sense of the word, because he exposes himself to the most terrible risk and leads the life of a martyr, full of suffering and incredible labour. He is a fanatic, and fanaticism leads him towards transformation into a complete Jesuit . . . Yet despite all this Nechaev is a force, because he represents colossal energy.[12]

There is something comical in the extreme indignation with which Bakunin described Nechaev's methods: methods which he had himself propagated for years, and which, indeed, they had jointly set forth in the *Revolutionary Catechism*. The reason for this unwonted upsurge of moral rectitude was really quite simple. Bakunin had preached the destruction of the old order; his ringing phrases, prophesying dire retribution and promising rivers of blood and hundreds of guillotines, had resounded throughout Europe, scaring the wits out of the bourgeoisie; he lived in an atmosphere of unending plots, conspiracies, intrigues, assassinations, denunciations, of spying and counter-spying; he was intoxicated by his own revolutionary manifestoes and bloodcurdling threats. But for all his personal bravery, for all his dare-devil exploits, the fabled career of the international revolutionary never amounted to much more than a lot of brave but empty phrases. And in Sergei Nechaev, Bakunin met a man who actually meant every word that he said – that they both said. Bakunin was a romantic revolutionary – Nechaev a cold and practical politician; Bakunin declaimed about ruthlessness – Nechaev practised it. Face to face with the flesh and blood incarnation of his rhetoric, Bakunin collapsed in horror. The man of his dreams had turned out to be a figure from a nightmare.

But time was already running out for Nechaev. Despite his constant changes of identity and of domicile, the Russian secret police (almost as efficient abroad as at home) had discovered his whereabouts. The Russian government officially demanded his extradition on a murder charge. In August 1872 Nechaev was arrested in Zurich. Fresh attempts were made to save him, fresh petitions sent around, fresh progressive professors pressed to heed the calls of conscience and intercede for the intrepid young revolutionary. Even Bakunin swallowed his outraged feelings and mounted a campaign on Nechaev's behalf. It was no good: by a vote of four to three the cantonal council decided to extradite Nechaev – on condition that he be tried not as a political, but as a common criminal. On 19 October he was taken to the Peter-Paul Fortress in St Petersburg.

The Tsar's government kept its word – after a fashion. Nechaev was indicted for murder and tried by jury in Moscow in January 1873. His conduct at the trial fully lived up to his heroic reputation. Refusing to answer any questions, he disdainfully announced: 'I do not recognize a Russian court's right to try me. I am an émigré, I am no longer a subject of the Russian Emperor, none of your legal formalities have any meaning for me' – and, as he was being carried out of the courtroom for obstruction, he managed a last shout: 'I am no longer a slave of your Tyrant!'[13] It was a clear-cut case, and the trial lasted only a few hours. Nechaev was sentenced to twenty years' hard labour in the mines, to be followed by life-long exile in Siberia. When the sentence was pronounced Nechaev merely shrugged his shoulders: 'A kangaroo court!'

The authorities had kept their promise: Nechaev was tried as a common criminal. But they had no intention of actually implementing his sentence – he was a man far too dangerous to be sent to do ordinary hard labour. In complete secrecy Nechaev was transported to the most redoubtable dungeon of all the Russias: the Alexei Ravelin of the Peter-Paul Fortress. It was, quite literally, a living death: his name was replaced by a number, he was allowed neither to send nor to receive letters, not a word about his fate could reach the public. He had simply disappeared from the face of the earth. When he failed to turn up in any of the convict settlements people naturally assumed that he had been secretly executed. According to every known precedent Nechaev had reached the end of the road.

The years passed. New events, new revolutionary outrages attracted the public's attention. Nechaev became no more than a fearsome memory. A new generation of revolutionaries grew up, the Men of the Seventies, for whom Nechaev was but a legend, a name from the distant past, arousing mixed emotions of revulsion and admiration. Then, suddenly, the impossible happened. One January evening of 1881 a member of the Executive Committee of the recently formed terrorist organization, *Narodnaya Volya*, the People's Will, arrived at a conspiratorial meeting, took a letter out of his pocket and nonchalantly explained: 'From Nechaev, from the Ravelin.' His comrades remained in their places, speechless,: a corpse had risen from the grave. Yet not only was Nechaev very much alive – eight years of the harshest prison in the world had not had the slightest effect upon this man of steel. Nechaev wrote as if he had only been arrested the day before, and as if these complete strangers had been known to him all his life. In the most matter-of-fact way possible he directed them to carry out his release; his detailed plan for the operation was eminently practical and businesslike.

The famous woman terrorist Vera Figner, regarded by all as the incarnation of honour and morality, was present at the meeting: many years later, having herself spent nearly twenty-five years in gaol, she described the feelings aroused by Nechaev's resurrection: 'The letter created an astonishing impression. Everything that had lain as a dark blot on Nechaev's reputation suddenly disappeared: the innocent blood he had spilt, the financial extortions, the blackmail, everything that had gone on in the name of "the ends justifying the means", all the falsehood that had obscured the revolutionary image of Nechaev. What remained was the mind, undimmed after long years of dungeon solitude; the will, unbroken under the weight of the punishment; the energy, intact after all the suffering he had endured. When Nechaev's address was read out to the Committee we all exclaimed, with immense fervour: "He must be released!"[14] The old magic was working again.

The story behind the letter was even more amazing than the effect it created. Nechaev had accomplished a feat unique in the history of Russia or of any other country: alone, in chains, isolated from the world, without money, without friends, without contacts, without even a name, he had, by sheer force of personality, suborned practically the entire staff of the Alexei Ravelin. Gradually, one by one, he had recruited the warders and the guards of Russia's top-security prison into an illegal revolutionary organization; none knew of the others' participation; all spied on each other and duly reported to Nechaev. 'Prisoner No. 5' gave them their orders; towards the end he became the *de facto* Governor of the Ravelin. It was through the guards, who were now regularly running errands for him, that Nechaev discovered the existence of the People's Will and established contact with them. The guards were to become the instruments of his escape.

It must have been a crushing blow to Nechaev to learn that his escape was to be postponed: after much heart-searching the Executive Committee decided that first it had to get on with the matter in hand, namely the assassination of the Emperor. Whatever his personal feelings, he accepted the decision unquestioningly (according to some versions, the Committee even asked Nechaev to make the choice himself, and he, like a true revolutionary, opted for the tyrant's execution in preference to his own release). Through his trusted gaoler-emissaries Nechaev took an active part in preparing the momentous enterprise, supplying the conspirators with advice about false manifestoes, the best methods of misleading public opinion, etc. The Tsar's assassination, followed by the speedy apprehension of almost every member of the People's Will, marked the end of Nechaev's hopes. A few months later a fellow-prisoner gave him away. The whole staff of the Ravelin was immediately replaced, dozens of warders and guards were arrested. At their trial not one of these simple men uttered a word of condemnation against Nechaev, to whom they invariably referred only as 'he' – Nechaev had forbidden them even to mention his name. 'Just try and refuse him whenever he gives an order,' explained one. 'It's enough for him just to look at you.'[15]

The authorities decided to put an end to Nechaev's activities, once and for all. Within a few months he was starved to death. Sergei Nechaev died on 21 November 1882, aged thirty-five.

This last episode of Nechaev's life is important only as an illustration of his incredible personality and of the devotion which his name inspired in a later and very different generation of revolutionaries. His active political career had actually come to an end with his trial and conviction. But his ghost has haunted Russia ever since. 'For' or 'against' Nechaevism: the question became the great dividing line between various revolutionary and 'progressive' trends. Few had the courage to acknowledge themselves openly as disciples of Nechaev – fewer still of the intelligentsia could damn him out of hand, any more than the illiterate soldiers who had fallen under his spell. It was not just the personality, but the extraordinary blend of selfless idealism and total lack of scruple that exerted such a powerful influence upon the whole course of Russian revolutionary history. For what Nechaev had done, after all, was to take the moral precepts expounded by Chernyshevsky and the other radical ideologues one step further, to their logical conclusion and their enactment in practice. Just as Dostoevsky's Smerdyakov had taken his half-brother Ivan Karamazov's preachings on the nullity of good or evil, his doctrine that 'If there is no God, then all is lawful', to *their* logical conclusions of patricide. And like Ivan Karamazov, the Russian intelligentsia as a whole sensed itself to be Nechaev's involuntary and not entirely unsympathetic accomplice.

Dostoevsky, in fact, was the man who understood and dissected the nature and the roots of Nechaevism better than anyone else to this day. The Nechaev affair was the greatest *cause célèbre* of the time; for the novelist it was a distillation of everything that was wrong, not just with the radical intelligentsia, but with Russian society as a whole. Even more: it was a portent of the future. As he saw it, the Nechaev case showed up the rottenness of educated Russian 'liberal' society, which had given birth to Nechaevism and which was driving the country to an inevitable appalling catastrophe. Dostoevsky avidly followed the newspaper accounts of the Nechaevites' trial; adding to them his own first-hand knowledge of the revolutionary mentality, he created *The Possessed*, possibly the greatest political novel ever written. Shortly after publication he described it as 'almost a historical study'.

The central character of *The Possessed* is the diabolical Pyotr Verkhovensky, easily recognizable as Nechaev (Dostoevsky frequently referred to him as 'my Nechaev'). Verkhovensky's methods are those of Nechaev; his political views are almost literal paraphrases of the *Revolutionary Catechism* and other Nechaevite writings (obligingly printed in full in the *Official Gazette*). Addressing his fellow-conspirators, Verkhovensky formulated the central problem of the Russian revolution, posed by every radical ideologist from Belinsky to Lenin:

I ask you which you prefer: the slow way, which consists in the composition of socialistic romances and the academic ordering of the destinies of humanity a thousand years hence, while despotism will swallow the savoury morsels which would almost fly into your mouths of themselves if you'd take a little trouble; or do you, whatever it may imply, prefer a quicker way which will at last untie your hands, and will let humanity make its own social organization in freedom and in action, not on paper? They shout 'a hundred million heads' [i.e. to be sacrificed for the revolution]; that may be only a metaphor; but why be afraid of it if, with the slow daydreams on paper, despotism in the course of some hundred years will devour not a hundred but five hundred million heads? Take note too that an incurable invalid will not be cured whatever prescriptions are written for him on paper. On the contrary, if there is delay, he will grow so corrupt that he will infect us too and contaminate all the fresh forces which one might still reckon upon now, so that we shall all at last come to grief together.

The future social order (a preview of Orwell's *Nineteen Eighty-Four*) is merely a blunter version of the ideals of Nechaev and some of his predecessors. It is described by Verkhovensky, who attributes its authorship to the fanatical Shigalev (the character based on Varfolomei Zaitsev):

He suggests a system of spying. Every member of society spies on the others, and it's his duty to inform against them. Everyone belongs to all and all to everyone. All are slaves and equal in their slavery. In extreme cases he advocates slander and murder, but the great thing about it is equality . . . There has never been either freedom or equality without despotism, but in the herd there is bound to be equality . . . The only thing wanting in the world is discipline. The thirst for culture is an aristocratic thirst. The moment you have family ties or love you get the desire for property. We will destroy that desire; we'll make use of drunkenness, slander, spying; we'll make use of incredible corruption; we'll stifle every genius in its infancy. We'll reduce all to a common denominator! Complete equality . . .! Only the necessary is necessary, that's the motto of the whole world henceforward. But it needs a shock. That's for us, the directors, to look after. Slaves must have directors. Absolute submission, absolute loss of individuality . . .

Finally, when taking leave of his fellow-conspirators after the murder of Shatov (Ivanov), Verkhovensky sets out the tasks of the organization:

One of the reasons why you have banded yourselves together into a separate branch of a free organization representing certain views was to support each other in the cause by your energy in any crisis and if need be to watch over one another. The highest responsibility is laid upon each of you. You are called upon to bring new life into the party,* which has grown decrepit and stinking with stagnation. Keep that always before your eyes to give you strength. All that you have to do meanwhile is to bring about the downfall of everything – both the government and its moral standards. None will be left but us, who have prepared themselves beforehand to take over the government. The intelligent we shall bring over to our side, and as for the fools, we shall mount upon their shoulders. You must not be shy of that. We've got to re-educate a generation to make them worthy of freedom. [Translated by Constance Garnett]

Using slander, spying, corruption, intrigue, drunkenness, crime, murder, working upon men's most evil instincts, Verkhovensky and his band wreak havoc in the peaceful provincial city where the novel is set. Order collapses; dark, elemental forces rise to the surface, the Governor goes mad; murder and arson reign; chaos engulfs all. The 'possessed' – Dostoevsky is referring to the Biblical parable of the Gadarene swine possessed by the devil – destroy society and themselves.

Dostoevsky's novel had a highly hostile critical reception. No wonder: the Russian quality press of his day was largely run by the 'progressive' intelligentsia, who rightly saw it as a powerful denunciation of their whole way of thinking. What infuriated them most was the novel's central idea: that the well-meaning, wishy-washy elderly liberal intellectuals, the remnants of the 'Men of the Forties', were directly responsible for the appearance of the ferocious young Nihilists. World literature contains no more searing indictment of the liberal mentality than that presented in *The Possessed*. Liberalism is epitomized – highly symbolically – by Stepan Verkhovensky, Pyotr's father

---

* Significantly, the 1957 Soviet edition of *The Possessed* – the only one to have appeared since the early post-revolutionary years – substitutes 'cause' for 'party': the obvious parallel is striking enough as it is.

(based on the historian Granovsky), and also by the famous writer Karmazinov (a wicked caricature of Turgenev). The elder Verkhovensky, a foolish, garrulous old man, horrified by the excesses of the new generation of radicals, has to acknowledge not only his physical but also his moral paternity. In anguish he exclaims that their basic idea 'is a true one, but that only makes it more awful. It's just our idea, exactly ours; we first sowed the seed, nurtured it, prepared the way, and, indeed, what could they say new, after us? But, heavens! How it's all expressed, distorted, mutilated! Were these the conclusions we were striving for? Who can understand the original idea in this?'

And, indeed, the progressive-minded Fathers had sowed the seed and prepared the way for revolution and destruction – and (as happened to Karmazinov) for their own brutal repudiation and extinction at the hands of the Sons they had nurtured. This is the message of *The Possessed*.

Dostoevsky includes every segment of Russian educated society in his sweeping indictment. Destructive influences, pernicious ideas, gradually boring away beneath the surface, undermining the nation's already shaken social stability, had reduced Russia to a state when, he says, 'the most worthless fellows suddenly gained predominant influence, began loudly criticizing everything sacred, though till then they had not dared to open their mouths, while the leading people, who had till then so satisfactorily kept the upper hand, began listening to them and holding their peace, some even simpering approval in a most shameless way'. He makes Pyotr Verkhovensky gleefully list the people who are unwittingly on his side and who are doing his work for him without even knowing it: 'the teacher who laughs with children at their God and at their cradle'; 'the prosecutor who trembles at a trial for fear he should not seem advanced enough'; the modish thinkers who believe 'that crime is no longer even insanity, but simply common sense, almost a duty; anyway, a gallant protest'.

Many people would argue today that Dostoevsky's approach to the wider implications of the Nechaev affair, which he saw as a piercing ray of light that mercilessly exposed the true state of Russian educated society, has been fully borne out by events. At the time, however, this analysis was almost universally rejected. Nearly every political writer and literary critic preferred to regard Nechaev as a hideous aberration. The *Nechaevshchina*, wrote the relatively 'moderate' Populist ideologist Nikolai Mikhailovsky, 'was a monstrosity in every respect',[16] and all hurried to agree with this assessment, regardless of political persuasion. The shudder of horror that passed through even the most radical elements of the intelligentsia as the gruesome details of Ivanov's murder unfolded in full public view was genuine enough. Understandably, they all dissociated themselves from Nechaev and his methods. But there was no getting away from it: the deed, however vile, *had* been committed in the name of the Cause; the methods, however detestable, *had* been employed to hasten the coming of the Revolution; the man himself, however frightening, was undoubtedly devoted to the same ideals as they themselves; the rejection of all conventional moral standards had long been accepted by all in theory, if not in practice. Inevitably, once the first shock had worn off, many came to take a kinder view of Nechaev, and even to profit by some of his ideas.

Later generations of revolutionaries could never quite make up their minds about Nechaev. The ambivalence shows in their judgments. 'However onerous the memory of Ivanov's murder and of the brazen use of the rule "the ends justify the means",' wrote Vera Figner, 'one cannot but be amazed by his strong will and powerful character, one must give credit to his selflessness: he had no personal ambition, and his devotion to the revolutionary cause was sincere and unbounded. Despite the absence of high moral qualities, there was about him something awe-inspiring and irresistible, exerting a kind of hypnotism upon ordinary people.'[17] Strangely enough, even Vladimir Burtsev, the famous organizer of numerous political assassinations in the early years of the twentieth century and head of the Socialist-Revolutionary Party's ruthless counter-intelligence service, also found it necessary to strike a tone of high moral righteousness when writing of Nechaev: 'His force of character, his energy and boundless devotion to the revolution all show him as an extraordinary personality. But his methods: his treatment of people, including comrades, as mere pawns, and his conviction that all means were permissible, including deceit and murder, carried the risk of introducing concepts and habits which might have proved fatal for the revolutionary movement.'[18] Nechaev became a kind of whipping-boy for the revolutionaries: so horrendous was his reputation (due largely to Dostoevsky), that they had to castigate his unscrupulousness in order to establish themselves as *bona fide* pure-minded idealists – while constantly remaining under the fascination of his personality and espousing principles not very far removed from his own.

'Nechaevism' was an accusation often used in the bitter in-fighting that prevailed among Russian revolutionary groups. Everyone understood what the term stood for. After 1904 it was addressed more and more frequently – and not entirely without reason – towards Lenin and his Bolsheviks. To do them justice, the Bolsheviks were the only group (apart from Nechaev's direct collaborators) proudly to acknowledge Nechaev – at least for a short time – as one of their predecessors. In his official *History of the Russian Revolutionary Movement*, published in 1924, Pokrovsky rightly points out that Nechaev was the first man to evolve 'the plan of a pre-appointed revolution ... which was later continually ridiculed by the Mensheviks, and which was carried out almost to the letter on 25 October 1917'. Nechaev's group, continued Pokrovsky, 'already contained in essence certain features of the future revolutionary organization which was moulded into the Bolshevik party. The indispensability of a conspiratorial organization, elements of planning and armed force, the idea of an uprising as the *modus operandi* – all this can already be found there.' Most important of all, as Lenin's favourite historiographer repeatedly stressed, was Nechaev's 'somewhat clumsy but prophetic idea of a predesigned uprising'. Pokrovsky's partiality for Nechaev led him so far as to dismiss the villainous ruse by which he had attempted to betray his political rival Natanson to the police with an indulgent chuckle: 'An interesting episode of the factional struggle of the time.'[19] A perfectly reasonable comment, considering that Lenin had used almost identical stratagems in his struggle with *his* enemies – and that in those early, innocent years it was still fashionable to glory in them.

Nechaev's official recognition as a precursor of Bolshevism, however well-founded, was short-lived. The rewriting of Russian revolutionary history had begun with the advent of Stalin, and Nechaev, not surprisingly, was one of its first victims. A notorious liar, impostor and murderer was on no account to be included in the family tree. Besides, Marx had savagely denounced Nechaev and the *Revolutionary Catechism* during his battle with Bakunin, and Engels – who, like Marx, was obsessed with visions of spies everywhere – had even written to a friend in 1872: 'Nechaev either is a Russian *agent-provocateur* or at any rate acts like one.'[20] So, after the victory of the revolution for which he had given his life, Nechaev once again became, first an object of execration and vilification, and then, for many years, simply an un-person, a non-existent being as far as the history books were concerned. Nor was Pokrovsky forgiven his championship of Nechaev's rightful claims. When the time came for his views to be disavowed, his school to be demolished, and his pupils to be shot, Pokrovsky's ill-advised candour regarding the indecently un-Marxist pioneers of Bolshevism was equated with high treason. 'It is not difficult to perceive,' snarled a contributor to the notorious symposium *Against the Historical Concepts of M. N. Pokrovsky*, 'that these remarks of Pokrovsky's fully concur with the slander of the fascist bandit Zinoviev, who unsuccessfully attempted to transform Lenin into a "peasant philosopher" – only to be unmasked by Comrade Stalin in 1925.'[21]

It is one of the minor ironies of the Russian revolution that the final destruction of Nechaev's reputation should have occurred at the height of the Great Purge of 1936–8: an event of which he would probably have wholeheartedly approved, conducted in accordance with the principles he himself had formulated. The possessed had devoured their prototype.

Not even then did the Nechaev saga come to an end. The dread ghost has not been laid yet. When, after Stalin's death, all the heroic figures of the revolutionary past were at last given their due, Nechaev alone – like Trotsky, another architect of the revolution – remained unrehabilitated. The references to him in current Soviet historical literature are invariably hostile. He is called 'an unscrupulous and dishonest intriguer, a monster of evil and egoism, a rogue and a careerist'.[22] The last part of this diatribe is completely untrue, but it reflects the grave dilemma posed by Nechaev: how can the Communists admit, not only that the man was both unscrupulous *and* selfless, dishonest *and* dedicated, but that the organizational principles he so outspokenly professed were nearer to their own than those of any other nineteenth-century rebel? Hence the lies and calumnies, far more hysterical than anything invented by the Tsar's authorities.

The trouble with Nechaev, from the point of view of posterity, is that he was exceptional only by reason of his daemonic personality and cynical straightforwardness (perhaps a strange word to use in this context, but nonetheless accurate). In every other respect he was an integral part of the revolutionary tradition. His was the tradition of Chernyshevsky and Pisarev, of Zaichnevsky and Ishutin; it was to be followed, as we shall see, by many others. The revolutionary amorality he practised and preached was hardly different in essence from the principles generally, if tacitly, accepted by the radical intelligentsia. Even his methods were indistinguishable from those of other groups to come. The only real departure was the resounding scandal of Ivanov's murder. But in Nechaev's case it did make all the difference: for this reason, and this reason alone, he could be treated (by Western and Communist historians alike) as an isolated, unique phenomenon.

The case for Nechaev as a typical, though exceptionally memorable, representative of Russian revolutionism is so strong that present-day Soviet historians can rebut it only by blatant (one might almost say Nechaevite) factual and textual distortions. For example: the author of the violent condemnation of Nechaev quoted above follows it by drawing a contrast between this 'monster' and his literary counterpart, Verkhovensky, and what he calls a true 'composite portrait' of a revolutionary of the seventies: the nameless heroine of Turgenev's 'poem in prose' *The Threshold*. A young girl about to enter a revolutionary organization is undergoing a preliminary test. 'Do you know what awaits you: cold, hunger, hatred, derision, contempt, insult, illness and even death?' 'I do.' 'Complete withdrawal and solitude?' 'I am ready.' 'Not only from your enemies – from your relatives and friends? Are you prepared for nameless sacrifice? You will perish, and nobody . . . nobody will even know whose memory to honour!' 'I desire neither gratitude nor pity. I need no name.' This, gushes the Soviet scholar, is true evidence of the 'moral grandeur of the fighters against autocracy' – how utterly unlike the squalor of the *Nechaevshchina*. But in his lengthy quotation from Turgenev he deliberately omits the key exchange: 'Are you prepared to commit a crime?' 'Yes, even a crime.'[23] In other words, the mentality of this pure and dedicated revolutionary is no different from that of her alleged 'antithesis' – Nechaev. Moreover, the whole interrogation bears the strongest possible resemblance to the *Revolutionary Catechism*. Here, as always, Turgenev is a faithful chronicler of his times (his attitude towards the girl herself is ambiguous, to say the least). What he really shows in this short piece (widely reprinted in the USSR, unlike *The Possessed*) is Nechaev's profound influence upon later generations of revolutionaries.

Yet there can be no doubt that for a time the shock of the Nechaev affair – just as the Karakozov case before it – turned most of the radical intelligentsia away from conspiracy. Their convictions remained unchanged: what was badly shaken was their faith in a centralized movement with purely political aims. Conspiracy led to moral degradation, politics led nowhere. Their new-found pessimism concerning the effectiveness of political action was strengthened by the defeat of the Paris Commune of 1871, which for a brief moment had rekindled the hopes of a successful socialist revolution. A new spirit arose among the youth, especially the students: away from politics, away from Jacobinist plotting, back to the grass-roots of traditional Populism. The reaction to the Nechaev affair in the early 1870s was, in a sense, a reaction against the Men of the Sixties. A whole decade, they felt, had been wasted; they were back at square one.

CHAPTER 15

Going to the People

Gradually the numbed survivors of the student crowds and of the wave of arrests that had followed the *Nechaevshchina* began to reassemble their scattered forces and to recover their sense of purpose. There would have to be a break with the past: new paths had to be found, new methods devised. The idea of accepting the existing social and political framework of society, of peaceful and useful activity towards its inevitable development into something better, never even entered their minds. The intelligentsia remained as irreconcilably opposed to society as it had been since its first appearance. It only sought new guidelines, new answers.

The radicals found their answers in the writings of a new prophet, Pyotr Lavrovich Lavrov. No longer a young man (he was born in 1823), Lavrov had taken a long time to arrive at revolution: an ex-artillery officer and professor at the Military Academy, he had dabbled in radical journalism and progressively become more involved in anti-government propaganda, until, inevitably, he was imprisoned and exiled in the wake of the Karakozov affair. In 1870 he came to Paris, and from then on until the end of his life (1900) conducted his revolutionary activities from abroad. Lavrov was dry, scholarly, reserved, rather pedantic, comfortable only among his books and manuscripts – in fact, totally unlike the popular image of a revolutionary leader. Apart from Herzen, he was probably the only important Russian radical ideologist whose ideas bore even a limited resemblance to Western concepts of liberalism and democracy. Perhaps that is why they left no lasting imprint on the Russian revolutionary movement, but it is also the reason why – for a brief and transient period,

367

in the special circumstances of the post-Nechaev disillusionment
– they enjoyed an overwhelming influence.

In 1868, before the débâcle, Lavrov began the serialized
publication, in St Petersburg, of his *Historical Letters*. They were
completed the next year, and appeared in book form (passed
by the censor) in 1870. The book was as earnest and as dull
as any of Chernyshevsky's writings. Nor was it very original:
a general study of the laws of intellectual and social progress,
based largely on the ideas of Comte, Spencer and Buckle. Yet
to the intelligentsia it came as a blinding revelation, for the
Historical Letters were a sustained and reasoned attack against
the Nihilism of the sixties, against Pisarev's vulgar idolization
of science, against the amorality of the conspiratorial groups
(without specifically mentioning any of these by name) – an
attack, moreover, from the impeccable position of a dignified
and ethical socialism. Ethics, indeed, were at the heart of Lavrov's
concepts of socialism and progress. Progress, he wrote, was the
factor which united private ethics and public activity. There
could be no progress without ethical values. The bearer of these
ethical values was the 'critically-thinking individual', whose task
it was to incorporate into society the 'ideal of true justice'. This
was the meaning of progress – but it could only be achieved
when the 'critically-thinking individual' (i.e. the revolutionary)
had himself acquired the necessary moral and intellectual values.
The key passage of Lavrov's book read:

> *The physical, intellectual and ethical development of the individual,*
> *the materialization of truth and justice in social structures* – such
> is the brief formula which, I believe, encompasses
> everything that can be regarded as progress.[1]

But the *Historical Letters* was no abstract theoretical work:
Lavrov had set out to formulate the position of the intelligentsia
in Russian society, and the tasks that confronted them. They
owed their education and their privileges to the sacrifices of
the long-suffering people, and it was their *moral* duty to repay
this enormous debt. Understandably, he was less explicit as
to how this was to be achieved, but, briefly put, the ponderous

book's message was: improve yourselves – and then improve the people:

> The time of unconscious sufferings and dreams has passed; the time of heroic activists and fanatical martyrs, of rash waste of forces and of useless sacrifices has passed. The time has arrived for calm and conscious workers, for calculated blows, for precise thinking, and for unremitting, patient activity.[2]

Not much of a revolutionary programme, one might think: in any Western country it would have been accepted as no more than a call for gradualist reform. But Lavrov left no shadow of a doubt that the 'unremitting, patient activity' was to be directed towards the total transformation of society and the achievement of socialism. His book was received with unparalleled enthusiasm, greater than anything since *What Is to Be Done?* The radical youthful intelligentsia had always been conformist to an extraordinary degree: for all their rebelliousness, they always expected to be told what to do, whether by Herzen, Chernyshevsky, Pisarev or Nechaev. Now, at last, their problems had once again been solved. The ardour with which radical youth seized upon Lavrov's teachings as their new creed is best conveyed by the words of one of the student activists of the time: 'The *Historical Letters* became not only the handbook of the youth of the seventies. No, it was our book of life, our revolutionary gospel, our philosophy of revolution!'[3]

The change in mood – like all changes in the Russian revolutionary movement – was startlingly rapid. No more conspiracies, no more talk of seizing power – the need now was to study, to discuss, to acquire knowledge, and then to pass it on to the people by means of *propaganda* (a new word that had suddenly sprung into vogue). Beginning from 1869 innumerable 'self-education circles' shot up in all the university cities. These were not just a means of study but a way of life; many of them became 'communes', with groups of young people of both sexes moving into ramshackle houses, holding what little property they had in common, and spending their time

– over vast quantities of tea and black bread – in collectively reading and discussing Russian and Western progressive philosophical and sociological works (the fact that most were enrolled as students weighed little with them – by that time the 'eternal student' had become an accepted part of Russian life, and academic study was the last thing the authorities expected of them). The most famous of these communes was the 'Vulfovka', situated on Vulfovskaya Street in St Petersburg; most of the future active Populist revolutionaries passed through it at one time or another. Similar communes flourished in Moscow, Kiev and other centres. But the principal institutions through which students were speedily involved in 'self-improvement' (and, in many cases, eventually in revolutionary work), were the so-called *zemlyachestva*, or associations of students from the same province or town. In a situation where the intellectual needs of a gigantic empire, sprawling over two continents, were served by only six universities (excluding the German and Polish foundations in the Western non-Russian provinces) – those of Moscow, St Petersburg, Kiev, Kharkov, Kazan and Odessa – it was unavoidable that students from one and the same, frequently remote part of the country should group together for comfort and nostalgia. The authorities encouraged the formation of *zemlyachestva*, believing that they would protect the unspoilt provincials from subversive metropolitan influences. The actual result was usually the reverse: the *zemlyachestva* became hotbeds of radical activity. In many cases, indeed, they served as the nuclei for illegal circles. It should not be thought, of course, that all the participants in the hectic 'self-education' endeavours of the early seventies went on to become fully fledged revolutionaries. The great majority, having in due course achieved their degrees, left for quiet posts and uneventful lives in the provinces; some became involved in local self-government *Zemstvo* work – while most remained disaffected and disgruntled *intelligenty*, contemptuous of their own 'petty-bourgeois' way of life, fondly cherishing and even passing on the youthful radical ideas they had retained, and applauding from afar the heroic revolutionary exploits of their former comrades. But a hard-core of what later came to be known as 'professional revolutionaries' soon graduated from these circles.

By far the most influential was the so-called 'Chaikovskist' circle. It was founded in St Petersburg in 1869 by Mark Natanson, Nechaev's sworn enemy, but acquired its name from its most prominent member, Nikolai Chaikovsky. Together with its affiliated groups the Chaikovskist circle came to include, during the four or five years of its existence, almost every leading revolutionary figure of the decade: Pyotr Kropotkin, Sergei Kravchinsky (Stepniak), Sergei Sinegub, Dmitry Rogachev in the capital; Lev Tikhomirov, Nikolai Morozov, Mikhail Frolenko, Nikolai Sablin in Moscow; Andrei Zhelyabov and Felix Volkhovsky in Odessa. The youngest of the Chaikovskists became Russia's most famous revolutionary heroine: Sofia Perovskaya, the organizer of the assassination of Alexander II in 1881.

At that early stage, however, the Chaikovskists were very far from thinking of assassinations or any other kinds of plot. They viewed the very idea with horror; as Kropotkin explained in his memoirs, the circle 'arose out of a desire to counter the Nechaevite methods'.[4] It was deliberately meant to be a free and easy affair, a loose association of like-minded people, without discipline, without rules, without leaders. An active member of the circle wrote many years later: 'The circle, organized along lines completely opposite to those of Nechaev's organization, with no rules or statutes or other formalities, was based exclusively upon affinity of feelings and views concerning the main questions, upon nobility and firmness of moral principles and sincere devotion to the people's cause. This naturally led to mutual trust, respect and genuine affection for each other. A circle based on such solid foundations needed neither statutes nor generals – these latter, indeed, it would never have tolerated for a moment.'[5]

Certainly that was how it seemed at the time in the first flush of newly discovered hope. Nor was there anything particularly subversive in the Chaikovskists' early efforts. Their primary concern was with what they called 'the book enterprise' (*knizhnoye delo*): the furtherance of self-education through the establishment of a network of students' libraries. To this end they purchased large quantities of legal radical publications at wholesale prices (many sympathetic publishers even offered them at half-price) and organized their distribution throughout the country. This perfectly licit enterprise soon put the Chaikovskists in touch with large numbers of students and ex-students, mainly teachers,who were to be of great use in coming years. But the young revolutionaries' faith in tame philanthropic activity did not last long. They were not interested in education for the sake of education; from the very beginning their aim was the education of cadres for a future 'Revolutionary socialist' or 'Populist' party. After a while they began to slip illegal publications into the batches of books sent out to the provinces; then they went on, with indifferent success, to establish a printing-press abroad. Along with the circle's rapid expansion came a corresponding radicalization of its basic principles. In essence these became little more than a recapitulation of the traditional tenets of revolutionary Populism. Professor Franco Venturi rightly points to the Chaikovskists' 'unanimous, deeply felt and deliberate repudiation of any expression of constitutionalism. They held the typically Populist conviction that any concessions to freedom would only have made it still more difficult to effect the quick transformation of Russia along Socialist lines. It was not just faith in the *obshchina* and the Socialist development of peasant communities that held this movement together, but rather the translation of this faith into political terms, and its opposition to any liberal tendencies.'[6] (Extraordinary though it may sound, the most distinguished Western student of Russian Populism regards this creed as an expression of the group's 'essential originality' – after two generations of radical intelligentsia had affirmed their undying devotion to the principles of anti-constitutionalism and anti-liberalism!)

Anyone untrained to differentiate between the subtle shadings of opinion within the Russian revolutionary movement might be led to conclude from this that the sole difference between extreme 'Jacobins' like Nechaev and 'moderate' anti-Nechaevites like the Chaikovskists lay in the timing and the means by which the revolution was to be attained: the final aim was more or less the same. Even as regards methods the distinctions were extremely delicate. The genuine divergence between the two factions concerned the question of centralized conspiratorial organization, espoused by the first and renounced by the second. As for the concept of *morality* accepted by *all* Russian revolutionary groups, its interpretation was somewhat dissimilar from the Western understanding of the term. The Chaikovskists, for instance, attached great importance to ethical considerations. Prince Kropotkin was to write of them in later years: 'Never in my life have I met a group of such ideally pure and morally impressive beings as the twenty or so people whom I met at the first session of the Chaikovskist circle.'[7] Almost every memoir draws the same picture of sublime morality. Yet when it came to obtaining funds for the establishment of an illegal press the Chaikovskists (or some of them, at any rate) felt no qualms about getting a young girl, Pisarev's sister, to prostitute herself to an old man for the needed sum; soon afterwards, in 1875, the girl committed suicide.[8] For every Russian revolutionary, in the final analysis, morality was subordinated to the 'people's cause'. Revolutionary ethics can cover a multitude of sins.

By the end of 1872 the Chaikovskists began to feel, not unreasonably, that they had already achieved creditable results: they had overcome the confusion and despair created by Nechaev, established a new system of revolutionary organization, rallied a substantial group of fresh and dedicated young people to the cause of liberation. It was time to move on from self-improvement to revolutionizing the people. Having discarded conspiracy, what they wanted most was a revolutionary journal: a new *Kolokol*, attuned to their sentiments, in touch with Russian developments, capable of supplying them, not with leadership – they rejected the very concept – but with instruction and guidance. After they failed to start a paper of their own they naturally turned for aid to Lavrov, who had been in constant contact with them throughout, and had followed their efforts with growing hope. Lavrov accepted their invitation, and in March 1873 the first issue of his journal appeared in Switzerland under the title of *Vperyod* (Forwards). For a number of years it was to remain the leading Russian revolutionary organ, widely read inside the country, and exercising an influence second only to Herzen's old paper. *Vperyod* was in no sense a party organ; its views were not accepted as compulsory directives – but, by and large, it did for a time reflect the main current of Populist thought and action. Lavrov's platform was to provide the ideological inspiration for the momentous events of 1873-5. It was set forth in the leading article of the first issue of *Vperyod*, called simply 'Our programme'.[9]

Lavrov began by tackling the vexed question of ends and means:

> The propagation of the truth cannot be attained by means of falsehood; the implementation of justice cannot be achieved by means either of exploitation or of the authoritative rule of personalities; victory over indolent self-gratification cannot be brought about by means of violent seizure of unearned wealth or the reversion of the right to self-indulgence from one person to another.

Yet after this eminently moderate exposition Lavrov went on to stress that 'in certain circumstances' it would inevitably be necessary, 'temporarily', to use both falsehood and violence *'against enemies'*. Such methods, though, were unthinkable among comrades:

> People who assert that *the end justifies the means* should always restrict this rule with a simple truism: *with the exception of means that undermine the end itself.* We unconditionally reject the use of *inexpedient* means.

No special analytical powers are required to see that Lavrov's formula was elastic to the point of double-talk: the end *does* justify the means – unless they happen to be inexpedient. Deceit and coercion can be used against the enemy – but who is to define the 'enemy'? Nechaev, after all, had only murdered an 'enemy'. But the basic inconsistency of Lavrov's ethical position passed completely unnoticed: for a revolutionary *intelligent,* educated on Chernyshevsky, it marked the height of moderation and morality.

The central element of Lavrov's programme was the socialist reconstruction of Russian society. Here his views, although following in the footsteps of earlier teachers, displayed an undoubted originality:

> The *social* question is for us the primary question: the most important task of the present time, and the sole possibility for a better future . . . The *political* question is subordinated to the social and especially to the economic questions. States, *as they exist today,* are hostile to the working-class movement, and they will all have finally to disintegrate and be replaced by a new social system . . .

It was at this point that Lavrov diverged from classical Populist theory. Although, from Herzen and Chernyshevsky onwards, most Populist authors (except the 'Jacobins') had emphasized the paramountcy of the 'social question' and called for the eventual abolition of the State, they were basically *étatistes* who believed in social transformation by political means, and, in particular, by means of the apparatus of State. Unlike them, when Lavrov wrote of 'social revolution' he meant a socialist transformation of society to be effected, not by political measures, but primarily by social developments. The *obshchina* – that miraculous, life-giving Russian institution – should be developed into the principal political and economical element of the social system; the country would be changed into a voluntary federation of small self-governing social units, of communes and associations. 'All existing centralizing political programmes are completely irreconcilable with our own.' Lavrov's beauteous vision of a free, Stateless Russia (perhaps the most unrealistic scheme ever hatched even by the proverbially impractical Russian intelligentsia), had many features in common with that of Bakunin. But the two prophets' paths sharply diverged when it came to the question of bringing about the ideal. Lavrov's concept of revolution was uncompromisingly opposed to Bakunin's (or to that of almost any other Populist ideologue):

Our prime postulate is that the reconstruction of Russian society should be carried out not only *with the aim* of the people's welfare, not only *for* the people, but also *by* the people. We believe that the modern Russian activist should renounce the obsolete conception that revolutionary ideas produced by a small but better educated minority group can be imposed upon the people – that the socialist-revolutionaries, having overthrown the central government by a well-timed onslaught, can then take its place and introduce a new system by legislative means, as a generous benefactor of the unprepared mass. We do not want any new coercive power in place of the old one, whatever the sources of this new power.

The future system, continued Lavrov, must be established in accordance with the conscious will of the majority. No minority, however civilized and well-meaning, has the right to enforce its concepts upon the people: all it can do is assist the people towards an understanding of their own interests and of the ways by which these can be realized. 'Only when the course of events will itself indicate the moment for revolution and the preparedness of the people – only then can one call upon the people to carry out this revolution.' But the only thing the intelligentsia can do to hasten that moment is to work, methodically and painstakingly, among the people, to gain the people's confidence, to understand the people's wishes, to establish a common classless language. A revolution is inevitable in Russia – but revolutions are not *made* artificially, they occur only as a result of complex historical processes. At the present time, concluded Lavrov, our mission is to *prepare* the revolution. How? The answer was ready:

A member of the civilized class, having armed himself with considerable knowledge and with an understanding of the people's needs, can *go to the people*. He will reject any participation in the present Russian state system; he will become an ordinary worker, one of those who suffer and struggle for their daily bread; and, if only he is capable of this, he will devote all his intellectual proficiency to the popular cause. [My italics.]

Go to the people, thundered Lavrov: tell them about their rights, show them how these rights are to be acquired, get them to understand that they possess the power to destroy the existing system and to establish a new social order.

At last the youthful intelligentsia, impatient for action, had received a slogan and a programme: go to the people! At last there was a practical job to be done, instead of just reading and trying to understand the ponderous and dreary works of Western philosophers and sociologists, none of whom seemed to have anything to say about the Russian peasant. 'Going to the people' was not an entirely novel idea – it had been put forward already by both Herzen and Bakunin – but it was Lavrov's message which got through. The effect was extraordinary: never before had a revolutionary slogan caught the imagination of practically the entire educated youth of the country. It inaugurated one of the most bizarre, and memorable, episodes of Russian revolutionary history.

Preparations for 'going to the people' got under way in the autumn of 1873. Students in the university cities struck up acquaintanceships with local factory-workers; not without difficulty, they began learning the language and the habits of the common people; the more conscientious even established workshops where they set out to master the crafts of carpenter, smith, wheelwright, etc. The most surprising feature of this movement was its genuinely spontaneous nature: there was no directing centre, no organization, no general plan. The Chaikovskists, who might have introduced some elements of unity, had very little to do with the movement – most of their leading members were arrested that same autumn. The whole venture consisted of thousands of selfless young men and women, acting on their own, all suddenly seized by the electrifying idea of 'going to the people'. They gathered in small groups to discuss plans, chart itineraries, arrange rendezvous, collect literature, and so on. That was about all the organization there was: inflamed with heady visions of finally meeting The People, those great natural socialists, and marching with them arm-in-arm towards a glorious future, they had no desire for any more formal arrangements. Nor can one speak of any ideological uniformity among those preparing to 'go to the people': the majority were 'Lavrovists' or 'propagandists', i.e. advocates of disseminating revolutionary knowledge among the people in preparation for the inevitable upheaval; some were 'Bakuninists' or 'agitators', who believed that a few inspired lectures would be enough to start off a *jacquerie* almost at once; others still were moved by no more than a vague feeling of guilt and a craving for good works. The one thing which united this motley assemblage was a boundless faith in the miraculous effects of 'going to the people'.

What, it is reasonable to ask, did they actually hope to achieve? A mixture of aims: to teach the people, to learn from the people, to find out how the people lived and what they thought, to share the sufferings of the people, to merge with the people and thereby acquire their trust, to make the people understand the full horror of their condition, to explain to the people the possibility of a better social order and the necessity of struggling to attain it, to galvanize the spontaneous revolutionary energies of the people and incite them to rebellion.

It was a beautiful dream, a fantasy born of the world of illusion created and inhabited by the intelligentsia. The dream was lived out – with disastrous consequences – in what came to be known as the Mad Summer of 1874.

Beginning in late spring, thousands of educated young men and women poured out of the cities to meet the people. They went alone or in small groups, making their way from village to village, with little bundles of books and belongings slung over their shoulders, walking or hitching rides in peasant carts, dressed in peasant clothes, doing their best to talk and act like peasants, yet also attempting to establish contact with local teachers and other potential sympathizers. They went, radiant with hope and joy, confident of a miracle; they were to preach the gospel of Socialism and Justice to the peasants who had awaited the message for so long, and the walls of tyranny would come tumbling down. It was not really a political movement at all, but another Children's Crusade. Many of its most enthusiastic participants were to understand this in later and sadder years. In his memoirs Sergei Kravchinsky (Stepniak) conveys the full flavour of 'going to the people':

> This movement can hardly be called political. It was, much rather, a kind of Crusade: infectious and all-absorbing, exactly like any *religious movement*. People were straining, not only to achieve certain practical aims, but also to fulfil a deeply felt need for *personal* moral purification . . . The propagandist of the Seventies was the type of person brought forth *by religious rather than revolutionary movements*. Socialism was his faith, the people – his god. However patently absurd this was, he firmly expected the revolution to take place at any moment – just as in the Middle Ages people would expect the Second Coming.[10]

Not since the great religious Schism of the seventeenth century had Russia witnessed a mass missionary campaign of such uncompromising faith, exaltation and ardour.

The disillusionment was speedy and shattering. After only a few weeks of work among 'the people' the student radicals were in complete despair. The peasants regarded them at best with incomprehension and suspicion, at worst with open hostility. All their cherished preconceptions had been proved wrong: they had 'gone to the people' – and the people had met them as unwanted interlopers. For the first time the intelligentsia realized that the abyss between them and the peasantry could not be bridged. Some, heartbroken, gave up after a month or so; others went on, trudging from village to village till the onset of autumn; a few stuck it out for nearly a year. But even the most innocent and ecstatic needed a very short time to arrive at the truth.

Innumerable letters sent during the summer of 1874 from various parts of the country all recounted the same tale of woe. Wherever they went they were faced with total lack of understanding, and, even more infuriating, with that curious mixture of obtuseness and cunning which the Russian peasant had evolved over the centuries for dealing with his social betters (the *'barin'* or 'master'). A young girl, Inna Ovchinnikova, wrote to a friend in August: 'Believe me, you can't even talk to them, all the time you feel you don't know enough to prove anything, even to refute their superstitions (and they are full of these), because they refer to facts which, they claim, they witnessed themselves, so there's nothing left to do but give up ... My pupils only like to listen to books about nature and dislike any works of fiction which touch upon social questions like factory life. They're interested only in the funny parts, and miss all the main things.'[11] A more experienced revolutionary, Solomon Aronzon, wrote in the same way: 'They listen all right, but they don't pass anything on, and talk remains talk. They don't take it to heart: it all goes in at one ear and out at the other.'[12]

Populist memoirs provide an inexhaustible fund of anecdotes illustrating the débâcle of 'going to the people'. The passage of time had mellowed even the fiercest revolutionaries, and looking back at it they saw the comical aspects of the improbable encounter. Osip Aptekman, who had begun his revolutionary career, while a medical student, with the Chaikovskists, and then spent a year working (as a carpenter) 'among the people', describes a number of colourful and revealing episodes. He began his propaganda after spending several weeks innocuously working in a Ukrainian village. One evening he gave a group of peasants a popular account of the terrible fate of the English peasantry, of enclosures and pauperization. They listened with absorption, occasionally breaking in with surprised remarks about these unspeakable goings-on. Then the senior member of the gathering began to speak. 'Yes, they've ill-treated the people over there. Ruined them. This is all the lords' doing, they've taken all the land for themselves. They had the power because they run all the affairs there. The same thing would have happened here – but the Tsar didn't allow it. Of course, we don't have too much land either, hardly enough to feed a chicken. But the Tsar will give us the land. Of course he will; you can't get on without land, can you? Who will pay the taxes? Who'll fill the treasury? And without a treasury, how can you rule the country? We'll be given the land, and that's for sure.' A lively discussion followed, and all agreed that 'We're much better off with our Tsar than any of those other countries, where the lords run everything.' Aptekman makes no attempt to hide his astonishment at the way the illiterate peasants managed to transform all his subversive propaganda into arguments for autocracy.[13]

He had a lot to learn about peasant attitudes. Some time later, and more than a thousand miles away, he was holding forth to a peasant meeting on the beauties of the future socialist society, where all the land would belong to the people, when he was interrupted by a triumphant exclamation: 'Won't it just be lovely when we divide the land! I'll hire two labourers and what a life I'll have!'[14] On another occasion, when Aptekman read out an article from the radical journal *Fatherland Notes* (*Otechestvennye Zapiski*) on the growing class differentiation among the peasantry, he aroused a furious response: 'Lies, it's all lies you're reading! It's the masters up to their tricks again. I'm telling you the truth: it's all them! They're envious that the peasant has begun to improve his position, that's why they're inventing stories about him . . . The masters would still like to return to the old days, but it's not in their power.'[15]

Needless to say, all this came as a startling revelation to the Populists. After years of discussing the 'people' from every possible angle, they did not have the faintest idea of what the real people were actually like. The idealized storybook vision of a nation of 'spontaneous socialists', ready at any moment to rise against the Tsar and all their other oppressors, vanished (for a time, at least). Aptekman was lucky: he only found himself misunderstood. Many others were simply handed over to the police by the irate peasants. Such, for instance, was the fate of one of the movement's leaders, Porfiry Voinaralsky. At a peasant meeting in Samara region he began by describing the government's misdeeds, and then went on to the solution: kill the authorities, the landowners and the priests, burn down the churches, throw out the Tsar, and take the land for your own. But what if the soldiers intervene? his listeners asked. They won't, he reassured them, because many of them support us. But, they went on, how can you exist without Tsar and authorities? For example, what if a bad man appears in the community: who will take care of him? The community can do it itself, he replied. But if there are ten or twenty bad men, the peasants persevered, then we won't be able to manage. At that point Voinaralsky lost his temper, called them a pack of fools, and explained that the French got along perfectly well without a Tsar. The peasants, their suspicions thoroughly aroused, began inquiring about his name and his papers. It was easy to get papers, he said airily, he had friends everywhere. The peasants sent for the police.[16] The story would be funny had it not ended tragically: Voinaralsky spent the next ten years in prison, and another thirteen years in Siberian exile.

These experiences were fairly typical; wherever they went, the enthusiastic young Populists met with the same reception. The remnants of the Crusade straggled home deeply disillusioned. In the words of the future terrorist leader Mikhail Popov, 'the hope that our propaganda would arouse the village people to active struggle, or at least inspire the peasantry with faith in the beneficial results of such a struggle: this hope failed. The peasant listened to the revolutionary just as he listens to the priest preaching about the Kingdom of Heaven – and, after the sermon, as soon as he left the church he went on living in exactly the same way as before the sermon. Many of those who had gone to the people returned with this conviction.'[17]

The episode of 'going to the people' ended in more than a moral débâcle: by the end of 1874 hundreds of active propagandists had been arrested. Some impression of the scope of the arrests, as well as the extent of Populist propaganda in the countryside in the 'Mad Summer', can be gained from the secret report compiled by the Minister of Justice, Count Pahlen, a copy of which was procured by the revolutionaries and published the next year in Geneva.[18] Subversive propaganda had been exposed in 37 provinces (*gubernii*), i.e. in the greater part of European Russia; criminal proceedings had been instituted against 770 persons (including 158 women): of these 265 were already in prison, 452 were under police surveillance, and 53 had not yet been caught. What genuinely astonished the Minister of Justice was not the large number of participants – the police had a fairly good idea of what was going on in the universities – but the widespread support and sympathy they enjoyed among the upper reaches of society. For the first time the authorities began to realize that they were faced not simply with the impetuous actions of a few misguided youngsters but with the deep-rooted disaffection of the educated and privileged classes. Count Pahlen (contrary to the generally accepted idea of the intense stupidity of Tsarist officialdom) fully appreciated the implications of this development – certainly far better than the sophisticated supporters of revolutionary upheaval.

'The investigation has shown,' he wrote to the Emperor, 'that many no longer young persons – fathers and mothers of families, well situated financially and holding honoured positions in society – not only failed to oppose [the young revolutionaries] but, on the contrary, offered them overt sympathy, aid and assistance. In their blind fanaticism they seem not to realize that the ultimate consequence of such actions would be the doom of society and of themselves.' The Minister listed a whole catalogue of seemingly inexplicable follies: the wife of a colonel in the Gendarmes helping her propagandist son with advice and information; a rich landowner and magistrate hiding one of the leading revolutionaries; a professor deliberately introducing a known propagandist to his students; the families of several State Councillors and generals (Perovskaya's family among them) warmly approving of their children's activities, etc. 'The propagandists' successes,' concluded the Minister bitterly, 'are due not so much to their own efforts and actions as to the ease with which their teachings penetrate into certain sectors of society and to the sympathy they meet there.'

Count Pahlen's official report fully confirmed the mordant indictment of Russian educated society contained in *The Possessed*: estranged – and growing ever more estranged – from the State, permeated with revolutionary, subversive and progressive ideas, exultantly anticipating the downfall of the existing order. It was a bleak outlook.

But if the authorities were alarmed, the revolutionaries were positively despondent. They had played their trump card; they had staked all on a venture which, they had convinced themselves, would lead to swift success – and they had lost. Their best people were put out of action; many were to spend years in gaol, coming up before a court only in 1877-8, at the so-called Trial of the 193. Worst of all, their whole concept of the revolution had collapsed: the peasants had simply refused to listen to them. Another half-hearted attempt at going to the people was made in 1875, but it soon petered out ingloriously. Clearly, all the ideas evolved in the preceding years would have to be scrapped and a completely new beginning made. Yet another radical break with the past was inevitable.

The propagandists returned to the cities; experiences were discussed; the great debate was on. 'All of us,' wrote Aptekman, 'were tormented by the same problems, all sought some way out of this transitional stage.' It was amazing, he went on, how rapidly, without any pre-arrangement, people were coming to identical conclusions about the future forms of revolutionary work. 'It had become clear that the propaganda of socialism in its full form could not be successful at the present stage of the people's development ... It was necessary to change our revolutionary activity among the people as regards agitation and organization. To this end we would have to establish, within the intelligentsia itself, a "strong power", i.e. a firm and comprehensive organization. These two points summed up the essence of all our fiery debates as well as their final conclusion. Life itself had forced these two principles upon us.'[19]

There were very few dissenters, mainly from among the orthodox Lavrovists. But their day had passed. Lavrov himself went on, preaching his doctrine of gradualism and at the same time trying to adapt his views to the changed temper of the times, but now his voice carried little authority. His remedy had been tried and found wanting. His former followers now turned upon him with the same fury (if not the same outrageous insolence) which Herzen had had to experience a decade earlier. The disillusionment with peaceful propaganda, the shock of finding themselves rejected by the people, the pain caused by seeing their comrades fall into the hands of the police, the shaming feeling of having made fools of themselves – for nothing, absolutely nothing: all this welter of emotions was expressed, with passion and barely controlled rage, in a letter written to Lavrov early in 1876 by Sergei Kravchinsky (Stepniak), one of the most highly regarded 'practical workers' of Populism:

> One must possess what is known as a revolutionary instinct: a quality that is not to be acquired by means of reason or logic . . . *In you this instinct is lacking.* You are a man of reason, not of passion. Well, that is insufficient . . .
>
> You are awaiting the time when the Russian people will be capable of rising with a *clear and conscious* programme of faultless purity. You are also waiting for them to rise *throughout the whole of Russia,* for only under *both* these conditions is the revolution of which you speak possible . . .
>
> What do you propose to do to bring this about? You advise us to go 'to the people', and propagandize, propagandize, propagandize – until finally a large enough part of the people has been won over by our propaganda to impart consciousness to the mass and provide leadership for the mass . . . Your universal panacea boils down to chatter . . .
>
> We believe neither in the possibility nor in the necessity

of the revolution that you are expecting. History provides no examples of a revolution beginning lucidly, consciously, 'scientifically' – as you expect of the greatest and most difficult of all: of the social revolution . . .

Likewise, we believe neither in the possibility nor in the necessity of a gigantic or all-Russian rebellion. Popular rebellions, with us as with other nations, have always begun from the rebellion of a small group, a small place . . .

Can propaganda create even a tiny revolutionary minority within the people? No, it is completely powerless to achieve this. It is ridiculous even to think of it. After all, we are but a tiny handful, while the people number 60 million. Our propaganda weapons are insignificant in the extreme, while our opponents' weapons of seduction are terrifying. We cannot change the thinking not only of one-sixtieth but even of one-six hundredth part of the mass . . .

And how long can we survive these terrible blood-lettings? We are already bankrupt. We have hardly anything left, we are playing our last cards. Today life is only just flickering; soon it will die out completely. Total reaction will follow. And this will drag on and on, until our youth becomes *embourgeoisé*, just as it became *embourgeoisé* in every other country where it was once revolutionary. And this is not too far off. The process is already taking place fairly rapidly, and only a *constitution* is missing for it to blossom out in full. And all the signs are that we won't have to wait too long for one . . .

That is what would inevitably happen were our intelligentsia to follow your organ: the revolution in Russia would be killed for several generations!

But this is not to be! The Russian intelligentsia is not following you. With great effort, feeling its way in the dark, it is discovering a new path, and the time is approaching when it will step onto it firmly, clearly and consciously . . .

Everyone will realize the necessity for *organization*. This is already beginning to be felt by all. Nobody will go to *disseminate propaganda* for a revolt – all will understand the absurdity of this. A revolt has to be organized. Such is the conclusion which I have arrived at by the hard way, together with many of my friends, who were themselves participants in the latest drama while it was still taking place in the towns and villages.[20]

Kravchinsky was writing in his own name only, but he expressed the bitter mood of his whole generation of revolutionaries. Without realizing it, he was repeating, almost word for word, the tirade of Dostoevsky's Pyotr Verkhovensky. His conclusions were the conclusions reached by the Men of the Seventies after the fiasco of 'going to the people'. Many, of course, took much longer time to draw the lessons of 1874: it is always difficult to rid oneself of cherished illusions, and in this case the illusions were based on the main body of Populist doctrine as evolved over the years. Lavrov's influence did not disappear overnight; he continued to argue his case (albeit in a somewhat modified form), and people continued to read and ponder his advice. But the magic was shattered. 'Lavrovism' remained a subject for academic debate, but it had, to all intents and purposes, ceased to exist as a basis for practical activity by the end of the seventies.

CHAPTER 16

Tkachev and the Roots of Leninism

The episode of 'going to the people' marked a decisive turning-point in the development of the revolutionary movement. For the first and only time the tradition founded by the Decembrists and fostered by Chernyshevsky and his disciples – the tradition of organized conspiracy, of élitist leadership of political action, the tradition of anti-constitutionalism and anti-liberalism, the tradition of trying to prevent the country's peaceful, Western, 'capitalist' evolution – had been broken. The intelligentsia had tried to win over the people to their side by means of gentle propaganda. The experiment was never to be repeated. The wheel had come full circle: back to the idea of a tight-knit conspiracy and the seizure of power in the name of the people. The experience of 1874 was crucial because it proved convincingly (within the revolutionary frame of reference) that any other method was fruitless. Kravchinsky's letter, so typical of the disenchanted writings of dozens of his comrades, showed the traditional fear of constitutionalism, liberalism and capitalism reasserting its old grip. The forces of evil would have to be fought and destroyed – by planning, organization, discipline, guile and, above all, by force.

The man who gave these ideas their fullest expression, who fashioned a whole practical theory of revolution out of them, and who was to leave an indelible mark upon the future development of the Russian revolutionary movement, was Pyotr Nikitich Tkachev. His name is barely mentioned in Soviet Russia today (and is practically unknown in the West). For this there are excellent reasons: Tkachev was the essential link between Chernyshevsky and Lenin, the legatee of Populism and the precursor of Bolshevism, the man who distilled the experience of the past into a forecast of the future. Of all the skeletons in the Bolshevik cupboard, Tkachev's is the most embarrassing – it rudely intervenes into the apostolic succession of Marx–Engels–Lenin. Yet, unlike Nechaev, Tkachev can hardly be written off as an unscrupulous adventurer. He was a considerable, forceful and original thinker; although generally regarded (by himself as well as others) as a Russian Jacobin, in actual fact he created a crude amalgam of Jacobinism, classical Populism and Marxism: a foretaste of things to come. Unrecognized in his lifetime, unhonoured after his death, he remains a central figure of the Russian revolutionary tradition.

Tkachev was born in 1844 into a petty nobleman's family. He joined the revolutionary movement in his teens, and was first arrested in 1861, during the famous St Petersburg students' strike. The next ten years of his life alternated between prison and journalism – a common enough combination. From the very beginning of his political and literary career Tkachev was a convinced Jacobin. As such, he stood outside the mainstream of the Populist movements of the 1860s, although he maintained rather vague connections with some of the revolutionary circles. The turning-point came when he met Sergei Nechaev, then beginning his meteoric ascent. For a short time the two were very close; together they wrote the *Programme of Revolutionary Action*, which called for the emergence of 'revolutionary prototypes' to hasten and lead the inevitable revolution (see pp. 338-9). Very little is known about the actual collaboration between Nechaev and Tkachev; although the cold and rational Tkachev seems never to have fallen under Nechaev's hypnotic spell, throughout his life he remained faithful to the principles they had jointly elaborated, and he never wavered in upholding Nechaev as a model for emulation – not even when practically every other revolutionary recoiled in horror from the sordid mess of the *Nechaevshchina*.

In March 1869 Tkachev was arrested, and two years later he was tried together with the other Nechaevites (though he was not even accused of complicity in Ivanov's murder). He was sentenced to sixteen months in gaol. In December 1873 the Chaikovskists helped to smuggle Tkachev out of the country and to get him to Switzerland. As an experienced journalist, he was expected to help Lavrov with the publication of *Vperyod*. But that was not quite how it worked out.

Tkachev had evolved his distinctive philosophy of revolution well before he went into self-imposed foreign exile. Like everybody else, he shared the fundamental tenets of the Populist creed: faith in the *obshchina*, in the advantages of Russia's backwardness, in the imminence of revolution, in the necessity of preventing capitalist development, in Russia's peculiar suitability for building socialism. Together with Zaichnevsky, Nechaev and the other Jacobins, he believed in a conspiratorial organization that would seize power by means of a coup d'état. His faith in the people was strictly limited, to say the least. But Tkachev was much more than a professional conspirator. To an even greater degree, perhaps, than Chernyshevsky, his revolutionary views were firmly grounded in a general philosophy of economic materialism. Nor was this the 'vulgar materialism' of Vogt and Moleschott, espoused by Pisarev: although it may be an exaggeration to call Tkachev the 'first Russian Marxist' (as Pokrovsky did in an exuberant moment), there is no doubt that he was one of the first serious Russian students and followers of the economic theory of Karl Marx. As early as 1865 Tkachev had written of Marx's *Zur Kritik der Politischen Ökonomie* (the first mention of Marx's book in the Russian press): 'This idea has now become common to practically all thinking and honest men, and no intelligent person could find any serious objection to it.'[1] In his scholarly writings Tkachev adhered to Marx's concept of the determining role of the economic factor in historical development.

All the more ironical, therefore, that Tkachev was soon to become the first man to contend against the application of Marx's theories to Russia. For while he accepted the general Marxist analysis of human society, he held very un-Marxist views concerning the future of his own country.

Tkachev's unorthodoxy, extreme even by Russian standards,

became apparent almost immediately after his arrival in Zurich. His collaboration with Lavrov was short-lived: Tkachev only had time to publish one article in *Vperyod* before it broke up. No other outcome was conceivable; not only were the two men utterly incompatible personally – they held diametrically opposed ideas on the nature and future development of the Russian revolution. Tkachev had mistrusted Lavrov for years; now he saw him as an unregenerate liberal who was poisoning Russia's youth with his gradualist precepts and actively retarding the growth of the revolutionary movement. Lavrov, then at the height of his fame and influence, in his turn regarded Tkachev as a distasteful upstart and intriguer, an atavistic and dangerous throwback to the dark days of Nechaev. The break, swift and spectacular, was to have far-reaching consequences.

Shortly upon arriving in Zurich Tkachev established contact with a small Russo-Polish group known as the *Cercle Slave*, which stood in opposition equally to Bakunin and Lavrov. Their views were fairly close to his own; in an anti-Lavrovist broadsheet they had expressed the opinion that 'to expect the initiative for progress to come from the majority is stupidity, if not treason'.[2] Tkachev found them congenial company, and it was probably with their material assistance that in April 1874 he published his first full-scale attack against Lavrov: the pamphlet 'The Tasks of Revolutionary Propaganda in Russia'. The great ideological battle that was to continue for six years, split the revolutionary movement into followers of Lavrov and Tkachev, and lead to the concise formulation of two opposing concepts of the revolution, had opened.

Tkachev began by a concentrated onslaught upon Lavrov's basic idea of preparing the revolution by educating the people (at the very moment when thousands of young Populists, full of high hopes, were preparing to 'go to the people'). This concept, Tkachev declared, was not only remote from any genuine revolutionary activity but would inevitably serve to destroy the opportunities for revolution. Addressing Lavrov directly (the pamphlet was sub-titled 'A Letter to the Editor of *Vperyod*') he wrote: 'For you the revolution means the realization in public life of the needs of the majority, as recognized and understood by the majority itself.' He quoted Lavrov's own words, according to which the revolution could take place 'only when the course of events will itself indicate the moment for revolution and the preparedness of the people'. But did he not see, continued Tkachev vehemently, that this was equivalent to denying the possibility or even the necessity of revolution? For if, by some miracle, the majority were ever to recognize its needs and to discover the means of achieving them – why, then no revolution would be required, no revolution would be possible, everything would take place gradually, along the path of 'peaceful progress', in an era of bloodless revolutions 'the idea of which has now become the basis of the West European working-class movement, the basis of the German programme of the International'.[3]

Against Lavrov's (and, by implication, Marx's) faith in the gradual revolutionary development of the toiling masses, founded on the inexorable workings of the laws of social progress, etc., Tkachev put forward his own revolutionary theory, adapted specifically to what he saw as Russia's peculiar circumstances. It consisted of three main propositions.

The first stated flatly that any real revolution could only be a minority movement:

Do you not understand that the difference between revolution (in the usual sense of the word) and peaceful progress is that the first is carried out by a minority, and the second by a majority . . . A violent revolution can take place only when the minority is no longer willing to wait until the majority itself recognizes its needs, and when it decides, so to speak, to impose this consciousness upon the majority, when it attempts to bring the people's muted but ever-present feeling of dissatisfaction to the point of explosion . . . And when this explosion takes place the minority tries to give it a sensible, rational shape, directs it towards certain aims.[4]

Tkachev's second principle concerned the imperative necessity of a revolution *as soon as possible*. It is at this point that we get the full flavour of his originality: his combination of Marxist social analysis with Jacobin revolutionism and Populist faith in the *obshchina*. Unlike all his predecessors, Tkachev believed that Russia was subordinated to the same laws of historical development as Europe – she was only a bit backward, but catching up fast. The persistence of the village community was a historical fluke which could not last much longer. The inference was clear: a speedy revolution, for which the circumstances were still uniquely propitious:

Have we the right to wait? Have we the right to spend time on re-education? Remember that every hour, every minute separating us from the revolution costs the people thousands of victims; even more, it diminishes the very probability of success. At present the strongest enemy confronting us is our government, with its armed forces and its vast material power. As yet there does not exist any intermediate force between the government and the people which could, for any length of time, stop and arrest the popular movement once it has begun.

The nobility are negligible as a social force; the *tiers état* is only beginning to develop into a Western-type bourgeoisie. But this favourable situation cannot last long: Russia is already moving 'in the same direction as the economic development of the Western European states'. The *obshchina* is beginning to dissolve; the peasantry is becoming stratified; modern industry is developing. In short, all the conditions exist for a rapid evolution of a bourgeoisie and a proletariat, and this would make the chances of a revolution more and more uncertain:

This is why we cannot wait. This is why we claim that in Russia a revolution is indispensable, and indispensable now, *at this moment*. We cannot permit any postponement, any delay. It is *now*, or perhaps very soon, *never*. Now the

393

circumstances are in our favour – within ten or twenty years they will be against us.[5]

Tkachev's third postulate derived logically from the first two. What was needed above all was a revolutionary party, and the émigré revolutionary journal would have to serve the needs of this party:

> The organ of this party has two obligations: first, it must spur on the party to action, elucidate the course of action, develop and defend its programme, promote its unity and its organization. Secondly, it must serve the party as a practical weapon in its struggle against the regime by means of revolutionary agitation.[6]

The (as yet non-existent) party, supported by its revolutionary journal, would conduct three types of political activity: organization, i.e. 'the unification of all separate, individual endeavours into a single, common, disciplined, orderly whole'; propaganda, or 'what your journal calls "the development among the people of a recognition of their rights and needs"'; and agitation, i.e. 'the direct incitement of the people to rebellion'. All three methods were equally valid and complementary: used in isolation, none would achieve the desired results. If we limit ourselves to instigating a rebellion, explained Tkachev, we could probably bring one about, but there would be little likelihood of its expanding into a genuine revolution. On the other hand, were we to organize a coup d'état we might quite possibly carry one out successfully – 'but it would not penetrate into the depths of the people's life, it would not arouse and agitate the lowest classes of society, it would only convulse the surface; in other words, it would not be in the least a popular revolution'.[7]

These remarks are of the utmost importance: they show that, contrary to the allegations made by both Soviet and Western historians (not to mention contemporary political figures), Tkachev was neither a follower of Bakunin nor of Blanqui. He repudiated the idea of a spontaneous peasant rebellion just as he rejected the concept of an isolated coup d'état. What he clearly stood for was an élitist, disciplined and conspiratorial party that would stir up and lead a great popular revolution. Tkachev concluded his pamphlet with an inspiring phrase:

The question 'what is to be done?' should no longer concern us. It has long been resolved. *Make the revolution!* How? In accordance with everyone's capabilities. Given a rational organization, no single isolated attempt, no single individual effort will be wasted.[8]

'The Tasks of Revolutionary Propaganda in Russia' was an extraordinary document. Not just because of the quality and originality of its ideas – though that alone would have ensured it an important place in Russian revolutionary literature – but because its main theses were to be repeated with astonishing precision, nearly thirty years later, by the greatest revolutionary leader of our age. And to the question which became the title of his most important book, 'What is to be done?' Lenin gave practically the same answer as Tkachev.

Not surprisingly, Tkachev's pamphlet had a highly hostile reception. It resurrected the spectre of Nechaev, it threatened to divert the revolution towards a course that was now being universally condemned. In the general atmosphere of great expectations engendered by 'going to the people' there was little chance that Tkachev's heretical views would gain any converts – yet Lavrov was shrewd enough to realize their potential attractiveness to the young intelligentsia. He was preaching the long-term, slow approach to revolution – they were impatient, emotional, frustrated, brought up on dreams of demolishing society and establishing socialism overnight. Their support could be lost as quickly as it had been gained. They had to be kept to the path of righteousness. The significance of Tkachev's manifesto can be judged by the fact that Lavrov found it necessary to publish a reply almost immediately in his pamphlet 'To the Russian Social-Revolutionary Youth'.[9]

Lavrov began by expressing his conviction that no one would thoughtlessly call upon the people to rebel simply because of a 'revolutionary itch'. But, just in case such a call might find followers, he went on to refute Tkachev's main theses. It was entirely wrong to believe that the development of capitalism would make a socialist revolution more difficult – did not the deeds of the European proletariat prove the contrary? It was quite incorrect to assert that the European working-class movement stood for 'bloodless revolution' – and he provided a long list of counter-proofs. Luckily for Lavrov, his readers knew even less about the European working-class movement than he, otherwise his facts would have convinced them of the correctness of Tkachev's case. The most shining examples of Red Revolutionism quoted by Lavrov were ... the peace-loving and law-abiding Joseph Arch, of the English National Agricultural Labourers' Union, and the German Social-Democratic Party. A few months later, at their unification congress in Gotha in February 1875, the German Social-Democrats adopted their famous programme (harshly but unavailingly criticized by Marx), announcing their intention 'to achieve a free state and a socialist society by all legal means', and explaining that socialism would come about 'through the establishment of productive co-operatives, with State aid and under the democratic control of the working people'. Tkachev's charge was not that far wrong.

Lavrov went on to affirm his faith in the revolution, but in a revolution different from that envisaged by Tkachev: 'The revolution must be popular, it must be social, it must be carried out by the people ... A revolution that is truly in the people's interest can be carried out only by the people, by the majority and not the minority.' A revolutionary party formed by the intelligentsia was necessary: to conduct propaganda and to help along the eventual uprising, but there was no need for any more centralization than the existing network of circles. As for the division of revolutionary activity into propaganda, agitation and organization, the idea was simply preposterous and only demonstrated Tkachev's morbid obsession with conspiracy. Lavrov, indeed, directly accused his opponent of attempting to revive the discredited and repugnant methods practised by Nechaev.

The central part of Lavrov's pamphlet was his powerful indictment of the idea of a minority revolution and of the minority dictatorship that he saw inevitably emerging from it. Written with passion and great moral dignity, today it reads even better than when first published:

History and psychology both prove that any unlimited power, any dictatorship, corrupts even the best people, and that even men of genius who wished to benefit their nations by decree could not succeed in this. Every dictatorship must surround itself by forces of compulsion, by blindly obedient weapons. Every dictatorship has been compelled to suppress by force not only the reactionaries but also the people who simply disagree with its methods. Every imposed dictatorship has had to spend more time, effort and energy in the struggle for power against its rivals than in implementing its programme with the aid of this power. The belief that a party, once it has seized dictatorial power, will then voluntarily renounce it, can be entertained only before the seizure: in the struggle of parties for power, in the turmoil of overt and covert intrigues, every minute will create a new imperative for the preservation of power, a new insurmountable obstacle to its renunciation. Dictatorship is torn from the hands of the dictators only by a new revolution.

Could our revolutionary youth ever agree to serve as the dais for the thrones of a few dictators who – even with the best will in the world – can only become a new source of social distress, but who would far more probably be not even selfless fanatics but men of vaulting ambitions, craving power for power's sake, craving power for themselves . . .?

Let the Russian Jacobins fight the government. We will not hinder them. We wish them well, and shall try to make use of their successes. But the party of the people's social revolution will always be their enemy as soon as any of them takes a step towards seizing the power that belongs to the people and to nobody else ... The power of the State must be transformed directly into the self-government of people's communities, people's meetings, people's circles. This is a question not of secondary but of primary importance. State power, whosoever wields it, is hostile to a socialist system of society. Any minority power means exploitation, and a dictatorship can mean nothing else. We cannot accept a programme of a dictatorial revolution as the programme of the social revolution. Not only will we fight the adherents of dictatorship tomorrow – we cannot go along with them today.[10]

Tkachev had received his reply. Needless to say, he remained utterly unrepentant. But now a far bigger gun was being trained upon him. Frederick Engels had just begun the publication, in the Leipzig social-democratic paper *Volksstaat*, of a leisurely series of articles on Polish, French and Russian émigré literature when someone (probably a member of Lavrov's circle, if not Lavrov himself) drew his attention to the new controversy. Engels was extremely annoyed: a friend of Nechaev, and *ipso facto* of the detested Bakunin, an unknown scribbler ignorant of scientific socialism, daring to attack Lavrov – a man who enjoyed the patronage of Engels and even the friendship of Karl Marx! He would certainly teach the whipper-snapper a sound lesson.

Engels decided to polish Tkachev off with a few well-chosen caustic phrases – an art in which he had hardly any equals. Obviously, the fellow did not merit the full-scale treatment reserved for really important people like Bakunin or Dühring; the article opened with some condescending remarks about 'friend Pyotr', or Lavrov (a decent and honourable chap but, like most Russians, insufficiently sound on Bakunin), before turning on Tkachev. 'A green and exceptionally immature schoolboy, a kind of Simple Simon of the Russian revolutionary youth,' wrote Engels derisively, 'with vast pretensions and totally insignificant achievements.' Everything about Tkachev – his views, his past associations, his relationship with Lavrov, his style – was held up to bitter mockery. Engels did not even bother to argue against Tkachev's theories: these, being in his view no more than 'endless repetitions of Bakuninist phrases', were beneath contempt. Poor Lavrov was chided for believing that these 'childish, dull and contradictory' notions could ever influence anybody, and for deeming them worthy of a long reply. As for Engels's own opinion:

> Here, in the European West, we would have put an end to all this childishness by the simple answer: if your people are ready for a revolution at any time, if you believe you have the right to summon them to make a revolution at any time, and if therefore you cannot wait any longer – then why do you continue to bore us with your prattling, why the hell don't you begin?

A robust rejoinder, even though it completely distorted Tkachev's actual approach to the revolution. But for Engels this was a trifling nicety: the incipient resurgence of Bakuninism-Nechaevism (as he persisted in treating Tkachev's manifesto) had to be nipped in the bud. Especially now, when the Russian movement had finally begun to develop along healthy lines, when the Russians were no longer able to hide their shady dealings from their Western comrades behind the spurious veil of 'special circumstances', and when 'the Russians will have to accept their inevitable international fate, because from now on their movement will be conducted under the eyes and under the control of the rest of Europe'. So let us have no more of this nonsense, warned the stern leader of the international working-class movement as he laid down the law for the unruly Russian revolutionaries.[11]

But, to the surprise of Engels and of everybody else, the 'ignorant schoolboy' refused to acknowledge defeat and came back with a stinging repartee, in the form of an 'Open Letter to Herr Frederick Engels'.[12] The arrogant, self-confident contempt with which Engels had treated the Russian revolutionary movement drove Tkachev to a fury of indignation. 'This is exactly how high-placed bureaucrats behave whenever they meet with any resistance. Their bureaucratic nature is incensed by people who disagree with them, who dare to have views different from those of the high-born.' Tkachev rightly accused Engels of attacking him primarily because he saw every Russian, even Lavrov, as a potential follower of Bakunin. He stated unequivocally that he, Tkachev, was no Bakuninist – despite his admiration for this 'greatest and most unselfish of revolutionaries' and his detestation of the methods employed by Marx and Engels to destroy Bakunin.

The trouble with 'Herr Engels', wrote Tkachev, was that for all his learning he knew nothing about Russia. 'Judging our programme from a German point of view (i.e. from the point of view of the social conditions of the German people) is just as absurd as examining the German programme from a Russian point of view.' The situation in Russia was completely different from that of any European country: Russia had no industrial proletariat, no freedom of the press, no representative bodies etc. There was, quite simply, no way of influencing the people and winning them over to the side of the revolution. Yet this did not mean that the chances of a successful revolution were smaller in Russia than in the West. On the contrary: we may lack your advantages, but we possess others that are infinitely more valuable:

> We have no urban proletariat: this, of course, is true – but then we have no bourgeoisie either. Between the suffering people and the oppressive despotism of the State there exists no middle class. Our working people will only have to fight the *political power*, for with us *the power of capital* is still in its infancy. You, dear Sir, should know that the struggle against the first is far easier than against the second.

There were other circumstances working in Russia's favour as well. The people were wedded to the idea of collective property, and therefore 'stand much nearer to socialism than the nations of Western Europe'. The revolutionary intelligentsia may be small and weak, but its opponents – the nobility, the clergy, the mercantile class – are weaker still. They have no independent standing of their own: their very existence is contingent on the power of the State. This was the heart of Tkachev's argument, the basis of his whole approach: the unique nature of the Russian State, which made it at once so powerful and so vulnerable. In the West, he explained (and here his reading of Marx served him in good stead), the State personified the economic interests of certain powerful social classes; it was firmly grounded, not only in the police and the army but in the whole closely interwoven texture of bourgeois society. In Europe the workers were confronted with the whole might of the capitalist system:

> In our country we have a reverse relationship: our social system is indebted for its existence to the State, to a State which, so to speak, hangs in the air, to a State which has nothing in common with the existing social structure, and whose roots are embedded not in the present but in the past . . .

> It is only from afar that our State creates the impression of might. It has no roots in the economic life of the people, it does not personify the interests of any class. It presses down equally upon all social classes . . . How little would be necessary for this State to fall apart. Yes, very little is needed for this – two or three military defeats, a peasant rebellion simultaneously in several provinces, an open rebellion in the capital . . .

For all these reasons, Tkachev concluded, Herr Engels should realize that what Russia required was not a Western-type mass working-class party, but a tight-knit, highly disciplined conspiratorial organization that would provide the masses with leadership in the overthrow of the old regime and the establishment of a new social order.

Tkachev's 'Jacobin' thesis regarding the fundamental weakness – and the all-importance – of the Russian State added a new dimension to the theories evolved by Herzen and Chernyshevsky. It came to exercise a profound influence upon successive generations of revolutionaries. His forecast of future developments, though delayed by some forty years, proved prophetic down almost to the smallest detail. Yet, as so often happens, this obscure publication would probably have remained unknown were it not for the intemperate and widely publicized reaction of the author's opponents. Tkachev's reputation as a theoretician of substance was firmly established after the appearance of Engels's lengthy counter-attack.

The 'Open Letter' had been read by Marx, who sent it on to Engels with an inscription in the margin: 'Take it on, but do it in a mocking tone. It is so stupid that Bakunin himself might have written it.'[13] Thus inspired, Engels turned all his vast erudition, his stylistic brilliance, wit, and formidable dialectical abilities upon the unknown Russian pamphleteer.

Engels's first reaction was hardly one of light mockery: he attacked Tkachev even more viciously and offensively than before. All the old jeers were repeated: 'Simple Simon', 'ignorant schoolboy', etc., and, above all, the supreme insult – 'a true Bakuninist'. Nothing could be more damning in Engels's eyes. At times Engels (who strongly disliked being contradicted) seemed unable to control his fury; all the statements made about him by Tkachev, he declared, 'are vile and insolent lies'. Yet it is quite clear that Engels's own understanding of his opponent's position, and of the state of the Russian revolutionary movement in general, was highly superficial. It was absurd, he wrote, to think that conspiracy was the only alternative open to the revolutionaries, and that the movement itself would remain largely limited to the intelligentsia. Why, look at the immense success of propaganda among the people! 'This is best proved by the fact that in the latest mass arrests in Russia the majority of victims were not educated people or students, but workers.'[14] Engels, alas, had substituted wishful thinking for the facts. In the two great 'propagandist' trials of 1877–8, the 'Trial of the 50' and the 'Trial of the 193', 209 of the defendants came from noble, bourgeois, military, bureaucratic or clerical families, while only 34 can be described as having a working-class or peasant background (and of these latter only a handful had ever actually engaged in physical labour).[15] The proof, if anything, strengthened Tkachev's case.

Having satisfactorily demolished the obscure Russian quill driver, Engels recovered from his rage. The last part of his series, printed in four issues of *Der Volksstaat* in 1875, was devoted to a serious Marxist analysis of social and economic conditions and trends in Russia. When he republished it later as a separate booklet under the title *Soziales in Russland* he even deleted the purely personal attack on Tkachev, substituting for it a brief preface with a contemptuous reference to 'hackneyed Bakuninist scribbling' which required no reasoned reply.

Engels's article remains a work of prime importance: the first detailed exposition of Marxist views on the future development of Russia.[16] He began by an uncompromising statement of the orthodox Marxist position:

> The bourgeoisie is just as much an indispensable precondition for the socialist revolution as the proletariat itself. Therefore a person capable of declaring that such a revolution is easier to carry out in a country which, *although* it has no proletariat, *in return* has no bourgeoisie either, only reveals that he still has to learn the ABC of socialism.

Contrary to what Tkachev had said, a bourgeoisie was already rapidly developing in Russia, and the government did possess powerful sources of support. Among these Engels singled out heavy industry, 'which only exists thanks to the protective tariffs bestowed upon it by the State', and 'the teeming army of bureaucrats which floods and plunders Russia, and which forms a genuine estate of the realm'. How then, asks Engels indignantly, can Mr Tkachev maintain that the Russian State 'has no roots in the economic life of the people, does not personify the interests of any class', that it 'hangs in the air'? Would it not be truer to say, he went on in his best sarcastic style, 'that it is not the Russian state but rather Mr Tkachev himself who is hanging in the air'? (Engels, apparently, failed to notice that his description of the social forces supporting

403

the Russian State only reinforced the strength of Tkachev's argument according to which 'our social system is indebted for its existence to the State'.)

Most of all, naturally, Engels was scandalized by the insistent Russian claim (the origin of which he correctly ascribed to Herzen) that, thanks to the survival of the village commune, the Russian revolution 'will be a socialist one, and that it will establish in Russia the social system towards which the West European socialist movement is directed – even before we shall have achieved it in the West'. The idea was so patently absurd that Engels spent no time on its refutation. The commune, he agreed, was indeed an interesting feature of Russian life, and might well play an important future role in bypassing the capitalist stage of development in agriculture. But, whatever the outcome, the Russians must at last take cognizance of one basic fact:

> This can only come about if – before the final disintegration of Russian communal property – Western Europe will experience a triumphant proletarian revolution which will then supply the Russian peasant with the means, especially the material means, necessary for the transition to a higher phase.

Tkachev, concluded Engels, was talking 'the most arrant nonsense'; Russia was infinitely further away from socialism than Western Europe, and would remain in that state until a proletarian revolution in the West came to her assistance. Though a revolution was probably inevitable in Russia in the fairly near future, it could not be anything more than a bourgeois revolution.

And that, thought Engels, was that: he had put Tkachev in his place, and also, with infinite tact and patience, shown the obstreperous and parochial Russians their country's real prospects for the future. Tkachev never replied, the argument was over, the truth had triumphed. To the end of his long life Engels never saw any reason to change his views; on the contrary, he found them constantly confirmed. Twenty years later, in 1894, not long before his death, Engels wrote a new Postscript to *Soziales in Russland* in which, with quiet satisfaction, he could point out how right he had been.[17] To be sure, in the heat of the polemic he had been somewhat unfair to Tkachev: the latter, he now saw, had not been a Bakuninist but a Blanquist, or, more precisely, a follower of the 'Panslavist *belletrist'* Herzen. Herzen, smiled Engels pityingly, who 'had been a Socialist at most in word', had built up the Russian peasant commune 'in order to present to the rotten West in an even more dazzling light his "holy" Russia and her mission – which was to rejuvenate and to resurrect, if necessary by force of arms, this putrescent and worn-out West'. The development of Russia over the past two decades had fully and finally exposed the absurdity of these ideas and the correctness of Engels's analysis. In the West capitalism had reached a stage of development when its extinction was now imminent, while backward peasant Russia had become even more of an historical anachronism:

> It is historically impossible for a society standing on a far lower stage of economic development to resolve the problems and the conflicts that arise and can only arise in a society standing on an infinitely higher stage of development . . .

> But it is not only possible but even inevitable that after the victory of the proletariat and the socialization of the means of production among the Western European nations, those countries which have just entered upon the path of capitalist production and have still retained tribal customs or their remnants will use these remnants of common ownership and the corresponding popular habits as a powerful instrument for shortening the process of their development towards a socialist society . . . But an inescapable precondition of this is the example and the active support of the West, which today still remains capitalist . . .

> Without the victory of the modern Western industrial proletariat present-day Russia can never achieve the

socialist transformation of society – neither through the *obshchina* nor through capitalism.

The great debate between Tkachev and Engels deserves a special place in history: it was the first open clash between Marxist and Populist views on the Russian revolution. It was to be repeated many times in the years to come; eventually, with the increasing grip of Marxism over the intelligentsia, both sides to the debate came to call themselves Marxists. Yet for nearly half a century the arguments put forward did little more than restate the basic positions taken up in 1874–5. At no time were the battle-lines drawn with greater clarity.

The outcome of the debate was a supreme example of what Engels himself liked to call 'the irony of history'. The overwhelming verdict of historians of the Russian revolutionary movement is that Engels won the argument hands down: his scholarly analysis, based upon a vast body of factual evidence, had made mincemeat of Tkachev's crude sloganeering. This, naturally, is the unanimous verdict of Soviet historians, who extol the debate as the first devastating theoretical exposure of Populism. Oddly enough, their opinion seems to be shared by many, if not most Western students. The following appraisal of Engels's article by a distinguished American scholar is fairly typical: 'In it Engels not only gave vent to a blistering attack upon the Russian Blanquist but virtually laid waste the foundation premises upon which the whole populist edifice rested.' Tkachev's programme, he goes on, was 'utterly demolished by Engels'.[18]

Rarely has scholastic mythology, even in our age, scored such a complete victory over plain common sense. Engels, a renowned political thinker, had proved his case with impeccable logic and learning, within the framework of a profound scientific theory of society which – as even its opponents agree – represents a majestic achievement of the human mind. Tkachev, on the other hand, had been able to back up his thesis with nothing but personal intuitions. The encounter was ludicrously mismatched, and Engels's victory could be in no doubt. In a certain sense, of course, it is quite true to say that Engels had demolished his antagonist – on the theoretical plane, in the sphere of abstract discussion. What seems to be overlooked is that Engels's analysis, for all its forensic beauty, proved to be utterly wrong in the light of the facts, and that the revolution which actually broke out in Russia some twenty years after Engels complacently closed the book developed in striking harmony with the unscientific ideas of the benighted Pyotr Tkachev. To add to the irony, it was carried out by men calling themselves disciples of Marx and Engels. Altogether, a remarkable instance of the triumph of theory over reality.

Tkachev himself refused to realize that he had been demolished; on the contrary, he appeared quite satisfied with the publicity given to his views. In November 1875 he brought out the first issue of his journal *Nabat* (The Tocsin). *Nabat* never achieved the circulation or the dominance of Lavrov's *Vperyod* – it is unlikely that more than a few hundred copies of any issue were ever smuggled into Russia – but, coming as it did at the very moment of disillusionment with Lavrovist gradualism, it acquired an intellectual influence out of any proportion to its circulation. Thanks to Tkachev, a new generation of Russian revolutionaries rediscovered the 'Jacobin' creed. The flame had been rekindled – it was never to go out again.

Tkachev's first editorial, written in his usual vigorous and blunt style, contained every essential element of his revolutionary programme. Russia – whatever the orthodox Populists chose to believe – had already entered the path of capitalist development. Economic progress was creating a host of new enemies, infinitely more dangerous to the revolutionary cause than anything they had had to contend with previously: 'Today our State is a fiction, a myth that has no roots in the people's life . . . But tomorrow all its present-day enemies will come to its support, tomorrow it will represent their interests, the interests of the *kulaks* and the rich peasants, the interests of private property, of trade and industry, of the emerging bourgeois world. Today the State is absolutely absurd and absurdly absolute – tomorrow it will become constitutionally moderate and calculatingly prudent.' There was no time to be lost: 'Hurry! Sound the tocsin! Sound the tocsin!'

But before a revolution could be carried out it was imperative to clarify its methods and aims. Anarchist ideas would have to be abandoned (here, at least, Tkachev was at one with Engels): the abolition of the State was a matter for the distant future, and in the meantime the Utopian dreamers of anarchism constituted a positive menace to the cause by dissipating its resources on fruitless ventures.

'The first and foremost task of the revolution consists solely in the seizure of state power and the transformation of the conservative State into a revolutionary State.' The revolution would be achieved by a minority – *a minority that was to retain power after it had been seized.* 'The minority, because of its superior intellectual and moral development, always has and always must have intellectual and moral power over the majority. Therefore the revolutionaries, the men of this minority . . . must inevitably possess, and, as long as they remain revolutionaries, cannot but possess power.'

The idea of a minority dictatorship, to be established after the victorious revolution, had already been propounded, among others, by Pestel and Zaichnevsky – but never before had it been put forward in such unemotional, matter-of-fact language. The seizure of power, Tkachev continued, was only the first step: the social revolution itself would be a long-drawn-out process, in the course of which the revolutionary government would, on the one hand, 'destroy the constitutionalist and reactionary elements of society', while at the same time introducing the socialist system by means of a series of economic, political and legal reforms. But these were all tasks for the future – what mattered at the moment was the seizure of power:

Our struggle will be successful only by a combination of the following conditions: centralization, strict discipline, rapidity, decisiveness, and unity of action. Any concessions, any hesitations, any compromises, any dispersal of leadership or decentralization of our forces will undermine their energy, paralyse their activity, and deprive the struggle of all chances of success.

Tkachev left no room for misunderstanding: the coup d'état could be carried out and the new regime established and defended only by a conspiratorial organization – 'a genuine organization, that would tightly knit together the disparate elements into a single living body, that would act in accordance with a single unified plan, that would be subordinated to a single unified leadership, that would be based on the centralization of power and the decentralization of revolutionary duties'.

Finally, though, a word of caution:

> Revolutionaries – while mindful of the conspiracy's aims – should never for one moment forget that these aims are unattainable without the direct or indirect support of the people ... An attack upon the centre of government and its capture by revolutionary forces which is not accompanied by a popular rebellion (even a local one), would need exceptionally favourable circumstances in order to achieve any positive and lasting results.[19]

The essence – and the innovatory character – of Tkachev's programme can be formulated in three basic points: the decisive role of a centralized and disciplined conspiratorial party; the necessity for a seizure of political power by a minority revolutionary organization; the establishment of a strong minority dictatorship which would introduce socialism by decree, from above. Clearly, this position had little in common with the theories then prevalent among Russian Populists (though they were all founded on the same general assumptions); equally clearly, Tkachev had developed the rudimentary 'Jacobinism' of Zaichnevsky and Nechaev into a powerful, comprehensive ideology of revolutionary action. Ever since Engels's outburst and down to the present day Tkachev has been persistently identified with anarchism and Bakunin.

The idea is patently absurd: although he felt it his duty to defend Bakunin from what he regarded as unjust and slanderous charges, Tkachev was, as seen above, utterly opposed to two of Bakunin's basic tenets – the abolition of the State, and the inevitability of a spontaneous popular revolution. Tkachev's programme was the antithesis of Bakuninism.

On the other hand, the repeated emphasis on the need for popular support and on the difference between a coup d'état and a revolution, illustrates how much Tkachev's views were at variance with those of Blanqui – another name facilely linked to his. The accusations of Bakuninism and Blanquism (although mutually incompatible) have both been hurled at Tkachev – and both must be judged incorrect. 'Revolution cannot be carried out without the people,' he wrote in his analysis of the failure of 'going to the people' (December 1875).[20]

Tkachev was (and still is) called a disciple of Blanqui because, like the latter, he openly preached minority revolution and minority dictatorship. The notion – or, at any rate, its undisguised expression – aroused a good deal of horror on all sides. Lavrov's attacks had been especially bitter. 'Every dictatorship,' he had written, 'even with the best will in the world . . . must surround itself by forces of compulsion, by blindly obedient weapons.' Tkachev's solution would merely open the door to 'men of vaulting ambitions, craving power for power's sake, craving power for themselves' (see p. 397).

The concept of minority leadership was, indeed, at the very heart of Tkachev's theory of revolution. But his approach to the problem was very different from that of Blanqui: he spoke not of a *minority revolt* but of a *revolution led by a minority*. Therefore he indignantly (if somewhat naively) rejected the accusations levelled against him. A revolution from above, he explained, could be called anti-popular only if the minority represented the interests of the bourgeoisie; when, however, as in their own case, the minority stood for the people – why, that was an entirely different matter!

In one of his most important essays, *Revolution and the State* (a title made world-famous by Lenin, with only the word-order reversed, in a pamphlet written exactly forty years later), Tkachev fervently defended the principle of dictatorship against its detractors:

> What right have you to believe that this minority – a minority which, partly by its social status, partly by its ideas, is steadfastly devoted to the people's interests – that such a minority, once it seizes power, would suddenly be transformed into a tyrant? You say that all power corrupts. But on what do you base this strange deduction . . .? Honest and decent men have never yet been corrupted by power.[21]

As evidence Tkachev referred to the examples of Robespierre, Cromwell, Washington – whereas men like Napoleon or Caesar had not been corrupted by power: they were intrinsically corrupt. It was, of course, an incredibly weak argument, and the fact that the hard-headed realist Tkachev had stooped to such arrant philosophical idealism was often cited as proof of his theories' essential inconsistency. The criticism is fully justified – yet has any other proponent of benevolent dictatorship ever been able to devise a formula for incorruptible absolute power? Even Lenin – a far more powerful mind than Tkachev – when finally, on his deathbed, confronted with the stark realities of corruption and arbitrary abuse, could invent no better solution than to double his Central Committee by co-opting fifty pure and undefiled workers from the factory bench.

What makes Tkachev stand out, like a portent of the future, from among all the Russian revolutionaries of the nineteenth century was not his defence of the indefensible but his closely reasoned arguments for a minority revolutionary dictatorship – arguments such as had never been heard before, either in Russia or anywhere else, but which were to be repeated later almost word for word, with shattering results. Tkachev was obliged to make the customary ritualistic obeisance to the *obshchina*, but he openly proclaimed his disbelief in its regenerative properties. Similar village communities, he pointed

411

out, had existed almost everywhere in the world. In Europe they had been destroyed by capitalism, and capitalism was already doing its work in Russia as well. Besides, what was this magical *obshchina*? The embryo of a potential socialist order, to be sure, but one that had been all but ossified by the agency of innate peasant conservatism. Tkachev had no illusions about either the peasantry or the commune: the first was a conservative class, and the second the embodiment of its conservative ideal.

It was time, he proclaimed, to end the ridiculous idealization of 'the people'. This would be of use primarily to the people themselves. 'We have no right to place exaggerated hopes and expectations upon the people. Enough of the stupid idea that the people, "left to themselves", can carry out a social revolution and themselves settle their future in the best possible way. The people are an indispensable factor of the social revolution, but only when the revolutionary minority takes the cause of this revolution into its own hands.'

The people, naturally, were not to blame for this state of affairs: illiteracy and backwardness, centuries of slavery and oppression, had made them incapable of evolving a revolutionary ideal. This ideal, together with the leadership necessary for its implementation, could only be brought to the people from the outside, by the educated revolutionary minority, by the intelligentsia. Then followed Tkachev's remarkable exposition of the relationship between masses and élite in the revolution and during the post-revolutionary period:

Our people's social ideal does not go beyond the fossilized forms of their life ... Beyond their traditional family relationships etc. they see nothing, know nothing and care about nothing. Just give them the chance to arrange their lives in accordance with their own desires, and you will soon discover that they won't introduce anything new. They will extend the accustomed forms of their life, their *obshchina*, their *mir*, their family, to those spheres from which they have now been pushed out under the influence of bourgeois progress – but that will be the whole extent of the people's reforming activities; we will be faced with the same old peasant *mir*, with its rigid, ossified principles and its immutable conservatism.

The final aim of the social revolution is the triumph of communism. In order to approach this aim, to prepare the ground for communism, we must introduce new elements, new factors . . . which are inherent exclusively in the socialist outlook of the revolutionary minority. That is why the ideal of this minority, broader and more revolutionary than the popular ideal, has to dominate over the latter during the revolution. The people are incapable of building, upon the ruins of the old, a new world that would be able to move and develop towards the communist ideal; therefore they cannot play any significant or leading part in building this new world. Such a part belongs solely to the revolutionary minority . . .

In its reforming activities the revolutionary minority should not count on the *active* support of the people. The latter's revolutionary role will come to an end the moment they demolish the institutions that directly oppress them, and destroy the tyrants who directly exploit them . . .

But the revolutionary minority must be able also to continue its work of revolutionary destruction in those spheres where it can hardly reckon on the genuine support and assistance of the popular majority. That is why it must possess might, power and authority. And the greater this might, the firmer and more energetic this power, the fuller and more comprehensive the implementation of the ideas of the social revolution, the easier it will be to avoid a conflict with the conservative elements of the people.

In short, the relationship of the revolutionary minority to the people, and the part played by the latter in the revolution, can be defined as follows: the revolutionary minority, having liberated the people from the grip of fear and terror of the authorities, provide them with the opportunity for demonstrating their destructive revolutionary force. Basing itself upon this force, skilfully guiding it towards the destruction of the immediate enemies of the revolution, the minority thereby demolishes the enemy's entrenched strongholds and deprives it of the means of resistance and counteraction. Then, utilizing its power and its authority, the minority introduces new, progressive-communistic elements into the people's life; it will shift the people's life off its age-old foundations, and rejuvenate its ossified and shrivelled forms . . .

The people can never save themselves. Neither in the present nor in the future could the people, left to themselves, carry out the social revolution. Only we, the revolutionary movement, can do this – and we must do it as soon as possible![22]

Tkachev could not have spelled out his doctrine in simpler terms: the people were to provide the mass force of the revolution, but they would be deprived of any say in its execution; a self-appointed élite, brought to power by the masses, would manipulate them towards the achievement of ends utterly alien to their traditions or desires. And, since the illiterate and backward people could never rise to an understanding of their own best interests, these ends would have to be imposed upon them *by force*. Tkachev had no qualms about applying compulsion to the people: after all, it would be for their own good, even though they were incapable of appreciating this. 'Once it has acquired power, the minority can force the majority – the inert, tradition-bound majority, which has not yet developed towards understanding the necessity for revolution and does not comprehend its aims and tasks – force this majority to reconstruct its life in accordance with its genuine interests, in accordance with the ideal of the best and most equitable type of society.'[23]

One of the curious features of the nineteenth-century Russian revolutionary movement was the line of division that ran through it. Broadly speaking, all its members were in general agreement with regard to their assessment of the situation, their attitude to the existing regime, their belief in socialism as the sole solution to Russia's problems. Unlike the European socialists, or the later Marxists in their own country, there were few, if any, ideological or doctrinal differences between them. Nor can they be easily fitted into the convenient European categories of 'extremists' and 'moderates': some of those most 'extremist' in methods were relatively 'moderate' in their aims, and vice versa (a source, among other things, of constant bafflement to the police, as well as to many Western students). They worked within a common framework of ideas – yet the divisions between the factions were clear-cut, bitter and lasting. What they boiled down to, in essence, were the questions: how much faith could be placed in the revolutionary potential of 'the people'? Did the people need the intelligentsia merely as guides and educators, or was it the revolutionary intelligentsia's function to do the people's job for them? To these questions the Jacobins gave one set of answers, the majority of orthodox Populists another. The disagreements may have concerned means rather than ends, but they were to result in widely diverging concepts of the revolution and the revolutionary State.

At no time were the opposing positions set out with greater clarity than in the controversy that raged between Tkachev and Lavrov throughout the 1870s. Tkachev's articles were nothing if not forthright. Of course, he wrote, the people were always ready for revolution – but they would only carry it out when they felt they could do so with impunity. 'All the purely popular revolutions, from the great Roman slave rebellions to the Paris Commune, without exception broke out at times when the ruling classes were overtaken by chaos, disorder, anarchy or divisions; when the hand of "supreme authority" began to tremble and falter.'[24] But this in itself was insufficient: the triumph of a spontaneous popular revolution could be made lasting only by means of tough, conscious, organized, disciplined leadership. Therefore 'the organization of a social-revolutionary party, its unity and the co-ordination of its activities is undoubtedly the first and absolutely essential step towards the practical implementation of the social revolution'.[25]

Lavrov was scandalized by Tkachev's ideas. The actual seizure of power, he pointed out, might well prove to be a fairly simple operation (as in earlier coups d'état) – but such a coup would remain no more than a purely *political* revolution, which could never achieve the *social* transformation of the country. Tkachev, in turn, derided Lavrov's objections. The man obviously did not understand what a social revolution was about: he thought it could be carried out instantaneously, whereas in fact it would require at least a generation and possibly even more. However that might be, a social revolution could only be initiated by a political one, by the establishment of a revolutionary government which would destroy the old order and create the preconditions for a profound transformation of society.

The Tkachev–Lavrov controversy may be justly regarded as the most significant of all the innumerable debates on the future paths of the Russian revolution. All the central issues were squarely faced; neither of the parties made any attempt to avoid them or to evade a direct answer. In contrast to earlier discussions, there was no blurring of the differences by reference to grandiloquent but meaningless generalized concepts; unlike later and even more ferocious debates (between Populists and Marxists, or Bolsheviks and Mensheviks), it was unencumbered by extraneous theories and jargon evolved in different circumstances and irrelevant to Russia's real problems. Despite the wide divergence in approach and temperament, both sides were absolutely honest; and both, in their own ways, were proved right forty years later. The 'realist' Tkachev correctly forecast the course of the Russian revolution but failed to discern the fatal pitfalls awaiting the revolutionary government; the 'idealist' Lavrov, while unrealistic in his assessments of the future, rightly foresaw the inevitable consequences of a minority revolution. To complete the paradox, both Tkachev and Lavrov were infinitely nearer the mark than any 'scientific' Marxian analysis and prediction – yet their arguments have been all but forgotten beneath the welter of chimerical, scholastic Marxist interpretation. Marxist dogma has served only to obfuscate the basic problems of the Russian revolution, the problems posed so starkly and uncompromisingly by Tkachev and Lavrov. Nowhere can one find a better explanation of 1917 and after.

The most thorough exposition of Lavrov's views on the revolution is contained in his long pamphlet 'The State Element in the Future Society'. The failure of 'going to the people' and the ensuing disillusionment had obviously caused Lavrov to rethink some of his earlier positions. Despite his natural inclinations, he now had to admit that it was impracticable to rely on pure spontaneity, on the exclusive power of education. Some degree of organization was unavoidable – but if it was not to be kept to the absolute minimum then the consequences could be dire indeed. This was the basic dilemma to which Lavrov sought a rational solution: how to organize a nationwide revolution throughout Russia without a centralized organization, how to establish power without a revolutionary government, how to run an effective body politic and a productive economy without a State? Above all, Lavrov feared the re-establishment of the State. Not because he was an anarchist, opposed to the institution of the State as such (or else he could hardly have maintained friendly relations with Marx and Engels), but because he understood and dreaded the immense force of the Russian State tradition. If the State was to re-emerge in any form, he felt, even in a revolutionary transmutation, then sooner or later the Old Adam of autocracy would reappear under some other name. Lavrov set out to square the circle – to determine the degree of 'State element' admissible in a stateless society.

Lavrov began by explaining how the revolution was to be carried out. Socialist groups would be established within the existing *obshchinas* and *artels*,* i.e. within the traditional organizations of popular co-operation and mutual aid; these groups, covering the whole of Russia or at least a large part of her territory, would be connected with each other, while

---

* *Artel:* a workmen's association based on communal principles, under an elected leader; it lived and worked together, and was paid as a group, sharing out the money equally.

retaining complete autonomy (Lavrov made no mention of a centre – apparently, none was envisaged), and would engage in propaganda and agitation among the masses. 'At the opportune historical moment these groups will, by common agreement, issue a simultaneous call for social revolution in various parts of Russia.' The uprisings, led by the socialist groups, would be joined by 'all those who have more or less clearly assimilated the tasks of working-class socialism', and supported by great masses of sympathizers who had already been won over by the revolutionaries' agitation. Large areas would simultaneously be gripped by peasant rebellion; the land would be seized and parcelled out, the landowners and rich kulaks killed or forced to flee. In the face of such a general conflagration the army (also propagandized by the revolutionaries) would prove unreliable, with part of it even joining the peasantry. Meanwhile, members of the 'social-revolutionary union' in the capitals and other large centres (mainly from the intelligentsia) would have immobilized or even taken over the administration. Thus, the people would have taken over power in most (if not all) of Russia; the revolution would have been carried out by the *majority*, upon the initiative of a large number of politically conscious groups, 'under the leadership of an *organized minority of the people* (including a small proportion of the intelligentsia)'. The revolution would immediately institute the basic principles of workers' socialism: 'common property, common labour, a federation of the toilers'.

This last was probably the most important of Lavrov's principles, for it contained his solution to the problem of a *stateless* national polity. The revolutionary groups within the traditional popular organizations would form the nuclei of a national federation of Russian revolutionary *obshchinas* and *artels*. 'This federation, evolved from the people itself, within its natural traditional elements, this federation of people's groups, having overthrown the old social order, will become the creator of a new workers' socialism.' The federation of equal and autonomous groups will socialize the means of production, organize universal compulsory communal labour, look after the needs of defence, etc. In other words, it would fulfil all the functions of the state without running the risk of becoming transformed into one itself.

It naturally followed from all this that there was no need for a special revolutionary organization: the revolutionaries would already be 'members of existing groups of *obshchinas* and *artels*, historically accepted by the people'. Quite simple, really. Moreover, there would not even be an actual seizure of power, since the social-revolutionary union would be composed of representatives of the people, and its influence would be based not on compulsion but upon popular trust. The people, however, though uniquely capable of carrying out the revolution, were in no position to plan its programme in advance – therefore the convinced and organized socialist-revolutionaries would, temporarily, have to perform certain functions of leadership, otherwise leadership might be seized by small groups of determined and even power-hungry men.

Alas for Lavrov: however much he wanted to exorcize the very concept of organization, the logic of his own argument inexorably drove him towards accepting – very unwillingly – the necessity for some kind of leadership. And if there was to be a leadership, even a temporary one, it would, equally inevitably, have to be a *minority*. Lavrov was too honest not to admit this, yet he was convinced that effective safeguards against the concentration of power in a few hands could be successfully evolved. For one thing, the leaders would be allowed to lead only insofar as they enjoyed the support of the masses; for another, they would regularly take part in physical labour together with all other members of society, thus widening the circle of leaders until it would embrace every citizen; finally, they 'would be subject to the strictest mutual control, which they must *voluntarily* accept as indispensable amongst themselves'. Mutual control among and between the autonomous revolutionary groups was seen by Lavrov as the principal guarantee against the concentration and abuse of power.

A certain degree of what Lavrov distastefully called 'State

element' was probably inevitable after the revolution – provided that it (*a*) did not influence relations *within* the revolutionary groups, (*b*) was introduced only in case of extreme necessity, and (*c*) remained under strict mutual control. There would have to be *some* central direction, at least at the first stages, but it would be limited to operating communications and transport between the various regions of the huge country, to preventing wanton destruction during the early heady months of the revolution, to building up and allocating food stockpiles for the prevention of famine, and to organizing the country's external security. Every other function of government would be exercised by the local autonomous units, i.e. by the people themselves. Naturally, all this would entail the establishment of some kind of central authority, of 'the revolutionary rule of a directing council, which would represent the rule of a minority'. Was this phrase, then, to mean the resurrection of the hated State? Not at all: 'The directors must remember that, however energetic their activities may be in the first moments, they have no *moral right* to preserve their dictatorship for a single minute longer than is necessary.' An admirable sentiment, further strengthened by Lavrov's conviction that the economic decrees of the socialist quasi-government could only be implemented with the willing co-operation of the masses, and that as soon as the basic task of socialization had been completed the revolutionary groups – their work being over – would hand over power to free associations of the people.

Such was the essence of Lavrov's plan for a socialist revolution and a socialist society, the core of his formula for abolition of the State. Despite the nobility and high-mindedness of his motives, despite the immense detail with which he elaborated his blueprint of the future ('The State Element in the Future Society' occupies 190 pages of Lavrov's *Collected Works*[26]), the plan was utterly unrealistic from beginning to end. Unlike almost all the other Russian revolutionary theoreticians, who were hardly concerned with the issue of individual freedom, and who blithely envisaged the State as the chief instrument for creating a classless egalitarian society, Lavrov was haunted by his fears of the State and of its possible transformation into an agency of revolutionary tyranny by a small group of determined and fanatical conspirators – fears which had been buttressed by the activities of Nechaev and the writings of Tkachev, as well as by recent disturbing developments inside Russia. Yet the sole guarantee against the enaction of his nightmare which Lavrov could conceive was, in the final analysis, the goodwill and moral purity of the revolutionaries themselves. Lavrov, the most libertarian (if the word is at all applicable) of the revolutionary ideologues, remained a prisoner of the Russian tradition and of the closed mind of the intelligentsia just as much as anyone else. One is struck by the total absence in his elaborate safeguards against dictatorship of such expressions as 'democracy', 'elections' or 'law'. These were all unmentionable, even unthinkable concepts, to Lavrov as to any other Russian revolutionary – they stood for capitalism and exploitation and inequality and injustice, and would be gloriously swept away, together with other reminders of class oppression, by the people's revolution. To be replaced by – what? Moral integrity, devotion, selflessness: the familiar personal qualities of Chernyshevsky's New Men would, it appeared, suffice to protect the emancipated people from any incipient dictators.

Nowhere can the fatal flaw that ran through the whole of Russian revolutionary thought – the distrust of democracy and the dislike of legality – be perceived more distinctly than in Lavrov's writings. For he, at least, understood the implications of revolutionary dictatorship and tried to come to grips with them (as did Pyotr Tkachev, in his own very different way). Lavrov remains a tragic figure: he saw the danger but failed to discover any remedy beyond empty phrases. His was the tragedy of the Russian revolution.

Lavrov's scheme collapsed as soon as he came to the question of the internal security of the new socialist order. This, he realized, was the most critical matter of all – too many earlier revolutions had led to tyranny via uncontrolled terror against their internal enemies. Yet the new social order would have to face the problem of the enemy within: the remnants of the former exploiting classes; the citizens who remained in the grip of the old mentality and were led to anti-social acts; the members of the social-revolutionary union who abused their power or even attempted to retain it longer than was absolutely necessary; the subversive agents sent into socialist Russia from capitalist and other hostile states. Obviously, the new order would have to ensure its own security. But how? Here again the Utopian dreamer Lavrov proved far more realistic than the hard-headed, practical, 'scientific' men, secure in their conviction that socialization and equality would automatically lead to freedom and justice for all. As he saw it, a minority revolution equipped with the machinery of suppression would inevitably result in the establishment of a monstrous tyranny. Lavrov painted a brilliantly prophetic picture of such a future 'socialist' state:

> Some might think it best to use the customary methods of the old society: to draw up a code of socialist laws with an appropriate section 'On Punishments'; to select from among the most reliable persons (in the main, naturally, from members of the social-revolutionary union) a 'public security' commission for the dispensation of justice and retribution; to organize a communal and territorial police corps of detectives to sniff out law-breaking and of guardians of propriety to look after 'order'; to place 'evidently dangerous' people under socialist police surveillance; to establish the requisite number of prisons, and, probably, of gallows, together with a corresponding assortment of socialist gaolers and executioners; and then, to implement *socialist legal justice*, set into motion this whole rejuvenated machine of the old order in the name of the principles of *workers' socialism*.

It would all come to pass, exactly as Lavrov had foretold. His diagnosis was faultless – the antidote he came up with was ludicrously inadequate. The new society should eschew legal institutions and special bodies for upholding law and order; the maintenance of internal security must be entrusted to the free initiative of the autonomous nuclei of society – to the workings of 'direct people's summary justice' (an odd echo of Nechaev's slogan). The members of the basic social units would be perfectly capable of defending their own communal interests and 'of undertaking, with regard to social criminals, such measures as they themselves regard to be most expedient'. As a praiseworthy example of such local initiatives, untrammelled by laws, Lavrov singled out ... the vigilante associations of the American Wild West. To be sure, he hastened to add, lynch law was repugnant – but only inasmuch as it was directed at the protection of private property. In a socialist society, where it would be fulfilling entirely different functions, this interesting prototype of 'people's summary justice' would acquire a new and immaculate moral justification.

Such, then, was Lavrov's ultimate safeguard against police despotism: mob rule. Given his premises, and his intellectual honesty, there probably could be no other solution. The Russian revolutionary idea left no room for peaceful evolution.

Lavrov's attempt to combine the revolutionary idea with the principles of abstract morality, to conjure up an organized revolution without an organization and a dictatorship without dictators, had led him into a morass of insoluble contradictions. No one saw this more clearly, or revelled in it more openly, than Tkachev. Consistent and logical as always, Tkachev brutally demolished the Lavrovian Utopia. But first he could not deny himself the pleasure of pointing out that Lavrov, albeit half-heartedly and hesitantly, had been compelled to adopt a number of his own, Tkachev's, ideas: ideas that only two or three years earlier he had scornfully dismissed as Nechaevite ravings. How gratifying, gloated Tkachev, to see Lavrov accepting the necessity of conspiracy, of force, of the seizure of power, of a revolutionary government, even – Heavens above! – of minority rule. In fact, concluded Tkachev triumphantly, Lavrov was now opposing the very basic principles that he had affirmed so passionately in 'To the Russian Social-Revolutionary Youth'. Only why this half-heartedness, why this hesitation, why these ridiculous scruples? A true revolutionary, once having entered upon his path, cannot stop half-way. What Lavrov feared most, what he so conscientiously sought to avert, were precisely the logical and inexorable conclusions of the revolutionary idea.

Lavrov agrees that a conspiracy is needed: but to be effective a conspiracy must be limited in numbers, highly centralized, organized and disciplined. A broad-based, loosely knit conspiracy, with a mass membership, as envisaged by Lavrov, ceases to be a conspiracy, and in no time falls victim to the police. Lavrov says that after the revolution power would belong to a minority – exactly what we had stated in our programme: 'it will belong to a prepared minority, namely to us, the socialist revolutionaries'.

After ironically welcoming Lavrov to the fold, Tkachev embarked upon a sustained critique of his opponent's plans for the future society. Every hazy moral assumption, every weak point, every inconsistency in Lavrov's argument was mercilessly laid open. Lavrov had written that 'the directors . . . have no *moral right* to preserve their dictatorship for a single minute longer than is necessary' – Tkachev bitingly commented: 'Necessary for *whom*? Necessary for *what*? Necessary *in whose opinion*? The author cautiously passes over all this in silence.' Lavrov, he went on, seems to believe that it will be sufficient to pass a few decrees abolishing private property and introducing universal social labour, and socialism would instantly take root among the people, thus making any further governmental activity superfluous. What nonsense: to imagine that 'the people' would renounce their age-old acquisitive habits, their lust for property, and be transformed into socialists overnight, simply by decree:

Practical revolutionaries – declared Tkachev – will certainly never act in accordance with our author's advice. If they once succeed in implementing the first part of his programme, i.e. in seizing revolutionary dictatorship in the insurgent communes, then we may be quite sure that they will not wish to relinquish it until the new order has put down fairly deep roots in our public life, until it has destroyed all its enemies and won for itself the sympathy of the majority.

Having settled that point, Tkachev passed on without trepidation to discuss Lavrov's oppressive nightmare: the question of the powers needed to destroy the revolution's internal enemies and to break down the deadening force of custom and tradition. 'This question is undoubtedly the most important of all. One can say without exaggeration that its decision will determine the whole future fate of the revolution, its success or failure, its triumph or defeat.' Tkachev coolly reproduced Lavrov's frightening vision of a police-socialist State. He refused to understand what all the excitement was about. Lavrov was worried that the use of repression would corrupt the new society and defile its ideals of justice – Tkachev had a simple answer, derived from Chernyshevsky and therefore irrefutable: 'Whatever is useful for society, whatever promotes the realization of human happiness, is just.' As for using the methods and machinery of repression of the old regime to crush the enemies of the revolution – why, what on earth was wrong with that? 'Nobody would dream of equating the two regimes, even though the *external* form of their activity, the legal machine which the one uses against society, and the other to its benefit, may be completely identical.' Surely even Lavrov, for all his squeamishness, could understand this elementary fact.

The only thing that really bothered Tkachev was the problem of efficiency. The Tsarist government, in his opinion, had not proved very competent at eliminating its enemies 'swiftly and irrevocably'; often it had created excessively favourable conditions for them; its legal system was full of dangerous loopholes and harmful procrastination. Well, the revolution would certainly do away with all this idiotic legalistic red tape; its security apparatus, directed at defending the interests not of the exploiters but of the whole people, would prove infinitely more resourceful and efficient than the old police machinery.

For Lavrov's own solution Tkachev, quite properly, had nothing but contempt. Basing the new order upon lynch law, he wrote, whatever its rationalization, was detestable, and could only lead to permanent fear, permanent insecurity, the permanent struggle of all against all: in other words, to a state of permanent civil war. Such a solution was not only 'vile hypocrisy' – it would mean chaos, anarchy, the inevitable defeat of the revolution. Lavrov had damned himself out of his own mouth; he had shown up the threadbareness of his blueprint far better than any critic could have done. Socialism could only be achieved through the seizure of power and the establishment of a minority dictatorship, based upon force, by an organized revolutionary party. This was the principal conclusion of Tkachev's polemical reply to Lavrov, entitled 'The Eve and the Aftermath of Revolution'.[27]

There were to be many other debates concerning the paths of the Russian revolution; few, however, did more than repeat the basic arguments of the Lavrov–Tkachev controversy. The battle-lines were drawn, the issues defined, the solutions put forward. Two conflicting conceptions had emerged within a single framework of thought; in one way or another, they were to dominate the Russian revolutionary movement for the next forty years.

Tkachev was quite convinced that he had finally won the argument. Things were going his way; events, both in Russia and abroad, were proving the correctness of his views. He spent the last remaining years of his active life in driving the lesson home. The collapse of the First International provided him with further proof of the futility of the old methods. The German and English socialists, he wrote, had wasted their time in peaceful propaganda and the parliamentary struggle; the Anarchists had wasted their time in opposing any organization and in fostering individual initiatives. In effect, both were pinning their hopes upon the arrival of favourable circumstances – of circumstances which, it was now clear, would never come about. Both therefore were equally guilty of deceiving and corrupting the working classes by feeding them on false illusions and unfounded hopes. Nothing illustrated the bankruptcy of evolutionary socialism more strikingly than Bismarck's anti-socialist laws of October 1878 and the resultant ignominious débâcle of the largest and seemingly most powerful Social-Democratic party in the world, the party which had arrogated the right to teach everyone else the ABC of socialism (as Tkachev had good reason to remember). Now, when the crunch had come, the Germans made no attempt to put up even a token show of resistance. The lesson was clear: 'A secret and underground revolutionary organization, well-disciplined and directed towards the overthrow of the existing social order by means of an open and violent revolutionary coup – such, as the experience of the German socialist party has shown, should be the practical programme of all genuine and devoted revolutionaries.'[28]

The words quoted above came from one of Tkachev's last articles. The publication of *Nabat* was becoming increasingly difficult; in 1880 Tkachev moved to Paris, and soon afterwards the paper folded. From 1882 Tkachev was incapacitated by a mysterious illness diagnosed as 'paralysis of the brain'; he died four years later in a lunatic asylum. Among the speakers at his sparsely attended funeral was Lavrov, magnanimous to the last.

The question of Tkachev's actual influence upon the development of the Russian revolutionary movement has always been a subject for heated and partisan debate. He remains, next to Nechaev, the most controversial figure of the revolutionary tradition. Unlike Nechaev, he could hardly be labelled a monster of iniquity, yet his outspoken, even cynical views shocked many idealistic susceptibilities hardly less than did Nechaev's ferocious immorality. Practically every faction, therefore, vehemently and continually denied connections with 'Tkachevism' – the very expression became a term of abuse – and, whenever the suspicion arose, hastened to announce that any resemblance between their principles and Tkachev's was purely coincidental. This may seem strange, considering that the idea of the ends justifying the means had been generally, if tacitly, accepted by all since Chernyshevsky's day. But the trouble with Tkachev was that he happened to be a true rebel, unlike the highly conformist radical intelligentsia of his and later generations: a rebel not only against the Tsarist regime but against revolutionary orthodoxy as well. He was denounced and disclaimed in turn by orthodox Populists and orthodox Marxists, whereas the more unconventional representatives of the two main revolutionary strains – the terrorist *Narodnaya Volya* organization in one case, and the Bolsheviks in the other – never bothered to conceal their admiration for many of Tkachev's views. It so happened that, in the long run, only these latter counted. Much has been made of Tkachev's isolation from the mainstream of Populist and Marxist thought. This, though true, need concern us little: it was through *Narodnaya Volya*, and, to a far greater degree, through the Bolsheviks, that Tkachev left his lasting imprint upon Russia and the world.

Tkachev himself was in no doubt as to his influence upon the development of the revolutionary movement. Shortly before his fatal illness he wrote, in a private letter to a critic of his actions:

Within the limits of what was possible *Nabat* has fully accomplished its task, and accomplished it quite successfully. It has rendered invaluable assistance to the development of the revolutionary cause, and has considerably advanced that new revolutionary trend which has just produced such abundant practical results. We are reproached for having paid little heed to *Nabat*'s circulation inside Russia, for not having organized our own party in Russia, etc. But . . . I have never attached particular importance to the circulation of *Nabat* in Russia. *Nabat* was never an agitational revolutionary sheet; its task was limited to returning the revolutionaries to the sole correct practical ideas and principles of revolutionary action, which they were rejecting under the influence of anarchist and Lavrovite ravings. And *Nabat* could, and did, fulfil this task even without being disseminated in Russia. It was sufficient for only *several* revolutionaries to become acquainted with its programme and its main ideas . . . and then revolutionary activity would soon prove the wisdom and practicality of these ideas and spread them among the majority of revolutionaries. I know very well that few in Russia can get hold of *Nabat*. But its existence, its programme and its principles are known in almost all the revolutionary groups . . . The irrefutable truth of the ideas expressed in *Nabat* was so obvious to me that I did not doubt for a minute that they would prevail, that they would be put into practice, even if *Nabat* had not circulated beyond the borders of Switzerland, even if it had been published in only a few dozen copies . . . Such was my conviction – and the facts, as you can see, have fully justified it . . . This 'ridiculous comedy', as you term it, has inaugurated a veritable upheaval in the direction and the nature of the revolutionary party's activity.[29]

Tkachev had never been a vainglorious man, and what he wrote was no more than the truth. The 'respectable' Populists – as soon as they got the opportunity to write their memoirs – frequently referred to the minute circulation of *Nabat* inside Russia to prove that its influence was nugatory. Plekhanov, however (and, having become a Marxist, he had no particular axe to grind), gives a different picture: '*Nabat* had a tiny circulation in Russia – but the leading revolutionaries of the day got hold of it without any difficulty'[30] – and then shows that Tkachev's ascendancy over the leaders of *Narodnaya Volya* was much greater than they would have cared to admit. As we shall see, the period of Tkachev's disfavour did not last long, and the powerful illegal organizations established in Russia in the late 1870s and early 1880s – the first effective revolutionary parties in the country's history – did indeed develop towards an ever greater acceptance of his ideas. But the real measure of Tkachev's historical importance is his influence upon Vladimir Ilyich Lenin. Here again, the facts should be allowed to speak for themselves – yet it would be fitting at this point, when summing up Tkachev's achievement, to say a few words about the much-argued subject of Tkachev and Lenin.

The fundamental relationship between the two men's ideas was probably best analysed by Berdyaev:

> Tkachev should be recognized, more than anybody else, as Lenin's precursor ... He was one of the few Russian revolutionaries of the past, possibly the only one, to think about power, about its seizure and organization. He wanted the revolutionary socialist party to become the government, and in this he already closely resembled Lenin ...
>
> Tkachev, like Lenin, created a theory of a socialist revolution for Russia. The Russian revolution was compelled not to follow Western examples. This was connected with a specific problem in the history of Russian socialist thought: could Russia by-pass capitalist development and the rule of the bourgeoisie, could the revolution be socialist, could Marxism be applied to Russia without consideration for the peculiarities of the Russian path? Tkachev was right in his criticism of Engels – and his rightness was not the rightness of Populism against Marxism but the historical rightness of the Bolsheviks against the Mensheviks, of Lenin against Plekhanov. In Russia it was not the communist revolution but the liberal bourgeois revolution that proved to be a Utopia.[31]

In the light of history one can scarcely disagree with this judgment. The interesting question is to what degree, if any, Lenin was *directly* influenced by Tkachev's writings, so little known inside Russia, or whether the coincidence between the two theories was purely fortuitous. While no absolutely conclusive answer will ever be possible, a number of strong clues all point in a very definite direction.

To begin with, Lenin's few explicit published references to Tkachev were invariably favourable – in marked contrast to his comments on other Populist theoreticians (apart from

Chernyshevsky).* In his most important work, *What Is to Be Done?*, which marked his break with orthodox Russian Marxism, Lenin wrote, referring to *Narodnaya Volya*: 'The attempt to seize power, which was prepared by the preaching of Tkachev and carried out by means of the "terrifying" terror that did really terrify, had grandeur.'[32] (Significantly, Lenin laid his main stress on the Tkachevite element in the policy of *Narodnaya Volya*, the attempt to seize power, and not on the political terrorism that is almost uniformly singled out by other writers.) Beginning from the publication of his book, Lenin was increasingly attacked by his Marxist critics for being a follower of Tkachev, for replacing Marxism by Jacobinism. Lenin remained remarkably unperturbed in the face of these accusations – unlike his vehement defence against other charges of heresy – and never essayed a serious refutation. Indeed, he repeatedly expressed his admiration for Jacobinism: at the most critical moment of his career, in the summer of 1917, he published an article under the sarcastic title 'Can the working class be frightened by "Jacobinism"?'.

Further, there is positive evidence to suggest that during his formative period as a revolutionary Lenin was strongly influenced by 'Russian Jacobins' – the followers of Zaichnevsky as well as of Tkachev. In 1891–2, while banished to Samara, Lenin came into frequent contact and conducted lengthy discussions with exiled members of 'Jacobin' circles. One of them, Maria Golubeva-Yasneva, published her reminiscences in a Soviet Communist journal shortly after Lenin's death: 'Today, remembering my conversations with Vladimir Ilyich,

---

* This fact is all the more important since many writers on Lenin – and by no means only Communist ones – attempt to gloss over it or even flatly deny it. Thus, Louis Fischer in his widely acclaimed biography of Lenin bases a questionable and 'loaded' assumption upon an entirely incorrect statement: 'There is no evidence that Lenin was a follower of Tkachev, whom he mentions once – unfavourably' (L. Fischer, *The Life of Lenin*, London 1965, p. 45).

I come more than ever to the conclusion that the idea of the dictatorship of the proletariat had already occurred to him then. Not without reason did he talk to me so often about the question of the seizure of power (one of the points of our Jacobin programme).'[33]

The most formidable testimony of all is that of Vladimir Bonch-Bruevich, Lenin's close associate, old personal friend, and general factotum during the 1917 revolution and the Civil War. At the turn of the century Bonch-Bruevich had established a library of revolutionary literature in Geneva, largely for Lenin's use. Tkachev's works occupied a place of honour. In his memoirs Bonch-Bruevich wrote:

Vladimir Ilyich read through and examined most carefully all of this old revolutionary literature, paying particular attention to Tkachev and remarking that this writer was closer to our viewpoint than any of the others ... We collected articles that Tkachev had written and handed them over to Vladimir Ilyich. Not only did V.I. read these works by Tkachev, he also recommended that all of us familiarize ourselves with the valuable writings of this original thinker. More than once he asked newly-arrived comrades if they wished to study the illegal literature. 'Begin', V.I. would advise, 'by reading and familiarizing yourself with Tkachev's *Nabat* ... this is basic and will give you tremendous knowledge.'[34]

After this it is not surprising that Bonch-Bruevich (a considerable scholar himself) should have held unequivocal views concerning the relationship between Tkachev and Leninism: 'It is an irrefutable fact that the Russian revolution proceeded to a significant degree according to the ideas of Tkachev. The seizure of power was made at a time determined in advance by a revolutionary party organized on the principles of strict centralization and discipline. And this party, having seized power, operates in many respects as Tkachev advised.'[35] In the early revolutionary years the Bolsheviks were fairly generous with their acknowledgments to their predecessors;

not having yet become the prisoners of an ossified orthodoxy, they saw no reason to genuflect to a fanciful apostolic genealogy. Pokrovsky, the leading Marxist historian of the time, assigned Tkachev a central place in the Russian revolutionary tradition: he called him 'undoubtedly the first Russian Marxist'; he wrote of Tkachev's 'Marxist interpretation of history' and of his 'communism'; he referred to the 'Jacobins' as the 'Bolshevik wing' of the revolutionary movement.[36] When Pokrovsky spoke of Tkachev's 'Marxism' he meant, of course, his 'Leninism' – but the word itself had not yet been established, and terminological usage was still quite free-and-easy. Writing a few years later, when the Stalinist ideological freeze had already begun to set in, Tkachev's biographer Kozmin was somewhat more cautious in his expressions, though hardly in his estimation of Tkachev's historical role: 'Tkachev may not have been a Marxist, but certainly in the Russia of his day there was no one who absorbed the teaching of Marx as strongly and as deeply as he did ... Tkachev's gigantic historical merit is his persistent advocacy of the establishment of a united centralized party.'[37]

A little later Tkachev disappeared altogether. He was an awkward character to have around after the proclamation of the monotheistic doctrinal purity of Marxism-Leninism. The silence of the memory-hole was clearly the wisest policy – with Tkachev's recent partial reappearance (though not rehabilitation), Soviet historians have become oddly defensive and unsure of themselves, flailing out wildly at ideological opponents and their cunning diversions. The customary formula (to quote one of the newer and better Soviet books on Populism) runs as follows: 'The enemies of Bolshevism have often made accusations that V. I. Lenin inherited his tactics of the revolutionary seizure of power from Tkachev and the *Narodnaya Volya*. In actual fact there is nothing whatever in common between the Leninist teaching on the conquest of political power by the proletariat and the seizure of power by a conspiratorial organization of the intelligentsia.'[38] This peremptory declaration may pass, in the USSR, for a statement of historical fact;

elsewhere it merely sounds comical. As the author himself undoubtedly knows, there is all too much evidence for the close similarity between the ideas of Tkachev and of Lenin. This similarity becomes even more marked when one turns from the rarefied atmosphere of ideological debate to the field of active underground revolutionary struggle.

CHAPTER 17

Back to Politics

The argument between Lavrov and Tkachev over the strategy and tactics of the Russian revolution, although conducted on a theoretical plane, was very far from academic. It was fought out against the background of far-reaching changes taking place in Russia within the revolutionary movement itself. In the space of a bare two or three years the situation had been dramatically transformed: the demoralization and hopelessness engendered by the failure of 'going to the people' had given place to the greatest eruption of revolutionary activity experienced by nineteenth-century Russia. The ideologists had done their work; now it was the turn of the practical men. And very soon these were to prove themselves far more practical – far more skilful, resourceful, efficient and mature – than any of their predecessors. Populism was approaching its climactic period, the culmination of decades of apprenticeship.

The 'Mad Summer' of 1874 had dealt a heavy blow to the revolutionary intelligentsia. Many of its most active leaders were in gaol; others were returning, defeated and dispirited, to the cities which they had left with such high hopes only a few months earlier. What they had suffered was more than a defeat: it was the collapse of deep-felt beliefs, of plans carefully worked out over the years. Propaganda among the people had failed; the peasants had turned out not to be spontaneous socialists after all; new ideas and new methods were urgently needed. The course upon which they embarked, hesitantly at first and then with ever greater assurance, was the ineluctable outcome of their experiences: organization instead of spontaneity, centralization instead of indiscipline, political action instead of immediate social revolution. They learned their lessons the hard way – but the speed with which the small band of routed revolutionaries restored themselves into a force capable of terrorizing the mighty Imperial government is a remarkable tribute to their resilience and to their almost religious faith in the revolution.

There were, inevitably, a number of false starts and stillborn attempts. Practically the only lasting achievement of the propagandists, mainly of the Chaikovskists, had been the establishment of ties with industrial workers in some of the larger centres. Throughout the 1870s the industrialization of Russia was proceeding at an ever greater pace – and with it grew the workers' grievances and sense of solidarity. As in the case of other industrial revolutions, the condition of the working class was indescribably bad – perhaps even worse than elsewhere, in view of the general semi-Asiatic backwardness of Russia's political and social relationships. Greatly to their surprise, therefore, the revolutionaries found the workers much more willing to listen to them than the idolized peasantry. So it was, paradoxically, among the once-despised proletariat that the Populists began their process of recovery. More and more one finds the word 'worker' replacing 'peasant' or 'people' in Populist literature, until by the end of the decade the working class had come to be regarded as the intelligentsia's main base of support. But the methods employed were very different from those of 'going to the people': what the revolutionaries now sought was not instant spontaneous rebellion but the creation of tight-knit conspiratorial organizations, with selected workers as equal partners and active participators.

It was in the south, the present-day Ukraine, with its traditional rebelliousness, its heterogeneous population and its greater openness to the outside world, that the reconstruction of active Populism began. Small working-class circles were set up, first in Odessa, then in Kiev: the 'Union of Workers of South Russia' and two separate organizations both called the 'Workers' Union of South Russia'. None lasted for more than a few months – the police saw to that – but they managed to carry out several strikes and, more important in the long run, to implant the seeds of socialist ideas among the workers of the rapidly burgeoning industrial centres of South Russia.

Yet the new interest in industrial workers by no means implied the renunciation of deep-rooted Populist attitudes. On the contrary, the Populists were attracted to the proletariat not because they saw it as the Marxist demiurge of the future socialist society, but primarily because its concentration within a limited number of large industrial enterprises made the latter far more suitable foci than the sprawling and individualistic villages for the activities of disciplined conspiratorial groups led by outsiders. As the months passed it became ever clearer that the collapse of propaganda and the turn towards organization had fortified the time-honoured tendencies towards conspiracy and mystification. The first palpable indication of this, even before the establishment of a centralized all-Russian secret party, came in 1876–7, with the famous 'Chigirin affair'.

Two leading Populists, Stefanovich and Deutsch (the latter subsequently to become one of the founders of the Russian social-democratic movement), had illegally established themselves in the Chigirin district, some 150 miles from Kiev – an area well known for its history of agrarian disorders. In strictest secrecy they began handing out to carefully chosen peasants copies of a 'Secret Imperial Charter', signed and sealed by Alexander II and dated 19 February 1875, the fourteenth anniversary of the Emancipation Decree. Addressing himself to 'Our loyal peasants', the Emperor informed them that in 1861, 'We had emancipated you from bondage and granted you all the land without any payment, together with the forests and meadows that had until then unjustly belonged to the nobles alone'. But the nobility had thwarted the Imperial desire, and after twenty years of ceaseless and unavailing struggle the Emperor had come to the conclusion that he was unable to help the peasants without their own active assistance in overthrowing the nobles' yoke. 'Therefore We command you to unite in secret societies under the name of "Secret Militias" and to make preparations for rebellion ... Everyone who is ready to sacrifice his life in the great cause must take an oath of loyalty to the society of the Secret Militia. These societies are to be upheld in the strictest possible secrecy.' This was followed by detailed directions as to the structure of the Secret Militias (headed by a Council of Commissars under the Emperor's direct patronage), the initiation ceremony, etc.[1]

Needless to say, the whole thing was an elaborate and cynical hoax, the 'document' itself having been printed at one of the underground Populist presses. Yet, because its contents coincided with the persistent legend of a 'true' Emancipation Edict that had been stolen and falsified by the nobles, the effect was resounding. Chigirin was undoubtedly the Populists' sole successful venture at organizing the peasantry. Stefanovich and Deutsch soon managed to enlist about a thousand peasants in their organization, and even to keep it secret for several months. When the inevitable betrayal came, nearly a hundred illiterate, duped peasants were sentenced to convict labour or Siberian exile – most of them expressing somewhat uncharitable feelings towards the 'peasants' friends' who had so cruelly tricked them. The two principals were incarcerated in Kiev prison but soon released in a sensational escape engineered from outside by their comrades, and spirited out of the country.

The Chigirin affair was one of the more important events in Russian revolutionary history. The methods employed by Stefanovich and Deutsch can hardly be called novel: they went back to the tradition of the Decembrists, the Ishutinites, the Nechaevites. Moreover, an almost identical attempt had been made some dozen years earlier, in 1863, when a group of students had tried to rouse the peasants of the Kazan region by means of a forged Imperial manifesto that called upon them – in the Tsar's name – to seize the land and overthrow their oppressors. The reversion to these methods of blatant deceit casts a strange light, to say the least, upon the Populists' constant moralistic condemnation of Nechaev. All the more so since neither Stefanovich nor Deutsch ever expressed the slightest qualms or regrets over their actions; indeed, as we shall see, no sooner were they free than they began planning a repeat performance.

Of greater significance was the attitude towards the Chigirin affair and its moral implications taken up by the general revolutionary milieu. At this point one comes up – not for the first time – against a direct conflict between the historical evidence and the writings of historians. It becomes necessary therefore to say a few words concerning some peculiarities of the historiography of the Russian revolutionary movement. Almost all the non-Marxist historians of Populism – liberal, progressive-minded men, Russians as well as foreigners – have been extremely favourably disposed towards the subject of their research. It is difficult, after all, to preserve one's neutrality when writing about the struggle of such incredibly heroic and selfless young people against such an unquestionably corrupt and repressive regime. As a result even historians of the highest scholarly standards have consistently tended to prettify the movement, to justify its excesses, to turn a blind eye on its blemishes, to depict it as a kind of Russian equivalent of the familiar European liberal-democratic revolutionary movements of the nineteenth century. In this picture amorality and élitism are temporary aberrations, Nechaev an isolated phenomenon, Tkachev a man of very little influence, and so on.

Thus, the revolutionaries' response to the Chigirin affair poses a knotty problem for the friendly and conscientious historians of Populism. They have solved it fairly straightforwardly. The most distinguished non-Marxist Russian authority, Bogucharsky, wrote that 'a great many revolutionaries immediately took up an uncompromisingly hostile attitude to the methods employed by Stefanovich and Deutsch'.[2] Bogucharsky's tendency to play down the conspiratorial, élitist and anti-democratic elements of Populism was harshly criticized by Plekhanov, himself a leading revolutionary of the seventies[3] – yet his basic approach has survived to this day.

Professor Franco Venturi is even more unequivocal with regard to the Chigirin affair. In his monumental *Roots of Revolution* he writes: 'The vast majority of revolutionaries severely condemned this attempt to deceive the peasants.'[4] It must be said quite clearly that this statement is untrue, and could be disproved by a large body of evidence. But it will be sufficient to quote two unimpeachable sources in refutation of Venturi's thesis.

The prominent Populist Osip Aptekman writes in his memoirs: 'The experience of Stefanovich's popular-revolutionary organization created an immense impression upon the revolutionaries. They were completely blinded by the "Chigirin affair". I don't even mention our incorrigibly romantic Osinsky – even the calmer ones like Adrian Mikhailov were beside themselves in their fascination with this affair.' Aptekman goes on to describe how Osinsky's proposal to base the whole tactics of *Zemlya i Volya*, the new all-Russian revolutionary party, upon the Chigirin methods 'was sympathetically received by practically the majority of the Council', and rejected only after lively debates in the face of the unyielding opposition of Plekhanov and of Aptekman himself.[5]

Mikhail Popov provides even more striking confirmation of the lasting effects of the Chigirin affair. He is describing the historic 1879 congress of *Zemlya i Volya*: 'Suddenly there arrive from abroad Stefanovich and Deutsch; according to their information, there is sound reason to believe that a new peasant organization is possible in Chigirin, and that the peasants there are inclined towards revolution. Those Populists, among them the author of these words, who clearly understood that the revolutionary elements could be stopped from moving towards purely political activity only by the creation of some resounding affair among the peasantry, seized upon these hopes. This became the direct cause of the conflict between Populists and terrorists which led to the splitting-up of *Zemlya i Volya* into two parties.'[6] Ironically, over two years the situation had changed to such a degree that this time it was Plekhanov and the future nucleus of the Russian Marxist party who supported the 'Chigirinite' line.

In other words, the Chigirin affair had a profound influence upon the Populist movement (including its final split into two divergent factions); as the evidence shows, the objections to Stefanovich's tactics were based not on moral scruples but upon the inexpediency of dissipating the revolutionary forces in such ultimately fruitless ventures. To call this attitude one of 'severe condemnation' on the part of 'the vast majority of revolutionaries' is not only to distort the facts of one particular case but to misrepresent the whole political and moral outlook of the revolutionary intelligentsia. Courage, faith and selflessness are admirable qualities, but they do not nullify fanaticism, intolerance and unscrupulousness – nor should they be made to do so.

The Chigirin affair was an integral part of the process by which, step by laborious step, a centralized revolutionary party was being established. The Southern workers' organizations were minor landmarks along this road. Of greater importance was the so-called All-Russian Social-Revolutionary Organization, founded in 1875 by two rather odd groups. One was the community of Russian female students in Zurich, who were infuriated by their government's order to desist from further studies for fear of radicalization; the other, the hot-blooded Caucasian student *zemlyachestvo*, in Switzerland, which nursed its own grievances. The two decided to combine efforts and to transfer their activities to Russia. They travelled to Moscow, where they established contact with the remnants of the old revolutionary circles and succeeded in setting up several illegal factory groups (the indomitable girls, despite their sheltered upbringing, went to work in the factories as ordinary labourers – soon they were unrecognizable).

Considering the amateurish nature of the enterprise and its members' lack of experience, the 'All-Russian Social-Revolutionary Organization' represented remarkable progress towards discipline and centralization. Although the main work was that of propaganda, the methods employed were very different from those of 'going to the people'. The organization functioned in accordance with carefully worked-out written rules. These laid down the principles of full equality of the members, of all property being held in common, etc.; on the other hand, unlike the Chaikovskist approach, they provided

441

for a central leadership or 'administration', whose members were to be freed from factory work and whose decisions were binding.

The Organization existed for only a few months before the police broke it up. During this short period they set up cells in some of the industrial centres of the Moscow area – chiefly in Tula and Ivanovo-Voznesensk – and were in regular communication with revolutionary groups in St Petersburg and Kiev. What was even more important, they maintained contact with their émigré friends in Switzerland and France, from whom they received a steady flow of subversive publications. Among these was the paper *Rabotnik* (The Worker), the first Russian illegal periodical specifically devoted to working-class problems, fifteen issues of which appeared in all; it was remarkable mainly for its unrelenting hostility alike to liberalism and reform and to Jacobin conspiracy.

The authorities, even though they had succeeded in making short work of the Organization, were seriously worried by this development. They had thought that, with the exception of a few innocuous study-groups, the revolutionary movement had ceased to exist – and suddenly they were faced by this new type of association, with ordered regulations and discipline, and with fairly widespread contacts. The government decided to make an example of the All-Russian Social-Revolutionary Organization: almost all its active members were arrested and tried in one of the great political cases of the 1870s, the 'Trial of the 50'; the sensation of the trial was the worker Pyotr Alexeyev who, thanks to his eloquent and intrepid defence and his especially harsh sentence (ten years' hard labour), achieved countrywide fame as Russia's first working-class revolutionary.

Slowly the need for greater centralization, greater discipline, greater efficiency was being understood by the small bands of dedicated revolutionaries scattered over the vastness of European Russia. Every new failure, every new batch of arrests was driving the lesson home. The radical intelligentsia was few in numbers – at this rate of bloodletting soon there would be none left, and all hope for the revolution would be gone. The only way in which the process could be stopped was by organization and strict conspiracy. A new generation had grown up, colder, more rational, more practical than their elders. They preferred action to words. They still believed in miracles, but at least they no longer expected them to come out of the blue: they knew now that miracles required hard work and heavy sacrifice. Above all, they required unity.

The first all-Russian revolutionary party, *Zemlya i Volya* (Land and Liberty), was formed in St Petersburg in the autumn of 1876. It is impossible to establish the exact date and difficult even to reconstruct the circumstances of its birth. Its founders were good conspirators: they left hardly any documents lying around; police and judicial interrogation records are inadequate and often misleading; memoirs written thirty years later frequently contradict each other. But the precise details are hardly of crucial importance.

According to some accounts, the nucleus of the new organization was provided by a 'Northern Revolutionary-Populist Group' which had been leading a rather shadowy existence in the capital. Whether by chance or by invitation, a large number of representatives of various other revolutionary groups had gathered in St Petersburg in the autumn of 1876: the remnants of the Chaikovskists, village propagandists who were still at liberty, the survivors of the Moscow social-revolutionaries, Bakuninist 'rebels' from the South and South-East, enthusiastic young students. After the usual long discussions they agreed to set up a unified organization. At first it did not even have a name – *Zemlya i Volya* came later. The leading principals in the negotiations were our old acquaintance Mark Natanson for the Northerners, and Valerian Osinsky, the most prominent of the Southerners. But from the first the moving spirit of the new organization, the man who gradually transformed it into an efficient and disciplined conspiratorial party, was Alexander Mikhailov, then a twenty-one-year-old student.

Alexander Mikhailov's reputation as a revolutionary leader has been overshadowed by that of his friend Andrei Zhelyabov, the organizer of the assassination of Alexander II, nor did

Mikhailov himself ever evince the slightest craving for fame or acknowledgment. In fact, *Zemlya i Volya* and its successor, *Narodnaya Volya*, never had any accepted single leader – its leadership was always genuinely collective – but if one were to pick out the dominant personality it would undoubtedly be that of Alexander Mikhailov. He was no Nechaev: although a born leader, attractive and exercising an easy authority, he had none of Nechaev's personal magnetism or hypnotic force. Mikhailov's strength lay in his exceptional organizational talent (a commodity always in extremely short supply in Russian intelligentsia circles); he was a born organizer, a brilliant planner, a conspirator of genius, a master of every technique needed to implement and protect the bold activities of the revolutionary party in the face of the greatest detection campaign ever mounted by the world's most experienced political police. 'Wherever he was,' wrote Vera Figner, one of his closest colleagues, 'he always chose the people most fitted to carry out any one particular task, he united them into a group, he enforced discipline upon the group's members, he unceasingly demanded the fusion of all the separate individual wills and their subjection to the collective will.'[7] But Alexander Mikhailov was no mere apparatus-man – his was one of the most powerful minds in the party. He had a thorough knowledge of theory, and exerted considerable influence upon the ideological development of Populism, especially in the later stages, when *Narodnaya Volya* was moving ever closer towards acceptance of Tkachev's ideas.

In the first eighteen months of its existence *Zemlya i Volya* was still far from being the centralized, unified organization that it later became; the links between its component parts were fairly tenuous, the Southerners especially enjoying a large degree of autonomy. Yet even speaking of that early period one must agree with Lenin (no mean judge of such matters) when he wrote in *What Is to Be Done?*: 'The magnificent organization that the revolutionaries had in the seventies, and that should serve us as a model, was not established by the *Narodnaya Volya*, but by the *Zemlya i Volya*.'[8] It was indeed the model for Lenin's 'party of a new type' – and the party for which Tkachev had been ceaselessly calling.

The party's basic strategic and tactical principles were set forth in its first programme, adopted in 1876. It stated that the party's final aim was the achievement of the full anarchist ideal, i.e. the abolition of the State, but recognized that this would be a task for the distant future. The immediate aims of the revolution were threefold: (1) the abolition of private ownership of land, and its distribution among the peasants; (2) the restructuring of the social system on the basis of the village communes; (3) the right of self-determination, including independence, of the national minorities. This, the programme went on, was what the party meant by 'Land and Liberty'.

The tortured soul-searching over Russia's future path was now at an end: 'This formula can be implemented only by means of a violent revolution, to be carried out as speedily as possible.' Speed was of the essence, because 'the development of capitalism and the ever greater injection of the various poisons of bourgeois civilization into the people's life, under the guidance of the Russian government, are threatening to destroy the *obshchina* and to corrupt the popular way of thought'. The idea of urgently preventing capitalist development – 'demolished' by Engels only a few months earlier – was now officially adopted as the mainstay of the revolutionary programme.

As its main practical tasks the party sought to effect the unity of all revolutionary elements and organizations, and to achieve the *disorganization of the State*. Without this, it stated, even the best-planned and broadest-based revolution was doomed to failure. It was the first time that the theme of 'disorganization' had been clearly formulated; from then on every revolutionary action was increasingly subordinated to the awesome task of paralysing the Russian State.

The new party briefly listed the methods by which it intended to carry out its programme. First and foremost was the creation of a 'tight-knit and orderly organization of mature revolutionaries, prepared to act in accordance with the above programme, and enlisted both from the intelligentsia and from among the workers directly connected with it'. The party would establish contacts with oppressed religious sects, with industrial workers, and also (a curious concession to Bakuninism!) with 'freedom-loving' bands of robbers; it would conduct propaganda and agitation among the intelligentsia – 'who will at first provide the main recruiting-ground for our organization'; and it would get in touch with the liberals 'in order to exploit them in our interests'. The disorganization of the State was to be achieved by a combination of the following methods: (a) subversion within the armed forces; (b) suborning government officials; (c) 'the systematic extermination of the most pernicious or the most outstanding representatives of the government'; (d) 'when the day of reckoning comes – the mass extermination of the government and in general of everyone who upholds or who may uphold any regime repugnant to us'.[9] Never since Zaichnevsky had the slogan of mass political terror as an object of the revolution been put forward so bluntly: only now it had become the credo not of an individual fanatic but of an organized party.

Organization was, indeed, the main problem facing the new party, pledged to ending the disunity and spontaneity that had hitherto been the plague of the Russian revolutionary movement. The organizational statutes of 1876 have not survived; they are known to us only from the account in Aptekman's memoirs. 'The basis of the statute,' he writes, 'was the principle of strict and consistent centralization, with its logical extension towards conspiracy.' The party and its organizations were to be directed by a secret 'main circle', whose decisions were binding upon all members. The chief department of the main circle was the 'administration' or 'centre', seated in the capital; among its principal functions, apart from the day-to-day running of the whole organization, was the fabrication of passports and other false documents. However, it could not take any serious decisions without the consent of the 'Council', the party's supreme body. The composition of the Council was somewhat volatile: it included, besides the administration, all members of the main circle who happened to be in St Petersburg when the Council was in session.

The other sections of the main circle were the intelligentsia group, the working-class group, the village group, and the 'disorganizing group'. The last was gradually to become the most important section of all; originally its activities were limited to releasing arrested comrades and to protecting them while in gaol, as well as to 'self-defence', i.e. the liquidation of traitors and police agents. Needless to say, the disorganizing group worked in the utmost secrecy – even the administration and the Council could receive no more than general information concerning its actions.

According to Aptekman, there were twenty-five founding members of the 'central circle': although in theory all remained absolutely equal, the most prominent were Alexander Mikhailov, Mark Natanson, Valerian Osinsky, Alexei Oboleshev, Adrian Mikhailov, Dmitry Lizogub and Georgy Plekhanov. Several additional members were co-opted over the next two years, including Sofia Perovskaya, Vera Figner, Sergei Kravchinsky, Lev Tikhomirov and Nikolai Morozov.[10] The total membership of the party probably never exceeded two or three hundred.

Unknown to all, a new political force had made its appearance upon the Russian scene – in the long run it was to prove more important than the mighty Imperial government against which it was now pitting its puny resources. The revolutionary movement had taken a gigantic step forwards. Although numerically no greater than at any time in the past thirty years (probably even smaller, due to the recent large-scale arrests), it had at last overcome its dissensions and hesitations, and formed a unified, centralized, disciplined illegal party. The self-sacrificing work of so many earlier generations had finally borne fruit; the radical intelligentsia and the whole smouldering, dissatisfied 'educated class' of Russia had acquired a focus for their loyalty, their admiration, their vicarious gratification.

In the first eighteen months of its existence the new party showed few signs of the momentous influence it was to have upon future events. It made its first public showing in St

Petersburg on 6 December 1876, in the form of a mass demonstration held in the Square of Kazan Cathedral. The revolutionaries had hoped for a large working-class contingent – in the event only about two hundred workers turned up, many fewer than the assembled students. Still, a not inauspicious beginning. Plekhanov made a short speech (this was also his first appearance as a revolutionary leader), and one of the demonstrators unfurled a red banner with the words *Zemlya i Volya* inscribed upon it. From that moment on the slogan began to be accepted as the name of the new revolutionary party. The demonstration itself was swiftly and expertly broken up by the police; a large group of participants was arrested, tried, and sentenced to stiff terms in gaol. Nothing out of the ordinary, it seemed, had happened: just another routine disturbance.

Nor were the other activities of the *zemlevoltsy*, as they came to be called, originally very different from those of their predecessors. In the main they concentrated once again on fairly orthodox methods of propaganda among the people. True, their work was now conducted in a much more organized fashion: instead of scattering individually throughout the whole of European Russia, they decided to establish revolutionary 'colonies' in certain selected areas – mainly in the South-East, around Saratov, Tambov, Voronezh and Rostov, where, they fondly hoped, the traditions of the Pugachev uprising of a hundred years before were still alive, and where the embers of insurgency were waiting to be fanned into a fire. This was no second 'going to the people' with the aim of educating the masses; the 'colonies' were to become the nuclei (or 'bases', to use a later terminology) of the coming all-Russian revolution. The 'colonists' themselves received fairly regular instructions and reinforcements from their St Petersburg centre; they were much tougher and more experienced than the starry-eyed boys and girls of 1874; most of them were 'illegal', i.e. living with false papers. Yet despite all the organization, the careful planning and conspiracy, the results of this second venture were no more encouraging than the first. The peasants and the workers proved no more co-operative, their suspicions of the strangers had not lessened, the police were as watchful as ever. Gradually the 'colonies' broke up and their dispirited members began to return home. Once again something had gone wrong.

Then suddenly, almost miraculously, the whole situation was transformed. Events over which the revolutionaries had no control – external war and internal repression – had come to their aid. The scene was set for the greatest outburst of the nineteenth-century Russian revolutionism.

It all started in the Balkans. In July 1875 a popular uprising broke out in Herzegovina and Bosnia; the Turks proceeded to put it down by the customary methods. Next May Bulgaria rose in revolt; this was suppressed with even greater cruelty. Serbia and Montenegro, unable to watch the massacre of their kith and kin, declared war on Turkey. By September 1876 they had suffered total defeat. These events created considerable commotion throughout Europe. The slaughter of thousands of defenceless Christians – pretty small beer by the more advanced standards of our own century – was something which in those days could still arouse the civilized conscience to a high pitch of indignation. Mr Gladstone published his celebrated pamphlet *The Bulgarian Horrors and the Question of the East*: a powerful indictment of Turkey and (perhaps more to the point) of Disraeli's pro-Turkish policy. Everywhere people were asking the same question: how could such unspeakable outrages be happening in the second half of the nineteenth century, when mankind had finally overcome the savagery and superstition of the past and entered into an age of peace and plenty?

Nowhere did the Balkan events stir up as violent emotions as in Russia. After all, the victims of the Turkish atrocities were not only Christian but *Orthodox*, not just Europeans but *Slavs*. And had not Russia been for centuries the sole protector, the only hope of her oppressed Slavonic Christian brethren? An immense wave of Panslavist emotion swept the country. It transcended all political and class divisions. Once again the old 'Russian idea' – the mystical conviction that autocratic Russia embodied a unique mission of liberation – had been reborn.

The press, with one voice, called for war; public collections to aid the South Slav brethren were started in almost every town and village; hundreds of volunteers, including many serving officers, poured into the Balkans; the command of the Serbian army was taken over by the Russian general Chernyaev (with singular lack of success). Finally, in April 1877, a somewhat unwilling Russian government declared war upon Turkey.

The degree of national unity was truly impressive. In the peasants' consciousness there had never really been any other external foe but Turkey – the hated pagan power of the South, against whom Russia had already waged nine wars. All segments of 'official' and 'educated' society appeared to concur in this: Gladstone's pamphlet was immediately translated by the arch-reactionary Pobedonostsev; liberal and radical publications vied with each other in hysterical chauvinism; illegal revolutionary papers appearing abroad denounced Turkey as 'the age-old national enemy of the Russian people'. This last was perhaps the most astonishing development of all: the cause of the Southern Slavs was taken up by the revolutionary groups with even greater enthusiasm than that of the liberation of their own country.

Many, not least among the revolutionaries themselves, were rather surprised by their sudden adherence to the banner of Panslavism. In fact, however, the idea of liberating the 'oppressed' Slav peoples and uniting them with Russia in some sort of federation had been an important element of the Russian revolutionary tradition from its very beginning. (This was the main reason for Marx's profound distrust of almost all Russian revolutionary émigrés, whom he tended to lump together with the Tsarist government as equally zealous proponents of Russia's messianic mission.) One of the original Decembrist groups had been the so-called 'Society of United Slavs', formed in 1823 with a programme for freeing all the 'Slav lands' – these included Russia, Poland, Bohemia, Moravia, Hungary with Transylvania, Serbia, Moldavia, Wallachia, Dalmatia and Croatia – and uniting them in a single republican federation (the capital of which remained unspecified).[11] The 'United Slavs' were in composition the least aristocratic, and in outlook the most radical of all the Decembrists; shortly before the uprising they had merged with Pestel's Southern Society. During their interrogation a number of Decembrists spoke of their dream of a democratic Panslav federation. The combination of Panslavism and revolutionism was then exuberantly taken up by Bakunin, who in 1848 even convened a special Slav congress in Prague. In this respect at least he found many followers.

It may seem strange, even slightly comical, that the disaffected subjects of the most oppressive tyranny in the world should devote so much attention to the liberation of other peoples before they had obtained any modicum of freedom for their own. Here was one of those paradoxes in which the history of the Russian revolutionary movement abounded. It was composed of several strands of thought. Firstly, by fighting oppression in another country they were striking a blow against their own hated regime. Secondly, history had shown that wars, whether successful or not, were the most effective instruments for bringing about sweeping changes within Russia. Thirdly, in their messianic vision Russia could only become truly free by showing the rest of the world the path to salvation. Fourthly, it was a question of Slavs, of their own kith and kin, of their younger brothers now standing in such sore need of protection. And lastly – not to put too fine a point on it – there was a good deal of unconscious nationalism in the psychological make-up of the Russian revolutionary. *Zemlya i Volya* may have envisaged the notional concept of self-determination, but in practice it never showed any interest in the problems of Russia's national minorities. Other countries' oppressed Slavonic minorities were a very different matter indeed. Perhaps Marx was not all that far wrong . . .

Only one man raised his voice against the Panslav rampage of the Russian revolutionary youth: Lavrov. By entering the fray, warned *Vperyod*, they would help neither the South Slavs nor their own people; on the contrary, the growth of Russian influence abroad could only strengthen the position of the Imperial government inside its country. Besides, he continued rather less realistically, what was needed was not national but social liberation. Lavrov's position over the Southern Slav question finally undermined the great authority he had once possessed – just as had happened to Herzen fifteen years earlier, in the case of the Polish uprising. The *zemlevoltsy* and the other revolutionary groups were shocked by this callous disregard for the sufferings of their fellow-Slavs. They themselves embraced the Slav cause with limitless fervour. Many, including such prominent figures as Kravchinsky, fought with the Serbian army and the local insurgents; others, like Zhelyabov and the southern 'rebel' groups, organized the collection of funds and the dispatch of volunteers; a number of young women Populists served as nurses on the battlefields.

The Balkan events of 1875–8 marked a turning-point in the development of the Populist movement. It emerged from them with a new-found unity, a sense of solidarity proven in a great cause. Its members had acquired practical experience of fighting, of military methods and military discipline, of large-scale organization. The war itself, although only partially successful, had given some of the Southern Slav peoples freedom from absolute tyranny, and even equipped them with European-type constitutions – this brought home the poignant irony of continued despotism in Russia, the 'liberator-nation'. The idea of overthrowing autocracy by force became correspondingly much more popular, as did the idea of the primacy of political over social struggle.

Most important of all, the Russo–Turkish war produced a new crisis in the relations between government and 'educated society'. The initially poor showing of the Russian army against backward Asiatic Turkey – much remarked upon in Europe – created a deep feeling of national shame and frustration, while Russia's diplomatic defeat at the Congress of Berlin caused widespread revulsion against a government which had weakly retreated in the face of English threats. Russia's military, diplomatic and political reverse led the revolutionary movement to a fundamental reappraisal of its strategy. The conclusion was drawn that Imperial Russia, for all her appearance of might, was fatally sick – the proverbial Colossus with feet of clay – and that a small group of organized conspirators, unafraid of violence, was in a position to topple this infirm regime.

With that monumental tactlessness and unconcern for public opinion which so often characterized the Russian government's actions (attributable in part to the novelty of having any public opinion at all), it was this moment of greatest disesteem that the authorities chose for a new show of repression. The great wave of political trials of the 1860s had culminated in the Karakozov affair (1866); during the next ten years only two or three political cases were brought before the courts, none of which created much of an impression – the obvious exception being Nechaev and his accomplices. It came therefore as all the more of a shock to the 'educated public' and the radical intelligentsia when 1877 – that winter of Russian discontent – saw the holding, in swift succession, of three big political trials, each on a scale larger than anything since the days of the Decembrists. The trial of the Kazan Square demonstrators, twenty in all (January 1877), was followed by two of the most famous political trials in Russian history: the Trial of the 50 (February–March 1877), with its inordinately heavy sentences, and the Trial of the 193, also known as the 'Monster Trial', which dragged on for four months, from October 1877 to January 1878. Curiously enough, it was this last which aroused the most emotion, despite the comparative leniency of its sentences: five of the accused were condemned to ten years' hard labour, ten to nine years, three to five years; forty were exiled to Siberia, while the rest were set free (some had already been out on bail). Among those acquitted were the eventual organizers of the Tsar's assassination, Zhelyabov, Perovskaya and Sablin, together with such prominent future terrorists as Morozov and Tikhomirov. The extraordinary and widespread indignation provoked by the Trial of the 193 was due to several causes: the defendants were charged with nothing more serious than 'going to the people' and peaceful proselytizing; the great majority had already spent over three years in pre-trial detention; and, most staggering of all, the Tsar rejected the court's own humble appeal for commutation of all but one of the hard-labour terms, and insisted on confirming the original sentence in all its rigour.

CHAPTER 18

Discipline and Terrorism

The three political trials of 1877 caused bitter resentment among the revolutionaries. Later historians have, on the whole, shared their sense of outrage over the gross injustice of the Tsarist authorities. Yet for all the severity of the punishment, it might seem a trifle odd that people who were earnestly contemplating the wholesale massacre of their opponents should have felt themselves deeply wronged by a few prison sentences passed on their comrades, and odder still that this point should be consistently overlooked by those who condemn the Tsarist government for its inhumanity. *'Cet animal est très méchant, Quand on l'attaque il se défend'*: the sentiment concisely expresses the prevailing censorious attitude towards the reactionary Tsarist regime.

The lessons of the trials were first formulated openly in the courtroom by some of the accused themselves. We have tried peaceful means, they declared, we did nothing more than attempt to educate the people, to tell them the truth about their lives. For this we are being sent to hard labour. From now on therefore all avenues of peaceful political activity are closed to us, and those who follow in our footsteps will have to devise entirely different means of struggle.

That about summed it up. Reading their comrades' defiant speeches, helplessly watching them being transported in chains to Siberia, the *zemlevoltsy* finally turned from talk to action. A terrible beauty is born. Everything that had happened in the past two years: the founding of the party, the uplift of the South Slav war, the humiliation of the government, the savage campaign of repression, the failure of propaganda, the thirst for revenge, the demands of self-defence, the need for decisive and speedy action – all fused into a new strategy of revolutionary

455

violence. No debates were held on the subject, no resolutions passed. All instinctively understood. The Trial of the 193 ended on 23 January 1878, and the next day Vera Zasulich fired a pistol point-blank at the Governor of St Petersburg, General Trepov. She missed, and was arrested on the spot. Zasulich's shot opened an incredible period of Russian history: a period of practically open civil war between the government and a handful of revolutionaries, which was to last for the better part of four years.

Soviet historians have had considerable difficulty in evolving a satisfactory interpretation of this weird episode: Marxist dogma has proved totally irreconcilable with the facts. During the Stalinist period one of the fundamental tenets of Soviet historiography (based on a single fleeting reference in one of Lenin's articles) was the existence in Russia in 1879-80 of a 'revolutionary situation'. This 'revolutionary situation' was supposed to consist of two weighty social elements: (a) 'the intensification of the contradictions between the multi-million masses of the peasantry and the class of landowning nobility which ruled the country's economic and political life'; and (b) 'the appearance of a new and higher type of social warfare: the struggle of the young Russian proletariat against capitalist exploitation.' It was 'the intensification of these social contradictions that determined the emergence of a general national crisis'.[1] For thirty years this remained Holy Writ; the Populists were mentioned, disapprovingly, only in passing, and their efforts were derided; one of the main accusations (usually followed by capital charges) against Pokrovsky and the early Marxist historians was their denial of the 1879-80 'revolutionary situation' and their attribution of the outbreak of revolutionary violence to the 'petty-bourgeois' Populists.

The theory of the 'revolutionary situation of 1879-80' became a prime victim of de-Stalinization. Cautiously, step by step, Soviet historians have begun to show that the once sacrosanct concept ran flagrantly counter to all historical facts. Today it is generally admitted that – unlike the 'revolutionary situation' of 1858-61, for which something of a case can be made out

– mass peasant and worker disturbances were negligible in 1878–82 (the period of crisis has itself been broadened, to accord with reality). Recent Soviet calculations[2] of the number of agrarian disorders show the striking contrast between the two periods:

1859 :	161	1878 :	31
1860 :	186	1879 :	46
1861 :	1859	1880 :	13
1862 :	864	1881 :	17
1863 :	509	1882 :	29
	3579		136

The figures for the first period are almost *twenty* times those for 1878–82. By Russian standards an average of twenty-seven peasant disturbances per year represented the height of tranquillity. To drive home the utter insignificance of the Russian peasant movement during the period of the 'revolutionary situation' a Soviet author aptly compares it with the contemporaneous Land War in Ireland – a country with a minute fraction of Russia's territory and population. He quotes the figures for Irish agrarian outrages contained in the *Report* of the Special Commission established by Parliament:

1878 :	301
1879 :	863
1880 :	2589
1881 :	4439
1882 :	3432
	11,624

Even after excluding such minor outrages as window-breaking, the Irish figure for 1880 *alone* is nearly ten times greater than the Russian total for the same period (see above).[3] So much for the legend of a peasantry seething with revolt, or experiencing a powerful 'intensification of contradictions'. Nor do the figures for industrial disputes[4] provide the slightest confirmation for the existence of anything resembling a 'revolutionary situation':

1877 : 16
1878 : 44
1879 : 54
1880 : 26
1881 : 25
1882 : 22

187

In other words, as the facts conclusively prove, the mass revolutionary movement of the workers and peasants was no more than a figment of the Marxist imagination. It was non-existent.

The question of the 'revolutionary situation of 1879–80', despite its seemingly esoteric nature, is not really an academic debate: the problems it poses are purely political (as Stalin and his ideologues well understood). They boil down to the central issue of the Russian revolutionary movement, of the 1917 revolution, and of Russia's whole twentieth-century history. On the one hand, there can be no doubt that an extremely grave political crisis did develop in Russia in 1878–81, a crisis created by the revolutionary movement and resulting in the near-paralysis of government. On the other hand, equally obviously the great mass of the population remained uninvolved in, and even largely hostile to, revolutionary activity. How is the conundrum to be explained? Soviet historians have latterly reconciled themselves to a decidedly un-Marxist interpretation. 'The peculiarity of the socio-political situation of the late 1870s,' writes one, 'is the fact that the crisis of autocracy was *directly* caused not so much by the struggle of the popular masses as by the actions of a party expressing the interests of these masses.'[5] Another and later author goes even further: 'Although in the final analysis the second revolutionary situation was

458

brought about by the various objective factors, including the heightened excitement of the masses generated by the Russo–Turkish war of 1877–8, the primary cause of the crisis of autocracy was the desperate anti-governmental struggle of the revolutionary intelligentsia, whose activities reflected the protest of the people.'[6] It is worthy of note that the intelligentsia no longer even 'expresses', but merely 'reflects' the interests of the people.

Such a diagnosis of the revolutionary crisis of 1878–82 – and, stripped of its Marxist verbiage, it has to be accepted as the correct one – carries profound political and historical implications. It means that contrary to all orthodox Marxist thinking, the peculiar conditions in Russia really did make it possible, given certain favourable external factors, for a tiny group of revolutionary intelligentsia conspirators to create a deep-seated political crisis, to convulse the whole body politic, to undermine the government and nearly bring it to its knees *in the absence of a mass movement or even of mass support*. The lesson was not lost on a later generation of revolutionaries.

Vera Zasulich's shot was symbolic of the new turn of events: not only did it mark the beginning of the wave of terrorism, it also indicated the extent of the sympathy enjoyed by the terrorists amongst Russian 'educated society'. The government decided to revert to its erstwhile liberalism; the case was tried by jury, in a court presided over by the famous liberal lawyer A. F. Koni. Zasulich defended her act as justified vengeance for the flogging of an arrested student by Trepov's order: the jury, not content with accepting her plea, refused even to recognize that she had fired a shot and acquitted her absolutely, much to the authorities' dismay. The verdict was immensely popular. In his diary the distinguished statesman D. A. Milyutin, Minister of War and author of the military reforms, noted that 'a great many, [here Milyutin crossed out his original text: 'even the majority, including numerous high-society ladies and officials'] if not the majority, were delighted by the court's verdict of acquittal'.[7] A spontaneous demonstration gathered to meet Zasulich outside the courthouse; when the bewildered police attempted to rearrest her she was hustled away in the crowd. The government had learnt its lesson: from then on all cases of terrorism were tried by special tribunals.

Zasulich had merely fired the opening shot of a campaign that was to increase in intensity with every passing month. In February Osinsky with two comrades attempted to kill an assistant public prosecutor; in May, also in Kiev, the terrorists succeeded in assassinating a gendarme (secret police) officer, Baron Geiking. Several police agents and informers were killed. A new and alarming phenomenon had appeared: the revolutionaries' armed resistance to arrest and police raids. On 30 January a group of active Populists led by Kovalsky shot it out with the police during a raid on their illegal printing-press in Odessa. Kovalsky was executed (the first political execution since Karakozov), but gun battles were becoming ever more commonplace.

It was in these early months of 1878 that the authorities first heard of a new revolutionary organization, the 'Executive Committee of the Popular-Revolutionary Party', which had made its appearance in the South, the area of greatest terrorist activity. What they could not know was that no such body existed in reality: the affair was a typical piece of revolutionary mystification. The *zemlevoltsy* had already begun to issue public announcements after each action, and also to send threatening letters to chosen victims; in order to increase the psychological effect Osinsky decided to have them signed in the name of an imaginary 'Executive Committee'. Each publication was stamped with a special seal incorporating a design of crossed revolver, dagger and axe. The idea was soon taken up by the Northern *zemlevoltsy* as well. At that stage the Executive Committee had no separate existence and no set membership; it corresponded more or less to the 'disorganizing group' of the 'main circle' of *Zemlya i Volya*. But what began as an ingenious hoax was soon to acquire a terrifying reality.

On 4 August 1878 the terrorists carried out their most daring exploit to date: the chief of the Imperial secret police, General Mezentsev, was stabbed to death in broad daylight in St

Petersburg by Sergei Kravchinsky – who then made a clean getaway. The government, its nerves already on edge, was stunned. Milyutin wrote in his diary about 'the secret society's satanic plan of terrorizing the whole administration'. And, he added, 'the plan is beginning to succeed'.[8] The authority of the government, incapable of catching the terrorists and even of protecting its own highest officials, was visibly wilting. Something obviously had to be done, but they were completely unequipped for dealing with such an unprecedented situation. The degree of the government's discomposure can be gauged from the fact that five days after Mezentsev's assassination it issued an appeal to the people – possibly the first occasion in the history of Russian autocracy that such a step had been undertaken during peacetime. After describing (somewhat disingenuously) the government's long-suffering forbearance towards the purveyors of sedition and subversion, the proclamation went on:

> Now the Government's patience is finally exhausted . . . The Government can not and should not treat people who scorn the law and trample on everything dear and sacred to the Russian nation in the same way as it treats loyal subjects of the Russian Monarch. Still less can it remain indifferent in the face of bloody crimes . . .
>
> Accordingly, the Government will from now on, with unyielding firmness and rigour, punish all those who are shown to be guilty of, or implicated in, evil designs against the existing State order, against the basic principles of social and family life, and against the rights of property consecrated by law . . .
>
> The Government therefore deems it necessary to call upon the support of all classes of the Russian nation and upon their assistance in its efforts to eradicate this evil together with its underlying doctrine, which is being imposed upon the people by means of the most erroneous notions and the most terrible crimes.[9]

The appeal achieved an effect directly contrary to its authors' intentions. The government had admitted its helplessness – or so everybody interpreted the appeal: a most dangerous thing for any despotic government to do. Disaffection within 'society' grew still further: the invisible and omnipotent terrorists became all the rage in the fashionable salons and among the liberal thinkers. The government was treated with open contempt. As for the revolutionaries themselves, their jubilation knew no bounds; they were determined to press on with the job. A few days after the appearance of the proclamation the police discovered a plot to blow up the Emperor's train outside Nikolaev; two participants were hanged. The terrorists were beginning to sustain losses, but there was always a willing supply of fresh recruits. The campaign of terrorism reached its peak in the spring of 1879. On 9 March the Governor of Kharkov, Prince Kropotkin (the famous revolutionary's cousin), was assassinated; four days later an unsuccessful attempt was carried out on the life of the newly appointed chief of secret police, Drenteln. And on 2 April 1879 the *zemlevolets* Soloviev (with Alexander Mikhailov watching nearby) fired five shots at Alexander II, who managed to get away unscathed.

Soloviev's attempt seemed to arouse the authorities from their state of stupefaction. Governors-General were appointed in St Petersburg, Kharkov and Odessa (previously ruled by Governors – the only Governor-Generalships had been those of Moscow, Kiev and Warsaw) with virtually plenipotentiary powers; the posts went to the most distinguished generals of the late Turkish war. Russia was, to all intents and purposes, divided into six territorial military dictatorships and ruled by martial law. The police were also learning to cope with the new challenge: one by one the most active terrorists were falling into their hands. During the first eight months of 1879 sixteen men were hanged, several more were killed while resisting arrest, and many others sent to a fairly speedy death in prison. Although the police remained unaware of the fact, by the autumn they had broken the back of the Southern terrorist organization; only two of the men associated with the first 'Executive Committee' remained at large.

The open warfare between police and revolutionaries was stirring public opinion to a state of feverish excitement. Student disorders broke out in St Petersburg, Moscow and Kharkov. The authorities were forced to recognize the complete failure of the appeal launched after the Mezentsev assassination. When the moment of crisis arrived the Russian 'educated class' – the people of wealth, upbringing, social standing and influence – openly showed their hostility towards the State. The long-standing domination of intellectual life by the radical intelligentsia and its 'progressive' ideas had led to a profound breach between government and 'society'; the increasingly obsolete autocratic regime, based upon Asiatic methods of rule, had neither the means nor the time to repair this breach. A few random shots were sufficient to show up the full gravity of the situation.

A 'Special Board' had been set up to deal with the revolutionary movement (its title was to acquire a far more sinister significance under the Communist successor to the Tsarist regime); on 4 June 1879 its chairman, Secretary of State P. A. Valuev, a highly intelligent and not illiberal statesman, reported to the Emperor: 'Specially worthy of attention is the almost complete failure of the educated classes to support the government in its fight against a relatively small band of evil-doers.'[10] In his private diary Valuev expressed a much gloomier view: 'One feels the ground trembling, the edifice is in danger of collapse.'[11] Milyutin was no less pessimistic in his diary: 'Public opinion in Russia is extremely hostile towards the government.' In St Petersburg, he wrote, one could sense 'a strange atmosphere: even in the highest government circles they are talking about the necessity for radical reforms, one even hears the word constitution, no one has any faith in the stability of the existing order of things'.[12] The astonishing success of the terrorists in singlehandedly precipitating a general political crisis was perhaps most perceptively described in a memorandum prepared for the Tsarevich Alexander: 'The Nihilists . . . have grown into a dangerous enemy. They are being regarded as a belligerent. They have discomposed the State more than either

Bismarck or Beaconsfield could have done. And after each seditious attack the charm of State power grows ever dimmer.'[13]

The 'charm of State power' was indeed growing perceptibly dimmer. Doubts about the wisdom of further repression, even about the immutability of absolute autocracy, were beginning to penetrate into the highest and unquestionably loyal circles of the bureaucracy and the military command. General Gurko, a renowned war hero and Governor-General of St Petersburg, caused a scandal by commuting the death sentence passed on Drenteln's would-be assassin. In explanation he stated that 'there have been enough executions as it is, we cannot follow this path in perpetuity'. Alexander II wrote a brusque comment on the margin of the report dealing with this matter: 'Acted under the influence of old women and scribblers.'[14] Despite these occasional lapses, however, the military and civil apparatus of State – the mainstay of the regime – stood firm.

Much more significantly, the toiling masses, with the exception of a very small number or worker-revolutionaries, never showed any signs of sympathy for the men and women who were staking their lives, as they believed, on the people's behalf. Popular reactions to terrorism ranged from violent condemnation to irritation or, at best, indifference. The Emperor remained sacrosanct as the 'Liberator-Tsar', while the educated revolutionaries represented, in the eyes of the peasants, the very people who were hoping to enslave them again. Soloviev's attempt aroused particularly strong indignation. The general attitude was best expressed by an ordinary worker: 'It's the nobles again, because the Tsar has freed the peasants.'[15]

Turgenev, that magnificent chronicler of Russian life, has provided us with the most faithful portrayal of the relationship between the people and the revolutionaries during the period of active terrorism. The collision between the two worlds of the intelligentsia and the people is described laconically and with a fine ear for reality in Turgenev's short sketch *The Labourer and the Fine Gentleman* (April 1878). The Fine Gentleman, who has just served six years in prison for fighting in the Labourer's cause, appeals to the latter for support – the Labourer dismisses him contemptuously: 'Serves you right for rioting!' When the Fine Gentleman is finally hanged the Labourer attends the execution, muttering 'That's what comes of rioting'; his sole concern is to get hold of a piece of the hangman's rope as a lucky charm. The novelist's observations are fully confirmed by the available documentary evidence. Irony piled upon irony: it is impossible to say which chasm was deeper, the one between the revolutionaries and the people whom they believed they represented, or that which divided the government from the educated classes whose interests it was defending. At least the government assessed its predicament more realistically than the revolutionaries did theirs. But then with the intelligentsia theory habitually took precedence over reality, and the years of the most intensive practical activity were also a crucial period in the shaping of the revolutionary ideology.

The Russian revolutionary upsurge of the 1870s has always aroused tremendous interest in the West. Although the whole world was at that time passing through one of its regular phases of political violence, with acts of terrorism taking place practically in every country including Great Britain (1878 alone saw two attempts to assassinate the German Emperor and one apiece against the lives of the Kings of Italy and Spain), the Russian experience has been generally, and rightly, treated as exceptional. In no other country was terrorism the deliberate strategy of an organized political party, nowhere else did it manage to throw the whole machinery of government into disarray, and Russia was the only country where the terrorists enjoyed general sympathy among the educated and well-to-do classes. But the widespread and continuing interest in Russian terrorism, and the large body of literature that it has evoked, have in some respects hindered a proper understanding of this phenomenon. The almost exclusive concentration on terrorism and its direct effects has obscured those organizational and ideological developments within *Zemlya i Volya* and its successors which proved, in the long run, to be of infinitely greater historical significance.

The originality of the terrorist campaign launched in 1878

lay not so much in its methods as in the fact that this was the first sustained and organized anti-governmental political activity of any kind in Russian history. Under the long-awaited stimulus of direct action *Zemlya i Volya* was transformed from a motley collection of disparate groups and individuals into a unified and disciplined political party. The reorganization of *Zemlya i Volya* took place in the spring of 1878, under the firm but unobtrusive direction of Alexander Mikhailov. The Council of *Zemlya i Volya* met in April–May 1878, in a radically changed political atmosphere; on Mikhailov's insistence it adopted the final text of the party's programme and organizational statutes. The programme was almost identical with the original draft of 1876: the statutes, however, were called 'a revised and supplemented version' of the original blueprint. It defined the party's 'immediate aim', somewhat vaguely, as 'the accomplishment of a popular rebellion in the nearest possible future, to implement the people's present desires'. The key part of the statutes was concerned with basic organizational principles. It required 'the unconditional dedication to the organization by each member of all their energy, means, bonds, sympathies and dislikes, even of their lives'; 'the acceptance by every member of the general programme of practical activity and their obligation to work in accordance with it'; the absence of private property among members of the Main Circle; complete secrecy concerning all the organization's affairs; 'the subjugation of the minority to the majority and of the member to the circle'; the elimination among members of all personal likes and dislikes; the acceptance of the principle that 'the end justifies the means' (with an ambiguous conscience-salving proviso: 'excepting those cases when the means resorted to might undermine the authority of the organization').

Taken together, the organizational principles leave little doubt that *Zemlya i Volya* had adopted Nechaev's precepts. The habit of treating Nechaevism as an isolated aberration in the history of the Russian revolutionary movement has been so ingrained over a century that contemporaries and historians alike have consistently refused to accept the evidence of their senses. Yet the 1878 statutes, deliberately or not, are a clear restatement of the *Revolutionary Catechism* – cooler, more businesslike, devoid of the original's passion – but nonetheless indistinguishable from it in spirit. The only essential difference (apart from the peculiar personality of Nechaev) was that whereas in Nechaev's case the revolutionary party remained no more than an elaborate fantasy, ten years later it had become very much a reality.

The party was to be highly centralized in structure – Mikhailov's will had prevailed. Leadership was concentrated in the Main Circle, composed of what came to be known later as 'professional revolutionaries'; its functions included the establishment of subsidiary territorial and functional groups and 'control over the activity of the groups and of each individual member' – encompassing their private lives as far as was deemed necessary. In theory any member of the Main Circle had the right to leave the organization – but disclosure of its secrets would be punished by death. The Main Circle, however, was too unwieldy a body for day-to-day operational administration: to this end it would elect a Commission with wide-ranging powers for an indeterminate spell of office. We do not know whether a Commission was actually elected or not – the arrangements were still fairly haphazard. Nor was there much clarity regarding the activities of the territorial and functional groups: these were to remain autonomous in their internal affairs, but actually, unbeknown to them, would be guided by delegated members of the Main Circle. An intricate structure but, considering the novelty of political organization in Russia, a very effective one when put into practice.[16]

What the *zemlevoltsy* did not perhaps sufficiently appreciate at the beginning was that the establishment of an organized political party in place of the previously ill-defined Populist movement would inevitably involve them more and more in *political* activities: political in aims as well as in means. This became for many a cause of deep unhappiness; in the end it was to lead to the break-up of *Zemlya i Volya*. The whole mentality of the Populists was still steeped in the old ways of thought: political action was fruitless, a political revolution would achieve nothing, only a social revolution could bring happiness to the people. Within this rather muddled theoretical framework social action (good) could not be reconciled with political work (bad); the magic word 'socialist' meant the antithesis of 'political'. The change-over to politics was a painful process, but it happened so fast that some of the staunchest Populists were rabid 'politicals' before they had even realized it.

The only method of political struggle open to them was assassination. They stumbled upon it almost by chance. The first acts of terrorism were unplanned: they were carried out to avenge maltreated or executed comrades, or in self-defence. The political crisis precipitated by these acts surpassed the terrorists' wildest dreams. Suddenly it began to dawn upon them that terror might be the one political weapon by which the revolution could be accomplished. A bare year passed after Vera Zasulich's shot, and the party's semi-official illegal periodical, *Listok Zemli i Voli* (News sheet of *Zemlya i Volya*) was exultantly writing:

> Political assassination is the accomplishment of the revolution in the here and now . . . Political assassination is the most formidable weapon against our enemies, a weapon which they cannot deflect either by mighty armies or by legions of spies. That is why our enemies fear it.
>
> That is why three or four successful political murders have forced our government to introduce martial law, to increase the secret police establishment, to post Cossacks in the streets, to send policemen to the villages: in other words, to carry out such somersaults as the autocracy has not been made to do either by years of propaganda, or by centuries of discontent throughout Russia, or by disturbances among the young, or by the curses of thousands of victims done to death by *katorga* or exile . . . That is why we accept political assassination as one of the main methods of struggle against despotism.[17]

This view was by no means unanimously shared, but most of the party gradually accepted it. How could they do otherwise when it was so manifestly true? As already mentioned above, no specific decision on terror was ever formally adopted, but the theme of terror as a political weapon in a political struggle came to dominate the activities and the publications of *Zemlya i Volya*. But this, in turn, raised new and even more contentious problems. If the struggle was going to be political, what were to be its aims? 'Land and Freedom' were enshrined in the party's name. 'Land' was straightforward – but 'Freedom' allowed of a multiplicity of meanings. The one meaning which no Populist would ever accept was political reform and the granting of constitutional rights, i.e. the introduction of the abhorred bourgeois democracy. It is strange that, in the face of all the evidence, many Western historians should persist in regarding Populism as a libertarian movement, and the *zemlevoltsy* as curious Russian counterparts of the Chartists.

Stranger still, this misconception was shared by the respectable Russian liberals of the day. The events of the late 1870s – the Russo–Turkish war and the upsurge of revolutionary activity – had galvanized the 'liberal' movement that was beginning to evolve within the *Zemstvos*. The leaders of three *Zemstvos* (Chernigov, Tver and Kharkov) even sent loyal addresses to the Emperor, asking him to grant Russia the same constitutional liberties that had just been bestowed on Bulgaria (coming on the crest of the wave of police repression, the addresses proved singularly ill-timed, and their authors were sent into administrative exile). The Russian liberals, up to and including 1917, always assumed a basic affinity between themselves and the revolutionaries, whom (much to their later regret) they consistently treated as no more than the somewhat over-enthusiastic Left wing of the broad liberation movement. The liberals had secretly welcomed the opening of the terrorist campaign – *that* would bring the government to its senses at last! – and were especially pleased by the Populists' switch to the political struggle. Now, however, they were concerned lest the terrorists go too far and endanger the important concessions which, they felt, the enfeebled government was on the verge of making. In December 1878 two prominent liberals (one of them, I. I. Petrunkevich, was to become a leader of the Constitutional-Democrat or 'Cadet' Party in the early years of the twentieth century) held a clandestine meeting with a group of Southern terrorists led by Osinsky; they suggested a temporary pause in terrorism and a concerted campaign for a constitution. The *zemlevoltsy* angrily rejected the offer: in their own words, they would no nothing to help 'Messrs the Liberals to achieve a constitution and thereby to oppress the people hand-in-glove with the bourgeoisie'.[18]

The liberals proved tenacious: a few months later Petrunkevich negotiated along similar lines with Nikolai Mikhailovsky, the famous radical journalist and legal spokesman for the revolutionary Populists (acknowledged as such even by the police – an interesting sidelight on Russian life). Mikhailovsky forcefully put forward the revolutionary case: 'What the people wants is not a constitution but the land. Still less does it want a constitution achieved by the nobility, and therefore primarily in the interests of the nobility, which are always directly opposed to the people's interests. Once in possession of the land the people will, in its own good time, create the political forms that correspond to its genuine interests – political forms in which there will certainly be no room for privileges ... Political reform will only be utilized by the privileged classes, to the detriment of the popular mass.'[19]

This was no more than a restatement of the classical Populist doctrine as originally formulated by Herzen, Chernyshevsky, Lavrov, and Mikhailovsky himself. The *zemlevolets* concept of 'Liberty' was, understandably, rather fuzzy – nobody had ever thought of the thing as being much more than the automatic corollary of 'Land' – yet on one score they were quite determined: it would not mean the introduction of Western bourgeois constitutional freedoms. Such a cure would be even worse than the disease.

Zemlya i Volya was moving over into the arena of political struggle, but the only political solution it was ready to discuss was still the one which it utterly refused to contemplate in practice. The efforts of the liberals to cash in on the revolutionaries' successes filled them with apprehension. Could it be that by toppling the autocracy they were merely helping to bring in a new and even more horrendous system of oppression? Warnings about the calamitous consequences of constitutional reforms filled the pages of the revolutionary Populist periodicals that began to appear, both inside Russia and abroad, from early 1878. The first such paper was *Obshchina*, published in Switzerland. From its pages, shortly after Vera Zasulich's acquittal, Kravchinsky issued a disturbing appeal: 'Beware! Like a flock of crows which smell a rotting corpse, new enemies are arising on all sides. These enemies are the bourgeoisie. In the past all the bourgeoisie has been capable of was fear, waiting like a coward for us socialist revolutionaries to destroy what it sprinkled with hatred and incense.' But now the danger was far greater – with the autocratic regime fatally weakened (thanks to the revolutionaries' efforts), the bourgeoisie might move in to establish a capitalist system. And all knew what that would mean from the example of the Paris Commune: 'The same fate awaits us if we give the Russian bourgeoisie time to stifle us.'[20]

The point was drawn even more sharply in the leading article of the next issue of *Obshchina*:

Not one of the groups which have so far appeared before the court of the Russian government has given any reason to doubt the purity of its socialist programme and its open hostility to constitutionalism. The latest trials, as well as the programme of the journal *Nachalo* – whose appearance we welcome as a new proof of the strength of the socialist party – all show a clear understanding of the programme of the socialist-federalists . . .

The corner-stone of constitutionalism is the right of the nation's representatives to debate the budget and to control expenditures. Excellent. Well now, will these debates make life any easier for the peasants and working-people? Will their tax load grow less? No, dear reader, rather than grow less it will increase still further. The liberals even have a saying, according to which the more liberal the government, the more expensive it is for its country, i.e. for the people, which invariably pays all the expenses of the State, and of the nobility, and of the bourgeoisie – in short, of all the idle population of the country, *of all the fantastic needs of bourgeois civilization*.[21]

The same unremitting hostility to constitutionalism and political reform marked most of the articles in *Nachalo* (The Beginning), the journal referred to in the above quotation. *Nachalo* was the first regular publication of *Zemlya i Volya* itself, and the first illegal periodical ever to be printed inside Russia; it began to appear in March 1878. Two months later it wrote: 'We can only laugh at those would-be "benefactors" of the people who wish to bestow the "principle" of a constitution upon the people. This principle would amount only to the replacement of one type of exploiter by another . . . Naturally, such a principle could never be accepted or even defended by socialists.'[22] Curiously enough, both these articles were directed against an anonymous pamphlet in favour of a constitution, the author of which (unknown to his critics) was none other than Mikhailovsky, the very same Mikhailovsky who was shortly to spurn the liberals' constitutionalist advances with such righteous indignation. Mikhailovsky was a man of the highest moral probity, and these baffling contradictions can on no account be explained by lack of principle, nor by mystification *à la* Nechaev. Rather, he reflected the general uncertainty with regard to political aims which was then prevailing among the Populist revolutionaries. Even *Obshchina* published one or two articles suggesting that constitutional reforms might not be altogether unbeneficial. After all, had not the programme of *Zemlya i Volya* spoken of the desirability of 'exploiting the liberals in our interests'?

Formulating a policy for practical action proved very different from theorizing in the abstract. The revolutionary movement had entered into an entirely new phase, with unexpected repercussions upon the whole of Russian society; a new situation had been created, new forces set in motion. 'Disorganizing the State' was no longer sufficient as a slogan – a new political strategy was obviously required. The social aims of the movement were coming into conflict with its political achievements. Slowly the majority of *zemlevoltsy* were groping towards the only possible solution of their dilemma, the solution already put forward by Tkachev and the earlier Jacobins: the idea of a political overturn directed at preventing the development of constitutionalism and capitalism, even before the people had taken over the land and made their own decisions regarding order.

This evolution was clearly signalled by the editorial of the first issue of the party's official organ, *Zemlya i Volya,* dated 25 October 1878 (thirty-nine years to the day before the Bolshevik Revolution):

> To devote all our forces to the struggle against the government would mean to abandon our direct and constant aim in favour of chasing after an incidental and temporary one. Such a direction of our activity would also be a tremendous error from the point of view of the party's tactics. The downfall óf our present political system *is no longer in the slightest doubt.* One does not have to be a prophet to forecast it. *The only question is the day and the hour of this happening.* The present system, stricken from all sides, will fall and give way to a more modern constitutional system which, like any other constitution, will promote into the foreground the privileged classes of landowners, merchants and manufacturers – all the owners of movable capital and real estate, or the bourgeoisie in the economic sense of the word. At present they are disunited and therefore powerless, but constitutional freedom, however pitiful it may be, will be sure at any rate to give them the opportunity to organize a powerful party, whose first act will be the proclamation of a crusade against us socialists – their most dangerous enemies.[23]

The tone of urgency was unmistakable: it was to grow in

intensity with every passing month. The new paper's editorial line diverged increasingly from the traditional Populist outlook. Largely under the influence of Marxist ideas imported from the West, it no longer attempted to deny the fact of capitalist development in Russia. On the contrary, it asserted that Russia had, in effect, been a bourgeois society since 1861 – and used this as an additional argument in favour of speedy socialist revolution. Since we already have capitalism, it reasoned, we possess the basic Marxist precondition for socialism, yet nowhere does it follow that socialism can come only in the most highly developed capitalist countries. True, the collective form of production inherent in capitalist industry, which Marx saw as the prerequisite for introducing. collective forms of property, existed in Russia only in its most rudimentary form – but as an effective substitute we had the collective form of production of the *obshchina*, which corresponded to the functions of large-scale industry in the Marxian scheme. Therefore the argument of the liberals – always ready to cite Scripture for their purpose – according to which Russia had to pass through a long period of capitalist development, was totally wrong and misleading (and merely provided additional proof of the liberals' wickedness). Whichever way one looked at it, the Russian political and social order was ripe for destruction.

The 'political' tendency within *Zemlya i Volya* was considerably strengthened after the appearance in March 1879 of the first issue of a new illegal journal, *Vestnik Zemli i Voli*. It was edited by Tikhomirov and Morozov, two of the party's most formidable intellects, both by this time convinced terrorists. Although their views on the ultimate political aims were still undefined they began campaigning for the party to concentrate all its resources on terrorism. Their arguments were by no means limited to the theoretical plane; as they pointed out, probably correctly, from the purely practical point of view it was courting disaster for the party to dissipate its strength in a variety of activities – propaganda, village colonies, etc. Only one method had proved efficacious, and it should be pursued with every ounce of energy at the party's command. Three years later Tikhomirov described this episode as follows: 'In 1879 part of the *zemlevoltsy* – convinced that in our conditions disregard of the political element and retreat before the government in the struggle that had already begun was equivalent to the party's suicide – began to alter the previous nature of their activities. Those who held this view soon became convinced of the necessity to change the whole programme and to build up their forces until they were in a position to offer strong resistance to the government; if it continued to cling to its system then a coup d'état should become the party's direct aim.'[24] Strange to say, this revolutionary innovation was derided by the others as rabid constitutionalism – to such an extent had the very concept of 'politics' become identified in the Populist mind with those of 'constitutionalism', 'reform', 'liberalism' and such-like detestable things.

Listok Zemli i Voli pursued a line noticeably different from that of the party's other publications. In its communiqués concerning terrorist actions it prominently featured a mysterious 'Executive Committee', thus continuing the practice of the now almost defunct Southern terrorist groups. The followers of Tikhomirov and Morozov were beginning to function as an organized faction within the party. This incipient 'Left wing' was strongly opposed by the orthodox Populists (now re-invigorated with an injection of Marxism), or the so-called 'villagists' (*derevenshchiki*), who hoped to confine terrorism to acts of self-defence and to turn the party's main attention once again to its proper field of work, the countryside. The differences between the two wings concerned fundamental questions of policy; they were inherent in the contradictory nature of Populist doctrine; and now, with the political crisis in the country that had been precipitated by the Populists themselves coming to a head, they proved irreconcilable. Which was to come first, political or social revolution? Such was the issue upon which *Zemlya i Volya* broke up.

Alexander Mikhailov himself hardly participated in the controversy. He was far too busily engaged in day-to-day conspiratorial work; using every device and stratagem evolved by his predecessors over the past fifty-odd years, and adding his own inimitable touch of genius, Mikhailov developed the technique of conspiracy into a fine art. Without him the party could never have survived the relentless nationwide hunt launched by the police – thanks to him it managed not only to preserve its organization and leading cadre intact, but also to ensure a constant flow of dedicated new recruits, to obtain all the money it needed, and to embark upon a series of ever more audacious ventures. Possibly Mikhailov's most successful coup was the planting of a trusted agent into the central office of the secret police: for two years, until his own accidental arrest in November 1880, he received a constant flow of top-secret information, enabling him always to keep one step ahead of the police. 'Alexander Mikhailov was the soul of the organization,' wrote Tikhomirov years later. 'He united everyone, went everywhere, knew everything, directed everything.'[25] By temperament an organizer and a man of action, Mikhailov was naturally inclined towards terrorism; indeed, he had personally sanctioned Soloviev's attempt against the Tsar despite the misgivings of most of his comrades. Yet, having built up *Zemlya i Volya* into the most redoubtable revolutionary organization Russia had every known, he above all was loath to see it succumb to internal dissensions. 'We must keep the "old firm" going,' was his unvarying refrain. His attempts at reconciliation proved fruitless, and when he finally realized the impossibility of accommodating two basically contradictory policies within a single party he threw all his immense authority behind the terrorists.

In a final effort to re-establish the unity of the party it was decided to hold a congress in June 1879 in Voronezh. The 'political group', however, was determined to push its policies through even at the price of an open split. They left nothing to chance. A few days before the congress was due to open, between 17 and 21 June, the 'politicals' held a separate meeting of their own in Lipetsk. Eleven men and women took part: five members of the St Petersburg centre, including Mikhailov,

Tikhomirov and Morozov, and six specially invited and carefully selected 'provincials'. Among them was Andrei Zhelyabov.

The minutes of the Lipetsk meeting have not survived, and the proceedings can only be reconstructed from often conflicting memoirs and legal records. Almost all the sources agree – despite certain discrepancies as to detail – that the meeting reached the following broad decisions: (*a*) the reconstructed party would be based on the highest degree of centralization; (*b*) its main object was to be a political revolution by means of a coup d'état; (*c*) the best method by which this could be achieved, and therefore the party's immediate task, was the assassination of the Emperor Alexander II. These principles determined the course of the revolutionary movement over the next two years: their influence upon future generations of revolutionaries can hardly be overestimated.

The Lipetsk conspirators (double conspirators, since they were conspiring against their own party as well as the State) decided to assume the name of 'Executive Committee of the Social-Revolutionary Party'. What had begun as a hoax was now a reality. A brief set of statutes was drafted (the only version extant was reproduced from memory in Morozov's memoirs). From the very first paragraph it struck a new tone: 'A person can become eligible for membership of the Executive Committee only if he agrees unconditionally to place his whole life and all his property at its disposal; therefore the question of withdrawal cannot even arise.' Another novelty was the rule (strictly adhered to thereafter) according to which in case of arrest no one was allowed to admit to membership of the Executive Committee, but could only call himself an 'agent' of the Committee. A simple yet effective conspiratorial principle, which for a long time led the police to vastly overestimate the organization's actual strength.[26] Finally, the meeting elected an Administration composed of Mikhailov, Tikhomirov and Frolenko; it was decided that Tikhomirov and Morozov were to edit the party's new periodical. After which the gathering moved over to Voronezh, where they were already awaited by most of the leading 'villagists'.

The Voronezh congress was a painful experience for all concerned. Old comrades who had risked their lives together, spent years in prison cells next to each other, who were tied by the strongest of personal bonds, had now reached the parting of the ways. Their distress was so great that they simply could not bring themselves to take the final irrevocable step. A vague compromise was hastily patched up – Plekhanov was the only man with sufficient fortitude to storm out of the meeting in protest against terrorism. The old programme of *Zemlya i Volya* was confirmed, propaganda and terrorism were to co-exist side by side. Nobody was happy. The sudden appearance of Stefanovich and Deutsch with their plans for a new Chigirin venture was the last straw; everyone realized that *Zemlya i Volya* was dead.

Two months after Voronezh the schism had been made final. The organization broke up into two parts, neither of which was allowed to keep the old title. The 'villagists' formed a group called *Chernyi Peredel* (Black Re-partition), the 'terrorists' or 'politicians' established *Narodnaya Volya*. The breaking-up of a long-standing association is always difficult – in this case it was complicated by the fact that the division did not take place (as is frequently implied) along the lines of 'moderates' *v.* 'extremists'. The Southern hotheads Stefanovich and Deutsch joined *Chernyi Peredel*, as did the initiator of the terrorist campaign, Vera Zasulich; on the other hand, such relatively sober-minded propagandists as Zhelyabov and Perovskaya entered *Narodnaya Volya*. The true line of division was the one which had plagued the Populist movement from its inception: political revolution *v.* social revolution.

A new phase had begun: the culmination of the great revolutionary upsurge of 1878–82. From now on *Narodnaya Volya* was the storm-centre. *Chernyi Peredel* hardly mattered – it was a stillborn organization. Its theoretical position was untenable, and most of its members, led by Plekhanov, began moving rapidly towards Marxism. The story of *Chernyi Peredel*, such as it is, belongs to the history of Marxism in Russia.

*

Narodnaya Volya is usually translated into English as 'People's Will'. This practice is to be regretted, since it leads not only to linguistic imprecision but to a considerable oversimplification, even distortion of the party's programme. The Russian word *'volya'* has a variety of meanings: among them are 'will', 'freedom', and 'power'. The party's name, whether deliberately or not, was ambiguous, and its members tended to interpret it in different ways, in accordance with their own ideological predilections. The varying interpretations of the party's name reflected the ideological divergences that still continued to exist, albeit in attenuated form, even after the break. The more traditionally minded Populists – convinced that 'the people were instinctive Socialists', who would, given the opportunity created by the revolutionaries, spontaneously establish socialism – stood for a party of the 'people's will' or the 'people's desire'. A small group of pure 'politicals' understood the party to be fighting for the 'people's freedom', i.e. for political rights. Most influential of all was the group standing for 'people's power': for a revolutionary dictatorship representing the interests of the people. The questions arising out of this ambiguity were never put forward in such a clear-cut form; definitions tended to criss-cross and even to coalesce; differing interpretations managed to live together peacefully, without ever upsetting the party's unity. It would appear that some kind of compromise was reached, according to which the party's ultimate aim was the implementation of the 'people's will' but its immediate object was the 'people's freedom', to be achieved through the establishment by revolutionary means of the 'people's power'.[27]

The organizational statutes adopted by the Executive Committee in the autumn of 1879 did not leave much scope for the theoretical arguments beloved by the Russian intelligentsia. *Narodnaya Volya* was to be a highly centralized, rigidly hierarchical, élitist and disciplined organization. The statutes, as Professor Venturi says, 'were closer to the model "conspiracy" which Tkachev and Zaichnevsky had conceived than to the earlier ones of *Zemlya i Volya*'[28] – and that is saying quite a lot. The statutes represented the final triumph of the organizational principles of the Jacobins, of Zaichnevsky, Nechaev and Tkachev. But even more interesting is the direct way in which they point towards the future: to the organizational structure of Lenin's Bolshevik Party.

The Executive Committee was to be the 'centre and leader' of the party. Its members, although equal in rights, unconditionally subjected themselves to the decisions of the majority; their property belonged to the Executive Committee, they were to work in complete solidarity and to accept the principle of 'all for each and each for all', they were to preserve complete secrecy regarding the party's affairs and to subdue all personal likes and dislikes in the party's interests; their obligations towards the Executive Committee 'take precedence over all other personal and social obligations'. Of especial significance is paragraph nine: the basic organizational principle of the party is declared to be 'elective centralism' (Lenin was to call it 'democratic centralism').[29]

The detailed provisions of the statutes (seventy-seven paragraphs in all), laying down precise rules for the acceptance of new members, the conduct of meetings, the relationship between groups and sub-groups, agents and sub-agents etc., are of little importance – if only because they were hardly ever implemented. What does deserve close attention is the circular on 'General principles of organization', compiled in 1880, largely by Zhelyabov, and widely distributed among the members and groups of *Narodnaya Volya*.[30] Here the basic principles are set out with admirable conciseness:

The organization of the *Narodnaya Volya* party consists of a network of small circles with common revolutionary aims; it is based on the principle of centralization of lower-level groups around groups of a higher level.

Each higher-level group complements itself by choosing from among the best elements of the lower-level groups.

All the circles of a given district are gathered around the Local Central Group. The party's whole organization is drawn together by a single centre – the Executive

Committee. All groups within the organization are united by a common programme, a common plan of action, community of forces and means. In the conduct of its own affairs each group is independent and has its own budget; it regularly gives a detailed account of its activities to its higher group. Each higher-level group regularly informs its sub-groups about the general state of affairs – within the limits of the rules of conspiracy . . .

Each Local Central Group is directly subordinated to the Executive Committee.

According to the General Principles, which were regarded as 'compulsory until the completion of the coup d'état', local groups had to receive the preliminary permission of the Executive Committee for almost any kind of political action, from terrorism to the publication of theoretical pamphlets. Moreover, individual groups were allowed to communicate with each other and with the Centre only through agents of the Executive Committee attached to each group.

The extent to which Lenin's 'democratic centralism' was anticipated by *Narodnaya Volya* is truly astonishing: nearly every one of Lenin's famed precepts is to be found, at least in prototype, in the General Principles. Without the experience of *Narodnaya Volya*, to which Lenin referred again and again in the most glowing phrases, it is hardly possible to imagine the invention of 'democratic centralism' or, indeed, the creation of a 'party of a new type'.

The programme of *Narodnaya Volya* was composed in September and October 1879 and remained in force throughout the whole period of the party's existence. At a number of crucial points it disagreed with the programme of *Zemlya i Volya*, and in almost every case the divergence showed a marked turn towards Jacobinism. It is without doubt one of the basic documents of the Russian revolutionary movement.[31]

The programme began by declaring that the members of *Narodnaya Volya* were both socialists and Populists. Their enemy was the main enemy of the people: the State, which 'creates and protects' the petty exploiters, which is both 'the largest capitalist force in the country' and 'the sole political oppressor of the people'. We see, the programme continued, 'that this State-bourgeois growth is supported exclusively by naked violence: by its military, police and bureaucratic organization – exactly like Genghis Khan's Mongols'. *Narodnaya Volya* used Marxist phraseology more than any earlier revolutionary group, yet its analysis of the nature of the Russian State was almost identical to that of Tkachev in his argument with Engels.

The main conclusion was stated with disarming frankness: 'Our immediate task is to relieve the people from the oppressive yoke of the present-day State, to carry out a political coup aimed at handing over power to the people.' Although the convening of a Constituent Assembly 'is, of course, a far from ideal form of expressing the people's will' they could think of nothing better, and had therefore decided to proceed with this after the revolution. There followed a list of eight points for the socialist reconstruction of State and society; significantly, these included neither the eventual abolition of the State nor the right of national self-determination. Otherwise they consisted of the familiar revolutionary demands.

The party was to concentrate on six main aspects of political work: propaganda and agitation; destruction and terrorism; the establishment and consolidation of new secret groups; the securing of influence and close links within the administration and the army, among society and the people in general. Especially the people – 'it must be prepared to support the coup as well as our fight in the elections after the coup, the object of which should be the exclusive return of people's [i.e. socialist-revolutionary] deputies.'

The key point of the action programme was the fifth, concerned with the realization of the coup: 'In view of the downtrodden state of the people, and because the government can by repressive measures long hold back the development of a general revolutionary movement, our party must take upon itself the initiative of the coup instead of waiting for the time when the people will be able to manage without it. As regards the methods for carrying out the coup . . . (This part of point five is not for publication.)'

Narodnaya Volya was both a political party and a conspiratorial society: it boldly proclaimed its aims but it could hardly afford to spell out its secret plans. These details, however, were provided in a highly confidential circular on 'The Party's Preparatory Work', distributed among the members and agents of the Executive Committee.[32] Here we have the fullest possible description of the party's revolutionary strategy and tactics. After dismissing the likelihood of the government's voluntary capitulation, the circular bluntly states that 'the party must specifically prepare itself for a rebellion':

It should prove possible to choose a favourable moment for the rebellion, under circumstances propitious to the plotters. Such propitious circumstances could be created by a popular revolt, an unsuccessful war, State bankruptcy, various complications of European policy, etc. The party should make full and prompt use of any such circumstances, but it must not base all its hopes upon their occurrence. The party must fulfil its tasks regardless of the situation . . .

The party must have the ability itself to create a favourable moment for action, to begin the action and to carry it through to the end. A skilfully executed system of terroristic measures, simultaneously destroying ten to fifteen men – the pillars of the present government–would cast the government into a state of panic and deprive it of the power to act; at the same time it would arouse the popular masses, i.e. create a favourable moment for attack. Such a moment would be used by fighting forces, gathered in advance, to begin the rebellion and to seize the main governmental offices. This attack should easily be successful if the party only ensures that the spearhead is supported by any considerable mass of workers, etc. To ensure success it is likewise imperative for the party to build up a position in the provinces strong enough either

to arouse them to action at the first news of the coup,
or at least to keep them neutral . . . [My italics.]

Sixthly, the party was to prepare for the convening of a
Constituent Assembly after the revolution. The precise
formulation of this point is of great importance – it provides
the first indication of the party's views on the post-revolutionary
government: 'However the over-turn is achieved, whether
through an independent revolution or by means of conspiracy,
the party's duty is to further the convening of a Constituent
Assembly and the handing over of power by the Provisional
Government that will be formed by the revolution or the
conspiracy.'

The programme ended with a restatement of the party's
ethical position: 'With regard to the government, as our enemy,
the end justifies the means; in other words, we accept as
permissible any means that lead to our end.'

The organizational and political principles of *Narodnaya Volya*,
as expounded in its statutes and programme, clearly indicate
that this most famous of nineteenth-century Russian
revolutionary parties had embraced every essential element of
'Russian Jacobinism'. For many years this has been denied by
historians both Western and Russian, with numerous references
to the Populism of the *narodovoltsy* and to Tkachev's Blanquism.
These arguments can hardly stand up to criticism: Tkachev,
too, was as much a residual Populist as the *narodovoltsy*, and
(as has been seen) he was no more of a Blanquist than they.
Today Soviet writers generally recognize the close affinity
between Jacobinism and the *Narodnaya Volya* – and bemoan it
as a dark spot on the latter's otherwise immaculate record.
Tkachev himself was the first to perceive the long-awaited
victory of his ideas. 'The final triumph of the principles of *Nabat*,'
he wrote in the letter quoted above (pp. 428-9), 'is embodied
in the formation of *Narodnaya Volya*, in the establishment of a
number of "Executive" and other committees, in the programme
of the Lipetsk congress, and, lastly, in a whole series of successful
and unsuccessful assassination attempts.'[33]

Tkachev was not a man given to exaggeration, and this was no idle boast. The illegal revolutionary groups' previous uniform hostility towards him had disappeared almost overnight. Plekhanov describes how Alexander Mikhailov, formerly a violent opponent of Tkachevism, completely revised his opinion of Tkachev's programme after Lipetsk.'[34] On Mikhailov's instructions Morozov established direct contact with Tkachev. Two of the Executive Committee's most dominant members, Tikhomirov and Maria Oshanina, were open and self-avowed Jacobins, and their influence was constantly increasing. Mikhailov and Zhelyabov tended to agree with their views more and more often. Many years later Plekhanov wrote to Engels that 'narodovolstvo was nothing more than ordinary Tkachevism (I refer to their printed propaganda: L. Tikhomirov, the theoretician of Narodnaya Volya, simply copied Tkachev's articles)'.[35]

The essential Jacobinism of Narodnaya Volya is best seen through its attitudes to the key issues raised by Tkachev. The original statutes and programme already contained passages that sound almost like paraphrases of Tkachev's ideas; during the next two or three years the publications of Narodnaya Volya indicated a movement towards acceptance of practically the whole Jacobin creed.

On the question of the nature of the Russian State the programme had already indicated complete agreement with Tkachev's interpretation as opposed to that of Engels. The Russian State, explained the first issue of the journal Narodnaya Volya in October 1879, was very different from Western States: it was not 'a commission of plenipotentiaries of the ruling classes', as Marxists described it, but an independent organization, hierarchical and disciplined, 'which would hold the people in economic and political slavery even if there were no privileged classes in existence'.[36] 'With us it is not the State which is a creation of the bourgeoisie, as in Europe, but on the contrary, the bourgeoisie is created by the State,' wrote Tikhomirov.[37] 'Remove this oppression,' added Narodnaya Volya No. 2, 'and, at a single blow, you will remove nine-tenths of the likelihood of a bourgeoisie being formed.'[38] Or, as Tkachev had put it in his debate with Engels, 'our social system is indebted for its existence to the State'.

From this flowed the second basic theoretical postulate (again faithfully following Tkachev's argument): the necessity to nip Russia's capitalist development in the bud, to act immediately, before the State had brought forth a far more dangerous enemy – the bourgeoisie. This was the central theme of the leading article of *Narodnaya Volya* No. 2:

> When it takes over power into its own hands, the bourgeoisie will of course be able to keep the people in slavery to a far greater extent than happens today. And it will find more efficient methods for paralysing our activities than the present government, which is unable to go beyond prison and the gallows.

This was a direct and ever-present danger, since the State might at any moment institute reforms handing over effective power to the bourgeoisie. Therefore it was imperative to act before 'it is too late, while there is a real possibility that power can in fact pass to the people. Now or never: that is our dilemma.'[39]

In its programme the Executive Committee still envisaged the possibility – though a fairly remote one – of a mass popular revolution. There is no indication that *Narodnaya Volya* ever took this contingency seriously into account. From the very beginning all its planning was based on the assumption that the people (because of their 'downtrodden state') were incapable of carrying out a revolution, and that the only practical option was the seizure of power by means of a coup d'état. Few, if any, had doubts on this score. Alexander Barannikov, a founder-member of the Executive Committee, testifying after his arrest in February 1881, explained that of the two conceivable ways of overthrowing the regime – 'either through conspiracy effected by the party, or by an independent, broad, popular, anti-governmental movement which would be joined by the party' – the first was 'undoubtedly preferable, since in that case the party would enjoy enormous authority, both during the struggle and after its victory. Therefore the party's principal method is a conspiracy headed by the Executive Committee.'[40]

This was confirmed by Maria Oshanina, who for a time, after the mass arrests of early 1881, practically directed the party's activities: 'Our members began to believe less and less in the people's ability to achieve anything on their own, and attached more and more importance to the revolutionaries' own initiative. Hence the change in the attitude to the seizure of power. Towards the end of the Committee's activity I can recall no one who held a negative attitude to the seizure of power.'[41]

Probably the most straightforward exposition of the party's strategy was contained in a letter of the Executive Committee sent to 'our comrades abroad' (members of *Chernyi Peredel*) in the latter half of 1881. This is one of the most interesting documents of *Narodnaya Volya*; its publication in 1925 raised a storm of protest from the surviving, much-mellowed *narodovoltsy*, who roundly declared it a forgery. Their denial was accepted by Western scholars; recent Soviet research has, however, confirmed the document's unquestionable authenticity.[42] The Executive Committee firmly laid down its principles:

From the very beginning *narodovolstvo* has been a movement of *immediate action, of a coup d'état* . . .

We believe that all the conditions for a revolution are already in existence, and that now we only have to prepare the coup itself, which will become the beginning of the revolution. The *coup d'état* is our 'to be or not to be'. If it takes place then the revolution immediately acquires a correct course. If it does not take place then the revolutionary movement might go astray, become distorted and lose most of its value. Therefore our aim is a *coup d'état*. It must be carried out. Our whole *raison d'être* is the seizure of power (either by us or by the labouring mass, it makes no difference), the overthrow of power; this can only be violent, and therefore requires force and force and even more force.[43]

The violent overthrow of the existing regime and the seizure of power by a small group of organized and disciplined revolutionaries was the cornerstone of the *Narodnaya Volya* strategy. Yet it would be a grave error to see the *narodovoltsy* as a band of Blanquist plotters, contemptuous of the people, concerned solely with a coup d'état and with capturing power at the top. Such a notion, however widespread it may be, is no more true of *Narodnaya Volya* than of Tkachev. They were certainly élitist, only they saw themselves, not as an élite group capable of seizing and holding power on their own, but as the *élite vanguard* of the masses who would inevitably follow their lead. All their programmatic documents state unequivocally that without mass support in the capital and in the provinces the enterprise was doomed to failure; the coup d'état itself was to be merely the initial phase of a profound political and social revolution, of a transformation of society.

The most distinctive feature of *Narodnaya Volya*, when compared to earlier Populist movements, was the ruthlessly consistent and unmuddled quality of its thinking. It never flinched from following up its theories to their logical conclusion. And the seizure of State power by coup d'état raised the central issue of every past argument: the nature of the revolutionary government. The *narodovoltsy* were convinced Statists – Zhelyabov was to declare this proudly at his trial; instead of abolishing the State they intended to use it as the prime weapon for carrying out the desired changes. But how and by whom was the revolutionary State to be run? *Narodnaya Volya* showed a shrewder understanding of the problem than any other Russian revolutionary party – including even the Bolsheviks, until they had been confronted with the practical tasks of establishing a new government.

The programme of *Narodnaya Volya* called – rather reluctantly – for the convening of a Constituent Assembly (often referred to alternatively by the old Russian term of *Zemsky Sobor*). Originally the idea was that the victorious party would forthwith hand over power to the Constituent Assembly, elected on the basis of universal suffrage. But very soon it became clear that,

if successful, the party would emerge as the country's leading
– indeed sole – organized political force. This was openly
acknowledged in the editorial of the fifth issue of *Narodnaya
Volya*, written by Nikolai Kibalchich and generally accepted as
one of the party's most important theoretical statements:

> When government centralization has been finally smashed
> by the wave of the popular movement, what social
> elements will show that they constitute real forces? Who
> will govern the course of events? Not the privileged classes,
> of course, for they are not united. Not the lawful parties,
> because they are disorganized. Only the people and the
> social-revolutionary party will constitute those
> fundamental forces on which the social and State
> organization of the future will depend.[44]

The party would itself form the revolutionary government.
This is put quite simply in the memoirs of Mikhail Ashenbrenner,
a leading figure of the military organization of *Narodnaya Volya*:
'The Executive Committee was to constitute the Provisional
Government.'[45] The party's views on its practical functions *qua*
government in turn underwent a certain evolution. At an early
stage it was hoped that these would be limited in scope. The
journal *Narodnaya Volya* attempted to forecast the situation that
would arise when the party had seized central power in the
State:

> What must it then do? Create a new structure for the
> State and decree the reforms which are indispensable? We
> say no. Only in the most unfortunate case, only if the
> body of the people were to show not even a spark of life,
> could such a step be considered necessary. In normal times
> the party would be obliged to use the power and means
> it had won so as to overturn the whole of Russia and
> to appeal everywhere to the people to realize its century-
> old demands. It would have to help the people with all
> its forces and retain control of the central power only so
> as to help the people to organize itself.[46]

Very soon the party had come to the conclusion that, popular participation or not, it would be the task of the government to carry out basic social and economic reforms *before* the convening of the Constituent Assembly, which would merely ratify the party's legislation. This position was first officially formulated in November 1880 in a basic constitutional document of the party – 'The programme of working-class members of *Narodnaya Volya*':

> When the rebellion achieves victory throughout the whole country, when the land, the factories and the plants have become the property of the people, and elective popular administration has been set up in the villages, towns and regions, when there is no other military force in the State except the people's militia – then the people will immediately send its representatives to the Union Government or Constituent Assembly, which, after dissolving the Provisional Government, shall confirm the people's gains and establish the all-Union system of State.[47]

A little later the party's journal spelled out in even more explicit terms the decisive role of the revolutionary Provisional Government in effecting the socio-economic transformation of the country:

> The provisional revolutionary government will carry out an economic revolution at the same time as it frees the people and creates new political institutions. It will do away with the right of private owners to the land and to the tools of heavy industry. And then the true representatives of the people, freed now of their political and economic bondage, will answer the summoning of the *Zemsky Sobor*. And the life of the people itself will be impregnably based on the will of the people.[48]

It will be noticed that the party continued to insist upon a Constituent Assembly even after the function assigned to it had been reduced to little more than a rubber-stamp. In part this was due to the genuine, if inexplicable, conviction of

Narodnaya Volya that in a free election it would gain ninety-nine per cent of the seats.[49] But one also has to speak here of an element of deliberate deception – the party was using a popular slogan (popular, at least, among the educated classes) to further its own ends. Revolutionary immorality has certain inexorable consequences, and not even the most high-minded and dedicated men and women are immune. When the ends justify the means one becomes progressively less fastidious about the means. The charge of cynicism has rarely, if ever, been brought against the *narodovoltsy*, yet what other word can be used to describe their own justification for the slogan of a Constituent Assembly, made in the letter of the Executive Committee to 'our comrades abroad' quoted above (no wonder the survivors protested against its publication)?

With regard to the *Zemsky Sobor*, we simply do not understand how you could have been seriously confused by our current agitational device. After all, we are demanding the *Zemsky Sobor* from the government, and not from life or from the revolution. From the revolution we naturally demand considerably more – for details see the programme of the Executive Committee (the content of our propaganda) and the workers' programme. Surely you don't expect us to demand of the government that it arrange things in the way we really want! This would be not only injudicious but useless as well – and anyway we have no desire to scare off the moderates. All in good time. At present the only thing we can *demand* is an appeal to the people. As for the actual results that we hope to achieve by this appeal – we don't have to proclaim them far and wide. We are not gammoning anyone, but it would be stupid to affront the moderates unnecessarily by telling them of the fate that awaits . . .

State power has always been in existence, and will probably always exist. That is why we pay no less attention to its organization than to the organization of economic relationships. The revolution will take place only when this power is in good hands – which is why we intend to seize it, since the people, as long as it is enslaved by innumerable conventions, is in any case incapable of holding it. If the coup d'état presents us with power we will not relinquish it until we have set the people on a firm footing. As for the future, we do not intend to transform this tutelage of the people into a permanent system, and as soon as the people has firmly settled down it will be our duty to convene the *Zemsky Sobor*, etc.[50]

Such, then, were the aims of *Narodnaya Volya*. It intended to overthrow the most powerful autocratic government in the world and to establish its own dictatorship with the object of introducing a socialist society. Its means were ridiculously disproportionate to its grandiose aspirations. The total membership of the Executive Committee throughout its existence (1879–84) was about forty; at no single time did it number more than twenty to twenty-two members. Apart from these there may have been two or three dozen 'agents' of the Executive Committee. In the country at large (Moscow, Kharkov, Odessa, Saratov, Kazan, Kiev, Tomsk and a few other cities) the party's local organizations, by the most optimistic Soviet calculations, had some 500 members in all. To this we might add three or four thousand sympathizers – ready to run errands, distribute leaflets, etc. – mainly among students. That was all.

The most astonishing aspect of *Narodnaya Volya* is not even the breathtaking audacity of the enterprise but the degree of its success. The Russian body politic was thrown into a state of complete turmoil, the government nearly brought to its knees. These results were achieved above all by meticulous planning and careful husbanding of scarce resources, by strict centralization, iron discipline and unquestioning subordination.

The crucial decision that was to determine all the activities of the Executive Committee had been taken at the moment of its formation. Having made a realistic appraisal of the scanty forces at its command, the Executive Committee resolved to concentrate them on a single object: the assassination of

Alexander II. This meant in practice the exclusion of almost every other kind of revolutionary activity. There was a certain amount of desultory propaganda among St Petersburg workers, a surprisingly large number of illegal publications were put out, and a few terroristic acts committed against police agents. Nothing more could be done until the main task had been fulfilled.

The decision to kill the Emperor had already been taken at the Lipetsk meeting after an uncharacteristically passionate speech by Alexander Mikhailov. On 26 August 1879 the Executive Committee of *Narodnaya Volya* formally condemned Alexander II to death. The hunt was on.

There was nothing irrational about this decision. Nor was it at all incompatible with their socialist outlook. Their analysis of the nature of the Russian State, of its complete dependence upon the autocracy, had resulted in the conclusion that the destruction of the autocrat would lead to the paralysis of the State, to the total demoralization of its machinery, to abject panic within the government, to widespread rebellions among the disaffected elements of the people. At the very least it would force the government to enter into negotiations with the revolutionaries and to make concessions that would embody the first stages of their programme.

In all, *Narodnaya Volya* made eight attempts upon the Emperor's life. Dynamite was the main weapon. The first attempt – to blow up the Imperial train outside Odessa – was abandoned when it was discovered that the Emperor had changed his route. A second effort, this time in Alexandrovsk, failed because of a technical mistake in assembling the electrical battery for detonating the explosion. On 19 November 1879 a train was finally blown up near a Moscow station – only it happened to be the train transporting the Emperor's retinue. The fourth attempt was nearly successful. Stepan Khalturin, one of the few active working-class members of *Narodnaya Volya*, had obtained a job as a carpenter in the Winter Palace. Bit by bit he transported about fifty kilograms of dynamite into the palace. On 5 February 1880 it was set off under the Imperial dining-room – but on that day the Emperor had an official reception and was late for his dinner. Ten soldiers and servants were killed and many more wounded.

The explosion in the Winter Palace caused an unparalleled sensation in Russia and abroad: the autocrat of all the Russias was no longer safe even in his own home! Rumours swept the capital – rumours of an imminent uprising, of a general massacre, of a dynamite attack on the whole of St Petersburg by means of 500 balloons. Fear seized the country. The government had to take extraordinary measures to cope with the new crisis – merely stepping up repression would achieve nothing (this conviction was strengthened by the inability of the police to discover the perpetrators of the outrage).

One week after the explosion the Emperor appointed a Supreme Executive Commission, charged with protecting the State order and the public peace. Its head was General Loris-Melikov, the Governor-General of Kharkov, named Minister of the Interior with direct control over the reorganized secret police force, previously split up between several departments of State. Martial law was introduced. Loris-Melikov became, in effect, dictator of Russia. He saw himself faced with the twofold task of suppressing the revolutionary movement and pacifying public opinion; he called his own regime 'the dictatorship of the heart'. The police establishment was increased; large additional funds were assigned to intelligence work and to propaganda and counter-propaganda abroad. On the other hand, direct police repression was markedly reduced: there were far fewer mass arrests, searches and exiles than in 1878–9. Loris-Melikov made vague references to reforms.

Russia certainly stood in need of reform. The open disaffection of public opinion, its generally sympathetic attitude towards the revolutionaries, were sufficient indications of this. What was most urgently required was at least some degree of participation in State affairs for the nobility and the rapidly developing bourgeoisie – this would have secured, in the first instance, a stable social basis for the regime and a bulwark against revolution. The urgency of reform was well understood by a number of people in the top ranks of the administration. Valuev had produced his own draft as long ago as 1863; it envisaged the establishment of a consultative Congress of State Representatives, elected by the *Zemstvos* and the large towns, alongside the State Council. On several occasions he brought his proposals to the Emperor's attention, each time to have them rejected. The Grand Duke Constantine was another would-be reformer; his suggestions were even more moderate than Valuev's, yet they met with the same fate. The most far-reaching of the plans for reform was composed by Milyutin – it even provided for a partially elected legislature. 'A legislative body subject to the Emperor's veto, a responsible Ministry, under a Chairman and with a collective policy, proper differentiation of the functions of the executive organs, a subordinate but, within the limits of its competence, independent local administration, and an independent judiciary – in sum, what Milyutin had in mind was a *Rechtsstaat* on the orderly, rational model of which Western European governments had provided some examples.'[51] A beautiful dream: there is no indication that Milyutin ever had the temerity even to submit his project to the Emperor.

In 1880, for a brief moment, a propitious climate had been created for a return to the reforming tendencies of the early years of the Emperor's reign. Government and public opinion alike seemed favourably inclined towards the idea of reform. Both had been given a severe shock by the revolutionary events of 1878-9: the government was seriously reconsidering the wisdom of its policy of ever-increasing suppression, while the 'educated classes', despite their fundamental sympathy for the revolutionaries, were beginning to feel a little uneasy about the latter's exclusive concentration on violence. Changes were in the air, and ever more frequent hints about an impending constitution began to appear in the Russian and Western press.

In another respect, too, the atmosphere was favourable for a policy of conciliation: for a whole year after the explosion in the Winter Palace no overt acts of terrorism had taken place (except for an attempt on the life of Loris-Melikov, for which

the Executive Committee expressly denied any responsibility).
True, three separate plans to kill the Emperor by means of
explosive charges placed in tunnels dug below streets and
beneath a bridge had been set in train, but they were all called
off for one reason or another, and the police only learnt about
them much later. It seemed as though Loris-Melikov's
conciliatory gestures were taking effect, and on 6 August 1880
the Supreme Executive Commission was abolished, its tasks
presumably fulfilled.

The proposals prepared many years before by Valuev and
the Grand Duke were now taken out of the archives, dusted
down, and discussed several times by the Special Board –
without any conclusion being reached. Everyone was fearful
to take the first step towards limiting autocracy. The deadlock
was broken by the 'dictator' himself. An indecisive and vain
man, with limited governmental experience, Loris-Melikov
nevertheless possessed a fairly shrewd insight into the nature
of the dilemma facing Russia. His meteoric rise had caused
intense jealousy among the old-established courtiers and State
officials, which partly explains their sour comments about his
plans – comments which have not been without influence upon
later historians. Yet there is little doubt that Loris-Melikov's
views did undergo considerable change during his period of
office. He had come to power, as he explained in his report
to the Emperor on 11 April 1880, in the conviction 'that if Russia
is today living through a dangerous crisis she can best be led
out of it by the determined autocratic will of the Monarch . . .
Today, as after the Crimean War, which left Russia in an even
more tense situation than the present one, all the attention,
all the hopes and desires of loving and thinking Russia, are
turned to Your Majesty's sacred person. Along with measures
of unrelenting severity towards the evil-doers it is necessary
to pass measures that would deprive the noisome false teachings
of their support, and assure support for the legal order . . .
Otherwise one villain would merely succeed another, and the
poison would be left there for future generations.' But Loris-
Melikov was firmly set against adopting any of the schemes

for popular representation that were then being put forward, whether based on Western models or on a resurrection of archaic Russian institutions: 'Such a measure would seem to be taken under the pressure of circumstances, and that is how it will be interpreted both in Russia and abroad.'[52] All he suggested at that stage was an alleviation of the most glaring instances of arbitrary power, improvements in the functioning of the universities, the courts and *Zemstvos*, etc.

Gradually, however, Loris-Melikov came around to the idea of more far-reaching reforms. His proposals were incorporated in his famous report of 28 January 1881, which soon came to be known as the 'Loris-Melikov Constitution'. It was very far from being a constitution in any Western sense of the word. Behind the lengthy, involved and repetitive bureaucratic phrases, all it involved was the setting up of two temporary preparatory Commissions: a Financial and a general Administrative and Economic Commission; their members were to be partly appointed by the Emperor and partly elected by the *Zemstvos*; they were to be allotted a limited field of activity, and their legislative proposals were to pass, via various stages, to the State Council – at which stage 'it might perhaps please Your Majesty to order the inclusion into it [the State Council], with full voting rights, of several, possibly ten to fifteen, representatives of public organizations who have displayed special qualifications, experience and talents'.[53]

This was the gist of Loris-Melikov's proposals. They were adopted by the Special Board, with some minor changes, on 16 February, and approved by the Emperor the next day. An official communiqué for publication by the Council of Ministers was composed, and awaited the Emperor's pleasure.

For nearly a century it has been the fashion among liberal writers to deride the Loris-Melikov 'Constitution' as woefully inadequate to cope with Russia's pressing needs. This may well be true, but it is difficult to see any other way, short of a revolution, by which the Emperor could have been induced to take the first steps towards limiting the principle of absolute autocracy. Loris-Melikov's proposals would have left autocracy intact – but they would have established embryonic representative institutions, and there can be little doubt that, given the facts of Russia's extremely rapid social and economic progress towards the end of the nineteenth century, these would soon have outgrown their original form and paved the way for proper constitutional development. After all, every existing constitutional system in the world was either established by revolution (or a series of revolutions), or evolved through a long process of limited reforms. Why should something different be expected of Russia, particularly when we know that a revolution would have been even less likely to establish constitutional government? Besides, our experience over the past fifty years has taught us that in many cases the most elaborate of written constitutions, equipped with every possible democratic right, may in practice mean far less than the reality of limited representative institutions and of restricted but clearly defined legal rights.

On this issue – as on quite a few others – it is possibly the revolutionaries who saw things in a more realistic light. Lenin himself wrote twenty years later that 'the implementation of Loris-Melikov's scheme *might* under certain conditions have become a step towards a constitution'.[54] As for the Executive Committee, the news of Loris-Melikov's plans gave rise to considerable alarm. The dreaded prospect of a constitutional, bourgeois Russia appeared on the horizon in a much more tangible form than ever before. They made no secret of their attitude:

At bottom it is by no means a stupid policy! To concentrate the forces of the government, to divide and weaken the opposition, to isolate the revolution, and to stifle all enemies one by one – all this is by no means stupid. Will the policies of the Armenian diplomat [Loris-Melikov] succeed? This will naturally depend on the amount of intelligence and civic sense that the Russians possess. Loris-Melikov's policy is entirely based on the stupidity and selfishness of society, of the young generation of liberals, and of the revolutionaries. We very much hope that his calculations will prove to be mistaken.[55]

But *Narodnaya Volya* was leaving nothing to chance – still less to the 'intelligence and civic sense' of their people. The hunt intensified. A new attempt on the Emperor's life was being carefully planned. The arrests of Alexander Mikhailov in November 1880 and of Zhelyabov on 27 February 1881 – only two days before the plan was due to be carried out – did not deter them. Sofia Perovskaya took charge of the operation. Zhelyabov gave nothing away under interrogation (contrary to the rumours assiduously spread by the revolutionaries, and eagerly accepted by Russian society and the outside world, since the beginning of the nineteenth century no political prisoners were ever tortured in Russia – it was left for the revolution to institute this practice).

The terrorists finally caught up with their royal quarry. At half past twelve on 1 March 1881 the Emperor received Loris-Melikov and approved the text of the communiqué to be adopted by the Council of Ministers on 4 March. Afterwards he left the palace for his regular review of the troops. The terrorists were awaiting him. The first bomb missed; the Emperor incautiously left his sleigh to interview the assassin. He had just taken a few steps back when the second bomb exploded. When the smoke cleared the Emperor was discovered lying on his back, the lower part of his body torn to tatters. He was carried back to the palace and died less than two hours later. The hunt was at an end.

But the revolution did not take place. Much to their surprise, the *narodovoltsy* detected no signs of rebelliousness. St Petersburg and the country remained quiet, stunned by the news. After the shock of disbelief had passed, grief and fury reigned among the peasants. The nobles and the 'educated ones' had killed the Tsar who had given them their freedom; now they were going to reintroduce slavery. In many parts of the country the peasants attacked anyone who looked like an educated person, and even the police who tried to protect them.[56] The government's first task was to restore some semblance of order and confidence by repeated denials of any intention of revoking the late Emperor's Emancipation Decree.

Other tasks were even more pressing. One of the two bomb-throwers was killed on the spot, the other, a nineteen-year-old youth called Rysakov, began to give evidence immediately after his arrest. Within ten days all the conspirators were either caught or killed while resisting arrest. They had prepared no follow-up to the assassination, and nothing happened. Their calculations had been wrong.

On 10 March the Executive Committee published its letter to the new Emperor, Alexander III. It called upon him voluntarily to transfer supreme power to the people, and, as a first step, to release all political prisoners and to convene a Constituent Assembly of freely elected representatives of the Russian people. They received no reply: it is surprising that they even expected one. Morozov himself wrote years later: 'As for the letter to Alexander III, it stood in such marked contrast to the regicide just committed that even Alexander III could not believe it.'[57]

Not that the government left the public in any doubt as to its views. It neither collapsed nor panicked. Loris-Melikov made one pathetic attempt to get his proposals accepted by the new Tsar. On 6 March they were discussed by a conference under the chairmanship of Alexander III himself, and rejected practically unanimously. Loris-Melikov was finished. The meeting was dominated by the man who was to play a decisive part throughout the new reign, and to make it into one of the most reactionary periods of Russian history, comparable only to the years of Nicholas I: the Procurator of the Holy Synod, Konstantin Pobedonostsev. He ended his speech with an impassioned appeal: 'Sire, at such a terrible moment it is necessary to think, not of the establishment of a new talking-shop for the voicing of new subversive speeches, but of action. We must act!'[58] On 29 April the Emperor published a Manifesto declaring his unwavering hostility to any ideas of constitutionalism or reform; it became the keystone of the new reign.

The direct organizers and participants of the assassination of Alexander II – Zhelyabov, Perovskaya, Kibalchich, Timofei Mikhailov and Rysakov – had been publicly hanged on 3 April. Four of them embraced each other for the last time on the scaffold – even in the face of death they turned their backs on the wretched Rysakov.

Only eight members of the Executive Committee remained at large. They co-opted new people, but now the authorities were fiercely determined to destroy the organization once and for all. By the end of 1883 *Narodnaya Volya* had, to all intents and purposes, ceased to exist. The one member at liberty was Tikhomirov; he had gone abroad, and a few years later renounced his revolutionary views.

Narodnaya Volya destroyed itself by achieving its supreme triumph. Its history is usually referred to as a glorious failure. What had it gained for the Russian people? Nothing. It had merely frittered away its members' lives in acts of individual terrorism that were inevitably doomed to failure. Such is the conventional view. It is wrong. In terms of its own purposes *Narodnaya Volya* was completely successful. It had sacrificed itself on the bloodstained altar of revolution, but in death it was triumphant. The revolution had won the race for time. The main aim had been accomplished: Russia's constitutional, bourgeois development had been stopped. It was only resumed twenty-five years later, and by then it was too late.

CHAPTER 19

The Marxist-Populist Dialectic

Marxism was a theory in search of a testing-ground, and Russia became the country to provide it with these facilities. The experiment has certainly worked: whether it has proved the validity of Marxist doctrine remains debatable. Yet whatever the degree of success in imposing the Marxist structure upon Russia, this could not have been achieved without substantially adapting it to the country's native traditions. Short of foreign conquest, no political order can survive for any length of time without having roots in the nation's past. No revolution can succeed without such roots. This applies to the Russian revolution as much as to any other. That the State born of the immense convulsion of 1917 has preserved an essential continuity with pre-revolutionary Russia nobody would deny. What is less generally realized is the basic continuity of the Russian revolutionary movement itself: the adaptation of Marxism, originally imported from the West, to a well-established indigenous revolutionary tradition. This process of adjusting Marxism to the peculiar conditions of Russia – a process without which Marxism would today be no more than a half-forgotten sociological theory – began long before 1917.

The history of the spread of Marxism and the growth of the Marxist movement in Russia has been described with a wealth of detail in a number of excellent specialist studies.[1] The full story requires no retelling. The historian's difficulty here is caused, as so often happens, not by the dearth but by the over-abundance of historical material. History is not simply an agglomeration of data, and the historian's task is not that of gathering as many facts on some given topic as he possibly can. The writing of history involves, above all, the art of selection. There is nothing invidious about this. 'The historian is

502

necessarily selective,' as E. H. Carr pointed out in his 1961 Macaulay Lectures:[2] every work of history, however limited the theme and comprehensive its treatment, is the product of ineluctable selection. The historian alone must decide which of the mass of facts at his disposal merit inclusion in his story, and which (the vast majority) are to be discarded as insignificant. It is a question not of bias but of judgment.

The 'pre-history' of the Bolshevik Revolution offers relatively fewer problems in this respect than most other topics of modern history. The study of Russian Marxism has become a flourishing field of academic research for one reason and one reason only: because of its bearings upon 1917. Without the Russian revolution these records would have remained to moulder untouched by human hand, never even achieving the status of historical facts. As with any historical experience, the growth of Russian Marxism was a multi-textured, complex process of intricate pattern. At the time it was impossible to foretell which line of development (if any) would emerge triumphant. The same considerations would apply, I imagine, to a study of the obscure doctrinal quarrels of Jewish sects in first-century Roman Palestine: apart from their role in the rise of Christianity they possess no intrinsic importance. Today we know which of the tortuous criss-crossing threads of Russian Marxism led to the greatest revolution of our time. I therefore offer no apology for limiting my account to an analysis of that particular line of development.

The history of Russia – precariously balanced in terms of geography, politics, social relationships, culture, between Europe and Asia – abounds from the very beginning in contradictions and paradoxes. The history of Marxism in Russia, of its appearance, growth and ultimate victory, contains perhaps even more elements of paradox than any other part of the story.

Marxism was a theory specifically designed for societies that had reached the highest degree of development. The socialist revolution, Marx argued, was to be the inevitable outcome of the development of the material productive forces of society, which would come into irreconcilable conflict with outmoded relations of production. It followed from this that socialist revolution could only come about in the most highly industrialized countries of the world. There was no short cut. As Marx himself wrote in one of the most famous passages of *The Critique of Political Economy*, 'No social order ever perishes before all the productive forces for which there is room in it have developed; and new, higher relations of production never appear before the material conditions of their existence have matured in the womb of the old society itself.'³ Thus orthodox, 'scientific' Marxism. By any reckoning the Russia of the late nineteenth century was worlds removed from the situation envisaged by Marx: a backward country with a primitive peasant economy, the rudiments of modern industry, and the mere embryo of a proletariat. Despite the rapid progress upon which Russia was then embarking she would obviously need many decades, probably well over a century, to catch up with, let alone overtake, the Western countries for whom Marx's prediction had been formulated. Yet it was Russia upon which Marxism soon took the firmest hold, and where the Marxist revolution first achieved victory – a bare generation after Marx's death.

Another paradox is nearly as strange: the attitude of the Founding Fathers towards the pioneers of Russian Marxism. Marx, usually so eager to support even the smallest band of disciples wherever they happened to appear, opposed the formation of a Russian Marxist group and was openly hostile to his bewildered Russian acolytes. Flying in the face not only of his general theory but also of his earlier views on Russia, Marx made no secret of his preference and his backing for those most un-Marxist revolutionaries, the Populists. So too, for a number of years, did Engels, loftily disregarding all the arguments he had only recently raised against Tkachev.

In the light of these facts it has become customary to speak of the 'ambiguity' or 'ambivalence' of Marx's attitude towards the Russian revolutionary movement (Soviet historians, for their part, have to resort to the most prodigious ideological contortions to explain it all away). Upon closer examination, however, the 'ambiguity' tends to dissolve and we discover a fairly clear-cut, even consistent attitude. But to grasp the entirely logical development of Marx's views on the Russian revolutionary movement we must see Marx as he really was: not as the dedicated, unworldly scholar of legend but as the no less dedicated practical revolutionary of reality. To this real Marx even poorish (by Marxist standards) revolutions were infinitely more valuable than the most brilliant theoretical contributions. Hence the motley collection of assorted revolutionaries of all shades and colours, of whom none shared Marx's ideas but all enjoyed his fervent support – from Kossuth and Garibaldi to the Communards and the Fenians. It was the expectation of revolution and the interests of the revolution that determined Marx's approach to Russia, with all its seemingly inexplicable changes of direction.

For thirty years, until the late 1870s, Marx's interest in Russia had been largely limited to two matters: his constant fear of Russian expansionism and almost paranoiac obsession with the omnipotence of the Russian government (Marx even suspected Palmerston of being in the Russians' pay), and the exigencies of his struggle with Bakunin for control of the International Workingmen's Association. Marx is often said to have been anti-Russian. The charge is unfair. He had the greatest respect for some Russian writers, notably Chernyshevsky; he learned Russian (an even rarer accomplishment in his day than it is in ours) when well into middle age, and read and appreciated Pushkin and others in the original. But under the circumstances it is not surprising that Marx's favourable comments on Russian affairs should have been few and far between.

More surprising, one might think, is the fact that Marx's theories were becoming well known and acquiring considerable weight within Russia itself. Marx's influence on Lavrov, Tkachev and other Populist ideologists has already been discussed. His writings were also penetrating into the academic world, where their earliest propagator was Russia's leading economist, N. I. Ziber. The very first foreign edition of *Das Kapital* was the Russian translation prepared by two prominent Populists, German

Lopatin and Nikolai Danielson, which appeared in March 1872. It was passed by the censors because, as they explained, while the author was undoubtedly a confirmed socialist, 'his exposition is far from accessible to the general public' and was 'put forward in a strictly mathematical scientific form'. Although *Capital* can hardly be called a runaway best-seller, the censors' judgment was badly at fault: the book had been printed in 3000 copies, of which 900 were sold in the first six weeks.[4] (The original German edition of 1867 had been limited to 1000 copies and took five years to sell out.)

Naturally, Marx would have preferred to see his magnum opus published in the countries that really mattered (it only appeared in France in 1875 and in England in 1887), yet he was wryly amused by the book's success in Russia, of all places, and boasted about it self-deprecatingly to his friends. Not that this led to any revision of his general attitude towards Russia. Ever since the Crimean War had revealed Russia's deep-rooted weaknesses Marx was vaguely expecting a revolution to break out there at any time (his dread of Russia, however, remained undiminished). Since his own social theory so obviously did not apply to Russia, Marx gave little thought to the precise form which a revolution there might take; he spoke indiscriminately about a peasant uprising or a palace coup or a combination of both. What he utterly refused to acknowledge was the revolutionary potential of the intelligentsia and the significance of Populism, which he contemptuously dismissed out of hand. Its ideas about the *obshchina* were patently absurd, and its leaders, particularly Bakunin and Herzen, at best trouble-making intriguers, possibly even police agents.

Marx was almost invariably scornful of Russian Populist revolutionaries. Typical of his attitude was a reference, in a letter to Engels in February 1870, to 'the schoolboy nihilism which is today fashionable among Russian students'.[5] Engels expressed himself even more strongly (and, in an odd way, presciently) on the subject, in a letter of 29 April 1870:

What a misfortune it would be for the world – were this

not an incredible lie [of Bakunin's T.S.] – to have in Russia 40,000 revolutionary students, who lack the backing of a proletariat or even a revolutionary peasantry, and who cannot hope for any career except the choice between Siberia and emigration to Western Europe. If anything could ruin the West European movement then it would be the importation of these 40,000 more or less educated, ambitious and starving Russian nihilists. These are all candidates for officers' posts – only without an army, and we would be expected to supply them with that. What a brilliant idea: to hand over the European proletariat under Russian command in order to establish unity in its ranks! But seriously, however much Bakunin may exaggerate, it is as clear as day that the danger exists. Holy Russia will annually spit out a certain number of these 'careerless' Russians, and they, under the pretext of *principe international*, will everywhere insinuate themselves among the workers, demand the leading position, introduce their personal intrigues – which are inevitable among Russians.[6]

This extremely hostile opinion can be partly explained by Marx's implacable hatred towards Bakunin and all those whom, rightly or wrongly, he regarded as Bakunin's allies. But Engels's theoretical broadside against Tkachev was not made in a fit of pique: it set forth a considered analysis (approved by Marx himself) of the future development of Russia and the Russian revolutionary movement, which left no room either for a conspiratorial coup d'état or for a short cut to socialism via the *obshchina*. Even in September 1877, after the open emergence of *Zemlya i Volya*, when Marx was hopefully diagnosing the 'complete disintegration' of all segments of Russian society, he could find words of praise only for the 'splendid Turks', and sneered that 'the foolish antics of the Russian students are mere symptoms, of no importance whatever in themselves'.[7]

Quite suddenly, a few months later, Marx came to reverse his entire attitude to the Russian revolution. From then on until Marx's death in 1883 (and in Engels's case, for several more years thereafter) the founders of Marxism consistently believed not only that the world revolution would begin in Russia, but also that it would be carried out by an élite conspiratorial organization, and that Russia had an excellent chance of by-passing the stage of capitalism and of achieving socialism earlier than any other country – thanks to the continued existence of the village commune! In other words, they had accepted practically the whole of the Populist case.

This extraordinary volte-face had not been preceded by any revision of the basic Marxist theoretical premise: its only explanation can be found in the changed state of Marx's mind, induced by a long period of bitter personal and political disappointment. The turning-point had come in 1871 with the tragic débâcle of the Paris Commune. However hard Marx tried to keep up appearances, his spirit was broken. For twenty-five years Marx had lived in the expectation of a proletarian revolution; everything he did or wrote was directed towards its imminent arrival. At last, in March 1871, the prophecy was fulfilled: the working class of the capital of Europe's largest and most revolutionary country had seized power. Less than two months later it was all over; no one had supported the Commune – and it fell, disabled by its own follies, drowned in blood by the government of Versailles.

Marx could not have known that there were to be no more proletarian revolutions in the West but some premonition may have entered his mind, for he never recovered from the blow. 'The Commune,' write the authors of a scholarly study of Marx's work in the International, 'marked a climax in Marx's life of which the last twelve years were strangely barren both in political activity and in theoretical work.'[8] A curious lassitude settled upon Marx; throughout these years he lived what can only be described as the life of a gentleman of leisure (financed by Engels). In effect he retired from active politics: at the Hague congress of the First International in September 1872 he carried through a resolution to close down the organization by which he had once set such great store and ship off what remained to America. The thing had lost all point, he explained, and was riddled through and through with Bakuninites. Besides, at last he would be free to return to the theoretical research that was his real life work, and to complete the remaining two volumes of *Capital*. He went on endlessly complaining about the strain of overwork, but when after his death Engels, as Marx's literary executor, finally gained access to his manuscripts he discovered to his amazement that Marx had left only rough and fragmentary notes for volumes 2 and 3 of *Capital*, almost all of which dated from the 1860s. During the last ten years of his life, apart from letters, Marx wrote only two short articles, an epilogue to an earlier work, prefaces to new German and Russian editions of *The Communist Manifesto* (jointly with Engels), and his *Critique of the Gotha Programme* (not for publication). That was all. His heart was no longer in his work. 'He had lost none of his intellectual and political acumen, but something had gone. He no longer had the capacity for sustained creative work. He was only fifty-three when the Commune fell, but this was the turning point in his life . . . Marx could not face the prospect of a long period of painfully slow development as he had faced it in his thirties.'9

There was little for Marx's comfort in the decade that followed the Commune. One by one the revolutionary lights went out in the West. The unification of Germany and Italy eliminated two great seed-beds of rebellion. Poland, too, remained quiescent, while Hungary achieved an accommodation with Austria. An unprecedented era of peace, prosperity and rising living standards had set in. Despite the depression of 1873, economic progress was gathering speed everywhere; industrialization, previously confined largely to Britain, was rapidly transforming Germany and the United States. But its social effects ran directly counter to all the Marxist assumptions: instead of increased impoverishment and sharper social strife the temperature of the class conflict was falling. Marx could find no consolation in any of the countries that had so recently seemed ripe for social revolution. After a short but savage period of counter-revolutionary terror the Third Republic in France settled down to a comfortably disreputable existence. The Fenian movement had been suppressed, and Marx gradually lost interest in Ireland: championship of the Irish cause, he had realized, was not exactly the best way to win support among the English working class. The English workers were what mattered, but the state of their revolutionary class-consciousness was such as to drive any Marxist to despair: the parliamentary reform of 1867 and the great reforming Acts of the 1870s had created a new social climate; the trade-union movement was resolutely turning its back on the idea of revolutionary struggle; in an article on 'The British Elections' (March 1874) Engels despondently acknowledged that the wily bourgeoisie had taken over almost all the Chartists' demands, and bitterly reviled his erstwhile British comrades from the General Council of the International as paid agents of the capitalist class.

Nor was the situation better elsewhere. During and after the American Civil War Marx had placed great hopes on the United States; he was convinced that the war would lead to a profound social revolution. Instead the country was soon caught up in the money-making orgy of the 'Gilded Age'. Yet the cruellest blow of all was delivered by the workers of Marx's native land, Germany. For a short time Marx spoke hopefully of 'the centre of revolution' having moved eastward, from France to Germany. Things were indeed looking up: in 1874 seven socialists were elected to the Reichstag, and the next year in Gotha the two rival socialist factions united into a single party under Marxist leadership. Then calamity struck. In 1878 the Reichstag passed Bismarck's anti-socialist law banning practically every social-democratic activity. And – to quote Marx's own words when describing Cromwell's dissolution of the Rump of the Long Parliament – not a dog barked: the German workers accepted the measure with complete equanimity, consoled no doubt by rapidly rising real wages and by Bismarck's newly invented social security system.

The degree of Marx's disillusionment can be gauged by the fact that ten years after the Paris Commune he no longer believed that it had been a real proletarian revolution, and saw the episode only as a colossal waste of life and effort. In a letter to the Dutch revolutionary Domela Nieuwenhuis Marx wrote: 'The Paris Commune ... was merely the rising of a city under exceptional conditions, and the majority of the Commune was in no sense socialist, nor could it be. However, with a small amount of common sense it could have reached a compromise with Versailles useful to the whole mass of the people – the only thing possible at that time.'[10]

One can hardly be surprised then that, coming when they did, the stirring items of news from Russia – the formation of a widespread illegal party, the involvement of workers in revolutionary activity, the gun battles, the strikes and demonstrations, the assassinations, the abject helplessness of the authorities – all the unmistakable signs of an imminent upheaval – should have pierced the atmosphere of unrelieved gloom like a brilliant ray of light. The old revolutionary's pulse quickened: once more there was hope. Perhaps revolution would come from the East – from even further East than he had imagined. What matter that events were developing not in accordance with his own theories, that they were proving his ideological opponents right? All that counted was the Deed, the Revolution, and the Russians were achieving miraculous results with their methods, while others, ideologically purer, had got nowhere. Perhaps the Russians had been right all the time? Perhaps there was no real contradiction between Marxist theory and Populist practice, which might supply the missing ingredient necessary for a concrete revolutionary situation? Come to that, perhaps even the theoretical ramblings about the *obshchina* had been soundly based? Anyway, it did not really matter – things would sort themselves out; that was what the laws of history were for. The Jacobin soul that had lain dormant since the heady days of 1848–50 once more awoke in Marx.

The first indication that Marx was revising his views on the village commune is found in a letter to Nikolai Mikhailovsky, then editor of the radical journal *Otechestvennye Zapiski*, written at the very end of 1877 but never posted (it was only discovered after Marx's death and first published, significantly, not by the

Marxists but by the remnants of the *narodovoltsy*). Mikhailovsky had written that Marx's theory denied the possibility of Russia bypassing the capitalist stage, and of socialism growing directly out of the village commune. Marx strongly repudiated any such interpretation of his writings. Never, he went on, had he implied that Russia must inevitably go through the stage of capitalism, or that his theory need necessarily fit every nation of the world. The key passage read: 'I have come to the following conclusion: If Russia continues along the path she has followed since 1861 then she will let slip the finest opportunity that history has ever offered any nation and will experience all the disastrous afflictions of the capitalist system.'[11]

The question of the *obshchina*, however, continued to bother Marx even after he had committed himself firmly – as will be shown further – to the cause of *Narodnaya Volya*. After all, it was a serious theoretical stumbling-block, and not a few would-be Russian followers were frightened away by his seemingly intransigent attitude towards their traditional sacred cow. In February 1881 Vera Zasulich wrote to Marx asking him point-blank about his views on the subject. The poor woman, whose ability to grasp the finer doctrinal points had never been very great, was now utterly confused. Some Russian Marxists, she explained, were saying that all nations would have to pass through the stage of capitalist development and that therefore the village commune was doomed to destruction. If this really was the conclusion to be drawn from *Capital* then obviously there was no sense in trying to preserve the *obshchina* and working towards a speedy revolutionary transformation of society on its basis: all activity should instead be concentrated on gaining influence among the working class, in the expectation of an eventual proletarian revolution after capitalism had had the time to develop fully. Would Citizen Marx please be so kind as to tell her how matters actually stood in this respect?[12]

Marx seized the opportunity. In his reply (8 March 1881) he did his best to dispel 'the misunderstanding with regard to my so-called theory'. Never, he wrote, had he suggested that his scheme of social development was universally applicable.

The analysis in *Capital* showed that the 'historical inevitability' of the capitalist phase 'was *precisely* limited to the countries of Western Europe'. It did not relate to Russia because the development of capitalism meant 'the transformation of one form of private property into another form of private property, whereas in the case of the Russian peasants it would be necessary, on the contrary, to transform their common property into private property'. Although *Capital* contained no specific references to the Russian commune, 'the special research that I have carried out on material from primary sources has convinced me that this *obshchina* is the fulcrum for Russia's social regeneration. But in order that it may fulfil this role it is necessary first of all to eliminate the pernicious influences to which it is subjected, and then to assure it of normal conditions for untrammelled development.' In other words, to carry out a revolution.[13]

Marx's letter to Zasulich was quite brief: some 400 words in all. But it was the product of strenuous work, of no less than four preliminary drafts which, taken together, are twenty times the length of the final text and represent the most detailed exposition of Marx's matured views on the *obshchina* and the future of Russia's revolutionary development. Marx devoted at least two weeks to the task: not so much composing a letter to an unfamiliar correspondent as working the problem out for himself, mulling over it, seeking an adequate solution to the very special case posed by Russia. It was the usual extremely thorough Marxian piece of work, a learned dissertation based on authorities from Tacitus to Sir Henry Maine. And, as usual, he found the answer – by skilfully incorporating the *obshchina* into his great vision of mankind's past, present and future.

Marx disowned the views attributed to him by followers of whom he had never heard. 'The process which I analysed . . . substituted one form of property for another. How could this be applied to Russia, where the land is not and never has been the husbandman's "private property"?' In Russia, unlike any Western country, 'common ownership of the land represents the natural basis for collective production and appropriation'.

To be sure, similar agricultural communities had existed at a particular stage in the historical development of every society. But the Russian commune differed from them all in certain crucial respects; for one thing, it was not based on blood ties, and thus retained vitality and potential for further growth. Everywhere else the 'archaic' agricultural community had disappeared. 'Why then should it escape this fate in Russia alone?' Because of an exceptional combination of circumstances: first, 'Russia is the only European country where the "agricultural commune" has survived to our day on a national scale,' and secondly, because the Russian communal system is not isolated artificially from the modern world (as, for example, in British India), and can thus adopt and utilize all the achievements of modern industry and technology. Of course, the *possibility* of a capitalist transformation should by no means be excluded. The commune, having maintained its vitality, continues to develop; at the present time it is approaching a crossroads. 'Either the element of private ownership that is contained within it overcomes the collective element, or the latter overcomes the former. It all depends upon the historical milieu.' But there is no *inevitability* about a capitalist development in Russia – rather, the contrary. In Russia's case the introduction of capitalism, far from being historically progressive, as everywhere else, would actually represent a retrograde step: 'It would mean the substitution of capitalist ownership for communist ownership.' Happily, Russia does not have to undergo the horrors of the capitalist system in order to enjoy the fruits of its development – any more than she would need to re-invent the machines, the railways, the banking and currency methods evolved in the West over the course of centuries. She can take over all the positive achievements of Western capitalism ready-made. But in her case – and only in her case – the capitalist system as such is uncalled-for.

Marx repeatedly drove home the central point of his argument: capitalism was an inevitable and necessary stage in the historical development of all civilized nations towards socialism – with the sole exception of Russia, which was in a unique position to bypass the stage of capitalism altogether and move directly into the socialist phase. The decisive factor that made this possible was the *obshchina*. 'It occupies a completely special place, unprecedented in history. Alone in Europe, it represents the organic, dominating form of village life of a vast empire. The common ownership of land is the natural basis for collective appropriation, while its historical milieu, namely the contemporaneous existence of capitalist production, provides it ready-made with the material means for organized wide-scale co-operative labour. It can therefore utilize all the positive attainments of the capitalist system without having to pass through its Caudine Forks.' Given the appropriate conditions, the *obshchina* 'could become the direct point of departure for the economic system towards which modern society is moving, without having had to commit suicide'. Marx was quite clear in his mind on the precondition for Russia's direct transition to socialism. 'What is needed to save the Russian *obshchina* is the Russian revolution ... If the revolution takes place at the proper time, if it concentrates all its forces on assuring the untrammelled development of the village commune, then this latter would shortly become the basic feature of the re-birth of Russian society and the basic feature of its superiority to the countries that remain under the yoke of capitalism.'[14]

The above is a compression of Marx's somewhat diffuse, at times repetitive meditations on this central question of Russian revolutionary doctrine. Whatever the merit of his arguments, however Marxian the phraseology in which they were couched, one point is beyond honest dispute: they stood in direct contradiction to the Marxist theory of social development. Without acknowledging it in so many words, Marx had revoked everything he and Engels had said for thirty years in their polemic with Populism, and accepted all the ideas hitherto held up to scorn: Russia's special predestination, her advantage over the capitalist West, the possibility of a non-capitalist road to socialism, the glories of the *obshchina* – all of it, without reserve. No wonder this document – Marx's last original contribution to the theory that bears his name – has ever since caused acute embarrassment to every ideological variety of Marxist. It undermined the very foundation of their doctrinal certainty in a rigid set of rules determining, with scientific precision, the whole evolution of human society. Hardly any of the latter-day Marxists have been able to match the revolutionary pragmatism of a man ever ready to rethink his basic views in the light of practical developments. When Marx wrote, in his celebrated Eleventh Thesis on Feuerbach, that 'the philosophers have only *interpreted* the world in various ways. The point, however, is to *change* it' – he meant exactly what he said. And he remained faithful to this principle all his life.

The revolutionary Populists were overjoyed at having their creed endorsed by the foremost Western socialist thinker. Marx and Engels made their changed attitude public early in 1882, in their Preface to a new Russian edition of *The Communist Manifesto*:

Now the question is: can the Russian *obshchina*, though greatly undermined, yet a form of the primeval common ownership of land, pass directly to the higher form of communist common ownership? Or on the contrary, must it first pass through the same process of dissolution as constitutes the historical evolution of the West?

The only answer to that possible today is this: If the Russian Revolution becomes the signal for a proletarian revolution in the West, so that both complement each other, the present Russian common ownership of land may serve as the starting-point for a communist development.[15]

The Preface, with its mention of a complementary proletarian revolution in the West, to be sparked off by Russia, was somewhat more cautious than Marx's letter to Zasulich. But the inference was clear. The Preface was first published, not in Plekhanov's new edition of the *Manifesto*, but three months earlier, less than a month after it had been written, in *Narodnaya Volya* No. 8–9, with an exultant footnote:

It gives us great pleasure to publish this Preface, in view

of the profound scientific and practical importance of the problems discussed. We are especially gratified to note the concluding words. We see in them confirmation of a cardinal thesis of the theory of *narodovolstvo* – confirmation based on the findings of such great scientific authorities as Marx and Engels. The long-awaited continuation of Marx's famous work (*Capital*) will undoubtedly give due space to elaborating the propositions which could only be touched upon in this Preface.[16]

The *narodovoltsy* had good grounds for their confidence, as Marx had promised them that he would write a detailed treatise on the *obshchina* (in the event, he never got round to it). By this time the close collaboration between Marx and Engels and *Narodnaya Volya* was in full swing. The founders of 'scientific socialism' now approved of the method of political assassination. The day after the death sentence had been passed on Zhelyabov and his comrades Marx described them to his daughter: 'They are sterling people through and through, without a melodramatic pose, simple, businesslike, heroic ... They try to show Europe that their *modus operandi* is a specifically Russian and historically inevitable method about which there is no more reason to moralize – for or against – than about the earthquake of Chios.'[17]

In the split between *Narodnaya Volya* and *Chernyi Peredel* Marx from the first unequivocally sided with the terrorists. He established direct contact with them early in 1880 through Lev Gartman, an agent of the Executive Committee just arrived in London. On 27 May 1880 Gartman wrote to the arch-terrorist Morozov: 'Choosing between the two organizations he has determinedly taken the side and supported the programme of the terrorists.' But Marx had understandable qualms about openly embracing the principles he had opposed for so many years. Two months later Gartman was reporting to Morozov: 'You shouldn't count on Marx, I mean, on getting his article. He won't write it. He will sympathize in private, so to speak, but not in print, because he says that the terrorists' programme is not socialist. In short, he is cautious.'[18] Marx was indeed cautious when it came to public expression of his new-found sympathies, but in private correspondence with friends he made no bones about his choice. On 5 November 1880 he informed one such old associate, F. A. Sorge, that in Russia 'we have a central committee of the terrorists, whose programme, recently published in Petersburg, has aroused the rage of the Russian anarchists in Switzerland, who in Geneva are publishing *Die schwartze Verteilung* (*Chernyi Peredel*). These people – the majority of them (not all) are those who left Russia voluntarily – have formed, in contrast to the terrorists who are risking their lives, a so-called propaganda party. (In order to conduct propaganda in Russia they go to Geneva! What a *quid pro quo*!)'[19] The spectacle of Marx – who had fled to London as a haven for his revolutionary activities in order to escape, at most, a short prison sentence – mocking Russian rebels for *voluntarily* evading the very real threat of execution, is an unedifying one, though fairly typical of his peculiar moral standards. Yet it also contained a much more poignant irony: the members of *Chernyi Peredel* were even then becoming orthodox Marxists – only to discover that Marx and Engels had meanwhile moved over towards accepting the basic Populist theses.

Marx had no patience with the idea of a 'so-called propaganda party' being formed, even in support of his own doctrines, at the very moment when a genuine activist revolutionary party existed inside Russia. With the revolution obviously due at any time he had more pressing matters to attend to. He was being regularly informed by the Executive Committee, via Gartman, about the latest current developments, including their preparations for a coup d'état. Marx, in turn, acted as a kind of foreign affairs consultant to the *narodovoltsy*, advising them on the best ways of influencing Western public opinion. He supplied their representatives with useful introductions to influential people, and took an active part in negotiations aimed at starting an English-language *narodovolets* newspaper in London (the idea fell through).[20]

The high regard in which Marx was held by *Narodnaya Volya*

found its expression in an official Address to him from the Executive Committee, dated 6 November 1880 and published a few weeks later in *L'Intransigeant*. Not even Marx's most devoted followers could have outdone the lavish panegyric: 'The progressive intelligentsia of Russia, ever attentive to European intellectual developments, has received the appearance of your scientific works with great enthusiasm. The most sterling tendencies of Russian life have found their scientific confirmation in these works. *Capital* has become a handbook for all educated people ... It is only natural that your name should have become indissolubly connected with the internal struggle in Russia.'[21] At about the same time Marx was sent a copy of the 'Programme of working-class members of *Narodnaya Volya*', which earned his full approval; indeed, there are strong, though not entirely conclusive, indications that he actually helped to edit this important statement of aims.

The eulogy of Marxist theory contained in the Address of the Executive Committee was not mere lip-service. Their alliance with Marx (for that is what it amounted to) was not confined to practical co-operation: Marx's approval of basic elements of Populist doctrine was more than matched by the eagerness of the *narodovoltsy* to study Marxism, to accept its tenets and to adapt them to Russian conditions. Classical Populism had been suspicious of Marxism because of its stress on political action, political organization and political revolution. Politics, wrote Lavrov and others, could never bring about the social revolution; the political struggle was of benefit only to the bourgeoisie, not the people; politics were incompatible with socialism. Now all was changed. *Zemlya i Volya* had split precisely over the issue of 'politics' *v.* 'propaganda', between the 'politicals' and the 'villagers'. *Narodnaya Volya* was established as a political organization; what repelled the 'villagers' were not its method of political assassination (some of the 'villagers' had been active terrorists themselves) but its unabashedly political aims: the preparation of a coup d'état and the seizure of power. As Zhelyabov declared, they were all statists. With this most difficult of hurdles overcome the sole obstacle between the *narodovoltsy* and Marxism was Marx's disbelief in 'Russian socialism' and the *obshchina*. Then that, too, was removed.

Given these modifications, Marxism undoubtedly possessed many attractions for the revolutionary Populist. It was a far more sophisticated doctrine than any home-grown product, it gave a convincing explanation of the relationship between political and social change, it exposed the horrors of the capitalist path. Above all, it was 'scientific'.

We have perhaps tended to underestimate the influence of Marxism upon the men and women of *Narodnaya Volya* (unconsciously following the lead of Soviet historiography, with its vested interest in emphasizing the divide between 'Populism' and 'Marxism-Leninism'). Not that the *narodovoltsy* ever became in any sense 'orthodox' Marxists – it is the very unorthodoxy of their peculiarly Russian approach that gives it its significance. Many elements of Marxism were taken over by them intact, some were adapted, still others misunderstood or misinterpreted. They had no inhibitions about this: after all, Marx himself had recognized their circumstances to be *sui generis*. The time at their disposal was strictly limited and the experiment short-lived. It was to be taken up later – with more lasting success.

The fusion of Marxism and the Russian revolutionary tradition produced a curious hybrid: not really a blend, rather a compound of easily distinguishable ingredients. Nevertheless, without the component of Marxism *Narodnaya Volya* could probably never have become more than just another group of terrorists. Writing many years later, Vera Figner conveys a vivid impression of the effect *Capital*, first read in 1881, had upon her. Figner's description of the strange medley of ideas and associations this produced could, one feels, apply just as well to later generations of Russian Marxists:

> The book had an exceptionally powerful impact upon me; this was, one might say, my second baptism in socialism. Marx's impassioned eloquence imprinted whole pages upon my memory in words of fire . . .

The knowledge that we feeble individuals were backed by a mighty historical process filled one with ecstasy and established such a firm foundation for the individual's activities that, it seemed, all the hardships of the struggle could be overcome.

I did not reconsider all my previous views or all the earlier influences; I did not readjust my ideas on the basis of Marx's theory. The previous views remained as the underlying stratum above which was deposited everything learnt from *Capital*. These two layers never intermingled, but in some mysterious fashion they fused together and doubled the power of conviction and the determination to struggle and to fight – to fight now, immediately, using those weapons which were at hand and which were called for by the reality around us.[22]

Narodnaya Volya was neither a monolithic nor an ideological party. Its members were in agreement regarding basic problems of strategy and tactics: beyond that there was hardly any attempt to draw up a unified and binding body of doctrine. However, some of the more thoughtful *narodovoltsy* did try to set their ideas into the wider framework of some general social philosophy. Marxism had an obvious appeal, yet their efforts to create a specifically Russian variety of Marxism resulted in something uncommonly like Tkachevism – just as Tkachev had arrived at his own views through an understanding of the Marxist laws of economic development and their application to Russia.

Nikolai Kibalchich perhaps came nearest to successfully welding the two disparate elements into a coherent and rational structure. His trenchant article on 'The Political Revolution and the Economic Question' set out the special predicament of the Russian revolutionary party: it had to achieve not only a social revolution but also the destruction of political despotism, a task already fulfilled in Europe by the bourgeoisie. But can a country's political structure influence its social system? There are three schools of thought with regard to this, explained Kibalchich.

The first, represented by Tkachev, are Jacobins, statists 'who wish to seize power in order to decree a political and social revolution, and to introduce socialist principles into the people's life from above', without the direct participation of the people. On the other hand there are those, like the *Chernyi Peredel* group, who deny the validity of political struggle altogether. The correct solution lies somewhere between these two extremes, in a combination of the political and social factors. 'This is the view accepted by our faction and our organ.' It is very close to the theories propounded by Marx, who has proved that all social systems are based on economic relationships, but who – unlike many of his pupils – also believes that political authority (as, for example, in the case of the Paris Commune) can be used as the agency of transformation of the social structure. After illustrating this last point with several examples from recent French history Kibalchich arrives at a clear-cut conclusion: 'Nobody can any longer doubt the feasibility of a political revolution which uses the State as a weapon for implementing the economic revolution.'

To be successful, such a revolution must be carried out in accordance with historical development and with the people's own desires. And at this stage Russia's special circumstances come into play. The Russian State, Kibalchich continues, shows very clearly how a political system can exert a crucial *negative* influence upon the social structure. 'The principles of the people's life are diametrically opposed to the principles upon which the present State is founded' (the contradiction between State and *obshchina* becomes the Russian counterpart to Marx's contradiction between productive forces and relations of production). Moreover, unlike Europe the Russian State has made impossible the development of privileged social classes or estates that could serve as its support. So when the super-centralized autocratic State is swept away by the tidal wave of revolution, which force will emerge as master of the situation? Certainly not the inchoate and unorganized property-owning classes. 'Only the people and the social-revolutionary party can be capable of determining the social and political system after the uprising. Therefore we come, once again, to the same conclusion: the main thrust of our party's destructive activity must be directed, at present and in the future, against the State – the principal, if not the only real force impeding the construction of a better society.'[23]

There is every indication that the majority of *Narodnaya Volya* agreed with Kibalchich's views. At first sight these are neither profound nor original. It had all been said before: Russia's unique revolutionary advantages over the capitalist West; the artificial and essentially fragile nature of the Russian State; the absence of a proper class structure that might otherwise serve as a barrier to revolution; the 'people's' spontaneously socialist psychology; the entirely practicable prospect of an overthrow of the State creating a social and political void which only the revolutionary party could fill; the job of 'bourgeois' reform devolving by default, almost as an aside, upon the socialist revolution. Nothing really new – all the issues had been, and were going to be, repeatedly argued over for decades. What distinguishes the creed of *Narodnaya Volya* from similar *professions de foi* is first the studied effort to dissociate it from both the Jacobin and the classical varieties of Populism and to align it with Marxist theory, and secondly its implicit acceptance by Marx and Engels.

Four weeks after the publication of Kibalchich's article Alexander II was dead and another month later Kibalchich himself was hanged. The backbone of *Narodnaya Volya* had been broken. But it took a long time for this to be realized, by enemy and friend alike. Marx's ardour for the impending Russian revolution remained undiminished till his death in March 1883. Engels was left the keeper of the conscience, with the self-imposed duty of preserving the heritage intact. In the year of Marx's death he had a long conversation with German Lopatin, just before the latter returned to Russia (in a vain attempt to re-establish *Narodnaya Volya*) and to twenty years in prison. Lopatin recorded the conversation in a letter to another member of the Executive Committee;[24] the correctness of his account was not disputed by Engels when he read it in print. Engels assured Lopatin of his continued faith in the *narodovoltsy*. He had particularly high praise for the letter sent to the new Tsar immediately after the act of 1 March 1881: 'Marx and I both thought the Committee's letter to Alexander III was truly splendid in the political sense it displayed no less than in its calm tone. It shows that there are people with statesmanlike minds among the revolutionaries.' As for the general state of Russia, Engels saw it as almost identical with that of France of 1789. There was nothing the Tsar could do to prevent a revolution from breaking out in the immediate future. 'The initiative of constructing a new social order belongs rightfully and properly,' declared Engels, 'to Russia.' It was a cheering thought, though hardly credible to anyone who, as some Russians were then doing, took a literal approach to the writings of Marx.

In no other country did orthodox Marxism have greater difficulty in getting off the ground than in Russia, for nowhere else were its opponents sustained by the personal authority of Marx and Engels themselves. That the venture survived and that Marxism in its European version achieved – for a time – a resounding victory over the proponents of 'Russian socialism' was due in large measure to the devotion and the untiring efforts of Georgy Valentinovich Plekhanov. But for many years it was heartbreaking, uphill work.

Plekhanov arrived in Geneva in January 1880, leaving behind him the life of a hunted underground revolutionary. He was to stay in the West for thirty-seven years. One issue of *Chernyi Peredel* had just appeared; two more were published in Switzerland (much to Marx's disgust). Then the group petered out, and with it the journal. Like Herzen so many years before, Plekhanov was transformed under the impact of Western Europe. Only in his case it had a totally different effect: instead of confirming his faith in a special Russian path to socialism it convinced him that Russia was inevitably subject to the same historical laws as the West, and that the road to socialist revolution could lead only through the development of capitalism. Plekhanov had discovered Marx – the old, the real Marx.

Strictly speaking, Plekhanov was familiar with some of Marx's writings even before emigrating. Like other Russian revolutionaries, he held Marx in great respect. But with the deeply ingrained Populism which led him to break away from *Zemlya i Volya* when it began to adopt the method of political terror, he stubbornly refused to believe that political action could lead to the socialist transformation of Russian society. Exposure to Europe, the first-hand experience of political liberty and of legal working-class movements, made him rapidly change his mind. Capitalism, he began to think, must come to Russia, and the people should have a revolutionary party properly equipped for the struggle under these changed circumstances. In January 1881, in the third and last issue of *Chernyi Peredel*, Plekhanov was already writing: 'The representatives of absolute monarchy will be replaced by representatives of the constitutional order, by exponents of the economic interests of the bourgeoisie. The struggle against these will be as inevitable for the people as were the earlier protests against the tyranny of absolutism . . . It is the bourgeoisie against which we shall have to fight. Its downfall can be brought closer only by the success of social-revolutionary propaganda, agitation and organization among the people.'[25] Upon which *Chernyi Peredel* closed down its activities, to give way to a new type of socialist organization. This, however, as Plekhanov came to discover, was much easier said than done.

CHAPTER 20

Towards the New-style Absolutism

Plekhanov must have already to some degree been disillusioned with Populism – it would be difficult otherwise to explain the suddenness of his conversion to Marxism. For Plekhanov, as for *Narodnaya Volya*, the most alluring feature of Marxism was its synthesis of political and social revolution. This offered a key towards solving the interminable argument between the two wings of the Russian revolutionary movement. (Plekhanov's interpretation of the relationship was very different from that of the *narodovoltsy*, but this is hardly surprising: Marxism, then as now, could mean many things to many men.) Plekhanov arrived at his moment of truth when reading the *Communist Manifesto* (strange to say, he had never read Marx's most famous book before). Here at last was the solution to Russia's problems. Russian conditions seemed very similar to those of Germany in 1848. Russia, too, would have to undergo a bourgeois revolution and a lengthy period of unfettered capitalist development, creating a new economy, a new society and a new system of relations of production. The old absolutist order would be destroyed by the triumphant bourgeoisie, as had happened everywhere else. But the bourgeoisie would also bring forth its own grave-digger, the industrial proletariat, the only class capable of accomplishing a socialist revolution and establishing a true classless society. The cold and unemotional Plekhanov was carried away by the magnificent phrases, the passionate conviction, the breathtaking universality of the Marxist analysis. It offered science instead of intuition, facts in place of feelings, certainty as a substitute for conjecture.

Russian Populism, with its narrow-minded parochial approach, seemed a very poor thing indeed by comparison.

Plekhanov's ready acceptance of Marxism had been prepared by the long years of failure. Going to the people, conspiracy, propaganda, terrorism: everything had been tried, and nothing had worked. Once again it was necessary to start from the beginning, only this time the movement would be based on the coherent, scientific world-outlook it had always lacked before, with such disastrous consequences. Besides, Plekhanov's considerable practical experience of revolutionary work in the field tended to confirm all Marx and Engels had written about the proletariat as the only class capable of evolving a revolutionary consciousness, and about the 'idiocy of rural life' having reduced the peasantry to an inert passive mass as far as revolution was concerned. The proletariat was the sole repository of hope – and that entailed the ineluctability of capitalist development for Russia.

The very same forecast for Russia's future, as Plekhanov now discovered with surprise, had been made several years before by Engels. One of the texts that most decisively influenced Plekhanov's turn towards Marxism was *Soziales in Russland* – Engels's polemic against Tkachev. The powerful logic, the skilfully marshalled arguments, completely convinced Plekhanov. He had always been an opponent of Tkachev; for him 'politics' had been epitomized by Tkachev and Nechaev; and now he discovered that there was another kind of revolutionary politics, founded not on conspiracy but on the laws of historical development, encompassing not a small élite but the whole working class, directed not at a coup d'état but at a great popular socialist revolution. The irony of the situation was that by then Marx and Engels had revised their views and, without explicitly saying so, conceded the argument to Tkachev and *Narodnaya Volya*. But Plekhanov, even when he learned with pain of this backsliding, remained loyal to his fundamentalist Marxism.

Plekhanov is often called 'the father of Russian Marxism'. The description is correct only in a certain sense. Marxism had exerted a substantial intellectual influence in Russia well before Plekhanov's conversion, and had shaped the thinking of many prominent revolutionaries. But none of them had regarded themselves as 'Marxists'. Indeed, few people did, anywhere in the world, during Marx's lifetime. His teachings had not yet acquired the form of a rigid doctrine, a unified and all-embracing body of faith known as 'scientific socialism', sub-divided into 'dialectical materialism' and 'historical materialism', neatly classified into laws and categories, providing a co-ordinated system of answers to every problem under the sun. This reverential orthodoxy hardly corresponded to the approach originally taken by Marx, an iconoclast with a restless and supple mind, who did not hesitate to adjust his theory to fit changing circumstances. (Russia provided an excellent example of his pragmatic handling of revolutionary politics.) One can sympathize with Marx and Engels when, towards the end of their lives, they saw their theories ossify into an inflexible dogma, administered by self-confident and unbending presbyters. In 1890 Engels scathingly wrote to Lafargue: 'In the last two or three years numerous students, *littérateurs* and other *déclassé* young bourgeois have flocked into the party ... All these gentlemen profess Marxism, but of a kind ... about which Marx used to say: "In that case I know only that I am not a Marxist myself!" And Marx would probably have described these gentlemen in the words used by Heine of his own imitators: "I sowed dragons and reaped only fleas".[1] Yet a major part of the responsibility for this ossification of Marxism must fall upon Marx himself – with his intolerance of dissent, his authoritarian disposition, his general insistence that his followers cleave to the path of righteousness.

One such follower was Plekhanov (though Engels's strictures were obviously not meant to apply to a man of his stature). Marxism appealed to Plekhanov because of the breadth of its intellectual approach; both his Russian background and his temperament predisposed him to ready acceptance of the authoritarianism inherent in Marxist doctrine. Plekhanov, the first real Russian Marxist, became the very embodiment of orthodox Marxism.

In the Russian context 'orthodox Marxism', as opposed to the other schools of thought influenced by Marx, meant full agreement with the European interpretation of Marxism, the denial of a specifically Russian path to socialism, the acknowledgment of the universality of the Western historical pattern and the inevitability of capitalist development and bourgeois revolution as preconditions for the eventual proletarian revolution. It was a genuinely revolutionary doctrine – as opposed to later revisionist glosses violently denounced by Plekhanov and the orthodox – but it set its face firmly against 'unscientific' and 'adventurist' trends like Populism, which could only delay the growth of a true working-class socialist movement. As a backward peasant country with hardly any proletariat to speak of, Russia was again relegated to her proper place in the scheme of things, well behind the advanced industrialized nations of the West. Revolution would come, but only when the conditions formulated by Marx were ripe for it. Meanwhile Marxists would work to prepare for the day – primarily by propagating their views as widely as possible.

Plekhanov's importance in Russian history has probably been overrated. It is deliberately magnified by official Soviet historiography, which builds him up as the vital link between Marx and Lenin. His actual achievements, though considerable, should be viewed realistically. He translated many of the works of Marx and Engels and thus made them accessible (somewhat later) to the Russian public. He was himself an important and internationally recognized Marxist theoretician – in other words, a leading exegetist of orthodox Marxism. Some of his books represent significant contributions to Marxist theory. He combined great erudition with brilliant intelligence and a scholarly mind. But similar statements could be made of others in that Golden Age of Marxism around the turn of the century: Plekhanov's claim to lasting greatness rests essentially on the role he played in the development of a Marxist revolutionary movement in Russia.

Plekhanov was the first to undertake a systematic Marxist analysis of the situation in Russia. He conducted it in strictly orthodox terms; Russia, he believed, had already stepped on to the capitalist road, and there was no sense in pretending otherwise. History could not be turned back: its laws applied to Russia no less than to any other country. He did not adapt Marxism to Russia, because he did not think that it could be or should be adapted to suit any particular set of circumstances – immutable social laws could not be bent to serve one's convenience – but neither did he tamper with the evidence. What Plekhanov did was to arrange all the relevant facts in their proper Marxist configuration, and fit Russia's social development securely into the Marxist pattern. In this he succeeded superlatively well. Plekhanov's analysis provided Lenin and the Bolsheviks with the general *theoretical* framework indispensable for their activities; they were never to abandon or even modify it to any significant degree, regardless of the stormy vicissitudes of politics. That is the measure of Plekhanov's success. And of his failure – for as the years passed and his view of Russian society gained ever wider acceptance he began increasingly to doubt the applicability of the Marxist method to the Russian past, or, for that matter, the future.

Plekhanov's career as a practical politician is marked by the same ambiguity. He founded the first Russian Marxist group properly to be so called, but it hardly amounted to anything in terms of real influence; other, roughly contemporaneous Marxist groups were far more important, but it was Plekhanov's which was later chosen to be lifted from obscurity by the men who were his bitterest political enemies; he presided over the formation of a united Russian socialist party – only to see it being immediately torn asunder, and to stand aloof from the internecine strife; he cut a great figure at meetings of international socialist organizations, but he never had the backing of a national party of his own. His life ended on a note of the utmost tragedy, as a man once again hounded out of his country – only this time by his own pupils, by Lenin, who had seized power a few months before his death and established a system embodying every principle which he abhorred and against which he had warned, yet professing to be constructed on the basis of Plekhanov's own writings. Like Herzen, Plekhanov realized the truth too late.

In the 1880s Plekhanov was convinced that he had found the truth at last. Marx, he knew, was against applying Marxism to Russia. That made matters rather difficult. It may have been only a coincidence, but Plekhanov formed his group, the 'Emancipation of Labour', devoted specifically to this purpose, a few months after Marx's death, in September 1883. The printed notice of the formation of the group and of its publishing enterprise, the Library of Contemporary Socialism, was sent to Engels by Vera Zasulich, together with a letter in which she asked Marx's literary executor for the privilege of publishing the second volume of *Capital*. Engels sent a decidedly cold reply. The political situation in Russia, he informed Zasulich, was now such that the crisis could come at any day. 'I even believe it probable that Russia will achieve freedom of the press earlier than Germany.' In these circumstances the coveted right should belong to Lopatin, who had translated part of the first volume.[2] The clear implications of Engels's letter, its scorn for a fruitless Marxist propaganda venture undertaken on the eve of a real revolution and its open preference for *Narodnaya Volya*, were hardly lost upon Plekhanov. Engels made no other reference to the momentous occasion of the formation of the first Russian Marxist group, apart from a jocular remark, in a letter to Eduard Bernstein written the same day, about poor old Lavrov's chagrin at having lost yet another batch of disciples. Otherwise Engels took no cognizance of the Emancipation of Labour: instead, he continued to cultivate his relationships with the Populists.

One must admire the fortitude with which Plekhanov, rudely cold-shouldered by Marx's acknowledged successor, persevered in his thankless task of bringing Marxism to Russia. At its inception the Emancipation of Labour group numbered only five members: Plekhanov himself, Pavel Axelrod, Vera Zasulich, Lev Deutsch and Vasily Ignatov. Within two years its strength was cut down to three: Ignatov died, and Deutsch was arrested in Germany and extradited to Russia. For the next decade it was these three people – in practical terms, Plekhanov and Axelrod alone – who represented what there was of Russian orthodox Marxism. They translated and published the works of Marx and Engels, wrote books and pamphlets of their own. Despite all the rebuffs they were convinced that some day their labours would bear fruit. And they were right.

Plekhanov saw as his first object the refutation of Populism and of the whole concept of a specifically Russian path to socialism. Events, he was convinced, had already proved the fallaciousness of this idea: capitalism had come to Russia, and its development could not be stopped. Nor should it be stopped, even if this were possible, for without capitalism there could be no proletarian revolution. 'Plekhanov's mission – as he conceived it – consisted in carrying out in Russia the fundamental task Marx had accomplished some decades earlier in the West: to effect a transformation of socialism, shifting it from a "Utopian" to a "scientific" basis.'[3]

Narodnaya Volya was in its death-throes, and however deeply Plekhanov, watching its agony from afar, sympathized with his old comrades, he felt he owed a duty to the revolutionary movement that transcended sentiment or personal attachments. The revolution had to be resurrected, and this could be achieved only on the basis of an entirely new approach. Plekhanov's conversion to Marxism, and with it, to political activity, had led to a temporary reconciliation with the remnants of *Narodnaya Volya*. For a time, after the dissolution of *Chernyi Peredel*, the two groups were even planning the joint publication of a new journal called *Vestnik Narodnoi Voli* (Courier of *Narodnaya Volya*). Its editor was to be Lev Tikhomirov, the most uncompromising of the 'politicals' and the last member of the original Executive Committee to remain at large. Plekhanov prepared a long article for the journal's first issue: a detailed and outspokenly Marxist critique of the theory and practice of Populism. Though never noted for his own generosity to dissenters, Plekhanov expected the piece to be published as a legitimate contribution to an important debate. Tikhomirov, supported by Lavrov and a few others, regarded it as little short of treachery towards the memory of their martyrs. The article was rejected – the rift had become complete and final. Shortly afterwards Plekhanov brought it out, under the title *Socialism and Political Struggle*, as a separate pamphlet, the first in his Library of Contemporary Socialism.[4]

Socialism and Political Struggle opened the second of the great debates between Populism and Marxism – only this time, unlike the encounter between Engels and Tkachev, the Marxist case was presented by a Russian. The second round was remarkably similar to the first; what Plekhanov lacked in authority and self-assurance he made up for in better knowledge of Russian reality. Everything Engels had written was now confirmed by practical experience. Populism had been proved wrong: both its classical variety, which denied the role of the State and the importance of politics and saw the revolution purely as a social and economic upheaval (a view which, Plekhanov admitted, he had himself shared), and the Jacobin school of *Narodnaya Volya*, with its exclusive concentration on the seizure of political power. The fatal weakness inherent in both main trends of Populism was their lack of a comprehensive theory of society. This had led them to idealize certain superficial features of Russian life, to romanticize the idea of instant insurgency – and to sustain repeated heavy defeats.

'There can be no revolutionary movement without a revolutionary theory,' wrote Plekhanov. And the only scientific theory of revolution was that discovered by Marx and Engels. Surely by now it should be clear to all that Marx's laws of economic development applied to Russia just as much as to any other part of the world! True, Plekhanov still allowed for the possibility that Russia might not have to undergo *all* the phases of capitalist development, that some Russian peculiarities were not incompatible with the general Marxist scheme; he even quoted Marx and Engels, in their new Preface to the *Communist Manifesto*, to show that, given the support of a proletarian revolution in the West, the village commune *might* provide the Russian path to socialism (he could hardly do less). These slight concessions to his pre-Marxist past were soon eliminated by Plekhanov, and his later writings revealed no flaws in the immaculateness of the Marxist orthodoxy. But even in this earliest Marxist work Plekhanov unequivocally declared that 'Russian revolutionaries must accept the point of view of Western social-democracy and make a complete break with "insurgency" theories.'

Socialism and Political Struggle was not an abstract theoretical exercise but a revolutionary tract, and Plekhanov's central argument concerned the conditions for a successful revolution. We have always, he wrote, exaggerated our own strength and underestimated the enemy's power of resistance. The time had come to say point-blank that there could be no socialist revolution in Russia in the foreseeable future. Russia's social and economic development had lagged far behind that of the West, and it was ridiculous even to think that she could suddenly outdistance Europe and reach socialism ahead of the West. 'The socialist organization of production presupposes a type of economic relationship which would make this organization the logical conclusion of the country's whole preceding development ... In present-day Russia the objective social conditions of production are as yet insufficiently developed for socialist organization.' Until the conditions necessary for socialist revolution matured within the body of Russian society the revolutionaries' task would consist of expediting this process and eliminating the obstacles in its path, 'and not of inventing socialist experiments and vivisections, the outcome of which is always highly uncertain, to say the least'.

A bleak outlook for an ardent young revolutionary. But what was the alternative? The seizure of power by a revolutionary government and the introduction of socialism by decree, as envisaged by *Narodnaya Volya*? Plekhanov dismissed the idea as 'fantasy'. Such a government, were it ever to be established, would no doubt represent itself as the dictatorship of the working class. 'But the dictatorship of a class is as remote from the dictatorship of a group of *raznochinets* revolutionaries as heaven is from earth.' A dictatorship of the proletariat can only be brought about by a highly developed and politically experienced working class, liberated from ancient prejudices, educated in socialist ideas and conscious of its own power. 'But *such* a proletariat would obviously *never permit* the seizure of power even by the sincerest of well-wishers ... A proletariat which has understood the conditions necessary for its emancipation and achieved the requisite maturity will take state power into its own hands.'

Plekhanov did not, either then or at any later time, even try to explain how this consummation was to come about, how the proletariat would succeed in operating its dictatorship *by the class as a whole*, without allowing power to be exercised by individuals – as power has been exercised, in one way or another, in every known type of polity. Not only did he not face the issue – he simply refused to recognize its existence. The laws of history were to take their course, and when conditions were ripe a proletarian revolution would take place, establish its dictatorship and proceed to create a classless society. That, as far as he was concerned, was the end of it. In actual fact, of course, it was not: Plekhanov had merely set a conundrum which neither he nor any of his followers was able to solve. To be fair to Plekhanov, the same lofty approach to practical problems of power and administration under the new order had been taken by Marx and Engels. Lavrov and Tkachev, for all their theoretical limitations, at least discerned the possible importance of the human factor in the running of the revolutionary government: Marxism has never been able to come to terms with this very unscientific consideration.

Yet Plekhanov did possess a strangely prophetic insight into the nature of the Russian revolution that was denied Marx and Engels, for all their superior intellectual equipment. In *Socialism and Political Struggle* he first voiced an apprehension which, however implausible he found it, he was to repeat several times in the course of the years. What would happen, he asked, if a small revolutionary group did, contrary to all expectations, actually seize and retain power? Two possibilities were open: 'Either it will have to stand by, helplessly watching the gradual decay of the "economic equality" it had established, or it will be compelled to *organize* national production.' The revolutionary government would be more likely to choose the second path. In that case, because of Russia's backwardness, 'it will have to seek salvation in the ideals of a "patriarchal and authoritarian communism", the only modification of these ideals being that national production will be managed, not by the Peruvian "Sons of the Sun" and their officials, but by a socialist caste.' But no – Plekhanov immediately cast off the horrifying vision: the Russian people even in their present state would not stand for 'Inca communism', and such a thing was patently impossible anywhere in the enlightened nineteenth century or the even more highly civilized twentieth century. There was nothing for it but the hard slog of fighting for political freedom within a bourgeois system and educating the proletariat for a proper socialist revolution.

Plekhanov probably intended to provoke a general debate that would settle, once and for all (on a theoretical level), the vexed question of Russia's future social and revolutionary development. He did not have to wait long. A few months later Tikhomirov published a lengthy pamphlet, *What Do We Expect of the Revolution?*, strongly attacking Plekhanov's Marxist interpretation of Russian reality. In 1885 Plekhanov replied with a full-scale book, *Our Differences*, perhaps his most important and original contribution to the Marxist cause.[5] Russian Marxism should, properly speaking, be dated from the appearance of *Our Differences* rather than the formation of the Emancipation of Labour group. The book contained every essential aspect of the Marxist case as it was to be argued (by all factions) over the next thirty years; there was very little, apart from detail, that Lenin and other later luminaries could add to Plekhanov's theoretical analysis. Lenin himself always generously acknowledged his movement's profound debt to Plekhanov's pioneering work; to this day *Our Differences* is enshrined in the Soviet Union as the foundation-stone of Russian Marxism.

The debate between Plekhanov and Tikhomirov is generally regarded as marking the decisive, if not the final victory of

Marxism over Populism. This judgment is correct, in a certain sense – in the same sense in which it can be said that Engels had defeated Tkachev ten years earlier. The debate followed the main lines of the Engels – Tkachev polemic: it covered roughly the same ground, and the opponents used arguments very similar to those of their predecessors. The resemblance was deliberately heightened by Plekhanov's copious use of quotations from *Soziales in Russland*. The antagonists, though rather lesser men than the original pair, were both powerful polemicists, fully conversant with the matter under debate. They had the advantage of being able to draw fresh arguments from another decade of Russian development, especially eventful in the revolutionary field. And at the end of the day the verdict must be the same: Plekhanov won the (theoretical) debate with flying colours, but, in the long run, lost the argument. For all his erudition Plekhanov proved quite wrong in every prediction concerning Russia's future. Tikhomirov was the better forecaster. But legend, not fact, is the stuff of much of twentieth-century history, and legend has it that, just as Marxism was finally triumphant in Russia, so along the road Plekhanov won a famous victory over the Populists.

Our Differences set out to prove that Russian history was subject to the universal Marxist laws, and that capitalism was developing in Russia just as it had developed earlier in the West. The Populist assumptions about the *obshchina* leading directly to socialism were fallacious. Plekhanov examined the evolution of the basic Populist ideas through the writings of Herzen, Chernyshevsky and Bakunin. He did not think much of any of them except Chernyshevsky (neither had Marx), but even Chernyshevsky, despite his great merits, had been wrong on the main issues. Then he came to Tkachev. In essence, the whole of Plekhanov's argument was conducted against Tkachev and Russian 'Blanquism'. The Populist propagandists, or classical Populists, no longer presented a serious ideological challenge: they had either faded away, or gone over to Marxism (like Plekhanov himself) or ceased being revolutionary. Tkachevism was another matter. Plekhanov, with the acute political perception which made him such a formidable figure, had seen that Tkachev was the crucial link between the old and the new Populism; that this man – derided by all, living in isolation, lacking any organized following – had had a decisive impact upon the young 'politicals', in particular on *Narodnaya Volya*. Unlike later historians, bemused by years of ideological hair-splitting, Plekhanov recognized Tkachevism as the theoretical creed of *Narodnaya Volya*.

'The literary activity of *Narodnaya Volya*,' he wrote, 'consists of reiterating, with various modulations, the teachings of Tkachev. The only difference is that Tkachev placed "the present critical moment" in the early seventies, while the writers of *Narodnaya Volya* locate it in the late seventies – early eighties. Russian Blanquism, completely lacking in what the Germans call "historical sense", has been shifting and will, with the greatest of ease, go on shifting its idea of a "moment" specially propitious for the social revolution, from one decade to another. Having been proved a false prophet in the eighties, it will stubbornly renew its prophecies in ten, or twenty, or thirty years' time.' In the light of later events this last statement of Plekhanov's can hardly be called a false prophecy.

Plekhanov was likewise right in discerning, as the central and most distinctive tenet of the *narodovolets* programme, not political terrorism but the seizure of political power. That was what made it so attractive: it combined the traditional Populist belief in a special Russian path to socialism with acceptance of the need for political action and with a clear-cut concept of revolution. Why, even Lavrov, the erstwhile determined foe of Blanquism, was now standing shoulder to shoulder with Tikhomirov – and Plekhanov got a lot of fun out of quoting, with a great show of approbation, from Lavrov's long-ago philippics against Tkachev. That was why Populism in its new, political incarnation could only be refuted by Marxism, which possessed most of its attractions, together with the added advantage of a solid 'scientific' base.

Plekhanov took up Tikhomirov's challenge on the three central issues facing the Russian revolutionary movement. The first was the question of whether capitalism was an historically progressive force, a universally necessary precondition of the socialist revolution. Tikhomirov had flatly denied this:

> With regard to the development of large-scale production one is entitled to doubt whether the paths of history to date have been the best possible and the only possible ones for all nations and all times ... It is quite true that in the history of certain European nations capitalism, having created a multitude of evils and misfortunes, has also among its consequences brought forth something good, namely large-scale production, which has to some degree prepared the ground for socialism. But from this it by no means follows that other countries, such as Russia, might not find other ways for the development of large-scale production ... Everything leads one to the conclusion that the method of collectivizing labour invented by capitalism is one of the worst methods imaginable: while on the one hand it did in many respects prepare the ground for a possible socialist system, its other aspects considerably retard the coming of socialism.

Such statements were fairly easy to refute for a well-read Marxist – in theoretical terms, of course. Marx and Engels, explained Plekhanov patiently, had proved beyond the shadow of a doubt that capitalism, for all its evils (and who had done more to expose its evils than they?), was an historically progressive force. Not only because it established industries, built railways and furrowed the oceans with its steamships, not even because it replaced an antiquated and obsolete feudal system, but above all because it was the indispensable precursor of socialism. The preconditions for socialism could mature only within a capitalist order. Plekhanov's case was skilfully argued, and illustrated with numerous historical examples and quotations from the *Communist Manifesto* and other Marxist writings. Naturally, he continued, history does not repeat itself, and the development of capitalism and the triumph of socialism in Russia would not be simple repetitions of similar processes elsewhere. For one thing, a proletarian revolution in England or France would greatly shorten the reign of capitalism throughout the civilized world. 'But all that belongs to the future, removed from us by a more or less lengthy period of time in the course of which our capitalism can become and, as we see, is already becoming the omnipotent ruler of Russia.'

This last was the crux of Plekhanov's argument. Anyone could say that capitalism played an historically progressive role: the obvious answer was that such a role remained strictly limited to the West, where capitalism actually existed. Tikhomirov had poured scorn on all those who believed that 'in order to create the material conditions for the possibility of a socialist system Russia is obliged to pass through the stage of capitalism'. The time-honoured Populist case could be demolished only by proving that capitalism already was the dominant force in Russia's economic and social life. This Plekhanov now proceeded to do. Must Russia go through the school of capitalism? he asked. Step by step, using every piece of available evidence, citing statistical handbooks, governmental legislation, sociological surveys and official publications (though bemoaning the absence of anything like the English Blue Books that had made Marx's task so much easier than his own), Plekhanov showed that capitalism had already taken root in the Russian economy. Tikhomirov had himself stated that there were 800,000 industrial workers in Russia; although Plekhanov believed the real figure to be much higher he was ready to accept Tikhomirov's statistic as proof that the creation of an industrial proletariat had passed the point of no return. He compiled quite an impressive picture of the growth of Russian industrial production – predominantly in textile manufacturing, but with a healthy start being made in heavy industry. As for the village commune, that repository of Populist hopes, Plekhanov had become convinced that it was already well on the way to disintegration, under the inexorable pressure of the profit motive and of new agricultural techniques. The principle of the regular redistribution of land was increasingly falling into abeyance and communal land passing into *de facto* private ownership.

'If, having said all this,' concluded Plekhanov, 'we were to ask once again: "Will Russia pass through the school of capitalism?", our unhesitating answer would be another question: Why should she not complete a school which she is *already attending?*' Capitalism, in short, had come to stay, and it was futile to argue about the possibilities of avoiding or by-passing it.

Plekhanov's facts (allowing for the imperfection of Russian statistics) were essentially correct. So too, as the ensuing thirty years proved, were his predictions regarding rapid industrial progress and the development of rural property relationships. Yet there was a crucial flaw in his argument, deriving from the overoptimistic economic determinism typical of almost all post-Marxian Marxists and especially of Plekhanov. History would have to run its course: the material means of production would develop, and as a result feudalism would be supplanted by capitalism, the peasantry and petty bourgeoisie become proletarianized, old social patterns and ways of thought be destroyed and replaced by proletarian class-consciousness, etc. That was what had occurred in the West, the homeland of the industrial society, and since industrialization was being carried out in Russia by the same methods, with the use of the technology and machinery perfected in the West, it stood to reason that the results would also be the same. In our time this very idea has been widely propagated – with far less justification, and by non-Marxists at that – as the doctrine of 'convergence', the idea that any industrial society is much the same as any other. What matters is the fact of industrialization. But that is not how things happen in the real, as opposed to the theoretical, world. For one thing, Russia had never known the feudal order: over the centuries she had evolved a social structure and a system of institutions peculiarly her own and to which Western criteria did not necessarily apply; she had a considerable experience in refashioning Western acquisitions and adjusting them to her own unique character. Plekhanov came to understand this better in later years, but Tkachev and his followers, limited though their outlook may have been, had an instinctive awareness of the great distance separating their country from the European model.

The future of Russia, Plekhanov firmly declared, would bring 'first of all the triumph of the bourgeoisie and the beginning of the political and economic emancipation of the working class'. That was not how Tikhomirov saw it. His analysis of the Russian social structure, and hence of the coming revolution, was practically identical with Tkachev's: 'Our supreme authority, according to popular belief, is representative of the whole people, and not just of some social class. The Tsars' power has been maintained only due to the steadfastness of this conviction.' The transition from the idea of the sovereignty of the Tsar to that of the people would not be too difficult to effect. In France, Tikhomirov continued, the people had gone on directly from an absolute monarchy to the concept of the *peuple souverain*, but the actual implementation of popular sovereignty had been prevented by the existence of a well-entrenched bourgeoisie. Russia had no bourgeoisie, and therefore nothing could thwart the triumph of the revolution – 'unless autocracy survives long enough for the bourgeoisie to acquire sufficient strength for the reorganization of all our production along capitalist lines'. The contingency was fairly unlikely: 'Russia in her present chaotic state can hardly wait until the bourgeoisie constitutes itself into a force capable of reducing this chaos to some order, even a bourgeois order. . . . If the present system collapses before this happens then the bourgeoisie has no chance of seizing political power.'

Plekhanov was at his most ironic in dealing with Tikhomirov's unscientific flights of fancy. He could not help pitying a person so blinded by his obsessions as actually to believe that the victory of socialism was easier in backward, semi-Asiatic Russia than in the developed, capitalist West. 'The subjects of the Persian Shah, the Egyptian Khedive and the Chinese Emperor have the same absurd notions about their supreme authority as the Russian peasants. Does it follow then that the Persians, the Egyptians and the Chinese will go over with the same ease to the "concept of the *peuple souverain*"? If so, then the further Eastward we move the nearer we come to popular sovereignty.'

Irony is a dangerous weapon: it can play strange tricks with those who use it. Plekhanov thought that by his *reductio ad absurdum* he had exposed the utter preposterousness of Tikhomirov's ideas. In reality the joke was on him. However ridiculous this may have sounded in the ordered, rational, European world in which Marxism was born and flourished, Plekhanov's mock forecast has come true, almost to the letter: it is the subjects of the Russian Tsar, the Chinese Emperor, the Egyptian Khedive, and of sundry other Asiatic potentates, who have established socialist systems on one or another Marxist model – while the industrial proletariat of the West lost any revolutionary spirit it may once have possessed.

In the final argument, concerning the feasibility and probable outcome of a revolutionary coup, 'science' was once again opposed to 'intuition'. Tikhomirov had written: 'There can be no doubt that what determines the question of the seizure of power by any revolutionary force is, above all, whether the existing government is sufficiently disorganized, debilitated and unpopular. If all these conditions exist then a coup d'état presents nothing impossible or even particularly difficult.' The seizure of power by the revolutionary party, Tikhomirov concluded, would become the starting-point for the 'socialist organization of Russia'.

To Plekhanov's mind this was not just nonsense but dangerous nonsense. The Blanquist coup envisaged by Tikhomirov would be a travesty of a real socialist revolution. No Marxist could have anything to do with such a thing: 'The social-democrat wants the worker *to make* his revolution himself; the Blanquist requires the worker *to support* a revolution begun and led on his behalf and in his name by others.' Tikhomirov had promised that the provisional revolutionary government would not cling on to power but, after expropriating all large-scale property, would hand it over to a freely elected popular assembly, which could then determine policy in accordance with the people's expressed wishes. Plekhanov, orthodox Marxist that he was, rejected the possibility of a minority coup with a democratic dénouement. Were the revolution to take place while Russia still remained a backward peasant nation, the 'people', i.e. the peasantry, though warmly welcoming the confiscation of landlords' estates, would certainly not vote in favour of introducing a communist economic system. Instead they would happily settle down to private farming, to extracting the maximum profit, to exploiting each other, and to a new pattern of inequality. No revolutionary government could allow this to happen, and therefore, lacking a mass working-class base, it would have to retain dictatorial control. And once again Plekhanov saw the realization of this disturbing vision: 'Once accomplished, the revolution could result in a political monstrosity similar to the ancient Chinese or Peruvian empires, or in other words in a renovated Tsarist despotism with a communist lining.' Whichever way one looked at it, therefore, socialism could only be established by the proletariat – the product and the eventual master of collectivized industrial production.

Looking back at the great debate between Marxism and Populism from the vantage-point of the present day we can see that, as so often happens, both sides were proved right, each in their own peculiar way. The two prophecies merged together in 1917. But at the time there seemed little doubt as to the winner. Tikhomirov's emotional appeal to an heroic tradition and an ineffectual faith was no match for Plekhanov's cold logic and 'scientific' analysis. Populist theory was demolished. Or so it appeared on the surface.

Curiously enough, *Our Differences* was least appreciated in the quarter where it might have been expected to arouse the greatest enthusiasm. Engels had shown no interest in the activities of the Russian Marxists, and Plekhanov could hardly have expected him to give the book his stamp of approval. The usual haughty and aloof Plekhanov was frankly terrified of Engels. The two men had no direct contact before a brief meeting in 1889; it was only another four years later that

Plekhanov plucked up the courage to open a correspondence – invariably addressing Engels as 'Dear Teacher', until the old man irritably told him to cut out the nonsense. In 1885, at the time of the publication of *Our Differences*, Plekhanov wistfully wrote to Axelrod: 'Never mind, don't give up – some day, I am sure, all will be well, and we shall travel together to London to report to the Chief [Engels].'[6] It all seemed a fairly remote hope then; Plekhanov did not even dare send Engels his book directly, but only through an intermediary in the person of Zasulich (whose great revolutionary reputation assured her easy access to Engels and other socialist leaders).

Engels's reaction to *Our Differences* was frigid, almost hostile; it must have surpassed poor Plekhanov's worst forebodings. His reply to Zasulich was an astonishing document – an outspoken defence of revolutionary pragmatism against the most hallowed precepts of Marxist theory.[7] It began with a cursory expression of his pride at seeing a Marxist party established among the revolutionary youth of Russia. Then, in considerable detail, it explained why Engels was giving his wholehearted support to the adversaries of this party.

Marx's theory of history, wrote Engels, provided the cardinal means for discovering the correct revolutionary tactic. This should be done by applying the theory to the concrete economic and political circumstances of any given country. Naturally, to find the solution one should be familiar with all these circumstances: 'As for me, I know too little about the present situation in Russia to set myself up as a competent judge of specific questions of the tactics to be followed there at any particular moment.' Nor, continued Engels, was he *au fait* with the policies of the revolutionary party – he had had hardly any information about this from any of his Russian friends for many years. Though the last assertion was not, strictly speaking, true, Engels's cautious attitude could well have been excused by an understandable reluctance to become embroiled in Russian émigré quarrels. Yet, having made his disclaimer, Engels immediately plunged into an impassioned harangue on the unique opportunity presented to Russia by history, a harangue that left no doubt as to his views on the Russian revolution:

> Everything that I know or think I know about the situation in Russia leads me to believe that the Russians are approaching their 1789: the revolution *must* break out within a definite period of time, but it *might* break out any day. In these circumstances the country is like a charged grenade which only requires a fuse to set it off. Especially since 13 March [1 March 1881 old style: the assassination of Alexander II]. This is one of those exceptional cases when a handful of people can *make* a revolution. In other words, by a small push they can bring down a whole system which is at present barely maintaining an uncertain balance, . . . and by a single act, insignificant in itself, liberate explosive forces which it would then be impossible to tame. And if ever the Blanquist fantasy of convulsing an entire society by means of a small conspiracy had any chance of success then the place is undoubtedly Petersburg. Once the gunpowder is lit, once the forces are freed and the people's energy transformed from potential into kinetic . . . then the people who have lit the fuse will be thrown aside by the explosion, which will prove to be a thousand times stronger than they, and will seek egress for itself wherever it can, depending on the economic forces and resistances.

> Suppose these people believe that they can seize power. Well, what of it? Let them just make the breach which will destroy the dam – the flood will soon put an end to their illusions. But suppose these illusions will further strengthen their willpower: would that give us any cause for complaint? People who boast that they *have made* a revolution always realize the next day that they did not know what they were doing, that the revolution they *had made* was quite different from the one they intended to make. This is what Hegel called the irony of history, an

irony which few historical figures have managed to avoid . . .

In my opinion what Russia needs most is a jolt that would set the revolution off. Whether the signal is given by one or the other faction, whether this takes place under one or another flag – I attach little importance to all this. If it is a court conspiracy then it will be swept away the very next day. A country where the situation is so charged with tension; where revolutionary elements have accumulated to such a degree; where the economic conditions of the vast mass of the population become more and more intolerable every day; where every stage of social development is represented, from the primitive village commune to modern large-scale industry and moguls of finance; and where all these contradictions are forcibly repressed by a despotism that has no equals, a despotism that is becoming more and more intolerable to the youth, the embodiment of the nation's intelligence and dignity – when 1789 comes to such a country then 1793 will not be slow to follow.

Engels's letter of 23 April 1885 to Vera Zasulich is a key document towards understanding the development of revolutionary Marxism in the nineteenth and twentieth centuries. Yet it has never been accorded its rightful place; historians, for a variety of reasons, have evaded the issues it poses. It is never properly discussed even in specialist works devoted to the period in question or the personalities involved. Thus, the author of the first full-length biography of Plekhanov goes to considerable effort to steer clear of the letter: it is only mentioned in passing as having been 'notable for its ambivalence' (the last word, one would think, to describe Engels's trenchant observations), and not even vouchsafed the dignity of direct quotation.[8] Not that the letter itself is unknown to students of Marxism – sections of it are cited quite often, especially the passage dealing with the irony of history. It is the letter as a whole that remains ignored.

This studied disregard might be justified in the case of a fleeting *obiter dictum* – as it is, far too many elaborate theoretical edifices are constructed upon chance remarks of Marx or Engels – but in fact Engels was giving voice to views which he and Marx had held and expressed consistently since 1877. These were the mature conclusions of a man at the height of his intellectual powers.

Engels's statement carries far-reaching implications. Not only was it a deliberate rebuff to Plekhanov, it was a straightforward acceptance of Tkachev's Jacobin thesis, which had been the object of Engels's savage attack ten years before. Engels bluntly advocated a Blanquist coup as the best and the most likely solution to Russia's problems. An exquisite irony: the co-founder of Marxism vehemently defending Blanquism from its Marxist critics! Engels accepted every essential feature of the Jacobin and *narodovolets* outlook: the glorification of youth, the cult of willpower, the primacy of politics over economics, the advantages of backwardness. He went even further: it did not really matter, he said, who made the revolution and with what purpose. Russia was pregnant with revolution, and if theory was an obstacle to delivery then theory should be cast aside. Engels put it even more ruthlessly in private conversation: what Russia needed, he remarked in 1885, was 'not a programme but a revolution'.[9] Revolution always took precedence over theory with Marx and Engels, who loved to quote Goethe:

> Grau, teurer Freund, ist alle Theorie
> Und grün des Lebens goldner Baum.

(All theory, dear friend, is grey, but the golden tree of life springs ever green.)

Some authors believe that Engels desired a revolution in Russia merely because it would spark off a conflagration in the West.[10] Engels's letter to Zasulich gives no indication of any such thing; nor, with the single exception of the 'official' 1882 Preface to the *Communist Manifesto*, do any of his or Marx's remarks on Russia during this period. In 1885 Engels was not even concerned with the theoretical ramifications of the future of the *obshchina*. What did it matter? Only the revolution counted – that, and nothing else. If its leaders had the determination and strength to impose their will upon the revolution, well and good – if not, it would find its own ways, and what they were, no one could foretell. Let the revolution begin: that was all he desired.

Nearly forty years later Lenin, the man who had led the Russian revolution to victory, lay on his deathbed, drawing up the balance-sheet of his five years in power, surveying the achievements and follies of his revolution, ruminating on its unfathomable ways. An orthodox Marxist had just published a work criticizing him for having embarked on a revolution in a country manifestly unprepared for one – and the dying Lenin, in one of his last notes, replied by quoting Napoleon's maxim: *On s'engage et puis . . . on voit.* That was how he had done it, and that was how Engels had expected it to be done. In the light of Engels's letter to Zasulich, and of all his and Marx's remarks on the subject over a number of years, it is difficult to sustain the view that the Bolshevik revolution of 1917 was carried out in breach of the principles of Marxism.

However, by the time Lenin seized power Engels's 'insurrectionist' views had long been consigned to oblivion by a new generation of orthodox determinist Marxists, who preferred confidently to await the predestined fruits of revolution without having to go through its terrible stresses. Towards the end of his life Engels had himself reluctantly returned to more conventional doctrine. His enthusiasm for the Russian revolution gradually subsided. The harsh facts had to be faced: there was no revolutionary situation in Russia, and the revolutionary movement had been destroyed. From the mid-eighties Russia was quiescent as she had never been for thirty years. There was nothing left for Engels but to reconcile himself to yet another disappointment, the latest of so many. It took him several years to accept Plekhanov's Marxist thesis on the inevitability of a slow process of capitalist development for Russia; only in 1892 could he bring himself to write sadly to Danielson: 'I am afraid we shall now have to think of your *obshchina* as a dream of the irretrievable past, and base our future calculations on a capitalist Russia. We shall certainly thus have lost a great opportunity, but there is nothing one can do against the economic facts of life ... Whether we like them or not, these facts will remain in existence, and the sooner we discard our likes and dislikes the better able we will be to judge both the facts and their consequences ... I do not see how the results of the industrial revolution that is taking place before our eyes in Russia can be in any way different from what has happened or is happening in England, Germany, America ... Capitalist production is preparing its own doom, and you can be assured that it will be the same in Russia.'[11]

So convinced had Engels now become – to no small degree under the influence of Plekhanov's writings – of the inescapable nature of prolonged capitalist development for Russia that in 1894 he re-published the full text of his polemic against Tkachev, together with a Postscript in which he comfortably concluded that all his twenty-year-old arguments against the ideas of a Blanquist coup and of Russia achieving socialism earlier than the West had withstood the test of time (see p. 403). He had some explaining to do – it was sufficiently well known that in the intervening period he and Marx had undergone a change of heart. This Engels now attributed to the fact that in 1877 there had been two actual governments in Russia (a state of affairs, one might think, similar to that described in 1917 by Lenin as 'dual power'): the governments of the Tsar and the Executive Committee. The latter's power was growing daily, and there was good reason to expect a revolution at any moment. Hence the about-turn performed by Marx and Engels. Engels made no reference to his own recent Blanquist phase, when he had implicitly accepted Tkachev's analysis, and dismissed the *narodovoltsy* as brave but sadly misguided men: 'These people, who numbered only a few hundred, but who by their self-sacrifice and courage reduced Tsarist absolutism to a state where it already had to think about the possibility and the conditions of surrender – people like that will not be taken by us before a tribunal for believing their Russian nation to be the chosen people of the social revolution. But this does not by any means lead us to share their illusions. The time for chosen peoples is irrevocably past.'[12]

All that was now done with. Yet even though Engels had returned from his ideological wanderings back to rigid Marxist ground he retained some sentimental attachment to the faded hopes of yesteryear. To the end of his days he stubbornly refused to make public statements critical of contemporary Populism. Only a few months before his death in 1895 Engels politely but firmly told Plekhanov that he would not let himself be dragged into a dispute with Danielson, by then one of the Russian Marxists' chief opponents – indeed, till the last he maintained a friendly and prolific correspondence with Danielson.

Engels had changed: so, it seemed, had Russia herself. The eighties marked a definite break with the preceding decades. Twenty years of revolutionary upsurge had come to an end. The remaining members of *Narodnaya Volya* were relentlessly hunted down. The great revolutionary movement which had convulsed Russia for a generation was extinguished. Similar calamities had befallen it in the past and each time it had risen triumphant from the ashes. But this time liberal sympathizers inside Russia and émigrés abroad awaited a new resurrection in vain. Revolutionary Populism was dead.

There were a few half-hearted and amateurish attempts to re-establish the famous organization; the police had no difficulty in dealing with them. One of these ineffectual student conspiracies, aimed at assassinating Alexander III on the sixth anniversary of his father's death, has been enshrined in history for an entirely extraneous reason: among the names of the five executed plotters was that of Alexander Ulyanov, Lenin's elder brother.

Nothing symbolized the collapse of the old hopes more tellingly than the defection of Lev Tikhomirov himself. In 1888, after several years of tortured reappraisal, the former apostle of terrorism announced his break with the revolutionary movement and published a sensational pamphlet, 'Why I have ceased being a Revolutionary'. Tikhomirov appealed to the Emperor for a pardon and returned to Russia, where he became a successful Right-wing journalist. Though such a total conversion was comparatively rare, many other members of the intelligentsia turned away from their beliefs in despair. Almost all felt that their worst fear had come true. The revolution had missed the boat, and there was to be no second chance.

For the radical intelligentsia the future looked bleak indeed. A long period of reaction set in. The reign of Alexander III (1881–94) is generally regarded as one of the most retrogressive epochs of Russian history, comparable only to that of Nicholas I. A British historian by no means in sympathy with 'progressive' Russian intellectual trends has described it as follows: 'The main characteristics of the last two decades of the century, extending into the next reign and indeed up to the war with Japan in 1904, are stagnation in agriculture, progress in industry, retrogression in education, russification of the non-Russian half of the empire's population, and an overall attitude of nostalgic, obscurantist and narrowly bureaucratic paternalism.'[13]

The characterization can hardly be disputed. Nor is there any cause for surprise at such a course of events. The assassination of Alexander II, the Emancipator-Tsar, by a group of revolutionaries – an act without precedent in Russian history – came as a profound shock to almost all classes of the population. Reaction was inevitable. The new Emperor possessed a strong will and a firm purpose; though by no means unintelligent, he was also coarse and narrow-minded. It did not need much to convince him that the roots of the tragedy lay in the exaggerated pace of reforms, and that his divine mission was the restoration of order, the extirpation of sedition, and the revival of autocracy in all its ancient glory.

The man who set Alexander III upon the course from which he never wavered, and who dominated Russia for much of the next quarter-century, was Konstantin Petrovich Pobedonostsev, the Procurator of the Holy Synod. Pobedonostsev, in the words of one of Alexander Blok's most famous poems, was the magician who looked Russia in the eyes and put her to sleep. He was undoubtedly one of the outstanding statesmen of Imperial Russia, combining formidable intellectual powers and wide erudition with an almost fanatical religious faith and a visionary devotion to the ideals of Russian nationalism and the autocracy. Pobedonostsev became the most dangerous opponent that the revolutionary intelligentsia had yet encountered.

Russia, Pobedonostsev believed, had to be brought rapidly to her senses. The alternative was disaster. He had no illusions about the disaffection of most of the educated class; if anything, he tended to be thoroughly pessimistic regarding the rottenness of the whole of Russian society. Salvation could come only through a renewal of the mystical unity between a rejuvenated autocracy and an undefiled people. And salvation would have to come fairly soon if the seeds of sedition were not to take root. Pobedonostsev had no personal ambition; his sole care was the greatness of autocratic, Orthodox Russia; he never occupied the centre of the stage and preferred to remain in the shadow (the shadow that he himself cast over Russia, according to Blok). Reform was no antidote to revolution – that had been proved by bitter experience. The only way the sick country could be cured was by bringing the intelligentsia to heel and providing a new content to intellectual life.

The 'reaction' inspired by Pobedonostsev horrified contemporary public opinion. Today, with a wealth of rather sterner experience behind us, it is permissible to take a calmer view of the reign of Alexander III. By twentieth-century standards the reaction of the 1880s was a mild enough affair. There was nothing even faintly resembling a 'White Terror' (though this misleading phrase has sometimes been used to describe the 1880s); nobody was executed apart from proven regicides or plotters of regicide, nobody sent to gaol or into exile but actual members of illegal revolutionary conspiracies. But compared to the febrile liberalism of the preceding reign the new reality seemed immeasurably harsh.

Not surprisingly, Pobedonostsev's counter-offensive was aimed above all at the hotbed of sedition, the country's educational system. The enlightened University Statute of 1863 was abrogated and replaced by a new one, severely curtailing the autonomy of the universities. In June 1887 Delyanov, Minister of Education since October 1881, issued a notorious circular barring access to secondary education for 'children of coachmen, servants, cooks, washerwomen, small shopkeepers, and persons of a similar type', with the possible exception of children of unusual ability. To make the proscription more effective, secondary-school fees were substantially raised. It is difficult to discover the rationale behind this most obsessively retrograde of all the new government's measures: they wished to keep persons of humble origin as far as possible out of the universities, yet they knew only too well – Pobedonostsev made no secret of the fact in his own writings – that the great majority of the revolutionaries had come from 'good' social backgrounds. In the long run the new regulations had little practical effect, especially in view of the considerable expansion of primary education that was being simultaneously carried out: they served only to embitter the intelligentsia still further.

Reaction became the order of the day in all fields of public life. Local self-government bodies, which were just beginning to acquire a semblance of vitality, saw their activities restricted. Censorship became stricter and some liberal journals were closed down. Russification of the national minorities was stepped up and repressive measures taken against the Jews (antisemitic pogroms broke out here and there, with some loss of life, but these were quickly put down by the police, who had little liking for Jews but even less for spontaneous popular initiatives of any kind). The bureaucracy, the indestructible mainstay of autocratic Russia, though somewhat shaken by the reforms of Alexander II, was coming into its own again. A real autocrat was on the throne and all, it seemed, was well with Russia.

There were sounder reasons as well for the government's revived self-confidence. At long last the country was at peace with the world: Alexander III remains the only monarch in Russian history whose reign passed without foreign war of any kind. This unique circumstance was due more to the generally peaceful state of European politics than to the Emperor's personal qualities, but Alexander received the credit for it and became enshrined in the folk consciousness as the 'Tsar-Peacemaker'. Russia made the most of the welcome respite – it was during Alexander's reign that she took the first firm steps towards industrialization. Textiles remained the main industrial field, but heavy industry was fast catching up. The modern foundations of a powerful metallurgy were laid down, largely with the aid of Western capital, in and around the Donets basin in South Russia. Pig-iron production increased fivefold between 1887 and 1900, from 36 to 177 million *poods* (1 *pood* = 16.38 kg); during the same period coal production in the Donets basin alone jumped from 125 to 671 million *poods*. As in many other countries, a considerable impetus to heavy industrial growth was provided by railway construction, for which Russia's vast spaces promised limitless scope. After a rather hesitant start the promise began to be fulfilled in the 1890s: the total length of railway track grew from 10.7 thousand km in 1870 to 22.8 in 1880, 30.6 in 1890 and 53.2 thousand km in 1900.[14] To be sure, in these traditional fields of industry and transport Russia still had a long way to go before she could catch up with more advanced countries; when it came to completely new industries, where all started more or less from scratch, Russia showed that she was in a position even to forge ahead of the rest. Thus in the 1890s, thanks to the Baku oilfields, Russia became the world's second largest oil producer.

A significant feature of Russian industrial development, much remarked upon by Marxists, was the large size (by general European standards) of the average industrial enterprise, as reflected in the high level of concentration of labour. According to one authoritative calculation, the number of factories actually declined between 1879 and 1900, from 27,927 to 23,296, whereas their labour force increased from 690,000 to over two million. The average number of workers per factory grew from 25 to 90, the average output in roubles, from 32.5 to 130,000.[15] Whatever interpretation is placed upon these figures, they undoubtedly show that Russian manufacture had passed well out of the cottage stage and that an emerging modern industrial working class was being concentrated in both the old and the new centres of industry.

The old prophecies were coming true: the industrial revolution was producing an industrial proletariat. It is worthy of note that the authorities were far less perturbed by this development than the Populists, who stubbornly refused to face a changing reality. Russia was not a bourgeois country – she had remained an Oriental-style autocracy – and unlike, say, Britain, France or the United States during their respective industrial revolutions, the Russian State never became identified, even temporarily, with the interests of the newly enriched industrialists. All the Tsar's subjects were equal – not before the law, for no such concept could exist, but in the sight of the autocrat and his faithful servants. Indeed, some influential elements of the bureaucracy, most notably within the ranks of the political police, felt more in sympathy with the savagely exploited workers than with the *nouveaux riches*. A curious attitude, composed of varying strands: well-bred disdain for the *parvenu*; Slavophile notions of a mystical oneness between Tsar and people which was now in danger of being broken up by the intervention of capital; a prudent desire to limit, as far as was possible, the causes of popular discontent. It was to produce many bizarre twists of policy, complicated intrigues and counter-intrigues, in the last quarter-century of the Russian monarchy. An early and paradoxical result was the introduction in ultra-reactionary Russia of a system of labour legislation undoubtedly enlightened and even progressive by the standards of any other incipient industrial revolution. As early as 1882 the employment of children under twelve was prohibited and the work-day of those between twelve and fifteen limited to eight hours; the next few years saw laws on school attendance for adolescent workers and the prohibition of night work for women and adolescents. A great step was taken in July 1897 with the imposition of a maximum working day of eleven and a half hours for all workers, regardless of sex or age, and of ten hours for workers engaged in night work. To ensure compliance with the new legislation a factory inspectorate was established in the mid-1880s under the Ministry of Finance; the factory inspectors soon proved to be efficient and incorruptible – exemplars of the new type of bureaucrat gradually coming to the fore – and showed no hesitation in exposing abuses and overcoming the prevarication and opposition of the employers.

The idea that until the revolution of 1917 Russia lagged far behind the West in every respect (with the exception of literature and the arts) is by now widely and unquestionably accepted. Yet it is by no means true with regard to many spheres of life. Labour legislation is a case in point – here Russia's record compared quite favourably with that of other countries. Only Britain and Germany had more uniformly advanced laws. It should be remembered though that in Russia labour legislation began with the industrial revolution, whereas in England the first timid acts of State intervention came only after industrialization had been in full swing for decades. Even Germany, renowned for her Bismarckian enlightenment, came out worse in some areas; thus, night work for women was prohibited only in 1891. As for France, the ten-hour working day was only introduced in 1900 and the institution of factory inspectors (less effective in practice than their Russian counterparts) in 1883; the eight-hour work-day for children aged eight to twelve and twelve hours for those between twelve and sixteen had been prescribed in the 1840s but this remained a dead letter for much of the century. In the United States child labour from the age of ten was legal until the 1880s, while a work-day of ten to eleven hours was almost universal.

That the Russian government should have intervened energetically in codifying the labourers' rights at the very outset of the industrial revolution is deserving of attention, but not as any sign of particular virtue. It was part and parcel of the government's general policy with regard to industrial development. In Russia there could be no question of laissez-faire capitalism, of untrammelled private enterprise or free competition. As in every other process thoughout Russian history, the State was the dominant factor in industrialization.

The development of modern heavy industry was not only welcomed – it was encouraged, supported, impelled, in many important respects even controlled by the State. Industry grew behind a heavy wall of protective tariffs, nurtured by subventions and fiscal and other privileges. The Ministry of Finance had a finger in every entrepreneurial pie. Not only did it award lucrative contracts in accordance with its own plans and priorities; its officials possessed far-reaching powers of inspection, and it even initiated the establishment of syndicates and of industrialists' congresses – under the chairmanship of governmental representatives. Joint advisory bodies for various fields of industry, composed of officials and businessmen, were set up under the Ministry.

Russia was undergoing an industrialization of a new type, one which was to become predominant in the twentieth century: industrialization directed largely by the State and aimed not at private profit but at advancing the interests of the State, in other words at strengthening the country's political system and enhancing its military might. The English industrial revolution, the first in history, was the only one ever carried out on the basis of the pure principles of laissez-faire capitalism. Its imitators, who started off at the relatively high level of technology achieved by the British in a casual and unsystematic way, required greater resources, more planning and organization, and, in one way or another, some measure of State support. The later industrialization began the greater the degree of State intervention. Germany, one of the later but possibly the most successful of the industrialized nations, provides a striking example. But, as E. H. Carr has pointed out, 'in the incipient Russian industrial revolution of the eighteen-nineties a further stage was reached. The motive of industrialization was not private profit, but national interest; it was the work predominantly not of individual *entrepreneurs*, but of large units; the main impetus came not from the bourgeoisie, or from any sector of it, but from the State. The march of history had radically changed, and in some respects inverted, the original features of the industrial revolution.'[16] (This would apply equally to Japan, where the industrial revolution began roughly at the same time as in Russia.)

The policy of rapid industrialization in the name of *raison d'état* was consciously evolved and deliberately applied by the government; the credit for its inception and striking early successes belongs above all to Sergei Yulievich Witte, the brilliant administrator and far-sighted statesman who was Russia's Minister of Finance from 1892 to 1903 and who in 1905 became her first Prime Minister. Witte set out his views on the decisive role of the State in the country's social and economic development in his first budget report (1893): 'In the understanding of the Russian people the sincere conviction prevails that it is within the power of government authority to be concerned with everything touching the welfare and the needs of the people.'[17] Witte justified his policy of rapid industrialization – in the report 'On the Condition of our Industry', prepared for the Emperor in February 1900 – with the same arguments, almost in the same phrases as his Bolshevik successors some thirty years later:

International competition does not wait. If we do not take energetic and decisive measures so that in the course of the next decades our industry will be able to satisfy the needs of Russia and of the Asiatic countries which are – or should be – under our influence, then the rapidly growing foreign industries will break through our tariff barriers and establish themselves in our fatherland and in the Asiatic countries mentioned above and drive their roots into the depths of our economy. This may gradually clear the way also for triumphant political penetration by foreign powers . . . It is possible that the slow growth of our industries will endanger the fulfilment of the great political tasks of the monarchy. Our economic backwardness may lead to political and cultural backwardness as well.[18]

The achievement of pre-revolutionary Russian industrialization was impressive by any yardstick. During eighteen of the last twenty-five years before the outbreak of war Russia showed the highest rate of industrial growth in the world. In 1913 she was already overtaking France as the world's fourth industrial Power – twenty years earlier her industrial production had been only one-third that of France. Russia was rapidly catching up with the rest of the world. Everything, it seemed, was changing. But in fact industrial development, far from strengthening the autocracy, served to cast a merciless light upon its fundamental weaknesses. The contrast between twentieth-century industry and seventeenth-century political and social institutions could hardly be more glaring. Underneath the bustle of an industrializing society the old Russia remained essentially unchanged. It assimilated industrialization as earlier it had assimilated the reforms of Alexander II, and even earlier, the innovations of Peter the Great. Russia was still in the grip of her past, as firmly as ever. Kliuchevsky pointed this out in his 1904 speech: few paid any attention.

The position remained much as it had been a century before, in Speransky's time. Autocracy was still the country's sole political institution, the omnipotent State her only political tradition. To this had been added the idea of revolution as the single possible method of political opposition. The social structure remained inchoate and fragmentary: the State allowed for no limitations on its absolute powers. Thus the glittering surface of Imperial Russia concealed a gaping void. The stability embodied by the autocrat had disappeared. Peasant emancipation had meant the irrevocable passing of the old social order. No substitute had been created.

The State was the Emperor, and, just as for centuries past, it was the Emperor's character and outlook that determined the direction of the nation's development. The liberal Alexander II was followed by the reactionary Alexander III, and a great opportunity was lost. Alexander III thought it would be sufficient to stop the clock and set it back a little. In another age this might have worked, but time was quickening as the world stepped into the twentieth century. Russia could not opt out. If she wanted to survive as a Great Power she had to modernize herself. Industrialization was not enough – Witte's vision proved too limited. Two alternatives stood before Russia: either a sweeping transformation along West European lines, or the invention of an entirely new system adaptable to the needs of a modern industrial society. The Tsars failed to do the first; others were waiting in the wings to attempt the second.

The reign of Alexander III was a period of reaction pure and simple. Pobedonostsev erected the idea of negation into a basic political principle: the spread of revolutionary ideas was to be stopped by administrative action. Pobedonostsev and his colleagues believed that in due course public life would be 'purified' and a healthier atmosphere created. Nothing much was done towards attaining this aim, and it seems highly unlikely that Pobedonostsev could have succeeded in turning the revolutionary tide back even had his royal master reigned as long as any of the last three Emperors. In the event, Alexander III died after only thirteen years of rule, in 1894, unexpectedly, at the age of forty-nine. His successor, the Tsarevich Nicholas, was known to be weak of character and limited in his grasp of affairs. He did his best to maintain his father's policies, but that best was no longer good enough. An infirm hand was guiding the Russian ship of State during the most critical period of its history.

Time had been lost, with nothing to show for it. The government had failed to come up with a single political idea around which public opinion could be rallied. And now that the period of immobility was drawing to a close it became clear that the radical forces had survived in far better shape than expected. They had merely gone to ground and given up overt propaganda; when they re-emerged it was in circumstances more favourable than those of 1881. A new generation of intelligentsia had grown up, ignorant of the turmoil of the 1870s, contemptuous of the regime, eager to take over the struggle from their elders. The shrewder members of Pobedonostsev's circle had no illusions as to the extent of their failure. Tikhomirov poured his despair into his diary upon hearing that the Emperor was dying:

> Terrible sadness . . . God is depriving us of this firm hand at such a decisive yet indeterminate moment! In the past thirteen years everything quietened down and became permeated with confidence in the stability of the existing order. Its enemies had to reconcile themselves to the hopelessness of any idea of overthrowing it. During the last five or six years something new has even begun to grow. But these are tiny growths as yet, and it will be easy to destroy them.
>
> Had the Emperor lived for another ten years he would have created an epoch in Russian history. But now?
>
> I can't expect anything good. Russia has made bad use of the time she had. But, without complaining, I must still say in all fairness that this time granted to Russia was terribly short, far too short . . .
>
> There is nothing to be seen on the horizon: neither talents nor leaders, not a single figure about whom it would be possible to say: here is a centre for uniting our forces. On the other hand, the remnants of the past – of the liberal revolutionary past – have survived these thirteen years, quietly and without victories, but with their closed ranks and strict discipline having preserved all their positions, preserved even the men, the establishments, the banners around which whole armies could be raised tomorrow.[19]

Tikhomirov was describing, not some hypothetical future but the new reality about him. The placidity of which he wrote had begun to disappear even before the death of Alexander III.

In 1891 the crops failed over large areas of European Russia. Famine set in, then cholera. Such calamities were by no means unknown in Russia, but nothing on the scale of 1891–2 had ever happened within living memory. Half a million people died, possibly more. Russian society was profoundly shocked – or rather, ashamed that such an uncivilized, uncultured thing could happen in their country, before the eyes of the whole world, in the last decade of the rational and scientific nineteenth century. The government evoked general disgust by its incompetence and its inability to control the spread of the disaster or to organize proper relief work.

The harvest failure of 1891 had several important consequences. It inflicted a heavy blow to the self-confidence of the authorities, so recently and so laboriously restored, and made the bureaucracy into a figure of fun. It rejuvenated the *Zemstvos* and enabled the intelligentsia, quite legitimately, to set up a network of voluntary charitable associations for combating the disaster – the authorities, having failed themselves, were in no position to object. Finally, criticism of government actions, once permitted even in limited form, soon grew into wholesale questioning of the legitimacy of the social order and into the theoretical search for alternatives. Quiescence was at an end and Russia entered a new period of intense debate. Twentieth-century Russia grew out of this debate; the men of the new revolutionary generation that now came to the fore were to become the men of 1917.

Every day brought its quota of exciting and hitherto unimaginable news. Here a society for the study of labour statistics was founded, there a progressive publishing house established, in a third place students were teaching industrial workers the ABC. New books were appearing all the time. And everywhere there was constant talk, talk, talk.

The intelligentsia did not simply take up the debate where it had been broken off ten to fifteen years before. Many things had changed in Russia; new explanations, new theories were called for. Very soon it became apparent that Marxism would be the dominant intellectual influence. The question that had once been so hotly argued – would or would not capitalism come to Russia? – was now, it seemed, no longer open to debate: capitalism was there already. The Populists, or neo-Populists, could do no more than fight a rather pathetic rearguard action on behalf of the *obshchina*. Marxism became all the rage; it was chic, it was fashionable, it was discussed everywhere, from

563

secondary-school common rooms to society salons. A brilliant group of young university professors, the so-called Legal Marxists – Struve, Tugan-Baranovsky, Berdyaev, Bulgakov and others – were openly preaching the Marxist gospel to crowded lecture rooms. Theirs was not a very revolutionary kind of Marxism – capitalism was for them a beneficial and progressive force, inevitable and desirable in itself; backward Russia would require the services of capitalism for so long ahead that there was not much sense in discussing the merits of socialism. The leading spirit among the Legal Marxists was Pyotr Struve; Russia, he wrote, would have to learn culture from capitalism.

What the authorities feared was Populism and a resurgence of terrorism; they were positively grateful to the Marxists for having deflected public attention to themselves. An abstruse scientific theory based on a rigorous system of evidence and directed at the distant future could hardly present much of a danger. So the censors showed themselves remarkably broad-minded with regard to the publication of Marxist works, and the police looked indulgently aside when young students explained the basic principles of Marxism to small groups of workers.

The triumphant march of Marxism among the intelligentsia was above all a personal triumph for Plekhanov. At last his faithfulness and pertinacity were rewarded. The years of solitude were over; he was no longer an outcast, and the Emancipation of Labour group was acquiring undreamt-of influence. Contacts with Russia, non-existent for years, now became almost too numerous to handle; dozens of young Marxist intellectuals travelled abroad specially to visit Plekhanov. With their assistance Plekhanov achieved, in late 1894, his most resounding success to date: the legal publication, inside Russia herself, of his magnificently lucid exposition of Marxism, under the *nom de plume* of Bel'tov and the undecipherable title of *On the Question of the Development of the Monistic View of History*. The edition was sold out in less than three weeks.

Plekhanov naturally saw all this as a straightforward justification of his Marxist analysis of Russian society. The development of the material means of production (i.e. industrialization) was creating a system of capitalist productive relationships, just as he had forecast. The capitalist *basis* had been laid down; now a capitalist *superstructure* was going up. This was how it should be, and in due course the time would come for a socialist basis and superstructure. Meanwhile the task was to prepare for that day by disseminating the ideas of socialism as widely as possible.

Yet, whether or not the Marxist scheme is correct with regard to any other country, Plekhanov was undoubtedly wrong when applying it to Russia. Throughout Russian history the State, or part of the Marxian 'superstructure', had been the force that created and shaped the economic 'basis' – and not the other way around. Capitalism and socialism were to be no exceptions. This had been understood by an earlier generation of Russian revolutionaries: Tkachev and the *narodovoltsy* saw Russian socialism as a creation of the revolutionary State, and the less capitalism there existed the easier the task would be. With the great upsurge of Marxism at the turn of the century Plekhanov no doubt believed that this debate had been decided once and for all in his favour. Here too he was mistaken.

The most important event of the decade passed, as often happens, completely unnoticed. In mid-September 1893 a young lawyer from Samara arrived in St Petersburg with the object of setting up a practice. His name was Vladimir Ilyich Ulyanov, and although he began his revolutionary activity almost immediately it was some time before he adopted the pseudonym of Lenin.

Twenty-three and a half years later Lenin made another and very different arrival to the capital. He was met by an official welcoming committee, by adoring and devoted comrades, by massed brass bands and huge crowds of workers and soldiers. Another seven months – and Lenin was leader of a victorious revolution and master of Russia. The Revolution had taken over the State, and the two strands of the Russian tradition had been finally fused into one.

NOTES

Chapter 1: The Sleeping Past

1 Marquis de Custine, *Nikolayevskaya Rossiya*, Moscow, 1930, p. 3.
2 Marquis de Custine, *The Empire of the Czar*, London, 1843, vol. I, pp. xvii, 161, 184, 185–6; vol. II, pp. 9, 10, 18, 150, 152, 190–1; vol. III, pp. 61, 207, 227–8, 294, 298.
3 Ibid., vol. III, p. 353.
4 André Gide, *Back from the USSR*, London, 1937, p. 15.
5 Ibid., pp. 46, 48, 49, 50, 62–3, 65, 66, 69, 79–80.
6 Sigismund von Herberstein, *Notes upon Russia*, London, 1851, vol. I, pp. 30, 32.
7 Giles Fletcher, *Of the Russe Common Wealth*, London, 1856, pp. 26–7.
8 Adam Olearius, *The voyages and travels of the Ambassadors sent by Frederick Duke of Holstein to the Great Duke of Muscovy and the King of Persia*, London, 1662, p. 95.
9 Ibid., pp. 95–6.
10 V. Kliuchevsky, *Ocherki i rechi (Vtoroi sbornik statei)*, Petrograd, 1918, p. 50.

Chapter 2: The Mongol Heritage

1 F. J. Turner, *The Frontier in American History*, New York, 1920, pp. ii, 3, 38.
2 S. M. Solovyov, *Sobranie sochinenii*, St Petersburg, n.d., p. 764.
3 V. Kliuchevsky, *Kurs russkoi istorii*, Moscow, 1937, vol. I, p. 21.
4 G. Vernadsky, *The Mongols and Russia*, Yale, 1953, p. 92.
5 Ibid., p. 105.
6 N. M. Karamzin, *Istoriya gosudarstva rossiiskogo*, St Petersburg, 1892, vol. V. pp. 227, 235.
7 V. Kliuchevsky, *Kurs russkoi istorii*, vol. II, pp. 44–5.
8 *Karamzin's Memoir on Ancient and Modern Russia*. Edited by R. Pipes, Cambridge, Mass., 1959, p. 109.
9 G. Vernadsky, *A History of Russia*, New York, 1944, p. 56.
10 Quoted in G. Vernadsky, *The Mongols and Russia*, p. 389.
11 N. Berdyaev, *Istoki i smysl russkogo kommunizma*, Paris, 1955. p. 7.
12 Karl Marx, 'Revelations of the diplomatic history of the 18th Century',

The Free Press, London, vol. IV, no. 26, 4 Feb. 1857; vol. IV, no. 29, 25 Feb. 1857.

13 A. D. Gradovsky, *Istoriya mestnogo upravleniya v Rossii*, St Petersburg, 1868, pp. 32–3. Quoted in Kliuchevsky, *Kurs russkoi istorii*, vol. II, p. 231.

14 Vernadsky, *The Mongols and Russia*, pp. 336–7, 367, 390.

Chapter 3: Independence and Despotism

1 S. Solovyov, *Istoriya Rossii s drevneishikh vremen*, St Petersburg, n.d., Book 2, p. 484.

2 Herberstein. op, cit., pp. 95–6.

3 Kliuchevsky, *Kurs russkoi istorii*, vol. II, p. 225.

4 Wittfogel, op. cit., p. 59.

5 J. F. C. Fuller, *Decisive Battles of the Western World*, London, 1957, vol. I, p. 464.

6 Ibid., p. 409.

7 Kliuchevsky, *Kurs russkoi istorii*, vol. II, p. 228.

8 P. Miliukov, *Ocherki po istorii russkoi kul'tury*, vol. III, 3rd ed., St Petersburg, 1909, pp. 22–3.

9 Kliuchevsky, *Istoriya soslovii v Rossii*. In *Sochineniya*, vol. VI, Moscow, 1959, p. 462.

10 Kliuchevsky, *Kurs russkoi istorii*, vol. III, pp. 15–16.

11 Ibid., pp. 135, 138.

12 *Karamzin's Memoir on Ancient and Modern Russia*, p. 115.

13 *Seven Britons in Imperial Russia, 1698–1812*. Edited by P. Putnam, Princeton, 1952, p. 148.

14 *The correspondence between Prince A. M. Kurbsky and Tsar Ivan IV of Russia 1564–1579*. Edited by J. L. I. Fennell, Cambridge, 1955, pp. 25, 27, 47, 67, 107, 127. (One or two words in the translation have been changed to make them correspond more closely to the original.)

15 *Sochineniya I. Peresvetova*. Edited by A. A. Zimin, Moscow-Leningrad, 1956, p. 161.

16 Ibid., pp. 167, 219.

17 *The correspondence between Prince Kurbsky and Tsar Ivan IV*, p. 59.

18 Kliuchevsky, *Kurs russkoi istorii*, vol. II, p. 408.

19 Giles Fletcher, op. cit., pp. 27, 30, 31.

20 Olearius, op. cit., p. 96.

21 Kliuchevsky, *Kurs russkoi istorii*, vol. III, p. 11.

Chapter 4: The State over Society

1 Miliukov, op. cit., vol. I, pp. 137–8.

2 Ibid., p. 225.

3 G. V. Plekhanov, *Istoriya russkoi obshchestvennoi mysli*, Book I, Moscow-Leningrad, 1925, pp. 88, 96.
4 *Sochineniya I. Peresvetova*, p. 67.
5 Fletcher, op. cit., pp. 32-3, 34.
6 Cyril E. Black, 'The nature of Imperial Russian society'. In *The Development of the USSR*. Edited by Donald W. Treadgold, Seattle, 1964, p. 179.
7 I. T. Pososhkov, *Kniga o skudosti i bogatstve*, Moscow, 1951, pp. 178, 222.
8 Miliukov, op. cit., vol. I, p. 268.
9 Fletcher, op. cit., pp. 60-1.
10 Olearius, op. cit., p. 85.
11 Kliuchevsky, *Kurs russkoi istorii*, vol. III, p. 199.
12 Miliukov, op. cit., vol. I, pp. 255-6.

Chapter 5: The Institutionalization of the Autocracy

1 *The Cambridge Economic History of Europe*, vol. I, London, 1941, p. 419.
2 B. Chicherin, *Opyty po istorii russkago prava*, Moscow, 1858, pp. 227-8.
3 Fletcher, op. cit., p. 62.
4 Miliukov, op. cit., vol. I, pp. 25, 83, 242-3.
5 Kliuchevsky, *Kurs russkoi istorii*, vol. III, p. 155.
6 Kliuchevsky, *Istoriya soslovii v Rossii*. In *Sochineniya*, vol. VI, pp. 372, 375.
7 Herberstein, op. cit., vol. I, p. 95.
8 Olearius, op. cit., p. 83.
9 *Karamzin's Memoir*, p. 185.
10 Berdyaev, op. cit., p. 10.
11 Miliukov, op. cit., vol. III, p. 91.
12 Solovyov, *Istoriya Rossii*, Book II, p. 1258.
13 Fletcher, op. cit., p. 55.
14 Kliuchevsky, *Kurs russkoi istorii*, vol. III, p. 143.
15 Grigory Kotoshikhin, *O Rossii v tsarstvovanie Alexeya Mikhailovicha*, 4th ed., St Petersburg, 1906, p. 185.
16 Miliukov, op. cit., vol. II, p. 39.
17 *The correspondence between Prince Kurbsky and Tsar Ivan IV*, p. 215.
18 Fletcher, op. cit., p. 63.
19 Olearius, op. cit., p. 95.
20 Solovyov, *Istoriya Rossii*, Book II, pp. 1130, 1174-9.
21 Kotoshikhin, op. cit., p. 53.
22 Solovyov, *Istoriya Rossii*, Book II, p. 1258.
23 Miliukov, op. cit., vol. III, p. 84.
24 Jurij Križanić, *Politika*, Moscow, 1965, pp. 482, 490, 540, 555, 558, 564.
25 Pososhkov, op. cit., pp. 107-8.
26 Kliuchevsky, *Kurs russkoi istorii*, vol. III, p. 319.
27 Wittfogel, op. cit., p. 92.

28 Herberstein, op. cit., p. 58.
29 Michael Cherniavsky, *Tsar and People. Studies in Russian Myths*, Yale, 1961, p. 33.
30 M. Dyakonov, *Ocherki obshchestvennogo i gosudarstvennogo stroya drevnei Rusi*, 4th ed., Moscow-Leningrad, 1926, p. 321.
31 V. Dal', *Poslovitsy russkogo naroda*, Moscow, 1957, pp. 243–4.
32 Dyakonov, op. cit., p. 319.
33 Miliukov, op. cit., vol, II, p. 23.
34 Karl Marx, 'Revelations of the diplomatic history of the 18th Century', *The Free Press*, London, vol. IV, no. 34, 1 April 1857.
35 Quoted in M. Cherniavsky, op. cit., p. 167.
36 K. Leontiev, 'Vostok, Rossiya i Slavyanstvo'. In *Sobranie sochinenii*, vol. V, Moscow, 1912, pp. 29–30, 107–8.
37 F. M. Dostoevsky, *The Diary of a Writer*. Translated and annotated by Boris Brasol, London, 1949, vol. II, pp. 565, 566, 578, 582, 632, 695.
38 *Karamzin's Memoir*, p. 123.

Chapter 6: Interpretations: Feudal and 'Asiatic'

1 Kliuchevsky, *Kurs russkoi istorii*, vol II, pp. 423–4.
2 Marc Bloch, *Feudal Society*, London, 1961, p. 446.
3 Ibid., pp. 148, 282.
4 F. Pollock and F. W. Maitland, *A History of English Law*, 2nd ed., Cambridge, 1923, vol. I, pp. 66–7.
5 *Feudalism in History*. Edited by Rushton Coulborn, Princeton, 1956, pp. 4–5.
6 *The Cambridge Economic History of Europe*, vol. I, p. 427.
7 Bloch, op. cit., pp. 228, 451.
8 Ibid., p. 451.
9 Jean Bodin, *Six Books of the Commonwealth*. Translated by M. J. Tooley, 1955, p. 107.
10 Geoffrey Barraclough, *History in a Changing World*, Oxford, 1957, p. 148.
11 Custine, op. cit., vol. II, p. 257.
12 Montesquieu, *The Spirit of Laws*, London, 1897, vol. I, pp. 8, 27, 29, 62, 65, 79.
13 Ibid., pp. 64, 231, 258, 322.
14 G. W. F. Hegel, *Lectures on the Philosophy of History*, London, 1861, pp. 130, 133–4, 137, 145.
15 For a detailed exposition of the progressive convolutions of Marxist thought on the 'Oriental mode of production' see the brilliant and controversial study of *Oriental Despotism*, by Karl A. Wittfogel (Yale, 1957).
16 N. P. Pavlov-Silvansky, *Gosudarevy sluzhilye liudi, liudi kabal'nye i zakladnye*, 2nd ed., St Petersburg, 1909, p. 223. (The last sentence contains a quotation from the 1649 *Ulozhenie*.)

17 Wittfogel, op. cit., pp. 26, 27, 49.
18 *Feudalism in History*, p. 58.
19 Wittfogel, op. cit., p. 321.
20 Stanislav Andreski, *Elements of Comparative Sociology*, London, 1964, p. 166.
21 Wittfogel, op. cit., p. 225.
22 Fletcher, op. cit., p. 26.
23 Križanić, op. cit., p. 608.
24 Pososhkov, op. cit., p. 81.
25 Quoted in *The Development of the USSR*. Edited by Donald W. Treadgold, Seattle, 1964, p. 326.
26 B. Chicherin, *O narodnom predstavitel'stve*, Moscow, 1866, p. 531.
27 Kliuchevsky, *Kurs russkoi istorii*, vol. II, p. 196; vol. III, p. 57; vol. IV, p. 352.
28 Miliukov, op. cit., vol. I, p. 147.
29 Plekhanov, *Istoriya russkoi obshchestvennoi mysli*, Book I, pp. 77, 99–100, 246.
30 Leon Trotsky, *The History of the Russian Revolution*. Translated by Max Eastman, London, 1934, vol. I, p. 474.

Chapter 7: The Petrine Watershed

1 Kliuchevsky, *Kurs russkoi istorii*, vol. IV, p. 92.
2 Solovyov, *Istoriya Rossii*, Book IV, p. 172.
3 Miliukov, op. cit., vol. III, p. 157.
4 Kliuchevsky, *Kurs russkoi istorii*, vol. IV, pp. 123, 223.
5 Ibid., p. 224.
6 *Readings in Russian Civilization*. Edited by T. Riha, Chicago, 1964, p. 85.
7 Miliukov, op. cit., vol. III, p. 150.
8 Solovyov, *Istoriya Rossii*, Book IV, pp. 782–3.
9 Kliuchevsky, *Kurs russkoi istorii*, vol. IV, pp. 47–8, 233.
10 Miliukov, op. cit., vol. I, pp. 24–7.
11 Solovyov, *Istoriya Rossii*, Book IV, pp. 276–7.
12 Cf. A. S. Pushkin, *Istoriya Petra Velikogo*, 1721, var. editions.
13 Quoted in Plekhanov, *Sochineniya*, vol. XXI, p. 52.
14 V. N. Tatishchev, *Razgovor o pol'ze nauk i uchilishch*, Moscow, 1887, pp. 137–8.
15 Pososhkov, op. cit., pp. 219, 237–9, 242.
16 A. I. Herzen, *Byloye i dumy*, Moscow, 1947, p. 46.
17 Kliuchevsky, *Kurs russkoi istorii*, vol. IV, pp. 92–3, 222–3, 232.
18 Plekhanov, *Sochineniya*, vol. XXI, p. 37.

Chapter 8: The Eighteenth Century: Enlightenment and Enslavement

1 Solovyov, *Istoriya Rossii*, Book IV, pp. 834-40.
2 Ibid., Book VI, p. 378.
3 Kliuchevsky, *Kurs russkoi istorii*, vol. V, p. 152.
4 Quoted in ibid., p. 101.
5 Miliukov, op. cit., vol. I, p. 234.
6 Geroid T. Robinson, *Rural Russia under the Old Regime*, London, 1932, p. 63; Kliuchevsky, *Kurs russkoi istorii*, vol. V, pp. 114-15.
7 Solovyov, *Istoriya Rossii*, Book VI, p. 378.
8 *Istoriya Rossii v XIX - omveke*. Izdatel'stvo bratiev Granat, St Petersburg (1907), vol. I, p. 8.
9 Solovyov, *Istoriya Rossii*, Book VI, p. 397.
10 Kenneth M. Stamp, *The Peculiar Institution. Slavery in the Ante-Bellum South*, New York, 1956, pp. 192, 217-19, 225.
11 Ibid., pp. 86-7, 421, 430.
12 Samuel E. Morison and Henry S. Commager, *The Growth of the American Republic*, New York, 1954, vol. I, p. 549.
13 Ivan Boltin, *Primechaniya na istoriyu drevniya i nyneshniya Rossii g. Leklerka*, St Petersburg, 1788, vol. II, p. 383.
14 A. S. Pushkin, *Puteshestvie iz Moskvy v Peterburg*, var. editions.
15 *Encyclopedia of American History*. Edited by Richard B. Morris, New York, 1953, pp. 443, 516; Stamp, op. cit., p. 30.
16 Bossuet, *Oeuvres complètes*, vol. XXIV, Paris, 1885, pp. 104-6.
17 M. M. Bogoslovsky, *Byt i nravy russkago dvorianstva v pervoi polovine XVIII veka*, Moscow, 1904, pp. 37-8.
18 Alexander Herzen, *From the Other Shore* and *The Russian People and Socialism*, London, 1956, pp. 12-14.
19 Solovyov, *Istoriya Rossii*, Book VI, pp. 338-9.
20 Quoted in Plekhanov, *Sochineniya*, vol. XXII, p. 65.
21 D. I. Fonvizin, *Sobranie sochinenii*, Moscow-Leningrad, 1959, vol. II, pp. 485-6, 508.
22 Kliuchevsky, *Kurs russkoi istorii*, vol. V, p. 220.

Chapter 9: Alexander I and Nicholas I

1 M. M. Speransky, *Proekty i zapiski*, Moscow-Leningrad, 1961, pp. 18, 21, 43, 45, 56, 118, 119, 140, 142, 147, 163, 178.
2 *Karamzin's Memoir*, p. 139.
3 Custine, op. cit., vol. II, pp. 146, 147, 149.
4 Kiuchevsky, *Kurs russkoi istorii*, vol. III, p. 8.
5 Ibid., vol. V, p. 344.
6 Quoted in Miliukov, op. cit., vol. I, p. 238.
7 *Istoriya Rossii v XIX veke*, vol. I, p. 443.

8 Ibid., vol. IV, p. 5.
9 *Karamzin's Memoir*, p. 166.
10 Berdyaev, op. cit., p. 63.

Chapter 10: The Intelligentsia

1 *Vekhi. Sbornik statei o russkoi intelligentsii*, Moscow, 1909, pp. 24–5.
2 M. Malia in *The Russian Intelligentsia*. Edited by R. Pipes, New York, 1961, p. 4.
3 Quoted in R. Ivanov-Razumnik, *Istoriya russkoi obshchestvennoi mysli*, vol. I, St Petersburg, 1907, p. 1.
4 *Intelligentsia v Rossii. Sbornik statei*, St Petersburg, 1910, p. 128.
5 N. Berdyaev, *Istoki i smysl russkogo kommunizma*, Paris, 1955, p. 17.
6 V. G. Belinsky, *Polnoye sobraniye sochinenii*, vol. X, Moscow, 1956, pp. 217–18.
7 N. K. Mikhailovsky, *Sochineniya*, vol. I, St Petersburg, 1896, p. 868.
8 *Vekhi*, p. 29.
9 N. K. Mikhailovsky, *Sochineniya*, vol. IV, p. 952.
10 Richard Hare, *Pioneers of Russian Social Thought*, Oxford, 1951, p. 34.
11 Among the most melancholy monuments to this immutable obsession are some of the writings of Russian émigrés, who, decades after 1917, persist in apotheosizing the revolutionary movement with an utter disregard for its actual results. Of particular interest in this respect are: Theodore Dan, *The Origins of Bolshevism*, London, 1964; and B. Elkin, 'The Russian intelligentsia on the eve of Revolution', in *The Russian Intelligentsia*, New York, 1961.
12 N. G. Chernyshevsky, *Polnoye sobraniye sochinenii v 15-i tomakh*, Moscow, 1939, vol. I, p. 357.
13 A. V. Nikitenko, *Moya povest' o samom sebe*, vol. II, St Petersburg, 1905, p. 78.
14 N. G. Chernyshevsky, *Polnoye sobraniye sochinenii v 10-i tomakh*, St Petersburg, 1906, vol. VI, p. 491.
15 Quoted in J. L. Talmon, *The Origins of Totalitarian Democracy*, New York, London, 1961, pp. 47–8.
16 G. V. Plekhanov, *Sochineniya*, vol. II, Leningrad-Moscow, 1925, p. 132.
17 Alexander Herzen, *From the Other Shore* and *The Russian People and Socialism*, London, 1956, p. 199.
18 Yu. M. Steklov, *N. G. Chernyshevsky*, Moscow-Leningrad, 1928, vol. II, p. 7.
19 A. V. Nikitenko, op. cit., vol. II, pp. 48, 107.
20 A. I. Herzen, *Polnoye sobraniye sochinenii i pisem*. Edited by M. K. Lemke, Petrograd, 1919, vol. VIII, pp. 45–6.
21 Nikitenko, op. cit., vol. II, pp. 54–5.

22 *Vekhi*, p. 44.
23 Ibid., pp. 6-7.
24 Quoted in R. Hare, op. cit., p. 33.
25 D. I. Pisarev, *Sochineniya*, vol. III, Moscow, 1956, pp. 105, 114.
26 Chernyshevsky, *Polnoye sobraniye sochinenii* (1906), vol. V, p. 408.
27 Ibid., vol. VIII, pp. 37-8.
28 Yu. M. Steklov, op. cit., vol. II, p. 85.
29 Ibid., pp. 52, 97.
30 Pisarev, op. cit., p. 126.
31 Ibid., p. 129.
32 Ivanov-Razumnik, op. cit., vol. I, p. 33.
33 Chernyshevsky, *Polnoye sobraniye sochinenii* (1906), vol. VIII, p. 37.
34 Pisarev, op. cit., p. 289.
35 Herzen, *From the Other Shore*, p. 200.
36 Quoted by Professor Leonard Schapiro in *The Russian Intelligentsia*, p. 20.
37 Chernyshevsky, *Polnoye sobraniye sochinenii* (1906), vol. IV, pp. 157-8, 204.
38 Mikhailovsky, op. cit., vol. IV, pp. 949-50.
39 Chernyshevsky, *Polnoye sobraniye sochinenii* (1906), vol. IV, p. 156.
40 V. A. Zaitsev, *Izbrannye sochineniya*, Moscow, 1934, vol. I, p. 319.
41 Chernyshevsky, *Polnoye sobraniye sochinenii* (1906), vol. IV, p. 156.
42 Quoted in R. Hare, op. cit., p. 118.
43 Chernyshevsky, *Polnoye sobraniye sochinenii* (1939), vol. I, p. 121.
44 Hannah Arendt, *The Origins of Totalitarianism*, 2nd ed., New York, 1958, pp. 311-27.
45 *Intelligentsia v Rossii*, p. 117.
46 George Lichtheim, *Marxism*, London, 1964, p. 398.

Chapter 11: The Early Revolutionaries: the Decembrists to Herzen

1 V. I. Lenin, *Sochineniya*, 3rd ed., vol. XV, p. 468. All further quotations from Lenin, except where otherwise stated, are taken from the third Russian edition of his Works (Moscow, 1926-1935).
2 *Vosstaniye Dekabristov. Dokumenty*, vol. VII, Moscow, 1958, p. 157.
3 M. Nechkina, *Dvizheniye Dekabristov*, vol. II, Moscow, 1957, p. 419.
4 *Vosstaniye Dekabristov*, vol. VII, pp. 204-5.
5 Ibid., p. 671.
6 R. Hare, *Pioneers of Russian Social Thought*, Oxford, 1951, p. 4.
7 Quoted in *Istoriya Rossii v XIX-om veke*, Izdatel'stvo bratiev Granat, St Petersburg (1907), vol. I, p. 465.
8 F. M. Dostoevsky, *The Diary of a Writer*, London, 1949, vol. 2, p. 962.
9 V. G. Belinsky, *Polnoye sobraniye sochinenii*, vol. XII, Moscow, 1956, p. 433.
10 Ibid., vol. III, Moscow, 1953, pp. 500-1.
11 Ibid., vol. XI, Moscow, 1956, pp. 148-50.

12 Ibid., vol. V, Moscow, 1954, pp. 140-7.

13 Ibid., vol. XII, Moscow, 1956, pp. 467-8.

14 M. N. Pokrovsky, *Ocherki russkogo revolyutsionnogo dvizheniya XIX-XX vv.*, Moscow, 1924, p. 54.

15 Dostoevsky, op. cit., vol. II, p. 580.

16 A. I. Herzen, *Byloye i dumy*, Moscow, 1947, p. 354.

17 Ibid., p. 358.

18 A. I. Herzen, *Polnoye sobraniye sochinenii i pisem.* Edited by M. K. Lemke, Petrograd, 1919, vol. V, p. 113.

19 Ibid., vol. XV, pp. 248, 256, 292.

20 Martin Malia, *Alexander Herzen and the Birth of Russian Socialism 1812-1855*, Harvard, 1961, p. 354.

21 P. Chaadayev, *Filosoficheskiye pis'ma*, Moscow, 1908, pp. 100, 104.

22 A. Herzen, *From the Other Shore*, and *The Russian People and Socialism*, London, 1956, p. 179; A. I. Herzen, *Polnoye sobraniye sochinenii i pisem*, vol. V, pp. 111-13; vol. VIII, pp. 45-7; vol. XV, pp. 304-5; vol. XI, p. 231.

23 Ibid., vol. VII, pp. 396-7.

24 A. Herzen, *From the Other Shore*, pp. 183-6; *Polnoye sobraniye sochinenii i pisem*, vol. VIII, pp. 33, 48-9, 491-4; vol. XI, p. 232.

25 M. O. Gershenzon, *Istoriya molodoi Rossii*, Moscow-Petrograd, 1923, p. 285.

26 Herzen, *Polnoye sobraniye . . .*, vol. XV, pp. 306-9.

27 N. V. Shelgunov, *Vospominaniya*, Moscow-Petrograd, 1923, pp. 67-8.

28 Herzen, *Polnoye sobraniye . . .*, vol. III, p. 128.

29 Ibid., vol. IX, pp. 1-2.

Chapter 12: The Second Generation: Chernyshevsky

1 Quoted in Yu. M. Steklov, *N. G. Chernyshevsky*, Moscow-Leningrad, 1928, vol. I, p. 169.

2 Ibid., vol. II, p. 38.

3 Ibid., p. 30.

4 I. S. Turgenev, *Sobraniye sochinenii*, vol. 12, Moscow, 1958, p. 247.

5 Steklov, op. cit., vol. II, p. 19.

6 Ibid., vol. I, p. 158.

7 P. Kropotkin, *Idealy i deistvitel'nost' v russkoi literature*, St Petersburg, 1907, p. 307.

8 G. V. Plekhanov, *Sochineniya*, vol. V. pp. 114-15.

9 Quoted in Vladimir Dedijer, *The Road to Sarajevo*, London, 1967, p. 178.

10 N. G. Chernyshevsky, *Polnoye sobraniye sochinenii v 10-i tomakh*, St Petersburg, 1906, vol. IV, p. 329.

11 Ibid., vol. III, pp. 183-6.

12 N. G. Chernyshevsky, *Polnoye sobraniye sochinenii v 15-i tomakh*, Moscow, 1939, vol. I, p. 356.

13 Chernyshevsky, *Polnoye sobraniye sochinenii v 10-i tomakh* (1906), vol. VI, p. 491.

14 Steklov, op. cit., vol. II, p. 98.

15 Franco Venturi, *Roots of Revolution*, London (1960), p. 139.

16 Chernyshevsky, *Polnoye sobraniye sochinenii v 10-i tomakh* (1906), vol. VIII, p. 198.

17 Ibid., vol. II, pp. 121–2.

18 N. Valentinov, *Vstrechi s Leninym*, New York, 1953, p. 103.

19 V. I. Lenin, *Sochineniya*, vol. XVII, pp. 224, 342.

20 Ibid., vol. XVII, p. 342; vol. XV, p. 144.

21 Valentinov, op. cit., p. 108.

Chapter 13: Nihilists

1 G. Dzhanshiev, *Iz epokhi velikikh reform*, Moscow, 1894, pp. 51–2.

2 A. V. Nikitenko, *Moya povest' o samom sebe*, St Petersburg, 1905, vol. II, pp. 38, 47.

3 M. Lemke, *Politicheskiye protsessy v Rossii 1860–kh gg.*, 2nd ed., Moscow, 1923, pp. 66–70.

4 For all quotations from 'Young Russia' see full text in Lemke, op. cit., pp. 510–18.

5 M. Pokrovsky, *Ocherki russkogo revolyutsionnogo dvizheniya XIX–XX vv.*, Moscow, 1924, pp. 59–61.

6 Yu. Steklov, *N. G. Chernyshevsky*, Moscow-Leningrad, 1928, vol. II, pp. 275–8.

7 Quoted in Franco Venturi, *Roots of Revolution*, London, 1960, p. 764.

8 Nikitenko, op. cit., p. 57.

9 D. Pisarev, *Sochineniya*, Moscow, 1956, vol. III, p. 21.

10 Ibid., p. 105.

11 Ibid., p. 10.

12 Ibid., pp. 376, 378, 415.

13 V. Zaitsev, *Izbrannye sochineniya*, Moscow, 1934, vol. I, pp. 216, 319.

14 Ibid., pp. 95–6.

15 'Byloye', No. 4/16, 1907, pp. 224–5; E. H. Carr, *The Romantic Exiles*, London, 1933, pp. 264–5.

16 *Pis'ma M. A. Bakunina k. A. I. Gertsenu i N. P. Ogarevu*, St Petersburg, 1906, p. 322.

17 A. I. Herzen, *Polnoye sobraniye sochinenii i pisem*. Edited by M. K. Lemke, vol. XXI, Petrograd, 1923, pp. 434–49.

Chapter 14: Nechaev and the Conspiratorial Principle

1 *Pokusheniye Karakozova. Sbornik dokumentov*, Moscow, 1928, p. 6.

2 Ibid., p. 10.

3 *Revolyutsionnoye dvizheniye 1860-kh gg. Sbornik*, Moscow, 1932, p. 138.

4 P. N. Tkachev, *Izbrannye sochineniya na sotsial'no-politicheskiye temy*, vol. I, Moscow, 1932, pp. 18–19; Venturi, op. cit., pp. 362–3.

5 E. H. Carr, *Michael Bakunin*, New York, 1961, p. 392.

6 *M. A. Bakunin: Statya A. I. Gertsena o Bakunine. Biograficheskii ocherk M. Dragomanova. Rechi i vozzvaniya* (St Petersburg), 1906, pp. 240–1.

7 Ibid., pp. 246–9.

8 Ibid., 252–7.

9 Ibid., pp. 262–8.

10 *Revolyutsionnoye dvizheniye 1860-kh gg.*, pp. 180–1.

11 Ibid., pp. 187–9, 210–11.

12 Yu. Steklov, *M. A. Bakunin*, vol. III, Moscow-Leningrad, 1927, pp. 541–3.

13 *Gosudarstvennyia prestupleniya v Rossii v XIX veke*. Edited by B. Bazilevsky (Bogucharsky), vol. I, St Petersburg, 1906, pp. 229–30.

14 Vera Figner, *Polnoye sobraniye sochinenii*, vol. I, Moscow, 1928, p. 230.

15 Ibid., p. 236.

16 'Otechestvennye Zapiski', 1873, No. 2, p. 323.

17 Vera Figner, op. cit., p. 235.

18 Vladimir Burtsev, *Za sto let (1800–1896)*, London, 1897, vol. I. p. 97.

19 M. Pokrovsky, op. cit., pp. 64–7.

20 K. Marx i F. Engels, *Sochineniya*, 1st ed., vol. XXVI, p. 208.

21 *Protiv istoricheskoi kontseptsii M. N. Pokrovskogo. Sbornik statei*, vol. I, Moscow, 1939, p. 442.

22 F. M. Dostoevsky, *Sobraniye sochinenii*, vol. 7, Moscow, 1957, p. 713.

23 Ibid., p. 714.

Chapter 15: Going to the People

1 P. L. Lavrov, *Izbrannye sochineniya na sotsial'no-politicheskiye temy*, vol. I, Moscow, 1934, p. 199.

2 Ibid., p. 255.

3 O. V. Aptekman, *Obshchestvo 'Zemlya i Volya' 70-kh gg.*, Petrograd, 1924, p. 123.

4 R. Kropotkin, *Zapiski revolyutsionera*, Moscow, 1918, p. 236.

5 N. A. Charushin, *O dadekom proshlom*, Moscow, 1926, pp. 85–6.

6 Venturi, op. cit., p. 485.

7 Kropotkin, op. cit., p. 238.

8 Venturi, op. cit., p. 793.

9 Lavrov, *Izbrannye sochineniya*, Moscow, 1934, vol. II, pp. 23–41.

10 S. Kravchinsky, *Podpol'naya Rossiya*, Moscow, 1906, pp. 15–17.

11 *Revolyutsionnoye narodnichestvo 70-kh godov XIX veka*. Sbornik dokumentov i materialov, vol. I, Moscow, 1964, pp. 266–7.

12 Ibid., pp. 277-8.
13 Aptekman, op. cit., pp. 144-5.
14 Ibid., p. 172.
15 Ibid., pp. 154-5.
16 *Revolyutsionnoye narodnichestvo* . . ., vol. I, pp. 294-5.
17 M. R. Popov, *Zapiski zemlevol'tsa*, Moscow, 1933, p. 60.
18 V. Bogucharsky, *Aktivnoye narodnichestvo semidesyatykh godov*, Moscow, 1912, pp. 173-7.
19 Aptekman, op. cit., pp. 179, 182-3.
20 Bogucharsky, op. cit., pp. 126-30.

Chapter 16: Tkachev and the Roots of Leninism

1 Tkachev, *Izbrannye sochineniya*, vol. I, p. 70.
2 Ibid., p. 24.
3 Tkachev, op. cit., vol. III, pp. 64-5.
4 Ibid.
5 Ibid., pp. 69-70.
6 Ibid., p. 76.
7 Ibid., pp. 84-5.
8 Ibid., p. 85.
9 Lavrov, op. cit., vol. III, pp. 335-72.
10 Ibid., pp. 360-1.
11 Marx i Engels, *Sochineniya*, 1st ed., vol. XV, pp. 231-40.
12 Tkachev, op. cit., vol. III, pp. 88-98.
13 *K. Marx, F. Engels i revolyutsionnaya Rossiya*, Moscow, 1967, p. 744.
14 Marx i Engels, *Sochineniya*, 1st ed., vol. XV, p. 248.
15 *Protsess 50-ti*, Moscow, 1906; *Gosudarstvennyia prestupleniya v Rossii v XIX veke*. Edited by B. Bazilevsky, vol. 3, *Protsess 193-kh*, St Petersburg, n.d.
16 Marx i Engels, *Sochineniya*, 1st ed., vol. XV, pp. 251-64.
17 Ibid., vol. XVI, part 2, pp. 388-401.
18 Samuel H. Baron, *Plekhanov*, London, 1963, pp. 66, 92.
19 Tkachev, op. cit., vol. III, pp. 220-9.
20 Ibid., p. 234.
21 Ibid., p. 251.
22 Ibid., pp. 264-8.
23 Ibid., p. 252.
24 Ibid., p. 244.
25 Ibid., p. 293.
26 Lavrov, op. cit., vol. IV, pp. 207-396.
27 Tkachev, op. cit., vol. III, pp. 360-81.
28 Ibid., p. 440.
29 'Byloye', 1907, No. 8/20, pp. 164-5.

30 G. V. Plekhanov, *Sochineniya*, vol. XXIV, Moscow-Leningrad, 1927, p. 155.
31 Nikolai Berdyaev, *Istoki i smysl russkogo kommunizma*, Paris, 1955, pp. 58-60.
32 V. I. Lenin, *What Is to Be Done?*, Moscow, 1964, p. 161.
33 *V. I. Lenin v Samare 1889-1893. Sbornik vospominanii*, Moscow, 1933, p. 69.
34 V. D. Bonch-Bruevich, *Izbrannye sochineniya*, vol. II, Moscow, 1962, pp. 314-16.
35 Ibid.
36 Pokrovsky, op. cit., pp. 62-4.
37 Tkachev, op. cit., vol. I, pp. 47, 52.
38 S. S. Volk, *Narodnaya Volya*, Moscow-Leningrad, 1966, p. 247.

Chapter 17: Back to Politics

1 'Byloye', 1906, No. 12, pp. 258-61.
2 V. Ya. Bogucharsky, *Iz istorii politicheskoi bor'by v 70-kh i 80-kh gg. XIX veka*, Moscow, 1912, p. 37.
3 Plekhanov, op. cit., vol. XXIV, pp. 131-60.
4 Venturi, op. cit., p. 584.
5 Aptekman, op. cit., pp. 281, 295.
6 Popov, op. cit., pp. 217-18.
7 A. P. Pribyleva-Korba and V. N. Figner, *Narodovolets Alexander Dmitriyevich Mikhailov*, Leningrad, 1925, p. 30.
8 Lenin, *What Is to Be Done?*, p. 126.
9 *Revolyutsionnoye narodnichestvo . . .*, vol. II, 1965, pp. 27-30.
10 Aptekman, op. cit., pp. 195-9.
11 M. V. Nechkina, *Dvizheniye dekabristov*, vol. II. Moscow, 1955, p. 149.

Chapter 18: Discipline and Terrorism

1 *Istoriya SSSR*, vol. II, ed. M. V. Nechkina, 2nd ed., Moscow, 1949, p. 666.
2 P. A. Zayonchkovsky, *Krizis samoderzhaviya na rubezhe 1870-80-kh godov*, Moscow, 1964, p. 10.
3 Volk, op. cit., p. 49.
4 *Rabocheye dvizheniye v Rossii v XIX veke*, vol. II, part 2, Moscow, 1950, pp. 644-76.
5 Zayonchkovsky, op. cit., p. 16.
6 Volk, op. cit., p. 63.
7 D. A. Milyutin, *Dnevnik*, vol. III, Moscow, 1950, p. 41.
8 Ibid., p. 85.
9 Bogucharsky, *Iz istorii politicheskoi bor'by*, pp. 19-21.
10 Quoted in Venturi, op. cit., p. 633.
11 P. A. Valuev, *Dnevnik 1877-1884*, Petrograd, 1919, p. 38.

12 Milyutin, op. cit., pp. 139, 148.
13 Volk, op. cit., pp. 61–2.
14 Ibid., p. 60.
15 Venturi, op. cit., p. 519.
16 *Revolyutsionnoye narodnichestvo* . . ., vol. II, pp. 34–42.
17 Quoted in Aptekman, op. cit., p. 357.
18 Volk, op. cit., p. 71.
19 Bogucharsky, *Iz istorii politicheskoi bor'by*, p. 399.
20 Quoted in Venturi, op. cit., pp. 610–11.
21 Bogucharsky, *Aktivnoye narodnichestvo*, p. 322.
22 Ibid., p. 321.
23 Ibid., p. 348.
24 'Byloye', 1906, No. 8, p. 109.
25 L. Tikhomirov, *Vospominaniya*, Moscow-Leningrad, 1927, p. 126.
26 N. A. Morozov, *Povesti moyei zhizni*, vol. II, Moscow, 1947, pp. 513–14.
27 Cf. Volk, op. cit., pp. 97–8.
28 Venturi, op. cit., p. 650.
29 *Revolyutsionnoye narodnichestvo* . . ., vol. II, p. 200.
30 Ibid., pp. 209–11.
31 Ibid., pp. 170–4.
32 Ibid., pp. 175–83.
33 'Byloye', 1907, No. 8/20, p. 165.
34 Plekhanov, op. cit., vol. XXIV, p. 155.
35 *K. Marx, F. Engels i revolyutsionnaya Rossiya*, p. 692.
36 *Literatura partii 'Narodnoi Voli'*, Moscow, 1906, p. 4.
37 Ibid., pp. 78–9.
38 Ibid., pp. 41.
39 Ibid., pp. 43–4.
40 *Narodovolets A. I. Barannikov v ego pis'makh*, Moscow, 1935, p. 140.
41 Volk, op. cit., p. 242.
42 Cf. *Revolyutsionnoye narodnichestvo* . . ., vol. II, p. 387.
43 Ibid., pp. 316–17.
44 *Literatura partii 'Narodnoi Voli'*, p. 172.
45 M. Yu. Ashenbrenner, *Voyennaya organizatsiya Narodnoi Voli*, Moscow, 1924, p. 97.
46 *Literatura partii 'Narodnoi Voli'*, p. 80.
47 *Revolyutsionnoye narodnichestvo* . . ., pp. 190–1.
48 *Literatura partii 'Narodnoi Voli'*, p. 247.
49 Plekhanov, op. cit., vol. II, p. 76.
50 *Revolyutsionnoye narodnichestvo* . . ., pp. 320–1.
51 Leonard Schapiro, *Rationalism and Nationalism in Russian Nineteenth-Century Political Thought*, Yale, 1967, pp. 123–4.
52 *I Marta 1881 goda*, Petrograd, 1918, pp. 158–9.
53 Ibid., p. 165.

54 Lenin, *Sochineniya*, 3rd ed., vol. IV, p. 136.
55 *Literatura partii 'Narodnoi Voli'*, p. 121.
56 Volk, op. cit., pp. 120-1.
57 Morozov, op. cit., p. 504.
58 'Byloye', 1906, No. 1, p. 194.

Chapter 19: The Marxist-Populist Dialectic

1 For exhaustive studies of various aspects of pre-revolutionary Russian Marxism see, inter alia: J. L. H. Keep, *The Rise of Social Democracy in Russia*, Oxford, 1963; L. H. Haimson, *The Russian Marxists and the Origins of Bolshevism*, Harvard, 1955; S. H. Baron, *Plekhanov*, London, 1963; R. Kindersley, *The First Russian Revisionists*, Oxford, 1962. The most comprehensive official Soviet account is contained in *Istoriya kommunisticheskoi partii Sovietskogo Soyuza*, vol. I (1883-1903), Moscow, 1964.
2 E. H. Carr, *What is History?*, London, 1961, p. 6.
3 K. Marx and F. Engels, *Selected Works in One Volume*, London, 1968, p. 183.
4 *K. Marx, F. Engels i revolyutsionnaya Rossiya*, Moscow, 1967, p. 244.
5 K. Marx, F. Engels, *Sochineniya*, 1st ed., vol. XXIV, Moscow, 1931, p. 292.
6 Ibid., p. 327.
7 Ibid., vol. XXVI, p. 480.
8 H. Collins and C. Abramsky, *Karl Marx and the British Labour Movement*, London, 1965, p. 296.
9 Ibid., p. 298.
10 K. Marx, F. Engels, *Sochineniya*, vol. XXVII, p. 116.
11 Ibid., vol. XV, p. 376.
12 *K. Marx, F. Engels i revolyutsionnaya Rossiya*, pp. 434-5.
13 K. Marx, F. Engels, *Sochineniya*, vol. XXVII, pp. 117-18.
14 Ibid., pp. 677-97.
15 K. Marx, F. Engels, *Manifesto of the Communist Party*, Moscow, n.d., p. 12.
16 *Literatura partii 'Narodnoi Voli'*, Paris, 1905, p. 558.
17 K. Marx, F. Engels, *Sochineniya*, vol. XXVII, p. 128.
18 S. S. Volk, *Narodnaya Volya*, Moscow-Leningrad, 1966, p. 441.
19 K. Marx, F. Engels, *Sochineniya*, vol. XXVII, p. 100.
20 Volk, op. cit., pp. 440-3.
21 *K. Marx, F. Engels i revolyutsionnaya Rossiya*, p. 427.
22 V. Figner, *Polnoye sobraniye sochinenii*, vol. V, Moscow, 1919, pp. 109-12.
23 *Literatura partii 'Narodnoi Voli'*, pp. 336-42.
24 The most complete text of Lopatin's letter was published by V. Figner in 'Golos minuvshego', 1923, No. 2, pp. 146-8. See Volk, op. cit., pp. 436-8.
25 G. V. Plekhanov, *Sochineniya*, vol. I, p. 135.

Chapter 20: Towards the New-style Absolutism

1 K. Marx, F. Engels, *Sochineniya,* vol. XXVIII, pp. 254–5.
2 Ibid., vol. XXVII, p. 335.
3 Baron, *Plekhanov,* p. 95.
4 Plekhanov, *Sochineniya,* vol. II, pp. 25–88.
5 Ibid., pp. 89–356.
6 *Perepiska C. V. Plekhanova i P. B. Axel'roda,* vol. I, Moscow, 1925, p. 21.
7 K. Marx, F. Engels, *Sochineniya,* vol. XXVII, pp. 461–3.
8 Baron, op. cit., p. 123.
9 Keep, op. cit., p. 19.
10 Ibid.
11 K. Marx, F. Engels, *Sochineniya,* vol. XXIX, pp. 38, 65, 129–30.
12 Ibid., vol. XVI, part 2, p. 399.
13 H. Seton-Watson, *The Russian Empire 1801–1917,* Oxford, 1967, p. 466.
14 P. A. Khromov, *Ekonomicheskoye razvitie v XIX–XX vekakh (1800–1917),* Moscow, 1950, pp. 456–62.
15 P. Miliukov, *Ocherki po istorii russkoi kul'tury,* vol. I, p. 95.
16 E. H. Carr, *Foundations of a Planned Economy 1926–1929,* vol. II, London, 1971, p. 443.
17 Cit. in T. H. von Laue, *Sergei Witte and the Industrialization of Russia,* New York, 1963, p. 34.
18 Ibid., p. 3.
19 L. Tikhomirov, *Vospominaniya,* Moscow-Leningrad, 1927, pp. 424–5.

Index

Aksakov, Ivan, 192, 253
Aksakov, Konstantin, 230
Alexander I (the Blessed), 172, 173–8,
   243; accession, 173; policies, 178;
   succession, 178
Alexander II, 464, 523, 554, 560;
   emancipation of serfs, 279, 302;
   reforms, 302–3; assassination
   attempts, 332, 462, 477, 493;
   assassination, 371, 499
Alexander III (Tsar-Peacemaker), 500,
   551, 552, 554, 555, 560–1
All-Russia Social-Revolutionary
   Organization, 441–2
Anarchism, 235, 294
Anne, Empress, 164
Apanage system, 18, 38, 44, 50, 51
Aptekman, Osip, 380–1, 384, 440, 447
Arakcheev, Count, 178
Army, regular, 127; Guards
   regiments, 127, 151
Aronzon, Solomon, 380
Arson, 320
Asia, 11, 13
Ashenbrenner, Mikhail, 489
Assassination, 332, 334–7, 456, 460–1,
   462, 468
Astrakhan, 31
Austria, 179
Autocracy, 8, 37, 40–2, 82–3, 142, 165–
   8, 173, 177–8, 560; Empress Anne,
   164
Axelrod, Pavel, 531–2, 545

Bakunin, Mikhail, 218, 283, 294, 329,
   342, 343, 391, 537; career, 340–2;
   relations with Nechaev, 340, 341–8,
   350–4; 'To the Officers of the
   Russian Army', 344; imagined

parties, 344–5; *Narodnaya Rasprava*,
   348
Balkan uprising, 449–53
Barannikov, Alexander, 486
Belgorod, 35
Belinsky, Vissarion, 195, 214, 220, 224,
   255–60, 262, 266, 280
Bel'tov (Plekhanov), 564
Berdyaev, 25, 73, 184, 192, 219
Blackstone, 154
Blanquism, 410, 488, 537, 538, 543, 550
Blok, Alexander, 10, 36, 185–6
Boborykin, 190
Bolshevik Party, 240, 315, 317, 362
Bonch-Bruevich, 432
Bourgeoisie, 232–3, 266, 471–2
Büchner, 226
Bureaucracy, 181, 182
Byzantium, 54

Capital punishment, 28
Capitalism, 233, 532, 540; theory of,
   292–3, 512, 514–15, 533–4;
   development in Russia, 304, 308–9,
   474
Catherine the Great, 153, 154, 155,
   157, 167, 168, 169, 177
Censorship, 168–9, 178, 194, 277, 303,
   336, 554
Census, 27
Chaadayev, Pytor, 119, 181, 224, 255,
   269
Chaikovsky, Nikolai, 371;
   Chaikovskists, 371–3
Checkov, 213, 224
Chernyi Peredel, 478, 487, 517, 518, 522,
   524, 525, 532
Chernyshevsky, Nikolai Gavrilovich,

195, 205, 207, 211, 214, 221-4, 225, 227, 231, 232, 236, 262, 280, 281, 282-301, 315-16, 319, 333, 537; compared with Herzen, 282, 283, 284, 292, 298; influence, 282-3, 298-301; as a literary critic, 284, 286; Turgenev on, 285; Tolstoy on, 285; *What Is to Be Done?*, 286-92; New men, 289-92, 295, 297; on capitalism, 292-3; on socialism, 290-2, 293; on *obshchina*, 292; on revolution, 293-6; on peasants, 295; on authoritarian state, 295; on post-revolutionary state, 295; political views, 295-6; on democracy, 295-8; on Peter the Great, 298; patriotism, 298; Lenin on, 300-1; trial, 321
Chigirin Affair, 437-41
China, war with, 32
Church, 42, 43, 140-1; Metropolitan, 23, 86; Orthodox Church, 86-95; fusion with State, 85-9; schism, 90-2; Old Believers, 90
Colonizing activities, 15, 17-18, 35
Congress of State Representatives, 495
Conspiracy, 337, 339, 340, 348, 388, 390
Constantine, Grand Duke, 495
Constantine (brother of Nicholas I), 243-4
Constitution, 472, 475
Corporal punishment, 28, 75, 303
Cossacks, 31-2, 156
Crimean War, 179, 184, 197, 250
Custine, Marquis de, 3-5, 7, 179

Danielson, 549-51
Decembrists, 178, 180, 183, 240-50, 251, 261, 262, 263; Decembrist poets, 181; *Russkaya Pravda*, 242, 245; 'Southern Society', 242, 451; pan-Slavism, 450-1
Defence, 50
Denikin, General, 194
Desna river, 35
Deutsch, Lev, 437, 440, 478, 531
Dnieper, 35

Dobrolyubov, Nikolai Alexandrovich, 195, 214, 224, 284, 322
Dostoevsky, Fyodor, 181, 223, 261, 356-7; *The Possessed*, 199, 261, 325, 327, 357, 360
Duma, 303

Economic materialism, 390
Education, 191, 336
Elected legislature, 495
Engels, F., 233, 531; relations with Tkachev, 398-407, 507, 527, 537, 548, 550; on conspiracy, 402; on propaganda, 402; analysis of Russian position, 402-6, 527, 548, 549-51; *Soziales in Russland*, 403, 405, 527; attitude to Russian Marxism, 504, 522-5, 529, 531-2
England, 234
Europe, comparison with, 8, 9, 10, 15, 16, 47-53; influence of, 11; reaction to, 169
Europeanization, 123, 126, 135, 142-3, 144-5, 149
Executive Committee of the Popular-Revolutionary Party, 460, 462
Executive Committee of the Social-Revolutionary Party, 477

False Dmitry, 97
Famine, 562-3
Fedoseyev, 333
Feudal system, 16-19
Fichte, 197
Figner, Vera, 354, 447, 520
Fletcher, Giles, 8, 47, 53
Fonvizin, Denis, 169
Fourier, Charles, 260
Foreign travel, 76, 77, 78, 79
Foreign visitors, 76
France, 179; idea of Russia, 169-71; revolution, 171, 172; revolution (1848), 265, 508-9
Frolenko, Mikhail, 371, 477
Frontier factor, 13, 14

Gartman, Lev, 517, 518
Geiking, Baron, 000
Genghis Khan, 19

Geographical factors, 10, 13
Germany, 509
Gide, André, 5, 7, 9
Gladstone, William, 449, 450
Godunov, Boris, 78
Golubeva-Yasneva, 431
Governor-Generals, 462
Granovsky, 255, 264
Gurko, General, 464

Haxthausen, Baron August von, 271
Hegel, 197, 251
Herberstein, Baron Sigismund von, 8, 34, 177
Herzen, Alexander Ivanovich, 3, 195, 206, 213, 240, 242, 249, 262-81, 335, 537; 'Open Letter to Jules Michelet', 210; style, 262-3; character, 262-3; attitude to West, 262-3; Populism, 263, 329-31, 332; exile, 263; Europe, 263-6, 267, 268-9; Paris, 264-5; Socialism, 266; bourgeoisie, 266-7; capitalism, 266, 268; *obshchina*, 271-5; peasants, 274; influence of, 277; Free Russian Press, 277, 308; *Pole Star*, 277; *Kolokol*, 277-8; Letters to Alexander II, 279; attitude to Peter the Great, 280-1; *Revolution in Russia*, 280; on Jacobins and Nihilists, 328-31; 'To An Old Friend', 329
Historical inevitability, 268-9
Historians, theories, 108, 119, 147; Soviet, 43, 224, 315, 364, 456-7
Hungarian Revolution (1848-1849), 179

Ignatov, 531
Industry, 70, 136-8, 436, 555-61
Intelligentsia, 190-239; alienation from society, 192, 237-8; in literature, 196; 'Men of the Forties' (Fathers), 197, 201, 264, 282; 'Men of the Sixties' (Sons), 199, 200, 223, 226, 281, 282, 284, 319, 321, 326; guilt, 200, 201-2; attitude to peasants, 201, 375-85; *raznochintsy* (students), 201, 240, 281, 287, 318, 327; attitude to Russia, 198-9, 227;

idea of the people, 204-7, 230, 234; intolerance, 211-12; martyrdom, 213, 222; youth, 214-18; approach to culture, 220, 224; morality, 221-2; attitude to science, 224-6; rationalism, 226; legal ideas, 228, 229, 230-1; traditionalism, 228; Slavophiles, 10, 147, 229, 233, 235, 251-5, 260, 268-9, 271, 272, 325; Westerners, 10, 147, 229, 233, 236, 251, 254-9, 262, 269, 271, 325; political attitudes, 232; egalitarianism, 232-3, 234, 239; capitalism, 233; proletariat, 228; on education, 234; on Western liberalism, 234; Statism, 235; on bourgeoisie, 239
Invasions, 15, 17, 19, 21, 22
Ishutin, 332-5
Isidore, Metropolitan, 87
Ivan I (Kalita), 22
Ivan III (The Great), 28, 29, 39, 50
Ivan IV (The Terrible), 32, 35, 37, 40-8, 51, 65, 177; political views, 40-3; mass-murder, 44; sacking of Novgorod, 44; reputation, 45-6

Jacobinism (Russian), 245, 280, 297, 310, 315, 316, 327, 338, 389, 484, 485
Jews, 554
Jury, trial by, 303

Kantemir, 164
Karakozov, Dmitry, 332, 334, 335, 336, 337, 340, 367
Karamzin, 177, 188
Kazan, 31
Khalturin, Stepan, 493
Kharkov, 35
Khazars, 17
Khomyakov, 224, 235, 252
Kibalchich, Nikolia, 489, 501, 521-3; 'The Political Revolution and the Economic Question', 521-3
Kiev, 16, 17, 28; Kievan State, 16-17, 25; Grand Duke of, 18
Kirevsky, 252
Kliuchevsky, 11, 119
Knyazhnin, 169

Kolachevsky, 349
Komissarov, 335
Koni, A.F., 459
Konstantin Brothers, 252
Kostomarov, 181
Kovalsky, 460
Kozelsk, 34
Krasnoyarsk, 35
Kravchinsky, Sergei (Stepniak), 371, 379, 385-7, 447, 461, 471
Križanić, Jurij, 82-4, 235,
Kropotkin, Prince, 373
Kropotkin, Pytor, 283, 287, 371
Kurbsky, Prince, 40-1
Kursk, 35

Labour, 18, 55-8, 555-6; compensation for, 302; legislation, 557;
Lafargue, 528
Land, 17, 18, 26, 470; Land/service system (Pomestie), 26, 49-51, 52, 53, 54, 56, 65; hereditary, 67, 132; State ownership, 49-51; sold to serfs, 000
Landowners, 60-1; full ownership, 152; compensation, 302
Language, 90
Lavrov, Pyotr Lavrovich, 195, 367-9, 374-7 387, 391, 451, 532, 538; exile, 367; Historical Letters, 368-9; attack on nihilism, 368; on propaganda, 369, 384; on students, 370-1; Vperyod, 374; on Chaikovskists, 374; on Going to the People, 376-85, 416; relations with Tkachev, 391-8, 423-8; 'To the Russian Social-Revolutionary Youth', 395-7; on capitalism, 397; on revolution, 397-8, 415, 417-21; on dictatorship, 397; 'The State Element in the Future Society', 417, 420; State organizations, 417-18, 419, 420; socialist groups, 417-19; on obshchina, 418-19; moral integrity, 421; on internal security, 422-3; on conspiracy, 424
Legal system: Code of Laws (Ulozhenie), 65-75; reforms, 303; trial by jury, 303; judges, 303; independent bar, 303

Lenin (Vladimire Ilyich Ulyanov), 194, 219, 223, 240, 498, 549, 565; What Is to Be Done?, 431, 444; on Tkachev, 430-4
Leontiev, Konstantin, 224
Lermontov, 181, 185
Liberals, 469, 475
Listok Zemli i Voli, 468
Literature, 168, 181, 184-5, 19-6, 251
Literary critics, 195, 322
Literary journals, 194
Lithuania, 20, 28; war with, 31
Lizogub, Dmitry, 447
Local administration, 153, 303
Lopatin, German, 523
Loris-Melikov, General, 494, 495, 496, 497, 498, 499, 500

Martial law, 461-2, 494
Marx, Karl, 223, 233, 266, 271, 401, 527-9; Zur Kritik der Politischen Ökonomie, 390; on the socialist revolution, 503; attitude to Russian revolutionaries, 504-7, 507-12, 517-19, 523, 527; as practical revolutionary, 505; relations with Bakunin, 505, 507, 608-9; Das Kapital, 509, 512, 513, 520; on obshchina, 506, 511, 512, 513-16, 520; on Paris Commune, 508, 510-11; final years, 509-11; Hague Congress of First International, 508; on failure of revolution in Europe, 509-11; on social effects of industrialization, 509; on revolution in France, 509; interest in Fenians, 509-10; on revolution in Britain and Germany, 510; on capitalism, 513, 514-15; on ownership of land, 513-14; The Communist Manifesto, 516-17, 526, 533, 548; relations with Tkachev, 521; death, 531
Marxism and Marxists, 233, 239, 474, 512-13, 515-16; Marxism in Russia, 502-5, 518, 524, 529, 563-5; necessity of industrialized society,

503-4; synthesis of political and social revolution, 526; Legal Marxists, 564

Mass man, 238

Maxim the Greek, 77

Menshikov, 156

Mezentsev, General, 460-1, 463

Migration, 31

Mikhailov, Adrian, 447

Mikhailov, Alexander, 443-4, 447, 462, 466, 475-6, 477, 485, 499

Mikhailov, Mikhail, 308, 314, 320; 'To the Young Generation', 308, 314-15, 317

Mikhailov, Timofei, 501

Mikhailovich, Alexei, 65

Mikhailovsky, Nikolai, 195, 201, 202, 214, 231, 470, 472, 511

Military service, 27, 33, 49-50, 51-2, 130, 151; regular army, 127-8; abolition of compulsory service, 152, 155

Miliukov, Paul, 192, 238

Milyutin, 462, 463, 495

Mir (see Obshchina)

Moleschott, 225, 390

Mongols, 13-29, 46; Mongol rule, 15, 117; invasion, 19, 22-3; Empire, 20, 22, 24; law code, 20; Mongol influence, 27-9

Morozov, Nikolai, 371, 447, 474, 475, 477, 485, 517

Moscow, 32-3, 35; rise to supremacy, 22-4, 38-9; Grand Dukes, 23; liberation from Poland, 67

Muscovy, 9, 25-9, 31, 37, 52-3, 128; independence from Mongols, 28, 38; political and social system, 49-98; compared with European feudalism, 100-9; compared with Asiatic empires, 109-21; compared with China, 111-12

Nabat, 428, 484

Nachalo, 471

Napoleon, 178, 179

Narodnaya Volya, 354, 428, 429, 431, 433, 444, 478-501, 512, 516, 517, 519, 523, 531-2, 538, 551; name, 479; statutes, 480; Executive Committee, 480, 481, 486-7, 492, 496; 'General Principals of Organization', 480-1; link with Lenin, 481; political work, 482, 519; conspiracy, 483; 'The Party's Preparatory Work', 483-4; Tkachev, link with, 484-5, 488; Jacobins, 485; on mass revolution, 487; strategy, 487; as an élite, 488; on the State, 488; Constituent Assembly, 488-90, 491; on government, 489-90, 491-2; members, 492; assassination of Alexander II, 492-4, 501; relations with Marx, 517-21; relations with Engels, 517, 523-4, 531

Narym, 35

Natanson, Mark, 349, 447

Nationalism, 169

National assembly, 312

Navy, 128

Nechaev, Sergei Gennadievich, 337-66, 389; reaction to, 337, 349, 356, 361-2, 467; birth, 338; education, 338; enters revolutionary circules, 338; revolutionary theory, 339; Programme of Revolutionary Action, 339; in Switzerland, 340, 350; relations with Mikhail Bakunin, 340, 341-8, 350-3; Narodnaya Rasprava, 342, 348; How the Revolutionary Question Presents Itself (written with Bakunin), 343; Principles of Revolution (written with Bakunin), 343; Revolutionary Catechism (written with Bakunin), 345-8, 350, 352, 357, 365; return to Russia, 348; World Revolutionary Union, 348; murder of Ivanov, 349-50; escape, 349; trial of Nechaevites, 349-50; extradition, 353; trial and imprisonment, 353-6; death, 356; Dostoevsky's description, 357-61; precursor of Bolshevism, 363-5

Nekrasov, 284-5, 335

'New Men', 289-92, 295, 297, 325 (see also Chernyshevsky)

Nicholas I, 7, 178-86, 222, 243, 249-50,

261, 271; police state, 180, 181, 197; attitude to writers, 181; death, 277
Nicholas II, 561
Nihilism, 218, 321-31
Nikitenko, Professor, 194, 212, 216, 307, 319-20
Nikon, Patriarch, 90
Nizhne-Kolymsk, 35
Nizhny-Novgorod, 24, 34
Nobility, 54-5, 67, 152-6, 303; Boyars, 37, 44, 45, 50; reform, 129-30; ranks of, 131, 138, 154; in local administration, 153-4; Charter of the Nobility, 155, 165, 171; obligation to State service removed, 152, 155; exemption from taxation, 155; exemption from corporal punishment, 155; trial by peers, 155; reliance on monarch, 155; end as a ruling class, 182-3; bureaucratization, 182
Nomads, 17
Novgorod, 29, 50; sacking of, 44
Novikov, 169

Obdorsk, 35
Oboleshev, Alexei, 447
Obshchina (paper), 471
Obshchina (village community), 62-4, 271-5, 281, 292, 375, 393-413, 418-19, 506, 511, 512, 513-15, 520, 533, 549
Ogarev, Nikolai, 249, 275-7
Oil, 555
Oka river, 33, 34
Okhotsk, 35
Olearius, Adam, 9, 36
Oprichniki (*see* Police, Secret)
Orel, 35
Oshanina, Maria, 316, 485, 487
Osinsky, Valerian, 447, 460, 470
Ovchinnikova, Inna, 380

Pahlen, Count, 383, 384
Palmerston, 179
Panslavism, 450-2
Passports, 138
Paul I, 165, 171, 172
Peasants, 55-7, 68, 133-4, 151, 155-64,

171, 303; Reform, 11, 308; uprisings, 97, 153, 295, 320, 457-8; sale of peasants, 134, 156; increase in bondage, 156; taxation, 156; alienation from nobility, 162-3; reaction to revolutionaries, 464; emancipation, 183-4 (*see also* Serfs and Slavery)
Pechenegs, 17
Penza, 35
Peresvetov, Ivan, 42, 235
Perovskaya, Sofia, 371, 447, 478, 499, 501
Persia, war with, 123
Pestel, Colonel Pavel, 242, 245, 246, 247
Peter the Great, 11, 45, 79, 122-48, 258; impact on Russia, 139-40; physical attributes, 122; military career, 122-3, 126; Westernizing influence, 123, 126, 135, 142-5; cruelty, 123, 124; attitude to Russia, 124; reputation, 125; accession, 126; foreign policy, 128; education policy, 129; serfs, 156
Peter II, 164
Petrashevsky, Milhail, 260-2
Petrine Reform, 125-48, 177; military reform, 126-9, 180, 182; educational reform, 129, 130; civil administration, 129; nobility, 129-32; industry, 136-8; Church, 140-1; Law of Succession, 149-50
Petrunkevich, I. I., 470
Pisarev, Dmitry Ivanovich, 195, 214, 225, 227, 322-6
Plekhanov, Georgy Valentinovich, 120, 288, 440, 447, 478, 485, 524-5, 526-48, 564, 565; influence of Europe, 524-5, on Marxism, 525, 528-32, 564-5; break with *Zemlya i Volya*, 525; conversion to Marxism, 526-9, 532; relations with Engels, 527, 544-5, 547-8, 549; relations with Tkachev, 527; relations with Nechaev, 527; importance in Russian history, 529; Emancipation of Labour', 531; on Populism, 532, 533, 537-8; *Socialism and Political*

Struggle, 533, 534; on the proletariat, 535, 540; relations with Tikhomirov, 536–7, 538–44; *Our Differences*, 536–8, 544; *On the Question of the Development of the Monistic View of Russia*, 564

Pobedonostev, Konstantin, 304, 450, 500, 552–4, 561

Pogodin, Professor, 194, 228

Pokrovsky, 261, 315

Poland, 20, 28; war against, 31 revolution in, 509

Pole Star, 249

Polezhaev, 185

Police, 178, 320–1; secret police, 180, 320–1; political police, 45, 51, 75

Police State, 180, 181, 197, 246

Political trials, 455–6, 459

Polovtsy, 17

Pomestie (*see* Land)

Popov, Mikhail, 000

Poppel, Nicholas, 76

Popular Assembly, 46

Population, 140

Populists, 140, 206, 263, 271, 274, 275, 280–1, 282, 299, 306, 308, 309, 315, 317, 318, 323, 332, 337, 366, 370, 372, 375–85, 435, 436, 437, 439, 469, 470, 551, 563, 564

Pososhkov, 143, 235

Potemkin, 156

Pretenders, 97

Prokopovich, Feofan, 142, 164

Proletariat, 233, 292, 437

Proletarian nations, 271

Propaganda, 141–2, 375–84, 388, 435, 437

Prussia, 179

Pskov, 51

Pugachev, Emelian, 153, 295

Pushkin, 153, 181

Rabotnik, 442

Radishchev, Alexander: *Journey from Petersburg to Moscow*, 161, 169, 196

Razin, Stenka, 295

Raznochintsy (*see* Intelligentsia)

Razumovsky, Kiril, 156

Revolutionary idea, 189, 192, 203–6, 296–7

Revolutionary movement (*see also* specific groups), 240, 305–6, 435; remoteness from people, 243, 357; conspiratorial tradition, 244; revolutionary élite, 291, 313; nineteenth century, 414–38; amorality, 438–41, 491; centralized party, 441; political reform, 467–70, 472, 473, 474, 477; late nineteenth century, 458, 563

Revolution 1917, 11

Riazan, 51

Rogachev, Dmitry, 371

Romanov dynasty, 65, 67, 73

Rurik, House of, 17, 18, 65

Rus, 17, 18

Russia, 7, 16–17, 24, 36–7, 41–2, 141–2, 177; unification of, 24, 28; idea of Russia, 79–83, 93–8, 141, 202; domination in Europe, 179; official ideology, 250

Rysakov, 500, 501

Sablin, 371

St Petersburg, building of, 139–40, 166; University, 306–8

Saltykov-Shchedrin, 180, 230

Samarin, 252

Saratov, 35

Schelling, 197, 251

Serfs and serfdom, 55–61, 65, 68, 152–64; State serfs, 133–4, 156; right to hold, 152; appropriation of, 156; Conditions of Bondage, 156–7; right to kill, 157–8; 1767 Code, 157; comparison with USA, 159–61, 163–4; emancipation, 302–3, 306 (*see also* Peasants and Slavery)

Serno-Solovievich, Alexander, 328, 335

Serno-Solovievich, Nikolai, 321

Serpukhov, 34

Shelgunov, Nikolai, 278

Shevchenko, 181

Siberia, 31, 35

Simbirsk, 35

Sinegub, Sergei, 371

Slavery, 17, 32, 52, 58, 157, 159–61, 163–4, 183, 302

Slavophiles (*see* Intelligentsia)

Socialism, 260, 271, 272, 274, 289, 319, 368, 369 (*see also* 'New Men')

Social system, 65–98, 145; categories, 66; mobility, 193–4

Soloviev, 462, 464

Solovyov, Vladimir, 224

Sorge, F. A., 518

South Africa, 16

Sovremennik, 285, 287, 321, 336

Soviet system, 190; continuity with pre-Revolutionary Russia, 502

Special Board, 463, 496

Speransky, M. M., 173–8, 193, 228

Speshnev, Nikolai, 261

Stankevich, 255

State Council, 495

State, service, 49–64, 65, 66, 71–3, 153–4; obligation relaxed, 152, 155; supremacy, 49–64, 164, 560; repression by, 455, 460, 461–3; appeal to people, 461–2, 463; reform, 494–501

Statute of Bondage, 147

Stefanovich, 437, 440, 478

Steklov, 315

Stolypin, 304

Students, 214–15, 216, 321, 377–85, 463 (*see also* Intelligentsia)

Succession, 149–50, 178

Supreme Executive Commission, 494, 496

Sweden, war with, 31

Tambov, 35

Tartars, 31–4 (*see also* Mongols)

Tatishchev, 164

Taxation, 27, 57, 60

Terrorism, 460–2, 463, 465–9, 474, 478 (*see also* Assassination)

Tikhomirov, Lev, 371, 447, 474, 475, 477, 485, 532, 536–7, 538–43, 551–2, 561–2; 'Why I have ceased being a Revolutionary', 551–2

Time of Troubles (1605–1613), 65, 67, 177

Timofeyevich, Yermak, 31

Tiumen, 35

Tkachev, Pyotr, 388–434, 484–5; relations with Nechaev, 339, 389; *Programme of Revolutionary Action*, 339, 389; link with Lenin, 388, 429–34; precursor of Bolshevism, 388; birth, 389; career, 389; as journalist, 389; revolutionary theory, 390–1, 392–5, 408–15; student of Marx, 390; relations with Lavrov, 391–8, 415–16, 423–7, 537, 565; Cercle Slave, 391; on revolutionary élite, 392, 395, 411–16; need for quick revolution, 393, 407–8; *obshchina*, 393, 411; 'The Tasks of Revolutionary Propaganda in Russia', 392–5; relations with Engels, 398–40; 'Open Letter to Herr Frederick Engels', 399–403; *Nabat*, 407, 427; on Jacobinism, 407; on capitalism, 407; on minority dictatorship, 410–16, 426; on need for popular support, 410; attitude to the people, 412–15; on internal security, 425–6; 'The Eve and the Aftermath of Revolution', 406; influence of, 427–9, 433; Soviet historians, 433

Tobolsk, 35

Tocqueville, Alexis de, 179

Tolstoy, Count Dmitry, 336

Tolstoy, Leo, 224, 285

Tomsk, 35

Torture, 28, 499

Townspeople, 68–70, 155, 183, 303

Trepov, General, 456

Tribal system, 18

Trubetskoy, Sergei, 224

Tsar, 25, 37, 92, 143

Tula, 34

Turgenev, 162, 190, 208, 224, 255, 276, 285; *Fathers and Sons*, 197, 199, 322; *Virgin Soil*, 318; *The Labourer and the Fine Gentleman*, 464

Turkey, 42, 54, 179, 449; war with, 123, 126, 449–52

Tver, 22, 28, 51

Tyutchev, 223

Ukraine, 31-2, 156
Ulozhenie (*see* Legal system)
Ulyanov, I. N., 194
Ulyanov, Vladimir Ilyich (*see* Lenin)
United States, comparison with, 13-14, 16
Universities, 178, 198, 303, 306-7, 554
Urals, 32
Uspensky, Gleb, 180
Uvarov, 252

Valuev, P. A., 463, 495
Vasily II, 24
Vestnik Narodnoi Voli, 532
Vestnik Zemli i Voli, 474
Vladimir, Grand Duke, 18, 23
Vogt, 226, 390
Voinaralsky, Porfiry, 382
Volga, 35
Volkhovsky, Felix, 371
Voronezh, 35
Vorovsky, 301
Votchina, 50, 52
Vulfovka Commune, 370

Wars, 30-6, 65, 554; Poland, 31;
Lithuania, 31; Sweden, 31; China,
32; Tartars, 31-5; Crimean, 179, 184,
197, 250
Water: theory of the hydraulic State,
114
Western democracy, comparisons
with, 217

Westerners (*see* Intelligentsia)
What Is to Be Done? (by
Chernychevsky), 286-92, 369
What Is to Be Done? (by Lenin), 431,
444
Witte, Sergei Yulievich, 304, 559
Wittfogel, Professor Karl, 114-30

Yakutsk, 35
Yasa (*see* Mongol law code)
Yevdokimov, General, 193-4
Yeniseisk, 35

Zaichnevsky, Pyotr, 310-17, 390;
'Young Russia', 310-15, 316-17
Zaitsev, Varfolomei, 234, 325-7
Zasulich, Vera, 456, 459-60, 471, 478,
512, 513; relations with Engels,
545-8, 549
Zemlya i Volya, 321, 440, 443, 444-8,
451, 460, 465, 466, 467, 468, 469, 470,
472, 473, 474, 475, 479, 481, 507;
aims, 445-6, 466-7; Congress in
Voronezh, 477-8; meeting in
Lipetsk, 476-7, 484; split in party,
478, 519
Zemlya i Volya (paper), 473-4
Zemsky Sobor, 46, 47, 73-4, 488, 491-2
Zemstvos, 303, 370, 469
Zhelyabov, Andrei, 371, 477, 478, 480,
499, 501